The
Constitution
in
Congress

The Constitution in Congress

The Federalist Period

1789–1801

David P. Currie

The University of Chicago Press • Chicago and London

DAVID P. CURRIE is the Edward H. Levi Distinguished Service Professor of Law at the University of Chicago. His award-winning, two-volume history, *The Constitution in the Supreme Court,* is also available from the University of Chicago Press.

The University of Chicago Press, Chicago 60637
The University of Chicago Press, Ltd., London
© 1997 by The University of Chicago
All rights reserved. Published 1997
Printed in the United States of America

06 05 04 03 02 01 00 99 98 97   12345

ISBN: 0–226–13114–9 (cloth)

Library of Congress Cataloging-in-Publication Data

Currie, David P.
    The Constitution in Congress : the Federalist period, 1789–1801 / David P. Currie.
        p.   cm.
    Includes bibliographical references and index.
    ISBN 0-226-13114-9 (cloth : alk. paper)
    1. United States—Constitutional history.   2. Law—United States—History.   3.
Legislative power—United States—History.   4. Executive power—United States—
History.   5. United States—Constitutional law—Interpretation and construction—History.
6. United States.   Congress—History.   I. Title.
KF4541.C834 1997
342.73'029—dc21   96-51493
                                                                            CIP

♾ The paper used in this publication meets the minimum requirements of the American National Standard for Information Sciences—Permanence of Paper for Printed Library Materials, ANSI Z39.48-1984.

Contents

PREFACE   ix

ABBREVIATIONS AND SHORTENED TITLES   xiii

Part One: The First Congress, 1789–1791

INTRODUCTION TO PART ONE   3

CHAPTER 1: THE NEW GOVERNMENT   7

    I. Congress   7
      A. Rules   9
      B. Records   10
      C. Officers   11
      D. Oaths   13
      E. Instructions   15
      F. Qualifications   16
      G. Elections   17
      H. Enumeration   19
      I. Investigation   20
    II. The Special Role of the Senate   21
      A. The French Consular Convention   22
      B. The Fishbourn Affair   23
      C. The Southern Indians   24
      D. The Fort Harmar Treaties   26
    III. The Executive Branch   28
      A. The President's Role in Legislation   29
      B. Emoluments and Titles   32

C. The Department of Foreign Affairs   36
D. Other Officers   41
IV.   The Courts   47
A. The Lower Federal Courts   47
B. The Supreme Court   52

CHAPTER 2: SUBSTANTIVE LEGISLATION   55

I.   Taxes and Trade   55
A. Tariffs and Tonnage   55
B. Whiskey   60
C. Ship Licensing   62
D. Inspection Laws   63
E. Seamen   65
F. The Slave Trade   66
II.   Spending   68
A. Appropriations   68
B. Lighthouses   69
C. Other Spending Proposals   71
III.   The Public Credit   73
A. Paper Money   74
B. The Question of Full Payment   74
C. The Assumption of State Debts   76
IV.   The Bank of the United States   78
V.   Military, Indian, and Foreign Affairs   81
A. Soldiers   81
B. Indians   85
C. Pirates   87
VI.   Miscellany   88
A. Naturalization   88
B. Patents and Copyrights   90
C. Crimes   93
D. States   97
E. Territories   103
F. The Seat of Government   107
VII.   The Bill of Rights   110

CONCLUSION TO PART ONE   116

Part Two: The Federalists, 1791–1801

INTRODUCTION TO PART TWO   125

CHAPTER 3: THE SECOND CONGRESS, 1791–1793   128

I.   Congress   128

Contents

II. The President   136
   A. The Electoral College   136
   B. Succession   139
   C. Special Elections   144
III. The Post Office   146
   A. Delegation   146
   B. Federalism and Other Problems   150
IV. The Mint   152
V. The Courts   154
VI. The Militia   157
   A. Organization   157
   B. Employment   160
VII. The Army   163
VIII. The Treasury   164
IX. Codfish   168
X. Fugitives   170
XI. Summary   171

CHAPTER 4: THE THIRD CONGRESS, 1793–1795   172

I. Neutrality   174
   A. The Proclamation   174
   B. The Aftermath   180
II. Defense   183
   A. The Scope of Federal Authority   183
   B. The President and Congress   186
III. St. Domingo   188
IV. Insurrection   189
V. Citizenship   192
VI. The Eleventh Amendment   195
VII. The District of New Hampshire   198
VIII. The Southwest Delegate   200
IX. The Flag   204

CHAPTER 5: THE FOURTH CONGRESS, 1795–1797   206

I. The Jay Treaty   209
   A. Negotiation and Approval   209
   B. The Role of the House   211
II. Tennessee   217
III. Congressional Powers   222
   A. Spending—Again   222
   B. Direct Taxes   225
   C. Perils of the Deep   227
   D. Kidnapping and the Right to Petition   229
IV. Randall and Whitney   232

CHAPTER 6: THE FIFTH AND SIXTH CONGRESSES, 1797–1801   239

    I. Troubles with France   239
        A. Declaring the Peace   241
        B. The Provisional Army   244
        C. Volunteers   248
        D. The French Treaties   250
   II. The Enemy Within   253
        A. Aliens   254
        B. Sedition   260
        C. The Expulsion of Matthew Lyon   263
        D. The Cases of Duane and Randolph   266
        E. All's Well That Ends Well   269
  III. Odds and Ends   274
        A. The Impeachment of Senator Blount   275
        B. Mr. Pinckney's Gifts   281
        C. The Mississippi Territory   284
        D. The District of Columbia   286
  IV. The Election of 1800   288
        A. The Grand Committee   288
        B. Mr. Bayard's Conscience   292

CONCLUSION   296

APPENDIX: THE CONSTITUTION OF THE UNITED STATES   299

INDEX   315

Preface

Judicial review of legislative and executive action has been such a success in the United States that we tend to look only to the courts for guidance in interpreting the Constitution. The stock of judicial precedents is rich, accessible, and familiar, but it does not exhaust the relevant materials. Members of Congress and executive officers, no less than judges, swear to uphold the Constitution, and they interpret it every day in making and applying the law.[1] Like judges, they often engage in extensive and enlightening debates over the constitutional issues that confront them. Like judges, they also leave voluminous records of their deliberations—from statutes and legislative hearings, reports, and debates to presidential messages, proclamations, and opinions of the Attorneys General, to mention only a few.

The very profusion of this material means that one must often do a good deal of sifting in order to uncover the treasure. Yet that was equally true at Sutter's Mill, and here too there is plenty to be uncovered. At the very least, legislative and executive records are apt to afford a useful preview of later judicial controversy, since courts rarely intervene before the other branches have made their decision. Moreover, especially in the early days, many years would often pass before the courts were called upon to reexamine leg-

---

[1]"[T]he whole business of legislation," said Representative Theodore Sedgwick in 1791, "was a practical construction of the powers of the Legislature . . . ." 2 Annals of Congress 1960 (Gales & Seaton, eds, 1834) [hereafter cited as Annals]. See generally Jefferson Powell, ed, Languages of Power: A Source Book of Early American Constitutional History xi–xii (Carolina Academic Press, 1991); Frank H. Easterbrook, Presidential Review, 40 Case W Res L Rev 905 (1989–90). Volumes 1 and 2 of the Annals of Congress appear in two separate compilations, one edited by Gales alone, the other by Gales and Seaton. Pagination differs from one set to the other. All citations in this book are to the Gales & Seaton edition. The Annals themselves are incomplete; I have supplemented them where necessary with references to other contemporaneous accounts currently being collected in volumes 10–14 of the Documentary History of the First Federal Congress (Johns Hopkins, 1972–) [hereafter cited as Doc Hist].

islative or executive acts. Before 1800 nearly all of our constitutional law was made by Congress or the President, and so was much of it thereafter. Indeed a number of constitutional issues of the first importance have *never* been resolved by judges; what we know of their solution we owe to the legislative and executive branches, whose interpretations have established traditions almost as hallowed in some cases as the Constitution itself.

Legislative and executive opinions respecting some of the great controversies are widely known. The President's right to remove executive officers[2] and Congress's power to establish a bank[3] are two early examples. In the main, however, legislative and executive precedents are less familiar than judicial ones.[4]

Historians and political scientists, of course, have written extensively about the issues that confronted Congress during the Federalist period. It would be more than presumptuous for a legal scholar to attempt to improve upon their work. My aim is to discuss the same material from a legal perspective, for constitutional questions are, among other things, legal questions. I am interested in congressional and executive interpretations of the Constitution precisely because and to the extent that they contribute to the development of legal doctrine; from that point of view they have not received the attention they deserve.

The aim of this study is to begin to remedy that deficiency, in the conviction that both Congress and the Executive have a great deal to tell us about the Constitution.

Portions of this book originally appeared in the form of articles in the University of Chicago Roundtable (chap. 1), the University of Chicago Law Review (chaps. 2 and 4), and the Northwestern University Law Review (chap. 3), to all of which thanks are extended for permission to reprint. See David P. Currie, The Constitution in Congress: The First Congress and the Structure of Government, 1789–1791, 2 U Chi L Sch Roundtable 161 (1995), © 1995 by The University of Chicago; Substantive Issues in the First Congress, 1789–1791, 61 U Chi L Rev. 775 (1994), © 1994 by The University of Chicago; The Second Congress, 1791–1793, 90 Nw UL Rev 606 (1996), © 1996 by Northwestern University Law School; The Third Congress, 1793–1795, 63 U Chi L Rev 1 (1996), © 1996 by The University of Chicago.

I should also like to thank the Kirkland & Ellis Faculty Research Fund, the Mayer, Brown & Platt Faculty Research Fund, the Morton C. Seeley Fund, the Raymond & Nancy Goodman Feldman Fund, and the Sonnenschein Faculty Research Fund for finan-

---

[2]See chapter 1.

[3]See chapter 2.

[4]See, e.g., Stanley Elkins & Eric McKitrick, The Age of Federalism (Oxford, 1993) [hereafter cited as Elkins & McKitrick]; John Miller, The Federalist Era: 1789–1801 (Harper & Brothers, 1960) [hereafter cited as Miller]; Leonard D. White, The Federalists: A Study in Administrative History (MacMillan, 1948) [hereafter cited as White]; Forrest McDonald, The Presidency of George Washington (Kansas, 1974) [hereafter cited as McDonald, Washington]; Ralph Adams Brown, The Presidency of John Adams (Kansas, 1975); Stephen G. Kurtz, The Presidency of John Adams (Pennsylvania, 1957); Irving Brant, James Madison: Father of the Constitution, 1787–1800 (Bobbs-Merrill, 1950) [hereafter cited as Brant]; James Thomas Flexner, George Washington and the New Nation (1783–1793) (Little Brown, 1970) and George Washington: Anguish and Farewell (1793–1799) (Little, Brown 1972); Dumas Malone, Jefferson and the Rights of Man (Little Brown, 1951) and Jefferson and the Ordeal of Liberty (Little, Brown, 1962); Forrest McDonald, Alexander Hamilton: A Biography (Norton, 1979) [hereafter cited as McDonald, Hamilton].

cial support; Charlene Bangs Bickford, Kenneth R. Bowling, and Helen E. Veit of the First Federal Congress Project for access to hitherto unpublished reports of the debates; Mark Anderson, Greg D. Andres, Julie Conner, Elizabeth Klein Frumkin, Valerie Ross, Jennipher Rutledge Martinez, Philip Shaikun, and Jim Young for seminar papers that stimulated my thinking on the issues here discussed; Akhil Reed Amar, Kenneth Bowling, Gerhard Casper, Barbara Flynn Currie, Frank Easterbrook, Philip B. Kurland, Lawrence Lessig, Richard Posner, Richard Ross, and David Strauss for invaluable advice and encouragement; and Keith Garza, Dianne Kueck, and Shambie Singer for exemplary research assistance.

Abbreviations and Shortened Titles

Am St Papers	American State Papers (Gales & Seaton, 1832)
Ames Works	Seth Ames, ed, Works of Fisher Ames (Little, Brown, 1854)
Amory	Thomas C. Amory, Military Services and Public Life of Major-General John Sullivan (Wiggin & Lunt, 1868)
Annals	Annals of Congress (Gales & Seaton, eds, 1834)
Biographical Directory	Biographical Directory of the United States Congress 1774–1989 (Government Printing Office, bicentennial ed 1989)
Brant	Irving Brant, James Madison: Father of the Constitution, 1787–1800 (Bobbs-Merrill, 1950)
Contested Elections	M. St. Clair Clarke & David A. Hall, Cases of Contested Elections in Congress (Gales & Seaton, 1834)
Doc Hist	Documentary History of the First Federal Congress (Johns Hopkins, 1972–)
Elkins & McKitrick	Stanley Elkins & Eric McKitrick, The Age of Federalism (Oxford, 1993)
Elliot's Debates	Jonathan Elliot, The Debates in the Several State Conventions on the Adoption of the Federal Constitution (2d ed 1836)

Farrand	Max Farrand, ed, The Records of the Federal Convention of 1787 (Yale, 2d ed 1937)
The Federalist	Jacob E. Cooke, ed, The Federalist (Wesleyan, 1961)
The First Hundred Years	David P. Currie, The Constitution in the Supreme Court: The First Hundred Years, 1789–1888 (Chicago, 1985)
Gallatin Writings	Henry Adams, ed, Writings of Albert Gallatin (Antiquarian Press, 1960) (first published in 1879)
Hamilton Papers	Harold C. Syrett & Jacob E. Cooke, eds, The Papers of Alexander Hamilton (Columbia, 1961–1979)
Haynes	George H. Haynes, The Senate of the United States: Its History and Practice (Russell & Russell, 1960)
Jay Papers	Henry P. Johnston, ed, The Correspondence and Public Papers of John Jay (Putnam, 1891)
J Cont Cong	Journals of the Continental Congress, 1774–1789 (Government Printing Office, 1937)
Jefferson Papers	Julian Boyd, ed, The Papers of Thomas Jefferson (Princeton, 1961–)
Jefferson Writings (Ford ed)	Paul Leicester Ford, ed, The Writings of Thomas Jefferson (Putnam, 1896)
Jefferson Writings (Wash ed)	H.A. Washington, ed, The Writings of Thomas Jefferson (Riker, Thorne, 1854)
Kent	James Kent, Commentaries on American Law (Da Capo, 1971) (first published in 1826)
Madison Papers	Charles Hobson, et al, eds, The Papers of James Madison (Chicago and Virginia, 1962–1991)
McDonald, Hamilton	Forrest McDonald, Alexander Hamilton: A Biography (Norton, 1979)
McDonald, Washington	Forrest McDonald, The Presidency of George Washington (Kansas, 1974)
Miller	John Miller, The Federalist Era: 1789–1801 (Harper & Brothers, 1960)
Op AG	Opinions of the Attorneys General of the United States (Robert Farnham, 1852–)
Rawle	William Rawle, A View of the Constitution of the United States of America (Philip H. Nicklin, 2d ed 1829)

Richardson	James D. Richardson, A Compilation of the Messages and Papers of the Presidents (US Congress, 1900)
The Second Century	David P. Currie, The Constitution in the Supreme Court: The Second Century, 1888–1986 (Chicago, 1990)
Senate Executive Journal	Journal of the Executive Proceedings of the Senate (Duff Green, 1828)
Sharp	James Roger Sharp, American Politics in the Early Republic (Yale, 1993)
Story	Joseph Story, Commentaries on the Constitution of the United States (Brown, Shattuck & Co., 1833)
Swanstrom	Roy Swanstrom, The United States Senate, 1787–1801 (reprinted as S Doc No 100–31 (1988))
Tucker's Blackstone	St. George Tucker, ed, Blackstone's Commentaries on the Laws of England (Birch & Small, 1803)
Washington Diaries	John C. Fitzpatrick, ed, The Diaries of George Washington, 1748–1799 (Houghton Mifflin, 1925)
Washington Papers	W. Abbott, ed, The Papers of George Washington (Presidential Series) (Virginia, 1987)
Washington Writings	John C. Fitzpatrick, ed, The Writings of George Washington (Government Printing Office, 1939)
White	Leonard D. White, The Federalists: A Study in Administrative History (Macmillan, 1948)
Whittemore	Charles P. Whittemore, A General of the Revolution: John Sullivan of New Hampshire (Columbia, 1961)
Works of John Adams	Charles Francis Adams, ed., The Works of John Adams (Little, Brown, 1851)

Part One

The First Congress
1789–1791

Introduction to Part One

New Hampshire, the decisive ninth state under Article VII, ratified the Philadelphia Constitution on June 21, 1788.[1] Elections were held pursuant to rules specified by the outgoing Confederation Congress,[2] and the new House and Senate convened in New York on March 4, 1789. It took a month and more than one stern summons to produce a Senate quorum,[3] and neither North Carolina nor Rhode Island had yet signed on. By April, however, both Houses were in business; and their business was to set up the government of the United States.

For the Constitution, as Chief Justice Marshall would later remind us, laid down only the "great outlines" of the governmental structure;[4] translating the generalities of this noble instrument into concrete and functioning institutions was deliberately left to Congress. The task was one partly of interpretation and partly of interstitial creation, for the Framers had been too wise to attempt to regulate all the details themselves—although for obvious reasons the structural provisions are among the most specific in the entire document. Thus in a very real sense it can be said that the First Congress was a sort of continuing constitutional convention, and not simply because so many of its members—

[1] See Roscoe R. Hill, ed, 34 Journals of the Continental Congress, 1774–1789, 281 (Government Printing Office, 1937) [hereafter cited as J Cont Cong]; John P. Butler, 5 The Papers of the Continental Congress 1774–1789, 658 (Government Printing Office, 1978).

[2] 34 J Cont Cong at 523 (Sept 13, 1788).

[3] See 1 Annals at 15–16. Article I, § 5 permits each House to authorize a number not constituting a quorum "to compel the attendance of absent members," but since the Senate had never met before it had made no such authorization. Fisher Ames, a Massachusetts Representative who would soon emerge as one of the leaders of the House, expressed his dismay at the lackadaisical attitude of his colleagues: "We lose £1,000 a day revenue. We lose credit, spirit, everything. The public will forget the government before it is born." Letter of Fisher Ames to George Richards Minot, Mar 25, 1789, in Seth Ames, ed, 1 Works of Fisher Ames 32 (Little, Brown, 1854) [hereafter cited as Ames Works].

[4] McCulloch v Maryland, 17 US 316, 407 (1819).

James Madison, Oliver Ellsworth, Elbridge Gerry, Rufus King, Robert Morris, and William Paterson being only the most conspicuous examples—had helped to compose or to ratify the Constitution itself.[5]

On April 6 the votes of the presidential electors were counted before a joint session of both Houses, as Article II prescribed. In accord with that provision, each of the sixty-nine electors had cast two votes. As expected, each had given one vote to George Washington; John Adams was second with thirty-four votes and thus became Vice-President.[6] Acutely aware that everything he or Congress did would set a precedent,[7] Washington urged the legislators to permit "no local prejudices or attachments, no separate views, nor party animosities" to distract them from laying the foundations of national policy "in the pure and immutable principles of private morality."[8] With that he left them to do their work; and work they did.

The First Congress determined its own procedures, established the great executive departments, and set up the federal judiciary. It enacted a system of taxation, provided for payment of Revolutionary debts, and erected a national bank. It made provision for national defense, regulated relations with Indian tribes, and (in the Senate) advised the President on foreign affairs. It passed statutes respecting naturalization, patents and copyrights, and federal crimes.[9] It regulated relations among existing states and admitted new ones while providing for the administration of territories and the establishment of a permanent seat of government.

In doing all this Congress interpreted a surprising number of provisions of the

[5]See Miller at 5; Charles A. Beard, Economic Origins of Jeffersonian Democracy 99 (MacMillan, 1927); Andrew McLaughlin, A Constitutional History of the United States 225 (Appleton-Century-Crofts, 1935); George Ticknor Curtis, 2 Constitutional History of the United States 84 (1896). Invaluable information about the members of the First and later Congresses is collected in the Biographical Directory of the United States Congress 1774–1989 (Government Printing Office, bicentennial ed 1989) [hereafter cited as Biographical Directory].

[6]See 1 Annals at 17. The remaining 35 votes were scattered among 10 candidates, of whom John Jay received the most with 9.

[7]"I walk," Washington wrote on one early occasion, "on untrodden ground." Letter of George Washington to Catherine Macaulay Graham, Jan 9, 1790, in John C. Fitzpatrick, ed, 30 The Writings of George Washington 495, 496 (Government Printing Office, 1939) [hereafter cited as Washington Writings]. See also Washington's letter of May 5, 1789, asking Madison to draft a response to the House's reply to his inaugural address: "As the first of every thing, in *our situation* will serve to establish a Precedent, it is devoutly wished on my part, that these precedents may be fixed on true principles." W. Abbott, ed, 2 The Papers of George Washington (Presidential Series) 216–17 (University Press of Virginia, 1987) [hereafter cited as Washington Papers]. Madison echoed these sentiments in the debate over presidential removal: "The decision that is at this time made, will become the permanent exposition of the constitution . . . ." 1 Annals at 514.

[8]1 Annals at 27–29. He did not mention Pareto optimality. Tsk, tsk.

[9]Representative Hartley moved at one point during the First Congress that a committee be directed to bring in a bankruptcy bill as well, arguing that "the Constitution *required* that an act should be passed on the subject." 1 Annals at 1143–44 (emphasis added). Smith suggested that it would be better "to defer the business till the public debt should be funded, and banks established, without which it was difficult to conceive how arrangements could be made to facilitate the payment of debts, or the operation of such a law," and Hartley agreed. Id at 1144. For Maclay's argument in the Senate that the bankruptcy power applied only to debts of "the Trading part of the community" see 9 Doc Hist at 225. See also 2 Annals at 1816, postponing consideration of a report from the Secretary of State on weights and measures (id at 1781) pending the outcome of British and French efforts to agree on a new set of international standards. The report itself appears in Julian Boyd, ed, 16 The Papers of Thomas Jefferson 650 (Princeton, 1961) [hereafter cited as Jefferson Papers].

Constitution, finding time along the way to propose not ten but twelve additional articles to improve the document itself. By the time the First Congress adjourned in 1791 the country had a much clearer idea of what the Constitution meant than it had had when that body had first met in 1789.[10]

[10]For a concise summary of the work of the First Congress see Charlene Bangs Bickford & Kenneth R. Bowling, Birth of the Nation: The First Federal Congress, 1789–91 (First Federal Congress Project, 1989). See also Kenneth R. Bowling, Politics in the First Congress, 1789–1791 (Garland, 1990).

1

The New Government

I. CONGRESS

The Constitution had a good deal to say about the structure and proceedings of Congress. Seats in the House of Representatives were to be apportioned among the states according to population and filled for two years by popular elections in which voter qualifications were tied to those set by state law.[1] Each state legislature was to choose two Senators for staggered six-year terms.[2] Distinct age, citizenship, and residence requirements were prescribed for Representatives and for Senators, and provision was made for filling vacancies.[3] The "times, places, and manner" of elections were to be determined by state law, unless Congress—"except as to the places of choosing Senators"—should otherwise provide.[4] Individual members were entitled to compensation determined by law,[5] enjoyed a

---

[1] US Const, Art I, § 2.

[2] Id, § 3.

[3] Id, §§ 2, 3. In each case there was to be a special election to fill the remainder of the term; for the Senate there were to be interim appointments by the executive as well.

[4] Id, § 4.

[5] Congress voted its members a salary of $6.00 for each day they were in session plus travel expenses, providing a $1.00 raise for Senators in 1795. 1 Stat 70–71 (Sept 22, 1789). The differential between the two Houses provoked a lively and entertaining debate, but the only constitutional argument made in this connection was Representative Burke's insistence that disagreement between the House and Senate not prevent fulfillment of the obligation imposed by Article I, § 6 to provide some compensation to the members. See 1 Annals at 676–84, 705–10, 923–26. See also Rep. Gerry's contention, id at 706–09, that legislative independence required that members of Congress be fully compensated for their services. One of the twelve constitutional amendments proposed by the First Congress would have provided that no increase in congressional salaries could take effect until after the next election, in order to keep the members from lining their own pockets; 200 years elapsed before it was ratified by three fourths of the states, and its present status is disputed. See 1 Annals at 756–57; 2 id at 2033–40; see also chapter 2.

limited immunity from arrest while in session, and "for any speech or debate in either House" were not to be "questioned in any other place."[6]

Congress itself was to meet "at least once in every year."[7] A majority of each House would constitute a quorum,[8] and each member was to be "bound by oath or affirmation to support this Constitution."[9] Each House was authorized to judge "the elections, returns and qualifications of its own members,"[10] to select its own officers[11] (except that the Vice-President was made President of the Senate),[12] to punish disorderly members, and (by a two-thirds vote) "to expel a member."[13] Each House was required to "keep a journal of its proceedings";[14] neither was permitted to "adjourn for more than three days, nor to any other place," without the other's consent;[15] the President was empowered to convene one or both Houses "on extraordinary occasions."[16] Legislation required the agreement of both Houses and was subject to a suspensive presidential veto.[17]

As intricate as these provisions were, they obviously did not regulate every procedural detail; and consequently each House was also authorized to "determine the rules of its proceedings."[18]

[6] US Const, Art I, § 6.

[7] Id, § 4. This meeting was to take place "on the first Monday in December, unless [Congress] shall by law appoint a different day." Id. When Congress adjourned its first session on September 29, 1789, it enacted a statute providing for a second session beginning on the first Monday of January, 1790. See 1 Annals at 96, 964; 1 Stat 96. See also 1 Annals at 1074, adjourning the second session on August 12, 1790, to meet again the first Monday in December of the same year, without embodying the decision in statutory form. Thus the First Congress sat for three sessions in the space of two years, adjourning for the last time on March 3, 1791 (2 Annals at 1826), two years after the date set for the commencement of its first session. For debate over the constitutionality of a resolution to fix March 4, 1789 as the date on which the terms of members of the First Congress had begun see id at 1636–38 and 1 Annals at 1010–11.

When the second session began, Congress had to confront the interesting question of what to do about matters left unresolved at the end of the preceding meeting. Representatives Lee, Page, and White argued that Congress should follow the British Parliament's practice of considering all unfinished business de novo. 1 Annals at 1084–88. Hartley responded that royal prorogation of Parliament was more final than voluntary adjournment of Congress and objected to the waste of effort involved in repeating work done in a previous session. Id at 1092–94. For the time being, however, both Houses voted to treat each session as an independent unit. Id at 1110–12. The end of a session wiped any unfinished business from the table; bills could not become law without being passed by both Houses within a single session. See id at 1115–18. For Maclay's report of parallel Senate deliberations on this issue see 9 Doc Hist at 185–91.

[8] US Const, Art I, § 5.

[9] Id, Art VI.

[10] Id, Art I, § 5.

[11] Id, §§ 2, 3.

[12] Id, § 3.

[13] Id, § 5.

[14] Id.

[15] Id.

[16] Id, Art II, § 3. President Washington called a special session of the Senate on March 4, 1791, chiefly to secure confirmation of appointments to federal offices in Vermont. See chapter 2. Whether Congress had inherent authority to call itself into special session ("[t]he Congress shall assemble *at least* once in every year"), or whether it could authorize itself to do so by setting a flexible date for its next meeting ("such meeting shall be on the first Monday in December, unless they shall by law appoint a different day"), the First Congress did not have to decide. See US Const, Art I, § 4.

[17] Id, § 7.

[18] Id, § 5.

A.   Rules

Deliberative bodies can scarcely function without procedural rules, and one of the first acts of each House was to adopt them.[19] The rules were simple, but they established a number ·of important precedents.

Both Houses provided that bills should be read three times and might be referred to committees.[20] The former provision could be said to encumber the legislative process and the latter to restrict the participation of individual members.[21] Nevertheless both served to improve the quality of legislation, the one by inhibiting impulsive action and the other by permitting a division of labor.[22] Moreover, both were sanctified by long tradition,[23] so that neither could well be said on its face to impair the constitutional principle of representative government.

The House rules imposed additional restrictions, requiring that leave be obtained in order to introduce a bill or speak more than twice on the same question and forbidding members to vote on matters in which they were "immediately and particularly interested."[24] If these provisions can be defended, it is on the ground that they went no further

---

[19]See 1 Annals at 20–21 (Senate); 102–06, 127–28 (House). See also id at 19 (conference procedure for resolving disagreements between the two Houses).

[20]Senate committees were to be elected by the members, House committees generally appointed by the Speaker. Both Houses optimistically prohibited reading and conversing while others were addressing the assembly. Id at 20–21 (Senate); id at 103 (House).

[21]In accord with British precedent, the original Senate practice was that "a Senator who opposed the basic purpose of a bill was not to be appointed to the committee considering it." Roy Swanstrom, The United States Senate, 1787–1801 228 (reprinted as S Doc No 100–31 (1988)) [hereafter cited as Swanstrom]. Thus "[i]n 1790 Hamilton's friends made certain that no opponents of the Secretary's program were named to the committee preparing the bill to establish the Bank of the United States." Id. Yet nobody seems to have complained; "committees were regarded merely as instrumentalities to accomplish the purposes of the Senate majority." Id at 229.

[22]See James Kent, 1 Commentaries on American Law 224 (Da Capo Press Reprint ed, 1971) (first published in 1826) [hereafter cited as Kent] (defending the three–readings requirement as "prudently intended to guard against surprise or imposition").

[23]The English Parliament has assigned potential legislation to committees and required bills to be read three times before passage since at least the late 16th century. See Sir Thomas Smith, De Republica Anglorum 38–39 (1583, reprinted by De Capo Press 1970); George Petyt, Treatise of the Law and Custom of the Parliaments of England 186 (1689, reprinted by Scholarly Resources 1974). The Continental Congress continued these traditions. On its second day of deliberation that body created two committees, one "to State the rights of the Colonies in general" and the other "to examine & report the several Statutes, which affect the trade and Manufactures of the colonies." 1 J Cont Cong 26 (Sept 6, 1774). The Continental Congress officially began requiring bills to be read three times before passage on May 4, 1781. 20 id at 477–78.

[24]The practice of requiring leave for multiple speeches was common to both Parliament and the Continental Congress. See Smith, De Republica Anglorum at 159 (cited in note 23); 1 J Cont Cong at 26. Although the Continental Congress did not speak directly to the issue of conflicts of interest, Jefferson cited ancient authority for such a rule in his famous Manual of Parliamentary Practice (1800), in H.A. Washington, ed, 9 The Writings of Thomas Jefferson 3, 29 (Riker, Thorne, 1854) [hereafter cited as Jefferson Writings (Wash ed)]:

> Where the private interests of a member are concerned in a bill or question he is to withdraw. And where such an interest has appeared, his voice has been disallowed, even after a division. In a case so contrary not only to the laws of decency, but to the fundamental principles of the social compact, which denies to any man to be a judge in his own cause, it is

than was necessary if business was to be conducted efficiently and fairly. Nobody is recorded as objecting that either the House or the Senate rules unconstitutionally limited the rights of individual members.[25]

B.   Records

Article I, § 5 requires each House to "keep a journal of its Proceedings" and to publish those parts of it not requiring secrecy. It does not say that congressional deliberations must be open to the public, and the Senate chose to operate behind closed doors for several years[26] despite repeated arguments that the blanket exclusion of the public was inconsistent with the principle of popular government on which the Constitution was based.[27]

Moreover, neither chamber interpreted the journal provision to require a verbatim transcript of its proceedings.[28] Senate debates were not reported at all until the public was finally admitted to hear them, and House debates made it into print only because it was in the interest of private entrepreneurs to record them.[29] Senator William Maclay of Pennsylvania made notes of some of the deliberations in the upper House,[30] but they were sketchy and unpublished; and there are significant gaps in the coverage of House proceed-

---

for the honor of the House that this rule of immemorial observance should be strictly adhered to. 2 Hats. 119, 121; 6 Grey, 368.

John Adams, then a delegate to the Continental Congress, told of an attempt to prevent him from voting on matters concerning the Colonies' independence from Great Britain because he held an office under the new government of Massachusetts and, therefore, was "interested" in the question. Charles Francis Adams, 3 The Works of John Adams 25–28 (Little, Brown, 1851) [hereafter cited as Works of John Adams]; 4 J Cont Cong at 125–27. Presumably the conflict of interest provision adopted by the first House of Representatives did not forbid farmers to vote on measures affecting farming; if it did it would be difficult to reconcile with the principle of representative government.

[25]Senator Maclay did raise objections with constitutional implications to the rule providing for referring bills passed by both Houses to a joint committee for reconciliation and correction of errors. 1 Annals at 58–59. This procedure, he argued, gave the committee effective "power to alter the bill"—and thus, he seemed to be saying, to usurp the legislative function. See 9 Doc Hist at 197.

[26]See 1 Annals at 15.

[27]See, e.g., 1 id at 1005; 2 id at 1810–12; 9 Doc Hist at 389. The argument for closed doors was to promote uninhibited discussion; the result was to make the House the center of attention. See Harry Ammon, James Monroe: The Quest for National Identity 82, 84 (McGraw–Hill, 1971). In keeping its doors closed, however, "[t]he Senate was merely following in the footsteps of its predecessor, the Congress of the Confederation." Swanstrom at 68. See generally id at 238–52.

[28]It does expressly require publication of the yeas and nays whenever requested by one fifth of the members present, and both Houses complied with this provision. See, e.g., 1 Annals at 51 (Senate); id at 380 (House).

[29]Recognizing the value of public records of its debates, the House argued over whether to allow private reporters to sit on the floor instead of in the public gallery in order to minimize errors (one reporter had converted a regulation of harbors into a regulation of barbers)—but was unwilling to give them official sanction lest reporting errors be attributed to the House itself. See 1 Annals at 1095–98. Reporting before the days of microphones and stenographic machines was a difficult business at best; Senator Maclay complained that the official Senate Journal, which contained only the formal actions of that body and a few messages from outsiders, revealed "neither System nor Integrity." 9 Doc Hist at 181.

[30]See The Diary of William Maclay and Other Notes on Senate Debates, reprinted in 9 Doc Hist. Unfortunately for posterity, Maclay was not reelected to the Senate in 1790. Id at xvi.

ings as well.[31] Nobody seems to have argued, as one might be tempted to argue today, that a full and accurate public record was indispensable to informed electoral decision and thus embraced within the journal requirement or even—despite the possible negative inference from that provision—that it was implicit in the clauses providing for congressional elections.[32]

C. Officers

Even before adopting its procedural rules, the House of Representatives without reported debate had chosen Frederick Augustus Muhlenberg of Pennsylvania as its Speaker and John Beckley as Clerk, in accordance with Article I, § 2.[33] In the Senate, Vice-President Adams took his constitutional responsibilities seriously, not only presiding on a regular basis and breaking a number of ties with his casting vote but participating in debate as well.[34] Interpreting quite literally the provision authorizing it to elect a President pro tempore "in the absence of the Vice President,"[35] the Senate declined to elect a permanent officer, making an ad hoc choice each time the Vice-President was unable to attend.[36]

The constitutionally mandated presence of the President's successor at the head of the Senate raised fears in some quarters of undue executive influence on the legislature.[37]

[31] The Annals of Congress for 1789–91 were taken primarily from Thomas Lloyd's Congressional Register (so long as it was published) and (thereafter) from John Fenno's Gazette of the United States. Other contemporary newspaper accounts are being collected and published as a part of the Documentary History of the First Congress, but they are incomplete too. One reporter's editor, for example, "had required him to put every day's proceedings into one paper, which forced much abbreviation." See White at 505. For further discussion of the inadequacies of the Annals see Charles F. Hobson, et al, eds, 12 The Papers of James Madison 63–64 (Virginia, 1979) [hereafter cited as Madison Papers]; 13 id at 6–8; James H. Hutson, The Creation of the Constitution: The Integrity of the Documentary Record, 65 Tex L Rev 1, 35–38 (1986).

[32] US Const, Art I, §§ 2, 3.

[33] 1 Annals at 100. Representative William Smith of South Carolina, who in a later Congress would have preferred Sedgwick as Speaker, nevertheless said of Muhlenberg: "We are very well pleased with him, as he is a candid & impartial Man." See Letter of William L. Smith to Edward Rutledge, Dec 6, 1793, in George C. Rogers, Jr., ed, The Letters of William Loughton Smith to Edward Rutledge, June 6, 1789 to April 28, 1794, pt 4, 70 SC Hist Mag 38, 49 (1969).

[34] See US Const, Art I, § 3; 1 Doc Hist at 86, 135, 181, 189, 318, 324, 325, 327, 341, 385, 387, 388, 449, 450, 456 (tiebreaking votes including the crucial bill acknowledging the President's authority to remove the Secretary of Foreign Affairs); 9 Doc Hist passim; id at 5: "The President [of the Senate] as usual made us two or three Speeches from the Chair." But see Swanstrom at 255 (arguing that Adams's intervention was generally limited to procedural matters and that, apart from the controversy over presidential removal, he seldom attempted to influence the Senators' votes).

[35] US Const, Art I, § 3.

[36] Before Adams took office, for example, the Senate had chosen John Langdon of New Hampshire as President "for the sole purpose of opening and counting the votes for President of the United States." 1 Annals at 16–17. Several months later, when Adams was briefly absent, Langdon was elected once again. Id at 59. See also Vice-President Jefferson's Manual of Parliamentary Practice (cited in note 24), 9 Jefferson Writings (Wash ed) at 17: "His office is understood to be determined on the Vice-President's appearing and taking the chair, or at the meeting of the Senate after the first recess." The temporary nature of the office prevented the President pro tem from exercising any significant influence on legislative policy, and the position was not coveted. See Swanstrom at 257–60.

[37] Both Gerry and George Mason had objected in the Convention on this ground. As Gerry put it, "[w]e might as well put the President himself at the head of the Legislature." See Max Farrand, ed, 2 The Records of the Federal Convention of 1787 536–37 (Yale, 2d ed 1937) [hereafter cited as Farrand]. See also George

There was nothing the Senate could do about the Vice-President's powers, which were plainly given him by Article I, § 3. An important symbolic issue was at stake, however, when Adams insisted on signing official Senate documents as "John Adams, Vice President." "Sir," Maclay recorded himself as saying, "we know you not as Vice President within this House. As President of the Senate only do we know you, as President of the Senate only can you sign or authenticate any Act of that body."[38] Acknowledging that Maclay appeared to express the sentiments of a majority, Adams so far modified his practice as to sign as both "Vice President of the United States and President of the Senate."[39] The controversy may seem trivial, but it was one of several early efforts by the Senate to establish its independence of the executive branch.

Wholly noncontroversial at the time, in contrast, were the appointments that have perhaps the most interest and significance for students of the Constitution today: Within a few days after they first convened, each House elected a chaplain.[40]

Under the Constitution as it then stood it might have been plausible enough to conclude that a chaplain was an appropriate "officer" for each chamber to select pursuant to Article I. After all, as Chief Justice Burger was to suggest nearly two centuries later, legislators obviously needed all the help they could get.[41] But the practice was continued not only after Congress had proposed a constitutional amendment forbidding the passage of any law "respecting an establishment of religion"[42] but also after the amendment had been ratified and had become law.[43]

As the Supreme Court would conclude long afterward,[44] this history strongly suggested that Congress itself did not understand the appointment of chaplains to offend the amendment it had just proposed. It is true that Congress might have overlooked the possible inconsistency, that the legislators were not the ultimate judges of the meaning of their handiwork, and that the states rather than Congress had given the amendment the force of law.[45] It is also true that the literal terms of the amendment did not apply, because in appointing chaplains Congress had passed no "law." But it seems unlikely that the framers of the establishment clause would have meant to permit each House to do by separate resolution that which they were forbidden to do jointly; the most probable inference seems to be that at the time nobody considered the mere appointment of chaplains an "establishment" of religion.

The possible implications of this understanding far transcend the piddling question

---

H. Haynes, 1 The Senate of the United States: Its History and Practice 204 (Russell & Russell, 1960) [hereafter cited as Haynes] (noting "the obvious violence which even this assignment did to the theory of the separation of powers").

[38]9 Doc Hist at 43.

[39]See id; 6 Doc Hist at 1609.

[40]See 1 Annals at 19, 24 (Senate); id at 242 (House).

[41]Wallace v Jaffree, 472 US 38, 85 (1985) (Burger, CJ, dissenting). On the other hand, nobody seemed to think it appropriate to appoint doctors or lawyers to tend to the legislators' medical or legal needs; tradition may well account for the distinction.

[42]US Const, Amend 1.

[43]See 3 Annals at 606 (Senate), 669 (House). See also Swanstrom at 185–86.

[44]Marsh v Chambers, 463 US 783, 786–88 (1983).

[45]See id at 813–17 (Brennan, J, dissenting).

of legislative chaplains. It has since become standard learning that the establishment clause forbids any public measure whose purpose or primary effect is religious or which fosters "an excessive government entanglement with religion."[46] The congressional decision with respect to chaplains seems to contradict this test on all three points, thus calling into question a number of subsequent Supreme Court holdings on such matters as school prayers and aid to parochial schools.[47] So does the resolution adopted by both Houses at the end of their very first session, calling on the President (as he did) to "recommend to the people of the United States a day of public thanksgiving and prayer" on which to acknowledge "the many and signal favors of Almighty God . . . ."[48] The original understanding thus appears to have been that the amendment did not forbid public endorsement of religion as such but only establishment as it had existed in England and in some of the states: the creation of a single official church.

D. Oaths

Another constitutional issue of considerable jurisprudential significance was raised when the First Congress confronted the humble problem of how to comply with Article VI's requirement that its members be "bound by oath or affirmation to support this Constitution," for Article VI said nothing about how or when the oath should be administered.[49]

Five days after achieving a quorum, the House adopted a resolution spelling out the form of the oath to be taken by its members.[50] Two days later, at the House's request, the Chief Justice of New York administered the oath in the form the resolution had prescribed.[51]

So far, so good; if the constitutional provision was to take effect, someone had to figure out the details of its implementation, and it made sense to conclude that the bodies to whose officers the requirement applied had implicit authority to do so—especially in light of the general rulemaking authority given to each House by Article I, § 5. At the same time it prescribed the form of the oath by resolution, however, the House appointed a committee to draft legislation on the same subject.[52]

---

[46]Lemon v Kurtzman, 403 US 602, 612–13 (1971).

[47]See, e.g., Engel v Vitale, 370 US 421 (1962) (state cannot compose prayers to be read aloud in public schools); Meek v Pittenger, 421 US 349 (1975) (state cannot provide educational equipment other than books to parochial schools). See also David P. Currie, The Constitution in the Supreme Court: The Second Century, 1888–1986 411, 531 (Chicago, 1990) [hereafter cited as The Second Century].

[48]1 Annals at 92. For President Washington's resulting proclamation see James D. Richardson, 1 A Compilation of the Messages and Papers of the Presidents 64 (US Congress, 1900) [hereafter cited as Richardson].

[49]Contrast US Const, Art II, § 1, which spells out the precise terms of the oath required of the President "[b]efore he enter on the execution of his office." This oath was administered to Washington by the Chancellor of New York before a joint session of Congress in the Senate Chamber. 1 Annals at 26–27. None of the latter details was prescribed by Article II.

[50]1 Annals at 101.

[51]Id at 106.

[52]Id at 101.

Insofar as legislators and legislative employees were concerned, such a statute could be explained as necessary and proper to the exercise of congressional powers, since neither members nor staff could function without taking the oath. Nor could there have been any constitutional objection to regulating the oath that Article VI required of federal executive and judicial officers, as the bill also did as it emerged from the House[53]—for the necessary and proper clause empowered Congress to enact legislation carrying into effect not only its own powers but also those vested in any other federal officer or department, and the regulation was as necessary for other officials as for members of Congress themselves.

The difficulty arose when the Senate amended the bill to prescribe the details of the oath to be taken by *state* officers, who were also subject to the requirement of Article VI. It was Elbridge Gerry of Massachusetts who raised the constitutional objection when the bill returned to the House, and it was a good one.[54] No clause of the Constitution, he argued, gave Congress authority to regulate the oath to be taken by state officers. It was therefore up to the states themselves to do so, and if they did not federal judges would annul their acts for want of constitutional authority to adopt them.[55]

John Laurance of New York replied that Congress had power to make "all laws necessary or proper to carry the declarations of the constitution into effect" and thus to implement Article VI,[56] but he was mistaken. As Gerry had already noted, Article I spoke only of laws needed to carry out the powers vested in some federal body.[57] New Jersey's Elias Boudinot had a better justification:

> The constitution said only that the officers of Government should be bound
> by oath, leaving to Congress to say what oath. In short it was the duty of
> the House . . . to detail the general principles laid down in the constitution,
> and reduce them to practice.[58]

In other words, Article VI itself implicitly authorized Congress to implement its provisions.

This was not a necessary conclusion. The principle that had justified the House in prescribing the form of the oath for its own personnel would have justified the states in doing the same for theirs. Indeed Article IV's explicit provision authorizing Congress to effectuate the full faith and credit clause[59] arguably strengthens the inference that when the Framers wanted Congress to implement constitutional provisions they said so. On the other hand, as Chief Justice Marshall would later tell us, the last thing the necessary and

---

[53]See 6 Doc Hist at 1611–13.

[54]Maclay, joined by Ellsworth, had made similar arguments in the Senate, and Madison expressed doubts in the House. See 9 Doc Hist at 9–10, 22–23; 10 Doc Hist at 270–71.

[55]1 Annals at 277–78. Gerry seemed to think this outcome ordained by the fact that the judges themselves were "bound to support the constitution." Id at 278. This was not only one of the earliest congressional affirmations of judicial review of both executive and legislative state action, but its rationale was broad enough to embrace federal action as well. Furthermore, its bottom line was surprisingly draconian; the Supreme Court never invalidated the acts of state legislatures on the ground that they had been unconstitutionally apportioned.

[56]1 Annals at 280.

[57]Id at 277.

[58]Id at 282.

[59]US Const, Art IV, § 1.

proper clause was meant to do was to limit the authority implicit in other constitutional provisions.[60] Like the sweeping clause itself, the power to flesh out full faith and credit may have been inserted out of an abundance of caution.

In any event, the statute as enacted regulated the oath to be taken by state as well as federal officers.[61] Four years later this action served as precedent for the far more significant Fugitive Slave Act,[62] which implemented a clause of Article IV that was as silent with respect to congressional authority as the oath provision of Article VI. It was in the emotionally charged context of fugitive slaves that the Supreme Court would ultimately accept Boudinot's argument of implied authority in the great case of *Prigg v. Pennsylvania*.[63]

E.   Instructions

From the beginning, members of the House were elected by the people themselves.[64] Members of the Senate, on the other hand, were chosen by state legislatures,[65] and it soon was suggested that they were mere agents subject to the instructions of those who had sent them. Maclay recorded in 1790 that South Carolina had instructed its Senators how to vote on the assumption of state debts, and he published an article urging other legislatures to follow this example.[66] The next year, when Virginia Senators relied on legislative instructions in moving once again to open Senate proceedings to the public, Ellsworth, Morris, and South Carolina's Ralph Izard protested.[67] The States had no more power to instruct Senators, Izard insisted, than electors had to instruct the President of the United States.[68]

Additional light was cast on this problem when South Carolina Representative

---

[60]McCulloch v Maryland, 17 US 316, 420 (1819).

[61]1 Stat 23 (June 1, 1789).

[62]1 Stat at 302 (Feb 12, 1793).

[63]41 US 539 (1842); see also David P. Currie, The Constitution in the Supreme Court: The First Hundred Years, 1789–1888 241–46 (Chicago, 1985) [hereafter cited as The First Hundred Years]. Although the issue was not explicitly debated, the oath controversy was also a precedent of sorts for a second constitutional problem raised by the 1793 statute providing for the return of fugitives. For the later statute expressly imposed duties on state officers to apprehend and return fugitives. By directing state officers to take a particular oath, the earlier law appeared to reflect the conviction that there was no barrier to its imposing duties on state officers if the regulation was otherwise within congressional power. Many years later the Supreme Court would find the imposition of such duties an infringement of implicit state sovereignty by analogy to the immunity principle of McCulloch v Maryland, 17 US 316 (1819). See Kentucky v Dennison, 65 US 66 (1860); The First Hundred Years at 245–47. More recently, with the fading of implicit immunities of all kinds, the Court has changed its mind. Puerto Rico v Branstad, 483 US 219, 230 (1987) (expressly overruling *Dennison*).

[64]US Const, Art I, § 2.

[65]Id, § 3.

[66]9 Doc Hist at 199, 219 (adding that reducing Senators to puppets might be a lesser evil than state defiance of laws passed contrary to state instructions). Several states did as Maclay advised. North Carolina's first Senators, however, defied their instructions on the ground that they were independent once elected, and Maclay's own legislature refused even to express opinions on issues pending before the Senate on the ground that state assemblies had no part to play in federal legislation. See Swanstrom at 162–71. In the House both Madison and William Smith of South Carolina indicated they understood Senators to be subject to state instructions. 2 Annals at 1904, 1913.

[67]9 Doc Hist at 388–89.

[68]Id at 388.

Thomas Tucker proposed a constitutional amendment guaranteeing the *people* the right "to instruct their Representatives."[69] Various speakers adverted with considerable force to the logistical difficulties involved in determining the sense of the people on particular issues. Others raised the more fundamental objection that binding instructions were inconsistent with the very idea of a deliberative body, and the proposal was roundly defeated.[70]

There is less difficulty, of course, in ascertaining the views of a state legislature than those of the population at large. Moreover, there are countries in which federal legislative issues are effectively debated and passed upon by bodies whose members are directly responsible to constituent states[71]—as members of Congress were under the Articles of Confederation.[72] Thus it was entirely plausible to argue that state election of Senators had been designed to preserve the tradition of a state check upon federal action[73]—even though the significant provision of the Articles permitting the states to recall their delegates[74] had been conspicuously omitted from the new Constitution.

The issue of state instructions to Senators was therefore both difficult and of transcendent importance. For better or worse, the question was never definitively resolved. It simmered for more than a century, only to be mooted in 1913 by the seventeenth amendment's provision that Senators too should be elected directly "by the people"[75]—a revision that was prompted by the desire for greater democracy but that profoundly altered the balance of power in our federal system.

F. Qualifications

"Each House," says Article I, § 5, "shall be the judge of the elections, returns and qualifications of its own members." Later events have confirmed that this clause poses a risk of arbitrary action against individual legislators,[76] but like the immunity provisions of the following section[77] it serves to guarantee the independence of Congress as a whole. Before

---

[69]1 Annals at 761. South Carolina's House of Representatives had attempted to instruct the state's representatives as well as its Senators to support federal assumption of state debts. Smith reported that Tucker, while willing to vote in accordance with the legislature's request, denied its right to bind him. See Letter of William L. Smith to Edward Rutledge, March 2, 1790, in Rogers, The Letters of William Loughton Smith (cited in note 33), 69 SC Hist Mag at 111. The resolution of the South Carolina House appears in id at 105 n 18.

[70]1 Annals at 761–76. The vote against Tucker's amendment was 41–10. Id at 776.

[71]See, e.g., Articles 50–51 of the Basic Law of the Federal Republic of Germany, under which a body composed of state executive officers plays a significant role in the enactment and enforcement of federal laws. For more details see David P. Currie, The Constitution of the Federal Republic of Germany 61–66 (Chicago, 1994).

[72]See Articles of Confederation, Art V, § 1: "[A] power [is] reserved to each state, to recall its delegates, or any of them, at any time within the year, and to send others in their stead, for the remainder of the year."

[73]See Swanstrom at 160–61. Both Rufus King and John Jay had affirmed the state legislatures' right to instruct Senators during the state ratifying conventions. See Jonathan Elliot, 2 The Debates in the Several State Conventions on the Adoption of the Federal Constitution 47, 283 (2d ed 1836) [hereafter cited as Elliot's Debates].

[74]See note 72.

[75]For an excellent discussion of this issue see Swanstrom at 154–72.

[76]See Powell v McCormack, 395 US 486 (1969) (giving the clause a narrow interpretation to minimize this danger).

[77]See US Const, Art I, § 6 (limited freedom from arrest and immunity for "any speech or debate in either House").

it had sat for a month, the House of Representatives was called upon to act under this provision.[78]

William Smith, elected as a Representative from South Carolina, had been born there before the Revolution. Having gone abroad to study, he was prevented by the war from returning until 1783. It was argued that when elected to the House in 1788 he had not been "seven years a citizen of the United States," as Article I, § 2 required.

The issue of who was a citizen of the United States was later to divide both the Supreme Court and the country,[79] and the Constitution did not define the term.[80] The members who spoke expressed a variety of views. Smith himself argued that South Carolina law made him a United States citizen,[81] and Richard Bland Lee of Virginia agreed.[82] James Jackson of Georgia, concerned lest the children of Tory loyalists be held citizens, refused to vote without proof that Smith had left South Carolina with the blessing of the state.[83]

Madison, as usual, was the most interesting. State law was determinative, he argued, to the extent it could be ascertained. When state law did not afford an explicit answer, the House "must be guided by principles of a general nature." Citizenship generally depended upon place of birth, and Smith had been born to South Carolina settlers in South Carolina. When a colony became independent, the allegiance of its citizens was transferred to the new state, wherever they might be; and "[s]o far as we can judge" these general principles were in accord with South Carolina law.[84]

Only one Representative voted to deny Mr. Smith his seat.[85] We do not know how many of his supporters were persuaded by Smith himself and how many by Madison, but the episode gave significant support both to the position that citizenship was based upon birthplace and that at least before 1789 it depended upon state law.

G.   Elections

Representative Smith did not contest the statement of facts in the petition challenging his eligibility,[86] and the House determined his case in plenary session. The very next day,

---

[78]See 1 Annals at 149, 175, 342–43, 412–25. A more complete report of this proceeding appears in M. St. Clair Clarke & David A. Hall, Cases of Contested Elections in Congress 23–37 (Gales & Seaton, 1834) [hereafter cited as Contested Elections].

[79]See Scott v Sandford, 60 US 393 (1857).

[80]The fourteenth amendment has since done so: "All persons born or naturalized in the United States and subject to the jurisdiction thereof, are citizens of the United States and of the State wherein they reside."

[81]1 Annals at 413–18. For a fuller statement of the facts see 10 Doc Hist at 765–72.

[82]1 Annals at 418–19. Smith reported that in private conversation Boudinot had insisted that the question was one of "civil Law" with which state law had nothing to do but that he had abandoned that position on finding "that the House were of a different opinion." See Letter of William L. Smith to Edward Rutledge, June 6, 1789, in Rogers, Letters of William Loughton Smith (cited in note 33), 69 SC Hist Mag at 3.

[83]1 Annals at 423–24.

[84]Id at 420–23.

[85]See id at 425. The dissenter was Jonathan Grout of Massachusetts, who apparently said nothing on this issue in debate—as he generally did on other issues as well. Cf David P. Currie, The Most Insignificant Justice: A Preliminary Inquiry, 50 U Chi L Rev 466 (1983).

[86]See 1 Annals at 413. Nevertheless both Laurance and Boudinot argued the case should be sent back to committee for further sifting of the evidence, in order to avoid burdening the House as a whole. See 10 Doc

however, when the entire New Jersey delegation was challenged on the basis of alleged irregularities in election procedure, a committee was appointed to take evidence and "report to the House all such facts as shall arise from the proofs and allegations of the respective parties."[87]

The committee in turn reported that it could not complete its task without the testimony of absent witnesses and that some of the petitioners had asked to be heard by counsel.[88] Various members spoke on each side of the counsel question without detailing their reasons, and the request was ultimately withdrawn.[89]

More basic was the question of what to do about witnesses. Fisher Ames of Massachusetts urged that judges of the New Jersey state courts be commissioned to take evidence on behalf of the House in order to avoid the inconvenience of bringing the witnesses to New York.[90] Boudinot, who was one of the challenged members, argued that this procedure would effectively deprive other parties of the right of cross-examination and require decision on a cold record.[91] New Hampshire's Samuel Livermore contended that the clause making the House "judge" of its members' elections required it to hear all the evidence itself.[92] Laurance, on the other hand, argued that the power to judge implied authority to "determine in what manner the investigation of such a subject shall be prosecuted."[93]

After this discussion, the reporter observes, it grew late, and the House adjourned.[94] The next entry, over a month later, informs us of a second committee report making certain findings of fact.[95] After considering this report, and after hearing speeches by Smith and Laurance for and against the validity of the election, the House determined that the challenged Representatives had been duly elected.[96]

The controversy over the New Jersey representatives thus raised a number of interesting constitutional questions regarding election contests—from the power to delegate responsibility and to gather evidence to the authority to co-opt state officers and the rights of parties to cross-examination and counsel. The sketchy record makes it difficult to say

---

Hist at 764–65; Contested Elections at 24–25.

[87] 1 Annals at 425. This case is reported in Contested Elections at 38–44. For the facts underlying the challenge see George A. Boyd, Elias Boudinot: Patriot and Statesman 1740–1821 154–55 (Princeton, 1952).

[88] 1 Annals at 663.

[89] Id at 663–67. See, e.g., id at 667: "Mr. Page . . . said, if the jurisdiction of the House was questioned, the parties had an indubitable right to be heard by counsel, and he hoped no gentleman would refuse the people of the United States a privilege of this important nature, which had always been enjoyed by the subjects of Great Britain." He did not say he found this right anywhere in the Constitution, but he did not seem to consider it a matter of legislative grace.

[90] Id at 664–65.

[91] Id at 664.

[92] Id at 666–67. Livermore and Thatcher had made the same argument in opposing recommitment of the challenge to Representative Smith. See 10 Doc Hist at 765; Contested Elections at 24–25.

[93] 1 Annals at 665. Lee argued that "the whole business" should be left to a committee in accordance with the practice of the British House of Commons because "the example of so old and so experienced a legislative body could be followed with safety and propriety." Id at 666.

[94] Id at 667.

[95] Id at 785–86.

[96] Id at 866–67; see 11 Doc Hist at 1394–99.

whether the House resolved any of these questions beyond concluding that it could employ a committee to report on the facts, but there was much force to Laurance's observation that, even apart from the House's express authority to adopt rules to govern its proceedings, a good deal of discretion in how to find facts was implicit in the provision making each House the judge of its members' elections.

H. Enumeration

The New Jersey controversy concerned only the manner of investigation; the Constitution left no doubt that House elections were an appropriate subject for House inquiry. A more basic question regarding the extent of congressional authority to acquire information arose when Congress turned to implementing the command of Article I, § 2 that a census be taken within three years after its first meeting.

In contrast to the oath requirement of Article VI, the census provision explicitly provided for congressional implementation: The enumeration was to be made "in such manner as [Congress] shall by law direct." The interesting question was the permissible scope of the information that was to be obtained.

The purpose of the enumeration, according to Article I, was to provide the basis for apportioning both congressional seats and direct taxes among the states "according to their respective numbers." Those numbers, the Constitution further provided, were to be determined by counting the number of "free persons," excluding "Indians not taxed," and adding "three fifths of all other persons"—that is, of the slaves.[97] As enacted, however, the census bill required that the population be further broken down by sex and by age—although neither of these characteristics was relevant to the purposes for which the Constitution required the enumeration to be made.[98] Indeed, at one point the bill had been even broader, requiring the census-takers to classify the population by occupation as well.[99] This requirement was later deleted, but both the earlier version and the statute itself raised the question whether Congress was not seeking more information than it had any right to demand.

It was the ubiquitous Madison who had promoted the idea of a census of occupations, and he had waxed enthusiastic over the utility of the information it would produce.[100] Several members objected, arguing among other things that the inquiry would serve no legitimate purpose and might lead the public to suspect ulterior congressional designs.[101]

Commendably, Madison made no effort to defend his additional questions on the basis of the census provision. His position was that knowledge of individual occupations would be useful to Congress in devising later substantive legislation:

---

[97]US Const, Art I, § 2. See also id, § 9: "No capitation, or other direct, tax shall be laid, unless in proportion to the census or enumeration herein before directed to be taken."

[98]1 Stat 101, § 1 (Mar 1, 1790).

[99]See 1 Annals at 1145–47.

[100]See id at 1115, 1145–46.

[101]See id at 1145–47 (Remarks of Reps. Livermore and Page); New York Daily Gazette, Jan 28, 1790 (Rep. White).

> I take it, sir, that in order to accommodate our laws to the real situation of
> our constituents, we ought to be acquainted with that situation. . . . If gen-
> tlemen have any doubts with respect to [the] utility [of this information], I
> cannot satisfy them in a better manner, than by referring them to the debates
> which took place on the bills intended collaterally to benefit the agricul-
> tural, commercial, and manufacturing parts of the community. Did they not
> wish then to know the relative proportion of each, and the exact number of
> every division, in order that they might rest their arguments on facts, in-
> stead of assertions and conjectures? Will any gentleman pretend to doubt
> but our regulations would have been better accommodated to the real state
> of society than they are?[102]

In short, the information that went beyond what was required for the apportionment of
representatives and taxes was necessary and proper to the informed enactment of legislation on various subjects within the express authority of Congress.

Similar arguments were later to support a broad power of congressional investigation.[103] The inclusion of questions concerning age and sex in the original census suggests
that Congress was already persuaded by the essence of Madison's position.[104]

I.   Investigation

Another question of the extent of congressional powers of inquiry arose soon after the
enumeration controversy when Senator Robert Morris of Pennsylvania asked that commissioners be appointed to investigate his own conduct as Superintendent of Finance under the Confederation.[105] The Senate sidestepped the constitutional problem by passing a
resolution requesting the President to appoint commissioners for the purpose.[106] In the
House, however, Connecticut's Roger Sherman provoked a minor storm by moving to
refer the investigation to a committee of five members of Congress.[107]

Gerry at once protested on constitutional grounds. Unlike the Confederation
Congress, he argued, the new House had only legislative powers; short of impeachment,
supervision of executive conduct was an executive matter entrusted exclusively to the

---

[102]1 Annals at 1146. See also id at 1115.

[103]McGrain v Daugherty, 273 US 135 (1927); The Second Century at 198.

[104]Madison did suggest that Congress ought not to inquire as to persons "who are employed in teaching
and inculcating the duties of religion" because "the General Government is proscribed from interfering, in
any manner whatever, in matters respecting religion; and it may be thought to do this, in ascertaining who
[are], and who are not ministers of the Gospel." 1 Annals at 1146. Not only does this passage reflect a healthy
recognition that the power of investigation was limited to matters of legitimate legislative concern; it also suggests a rather strict notion of what it meant to pass laws "respecting an establishment of religion, or prohibiting
the free exercise thereof." US Const, Amend I.

[105]See 1 Annals at 1168; 2 Annals at 2168–70.

[106]See 1 Annals at 1233. Maclay thought the whole business a sleazy effort by Morris to divert attention
from his personal financial difficulties by focusing on his unchallenged public accounts, but he raised no
constitutional objections to this procedure. See 9 Doc Hist at 199.

[107]2 Annals at 1514.

President.[108] Madison replied that the House had the right to "possess itself of the fullest information in order to doing justice to the country and to public officers," and the committee was appointed.[109] Thus within a year of its first meeting, in the face of an explicit constitutional challenge, the House of Representatives flatly asserted a broad power to investigate the conduct of a former executive in order to do "justice" to the officer and to the country as a whole.

No such authority, of course, was expressly given to either House. It had been easy enough to find authority to gather relevant information implicit in the powers to legislate and to resolve election disputes, and Gerry's argument reminds us that it was fairly implicit in the impeachment power too.[110] But neither Madison nor anyone else suggested that the investigation of Morris was relevant to an election contest, to an impeachment, or to any prospective legislation,[111] although the last argument could easily have been made.[112] Many years later the Supreme Court would convincingly conclude that "doing justice" was not enough to justify congressional inquiry; investigations designed simply to determine the existence of past wrongdoing were not ancillary to any legitimate congressional function.[113]

II.   THE SPECIAL ROLE OF THE SENATE

Apart from impeachment, the functions of the House of Representatives were restricted to those incident to legislation and to the quasi-legislative process of constitutional amendment. The Senate, on the other hand, was given a role to play in two important functions otherwise entrusted to the executive: the appointment of officers and the making of treaties. For Article II, § 2 empowered the President to make both appointments and treaties "by and with the advice and consent of the Senate"—requiring a two-thirds majority in the latter case.[114]

On May 25, 1789, as the reporter informs us, the Senate "for the first time, entered upon executive business" as it acknowledged the receipt of a communication from President Washington enclosing two Indian treaties concluded at Fort Harmar in January

[108]Id at 1515.

[109]See id at 1514–15. The Committee's report, filed nearly a year later, see id at 2017, recited that it was "impossible" to examine Morris's accounts in detail, enclosed copies of relevant documents for the members to peruse, and refrained from any commentary on the propriety of the conduct it had been appointed to explore. 13 Madison Papers at 392–93.

[110]See US Const, Art I, § 2: "The House of Representatives . . . shall have the sole power of impeachment."

[111]No impeachment inquiry had been instituted, and the likelihood of any such proceeding was reduced by the fact that Morris was no longer in office. Nor was there any suggestion that integrity was a qualification for election to the Senate or that Morris's conduct justified his expulsion under Article I, § 5.

[112]An understanding of past practices might well have led to new regulations designed to protect against the future abuse of authority. See Philip B. Kurland, Watergate and the Constitution 20–23 (Chicago, 1978).

[113]Kilbourn v Thompson, 103 US 168 (1881); The First Hundred Years at 436–38.

[114]Recognizing the distinct nature of these functions, the Senate kept its records of appointment and treaty matters in a separate Executive Journal, and executive matters were excluded from the 1794 resolution otherwise admitting the public to Senate deliberations, apparently on grounds of confidentiality. See 1 Annals at 15.

and an explanatory statement by Secretary of War Henry Knox.[115] A few weeks later, after what seems to have been a prolonged examination of the "fitness" of the nominee, the Senate consented to the appointment of William Short as chargé d'affaires in France during the absence of the Minister, Thomas Jefferson.[116]

Having thus moistened their toes, the President and the Senate rolled up their cuffs and waded into the task of defining their respective roles with respect to executive affairs.[117]

A.   The French Consular Convention

On July 21 the Senate requested John Jay, who as Secretary of Foreign Affairs under the Confederation was still in office, to appear and inform the Senators about a consular agreement that Jefferson had concluded with France in November, 1788.[118] The Secretary appeared and argued that the treaty should be approved.[119] The Senators agreed, unanimously resolving "[t]hat the Senate do consent to the said convention, and advise the President of the United States to ratify the same."[120]

This episode passed without recorded friction, but it set several interesting precedents. First, like the Indian treaties that still lay on the table, the consular agreement had been concluded before the first meeting of the new Congress; both the President and the Senate assumed that the advice and consent provision nevertheless applied. Second, the Senate explicitly gave advice as well as consent, imparting not only its own imprimatur but also an unequivocal suggestion as to how the President should exercise his authority to perform the distinct act of final ratification. The form of the resolution thus illustrates both the imprecision of the common reference to Senate "ratification" of treaties and the original understanding that the President retained discretion to withhold ratification after the Senate had given its consent.[121]

Finally, the consular incident demonstrates that the Senate understandably interpreted its treaty responsibilities to give it implicit power to acquire the information needed for their intelligent exercise and to confer in person with executive officers in order to obtain it.[122] Indeed, although the order respecting Jay's appearance was cautiously

---

[115]See id at 40–42. Knox, who had not yet been appointed Secretary of War under the new Constitution, was serving in that capacity by virtue of an appointment by the Confederation Congress. He was renominated September 11, 1789 and confirmed the next day. Id at 80, 81.

[116]See 2 Doc Hist at 8–9; 1 Annals at 47. Jefferson's aim was to spend a short time at home for rest and recreation. On September 26 he was nominated to be Secretary of State, and the Senate immediately consented to his appointment. Id at 93.

[117]"Before its final adjournment was reached, the twilight zone in which lie the Senate's so-called executive powers had been rather thoroughly explored and tentatively charted." 1 Haynes at 77.

[118]1 Annals at 52. The treaty itself appears at 8 Stat 106.

[119]1 Annals at 54–55.

[120]Id at 55.

[121]See Quincy Wright, The Control of American Foreign Relations 254 (MacMillan, 1922); 2 Haynes at 637–39; Joseph Story, 3 Commentaries on the Constitution of the United States § 1517 (Brown, Shattuck & Co., 1833) [hereafter cited as Story].

[122]"This direct and personal intercourse between the executive and the Senate is an indication of the feeling which seems to have been prevalent that the latter really was a council of advice upon treaties and appointments—a council which expected to discuss these matters directly with the other branch of govern-

phrased as a "request[]," the cruder terms employed a few days earlier in "order[ing]" that the Secretary furnish copies of relevant documents and report on the accuracy of a translation appeared to assert the additional right to employ compulsory process against a high executive official. Nevertheless the failure of either Jay or Washington to raise any objection based upon executive privilege cannot be taken to concede this important principle, since the President had directed the Secretary in advance to provide "whatever official Papers and information on the subject" the Senate might require.[123]

B. The Fishbourn Affair

A real ruckus erupted a few days later, however, when the Senate without recorded explanation rejected the nomination of Benjamin Fishbourn for the position of naval officer for the port of Savannah under the tariff law.[124] Washington went up in flames:

> Whatever may have been the reasons which induced your dissent, I am persuaded they were such as you deemed sufficient. Permit me to submit to your consideration whether, on occasions where the propriety of nominations appear [sic] questionable to you, it would not be expedient to communicate that circumstance to me, and thereby avail yourselves of the information which led me to make them, and which I would with pleasure lay before you.[125]

While bowing to the Senate's decision by nominating a substitute, the President went on to extol the virtues of his vanquished champion in an effort "to show that such a mode of proceeding" as he was suggesting "might be useful."[126]

Equally aware of the need for improved procedure, the Senate without waiting for Washington's reaction had appointed a committee to confer with him "on the mode of communication proper to be pursued between him and the Senate" in appointment and treaty matters, and a motion had been introduced to declare it "the opinion of the Senate that their advice, and consent to the appointment of Officers should be given in the presence of the President."[127] Making clear his own preference for written communications with respect to appointments lest his presence inhibit free discussion by the Senate, Washington told the committee he favored a flexible arrangement permitting com-

---

ment." Ralston Hayden, The Senate and Treaties, 1789–1817 6 (MacMillan, 1920).

[123]See Senate Executive Journal, 2 Doc Hist at 6–10.

[124]1 Annals at 60; 2 Doc Hist at 23–24. Fishbourn was one of 102 individuals nominated at the same time for various customs offices and the only one to be rejected. See id at 13–23; 1 Annals at 56–57, 61–62.

[125]Id at 61.

[126]Id at 61. To hear the President tell it, Fishbourn was highly qualified, having served his state as legislator, executive councillor, militia officer, and customs agent after fighting bravely under Washington himself during the Revolution. On the hypothesis that the nominee had somehow aroused the enmity of one or both of Georgia's own Senators, the episode has been cited as the first instance of the questionable practice that came to be known as senatorial courtesy; but there appears to be little evidence to support the hypothesis. See, e.g., 1 Haynes at 54; 2 id at 736–37 (repeating the suggestion); James Hart, The American Presidency in Action 1789 123–25 (MacMillan, 1948) (questioning it); Swanstrom at 102–03 (summarizing the debate). The nomination of Fishbourn's replacement was confirmed on the day it was received. See 1 Annals at 62.

[127]2 Doc Hist at 24.

munications in a variety of forms and forums as circumstances might require.[128]

On the strength of these consultations the Senate adopted a resolution expressly contemplating both written nominations and meetings with the President at any place he might select. If the President chose to come to the Senate Chamber, he would sit in the Vice-President's chair; but the Vice-President would still "be considered as at the head of the Senate" and most significantly would put all the questions, "either in the presence or absence of the President of the United States."[129] Thus once again the Senators insisted on asserting their independence: If the President elected to seek their advice in person, they were determined not to lose control of the proceeding.

C.   The Southern Indians

President Washington never took advantage of the opportunity to submit nominations in person,[130] but on the very day the resolution was adopted he peremptorily informed the Senators that he would meet them in their chamber at 11:30 the next morning "to advise with them on the Terms of the Treaty to be negotiated with the Southern Indians."[131] He appeared as scheduled with Secretary Knox in tow and laid before the Senate a detailed written statement of facts and questions in which he solicited the Senate's advice on what position to take in the coming negotiations.[132]

This intricate document was read aloud twice over the din of passing carriages,[133] and then Vice-President Adams began to ask for yes or no answers to the questions the President had posed. Maclay rose to object: "The business is new to the Senate, it is of importance, it is our duty to inform ourselves as well as possible on the subject." When he moved to refer the questions to a committee for that purpose, Washington "started up in a Violent fret" and remonstrated that "[t]his defeats every purpose of my coming here." Ultimately he agreed to postpone the remaining consultation until the following Monday, when after debating the merits of each question in Washington's presence the Senate gave him the requested advice.[134]

This famous confrontation resolved three critical questions regarding the Senate's authority with respect to treaties. First, both the President and the Senate plainly interpreted the power to advise and consent to include not merely approval of the finished product but also discussion in advance of the course of action to be pursued. The same understanding was evident the following year, when Washington asked the Senate what

---

[128]See id at 29; 30 Washington Writings at 373–79.

[129]See 1 Annals at 66–67; 2 Doc Hist at 29–30.

[130]See Swanstrom at 98.

[131]1 Annals at 67; 2 Doc Hist at 30. The President had already suggested the creation of a commission to negotiate with the Southern Indians, 1 Annals at 60; a statute had been passed to provide for its expenses, 1 Stat 54 (Aug 20, 1789); and the Senate had consented to the appointment of the three commissioners, 1 Annals at 66–67.

[132]Id at 67–71; 2 Doc Hist at 31–34.

[133]"I could tell it was something about indians," Maclay wrote after the first reading, "but was not master of one Sentence of it." 9 Doc Hist at 128.

[134]See id at 128–32.

he should do to resolve differences with Great Britain over our northeastern boundary and was advised if negotiation failed to propose that the matter be submitted to arbitration.[135] Thus the original understanding seems to have been that, at least with regard to treaties, the Senate would function as a true advisory council, not simply as a check on the arbitrary exercise of power.[136] Indeed in the waning days of the First Congress the President went so far as to ask and the Senate to give advice as to the *meaning* of an existing treaty, although this service scarcely seemed to have been embraced within the authority to advise and consent with respect to the making of treaties.[137]

It is noteworthy that no comparable practice emerged with regard to appointments; from the outset the President simply submitted the names and the Senate voted yes or no.[138] It has been suggested with some force that the text of Article II supported this discrepancy by making clear that it was the President alone who was to "nominate" officers; only their actual appointment required Senate participation.[139] On the other side it may be argued that this interpretation gives little effect to the explicit requirement that here as in the case of treaties the Senate provide the President not only with consent but with advice as well.

Second, as seemed to follow from their shared conception of the Senate's role as an

[135] 1 Annals at 980, 994. See also id at 1063–64, where the President asked and received permission to add a secret article respecting trade to the treaty with the Creeks that was in the process of negotiation pursuant to earlier Senate advice; id at 1072–73, where he asked the Senate whether to enforce the existing treaty with the Cherokees or negotiate a new one and was advised to do whichever "the tranquillity and interest of the United States may require."

[136] See Swanstrom at 93; Louis Henkin, Constitutionalism, Democracy, and Foreign Affairs 49–50 (Columbia, 1990). This is not to suggest that the special advisory function of the Senate raised any question as to the constitutionality of Washington's well–known practice of seeking advice on a variety of matters from Representative James Madison and others in addition to the Senate and the heads of departments whose opinions Article II expressly empowered him to obtain. See Swanstrom at 93–95; James Thomas Flexner, George Washington and the New Nation 1783–1793 214 (Little Brown, 1970); Ralph Ketcham, James Madison, A Biography 286–87, 315–17, 319–21 (MacMillan, 1971) (noting that during the first session of Congress, before department heads were appointed, Madison was in essence Washington's "aide, grand vizier, and prime minister"). The Justices of the Supreme Court were soon to invoke the Article II provision in support of their refusal to advise the President on abstract legal questions (see chapter 4), but it seems unlikely that the clauses giving the Senate and the Cabinet particular rights and duties in this regard were meant to deprive the President of the obvious benefits of talking to anyone else.

[137] 2 Annals at 1814–15. In early 1791, responding to a presidential message asking Congress to do "what to you shall seem most expedient" about "citizens of the United States in captivity at Algiers" (id at 1783), the Senate resolved to "advise and consent that the President . . . take such measures as he may think necessary for the redemption" of the captives "provided the expense shall not exceed forty thousand dollars." Id at 1795–96. Necessary "measures" to secure the release of prisoners might of course have included a treaty, but the Senate's approval was not so limited; this resolution too suggests the Senate may have shared Representative Sherman's expansive view that Article II required Senate participation "in every transaction which respects the business of negotiation with foreign powers." 1 Annals at 1122. For further discussion of the Algerian pirates see chapter 2.

[138] See the discussion of the Short and Fishbourn nominations, text at notes 116, 124–29. Madison, Jefferson, and Jay all advised Washington not to consult the Senate before making nominations. See John Fitzpatrick, 4 The Diaries of George Washington, 1748–1799, 122 (Houghton Mifflin, 1925) [hereafter cited as Washington Diaries] (Apr 27, 1790).

[139] Swanstrom at 113. See also Jacob E. Cooke, ed, The Federalist No 76 (Hamilton) (Wesleyan, 1961) [hereafter cited as The Federalist]: "In the act of nomination his judgment alone would be exercised."

advisory council, both parties plainly thought it appropriate for the President to consult with the Senate in person. Even when nothing was wanted beyond simple consent, as the Fishbourn controversy had shown, there was ample room for misunderstanding if the matter was handled entirely in writing; it seemed to go without saying that the flexibility of oral discussion would facilitate the giving of actual advice.

At the same time, however, Washington's method of seeking advice in the case of the Southern Indians posed a patent threat to the independence of the Senate in performing its advisory function. Washington had perceptively called attention to the problem himself when consulted by the Senate committee as to the proper means of communication on treaty and appointment matters.[140] If the Senate was to participate meaningfully in the exercise, it required an opportunity both to study the President's proposals and to discuss them when the President was not around.[141] "I saw no chance of a fair investigation," Maclay had whispered at one point to Morris, "while the President of the U.S. sat there with his Secretary at War, to support his Opinions and over awe the timid and neutral part of the Senate."[142]

In insisting on postponing their answers until they could study the President's inquiries on their own, the Senators assured themselves the autonomy without which they could hardly have performed the checking function contemplated by Article II; and thus the third result of the confrontation over the Southern Indians was to resolve apparently for all time a major issue of the balance of power between the two organs of government. The price of the Senate's victory was high, however, for Washington responded to his procedural defeat by resolving never to ask the Senate for advice in person again.[143]

D.   The Fort Harmar Treaties

When President Washington had presented the Indian treaties concluded at Fort Harmar to the Senate in May, he had not expressly asked for Senate consent. He had asked for advice, however, and Knox's accompanying letter had added that, if "the Senate of the United States should concur in their approbation" of the agreements, "it might be proper that the same should be ratified and published, with a proclamation enjoining an obser-

---

[140]See text at notes 127–28 supra.

[141]See Gerhard Casper, An Essay in Separation of Powers: Some Early Versions and Practices, 30 Wm & Mary L Rev 211, 226–27 (1989).

[142]9 Doc Hist at 130. See also Maclay's additional remarks to his own diary, id at 130–31: "[H]e wishes Us to see with the Eyes and hear with the ears of his Secretary only, the Secretary to advance the Premisses the President to draw Conclusions. and to bear down our deliberations with his personal Authority & Presence, form only will be left for Us—This will not do with Americans."

[143]See Swanstrom at 117–18; 3 Flexner, The New Nation at 216–18 (cited in note 136). It seems a pity that the parties were unable to agree on some means of preserving the advantages of face-to-face consultation while avoiding ignorance and intimidation. One way out might have been for the Senators after discussing the matter both among themselves and with the Chief Executive to vote by secret ballot, as they had done for a brief time on appointments, in order, as Maclay argued, to insulate them from fear of presidential or other reprisal. See 9 Doc Hist at 79–82. The resolution regulating the advice and consent procedure had repudiated that option by requiring the Senators to indicate their position viva voce. See 1 Annals at 67; Swanstrom at 98–99.

vance thereof."[144] On September 8, therefore, the Senate adopted a resolution advising the President "to execute and enjoin an observance of" one of the two treaties in question.[145]

Finding the suggestion that he "execute" the treaty ambiguous, the President posed a major question of law on which he requested further guidance. Did the Senate mean that he should ratify the agreement, or that he should enforce it without further ado because no ratification was required? "[A]s a check on the mistakes and indiscretions of ministers or commissioners," Washington observed, it had been the practice of nations "not to consider any treaty negotiated and signed by such officers as final and conclusive, until ratified by the sovereign or government from which they derive their powers."[146] He was "inclined to think it would be advisable" to adopt the same practice in dealing with Indian treaties, even though they were made by the chiefs themselves and thus required no ratification from the Indian side, since they were "formed on our part by the agency of subordinate officers." Like the responsible statesman he was, Washington thought it important "that this point should be well considered and settled, so that our national proceedings, in this respect, may become uniform, and be directed by fixed and stable principles."[147]

A Senate committee appointed to draft a reply argued against formal ratification on the ground of precedent: "The signature of treaties with the Indian nations has ever been considered as a full completion thereof," and the Senate's earlier resolution "authorizes the President of the United States to enjoin a due observance thereof."[148] This apparent effort to dispense with Presidential ratification while preserving the Senate's own veto power raised a serious issue of consistency, for if the negotiator's signature made a treaty binding there seemed to be no room for later Senate consent.[149]

Some of the thornier issues raised by this suggestion were avoided when the Senate rejected the committee's report and embraced the President's position by resolving to "advise and consent that the President of the United States ratify the treaty."[150] Implicit both in this resolution and in the committee report was the assumption that agreements

[144] 1 Annals at 42; 2 Washington Papers at 370–73, 391.

[145] 1 Annals at 79. The treaty approved was with the "Wiandot, Delaware, Ottawa, Chippewa, Pattawatima, and Sac Nations" and appears at 7 Stat 28. The second agreement, with five of the Six Nations of the Iroquois, was not approved until the second session out of concern lest it impair New York and Massachusetts claims to certain lands. See 1 Annals at 87; 7 Stat 33.

[146] See William Prescott, 3 The History of the Reign of Ferdinand & Isabella The Catholic 87–91 (Little, Brown, 1838) (tracing this practice to an unfortunate instance in which a Spanish emissary to France during their reign had grievously abused his authority).

[147] 1 Annals at 83. See Casper, 30 Wm & Mary L Rev at 260 (cited in note 141): "Washington . . . has found few matches among later Presidents in the deliberateness with which he worried about what was right for the government as a whole . . . ."

[148] 1 Annals at 84.

[149] Senate authority might have been reconciled with the finality of the negotiator's action if the Senate had given its approval in advance, but that was not what had happened. A requirement of subsequent approval by the Senate but not by the President might have been justified on the ground that only the President had consented in advance, but that was not what the committee said. These explanations assume either that the President could delegate the power to make treaties or that the Senate could give its consent in advance, or both; and both assumptions could be disputed.

[150] 1 Annals at 87.

with Indian tribes were "treaties" requiring Senate approval under Article II. Washington had made the same assumption in asking the Senate for advice about treating with the Southern Indians a few weeks before.[151] Moreover, as Knox's letter on that occasion had indicated, Congress had dealt with Indian nations by treaty throughout the Confederation period.[152] There was nothing in the language of Article II to suggest that either the President's power or that of the Senate was limited to agreements with foreign nations,[153] and there seemed as much reason to require Senate approval in the one case as in the other.

The Fort Harmar controversy thus established that treaties with Indian nations required both Senate consent and presidential ratification.[154] Thenceforth Indian treaties were subject to the same rules as treaties with foreign nations until Congress legislated to forbid the negotiation of further Indian agreements in 1871.[155]

III.   THE EXECUTIVE BRANCH

"The executive power," said Article II simply, "shall be vested in a President of the United States of America." There were detailed provisions for the President's election[156] and a brief description of his powers[157]—some of which, as we have seen, he was to share with the Senate.[158] There were provisions for his removal by an extraordinary Senate majority after impeachment by the House for "high crimes and misdemeanors"[159] and for his replacement in case the office became vacant.[160] Apart from prescribing the exact terms of the oath the President was to take before entering upon his duties,[161] however, Article II

[151]See text at notes 130–43.

[152]The Indian treaties concluded under the Confederation are reported in 7 Stat 13–27.

[153]Contrast US Const, Art I, § 8, cl 3, which expressly distinguishes between commerce with "foreign nations" and with "the Indian tribes," only to equate them again by empowering Congress to regulate both, and Art III, § 2, which distinguishes between foreign states and Indian nations by extending the judicial power to certain controversies involving the former without mentioning the latter. See Cherokee Nation v Georgia, 30 US 1 (1831); The First Hundred Years at 122–25.

[154]"The circumstances in which this decision was reached reveal how both the President and the Senate were feeling their way carefully and thoughtfully in the determination of the technique of treaty-making." Hayden, The Senate and Treaties at 12 (cited in note 122).

[155]16 Stat 544, 566 (March 3, 1871). This prohibition raised interesting constitutional questions of its own, but they belong to a later period.

[156]US Const, Art II, § 1.

[157]Id, §§ 2–3.

[158]See section II of this chapter.

[159]US Const, Art I, §§ 2–3; Art II, § 4. The Constitution did not expressly give the President any immunity from judicial process, as it did members of Congress (Art I, § 6). Nevertheless Maclay records Ellsworth and Adams as having argued privately that apart from impeachment all process against the President was implicitly forbidden because it would "Stop the Whole Machine of Government." When Maclay put the case of murder, the Vice-President replied that the example was unrealistic: In two centuries there had been no instance of murder by a European head of state. This was "very true in a retail way," Maclay noted in his diary; "they generally do these things on the great Scale." 9 Doc Hist at 168.

[160]US Const, Art II, § 1. There were interesting debates in the First Congress over a bill to provide for the exercise of presidential powers in the event that both the President and Vice-President were unable to act, but discussion will be postponed because the statute was not enacted until 1792. See 2 Annals at 1902–05, 1911–18; 1 Stat 239, 240 (Mar 1, 1792); see also chapter 3.

[161]US Const, Art II, § 1.

said very little about how the President was to perform his functions. It also said very little about the officers with whose assistance he was to perform them.[162]

A.   The President's Role in Legislation

President Washington's first official act after taking the oath prescribed by Article II, § 1
was to deliver an inaugural address.[163] One of the most conspicuous features of this speech
was the reticence with which he approached the duty imposed upon him by § 3 of the
same Article to "recommend to [Congress's] consideration such measures as he shall
judge necessary and expedient." Declining to propose "particular measures," he diffi-
dently commended to the legislators the list of their own constitutional powers, noting
specifically that it would be up to them to determine to what extent they should propose
amendments to the Constitution itself under Article V. He justified this passive attitude
by reference to "the circumstances under which I now meet you," by which he seems to
have meant the fact that both he and his auditors had just entered upon their duties.

When Congress assembled for its second session in January 1790, the President
came to address both Houses once again.[164] In fulfillment of his obligation under Article
II, § 3 periodically to "give to the Congress information of the state of the Union," he
congratulated the members on "the present favorable prospects of our public affairs,"
listed some accomplishments of the past months, and went on to identify additional matters deserving of congressional attention. This time he was somewhat more specific in
making recommendations for legislative action, calling attention to such matters as organization of the militia, defense against Indian depredations, and the need for legislation
respecting naturalization, currency, weights and measures, and the promotion of learning.

Even on this occasion, however, he confined himself largely to suggesting areas of
concern rather than particular solutions. Apart from urging Congress to act as the patent
clause expressly contemplated to encourage invention, the closest he came to making a
specific recommendation was to toss out the rather startling possibility of establishing a
national university. Yet this suggestion too was cautiously phrased as merely one of several options "well worthy of a place in the deliberations of the Legislature."[165]

Of course it was possible for Washington to package pointed recommendations in
deferential terms without disguising his own preferences, as he did in urging the third
session of the same Congress to consider "how far, and in what mode," it might be desirable to provide "such encouragements to our own navigation as will render our commerce and agriculture less dependent on foreign bottoms, which may fail us in the very
moments most interesting to both of these great objects."[166] But this fictionalization of

---

[162]For a thorough study of the actual structure and operations of the executive department under
Washington and Adams see Leonard D. White, The Federalists: A Study in Administrative History (Mac-
Millan, 1948) [hereafter cited as White].

[163]1 Annals at 27–29.

[164]Id at 969–71.

[165]Id at 970. See White at 54–56: "His messages went no further than to suggest subjects for consideration, and in no case did they contain any indication concerning the policy which he thought Congress should
pursue. . . . The first Congress went through its first session without any known suggestions from the
President."

[166]2 Annals at 1772. His position seemed no more difficult to discern when in the same speech he asked

deference may have represented the beginnings of a change of heart. For the unfeigned reticence of his initial address seems not to have been attributable solely to the "circumstances" with which he excused his silence on that occasion. With his usual punctiliousness Washington appeared at first to be afraid that concrete presidential proposals might unduly influence an autonomous branch of government.[167]

Fears of excessive executive influence also crept up in Congress. After Washington's second address, for example, Maclay complained to his diary about the "Servile" practice by which the Senate had elected to respond immediately to each suggestion made in a presidential speech:

> It was a Stale ministerial Trick in Britain, to get the Houses of parliament to chime in with the speech, and then consider them as pledged to support any Measure which could be grafted on the Speech. It was the Socratic mode of Argument introduced into politicks, to entrap men into Measures they were not aware of.[168]

Similarly, when the Postmaster General attached a proposed bill to a report submitted to the House of Representatives on behalf of the President, there were vociferous objections to its being read:

> Mr. Fitzsimons thought there was a degree of indelicacy, not to say impropriety, in permitting the Heads of Departments to bring bills before the House. He thought it was sufficient for them to make reports of facts, with their opinions thereon, and leave the rest to the discretion of the Legislature.[169]

Page added that "no bill ought to be read in the House that did not originate with its leave," and the report was referred to a committee for consideration.[170]

The concern for congressional autonomy was legitimate, but it did not justify Washington's initial fastidiousness. In the two instances just cited Congress sensibly responded by sending executive suggestions to committees[171] and by establishing that only

---

the legislators to consider whether there might be room for improvements in the judiciary system that they had just established "and, particularly, whether an uniform process of execution, on sentences issuing from the federal courts, be not desirable throughout all the States." Id. See also 1 Annals at 82 (requesting Congress to give the President authority to call out the militia); id at 975 (transmitting Secretary Knox's plan for organizing the militia; 4 Washington Diaries at 60 (Dec 19, 1789) (noting that he had sent Knox his thoughts on the militia question so that the Secretary could put them "into the form of a Bill").

[167]See Flexner, The New Nation at 221 (cited in note 16); McDonald, Washington at 78; James Hart, The American Presidency in Action 1789, 55–57 (MacMillan, 1948); Swanstrom at 260–62. According to Ralph Ketcham, Washington's original draft of his inaugural address had contained a "detailed legislative program" for Congress's consideration, which Madison omitted in rewriting the address out of a concern for separation of powers. Ralph Ketcham, James Madison, A Biography 277–78 (MacMillan, 1971). As late as February 1792 Washington wrote that "[m]otives of delicacy" had "uniformly restrained" him "from introducing any topick which relates to Legislative matters to members of either house of Congress, lest it should be suspected that he wished to influence the question before it." 31 Washington Writings at 493.

[168]9 Doc Hist at 181.

[169]1 Annals at 1114.

[170]Id.

[171]See id at 1094–95.

members could introduce bills, not by attempting to silence the President.[172] For there was nothing wrong with the President's making recommendations; that was what the Framers, cognizant of his opportunities for perceiving problems and possible solutions, had wisely encouraged him to do.[173] The increasingly assertive tone of Washington's first three addresses suggests that he was gradually coming to accept the significant advisory role that the Constitution envisioned for him in the legislative process.[174]

Apart from authority to convene special sessions of Congress and to resolve disputes between the two Houses as to the time of adjournment,[175] the President's remaining power with respect to legislation was the significant right to veto bills and other actions of both Houses, subject to override by a two-thirds vote in each chamber.[176] Washington vetoed no congressional action during the First Congress, though he seriously considered doing so in one important instance discussed below.[177] Here too, as with his right to propose legislation, he seems to have taken a singularly diffident view of his function, vetoing only two bills in eight years. Some have gone so far as to suggest that he initially

[172]On the other hand, when a provision in the Treasury bill that would have required the Secretary to "digest and report plans for the improvement and management of the revenue, and the support of the public credit" was branded "a dangerous innovation upon the constitutional privilege of this House" that would give him "an undue influence within these walls," it was watered down so that the Secretary would merely "digest and prepare" plans rather than report them—despite the sensible arguments of Benson and others that advice was useful and that nothing in the bill impaired the House's right to make the ultimate decision. Even the opponents of secretarial reports, however, had to concede that the President himself was entitled to make recommendations. See 1 Annals at 616–31; 1 Stat 65, § 2 (Sept 2, 1789); Casper, 30 Wm & Mary L Rev at 227–28 (cited in note 141). For the arguments of Gerry and Tucker that secretarial reports with respect to taxation would offend the Article I, § 7 provision that "all bills for raising revenue shall originate in the House" and the sensible responses of Madison and others see 11 Doc Hist at 1055–73.

[173]See William Rawle, A View of the Constitution of the United States of America 172 (Philip H. Nicklin, 2d ed 1829) [hereafter cited as Rawle].

[174]Moreover, the President's reticence did not seem to be shared by his Treasury Secretary; the plan for payment of revolutionary debts, the whiskey tax, and the national bank were all based upon reports submitted by Hamilton in response to House requests. See chapter 2. "It was not long," wrote Professor Corwin, "before the ever alert suspicion of Jefferson discovered that Hamilton's connection with Congress, whereby 'the whole action of the Legislature was . . . under the direction of the Treasury,' tended definitely to the overthrow of republican institutions." Edward S. Corwin, The President: Office and Powers 265–66 (NYU, 1940). For the more aggressive attitudes of Presidents Theodore Roosevelt, Woodrow Wilson, and Franklin Roosevelt toward the legislative process see id at 267–82; for discussion of the special relationship between the Treasury and Congress see text at notes 89–95.

[175]US Const, Art II, § 3. The latter power, wrote Corwin in 1940, "has never been used," while the former "has been used so often that the word 'extraordinary' in the constitutional clause has taken on a decidedly Pickwickian flavor." Corwin, Office and Powers at 289 (cited in note 174). For discussion of the first special session see chapter 2.

[176]US Const, Art I, § 7.

[177]See chapter 2 (discussing the national bank). Washington's hesitation regarding the bank bill induced him to ask Hamilton a procedural question of constitutional dimension: "To what precise period, by legal interpretation of the constitution, can the president retain [a bill] in his possession before it becomes a Law by the lapse of ten days?" Hamilton responded that the President had "ten days exclusive of that on which the Bill was delivered to you, and sundays," so that a bill presented on Monday might be returned a week from Friday "at any time while Congress are setting" [sic]—a plainly reasonable interpretation of Art I, § 7's provision for return "within ten days (Sundays excepted) after it shall have been presented to him." See Harold C. Styrett & Jacob E. Cooke, eds, 8 The Papers of Alexander Hamilton 134–35 (Columbia, 1965) [hereafter cited as Hamilton Papers]; McDonald, Hamilton at 204.

thought that a veto was appropriate only on constitutional grounds.[178] Neither the text nor the history of the veto provision seemed to support this restrictive interpretation,[179] and if Washington ever embraced it he changed his mind; for he vetoed a bill on pure policy grounds shortly before leaving office in 1797.[180]

Washington's understanding of the veto power was best summarized in a letter he wrote to Edmund Pendleton in 1793:

> You do me no more than justice when you suppose that from motives of respect to the Legislature (and I might add from my interpretation of the Constitution) I give my Signature to many Bills with which my Judgment is at variance. . . . From the nature of the Constitution, I must approve all the parts of a Bill, or reject it in toto. To do the latter can only be Justified upon the clear and obvious ground of propriety; and I never had such confidence in my own faculty of judging as to be over tenacious of the opinions I may have imbibed in doubtful cases.[181]

Not only does this passage reveal Washington's perception that in authorizing the President either to sign or return each "bill" the Constitution clearly excluded any possibility of an item veto. It also displays a degree of personal and institutional modesty far exceeding that of many of his successors who had so much more to be modest about.

B.   Emoluments and Titles

Article II, § 1 provided that the President should "receive for his services, a compensation, which shall neither be increased nor diminished during the period for which he shall have been elected," and that he should "not receive within that period any other emolu-

---

[178]See McDonald, Washington at 77 (stating flatly that this was Washington's view); Flexner, The New Nation at 281 (cited in note 136) (saying only that the President believed "a major function" of the veto was "to protect the Constitution"). Washington's first veto was of a 1792 bill apportioning congressional seats in a manner he thought contrary to the criteria laid down in Art 1, § 2. 1 Richardson at 124; see the discussion of this controversy in chapter 3. As early as 1789, however, he had asked Madison whether if Congress passed a bill equating Senate and House salaries he ought to return it—on the policy ground that he thought "there ought to be a difference in the wages of the members of the two branches of the Legislature." See 30 Writings of Washington at 394. Significantly, none of Washington's advisers seems to have doubted that the President *could* veto a bill on constitutional grounds, despite the widespread assumption that the courts could also review its constitutionality.

[179]See The Federalist No 73 (Hamilton), defending the President's veto not only as a check on encroachment upon executive prerogatives but also as a safeguard for the community "against the enaction of improper laws." But see Charles L. Black, Jr., Some Thoughts on the Veto, 40 L & Contemp Probs 87, 89–90 (1976), stressing the first half of Hamilton's argument in asserting an "original understanding that the veto would be used only rarely, and certainly not as a means of systematic policy control over the legislative branch . . . ." In England, where the veto was a vestige of the King's original legislative authority, it obviously was not limited to constitutional issues; and both the Crown and the Governors frequently vetoed colonial legislation on grounds other than conflict with the charters defining colonial authority. See Edward C. Mason, The Veto Power 15–18 (Russell & Russell, 1890).

[180]See 1 Richardson at 211–12; Corwin, Office and Powers at 284 (cited in note 174). Since this bill would have reduced the size of the army, Professor Black argued that its veto "may well be thought to fall within the category of defense of the presidential office . . . ." Black, 40 L & Contemp Probs at 90 (cited in note 179).

[181]Letter of George Washington to Edmund Pendleton, Sept 23, 1793, 33 Washington Writings at 94, 96.

ment from the United States, or any of them." Alexander Hamilton had explained the reasons for these provisions in the Federalist. "[A] power over a man's support" was "a power over his will"; the salary guarantee meant that Congress could "neither weaken [the President's] fortitude by operating upon his necessities; nor corrupt his integrity, by appealing to his avarice;" the ban on other emoluments assured that he would have "no pecuniary inducement to renounce or desert the independence intended for him by the Constitution."[182]

Washington caused something of a stir in his first inaugural address by disclaiming his constitutional compensation. His sense of duty, he announced, had always required him to serve his country without remuneration; and thus he requested Congress in making "estimates for the station in which I am placed" to provide only for payment of "such actual expenditures as the public good may be thought to require."[183]

Undeterred, Congress proceeded to debate and enact a statute providing the President with a $25,000 annual salary.[184] John Page of Virginia began the House discussion by denying that Washington had the right to refuse his pay: "[T]he constitution requires that he shall receive a compensation, and it is our duty to provide it."[185] This was not a frivolous argument, for the salary provision was not designed for the President's benefit. If the constitutional premise was that financial independence was a crucial barrier to corruption, an officer who impoverished himself by declining his wages endangered the public interest. Moreover, if Washington was right that he need not accept this money, there would always be the risk that a President's waiver was not truly voluntary; reading the Constitution to mean what it said would obviate the need for inquiry on this unpromising score.

Thus Congress determined that Washington would be compensated whether he liked it or not,[186] and the next question was how much to pay him. This too turned out to be a constitutional question. The House committee had proposed that in addition to his salary the President be given a separate allowance to pay for a house, furniture, secretaries, clerks, carriages and horses,[187] and Representative Laurance objected that this provision conferred an "emolument beyond the compensation contemplated in the constitution."[188] Of course, as Abraham Baldwin of Georgia responded, it could hardly matter whether the President's compensation was stated in one provision or in two.[189] Laurance's concern, however, went deeper. The question was whether payment of the

[182]The Federalist No 73.
[183]1 Annals at 29.
[184]1 Stat 72 (Sept 24, 1789).
[185]1 Annals at 659.

[186]Washington accepted the salary despite his inaugural address. See George Nordham, George Washington and Money 45 (University Press of America, 1982). In fact Washington was later criticized for consistently overdrawing his salary, although the reasons for his doing so are disputed. See id at 47–48 (arguing that the overdrafts were reimbursements for start-up expenses incurred by Washington personally); James Thomas Flexner, Washington: The Indispensable Man 338–39 (Little, Brown, 1974) (suggesting that Washington may have been ignorant of the situation because his secretaries kept the accounts). In any event, Washington bowed to public pressure and stopped taking salary advances. Nordham, supra, at 48.

[187]See 1 Annals at 658 (remarks of Rep. White).
[188]Id at 659.
[189]Id at 660.

President's expenses was compensation for his services at all, and if not whether it was a forbidden emolument.

Arguably it was neither. Strictly speaking it compensated the President not for services but for expenditures, and it did not make him wealthier as a result of holding office. But if that was true, argued Theodore Sedgwick of Massachusetts, there would be nothing to prevent Congress from increasing expense allowances at will; and thus "one of the most salutary clauses in the constitution [would] be rendered nugatory."[190] Internal Revenue agents have since developed tools for dealing with such problems, but there were additional objections to the expense provision.[191] Congress chose to avoid the hornet's nest by dropping all references to expenses and voting a salary intended to be high enough to cover them.[192]

The controversy over the practical question of how much the President should be paid, however, paled in comparison to the dispute that had raged at the very beginning over the purely formal question of how he should be addressed. In April 1789, apparently at the instigation of Vice-President Adams,[193] a joint committee was appointed to consider "what style or titles [if any] it will be proper to annex to the offices of President and

---

[190]Id at 659.

[191]This allocation could scarcely be justified as compensation, said Livermore, since Congress was directing the President how to spend it; and Congress had no business dictating "the style in which he shall live." 1 Annals at 661. "[N]o part of the constitution," Representative Stone added, "gives us a right to dictate to him on this head." Id. Laurance had already raised yet another objection with respect to the provision for secretaries and clerks: To set their salaries would make them officers of the United States, and to do so would infringe the President's "right to employ a confidential person in the management of those concerns, for which the constitution has made him responsible." Id at 659. See the discussion of inferior officers in the text at notes 100–05.

[192]See James F. Vivian, The President's Salary, ch 1 (Garland, 1993). The Constitution said nothing about the Vice-President's remuneration, but some monetary provision was obviously necessary and proper to the exercise of his powers. Fisher Ames went further, suggesting the Constitution *required* that the Vice-President be paid:

> Every man is eligible, by the constitution, to be chosen to this office; but if a competent support
> is not allowed, the choice will be confined to opulent characters. This is an aristocratic idea, and
> contravenes the spirit of the constitution.

1 Annals at 674.

Significantly, while making the Vice-President presiding officer of the Senate, the Constitution gave him no executive responsibility beyond being available in case the President was unable to act. See US Const, Art I, § 3; Art II, § 1. Consequently, when a House committee proposed that the Vice-President be paid $5,000 per year, John White of Virginia protested that there was nothing in the Constitution to ensure that he perform services deserving of that princely sum and moved to allow him the President's salary when acting as President and a per diem such as that provided to members of Congress when actually present in the Senate. 1 Annals at 658, 671.

If he had had anything to do with framing the Constitution, Page retorted, he might "never have thought of such an officer; but as we have got him, we must maintain him," and at a level befitting the dignity of his position. Unlike the members of Congress, Sedgwick argued, the Vice-President "ought to remain constantly at the seat of Government" in order "to take the reins . . when they fall out of the hands of the President"; and thus he would be unable to pursue any other occupation during his term. Id at 672. Madison, Ames, and Boudinot echoed these sentiments, and the $5,000 salary was approved. See id at 671–76; 1 Stat 72 (Sept 24, 1789).

[193]See 9 Doc Hist at 4, 27–29.

Vice-President of the United States."[194] The committee recommended that no titles be added to those specified in the Constitution,[195] and the House agreed.[196] The Senate balked,[197] and a Senate committee then proposed that the President be addressed as "His Highness, the President of the United States of America, and Protector of their Liberties."[198]

Maclay argued that any such title would be unconstitutional. The Constitution had "designated our Chief Magistrate by the Appellation of *The President of the U.S. of America*," and Congress could neither "add to [n]or diminish it, without infringing the Constitution." Moreover, Article I, § 9 expressly provided that "no title of nobility sh[ould] be granted by the United States"; "the appellations & Terms given to Nobility in the old World" were "contraband language" in this country.[199]

This quarrel may seem petty, but in adopting the nobility provision the Framers themselves had plainly recognized the importance of symbols. One thing both the Revolution and the Constitution were all about was to substitute a republic for an aristocracy, and to abjure exalted forms of address served to underline our commitment to that decision.[200] When the House refused to recede from its disagreement, the Senate passed a resolution sulkily affirming the desirability of additional titles in order "to assure a due respect for the majesty of the people of the United States" in intercourse with other nations[201] but yielding for the moment in the interest of "preserving harmony with the House of Representatives."[202] That was the last that was heard about His Highness the Protector of our Liberties; ever since the President has been simply "the President of the United States," as Article II provides.[203]

---

[194]1 Annals at 24, 25. In return for his pains Adams himself came to be referred to in private as "His Rotundity." See 9 Doc Hist at 33.

[195]See 1 Annals at 257; 9 Doc Hist at 29.

[196]1 Annals at 257.

[197]Id at 33–34.

[198]Id at 36. Maclay recorded a slightly different formulation: "His Highness the President of the United States of America and Protector of the rights of the same." 9 Doc Hist at 29.

[199]Id at 31. Page echoed these arguments in the House, 1 Annals at 331. As reported in the Convention by the Committee of Style, Article II would have provided that the "stile" of the executive officer should be "'The President of the United States of America;' and his title shall be 'His Excellency.'" See 2 Farrand at 572. The omission of this language, while unexplained, arguably lends force to Maclay's objection.

[200]See 1 Annals at 332 (Rep. Tucker); John Ferling, John Adams: A Life 302 (Tennessee, 1992). Tucker sounded slightly hysterical, however, in suggesting that the President's title might be the first step down the road to "a crown and hereditary succession." 1 Annals at 332. As Madison argued in urging his colleagues not to deny the Senate the courtesy of appointing a conference committee to iron out the disagreement between the two chambers, "I believe a President of the United States, clothed with all the powers given in the constitution, would not be a dangerous person to the liberties of America, if you were to load him with all the titles of Europe or Asia." Id at 333.

[201]Maclay reports that Adams at one point in the debate reminded the Senate that "there were Presidents of Fire Companies & of a Cricket Club." 9 Doc Hist at 28.

[202]1 Annals at 36.

[203]On the importance of symbols in the First Congress see Casper, 30 Wm & Mary L Rev at 224–25 (cited in note 141). See also Miller at 9–10, noting that the title controversy "consumed virtually all of the Senate's time from April 23 to May 14" and "revealed the existence of a dangerous fissure within the Federalist party."

C. The Department of Foreign Affairs

The greatest and best known struggle in the First Congress over the structure of government began on May 19, 1789, when Representative Boudinot moved to establish three executive departments to aid the President in carrying out his duties with respect to war, finance, and foreign affairs.[204]

Virtually no one disputed the necessity for some such legislation. Recognizing that the President could not perform the functions entrusted to him all by himself, Article II authorized him to obtain written advice from "the principal officer in each of the executive departments" and with Senate consent to appoint not only judges but also "ambassadors, other public ministers, and consuls" and "all other officers of the United States, whose appointments are not herein otherwise provided for, and which shall be established by law." Not only did these provisions make clear the expectation that additional executive offices and departments would be created; they made equally plain that Congress had power to create them as necessary and proper to the execution of various powers granted to the President and Congress.[205]

Madison gave the members something concrete to chew on by moving to establish a Department of Foreign Affairs to be headed by a Secretary who was to be "appointed by the President, by and with the advice and consent of the Senate" and "removable by the President."[206] Chew they did; over a month elapsed before the House passed a bill on the subject, and much of that time was spent in debating the constitutional conundrums posed by Madison's simple proposal.

Even the innocuous suggestion that the Secretary be appointed as Article II prescribed provoked dissent. To provide by law for the method of appointment, argued Smith of South Carolina, would convey the impression that Congress was "conferring power," when in fact the Constitution gave it no discretion; the statute should say nothing about appointment one way or the other.[207] Lee responded that Congress did have a choice, for Article II, § 2 expressly authorized Congress "to vest the appointment of . . . inferior officers" elsewhere. The Secretary, he contended, was an inferior officer, because his only function was to aid the President in performing his duties.[208] Under this interpre-

---

[204]See 1 Annals at 383–84. The Constitution is surprisingly sparse in respect to the President's foreign affairs authority, expressly giving him only power to receive foreign diplomats, to appoint our own, and to make treaties—and in the latter two cases requiring him to obtain the advice and consent of the Senate. See US Const, Art II, §§ 2–3. In requiring the Secretary of Foreign Affairs not only to carry on such dealings with our own and foreign ministers but also to conduct "such other matters respecting foreign affairs" as the President should direct, the First Congress appeared to share the modern conviction that a general authority over foreign affairs was either implicit in the unpromisingly drafted specific powers or the general provision vesting executive power in the President or inherent in the office itself. See 1 Stat 28, 29, § 1 (July 27, 1789); United States v Curtiss-Wright Export Corp., 299 US 304 (1936); The Second Century at 217–18 n 63.

[205]See 1 Annals at 383 (Rep. Boudinot). Senator Maclay thought the President should nominate officers without prior legislation establishing their offices. See 9 Doc Hist at 104–05. In the House, however, "that the principles of organization for the executive offices should be settled by legislation was taken for granted." Casper, 30 Wm. & Mary L Rev at 233 (cited in note 141). For further discussion of this question see text at notes 100–12.

[206]1 Annals at 385.

[207]Id at 386.

[208]Id.

tation the President alone could have been empowered to appoint everybody except Justices of the Supreme Court, and it was quickly repudiated. "The inferior officers mentioned in the constitution," said Smith, "are clerks and other subordinate persons," not the heads of departments; and the reference to appointment by the President and Senate was struck from Madison's proposal.[209]

Smith's second objection was to the provision making the Secretary "removable by the President." For Article II, § 4 provided that civil officers of the United States should be removed from office when convicted of high crimes and misdemeanors by the Senate; and that, Smith argued, meant there was no other way to remove them.[210] Madison sensibly replied that the impeachment provision had been designed to provide "a supplemental security for the good behavior of the public officers," not to limit the President's authority to discharge them,[211] and Smith's contrary interpretation received little support from other members.[212]

Theodorick Bland of Virginia had a more challenging basis for complaint about the provision for presidential removal. If the President could remove an officer whom the Senate had approved, he might circumvent the Senate's authority by giving a recess appointment to an individual whom the Senators had already rejected.[213] Bland therefore opined that "the same power that appointed had, or ought to have, the power of removal"; the Senate's power of consent extended not only to naming officers but to dismissing them as well.[214]

[209]Id at 386–87. As enacted the statute made no reference to the method of appointing the Secretary, but it did provide for a Chief Clerk to be appointed by the Secretary himself in accordance with the authority granted by Article II. 1 Stat 28, 29, § 2 (July 27, 1789). This incident may have some bearing on the Supreme Court's later decision that a special prosecutor essentially independent of executive, legislative, or judicial control could constitutionally be appointed by a panel of federal judges. Morrison v Olson, 487 US 654 (1988). Even if Lee's view had prevailed, it might still have been pertinent to ask to what other officer such a prosecutor could be described as "inferior." Maclay's interpretation went as far overboard in one direction as Lee's went in the other: He denied that the Chief Clerk was an "inferior officer," because in the absence of the Secretary he would run the Department. 9 Doc Hist at 118.

[210]1 Annals at 387.

[211]Id. See also id at 393 (Rep. Sylvester); The Federalist No 65 (Hamilton) (arguing that impeachment was "a bridle in the hands of the legislative body upon the executive servants of the government"). The further suggestion of Benson and Boudinot (1 Annals at 387–88, 390–91) that Smith's argument would give all officers the tenure during "good behavior" that Article III reserved for judges was clever but flawed, for even Smith's reading would permit Congress to set fixed terms for other officers. See id at 391–92 (Reps. Jackson and Smith).

[212]Benjamin Huntington of Connecticut broke his habitual silence to echo Smith's position, 1 Annals at 477. See also id at 540 (Rep. Page), 389 (Rep. Jackson) (adding that if either the House or the Senate had a constitutional role to play in removing officers it could not delegate the task to anyone else; for "every power recognised by the constitution must remain where it was placed by that instrument").

[213]See US Const, Art II, § 2, authorizing the President "to fill up all vacancies that may happen during the recess of the Senate, by granting commissions which shall expire at the end of their next session."

[214]1 Annals at 388–89. Livermore added the inevitable comparison to the treaty power: "I will not by any means suppose that gentlemen mean, when they argue in favor of removal by the President alone, to contemplate the extension of the power to the repeal of treaties." Id at 497. The extension that Livermore thought so absurd was endorsed by the court of appeals and the only Supreme Court Justice to reach the merits in Goldwater v Carter, 444 US 996, 1007 (1979) (Brennan, J, dissenting).

Hamilton had said as much in the Federalist,[215] but the words did not seem to support him; what Article II said was that the President should *appoint* officers with the advice and consent of the Senate. As Smith cogently observed, removal power was not implied in the authority to select the President, Vice-President, or members of Congress—not even, he noted interestingly, in the case of the Senate.[216] Moreover, the distinction the Constitution seemed to draw between appointment and removal of executive officers could easily be justified in terms of Hamilton's own explanation that the purpose of the provision was to "prevent[] the appointment of unfit characters," although he was right that a Senate check on removal would also "contribute to the stability of the administration."[217]

In the House debate Madison was quick to disown the position Hamilton had taken. "[O]ne of the most prominent features of the constitution" was the President's responsibility for executive affairs. The Senate had been given a say in the appointing process because as a collective body it had better knowledge of possible candidates than any individual could have; but that limitation was consistent with presidential responsibility because, unlike a senatorial veto on removal, it permitted "no person" to be "forced upon him as an assistant by any other branch of the Government."[218]

Several other members agreed with Bland,[219] but his motion that the proposal be amended to provide for removal "by and with the advice and consent of the Senate" was defeated.[220] It was Gerry who raised the third and final argument against Madison's proposal: Even if neither the impeachment clause nor the appointments clause prevented the President from removing the Secretary, nothing in the Constitution authorized him to do so; and he had only those powers which the Constitution conferred.[221]

There were two ways to repulse this attack, and both were employed. Laurance had already made the defense of confession and avoidance: Since the Constitution did not provide one way or the other, Congress was free—under the necessary and proper clause, as Thomas Hartley of Pennsylvania later added[222]—to give the President removal power or not, and it made sense to do so.[223] George Clymer of Pennsylvania, in contrast, took the high road of direct denial: "[T]he power of removal was an executive power" and thus was vested in the President "by the express words" of Article II.[224]

It was at this point that in the Committee of the Whole "[t]he question was . . . taken, and carried by a considerable majority, in favor of declaring the power of removal

[215]The Federalist No 77. Smith read this passage aloud with evident relish at a later point in the House discussion. See 1 Annals at 474.

[216]1 Annals at 392. See the discussion of the role of Senators as representatives of the states at notes 64–75.

[217]The Federalist Nos 76–77.

[218]1 Annals at 394–95.

[219]See, e.g., id at 389 (Rep. Jackson), 391 (Rep. White), 395–96 (Rep. Gerry).

[220]Id at 397–98.

[221]Id at 395. See also id at 475 (Rep. Smith): "I call upon gentlemen to show me where it is said that the President shall remove from office."

[222]Id at 500.

[223]Id at 392–93.

[224]Id at 397.

to be in the President."[225] The reader will observe that this resolution left the difference of opinion between Clymer and Laurance unresolved. It did not say whether the President had removal power because the Constitution had given it to him or because Congress in its discretion had chosen to confer it. The House did not have to answer that question in order to agree that the President could discharge the Secretary, but it would be crucial if Congress ever decided to prohibit presidential removal.

The debate was resumed a few weeks later, when a bill was presented to carry out the principles agreed to in the Committee of the Whole.[226] The House talked of nothing else for a week. In the process all the arguments that had been made before were repeated and enlarged upon. There were also a few new twists, however. In particular, the difference of opinion among the supporters of presidential removal was brought into the foreground, and the argument that the Constitution itself gave the President this authority was substantially reinforced.

When Madison endorsed Clymer's position that removal was an executive power vested in the President by Article II,[227] Smith and White leapt to the attack. There was nothing intrinsically executive about removal, Smith argued; he knew of no state in which the Governor had any such power.[228] Moreover, White contended, the Constitution did not give the President all powers that might abstractly be classified as executive: "[T]he executive powers so vested, are those enumerated in the constitution."[229]

The former argument was troubling, and the latter potentially fatal. For despite the conspicuous textual contrast between Article II and Article I, which expressly vested in Congress only those legislative powers "herein granted,"[230] it seemed unlikely that the Framers had meant to give the President blanket authority to do everything that could theoretically be termed executive, especially since the critical words of Article I had been inserted without explanation by the Committee of Style;[231] at the very least there seemed to be an implicit restriction to executive matters that could fairly be deemed of federal concern.

Nevertheless, as Fisher Ames pointed out, the case did not depend on the argument that removal was in itself an unenumerated executive function:

> The constitution places all executive power in the hands of the President, and could he personally execute all the laws, there would be no occasion for

---

[225]Id at 399.

[226]Id at 473.

[227]Id at 481. Madison had initially argued that the matter lay in the discretion of Congress, and he acknowledged his change of mind. See id at 389, 480.

[228]Id at 490.

[229]Id at 485.

[230]US Const, Art I, § 1. Article III is equally explicit, vesting the judicial power in specified courts and defining that power to embrace a finite list of disputes. John Adams recorded in his notes that Ellsworth relied on the absence of any such language in Article II in arguing to the Senate that the vesting clause gave the President removal power: "The executive power is granted; not the executive powers hereinafter enumerated and explained." 3 Works of John Adams at 409.

[231]See 2 Farrand at 547, 565, 590; Charles C. Thach, Jr., The Creation of the Presidency, 1775–1789, in 40 Johns Hopkins University Studies in Historical and Political Science 138–39 (1922).

establishing auxiliaries; but the circumscribed powers of human nature in one man, demand the aid of others. . . . He must therefore have assistants. But in order that he may be responsible to his country, he must have a choice in selecting his assistants, a control over them, with power to remove them when he finds the qualifications which induced their appointment cease to exist.[232]

In other words, removal authority was implicit in the *enumerated* powers of the President, because he could exercise none of them without subordinates subject to his supervision and control. Madison succinctly restated the point a few minutes later: "[I]f the officer when once appointed is not to depend upon the president for his official existence, . . . I confess I do not see how the president can take care that the laws be faithfully executed."[233]

It was at this point that Egbert Benson of New York offered an amendment that was to divide the supporters of presidential removal power. A proposal to specify the manner of *appointment* had already been dropped after it was argued to imply a power of choice foreclosed by Article II;[234] Benson made the same argument with respect to removal. That the Secretary was removable by the President was the command of the Constitution itself; to say the same thing in the statute was to suggest that the power was for Congress to give or withhold. The bill should therefore be amended to acknowledge the President's constitutional prerogative by providing that the Secretary's custodial duties should devolve upon his clerk "whenever the said officer shall be removed by the president."[235]

Sedgwick protested that it made no sense after having won the debate for the supporters of the removal power to quarrel over a purely academic question.[236] Nevertheless the question was put, and Benson prevailed. The words "whenever the said officer shall be removed by the President" were inserted,[237] and the words "to be removable by the President" were dropped.[238] Thus at first glance it might appear that the House had agreed with Benson that the Constitution itself gave the President the power of removal.[239]

Unfortunately the matter was not so simple. For better or worse, the two halves of Benson's proposal were put to the House separately. The members first voted thirty to eighteen to add Benson's "whenever" language. All those who had spoken in favor of presidential removal voted aye, whether they thought that Article II settled the question

---

[232]1 Annals at 492. George Read made the same argument in the Senate. See 3 Works of John Adams at 411.

[233]1 Annals at 516. Ames later repeated the point: "In the constitution the President is required to see the laws faithfully executed. He cannot do that without he has a control over officers appointed to aid him in the performance of his duty." Id at 561. To put the argument another way, to place the conduct of foreign affairs in the hands of an officer not subject to presidential control would offend Article II's command that the enumerated executive powers be vested in the President. See Morrison v Olson, 487 US 654 (1988) (Scalia, J, dissenting).

[234]See text at notes 51–53.

[235]1 Annals at 525–27.

[236]Id at 602.

[237]Id at 602–03.

[238]Id at 608.

[239]Chief Justice Taft took this view of the House's action in Myers v United States, 272 US 52, 112–14 (1926). See also John Marshall, 5 The Life of George Washington 231–32 (AMS, 1805).

or left the matter to Congress. The House then voted thirty-one to nineteen to drop the phrase "to be removable by the President." The numbers were virtually identical, but it was a different majority. For on this question the proponents of Article II power prevailed only because they were joined by a substantial number of members who had opposed presidential removal altogether.[240]

The original coalition was patched up again when it came time for the House to pass the amended bill,[241] and after a similar discussion in the Senate[242] Benson's "whenever" formula became law.[243] Thus it was the considered judgment of a majority in both Houses that the President could remove the Secretary of Foreign Affairs, but there was no consensus as to whether he got that authority from Congress or from the Constitution itself.[244]

D. Other Officers

Once the great controversy over presidential removal was resolved, Congress moved quickly to set up War and Treasury Departments, each headed by a Secretary whose tenure was described by the same "whenever" formula that had been so painstakingly worked out for the Secretary of Foreign Affairs.[245] In other respects, however, the statute governing the Treasury differed significantly from those setting up the other two departments. To begin with, the Treasury was not expressly designated an "executive" depart-

[240]Fifteen of the thirty members who voted to add "whenever" voted not to delete "to be removable"; sixteen of the eighteen who voted not to add "whenever" voted to delete "to be removable." These were the members who were opposed to presidential removal entirely. Only sixteen of the forty-eight who voted on both questions voted for both, that is, for Benson's substitution. Justice Brandeis worked this all out in his dissent in *Myers*, 272 US at 286–87. See also Corwin, Office and Powers at 87 (cited in note 174). That was not enough to make Brandeis right on the merits; my own view is that Ames's argument was overpowering. See The Second Century at 194–95.

[241]The final vote was twenty-nine to twenty-two. See 1 Annals at 614.

[242]See 9 Doc Hist at 114–15.

[243]1 Stat 28, 29, § 2, (July 27, 1789). Vice-President Adams had had to cast a tie-breaking vote in the Senate. See 9 Doc Hist at 115.

[244]"[T]he real significance of the debate," wrote Professor Casper, "lies in the multitude of views expressed about the significance and meaning of separation of powers." Casper, 30 Wm & Mary L Rev at 237 (cited in note 141).

[245]See 1 Annals at 412; 1 Stat 49 (Aug 7, 1789); 1 Stat 65 (Sept 2, 1789). The Treasury bill, however, also provided for a Comptroller whose duties included determining the validity of claims against the government. Because this task was more judicial than executive, Madison argued, the President should not control it; either the Comptroller should not be removable, or his decisions should be subject to Supreme Court review. 1 Annals at 635–37.

This proposal raised more difficulties than it resolved. It was by no means clear that the Comptroller's function was judicial; until the Treasury had rejected the claim, it was hard to find the adverse parties who characterized the ordinary judicial proceeding. Moreover, if the matter was judicial, Article III appeared to require that it be decided by a judge with tenure during good behavior and irreducible salary. Finally, unless the Comptroller could somehow be considered a judicial officer, it was not obvious how the Supreme Court could be empowered to review his decision; for under Article III, unless a state or a (foreign) diplomat was a party, the Supreme Court's jurisdiction was appellate, not original. Madison withdrew his motion after several colleagues spoke against it; as enacted the statute said nothing about the removal of inferior officers. See 1 Annals at 637–39; 1 Stat at 65, §1.

ment, as the others were.[246] Nor was the distinction purely stylistic, for the Treasury Secretary was given specific duties that made him in part an agent of Congress. For one thing, he was directed to make estimates of "public revenue" and "public expenditures," which formed the basis of taxing and spending legislation.[247] For another, he was instructed to report to either House "in person or in writing" on "all matters referred to him by the Senate or by the House of Representatives, or which shall appertain to his office."[248]

The debate on these provisions was marked by deep concern over undue executive influence on the House.[249] No one seems to have made the converse argument that they gave Congress excessive power over the executive; apparently Alexander Hamilton got exactly what he wanted.[250] Regardless of who was encroaching upon whom, the Treasury statute incarnated an officer with a mix of executive and legislative functions that was remarkable in a system of supposedly separate powers; "the Secretary . . . was seen as an indispensable, direct arm of the House . . . ."[251]

Foreign Affairs, War, and the Treasury were the only three executive departments set up by the First Congress. John Vining of Delaware proposed a Home Department with a variety of largely archival functions, but after a brief debate centered on a less than overwhelming cost argument many of these duties were added to those of the Secretary of Foreign Affairs, who was renamed the Secretary of State.[252] Pressed for time, Congress en-

---

[246]See 1 Stat 28, §1 (July 27, 1789) (Foreign Affairs); 1 Stat 49, §1 (Aug 7, 1789) (War); 1 Stat 65, §1 (Sept 2, 1789) (Treasury). Nor was the Treasury Secretary, like his two colleagues, explicitly directed to perform his duties "as the President . . . shall . . . order or instruct." Id.

[247]1 Stat at 65–66, §2. For some of the first results of this provision see the discussion of early appropriations in chapter 2.

[248]1 Stat at 65–66. Hamilton's famous reports on public credit, on the national bank, and on manufactures (see chapter 2) were made on the basis of this provision.

[249]See note 172.

[250]See McDonald, Hamilton at 133. In his book on the Washington Administration the same author argues that the aim of Congress in enacting these provisions was "to curtail the executive and aggrandize the House" but that the result was to enable Hamilton "to become, for practical purposes, an American 'prime minister.'" McDonald, Washington at 37.

[251]Casper, 30 Wm & Mary L Rev at 241 (cited in note 172) (adding that as soon as Hamilton was appointed the Committee on Ways and Means was disbanded and its functions "turned . . . over to him"). See also Corwin, Office and Powers at 79 (cited in note 174): "The State and War Departments are principally . . . organs of the President in the exercise of functions which are assigned him by the Constitution itself, while the Treasury Department is primarily an instrument for carrying into effect Congress's constitutional powers in the field of finance." For the suggestion that the distinctive Treasury provisions cast doubt on the thesis that the First Congress believed Article II required a unitary executive see Lawrence Lessig & Cass R. Sunstein, The President and the Administration, 94 Colum L Rev 1, 27–30 (1994).

Gerry's motion to replace the Treasury Secretary with a three-member board raised no constitutional question; it was defeated on the ground that the advantages of efficient administration outweighed the risk of abuse of authority. See 1 Annals at 400–12.

[252]See id at 692–95; 1 Stat 68 (Sept 15, 1789). Representative Vining observed that it was not obvious why it would be more expensive for the duties in question to be performed by a new Home Department than by anyone else. 1 Annals at 694. Nor was there any logical connection between these responsibilities and those initially assigned to the Secretary of Foreign Affairs; Huntington had suggested that the Secretary be chosen because at the moment he seemed to be "not so much overcharged with business but that he might attend to the major part of the duties mentioned." Id at 693. The implication seemed to be that by increasing his responsibilities Congress might avoid having to pay another Secretary's salary.

acted a temporary measure providing for appointment of a Postmaster General "subject to the direction of the President" but to carry out duties specified for his predecessors by the Confederation Congress.[253] The Judiciary Act provided for an Attorney General to render legal advice to the executive and to represent the United States before the Supreme Court and for District Attorneys to represent it elsewhere, but they were not part of any executive department, and the statute did not say who was to appoint or remove them.[254] In prescribing that each of the government's attorneys be "a meet person learned in the law" Congress significantly if sensibly restricted the President's discretion in selecting them. Nobody seems to have suggested that in so doing Congress offended the appointment provisions of Article II.[255]

Other proposals, however, raised important and interesting questions as to what was included in the President's powers of nomination and appointment. On several occasions Congress provided by statute for the appointment of officers inferior to the heads of departments.[256] From the beginning, however, there was evidence of an understanding that other public servants could be appointed although their offices had never been created by law.

---

[253] 1 Stat 70 (Sept 22, 1789); see 1 Annals at 923, 927–28.

[254] 1 Stat 73, 92–93, §35 (Sept 24, 1789). Indeed the District Attorneys were supervised not by the Attorney General but by the Secretary of State—a situation that hardly seemed conducive to the evolution of a uniform legal policy. See White at 406. Early drafts had provided that District Attorneys be appointed by the District Courts and the Attorney General by the Supreme Court. These provisions disappeared after Robert Livingston wrote (apparently to Ellsworth) suggesting that the Attorney General should be "appointed by the executive to which department he necessarily belongs." See Susan Low Bloch, The Early Role of the Attorney General in Our Constitutional Scheme: In the Beginning There Was Pragmatism, 1989 Duke LJ 561, 567, 571 n 32.

[255] The following April, however, Representative Scott moved to excise from a bill to regulate Indian commerce a requirement that the Superintendent of Indian Affairs be a military officer, arguing among other things that this restriction both "infringe[d] the power of the President" and "blended the civil and military characters." In response it was noted that "the President and Senate are restricted in their appointments of officers in several other departments," and the Attorney General was cited as an example. 2 Annals at 1575. When the bill was enacted, the military qualification had disappeared—the precedents suggested for reasons of policy rather than constitutional compulsion. 1 Stat 137, §1 (July 22, 1789). See Corwin, Office and Powers at 70–71 (cited in note 174) (noting the "vast variety of qualifications" laid down over the years for federal appointments but adding that it was "universally conceded that some choice, however small, must be left to the appointing authority").

A different issue respecting the appointment power arose during the second session in connection with a bill to create a commission to settle accounts between the United States and the states. Laurance and Gerry objected to the original draft of the bill on the ground that by designating the Secretary of the Treasury and the Comptroller as members of the commission it usurped the appointing authority vested in the President and Senate. Sedgwick retorted with considerable force that the Constitution did not forbid Congress to attach additional duties to existing offices, and Madison argued that, since the commission's functions were legislative, Congress could appoint its members. Nevertheless the offending language was removed—whether for reasons of policy or constitutional compulsion was not made clear. See New York Daily Gazette, June 2, 1790; Lloyd's Notes for June 1 & 2, 1790; Gazette of the United States, June 7, 1790; 1 Stat 178, § 1 (Aug 5, 1790).

[256] E.g., 1 Stat 28, 29, §2 (Chief Clerk in Department of Foreign Affairs); 1 Stat 49, 50, §2 (Chief Clerk in Department of War); 1 Stat 65, §1 (Comptroller, Auditor, Treasurer, Register, and Assistant to the Secretary of the Treasury). Under the authority conferred by the proviso to Article II, § 2, Congress provided for appointment of the two chief clerks and of the assistant by the respective Secretaries; it said nothing about their removal. See also 1 Stat 67, 68, §2 (Sept 11, 1789) (authorizing each of the three Secretaries to appoint "such clerks . . . as they shall find necessary").

One of Washington's first acts as President was to appoint Gouverneur Morris, entirely without statutory authority, as "a 'special agent' to explore the possibility of a commercial treaty with Great Britain."[257] Maclay once took the position that he should do the same with the Secretary of Foreign Affairs.[258] Laurance had gone even further in arguing that to set salaries for the President's secretaries and clerks would "infringe[] his right to employ a confidential person in the management of those concerns, for which the constitution has made him responsible."[259] Madison responded that the President had no power to create offices,[260] and there were other explanations for the omission of the contested provision; it thus cannot be said that Congress either accepted or rejected Laurance's interesting contention.

If Laurance's position could be defended on the ground that not every menial employee was an "officer of the United States" within the meaning of Article II,[261] the same could hardly be said of ambassadors, other public ministers, or consuls. Yet when Congress turned to providing for intercourse with other nations in 1790 it conspicuously refrained from creating any such posts at all, simply authorizing the President to draw up to $40,000 per year from the Treasury "for the support of such persons as he shall commission to serve the United States in foreign parts" and to pay their expenses.[262]

A closer look at the Constitution may suggest why. The assumption that it is Congress that is to determine which offices are to be filled derives in part from the necessary and proper clause and in part from Article II's reference to offices "which shall be established by law." That qualification, however, appears to apply only to "other officers of the United States, whose appointments are not herein otherwise provided for," not to the preceding and separate provision for the appointment of "ambassadors, other public ministers and consuls, [and] judges of the Supreme Court." The text thus gave some support to Smith's argument that the President and Senate should "determine when and where to send ambassadors and other public ministers; all that the House has to do is to make provision for their support."[263]

---

[257]See 30 Writings of Washington at 439–42; Miller at 13. Executive authority to make such appointments had long existed in England. See Corwin, Office and Powers at 65 (cited in note 174). See also id at 231 (arguing that appointments like that of Morris could "be reconciled with the Constitution only by invoking the Hamiltonian conception of residual executive power").

[258]9 Doc Hist at 104–05, adding that the appointment would be subject to Senate confirmation under Article II. But the requirement of Senate consent applies only to officers who are named in that Article or whose offices are established by law; to permit the President to appoint to additional offices not created by statute would allow him to circumvent the important check of Senate consent.

[259]1 Annals at 659.

[260]Id at 662.

[261]See Buckley v Valeo, 424 US 1, 126 n 162 (1976); Corwin, Office and Powers at 72 (cited in note 174) (criticizing the accepted distinction between "officers" and "employees" as a device for "circumventing the apparent purpose of the Constitution" with respect to the appointment of inferior officers).

[262]1 Stat 128, §1 (July 1, 1790).

[263]1 Annals at 1100. Accord id at 1101 (Rep. White). Sherman, on the other hand, "was inclined to think that the Legislature should determine how many ministers should be employed abroad." Id. Gerry had twice moved in the Convention to provide that offices could be established only by legislation, but without success; Madison had cryptically recorded that such a provision was "unnecessary." See 2 Farrand at 550, 553. Attorney General Cushing relied on the phrasing of the appointment provision in reaffirming Smith's conclusion in 1855. See 7 Op Att'y Gen 186, 193. Smith made clear that he viewed Congress's power of the purse as a "check" on Presidential discretion in this regard: If the House "were of opinion that all intercourse with

The textual argument applies to Justices as well as to diplomats, and Congress fixed the number of the former at six.[264] It may be that Congress thought it had the power but not the duty to fix the number of offices in both cases and chose to exercise its authority only in the case of the judges. The contrast may also suggest, however, that the constitutional principle that dissuaded Congress from creating particular diplomatic offices was found not in the second section of Article II but in the third.

For buried near the end of that section was an apparently innocuous provision directing the President to "receive ambassadors and other public ministers." This duty could have been construed in a purely ceremonial sense,[265] but it was not. It has long been understood that the decision to receive a foreign diplomat embodies a decision to recognize the government that dispatched him, and thus that the reception clause empowers the President to decide with which governments the United States shall have diplomatic relations.[266] For Congress to create an embassy to Lower Slobbovia would appear to conflict with this presidential responsibility; and thus it is arguable that, as Smith suggested, Congress could not have prescribed where our diplomats should be sent even if it had been so inclined.[267] All that the failure to establish specific diplomatic offices by statute can fairly be said to prove, however, is that Congress did not think the Constitution required it to do so before the President and Senate could fill them.[268]

Yet congressional reticence in this case was not confined to the question of what diplomatic offices should be established. The statute did not even prescribe what salary was to be paid to such envoys as the President, with Senate consent, might decide to

---

foreign nations should be cut off, they might decline to make provision for them . . . ." 1 Annals at 1100–01.

[264]1 Stat 73, § 1 (Sept 24, 1789).

[265]See The Federalist No 69 (Hamilton); Helvidius No 3, 15 Madison Papers at 95, 96–97.

[266]United States v Belmont, 301 US 324, 330 (1937). Cf the conclusion in Luther v Borden, 48 US 1 (1849), that it was for each House of Congress to decide, in determining the qualifications of its own members, whether the government that sent them was the legitimate government of the state.

[267]As Washington tells it, Madison, Jefferson, and Chief Justice John Jay followed this line of analysis to its logical conclusion: Not even the Senate had any say in determining where to send diplomats; its authority "extend[ed] no farther than to an approbation or disapprobation of the person nominated by the President, all the rest being Executive and vested in the President by the Constitution." 4 Washington Diaries at 122 (Apr 27, 1790). For Jefferson's written opinion to this effect see 16 Jefferson Papers at 378–82.

When a debate over the extent of the Senate's authority broke out over the appointment of three envoys to Britain, France, and the Netherlands in early 1792, Jefferson drafted a stern message reiterating that the President was sole judge of the question where diplomats should be sent, and of their appropriate rank as well. Jefferson noted on the draft a pointed reference to the President's power to receive ambassadors and other public ministers and the rhetorical question whether the Senate could reject a judicial nomination on the ground that no judge should be appointed. A meeting with a Senate committee resolved the particular dispute, and the message was not sent. See 23 Jefferson Papers at 10–15, 18–19.

[268]Ten months earlier, in appropriating $20,000 to cover the expenses of negotiating and treating with the Southern Indians, Congress had struck out a provision authorizing the appointment of not more than three commissioners to perform the contemplated negotiations after Sedgwick announced that "[h]e thought it a dangerous doctrine to be established, that the House had any authority to interfere in the management of treaties," although Tucker had argued that commissioners could not be appointed unless Congress first created their offices and Page that the appropriation power enabled Congress to determine how the money was to be spent. See 1 Annals at 716–30; 1 Stat 54 (Aug 20, 1789) (providing an allowance of eight dollars a day for "each of the commissioners who may be appointed for managing such negotiations and treaties").

appoint. It merely set upper limits to the sums that could be paid to individual officers and to the total that could be expended in a single year.[269]

The arguments on this provision had been largely a reprise of the controversy over presidential removal, ranging from the suggestion that the determination of salaries was incident to appointment or to treaty-making and thus could be made only by the President with Senate consent[270] to the position that it was an executive function entrusted to the President alone.[271] Thomas Scott of Pennsylvania, however, put forward a new argument that had not been available in the removal debate:

> I think disposing of, or giving away sums of public money, is a Legislative, not an Executive act, and cannot be performed in any other way than with all the formalities of Legislative authority.

Thus there was no point in arguing over whether salaries should be set by the President alone or with Senate consent, because "it would be improper to give it to either"; the setting of salaries being a legislative responsibility, Congress could not constitutionally delegate it to anyone else.[272]

This argument was given credence by the provision of Article I, § 9 that no money should be drawn from the Treasury "but in consequence of appropriations made by law." Of course it was true that the bill did authorize the withdrawal of funds from the Treasury, but the Constitution arguably required Congress to determine not only how much to spend but also how to spend it. Sedgwick replied that Congress had already recognized the necessity for discretionary spending authority in providing for military supply.[273] This exchange was an opening salvo in a continuing battle over the proper degree of specificity in congressional appropriations.[274]

As in the removal debate, Laurance took the position that the Constitution did not answer the question,[275] and this time the majority evidently agreed. In prescribing ceilings for the remuneration of various types of officers, Congress rejected the thesis that the Constitution reserved the matter to the President with or without consent of the Senate; in leaving it to the President to determine the appropriate compensation within those limits, it rejected the argument that salaries could be set only by statute. The bottom line seemed to be that Congress could decide one way or another under its authority to enact

---

[269]1 Annals at 1118.

[270]See id at 1119–20 (Reps. Lee and Stone); id at 1122–23 (Rep. Sherman (arguing that by virtue of these provisions the President and the Senate "ought to act jointly in every transaction which respects the business of negotiation with foreign powers"). Smith's reply was the one that had prevailed when the same argument was made with respect to removal: Article II gave the Senate a role in the appointment of officers but not in determining their salaries. Id at 1119.

[271]See id at 1124–25 (Rep. Benson).

[272]Id at 1127. See also Gazette of the United States, Jan 30, 1790 (Rep. Jackson).

[273]See 1 Annals at 1127–28: "How else could the business of the quartermasters' or commissaries' departments be performed . . . ?"

[274]See also chapter 2.

[275]1 Annals at 1121; Quincy Wright, The Control of American Foreign Relations 312–15, 324–34 (MacMillan, 1922).

laws necessary and proper to the execution of powers granted by the Constitution to various officers and departments of the federal government.[276]

IV. THE COURTS

Article III provided only the broad outlines of the structure and authority of the federal courts. The judicial power of the United States was to be vested in "one Supreme Court" and in "such inferior courts as the Congress may from time to time ordain and establish." The judges were to "hold their offices during good behavior," and their salaries could not be "diminished during their continuance in office." The judicial power was defined to extend to an impressively long list of "cases" and "controversies," prominent among which were federal-question, diversity, and admiralty cases and those to which the United States was a party. If a state or a foreign diplomat was a party, the Supreme Court was to have "original jurisdiction"; in all other enumerated cases it was to have "appellate jurisdiction, both as to law and fact, with such exceptions, and under such regulations, as the Congress shall make." The final provisions of Article III went on to guarantee a jury trial in criminal cases and to define treason.

Given the leanness of these constitutional provisions, the question of how Congress would implement them was of first importance. The Judiciary Act, largely crafted by Oliver Ellsworth in the Senate and adopted on September 24, 1789,[277] has been called "probably the most important and the most satisfactory Act ever passed by Congress."[278] Recorded debates were unfortunately meager,[279] but the act itself established a number of significant constitutional precedents.

A. The Lower Federal Courts

The one issue on which significant debate was reported arose when Tucker and Livermore argued on policy grounds that Congress ought to limit lower federal courts to the decision of admiralty cases.[280] Smith responded with the policy argument that Supreme Court review was inadequate to protect federal rights,[281] but he had constitutional arguments as

---

[276]Consistently with this analysis, Congress now regulates the salaries of diplomats while still leaving it to the President to determine where to send them. Foreign Service Act of 1980, 94 Stat 2071, 22 USC § 3921. For a period beginning in 1855, however, Congress also determined which countries were to receive diplomats. See 10 Stat 619 (Mar 1, 1855); Corwin, Office and Powers at 266 (cited in note 174). For reasons stated above, Attorney General Cushing thought this practice unconstitutional. See note 107.

[277]1 Stat 73. See William G. Brown, The Life of Oliver Ellsworth 184–86 (Da Capo 1970) (first printed in 1904).

[278]Justice Henry B. Brown, Address to the American Bar Association (Aug 20, 1911), cited in Charles Warren, 1 The Supreme Court in United States History 12 n 1 (Little, Brown, 1923). See also William H. Rehnquist, The Courts and the Constitution, 60 Temple LQ 829, 832 (1987).

[279]"Mr. Benson said, the Senate had employed a great deal of time in perfecting this bill, and he believed had done it tolerably well; besides, the session was now drawing to a close; he therefore wished as few alterations as possible to be made in it, lest they should not get it through before the adjournment." 1 Annals at 812.

[280]Id at 812–14, 826–28.

[281]"[I]t would be *felo da se* to trust the collection of the revenue of the United States to the State judicatures." Id at 830. See also id at 843–44 (Rep. Madison).

well. In extending the judicial power to enumerated categories of cases, he suggested, Article III required the erection of federal trial courts to determine them; and the tenure provision of the same Article forbade leaving those cases to state judges "who, in many instances, hold their places for a limited period."[282]

As Jackson argued, by vesting judicial power in the Supreme Court and "such inferior courts as the Congress may from time to time ordain and establish" Article III seemed to refute Smith's contentions by giving Congress discretion as to the establishment of inferior federal courts.[283] Smith argued that Congress's discretion extended only to how many inferior courts to establish, not to whether to establish them at all,[284] but the text certainly did not compel this conclusion. Moreover, the well-known history confirms that the wording ultimately adopted was a compromise between those who thought the Constitution should itself establish inferior courts and those who thought there should be only a Supreme Court—Wilson and Madison having justified the change of phrasing on the ground that "there was a distinction between establishing such tribunals absolutely, and giving a discretion to the Legislature to establish them."[285]

Since Congress decided to establish lower federal courts, it did not have to determine whether or not it was required to. The statute itself, however, clearly reveals Congress's conviction that nothing in the Constitution required it to give federal trial courts jurisdiction over all the cases and controversies enumerated in Article III. For apart from civil and criminal cases brought by the Government, the district courts were to sit basically in admiralty, and the circuit courts in diversity and alienage cases involving more than $500. There was no general grant of federal-question jurisdiction.[286]

Since Congress did not have to create lower courts at all, it might appear obvious that it did not have to give them jurisdiction over any particular category of cases.[287] As Justice Story was to demonstrate a generation later, however, the matter was not so simple. For while Article III gave Congress discretion as to the existence and powers of inferior federal courts, it also provided in ostensibly mandatory terms that "the judicial power shall extend" to the enumerated classes of cases. Arguably the two provisions should have been reconciled by concluding that the entire judicial power had to be vested

---

[282]Id at 831–32. See also id at 859–61 (Rep. Gerry). Despite his predictable objection to the creation of an "expensive and enormous" federal judiciary, Maclay surprisingly concluded at one point not only that the Constitution required federal jurisdiction over all federal-question cases but also that state courts would have no jurisdiction to decide them. 9 Doc Hist at 10, 85–87, 116.

[283]1 Annals at 833.

[284]Id at 849–50.

[285]1 Farrand at 124–25.

[286]1 Stat at 76–79, §§ 9–12. The district courts also had jurisdiction of actions "where an alien sues for a tort only in violation of the law of nations or a treaty of the United States" and of "suits against consuls or vice-consuls" (§ 9), while a claimant to land worth more than $500 under the grant of a state other than that in which the action was brought could remove to circuit court under § 12. For reliance on a semicolon to support the novel position that the jurisdictional minimum was inapplicable to diversity cases originally filed in federal court see Wilfred Ritz, Rewriting the History of the Judiciary Act of 1789 57 (Oklahoma, 1990).

[287]See Sheldon v Sill, 49 U.S. 441, 449 (1850) (upholding the clause of § 11 precluding jurisdiction when diversity of citizenship had been created by assignment of a chose in action): "[I]t would seem to follow, also, that, having a right to prescribe, Congress may withhold from any court of its creation jurisdiction of any of the enumerated controversies."

in *some* federal court: Congress could withhold jurisdiction of particular cases from the inferior courts only if it permitted the Supreme Court to hear them.[288]

Congress evidently disagreed, for the Judiciary Act did not satisfy this model. Diversity cases excluded from the circuit courts by the jurisdictional amount, for example, were excluded from the federal courts altogether, for the Supreme Court was given no authority to review state-court judgments in cases in which diversity was the sole basis of federal jurisdiction.[289] Thus Congress seems to have agreed with Maryland Representative Michael Stone that the courts were no more required to exercise the entire judicial power than Congress was required to exercise all the legislative authority conferred by Article I.[290]

One should not be too quick, however, to leap to the further conclusion that Congress thought it had complete discretion to exclude Article III cases from federal courts. As Story also observed, in contrast to federal-question, admiralty, and diplomatic cases the Constitution did not expressly extend the judicial power to "all" controversies between citizens of different states, and the difference in phrasing might have been deliberate: "The vital importance of all the cases enumerated in the first class to the national sovereignty, might warrant such a distinction."[291] The First Congress, Story added, seemed, "in a good degree, . . . to have adopted this distinction"; for "[i]n the first class of cases, the jurisdiction is not limited except by the subject matter; in the second, it is made materially to depend upon the value in controversy."[292]

Indeed the Judiciary Act came suggestively close to giving some federal court jurisdiction over all cases within the three categories in which Article III expressly employed the word "all." Section 9 empowered the district courts to hear "all civil causes of admiralty and maritime jurisdiction";[293] § 13 comprehensively confirmed the Supreme Court's original jurisdiction over cases affecting foreign diplomats;[294] § 25 authorized the Supreme Court to review state-court judgments in federal-question cases. Although that section was hedged about with a variety of restrictions,[295] it has been forcefully argued that at the

[288]Martin v Hunter's Lessee, 14 US 304, 330–33 (1816).

[289]See 1 Stat at 85–87, § 25. The same was true of Government civil cases involving less than $100, which were excluded from the district courts by § 9.

[290]1 Annals at 854–55.

[291]*Martin*, 14 US at 334. See also Akhil Reed Amar, A Neo-Federalist View of Article III: Separating the Two Tiers of Federal Jurisdiction, 65 BU L Rev 205 (1985); Akhil Reed Amar, Reports of My Death Are Greatly Exaggerated: A Reply, 138 U Pa L Rev 1651, 1658–60 (1990) (pointing out, among other things, the striking parallel between the categories of cases with respect to which Article III omitted the word "all" and those with respect to which an earlier draft would explicitly have left federal jurisdiction to the discretion of Congress).

[292]*Martin*, 14 US at 336.

[293]Criminal admiralty cases fell within exclusive federal jurisdiction under §§ 9 and 11.

[294]For reservations as to the completeness of this provision see Paul Bator, et al, Hart & Wechsler's The Federal Courts and the Federal System 386–87 n 41 (Foundation, 3d ed 1988) (pointing out, among other things, that there was no provision for removal or appeal if a foreign diplomat sued in state court).

[295]Supreme Court review was limited to questions concerning the "validity" of federal or state action or the "construction" of a constitutional provision, treaty, federal "statute," or "commission." 1 Stat at 85–87, § 25. Nothing was said about review of questions of federal common law (which as a modern concept was probably not envisioned at the time) or the *application* of federal law (which might have been subsumed under its "construction"). Most notably, review was provided only in cases in which the state court rejected the claim of federal right.

very least it fulfilled the central constitutional purpose of providing a federal forum to assure the vindication of federal rights.[296] Significantly, even opponents of broad federal jurisdiction tended to agree that federal courts should hear cases in these categories. As Livermore argued, "if we have a Supreme Court, to which appeals can be carried [in federal question cases], and an Admiralty Court for deciding cases of a maritime nature, our system will be useful and complete."[297] Thus, while the Judiciary Act clearly reveals Congress's belief that it was not required to extend federal jurisdiction to all cases or controversies enumerated in Article III, it does not seem to be a good precedent for congressional power to strip all federal courts of authority to remedy the denial of a federal right.

In conspicuously declining to give the federal trial courts jurisdiction over all of the controversies within federal judicial power and in expressly making the jurisdiction it did give them "concurrent with the courts of the several States" in most civil cases,[298] Congress clearly rejected any argument that the grant of judicial power in Article III was exclusive.[299] This conclusion does seem to follow from the Convention compromise, since it seems highly unlikely that the Framers intended the consequence of a congressional decision not to create lower federal courts to be that Article III cases outside the Supreme Court's narrow original jurisdiction could not be heard at all.[300] At the same time, the express statutory provisions making federal jurisdiction in criminal and maritime matters exclusive testify to Congress's reasonable conclusion that the exclusion of state courts might sometimes be necessary and proper to effectuating the purposes that the grant of federal judicial authority was meant to serve.[301]

The Judiciary Act scrupulously followed the Constitution in assigning to the inferior federal courts only the decision of "cases" and "controversies" that were traditionally judicial. In 1790, however, after Hamilton reported that many shipowners had incurred li-

[296]See Akhil Reed Amar, The Two-Tiered Structure of the Judiciary Act of 1789, 138 U Pa L Rev 1499, 1529–35 (1990) (arguing imaginatively that in one sense no appeal arises under federal law unless a federal right has been denied and that to uphold one party's federal right is generally to deny the other's). For criticism of this view see Daniel J. Meltzer, The History and Structure of Article III, 138 U Pa L Rev 1569 (1990); Martin H. Redish, Text, Structure, and Common Sense in the Interpretation of Article III, 138 U Pa L Rev 1633 (1990).

[297]1 Annals at 827. See also id at 832–35 (Rep. Jackson); Amar, 138 U Pa L Rev at 1549–59 (cited in note 296).

[298]See §§ 9, 11 (alien tort, government, diversity, and alienage cases). See also § 13 (original but not exclusive jurisdiction of Supreme Court in certain cases).

[299]Stone and Livermore made the interesting suggestion that the supremacy clause *required* state courts to entertain claims based on federal law, 1 Annals at 840–44, 863, but Congress cannot be said to have taken a position one way or another on this suggestion. Cf Testa v Katt, 330 US 386 (1947); General Oil Co v Crain, 209 US 211 (1908).

[300]Hamilton had anticipated this question in The Federalist, noting that federal jurisdiction would normally be concurrent because of the tradition that the courts of one sovereign regularly heard cases involving the laws of another. The Federalist No 82. Thus the compromise appears to dispose of Smith's tenure argument as well; apparently the Framers not unreasonably thought the countervailing interests of federalism outweighed any danger that state judges might not be sufficiently independent to decide cases without fear of reprisal, especially since there was little risk that they would be dominated by the President or Congress. See Thomas Krattenmaker, Article III and Judicial Independence: Why the New Bankruptcy Courts are Unconstitutional, 70 Geo L J 297, 304–05 (1981).

[301]See §§ 9–12 (also excluding the state courts from suits against consuls and vice-consuls) and the various provisions for exclusive original Supreme Court jurisdiction in § 13.

ability for penalties and forfeitures through ignorance of the recently enacted tariff and tonnage duties,[302] Congress directed district judges after adversarial proceedings to report the facts to the Secretary of the Treasury, who was given "power to mitigate or remit" any such penalty "if in his opinion the same was incurred without wilful negligence or any intention of fraud."[303] A Senate amendment to the original bill that would have vested mitigation authority in a committee of three Cabinet officers had been deleted after objections that it gave judicial power to the executive;[304] yet the act as adopted seemed both to leave this problem unresolved and to compound the difficulty by conferring advisory powers on the judges.[305]

In only two instances, moreover, did the Judiciary Act arguably give federal courts jurisdiction over judicial matters outside the enumeration of Article III. Most suspiciously, if the $500 minimum was satisfied, § 11 purported to give the circuit courts jurisdiction of all cases in which "an alien [was] a party," although the corresponding clause of the Constitution spoke only of controversies "between a State, or citizens thereof, and foreign states, citizens or subjects." There was no recorded debate on this provision. In light of the care exercised elsewhere in the statute to avoid exceeding the limits implicit in Article III's enumeration, the Supreme Court may well have been right to conclude that in this instance as well Congress had no intention of going beyond the constitutional provision.[306]

[302]See chapter 2.

[303]1 Stat 122–23, § 1 (May 26, 1790).

[304]2 Annals at 1525.

[305]Cf Hayburn's Case, 2 US 409 (1792) (also noted in chapter 3), where three circuit courts including five of the six Supreme Court Justices declared invalid a similar provision respecting military pensions. See also 1 Stat 186, § 2 (Aug 12, 1790), making the Chief Justice a member of a committee to supervise the repurchase of government obligations. Given the absence of any incompatibility clause comparable to that forbidding simultaneous exercise of legislative and executive functions (US Const, Art I, § 6), Congress evidently saw no constitutional impediment to giving the same officer both judicial and executive duties. See Mistretta v United States, 488 US 361 (1989); Russell Wheeler, Extrajudicial Activities of the Early Supreme Court, 1973 Sup Ct Rev 123; Mark Tushnet, Dual Office Holding and the Constitution: A View from Hayburn's Case, in Maeva Marcus, ed, Origins of the Federal Judiciary 196 (Oxford, 1992).

[306]Mossman v Higginson, 4 US 12 (1800); Hodgson v Bowerbank, 9 US 303 (1809); The First Hundred Years at 89–90, 29–30. As a stopgap measure, the overburdened legislators directed lower federal courts in common law cases to follow "the forms of writs and executions, . . . modes of process and rates of fees" prescribed by state law, but avoided any problem of delegating federal authority to the states by adopting only those forms, modes, and rates "now used or allowed" in state courts. The "forms and modes of proceedings" in equity and admiralty cases, in contrast, were to be "according to the course of the civil law"—a less precise reference that arguably left considerable room for judicial discretion. 1 Stat 93–94 (Sept 29, 1789). The necessary and proper clause seemed to give Congress authority to adopt procedural rules for federal courts, though judicial authority to do so was arguably implicit in Article III's grant of judicial power, and judicial independence might plausibly be argued to require that judicial authority be exclusive. See Wayman v Southard, 23 US 1, 22 (1825); The First Hundred Years at 117–19; People v Cox, 82 Ill 2d 268, 274–75, 412 NE2d 541, 544–45 (1980) (concluding that a statute contradicting a judicial rule of procedure would be void). § 34's celebrated requirement that "the laws of the several states" should generally "be regarded as rules of decision" in common law cases in federal court (1 Stat at 92) was to raise an interesting issue of interpretation. See Erie RR v Tompkins, 304 US 64, 79–80 (1938). Despite the Supreme Court's conclusion in that case that application of state law was required by the Constitution, the absence of recorded debate on the provision makes it impossible to say whether it was enacted on policy grounds or from a sense of constitutional compulsion.

More difficult to explain on this ground was § 9's interesting provision giving the district courts jurisdiction over "all causes where an alien sues for a tort only in violation of the law of nations or a treaty of the United States."[307] Some have argued that the precipitating cause of this enactment was an attack by one Frenchman on another, and the Second Circuit has recently upheld its application to a suit between two aliens on the ground that the case arose under federal law: "The constitutional basis for the Alien Tort Statute is the Law of Nations, which has always been part of the federal common law."[308]

B.   The Supreme Court

The Judiciary Act also resolved a number of interesting and important constitutional questions in defining the jurisdiction and powers of the Supreme Court. First, as already noted, § 25 confirmed the Court's authority to review federal questions decided by state courts—a conclusion hardly surprising in light of precedent under the relatively feeble Articles of Confederation[309] and the debates in the Constitutional Convention.[310] Second, both § 25 and § 22 reflected a broad view of Congress's power to make "exceptions" to the appellate jurisdiction of the Supreme Court. For as already indicated the former section provided for review of state judgments only in federal-question cases, while the latter made no provision for appellate review of federal criminal convictions. The argument that Congress was authorized to make exceptions only to Supreme Court review of factual determinations[311] was thus not the view of the First Congress. Nor was Congress of the

---

[307]1 Stat at 77.

[308]Filartiga v Pena-Irala, 630 F2d 876, 885 (2d Cir 1980). See Anne-Marie Burley, The Alien Tort Statute and the Judiciary Act of 1789: A Badge of Honor, 83 Am J Int'l L 461 (1989). An alternative modern explanation might be that by directing federal courts to apply the law of nations in alien tort actions Congress under its implicit foreign affairs authority had made it federal law or empowered the courts to adopt it as federal common law. Cf US Const, Art I, § 8, cl 10 (explicitly authorizing Congress to punish criminal offenses against the law of nations); Textile Workers v Lincoln Mills, 353 US 448 (1957) (upholding federal-question jurisdiction of an action to enforce a collective-bargaining agreement under § 301 of the Taft-Hartley Act, 29 USC § 185(a), on the basis of an implicit statutory grant of power to develop federal common law).

[309]One of the few federal courts provided for by that document was a court of appeal in prize cases. Because there was no corresponding federal trial court, the appeal court necessarily heard cases coming from state courts, and the Supreme Court approved this course in Penhallow v Doane's Administrators, 3 US 54 (1795). See The First Hundred Years at 49–51.

[310]Rutledge had argued against the creation of lower federal courts on the ground that Supreme Court review was adequate to assure both the vindication of federal rights and the uniformity of federal law. 1 Farrand at 124. The Supreme Court upheld § 25 in Martin v Hunter's Lessee, 14 US 303 (1816). See The First Hundred Years at 91–96.

[311]See Henry J. Merry, Scope of the Supreme Court's Appellate Jurisdiction: Historical Basis, 47 Minn L Rev 53 (1962). By providing for writ of error rather than appeal, the Act did limit Supreme Court review of the facts—not only in common law actions, as did the contemporaneously proposed seventh amendment, but in equity and admiralty cases too. 1 Stat at 84–87, §§ 22, 25. Professor Casper has described these provisions, along with those restricting equity powers and guaranteeing the civil jury, as elements in a general design of the First Congress to democratize and limit the courts—out of fears lthat the judges, made independent by Article III, might themselves exercise arbitrary power. See 1 Stat at 77, 80, 82, §§ 9, 12, 16; US Const, Amend 7; Gerhard Casper, The Judiciary Act of 1789 and Judicial Independence, in Marcus, Origins of the Federal Judiciary 281 (cited in note 305) (adding that five of the first eight amendments dealt with "matters mostly concerning the courts").

view that it could make no exceptions to the Supreme Court's jurisdiction without entrusting the excluded cases to some other federal court, for as also noted above the statute left significant categories of cases outside federal jurisdiction altogether.[312]

The original jurisdiction of the Supreme Court was defined essentially as in Article III itself, embracing cases in which states or foreign diplomats were parties.[313] Notably, however, the Supreme Court's jurisdiction in state cases was limited to "controversies of a civil nature," suggesting that Congress believed either that criminal cases fell outside the constitutional provision for "cases . . . in which a state shall be party" or that it was not required to vest in the Supreme Court the entire original jurisdiction defined by Article III. Both of these interpretations seem doubtful. For, although the disputes to which the judicial power was extended by virtue of the state's presence as a litigant were described by the arguably narrower term "controversies" rather than "cases," the Framers seemed to treat the two terms as equivalent in giving the Supreme Court original jurisdiction of "cases" to which a state was a party; and the reasons for jurisdiction seem as strong in criminal as in civil cases.[314] The explicit provision authorizing Congress to make exceptions to the *appellate* jurisdiction, moreover, casts considerable doubt on the alternative hypothesis that Congress may make exceptions from the original jurisdiction as well.[315]

Buried at the end of § 13 was a provision authorizing the Supreme Court to issue writs of mandamus "to any courts appointed, or persons holding office, under the authority of the United States." This was the provision that *Marbury v. Madison* struck down on the ground that Congress had no power to expand the original jurisdiction beyond those cases enumerated in Article III.[316] The constitutional question could easily have

---

[312]Nevertheless Congress was careful to insist that the Supreme Court be open in most if not all cases in which a state court had denied a federal claim, thus preserving to a substantial degree the Court's essential authority to keep states from infringing federal constitutional rights. See text at notes 292–96. Moreover, despite the absence of Supreme Court review of federal criminal convictions, the principle of judicial review that would be confirmed in *Marbury v Madison* ensured that even in such cases constitutional objections would be heard by *some* federal court. Arguably the most serious failing of the Judiciary Act from the standpoint of an adequate modern system of judicial review was the absence of any provision guaranteeing access to the courts to those injured by public officers who acted illegally without seeking judicial assistance. Cf 42 USC § 1983; 28 USC § 1343(a)(3) (1988). Apparently the First Congress thought no such provision was constitutionally required.

[313]1 Stat at 80–81, § 13. Cf US Const, Art III, § 2. Like that of the inferior courts, this jurisdiction was partly concurrent and partly exclusive. See text at notes 298–301. By essentially repeating the Constitution's general reference to matters "in which a State shall be Party," this section did nothing to resolve the question whether a state could be made defendant, and nothing was said on the subject during debate. See Chisholm v Georgia, 2 US 419 (1793).

[314]But see Wisconsin v Pelican Insurance Co., 127 US 265, 300 (1888).

[315]Nevertheless Attorney General Charles Lee advised the Secretary of State in 1797 that, although a prosecution for libeling a foreign ambassador was a "case[] affecting ambassadors" within the original-jurisdiction provision of Article III, the Supreme Court could not hear it because the statute provided only for suits by or against them: The Supreme Court had recently held that the judicial power "remains inactive and unexercisable until by law it is drawn into action." 1 Op AG 71, 74 (1797). The opinion to which he referred dealt with the appellate jurisdiction, to which Congress is expressly empowered to make "exceptions." Wiscart v D'Auchy, 3 US 321 (1796); The First Hundred Years at 25–28.

[316]Marbury v Madison, 5 US 137, 171–80 (1803).

gone the other way,[317] but it would be wrong to conclude that Congress interpreted Article III differently from the Court. For the authority to issue mandamus appears in a sentence otherwise dedicated to appellate jurisdiction; it seems likely that the mandamus power was meant to be appellate as well.[318]

In contrast to its later decision with respect to diplomatic appointments,[319] Congress set the number of Justices at six. This provision need not imply that Congress thought the Constitution required it to fix the number of Justices, since there were obvious reasons of policy for having precisely six. The figure was inconvenient, since as Jackson noted an even number would enhance the risk of stalemate.[320] But six Justices made sense in terms of Congress's additional decision to divide the country into three judicial circuits and to assign two Justices to each of the circuit courts.[321]

No one is reported as objecting at the time, but the Justices themselves were soon to protest against this additional assignment on both constitutional and practical grounds.[322] The most serious constitutional argument was that when sitting on circuit the Justices would be expected to act as trial judges in cases not within the Supreme Court's original jurisdiction. The response that in so doing they were not acting as the Supreme Court raised a constitutional difficulty of its own: If they were to exercise two offices, they arguably had to be given two appointments under Article II.

When these issues reached the Supreme Court in 1803, the Court upheld Congress's power to impose circuit duties on the Justices without reaching the merits: "[P]ractice and acquiescence under it for a period of several years, commencing with the organization of the judicial system, affords an irresistible answer, and has indeed fixed the construction."[323] The provision for circuit riding thus illustrates in starkest form the influence that congressional interpretation of the Constitution can have on the course of judicial decision.

---

[317]See Cohens v Virginia, 19 US 264, 399–402 (1821) (modifying the *Marbury* dictum); Börs v Preston, 111 US 252, 260 (1884) (holding Congress could constitutionally give the Court appellate jurisdiction where Article III said it should have original).

[318]See The First Hundred Years at 67–68.

[319]See text at notes 105–12.

[320]1 Annals at 812.

[321]1 Stat at 74–75, § 4.

[322]See 3 Story, § 1573 n 1.

[323]Stuart v Laird, 5 US 299, 309 (1803); The First Hundred Years at 74–77.

2

Substantive Legislation

Apart from questions of government organization, most of the permissible subjects of federal legislation were listed in Article I, § 8. They ranged from taxation and trade to military and monetary matters, from borrowing and bankruptcy to citizenship and copyrights, from patents and post offices to piracy. Articles I and IV empowered Congress to legislate for the seat of Government and for the Territories respectively. The latter Article added the power to admit new states and prescribe the effect of one state's judgments and acts in another, the former the authority to enact "all laws which shall be necessary and proper for carrying into execution" any powers granted to any officer or organ of the federal government.

Within its first few years, in accord with Washington's initial admonition,[1] Congress worked its way methodically through this list of powers. Even as it set up the Government itself, the First Congress made a good start on that project. In so doing it left us an invaluable set of annotations to the various grants of federal legislative power.

I. TAXES AND TRADE

A. Tariffs and Tonnage

No government can run without money, and the dependence of the old Congress on contributions from the states had been a principal source of discontent with the Articles of Confederation.[2] One of the central innovations of the Philadelphia Convention was the

---

[1] See chapter 1.

[2] See Articles of Confederation, Art VIII, 1 Stat 4, 6 (July 9, 1778); 1 Story, §§ 123–25; Merrill Jensen, The New Nation: A History of the United States During the Confederation, 1781–1789, 407–21 (Knopf, 1950).

general federal tax power conferred by the first clause of Article I, § 8: "The Congress shall have power to lay and collect taxes, duties, imposts and excises, to pay the debts and provide for the common defence and general welfare of the United States." "Direct" taxes were required to be apportioned among the states according to population;[3] "duties, imposts and excises" were to be "uniform throughout the United States."[4] Congress was forbidden to lay any tax or duty "on articles exported from any state," to discriminate by any revenue or trade measure in favor of the ports of any one state, or for twenty years to impose a tax of more than ten dollars a head on the importation of slaves.[5]

Congress thus had a wide choice of means for supporting the operations of the new Government. It decided to rely principally on customs duties on imported goods and tonnage duties on foreign and domestic vessels.[6]

The most striking feature of the tariff law was the candid admission in its first section that its purposes included not only the support of government and the payment of debts but also "the encouragement and protection of manufactures."[7] In April, 1789, as the House began debating the revenue question, it received a petition from a long list of Baltimore tradesmen complaining of the tendency of their fellow citizens to fritter away the nation's wealth "in the purchase of those articles, from foreigners, which our citizens, if properly encouraged, were fully competent to furnish" and urging Congress to "impos[e] on all foreign articles, which can be made in America, such duties as will give a just and decided preference to the[] labors" of American artisans and "discountenanc[e] that trade which tends so materially to injure them, and impoverish their country."[8]

These sentiments found many adherents in the House. Thomas Fitzsimons of Pennsylvania began by proposing specific duties on a long list of imported items from beer to nuts with the avowed purpose, among others, "to encourage the productions of our country, and protect our infant manufactures."[9] Hartley enthusiastically agreed,[10] Madison conceded that free trade was not an absolute principle,[11] and other members

[3]US Const, Art I, § 2, cl 3; Art I, § 9, cl 4.

[4]Art I, § 8, cl 1.

[5]Art I, § 9, cls 1, 5, & 6. Article I, § 7 required "[a]ll bills for raising revenue" to originate in the House of Representatives but permitted the Senate "to propose or concur with amendments as on other bills."

[6]1 Stat 24 (July 4, 1789) (tariffs); 1 Stat 27 (July 20, 1789) (tonnage). Customs duties had been the basis of a proposal for federal taxation made by the Confederation Congress in 1783, which, according to Madison, had "received, generally, the approbation of the several States . . . ." 1 Annals at 107.

In order to prevent interference with commerce or with federal revenue, Article I, § 10 forbade the states to impose tonnage duties or tariffs ("except what may be absolutely necessary for executing [their] inspection laws") "without the consent of Congress." The purpose and operation of this provision were illustrated in August, 1790, when Congress passed a statute consenting to tonnage duties imposed by three states for navigation improvements—the establishment of port wardens and the removal of obstructions from the Savannah River—that Congress had declined to finance out of the federal treasury. 1 Stat 184 (Aug 11, 1790); 9 Doc Hist at 349; see note 116.

[7]1 Stat at 25.

[8]1 American State Papers (Finance) 5 (Gales & Seaton, 1832) [hereafter cited as Am St Papers]. See also the similar petition from New York manufacturers, id at 9.

[9]1 Annals at 110–11. See also id at 150 (making a special plea for high duties to encourage the manufacture of malt liquor).

[10]Id at 114–15.

[11]Id at 115–19.

scrambled for a piece of the action. Clymer sought protection for steel and paper,[12] Moore and Hiester for hemp,[13] Carroll for glass,[14] Bland and Parker for Virginia coal.[15] Fisher Ames made quite a touching little oration on the virtues of cottage industries in advocating a protective tariff on nails.[16] Roger Sherman pleaded for a six-cent tariff on manufactured tobacco on the express ground that "the duty ought to amount to a prohibition," and he got it.[17]

There were objections to several of these suggestions,[18] but no one denied that Congress could constitutionally impose tariffs in order to stimulate domestic production, and it did so.[19] Fitzsimons suggested a plausible basis for this authority in urging a high duty on bohea tea "not only as a revenue but as a regulation of a commerce highly advantageous to the United States."[20] Our budding trade with China and India was clearly commerce, and higher duties on goods imported in foreign vessels would encourage American shipping.[21] Generalizing Fitzsimons's suggestion, § 5 of the statute provided a 10% discount on all customs charges for imports carried by American vessels.[22]

Fitzsimons's argument that differential duties for the promotion of American shipping constituted a regulation of foreign commerce suggested two interesting conclusions respecting the commerce power. First, a measure could qualify as a regulation of commerce even though it took the shape of a tax; not form but purpose and effect were determinative.[23] Second, the power to regulate commerce included the power to restrict it.

[12]Id at 153–54, 174.
[13]Id at 158.
[14]Id at 174.
[15]Id at 177.
[16]

> [I]t has become usual for the country people in this State to erect small forges in their chimney corners, and in winter, and on evenings when little other work could be done, great quantities of nails were made even by children; perhaps enough might be manufactured in this way to supply the continent.

Id at 163. See also id at 164.
[17]Id at 174; 1 Stat at 25.
[18]Various members suggested that high duties on hemp would be detrimental to rope manufacturers and to the shipping business. 1 Annals at 158–62. Bland opposed the inclusion of nails as unfair to the South, since the Northern states made only enough nails for their own consumption. Id at 163. Madison urged restraint both because he thought there should be a presumption of free trade and because he was afraid disputes over particular objects of protection might delay the crucial business of financing the Government. Id at 115–19. Many years later Madison would emphatically argue that the power to regulate commerce included the power to impose protective tariffs. See Letter of James Madison to Joseph C. Cabell, Sept 18, 1828, in Gaillard Hunt, ed, 9 The Writings of James Madison 316–40 (Putnam, 1910).
[19]"In its final form, the tariff of 1789 represented a compromise between the advocates of high protective duties and those who favored a tariff for revenue only . . . . [S]pecific duties ranging as high as 50 per cent were levied upon steel, ships, cordage, tobacco, salt, indigo, cloth, and so on." Miller at 15.
[20]1 Annals at 147.
[21]Id at 147–48.
[22]1 Stat at 27.
[23]For recognition in the Convention of the impracticability of distinguishing between commercial regulations and revenue measures see 2 Farrand at 276 (Madison). Later applications of Fitzsimons's principle include the Head Money Cases, 112 US 580, 595 (1884) (holding the requirement that duties be uniform inapplicable to a charge imposed on the landing of passengers from abroad on the ground that the exaction was

In the immediate context this was hardly surprising, since one justification for giving Congress authority to regulate foreign commerce had been to permit it to retaliate against and therefore to deter foreign restrictions.[24] But the First Congress's decision with respect to foreign commerce seemed likely also to affect the interpretation of the parallel clause regarding commerce among the several states, although the specific reason for giving this latter authority to Congress had been to enable it to remove obstacles to freedom of trade.[25]

The commerce-clause argument applied equally to a second major feature of the tax system adopted by the First Congress: tonnage duties that discriminated sharply between American and foreign vessels. Ships built in the United States and owned by U.S. citizens were to pay six cents per ton per year. Ships built here but owned by foreigners were to pay thirty cents per ton, and others fifty, each time they entered an American port.[26] Madison expressly supported discriminatory tonnage duties on the ground that they would encourage American shipping, thus bringing them too within the umbrella of the commerce clause as Fitzsimons had construed it.[27]

A further step would be necessary to find a commerce-power justification for duties designed to promote production, since neither agriculture nor industry was "commerce" within the ordinary meaning of the term.[28] In one sense that step was not difficult to take, since protective tariffs restrict commerce itself by increasing the price of exchange; but acceptance of this position would mean that Congress could regulate foreign commerce in

---

not a tax but a regulation of commerce), Henderson v Mayor of New York, 92 US 259, 273–74 (1876) (striking down a similar state law as impinging on the federal power to regulate foreign commerce), and Bailey v Drexel Furniture Co. (The Child Labor Tax Case), 259 US 20, 38–39 (1922) (striking down a federal tax as an effective regulation of child labor). See The First Hundred Years at 431–32, 405–08; The Second Century at 173.

[24]See The Federalist Nos 11, 22 (Hamilton); Madison's Preface to the Debates in the Convention of 1787, 3 Farrand at 539, 547.

[25]In support of this view see 3 Farrand at 542, 547–48; H.P. Hood & Sons v Du Mond, 336 US 525, 539 (1949). This issue was to divide the Court over 100 years later in the interstate context. See the various opinions in Champion v Ames (The Lottery Case), 188 US 321, 355, 371–72 (1903), and in Hammer v Dagenhart, 247 US 251, 272, 277 (1918); The Second Century at 28, 96–98.

[26]1 Stat at 27–28, § 1 (July 20, 1789). Representative Bland argued at one point that any tonnage tax laid on ships traveling between ports in the United States would offend Art I, § 9's provision that "vessels bound to, or from, one state" not "be obliged to enter, clear, or pay duties in another." More thoughtful colleagues pointed out that this language had been meant to preclude compulsory detours to third states, not to exempt the coasting trade from such duties altogether. See 10 Doc Hist at 408–11; 2 Farrand at 417.

[27]1 Annals at 196–97. See also Madison's letter to George Nicholas, July 5, 1789, 12 Madison Papers at 279, 280 ("a navigation act under the name of duties on tonnage"). Madison and others also defended high duties on British vessels (as well as a preference for French ships that was not adopted) on the ground of retaliation against British measures obstructing our own shipping—which Abraham Baldwin of Georgia insisted had been the whole point of the Annapolis and Philadelphia Conventions. 1 Annals at 184–96. In addition, one of Madison's reasons for encouraging American shipping was to facilitate eventual establishment of a Navy, and thus the discrimination might also be justified as necessary and proper to Congress's authority "to provide and maintain a navy." US Const, Art I, § 8, cl 13.

[28]See Marshall's definition in Gibbons v Ogden, 22 US 1, 83–84 (1824); United States v E.C. Knight Co., 156 US 1, 12 (1895); cf Carter v Carter Coal Co., 298 US 238, 297–310 (1936) (mining); see The Second Century at 22, 223–24.

order to encourage conduct it presumably could not regulate directly. That in itself would be a significantly broad interpretation of congressional power, and it would later be hotly disputed;[29] but it was less threatening to reserved state powers than the alternative explanation that the essentially unlimited tax power might likewise be used for ulterior ends.[30]

Many of the members who spoke during the debate on the tariff and tonnage laws seemed to think it appropriate to use the tax power itself for the promotion of goals unrelated to revenue. Few of the advocates of protection for domestic producers mentioned the commerce power. Ames said nothing about commerce in urging high tariffs for certain imports from Rhode Island in order to coerce that refractory state into joining the new Union.[31] Fitzsimons himself, the exponent of the commerce-clause thesis, bolstered his plea for high duties on liquor with an argument based entirely on health and morals: If the result was to discourage the consumption of alcoholic beverages, so much the better, because alcohol was "a luxury of the most mischievous kind."[32] Finally, in adopting a duty on tobacco products that had explicitly been justified as a prohibition Congress seemed to lend strength to the extreme position that taxes might be levied even when they served no revenue purpose at all.

Of course, as Justice Robert Jackson would later observe, economic incentives are inseparable from taxation: "[A]ll taxation has a tendency . . . to discourage the activity taxed."[33] Indeed, so far as the text is concerned, Article I could easily be read to permit Congress to levy taxes in order not only to pay the debts and provide for defense but also to promote "the general welfare"—in other words, for any reason that was good for the nation as a whole. On the other hand, indifference to the purpose and effect of measures cast in the form of taxes could obliterate the limitations on federal regulatory powers that

[29]See Champion v Ames (the Lottery Case), 188 US 321 (1903); Hammer v Dagenhart, 247 US 251 (1918); United States v Darby, 312 US 100 (1941); The Second Century at 28, 96–98, 238. Congress's acceptance of Sherman's prohibitive duty on manufactured tobacco products (see text accompanying note 17 supra) suggests the further conclusion that the power to regulate commerce includes the power to forbid it—another important issue at stake in the Lottery Case, 188 US at 354–62. Cf § 40 of the 1789 statute providing for enforcement of the tariff law, 1 Stat 29, 48–49 (July 31, 1789), which generally forbade the importation of goods subject to duty "in any other manner than by sea, []or in any ship or vessel less than thirty tons burthen," evidently on the ground that this prohibition (or regulation) was necessary and proper to the collection of revenue.

[30]See McCray v United States, 195 US 27 (1904); Bailey v Drexel Furniture Co. (the Child Labor Tax Case), 259 US 20 (1922); The Second Century at 30, 173–74.

[31]"He just stated that these articles were imported in considerable quantities from a neighboring State that had not yet adopted the constitution; and, perhaps, said he, our political situation is such as to make some regulation on this head necessary." 1 Annals at 162–63. Pressure on Rhode Island might conceivably have been defended as necessary and proper to protection of trade or revenues, to the conduct of foreign affairs, or even to the admission of additional states. See also the discussion of Rhode Island's status, text at notes 335–58.

[32]1 Annals at 204. See also id at 111 (noting that several items had been included in his initial list of specific duties in order to discourage their use). Madison made a similar argument in advocating the excise tax on whiskey that Congress adopted in 1791. See Daily Advertiser, Jan 12, 1791; text accompanying notes 36–56.

[33]United States v Kahriger, 345 US 22, 35 (1953) (concurring opinion).

were implicit in the initial enumeration and confirmed by the First Congress in proposing the tenth amendment.[34]

Because all the incentive provisions of the tariff and tonnage laws can be explained
on the narrower ground that they effectively regulated interstate or foreign commerce, neither of these statutes proves that the legislators believed they could accomplish by taxation that which they could not do directly.[35] At the very least, however, they demonstrate
that the First Congress took a broad view of the purposes for which it could regulate
commerce; and those who would later argue that the tax power could be exercised only
for revenue purposes would have a good deal of explaining to do.

B.   Whiskey

Before Congress had been in business two years, it felt obliged to tap additional sources
of revenue.[36] As several speakers had emphasized during the 1789 debates, there were limits to how high customs duties could be raised without provoking widespread smuggling.[37] Convinced that direct taxation "would be contrary to the sentiments of the majority of the people," Madison accordingly proposed an excise on the domestic production of
ardent spirits as "the least exceptionable" option.[38]

Whiskey producers were not so sure, and as usual some of their arguments took
constitutional shape. Jackson objected that the burden of the tax fell unequally on the
South, which had "no breweries or orchards to furnish a substitute" for whiskey.[39] Hugh
Williamson of North Carolina tied this argument to Article I's requirement that excises
be "uniform throughout the United States" and urged the House "to equalise them, by
proposing a tax on beer and cider."[40]

Similar arguments had been raised and rejected in the tariff debate,[41] and they were
rejected again as the whiskey tax was adopted.[42] Since the tariffs could be justified as reg-

---

[34]"The powers not delegated to the United States by the Constitution, nor prohibited by it to the States, are
reserved to the States respectively, or to the people." See also McCulloch v Maryland, 17 US 316, 405 (1819).
"[S]hould Congress, under the pretext of executing its powers, pass laws for the accomplishment of objects
not entrusted to the government; it would become the painful duty of this tribunal, should a case requiring such
a decision come before it, to say that such an act was not the law of the land." Id at 423.

[35]A provision in the act next to be discussed, however, did seem to be difficult to explain on any other
basis. The excise on domestic liquors discriminated against beverages made from foreign materials, apparently in order to encourage local production. See 1 Stat 199, 202–03, §§ 14–15 (Mar 3, 1791). Though foreign
materials must be imported before they can be turned into domestic whiskey, it might be stretching things to
call this discrimination a regulation of commerce.

[36]The reason was to finance the payment of interest on state debts that Congress had assumed in 1790.
See Hamilton's second report to the House of Representatives on public credit, Dec 13, 1790, 7 Hamilton
Papers at 225, 226. For discussion of the assumption controversy see text at notes 168–81.

[37]See, e.g., 1 Annals at 200–01 (Rep. Boudinot).

[38]2 Annals at 1894.

[39]Id at 1890.

[40]Id at 1906–07. See also id at 1908 (Rep. Parker). George Nicholas made the point clearly in a letter to
Madison: "The spirit of [the constitutional requirement] must be that it shall be uniform in fact as well as in
name." Letter of George Nicholas to James Madison, Sept 16, 1791, 14 Madison Papers at 75.

[41]See 1 Annals at 163 (Rep. Bland) (arguing that a duty on nails would impose an unequal burden on the
South because the Northern states manufactured their own); id at 170 (Rep. Madison) (conceding the importance of a fair distribution of actual burdens by insisting that although Westerners would bear a dispropor-

ulations of commerce, rejection of the inequality argument in that context might be explained on the unappetizing ground that Congress could evade the uniformity requirement by invoking some power other than that of taxation.[43] No such argument was available, however, in the case of the whiskey excise; Congress seems to have concluded both that the Constitution required only geographical uniformity (as suggested by the phrase "uniform throughout the United States") and that the tax was uniform because it was nondiscriminatory on its face.

To require that the actual burden of taxation be distributed equally throughout the nation would have posed formidable accounting difficulties, but Justice Nelson's later example of a New York tax impartially imposed on domestic and out-of-state cotton suggests the possibilities of abuse invited by limiting the inquiry to facial discrimination.[44] We had by no means heard the last of arguments that various constitutional guarantees required de facto as well as de jure equality.[45]

Other objections to the whiskey tax implicated provisions of the new Bill of Rights, which Congress had proposed in 1789 and which was ratified the same year the excise was adopted. Parker zeroed in on "the mode of collecting the tax," which he argued would "let loose a swarm of harpies" who would "range through the country, prying into every man's house and affairs."[46] The modern reader will take this argument as a reminder to measure the enforcement provisions of the statute against the fourth amendment's prohibition of "unreasonable searches and seizures."

In fact the act raised interesting questions in this regard, for in addition to authorizing the issuance of warrants to search any place where spirits were suspected of being fraudulently concealed[47] it empowered revenue agents to enter any registered distillery or warehouse in order to sample and measure the inventory, without any ground for suspicion and without procuring a warrant.[48] Whether it was the regulated nature of the business or the voluntary act of distilling or storing liquor in the face of the registration and inspection provisions that made this requirement reasonable no one bothered to say, but Congress evidently thought there was no constitutional problem.[49]

---

tionate share of the salt tax it was "almost the only tax they will have to pay"). Neither Bland nor Madison expressly invoked the uniformity provision in this debate. See also the related argument of Representative Laurance, id at 184–85, that tonnage duties would increase the price of exports and thus constituted an export tax forbidden by Art I, § 9. Parker seemed to echo this last contention in suggesting that the whiskey tax was "not any thing better than a tax on exports." Daily Advertiser, Jan 12, 1791.

[42]1 Stat 199, 202–03, §§ 14–15 (Mar 3, 1791).

[43]See the Head Money Cases, 112 US 580, 595 (1884); The First Hundred Years at 431–32.

[44]Woodruff v Parham, 75 US 123, 145–46 (1869) (dissenting opinion); The First Hundred Years at 337. In a later defense of the whiskey excise, Hamilton argued that there was not even de facto inequality, since the tax was passed on to consumers throughout the nation. Report on the Difficulties in the Execution of the Act Laying Duties on Distilled Spirits, Mar 5, 1792, 11 Hamilton Papers at 77, 97.

[45]See, for example, Washington v Davis, 426 US 229 (1976); The Second Century at 488–93.

[46]2 Annals at 1891–92.

[47]1 Stat at 207, § 32.

[48]Id at 206, § 29.

[49]See also §§ 23, 24 of the 1789 statute providing for the collection of tariff and tonnage duties, 1 Stat at 43, authorizing customs officers without warrant to "open and examine" packages "on suspicion of fraud" and "to enter any ship or vessel" suspected of concealing goods subject to duty while authorizing issuance of a warrant to search buildings under the same conditions. A supplemental collection law adopted the next year

Jackson perceived a distinct threat in the dreaded host of federal tax collectors and proposed to meet it "by adding a clause to prevent Inspectors, or any officers under them, from interfering, either directly or indirectly, in elections, further than giving their own votes."[50] Sherman and Livermore made clear that the objection was to "electioneering" by federal agents whose duties would afford them "such a knowledge of persons and characters, as will give them great advantages, and enable them to influence elections to a great degree."[51] Jackson added that his proposal was made more imperative by "the dangerous influence that some future Presidents would acquire, by virtue of the power which [they] will possess of removing these officers."[52]

John Vining of Delaware responded that Jackson's proposal was unconstitutional, as it would deprive revenue officers of the right "of speaking and writing their minds."[53] Maryland's Joshua Seney replied that no rights would be infringed because it "would be optional to accept the offices or not,"[54] but Jackson's motion to muzzle the revenuers was decisively rejected.[55]

Thus the First Congress gave us a concise but cogent preview of the arguments that were to be made many years later with respect to the constitutionality of the Hatch Act.[56] While there were plenty of other objections to stripping civil servants of rights fundamental to the operation of republican government, Vining provided us at the outset with powerful ammunition based on the speech and press guarantees that Congress itself had recently proposed.

C.   Ship Licensing

As we have seen, one argument in favor of protective tariffs was that they fell within Congress's power to regulate commerce. The First Congress did other interesting things under the commerce power as well.

Perhaps the best known commercial regulation of the First Congress was the 1789 law providing for registration or enrollment of ships belonging to citizens of the United States.[57] There was no requirement that ships be either registered or enrolled, but a registered or enrolled vessel was entitled to all privileges granted to U.S. vessels by federal law.[58] Upon payment of tonnage duties and the posting of security against "illicit trade or commerce," the owners of registered or enrolled vessels might obtain licenses to

---

went even further, authorizing customs officers to board and inspect any vessel entering the United States or within four leagues of the coast, without requiring even suspicion of any wrongdoing. 1 Stat 145, 175, § 64 (Aug 4, 1790). As acts almost contemporaneous with the proposal of the fourth amendment, these provisions too provide some evidence of what Congress thought constituted an unreasonable search.

[50]2 Annals at 1924–25.

[51]Id at 1925.

[52]Id.

[53]Id. See also Ames's suggestion that Jackson's proposal would "muzzle the mouths of freemen, and take away the use of their reason." Id at 1926.

[54]Id.

[55]Id at 1927.

[56]See United Public Workers v Mitchell, 330 US 75 (1947), The Second Century at 355; Civil Service Commission v Letter Carriers, 413 US 548 (1973).

[57]1 Stat 55, §§ 1, 22 (Sept 1, 1789).

[58]Id, §§ 1, 22.

engage in the "bank or whale fisheries" or in trade between different customs districts within the United States. There was no requirement that a license be obtained either, but any vessel of twenty tons or more engaging in these activities without a license was "subject to the same tonnage, and fees, as foreign ships or vessels."[59]

This section was the predecessor of the licensing provision that Chief Justice Marshall would later invoke in striking down a state steamboat monopoly in *Gibbons v. Ogden*.[60] The Annals reveal no recorded debate on the 1789 statute. Congress evidently was convinced that a regulation of transportation was a regulation of commerce, and Marshall relied heavily on Congress's view in upholding federal licensing: "[T]his power has been exercised from the commencement of the government . . . ."[61]

Interestingly, none of the provisions of the 1789 Act was expressly limited to vessels engaged in commerce with foreign nations or among the several states.[62] Possibly Congress thought that licensing of all ships owned by U.S. citizens was necessary and proper to the enforcement of import duties or to the collection of the tonnage taxes that were assessed even against local vessels; perhaps Congress simply overlooked the possibility that some ships subject to the law might be engaged in purely local commerce. In any event the text and context of the licensing provision strongly suggested that its purpose was to facilitate the collection of duties, not to confer a right to engage in interstate or foreign trade. The later statute from which Marshall drew the opposite conclusion was substantially similar in every relevant respect.[63]

D. Inspection Laws

In January 1790 Representative Sedgwick moved that a committee be appointed to explore means "to encourage the exports of the United States, and to guard against frauds in the same."[64] The export of inferior goods, he explained, had so "injured the reputation of the United States" that legislation was needed, and Congress had power to enact it under the commerce clause. The ninth section of Article I, he added, forbade Congress only to tax exports, not to regulate them; and the tenth section confirmed the authority of Congress by empowering it to revise and control state inspection laws.[65]

Sedgwick did not say just what sort of legislation he had in mind, but he was on sound ground in suggesting that exports were subjects of foreign commerce susceptible to

[59] Id at 61, § 23.

[60] 22 US 1 (1824).

[61] Id at 190.

[62] The license and enrollment provisions applied only to vessels traveling between districts or engaged in the "bank or whale fisheries," but several states contained more than one district (see 1 Stat 29–35), and fishing on the high seas does not always involve contact with other countries or states.

[63] See 1 Stat 305 (Feb 18, 1793); The First Hundred Years at 171–72. Thus the licensing law illustrates once again the intimate relation between Congress's powers to tax and to regulate commerce. The protective tariff was an example of a tax imposed for regulatory purposes; ship licensing was an example of regulation imposed to promote the collection of taxes. See also 1 Stat 145, 175, § 62 (Aug 4, 1790), authorizing the President to build as many as ten "boats or cutters . . . to be employed for the protection of the revenue," i.e., as necessary and proper to the collection of duties.

[64] 1 Annals at 1143.

[65] Id at 1142.

federal regulation. The argument that the power to regulate included the power to impose exactions that looked like taxes, strongly advanced during the tariff debates, raised the question whether the ban on export taxes ought to apply to some regulations as well; but it did not require the improbable conclusion that exports were wholly beyond the reach of a body expressly authorized to regulate commerce with other nations. Though the immediate effect of federal regulation might be to restrict the export of inferior items, its ultimate goal was to promote commerce; and in any event the tariff debate had suggested that the purpose of a commercial regulation was immaterial to its validity.[66]

Two months afterward, apparently in response to Sedgwick's proposal, Congress enacted a statute directing federal customs officials not to authorize any vessel to leave port without complying with state inspection laws.[67] Given the understanding that transportation was trade, to restrict the movement of ships was to regulate commerce. Like the licensing law, however, this statute was not expressly limited to vessels sailing to other states or nations. Furthermore, in contrast to the licensing and registration provisions, it could hardly be thought necessary and proper to the collection of federal taxes, since its immediate purpose was to enforce state law[68] in the ultimate interest of promoting trade.

The constitutional difficulty, however, went deeper. Even with respect to ships that were engaged in interstate or foreign commerce, it was not obvious that Congress could provide for federal enforcement of state law. Executing that law, Livermore argued, was a matter for the states themselves; the bill was "an unconstitutional interference . . . with the powers of the respective states."[69]

In two respects the threat to state interests was less than that posed by the tariff law. Not only was the ultimate purpose of the inspection provision the irreproachable goal of removing obstructions to commerce. In addition, while the tariff law contained provisions intended to discourage conduct permitted by state law, the inspection statute was designed to help the states to carry out their own policy.[70] Nevertheless both the provisions of the Judiciary Act for exclusive federal jurisdiction over certain classes of cases[71] and the traditional principle that one sovereign will not execute the penal laws of another[72] suggest that on occasion a sovereign might legitimately object to officious assistance in enforcing its own laws. Livermore seemed to be suggesting an implicit limitation somewhat akin to the intergovernmental immunity later recognized in *McCulloch v. Maryland*;[73] the majority seemed to think there was no such limitation.

The more serious objection, perhaps, lay elsewhere. The effect of requiring compliance with state inspection laws was to make changing state laws the measure of federal rights and thus arguably to delegate to state legislatures the power that the Constitution had conferred on Congress. Later statutes forbidding the transportation of liquor in violation of state law and adopting state criminal laws to govern federal reservations would

---

[66]See text at notes 25–35.

[67]1 Stat 106 (Apr 2, 1790).

[68]"[T]he object of the bill is to make it the duty of the collectors to attend to the execution of the State Inspection Laws . . . ." 2 Annals at 1527 (Rep. Smith).

[69]Id at 1527.

[70]See The Second Century at 175, discussing Brooks v United States, 267 US 432, 439 (1925).

[71]1 Stat 73, 76–79, §§ 9, 11 (Sept 24, 1789). See chapter 1.

[72]See Huntington v Attrill, 146 US 657, 669 (1892).

[73]17 US 316, 429–30 (1819).

pose similar problems.[74] The enactment of the inspection law suggests that the First Congress saw no constitutional obstacle to such cooperative uses of federal power.

E.   Seamen

Possibly the most ambitious exercise of the commerce power during the First Congress was the enactment in July 1790 of a comprehensive labor law for merchant seamen.[75] On the one hand this Act provided stringent sanctions against sailors who deserted or failed to report and those who harbored them.[76] On the other it guaranteed crew members a written contract, prompt payment of wages, adequate medicines and provender, and the right to require a leaky vessel to put into port for repairs.[77]

Unfortunately the Annals report no debate on these provisions. Their most plausible source of support was the commerce clause, and that was the basis on which they were subsequently explained.[78] It was not obvious, however, that a regulation of the care and feeding of seamen was a regulation of commerce. Transportation was commerce, as the ship licensing law implied, and crew members were engaged in transportation. Yet the law regulated not transportation itself but the labor relations of those who did the transporting.[79]

On the other hand, both the duties and the rights created by this law obviously promoted commerce by assuring that ships would be properly manned. If the bill did not regulate commerce itself, it could easily be found necessary and proper to the commerce power. In the early twentieth century, when Congress for similar reasons attempted to give railroad workers the right to join unions and to receive pensions, the Supreme Court held it had exceeded its powers.[80] The First Congress plainly took a broader view of its commerce clause authority.[81]

---

[74]See Clark Distilling Co. v Western Maryland Ry, 242 US 311, 326–32 (1917), The Second Century at 115 n 150; United States v Sharpnack, 355 US 286 (1958).

[75]1 Stat 131 (July 20, 1790).

[76]Id at 131–34, §§ 2, 4, 5, 7. Section 4's provision for private prosecution of persons harboring delinquent seamen (with the inducement of retaining half the penalty) has been cited as casting doubt on the argument that the Framers contemplated Presidential control of all federal executive functions. Lawrence Lessig & Cass Sunstein, The President and the Administration, 94 Colum L Rev 1, 20 n. 82 (1994).

[77]1 Stat at 131–35, §§ 1, 3, 6, 8, 9.

[78]See the discussion of the national bank, text at notes 182–205; St. George Tucker, ed, 1 Blackstone's Commentaries on the Laws of England 252 (Birch & Small, 1803) [hereafter cited as Tucker's Blackstone]. The reader may recall that much later the Supreme Court would find the enactment of statutes respecting the shipping business necessary and proper to the exercise of the admiralty jurisdiction conferred on federal courts pursuant to Article III. In re Garnett, 141 US 1, 12 (1891); The Second Century at 27 n 139. If the notion that laws facilitate the decision of cases seems reasonable enough, it also implies a fairly broad understanding of the words "necessary and proper." In any event there is no evidence in the Annals that Congress in enacting the seamen's law thought it was acting under the admiralty clause.

[79]Moreover, like the licensing law, the statute was not expressly limited to seamen engaged on vessels employed in commerce "with foreign nations, and among the several states, and with the Indian tribes."

[80]Adair v United States, 208 US 161 (1908); Railroad Retirement Board v Alton RR, 295 US 330 (1935); The Second Century at 27, 232–33.

[81]Three provisions of the seamen's statute raised federalism questions of a different sort by providing for participation of state officials in the enforcement of federal law. Section 2 made penalties payable to the owner by delinquent seamen "recoverable in any court, or before any justice or justices of any state, city,

F. The Slave Trade

The clouds of future storms darkened the halls of Congress in February 1790, when Representative Fitzsimons presented an address from an assembly of Quakers urging Congress to do something about the slave trade.[82] South Carolina's William Smith protested that the House should not even consider the petition because Article I, § 9 deprived Congress of the power to ban importation of slaves into existing states before 1808.[83] Madison appropriately responded that the same provision expressly permitted a federal tax not exceeding ten dollars a head[84] and suggested that Congress might also have authority to outlaw the transportation of slaves from Africa to the West Indies in American ships[85]—thus implying both that the transportation of slaves was commerce and that trade "with foreign nations" included trade by Americans between them.

Jackson of Georgia protested that anything done to suppress the slave trade might threaten slavery itself,[86] and the very next day a memorial signed by no less a personage than Benjamin Franklin urged Congress to take steps under unspecified powers to free the slaves.[87] Representatives from the deep South began to squeal like stuck pigs. Smith warned that emancipation would offend the constitutional ban on ex post facto legislation,[88] Tucker that it would bring about "civil war."[89] Baldwin declared that the requirement that direct taxes be apportioned according to the census was meant to prevent "any special tax upon negro slaves."[90] Madison responded that Congress had authority (under

---

town or county within the United States" having "cognizance of debts of equal value," while making no provision for federal jurisdiction. Section 3 "required" local justices of the peace, in places where no federal district judge resided, to resolve controversies between master and crew over the seaworthiness of a vessel. Id. Section 7 authorized "any justice of the peace within the United States" to issue warrants for the arrest of delinquent sailors and directed the justices upon a finding of delinquency to commit them "to the house of correction or common gaol of the city, town or place" pending departure of the vessel. Id at 134. A year earlier Congress had passed a resolution that "recommended" passage of state legislation permitting federal convicts to be housed in state jails (1 Stat 96 (Sept 23, 1789)), but the seamen's act seemed to be phrased as an order rather than a request. Cf Testa v Katt, 330 US 386, 394 (1947); New York v United States, 504 US 144 (1992).

[82] 1 Annals at 1224–25.

[83] Id at 1230.

[84] An earlier proposal to add such a tax to the tariff bill, ably seconded by Madison, had been withdrawn once it became evident that the controversy it engendered would delay passage of the bill itself. See id at 349–56. As Representative Parker said in introducing the amendment, its principal purpose was to "prevent, in some degree, this irrational and inhuman traffic" (id at 349); no one suggested that this purpose made the proposal unconstitutional.

[85] Id at 1226–27.

[86] Id at 1228.

[87] Id at 1239–40. In the brief debate on Parker's earlier proposal to tax the importation of slaves, Madison had made an argument that might have been extended to support the improbable conclusion that the war powers enabled Congress to abolish slavery: Any addition to the number of slaves diminished the capacity for self-defense, and anything that increased the danger of war was "a proper subject for the consideration of those charged with the general administration of the Government." Id at 354.

[88] Id at 1244, citing US Const, Art I, § 9.

[89] 1 Annals at 1240.

[90] Id at 1243, citing US Const, Art I, §§ 2, 9.

Article IV?) to regulate slavery in the western territory[91] and the introduction of slaves into new states that might be formed there.[92] Gerry suggested that Congress might raise money to purchase slaves and set them free by selling lands in the western territories.[93] The protesters were noisy but badly outnumbered; both petitions were referred to a committee for consideration.[94]

Predictably, the committee reported that Congress had no power to interfere with slavery itself, or to forbid importation of additional slaves to the original states before 1808. It added, however, that Congress did have authority to impose a ten-dollar tax on each slave imported, to forbid citizens to transport slaves between foreign countries, and "to make provision for the humane treatment of slaves" during the course of importation. The report concluded by urging that Congress exercise all these powers "for the humane objects of the memorialists, so far as they can be promoted on the principles of justice, humanity, and good policy."[95]

This committee report provoked another five days of heated debate. Aedanus Burke of South Carolina insisted that slavery was good for slaves and vilified the Quakers.[96] Smith enlarged upon Burke's remarks, trumpeted states' rights, and disparaged blacks in general.[97] Boudinot expatiated at length on the evils of slavery, acknowledged that there were serious limits to what Congress could do about it, and stood up for the petitioners.[98] The upshot was a report of the Committee of the Whole House restating the original committee's conclusions concerning the extent of congressional powers but omitting any reference to the desirability of their exercise.[99]

With that the House dropped the subject for the time being, but the spirit of dissension it had awakened had come to stay.

---

[91]"He adverted to the western country—and the cession of Georgia in which Congress have certainly the power to regulate the subject of slavery . . . ." Gazette of the United States, Feb 12, 1790.

[92]1 Annals at 1246.

[93]Id at 1247.

[94]Id. Representative Smith suggested privately that his defeat on this motion might have been a Pyrrhic one: "I think we so effectually tired the members out & embarrassed them that they will not be in a hurry to bring the subject on again." Letter of William L. Smith to Edward Rutledge, Feb 13, 1790, in George C. Rogers, Jr., ed, Letters of William Loughton Smith to Edward Rutledge, 69 South Carolina Historical Magazine 101, 104 (1968).

[95]2 Annals at 1465–66.

[96]Id at 1502.

[97]Id at 1503–14. "The Gentlemen from S. Carolina & Georgia," wrote Madison, "are intemperate beyond all example and even all decorum." Letter of James Madison to Benjamin Rush, Mar 20, 1790, 13 Madison Papers at 109.

[98]2 Annals at 1517–22. Though the Annals are particularly unhelpful on this score, other sources reveal a variety of attacks on particular conclusions in the committee report. Tucker argued that foreign commerce "can only mean betwixt this country and foreign countries," lest Congress have power to provide "that no person shall, when in a foreign country, buy himself a shirt or a coat." Smith protested that if Congress could regulate the conditions of transport it might effectively ban importation by prescribing that no more than one slave per two tons of burden be carried. Baldwin agreed with both of them, while Scott, at the opposite end of the spectrum, insisted that Congress could ban importation immediately because slaves were not "persons" within the meaning of the limitation in Art I, § 9. See New York Daily Gazette, Mar 23 and 26, 1790.

[99]2 Annals at 1523–25. The committee's recommendations with respect to the international slave trade were enacted in part in 1794. 1 Stat 347 (Mar 22, 1794); see chapter 4.

II. SPENDING

A. Appropriations

Federal spending raises challenging questions of separation of powers. For by virtue of the appropriations clause of Article I, § 9, the power of the purse extends to the disbursement as well as the raising of funds; both are subject to congressional control.[100]

As its decision not to specify the salaries of diplomatic officers illustrates,[101] the First Congress was not always very particular in defining how the money it appropriated should be spent. The basic appropriation statute for 1789, for example, provided $137,000 for the War Department, $190,000 to discharge old treasury warrants, $96,000 for veterans' pensions, and $216,000 "for defraying the expenses of the civil list," which included virtually everything else.[102] The corresponding law for the following year—although passed more or less in advance—granted precise sums for the payment of named debtors and for construction of a particular lighthouse, but it contained a military appropriation that appeared as general as that of the previous statute. Moreover, it allotted the President a $10,000 fund for "contingent charges of the government" without attaching any strings whatever.[103]

Maclay objected vehemently to Congress's failure to specify the objects of federal spending:

> The Appropriations were all in Gross, to the amount of Upwards of half a Million . . . . [T]he particulars are not mentioned. [T]he Estimate on which it was founded may be mislaid or changed. [I]n fact it is giving the Secretary the money for him to account for as he pleases. This is certainly all Wrong. [T]he estimate should have formed part of the bill or should have been recited in it.[104]

In what may have been a response to such criticism, the 1791 statute appropriated lump sums for the expenses of the civil list "as estimated by the Secretary of the Treasury, in the statement . . . accompanying his report to the House of Representatives"[105]—a formulation that represented a sea change in congressional control of expenditures if, as seems probable, it was intended to bind the Secretary to the allocation of funds that he had proposed.[106] It is certainly arguable that the revised formula more nearly captured the spirit of the constitutional provision.

---

[100]For the history of legislative control of expenditures in England and the states before adoption of the Constitution see Gerhard Casper, Appropriations of Power, 13 U Ark Little Rock L J 1, 3–8 (1990).

[101]See chapter 1.

[102]1 Stat 95 (Sept 29, 1789). Hamilton's detailed estimates, made in response to instructions from the House pursuant to the statute by which the Treasury Department was created, were the source of these figures. The sums appropriated for the civil list and for the War Department, however, were somewhat less than Hamilton had requested. See 5 Hamilton Papers at 379–92; 1 Annals at 894–95; 1 Stat 65, 65–66, § 2.

[103]1 Stat 104, 104–06 (Mar 26, 1790).

[104]9 Doc Hist at 225–26.

[105]1 Stat 190 (Feb 11, 1791).

[106]See Casper, 13 U Ark Little Rock LJ at 10–12 (cited in note 100); Lucius Wilmerding, Jr., The Spending Power: A History of the Efforts of Congress to Control Expenditures 22 (Yale, 1943). In fact the final version of the 1790 bill Maclay was protesting contained a similar clause, although no comparable lan-

B. Lighthouses

As already noted, one of the more specific provisions of the 1790 appropriation law granted a named sum to discharge obligations specified in a particular report, "including . . . a provision for building a light-house on Cape Henry in the State of Virginia."[107] Construction of the lighthouse had been authorized by a statute enacted in August of the preceding year.[108] The same legislation authorized federal spending to repair and maintain all "lighthouses, beacons, buoys and public piers" previously erected for navigational purposes at "any bay, inlet, harbor, or port of the United States" pending their prompt cession to the United States.[109]

Thus the aim of this enactment was to put the federal government in the business of constructing, operating, and financing a nationwide system of aids to navigation. The interesting question is where it got the authority to do so; for spending, like taxation, poses questions not only of separation of powers but of federalism as well.[110]

Observers in the late twentieth century are likely to think at once of the first clause of Article I, § 8, which empowers Congress "to lay and collect taxes, duties, imposts and excises, to pay the debts and provide for the common defense and general welfare of the United States." Acknowledging that the enumeration of congressional powers precludes interpreting this provision to support all legislation that promotes the general welfare, the modern Supreme Court has read it to justify taxation to acquire and expend funds for any such purpose[111]—and thus to confer a power that, as experience has taught, goes far to break down the Constitution's carefully crafted limitations on federal authority.[112]

It would be remarkable if the First Congress had entertained any such view of its powers, and in fact there were narrower and less sweeping arguments for the statute in question. The power of "exclusive legislation" over "places purchased" with state con-

---

guage seemed to qualify the War Department's appropriation until the next year. At the time Maclay wrote he was unaware of what the bill actually said. As he wrote in his diary, "I could not get a copy of it. I wished to have seen the particulars specifyed [sic] but such a hurry I never saw before." 9 Doc Hist at 226.

[107]1 Stat 104, 105, § 4 (Mar 26, 1790).

[108]1 Stat 53, 54, § 2 (Aug 7, 1789): "[A] lighthouse shall be erected near the entrance of the Chesapeake Bay, at such place . . . as the President . . . shall direct." The leeway permitted in selecting the site seems sufficiently narrow to obviate any serious objection that this provision delegated legislative power to the President. The absence of any specifications for the construction itself and the further provision directing the Secretary of the Treasury to fix the salaries of unspecified "persons appointed by the President" to look after the facilities showed that Congress believed it could give executive officers significant discretion in the management of government property, but even in these matters the Secretary and the President could fairly be said to be executing a policy decision made by Congress itself. Cf United States v Grimaud, 220 US 506, 521–22 (1911); The Second Century at 115 n 150.

[109]1 Stat at 53–54, § 1.

[110]At the time of the Convention, Maryland Delegate James McHenry had lamented in his notes that the Constitution did not appear to empower Congress to "erect light houses or clean out or preserve the navigation of harbours," although the expense was one that "ought to be borne . . . by the general treasury . . . ." 2 Farrand at 504 (emphasis omitted).

[111]United States v Butler, 297 US 1, 64–65 (1936).

[112]See The Second Century at 228–31; South Dakota v Dole, 483 US 203, 207, 212 (1987) (upholding a statute withholding federal highway funds from states that permitted the sale of alcoholic beverages to persons under 21 years of age).

sent "for the erection of forts, magazines, arsenals, dock-yards and other needful build-ings"[113] will not do the trick; even if buoys are buildings and the provision is not limited to strictly military facilities analogous to those specifically listed, this authority cannot easily be made to embrace expenditures to maintain installations not yet owned by the United States.[114] On the other hand, lighthouses and other navigational aids are as useful to naval vessels as they are to others; one might conceivably have argued even in 1789 that they were necessary and proper in order "to provide and maintain a [future] navy."[115]

The most obvious argument for federal navigational aids, however, was based on the commerce clause. Navigation is commerce, as Congress concluded in enacting the ship licensing law; buoys, beacons, and lighthouses promote interstate and foreign trade and thus are necessary and proper to carry out the purposes for which the commerce power was granted. This seemed to be Madison's theory in advocating that tonnage duties be imposed in order to support lighthouses, marine hospitals, "and other establishments in-cidental to commerce";[116] and Fitzsimons expressly embraced it in opposing Tucker's suggestion that the entire subject be left to the states.[117]

The immediate objection to this line of reasoning is that the construction and opera-tion of these establishments is not itself *regulation* of commerce, and not obviously nec-essary or proper for its regulation, which is what the Constitution seems literally to re-quire. In light of the patent relation between navigation aids and the purposes of the commerce provision, however, it may be appropriate not to parse the necessary and proper clause with all the ferocity of a medieval conveyancer. As somebody would soon admonish us, it was a constitution we were expounding.[118]

---

[113]US Const, Art I, § 8, cl 17.

[114]A modern lawyer would find a way: Repairs help to maintain the value of navigational aids and thus are necessary and proper to federal operation after the property is acquired. Cf Wickard v Filburn, 317 US 111, 128–29 (1942).

[115]US Const, Art I, § 8, cl 13.

[116]1 Annals at 183. In March of 1790 the House defeated a motion by Representative Jackson of Georgia to appropriate funds to pay for removing obstructions to navigation in the Savannah River. 2 Annals at 1499–1500. The proposed expenditure was necessary and proper to facilitate commerce in the same way a light-house was, and none of the recorded objections was on constitutional grounds. See Gazette of the United States, Mar 17, 1790 (Reps. Fitzsimons and Bland); Lloyd's Notes, Mar 15, 1790 (Rep. Boudinot). Congress evidently thought it better policy to let the state place the burden on those who benefited directly, for it con-sented to the imposition of a state tonnage tax. See note 6.

[117]See Daily Advertiser, July 17, 1789, 11 Doc Hist at 1130. Tucker replied, without elaboration, that "these establishments were not necessarily incidental to the power of commerce." Id. Not content to assert that federal action was both lawful and preferable, Fitzsimons went to far as to argue that the subject *could not* be left to the states, since "regulations respecting light houses and pilots were a part of the commercial system and had been given up by the states." Id. This view foreshadowed two centuries of litigation over the extent to which the grant of commerce power to Congress implicitly limited state authority.

[118]See McCulloch v Maryland, 17 US 316, 413–15 (1819). The last section of the same statute provided that "pilots in the bays, inlets, rivers, harbors and ports of the United States" should "continue to be regulated in conformity with the existing laws of the States . . . , or with such laws as the States may respectively here-after enact . . . until further legislative provision shall be made by Congress." 1 Stat at 54, § 4. Regulation of pilots was obviously relevant to the conduct of commerce, but by leaving the matter to future state regulation Congress left itself open to the argument that it could neither delegate the power to make federal law to the states (cf the discussion of federal enforcement of state inspection laws in the text at note 74) nor remove limitations on state authority that might be implicit in the commerce clause itself. See Cooley v Board of Port Wardens, 53 US 299, 313–21 (1852) (accepting the latter argument but holding that state law could constitu-

C. Other Spending Proposals

The First Congress considered three additional spending suggestions that could not so easily be justified. Their fate illustrates the diversity of views as to the extent of congressional authority to spend.

The first was the argument of two Virginia representatives that Congress should underwrite a private voyage to Baffin's Bay in search of a better understanding of the magnetic pole.[119] Neither explicitly identified the source of Congress's alleged authority. Page seemed to believe in a broad power to spend for the general welfare, for he said only that the knowledge to be obtained "would do honor to the American name."[120] In suggesting that the voyage might contribute to "improving the science of navigation,"[121] Madison appeared once again to conjure up the ubiquitous commerce clause—though the relation to commerce seemed more attenuated here than in the case of an honest-to-goodness lighthouse.[122] Ignoring the commerce power, Tucker expressed doubt whether the patent clause authorized Congress "to go further in rewarding the inventors of useful machines, or discoveries in sciences, than merely to secure to them for a time the right of making, publishing and vending them"[123]—a doubt solidly supported by the text of the provision. In the face of these uncertainties, and in view of "the present deranged state of our finances," the House agreed with the committee recommendation not to subsidize the voyage;[124] the constitutional question did not have to be decided.

The second spending suggestion was Washington's startling invitation to Congress in his first State of the Union message to promote "science and literature" either "by affording aids to seminaries of learning already established" or "by the institution of a national university."[125] Like Page and Madison, the President did not discuss the issue of congressional authority. His reference to the promotion of science suggests the same reliance on the patent clause that Tucker had so tellingly refuted a few months before, and any argument that support for education might produce information that would facilitate commerce seems even more attenuated here than in the chilly context of Baffin's Bay. Washington's additional observation that knowledge was conducive to stability and good government[126] might seem to imply that support for education was necessary and proper to the intelligent exercise of all federal powers, but he seemed to be discussing policy rather than authority. More probably, if he thought about the problem of power at

---

tionally be applied even without congressional consent). Contrast the express provisions of Art I, § 10 prohibiting state tariffs and tonnage duties in the absence of congressional approval, considered in note 6. For discussion of this issue see The First Hundred Years at 330–35.

[119] 1 Annals at 178–80 (Reps. Madison and Page).

[120] Id at 180.

[121] Id at 179.

[122] See Irving Brant, James Madison: Father of the Constitution, 1787–1800 332 (Bobbs-Merrill, 1950): "[A] ship captain did not need to know the cause of compass deviations in order to use the charts recording them. The fact was that [Madison] wanted to send out a purely scientific expedition, which could be justified only by a sweeping interpretation of the power to spend for the general welfare." A war powers argument would have been no less plausible but subject to the same objection.

[123] 1 Annals at 180.

[124] Id at 178, 180.

[125] Id at 970. See also chapter 1.

[126] Id.

all, he either assumed the university would be built at the seat of government[127] or gave a broad reading to the general welfare clause.[128] In any event Congress put the proposal on ice for the time being;[129] its constitutionality would be seriously debated a few years later.[130]

The final example of proposed federal spending was a committee recommendation in June 1790 that Congress authorize a loan of federal funds to rescue a glass factory that found itself in straitened circumstances.[131] In tones reminiscent of the famous Report on Manufactures that Hamilton was to file a year and a half afterward,[132] Vining argued that Congress possessed "a general power to encourage the arts and manufactures of the United States."[133] His terminology suggested he too had not looked closely enough at the actual terms of the patent clause.

Smith and Sherman doubted that Congress could "loan the money of their constituents,"[134] but as Boudinot said their objection seemed too broad.[135] Loans, no less than outright grants, might well be necessary and proper to the execution of some express federal authority; the difficulty lay in finding any power to which the support of a glass factory could fairly be deemed incidental. Of course glass was useful for commercial and military purposes, as well as to provide windows in all sorts of government buildings; but such an argument would leave little room for the powers that both the enumeration and the tenth amendment clearly acknowledged to be reserved only to the states. Ames's policy argument respecting the national interest in encouraging manufactures seemed to reflect a more straightforward reliance on the general welfare clause, which Boudinot, Seney, and Stone expressly invoked.[136]

---

[127]See US Const, Art I, § 8, cl 17: "Congress shall have power . . . [t]o exercise exclusive legislation in all cases whatsoever, over such district . . . as may . . . become the seat of the government of the United States."

[128]See Brant, James Madison at 289 (cited in note 122): "All of the power found afterward in the 'general welfare' clause was latent in this recommendation."

[129]In May 1790 William Smith moved to refer the President's suggestion to a committee for study. Stone objected that Congress had done all it could to encourage learning by providing for copyrights; Sherman added that the Convention had rejected a proposal to give Congress authority to establish a national university. 2 Annals at 1603–04. It had done so, in fact, after Gouverneur Morris had dismissed the suggestion as unnecessary, since "[t]he exclusive power at the Seat of Government, will reach the object." 2 Farrand at 616. Page "rather supposed" Congress had such authority and favored commitment in order to resolve the question, but "the House adjourned without a decision." 2 Annals at 1604.

[130]6 Annals at 1697–1711. See the discussion in chapter 5.

[131]2 Annals at 1685–86.

[132]1 Am St Papers (Finance) at 123; 10 Hamilton Papers at 230 (Dec 5, 1791). This report grew out of the additional suggestion in Washington's 1790 Annual Message that "[a] free people" should "promote such manufactures as tend to render them independent of others for essential, particularly military supplies." 1 Annals at 969. The House had referred this suggestion to Hamilton. House Journal, Jan 15, 1790, reprinted in 3 Doc Hist at 265.

[133]2 Annals at 1686.

[134]Id.

[135]Id. See also Lloyd's Notes, June 3, 1790 (Reps. Seney and Vining).

[136]See 2 Annals at 1687; Lloyd's Notes, June 3, 1790. Hamilton would be unequivocal in his recommendations to the Second Congress with respect to manufactures:

> Apart from the uniformity and apportionment requirements and the ban on export duties, the power to raise money is plenary, and indefinite; and the objects to which it may be appropriated are no less comprehensive, than the payment of the public debts and the providing for the com-

The committee's recommendation was rejected, but not all of the objections to the loan were on constitutional grounds. The question of the extent of federal spending powers had been raised and debated, but it had not yet been resolved.[137]

III. THE PUBLIC CREDIT

The Revolution had been fought in substantial part on credit, and many creditors had not been paid.[138] When a group of public creditors from Pennsylvania petitioned for relief, the House adopted a resolution declaring that "an adequate provision for the support of public credit" was "a matter of high importance to the national honor and prosperity" and directed the Secretary of the Treasury to propose an appropriate plan.[139]

The Secretary was Alexander Hamilton. His response was a lengthy Report on Public Credit,[140] the first in a remarkable series of reports in which the Secretary set forth his comprehensive and ambitious economic program.

The United States, wrote Hamilton, would need to borrow money in the future (as Article I, § 8 authorized Congress to do). They could borrow only if their credit was good; and their credit would be good only if they paid their debts. Thus satisfaction of existing claims was required not only by justice but by self-interest as well.[141] Money loaned by foreigners, he argued, should be paid back in full. The domestic debt, in contrast, should be refinanced rather than retired. Finally, Congress should also provide for paying off existing debts of individual states since it was in a better position to raise money—and since many state obligations had been incurred in the interest of common defense.[142]

Congress wrestled with Hamilton's proposals for nearly six months and ultimately adopted the essence of his suggestions.[143] In the process Washington's closest confidant

---

mon defence and "general Welfare." The terms "general Welfare" were doubtless intended to signify more than was expressed or imported in those which Preceded; otherwise numerous exigencies incident to the affairs of a Nation would have been left without a provision.

10 Hamilton Papers at 303 (emphasis omitted).

[137]The House's decision to furnish its members with newspapers at public expense, which could easily have been justified as necessary and proper to the informed exercise of the legislative function, was defended instead on the broader ground that the press deserved encouragement. See 1 Annals at 427; 2 Annals at 1580–82, 1835–36. Efforts to restrict the number of journals taken in the interest of economy were attacked as creating a risk of partiality—a preview of the problems that later were to complicate government support of arts and letters. See 2 Annals at 1581 (Rep. Gerry), 1835 (Rep. Madison).

[138]See 6 Hamilton Papers at 69.

[139]1 Annals at 939. The story of this whole controversy is ably and concisely told in McDonald, Washington at 47–75 and in Miller at 33–54. See also E. James Ferguson, The Power of the Purse 289–325 (North Carolina, 1961).

[140]6 Hamilton Papers at 65; 1 Am St Papers (Finance) at 15; 2 Annals at 2041 (Appendix).

[141]See also 1 Annals at 1171–77 (Rep. Boudinot, repeating Hamilton's arguments and concluding that Congress was bound by "honor, justice, and policy" to fund the existing debt); id at 1193–95 (Rep. Ames).

[142]See Miller at 37–40; McDonald, Hamilton at 167–68.

[143]1 Stat 138 (Aug 4, 1790). A proposal to empower the Secretary of the Treasury to borrow money in order to discharge foreign debts occasioned an interesting debate barely hinted at in the Annals. See 2 Annals at 1639. According to Lloyd's notes, when Madison objected that Congress should not sidestep the President by giving authority to his agent (see US Const, Art II, § 1!), Smith doubted whether Congress could delegate its power to the President at all. Huntington understandably replied that members of Congress were not ex-

became the leader of the opposition and the future capital was fixed on the banks of the Potomac. For present purposes, however, the most important aspect of the controversy is the interesting constitutional questions that it raised.

A.   Paper Money

Hamilton's argument against retiring the domestic debt was in part that public securities would promote trade by serving as currency and thus increasing the money supply.[144] The Constitution did not expressly say whether Congress had power to issue paper money. It did authorize Congress "to coin money,"[145] but securities are not coins. It did forbid states to issue "bills of credit" or to make anything but gold and silver legal tender,[146] but neither restriction seemed to forbid the circulation of promissory notes,[147] and neither applied to Congress.

Negotiable notes plainly facilitate borrowing and thus appear necessary and proper to the exercise of congressional power to borrow money. The Confederation Congress had issued such notes with common consent; nobody is recorded as doubting that the new Congress could do so too.[148]

B.   The Question of Full Payment

Paying debts is obviously necessary and proper to incurring them; people rarely lend money without reasonable assurance of getting it back. Article I leaves no doubt of this, for it explicitly empowers Congress to tax in order "to pay the debts of the United States."[149] Article VI removes any obstacle to the payment of debts contracted before the Constitution took effect: "All debts contracted and engagements entered into, before the adoption of this Constitution, shall be as valid against the United States under this Constitution, as under the Confederation."

Thus the important constitutional question raised by Hamilton's proposal to refinance the domestic federal debt was not whether Congress was permitted to provide for payment of pre-constitutional debts but whether it was required to do so. For several members of the House argued vigorously that at least some domestic creditors should not be given the full benefit of their bargain.

Livermore, for example, argued that many of these creditors were price-gouging suppliers who had taken advantage of the common necessity to extort exorbitant profits

---

pected "to turn borrowers themselves," while Laurance suggested that nothing needed to be said about who was to do the borrowing: Once Congress had passed a borrowing law, it was the President's duty to enforce it. Madison's view prevailed: The statute vested borrowing authority in the President. See Lloyd's Notes, May 19, 1790; 1 Stat 138, 139, §2.

[144]6 Hamilton Papers at 70–71; McDonald, Hamilton at 160.

[145]US Const, Art I, § 8, cl 5.

[146]Id, § 10.

[147]See Briscoe v Bank of Kentucky, 36 US 256, 299–300 (1837); The First Hundred Years at 206–08.

[148]See Kenneth W. Dam, The Legal Tender Cases, S Ct Rev 367, 382–90 (1981); James Willard Hurst, A Legal History of Money in the United States, 1774–1970 5–18 (Nebraska, 1973).

[149]For the answer to the alternative argument that this phrase confers a power independent of taxation see text at note 111 (discussing the parallel general welfare clause). In the case of debts it hardly matters; on either interpretation Congress can pay them.

and that (unlike foreign creditors) they had already been repaid in part by the benefits of independence.[150] Scott and others contended that Congress ought to distinguish between original holders such as soldiers who had given full value for their securities and later speculators who had bought them up on the cheap.[151]

Hamilton had already pointed out that any such depreciation would deprive the assignee of the benefit of his bargain, impair the value of future securities to the original holder, and increase the cost of borrowing to the government.[152] Several members of the House echoed his arguments[153] and raised constitutional objections as well.

Laurance, Smith, Ames, and Boudinot variously suggested that reducing the claims of assignees would impair the obligation of contract, offend the ex post facto clause, and take property without compensation.[154] Anticipating the obvious riposte that the contract clause applied only to the states,[155] they could only argue lamely that anything the states could not do must be forbidden to Congress as well.[156] Their remaining arguments were more plausible, since there was no doubt that the ex post facto and property provisions applied to the United States.[157] Anticipating *Calder v. Bull*, Madison nevertheless replied with some force that the separate provision precluding state impairment of contracts showed that the ex post facto clauses reached only criminal laws.[158] No one stopped to rebut the taking contention, but Madison's response was equally applicable here: Arguably the separate provisions respecting contracts and property implied that contractual rights did not come within the purview of the taking clause.[159]

Hamilton's more interesting argument,[160] repeated by Boudinot in the House,[161] was that discrimination against assignees of the original creditors was forbidden by Article VI, which made pre-constitutional debts "as valid against the United States under th[e] Constitution, as under the Confederation." As Seney pointed out, however, the text of this article refuted any notion that it gave preexisting debts any more protection than they had enjoyed under the Confederation;[162] and the Articles of Confederation had contained no provision forbidding Congress to renege on its obligations.[163]

---

[150]1 Annals at 1185–87.

[151]Id at 1205–06. See also id at 1224 (Rep. Burke). Madison offered a variant of this proposal that would have provided for payment in full to be divided between the original holder and the assignee in proportion to their respective investments. See id at 1233–38.

[152]6 Hamilton Papers at 73–77.

[153]See 1 Annals at 1212, 1238–39.

[154]Id at 1251, 1257, 1263, 1294.

[155]See US Const, Art I, § 10.

[156]See 1 Annals at 1251, 1257, 1294. Cf Bolling v Sharpe, 347 US 497 (1954) (reading the equal protection clause into the fifth amendment by the same questionable reasoning); The Second Century at 378–79.

[157]US Const, Art I, § 9 and Amend 5.

[158]1 Annals at 1311. See *Calder*, 3 US 386, 390 (1798); The First Hundred Years at 41–49.

[159]But cf Dartmouth College v Woodward, 17 US 518 (1819) (holding what appeared to be a taking of property a violation of the contract clause); The First Hundred Years at 141–45.

[160]6 Hamilton Papers at 77.

[161]1 Annals at 1190. See also McDonald, Hamilton at 178.

[162]2 Annals at 1323. See also New York Daily Gazette, Feb 25, 1790.

[163]Boudinot's final contention that to scale down payments to assignees would be to exercise judicial powers vested exclusively in the courts by Article III (1 Annals at 1294) had little to recommend it, since what was proposed was general legislation applicable to all existing domestic obligations. Contrast Fletcher v

Thus no convincing argument was made that Congress was constitutionally required to pay its debts in full. Moreover, despite the defeat of various motions to discriminate against assignees or suppliers of goods, the statute did not provide for full payment. While the new certificates issued in exchange for the old were to bear a full six percent, interest on one third of their value was to be paid only after the turn of the century;[164] and preconstitutional bills of credit (the discredited "continentals") were to be redeemed at the princely rate of 100 to 1.[165] As Sedgwick said, nobody was really for full payment;[166] and the Constitution did not seem to require it. Nearly 150 years would pass before the Supreme Court surprisingly concluded that it did.[167]

C.   The Assumption of State Debts

In both political and constitutional terms, the most fascinating controversy respecting public credit concerned Hamilton's proposal that Congress assume the debts of the several states. Predictably, those states which had already discharged the bulk of their obligations tended to be less than eager to help discharge the obligations of others.[168] Moreover, several Representatives recognized—as Hamilton is said to have intended—that federal assumption would enhance the power of the federal government relative to that of the states by reducing the necessity for state taxation.[169]

At the constitutional level, Stone began by observing that Article I empowered Congress to pay only the "debts . . . of the United States," not those of individual states.[170] Once state debts were assumed, of course, they would become debts of the United States; but that did not prove that Congress had the power to assume them. Nor was Article VI of much assistance in this regard, for as noted above it made debts good against the new Congress only to the extent they had been good against the old; it too seemed to apply only to obligations of the United States.

Peck, 10 US 87, 136 (1810), The First Hundred Years at 130–32, where Chief Justice Marshall suggested that statutory repudiation of a single contract was an exercise of judicial rather than legislative power.

[164]1 Stat at 140, § 4. Section 9 provided that the statute did not disparage the rights of creditors who chose not to make the exchange, but § 10 provided that they should receive the same interest as if they had done so. Id at 141–42. Except for the bills of credit noted below, the domestic debt had all been consolidated into securities bearing an interest rate of 6% before the Constitution was adopted. 6 Hamilton Papers at 84, 86.

[165]1 Stat at 140, § 3. The continentals had previously been officially devalued at a rate of 40 to 1. See 16 J Cont Cong 262–67 (Mar 18, 1780). See also Miller at 37; McDonald, Hamilton at 147.

[166]1 Annals at 1210–11. Hamilton himself had acknowledged that repudiation might be justified by "necessity." 6 Hamilton Papers at 68.

[167]See Perry v United States (the Gold Clause Cases), 294 US 330, 350–51, 357 (1935) (finding the duty to repay implicit in the power to borrow but taking it back by implausibly concluding that the complainants had suffered no harm). See The Second Century at 233–34.

[168]See 2 Annals at 1405 (Rep. White), 1427 (Rep. Madison). See also Madison's letter to Jefferson, Mar 8, 1790, 16 Jefferson Papers at 213, opposing assumption, which as devised would principally benefit South Carolina and Massachusetts and "would be peculiarly hard on Virginia." For a more sophisticated version of this argument see Ferguson, The Power of the Purse at 307–11 (cited in note 139).

[169]See, e.g., 2 Annals at 1359 (Rep. Stone); Miller at 40–41; McDonald, Hamilton at 167.

[170]2 Annals at 1361.

Sedgwick found authority for the assumption of state debts in a broad reading of the general welfare clause of Article I, § 8, which he said authorized Congress "to levy money in all instances where, in their opinion, the expenditure shall be for the 'general welfare'[:] . . . [I]f prudence, policy, and justice dictated the assumption of the State debts it must be for the general welfare that they should be assumed."[171] Even before Sedgwick spoke, however, Stone had branded as "dangerous" any argument that Congress could tax and spend for a purpose, however salutary, that was "not a constitutional object of their power";[172] and most defenders of assumption espoused a narrower justification.

The debts in question, Sherman argued, had been incurred for the most part (as Hamilton had noted) "for the common defence."[173] That defense had been the responsibility of Congress, but Congress had been unable to raise the requisite funds. Consequently the states had contracted obligations as agents of Congress; from the beginning the state debts had been "debts . . . of the United States."[174] Two former members of the constitutional convention relied on their recollection of its proceedings in support of their conflicting interpretations. Madison insisted that the Convention had decided not to assume state debts,[175] Gerry that it had taken for granted Congress would have power to do so.[176]

The House initially voted against assumption.[177] At that point Secretary of State Jefferson arranged an informal meeting between Hamilton and Madison, who as representative of a state that had paid most of its own debts had opposed assumption tooth and nail. The result was a compromise whereby in exchange for assumption of debts actually incurred for the common defense[178] Virginia was given both assurance of reimbursement for the sums it had already expended[179] and the future seat of the national government,[180]

---

[171] Id at 1382.

[172] Id at 1361.

[173] Id at 1365. See also 6 Hamilton Papers at 81–83.

[174] See also 2 Annals at 1371–72, 1397 (Rep. Gerry); id at 1407 (Rep. W. Smith); id at 1647–69 (Reps. Boudinot and Ames). The thesis that "debts" included quasi-contractual as well as contractual obligations received further support when Congress empowered federal commissioners appointed to settle accounts between the United States and individual states to recognize all claims "accrued for the general or particular defence during the war," whether or not "sanctioned by the resolves of Congress, or supported by regular vouchers," "according to the principles of general equity." 1 Stat 178, 179, § 3 (Aug 5, 1790).

[175] 2 Annals at 1591.

[176] Id at 1409–10. In fact the Convention record is ambiguous on this score. The original proposal would have given Congress authority to discharge both federal and state debts. 2 Farrand at 355–56. The reference to state obligations was omitted when the provision was altered to make payment of federal debts mandatory. Id at 377. The most that can be said with confidence is that the Framers decided not to *require* Congress to discharge state obligations.

[177] See 2 Annals at 1597; McDonald, Hamilton at 181.

[178] § 13 provided that no certificates would be redeemed if it was shown that they had not been issued for such a purpose. 1 Stat 143.

[179] 1 Stat at 143–44, §§ 17–18. See also 1 Stat 178, 179 (Aug 5, 1790) (establishing a board to settle accounts between the United States and individual states, with particular reference to claims "accrued for the general or particular defence during the war"). In light of these developments, Madison wrote to his father on July 31, "in a pecuniary light, the assumption is no longer of much consequence to Virginia." 13 Madison Papers at 285.

[180] See text at notes 413–30. For Jefferson's later account of the bargain see 17 Jefferson Papers at 205–07. Some insight into Jefferson's motives is afforded by a letter he wrote to Thomas Randolph on June 20, 1790: "[I]f they [Congress] separate without funding there is an end of the government." 16 Jefferson Papers at 540. See also Miller at 48–49; McDonald, Washington at 74–75.

but the breach between Madison and the Administration was never to be mended.[181]

IV.   THE BANK OF THE UNITED STATES

Resolution of the controversy over assumption of state debts brought the second session of the First Congress to a dramatic close. On the same day on which it approved the bill providing for payment of existing debts, however, the House asked the Secretary of the Treasury to propose "such further provision as may, in his opinion, be necessary for establishing the public credit."[182] Four months later, in December, 1790, Hamilton responded with two more of his impressive economic reports. The first, which proposed additional taxes on whiskey, has already been discussed.[183] The second, which is better known, framed the great constitutional issue that dominated the third session. For in this report Hamilton urged Congress to establish a national bank.[184]

The Constitution did not expressly authorize Congress to set up banks. Moreover, as Madison hastened to point out during the House debate, the Convention had rejected a proposal to authorize Congress to create corporations.[185] Gerry, who had invoked his own recollection of the Convention debates during the assumption controversy,[186] gave several of the reasons that have since been given for ignoring the debates[187] and sensibly added that the proposal before the Convention would have given Congress a general power of incorporation[188]—not authority to establish an institution that might be implicit in some other power explicitly granted to Congress.

Hamilton's report had not addressed the constitutional question, but it had spelled out the benefits that a bank would confer.[189] In the House, Fisher Ames took the lead in

---

[181]See Brant, Madison at 305 (cited in note 122): "Madison sacrificed his congressional leadership when he undertook the fight for Revolutionary War veterans and other small creditors against speculators in and out of Congress."

[182]2 Annals at 1763 (Aug 9, 1790).

[183]See text at notes 36–56.

[184]7 Hamilton Papers at 305; 1 Am St Papers (Finance) at 67; 2 Annals at 2082 (Appendix).

[185]Id at 1945. See Farrand at 615–16.

[186]See text at note 176.

[187]Noting the impropriety of relying "on the memory of the [delegates] for a history of their debates" and that "the opinions of the individual members . . . are not to be considered as the opinions of the Convention," Gerry added that the records of the state ratifying conventions were no better since they were "generally partial and mutilated." 2 Annals at 2004–05. See also Hamilton's later report to the President on the constitutionality of the Bank, 8 Hamilton Papers at 97, 111:

> [W]hatever may have been the intention of the framers of a constitution, . . . [it] is to be sought for in the instrument itself, according to the usual & established rules of construction . . . . If then a power to erect a corporation . . . be deducible by fair inference from the whole or any part of the . . . constitution . . . , arguments drawn from extrinsic circumstances, regarding the intention of the convention, must be rejected.

[188]"[T]he measure which [Madison] has referred to was a proposition merely to enable Congress to erect commercial corporations . . . ." 2 Annals at 2004–05. More precisely, the proposal initially made was limited to the construction of canals; Madison's attempt to enlarge it so as to authorize the grant of charters whenever "the interest of the U.S. might require & the legislative provisions of individual States may be incompetent" failed; and then the canal provision itself was voted down. See 2 Farrand at 615–16.

[189]7 Hamilton Papers at 305–42.

showing how these benefits brought the creation of the Bank within various categories of congressional authority.

Commerce, Ames argued, could hardly be carried on without banknotes; thus the Bank was implicit in the power to regulate commerce. Debts could hardly be paid without easy transfer of funds across the country; thus the Bank was implicit in the power to pay the debts. Wars could hardly be fought without a bank to facilitate the raising of money; thus the Bank was implicit in the various war powers. Money could not effectively be borrowed without a bank; thus the Bank was implicit in the power to borrow.[190] Congress had exercised implied authority from the beginning in taxing ships, building lighthouses, and regulating seamen, all on the theory that they were incident to the commerce power;[191] the necessary and proper clause confirmed that each grant of authority gave power to do whatever was needed to accomplish its goal.[192]

Sedgwick, Boudinot, and Gerry ably seconded these arguments.[193] Madison, who as Sedgwick noted had argued vigorously for the President's implicit power to remove executive officers,[194] was the principal spokesman against implicit authority to establish a bank.[195] This bill, he insisted, was not supported by the tax power, for it imposed no tax; nor by the power to borrow, for it borrowed no money. The general welfare clause, he continued, was not an independent grant of power but a limitation on the purposes for which taxes could be collected;[196] the necessary and proper clause was "merely declaratory of what would have resulted by unavoidable implication."

It was not enough, said Madison, that a measure might be "conducive" to the exercise of some express authority. Under such an interpretation manufacturing subsidies or

---

[190]2 Annals at 1956–59 (also invoking the tax power). Moreover, Ames contended, Congress could always set up a bank at the seat of government or in the Territories, where it had plenary powers, or to manage the Government's own property under Art IV, § 3. In suggesting that this property included the Government's shares in the bank, however, Ames seemed to be lifting himself by his bootstraps. Jackson went so far as to deny that Congress could establish a bank at any place subject to its exclusive jurisdiction, adding more persuasively that "if they should, they could not force the circulation of their paper one inch beyond the limits of those places." Id at 1968. See also id at 1985 (Rep. Stone) ("It would be equally reasonable to say, that France, because within the limits of her own dominions, . . . exercised exclusive legislation, that hence she had a right to legislate for the world"); Cohens v Virginia, 19 US 264, 440–47 (1821) (holding that a federal statute authorizing a lottery in the District of Columbia did not legalize ticket sales elsewhere because Congress would not be presumed to interfere with state penal laws).

[191]2 Annals at 1954.

[192]Id at 1959.

[193]Id at 1960–64 (Rep Sedgwick), 1970–79 (Rep. Boudinot), 1997–2006 (Rep. Gerry). "[T]he Constitution," said Sedgwick, "had expressly declared the ends of Legislation; but in almost every instance had left the means to the honest and sober discretion of the Legislature." Id at 1962.

[194]Id at 1960. For Madison's defense of presidential removal see chapter 1.

[195]2 Annals at 1944–52, 2008–12.

[196]To construe it more broadly, Madison insisted, "would render nugatory the enumeration of particular powers." 2 Annals at 1946. Moreover, he added, the general purposes listed in the tax provision "themselves were limited and explained by the particular enumeration subjoined." Id. The terms of this provision were "copied from the articles of Confederation; had it ever been pretended, that they were to be understood otherwise than as here explained?" Id. See Articles of Confederation, Art VIII: "All charges of war, and all other expenses that shall be incurred for the common defence or general welfare, . . . shall be defrayed out of a common treasury, which shall be supplied by the several States . . . ." See also The Federalist No 41 (Madison).

even a prohibition of state taxation might be held necessary and proper to the collection of federal taxes, since they would increase the ability to pay. "If implications, thus remote and thus multiplied, can be linked together, a chain may be formed that will reach every object within the whole compass of political economy;" and "[t]he essential characteristic of the Government, as composed of limited and enumerated powers, would be destroyed." A national bank, he concluded, was not necessary: "Its uses to the Government could be supplied by keeping the taxes a little in advance; by loans from individuals; [and] by the other Banks, over which the Government would have equal command . . . ."[197]

Madison was as eloquent on one side of the bank question as Ames had been on the other. The House approved the Bank by the lopsided vote of thirty-nine to twenty,[198] and the Senate agreed without calling the roll.[199] Disconcerted by Madison's arguments, Washington called upon Jefferson and Randolph for opinions,[200] which echoed Madison's position.[201] Hamilton then expanded on Ames's defense of the Bank,[202] and Washington signed the bill.[203]

As in the case of presidential removal power, the congressional and executive debate on the Bank thoroughly rehearsed the arguments that would inform the later judicial decision.[204] There was just one difference: Unlike Ames and Hamilton, Chief Justice Marshall never bothered to explain how the establishment of the Bank was necessary, proper, or even conducive to the execution of any of the powers expressly granted to Congress.[205]

[197]2 Annals at 1947. See also id at 1967–70 (Rep. Jackson), 1981–88 (Rep. Stone), 1989–97 (Rep. Giles) ("I have been taught to conceive that the true exposition of a necessary mean to produce a given end was that mean without which the end could not be produced."). For the argument that in opposing the Bank Madison was inconsistent with the broad view of implied powers he had taken as early as 1781 in a report to the Continental Congress, reiterated in the Federalist, and espoused in urging support for the expedition to Baffin's Bay, see Brant, Madison at 331–33 (cited in note 122) (adding that Madison "deliberately abandoned his majority leadership when he saw that the price of keeping it was to become a tool of financial oligarchy"). For a more cynical view see McDonald, Hamilton at 199–204 (arguing that Madison had nothing against the Bank itself but saw its 20-year charter as a possible means of frustrating the move of the national capital to the Potomac, in which he had a financial interest, and explaining Washington's hesitation in signing the bill on similar grounds). Accord Kenneth Bowling, The Bank Bill, the Capital City and President Washington, 1 Capitol Studies 59 (1972).

[198]2 Annals at 2012.

[199]Id at 1813.

[200]See US Const, Art II, § 2: "The President . . . may require the opinion, in writing, of the principal officer in each of the executive departments, upon any subject relating to the duties of their respective offices."

[201]Jefferson's opinion can be found in 19 Jefferson Papers at 275 (Feb 15, 1791), Randolph's in M. St. Clair Clarke & D.A. Hall, eds, Legislative and Documentary History of the Bank of the United States 86 (1832, reprinted by Augustus M. Kelley, 1967) and in Walter Dellinger and H. Jefferson Powell, The Constitutionality of the Bank Bill: The Attorney General's First Constitutional Law Opinions, 1994 Duke L J 110, 121–30. See also McDonald, Hamilton at 202.

[202]8 Hamilton Papers at 97–134. Clinton Rossiter has termed Hamilton's response "perhaps the most brilliant and influential one-man effort in the long history of American constitutional law." Alexander Hamilton and the Constitution 79–80 (Harcourt, Brace & World, 1964).

[203]1 Stat 191 (Feb 25, 1791). The preamble recited that the Bank would be "conducive to the successful conducting of the national finances," facilitate borrowing, and promote commerce. Id. For Madison's draft of a veto message on both constitutional and policy grounds see 13 Madison Papers at 395.

[204]See McCulloch v Maryland, 17 US 316 (1819).

[205]See The First Hundred Years at 164–65.

V. MILITARY, INDIAN, AND FOREIGN AFFAIRS

Having set up the Department of Foreign Affairs, renamed it the Department of State, and provided funds for diplomatic salaries,[206] the First Congress passed no other major legislation in the field of foreign affairs. Having established ground rules for the process of advice and consent, the Senate was asked to approve only a single foreign treaty, which had been concluded before the new Government began operations.[207] However, Congress did begin to create a new military establishment, confront a number of important constitutional issues in connection with the ticklish relations between the United States and the Indian tribes, and afford a preview of controversies to come as it began to wrestle with the question of what to do about the Barbary pirates.

A. Soldiers

On August 10, 1789, President Washington sent a message to the House regarding military troops then in the service of the United States. There were 672 of them, according to the accompanying report; they had been raised pursuant to resolutions of the Confederation Congress "in order to protect the frontiers from the depredations of the hostile Indians, to prevent all intrusions on the public lands, and to facilitate the surveying and selling of the same."[208] "As these important objects continue to require the aid of the troops," said the punctilious President, "it is necessary that the establishment thereof . . . be conformed by law to the constitution of the United States."[209]

Congress promptly obliged,[210] ratifying the previous establishment in all respects save "the mode of appointing the officers" (which was now governed by Article II), prescribing the form of the oath that may have been required by Article VI,[211] and—in response to another request by the President—authorizing him to call out "such part of the militia . . . as he may judge necessary" in order to protect against Indians on the frontier, as authorized by Article I.[212]

Protection of the frontier was the principal purpose for which Washington had requested authorization to keep the regular troops as well, yet the statute was notably silent about the purposes for which the soldiers might be employed. Maybe Congress thought approval of the original establishment implied endorsement of its purposes; maybe the members believed that once they had raised troops pursuant to Article I, § 8 it was up to the President as Commander in Chief to decide what to do with them[213]—subject of

---

[206]See chapter 1.

[207]Id. The treaty was a consular convention with France.

[208]1 Annals at 715.

[209]Id. See also 6 Doc Hist at 1995–98.

[210]1 Stat 95 (Sept 29, 1789).

[211]1 Stat at 96, § 3. It was not clear whether army officers were "executive officers" within the meaning of Article VI, and the statutory oath was required even of privates, who might not qualify as "officers" at all. It would not be difficult to conclude that for all military personnel an oath to support the Constitution was necessary and proper to the raising of troops or the governance of the army.

[212]1 Stat at 96, § 5. See 6 Doc Hist at 1999; US Const, Art I, § 8, cl 15 ("The Congress shall have power . . . to provide for calling forth the militia to execute the laws of the Union, suppress insurrections and repel invasions."). Note the breadth of discretion given the President—unavoidably—by this provision.

[213]See 1 Annals at 724 (Rep. Madison): "By the constitution, the President has the power of employing these troops in the protection of those parts [of the frontiers] which he thinks requires [sic] them most."

course to whatever limitation might be implicit in Article I's reservation to Congress of the power "to declare war."[214]

The 1789 legislation was obviously a temporary expedient, and in the following session Congress enacted a more comprehensive measure providing for a permanent military establishment.[215] In light of deteriorating relations with the Creek Indians,[216] the number of troops was increased to more than 1200 "able-bodied men, not under five feet six inches in height," and between eighteen and forty-six years of age.[217] The statute divided them into regiments and battalions, regulated their pay and rations, and provided pensions for the wounded—all of which was plainly necessary and proper to the raising and support of armies.[218] As under the 1789 statute, the Articles of War adopted under the Confederation were to govern until altered by Congress—but only insofar as they were consistent with the new Constitution.[219]

The most intriguing section of the 1790 Act was the last, which echoed the militia provision of its predecessor with one important difference: Now the President was empowered to call out the militia "for the purpose of aiding the troops" in protecting the frontiers.[220] The new phrasing was manifestly drafted in response to Secretary Knox's unequivocal recommendation that the regulars should bear the principal burden of frontier defense: "The œconomy of disciplined troops is always superior to militia while their efficacy is at least equal."[221]

Once again there was no doubt that the reason for raising additional soldiers was to protect against Indian depredations,[222] and this time Maclay confided to his diary that he

---

Accord Quincy Wright, The Control of American Foreign Relations 193–94 (Macmillan, 1922). Contrast Louis Henkin, Constitutionalism, Democracy, and Foreign Affairs 26 (Columbia, 1990): "The President's designation as Commander in Chief . . . appears to have implied no substantive authority to use the armed forces, whether for war (unless the United States were suddenly attacked) or for peacetime purposes, except as Congress directed."

[214]See US Const, Art I, § 8, cl 11; Art II, § 2, cl 1.

[215]1 Stat 119 (Apr 30, 1790). There was no reported discussion of this bill; much of the House debate was in secret. See 5 Doc Hist at 1278.

[216]See the report of Secretary Knox, 5 Doc Hist at 1279–84.

[217]1 Stat 119, §§ 1, 2. It did not seem to occur to anyone to suggest that any of these restrictions offended the "equal protection component" that modern wizards have conjured into the due process clause that Congress had proposed in 1789. See Bolling v Sharpe, 347 US 497, 499 (1954); The Second Century at 378–79.

[218]1 Stat at 119–21, §§ 3–11. Contrast once more the cramped interpretation of the commerce clause with respect to railroad workers' pensions in Railroad Retirement Board v Alton Railroad, 295 US 330 (1935) (discussed in text at note 80). Pensions were to be paid "at such rate . . . and under such regulations as directed by the President," but no more than half the normal pay. 1 Stat at 121, § 11. Once again significant discretion was conferred upon the President.

[219]1 Stat at 121, § 13. Art I, § 8, cl 14 empowers Congress "[t]o make rules for the government and regulation of the land and naval forces."

[220]1 Stat at 121, § 16. A separate bill for the uniform organization of the militia was hotly debated in the waning days of the First Congress but was not adopted until the Second. See 2 Annals at 1851–75; 1 Stat 271 (May 8, 1792). Discussion of the serious constitutional problems raised by this bill can be found in chapter 3.

[221]See 5 Doc Hist at 1281.

[222]See id at 1279–82. Knox had asked for an army of 5000 men in order "to be in a situation to punish all unprovoked aggressions" by the Creeks and if necessary "to march into their country and destroy their Towns." Id at 1280. He did not say whether he thought that once the troops were in place all this could be done without a declaration of war or other specific authorization by Congress. See id at 1356.

thought this purpose illegitimate. Armies were meant "for the Annoyance of an Enemy in their own Country"; Article I left the enforcement of laws, the suppression of insurrections, and the repulsion of invasions to the militia.[223] Congress was unimpressed by this contention, and the text hardly supports it; the militia provision can as easily be interpreted to permit the supplementary use of militia, and it would have been odd to forbid the raising of regular troops in a case of actual invasion.

More interesting was Maclay's related conclusion that the Constitution permitted no Troops to be "kept up in peace."[224] Whether the country was at peace at the time might have been disputed in view of the Indian raids that had prompted the President to seek legislation, but it was true that war had not been declared. Maclay appeared to be suggesting that Congress could not constitutionally raise troops until it had taken the more drastic step of declaring war.

Stated this baldly, the argument seems quite wrong; one would not expect the Framers to require the country to leap into war before preparing for it.[225] Perhaps in saying troops should not be "kept up" in peace Maclay meant only that there could be no "Standing Army," for which he feared the bill would "lay[] the foundation."[226] Standing armies had been a popular bugaboo of the Anti-Federalists, who had proposed to restrict them by constitutional amendment.[227] The ninth amendment stands as a perpetual warning against interpreting even the adoption of a limitation as implying the existence of congressional power,[228] but supporters of the Constitution had made quite clear that they understood it to permit the creation of a permanent military establishment. It was enough, Hamilton had written, that armies could not be raised or money expended for their support without statutory authority, and that even statutory appropriations for military purposes could not last longer than two years.[229]

Like its predecessor, the 1790 statute gave the President no express authority to employ the army to protect the frontiers. At the same time, the last section plainly assumed that the President already had that power. Since this time nothing was said about those resolutions of the Confederation Congress, the inference is strong that Congress thought the requisite authority inherent in the office of Commander-in-Chief.[230]

---

[223]9 Doc Hist at 230–31.

[224]Id at 231.

[225]See The Federalist No 25 (Hamilton) (deriding the prospect of "a nation incapacitated by its constitution to prepare for defence, before it was actually invaded").

[226]9 Doc Hist at 230–31.

[227]See 4 Doc Hist at 15 (New Hampshire), 17 (Virginia), 20 (New York). Burke of South Carolina offered an amendment in the House that would have required both "necessity" and a two-thirds vote for a standing army in peacetime, but it was defeated. 1 Annals at 780–81.

[228]See The First Hundred Years at 41–49 (discussing Calder v Bull, 3 US 386 (1798)).

[229]The Federalist Nos 24–29. See, e.g., No 28, at 178: "Independent of all other reasonings upon the subject, it is a full answer to those who require a more peremptory provision against military establishments in time of peace, that the whole power of the proposed government is to be in the hands of representatives of the people." Hamilton had specifically envisioned the continuing necessity "for keeping small garrisons" of regular troops "on our western frontier" for the very purposes proposed by Washington. The Federalist No 24, at 156.

[230]Indeed the formulation of § 16 is reminiscent of the provision respecting removal of the Secretary of Foreign Affairs, which was placed in the passive voice in order, as its sponsor argued, to avoid any implication that the authority was for Congress to confer or withhold. See chapter 1. Some 900 additional troops were

Moreover, both Secretary Knox and Washington himself seemed to think this authority extended to offensive operations undertaken in retaliation for Indian atrocities. Not long after enactment of the 1790 statute the President, without further congressional sanction, directed General Harmar to develop a plan employing both regular troops and militia to "extirpate" a band of marauders in the Northwest Territory.[231] As the Secretary later explained to Governor St. Clair, the aim of this expedition was to destroy the "Towns and Crops" of the Wabash Indians in order to exhibit "our power to punish them for their depredations."[232]

The operation was carried out, with heavy casualties.[233] Maclay thought the President had exceeded his powers: "A War has been actually undertaken against the Wabash Indians, without any Authority of Congress . . . ."[234] That Washington himself recognized there were limits to the powers of the Commander in Chief was indicated not long afterward, when he replied to an importunate Governor that he had been making preparations to conduct an offensive expedition against the Creeks "whenever Congress should decide that measure to be proper and necessary":

> The Constitution vests the power of declaring war with Congress; therefore no offensive expedition of importance can be undertaken until after they shall have deliberated on the subject, and authorized such a measure.[235]

We were to hear much more both of expeditions to chastise the Indians and of the division of military authority between Congress and the Commander in Chief.[236]

---

authorized the following year to reinforce the Southwest frontier; once again there was no express authority to employ the new troops for their intended purpose. See 1 Stat 222 (Mar 3, 1791); House Committee Report, 5 Doc Hist at 1422 (Feb 1, 1791).

[231] See Letter of Secretary Knox to General Harmar, June 7, 1790, 5 Doc Hist at 1348–50.

[232] Letter of Secretary Knox to Governor St. Clair, Sept 12, 1790, 5 Doc Hist at 1355, 1356.

[233] See Letter of General Harmar to Secretary Knox, Nov 4, 1790, 5 Doc Hist at 1359; James Ripley Jacobs, The Beginnings of the U.S. Army: 1783–1812 53–63 (Princeton, 1947); Richard H. Kohn, Eagle and Sword: The Federalists and the Creation of the Military Establishment in America, 1783–1802 99–107 (Free Press, 1975). President Washington informed Congress of this expedition (but not of its outcome) in his Annual Message of December 8, 1790. 2 Annals at 1770, 1771–72.

[234] 9 Doc Hist at 340.

[235] Letter of George Washington to William Moultrie, Aug 28, 1793, 33 Washington Writings at 73. See also 1 Tucker's Blackstone at 269–70 ("In England the right of making war is in the king. . . . With us the representatives of the people have the right to decide this important question"); Letter of Thomas Jefferson to James Madison, Sept 6, 1789, 15 Jefferson Papers at 392, 397 ("We have already given in example one effectual check to the Dog of war by transferring the power of letting him loose from the Executive to the Legislative body").

[236] The First Congress also authorized the President to purchase land at West Point on the Hudson River for the construction of a fort. 1 Stat 129 (July 5, 1790). Art I, § 8, cl 17 envisioned exclusive federal authority over lands ceded by the states for such purposes, but West Point was to be purchased from a private individual who had petitioned Congress for compensation after the Government occupied his property. See 6 Doc Hist at 2059–60. Plainly enough the statute was necessary and proper to national defense in view of the strategic importance of navigation on the river. See Report of the Secretary of the Treasury, June 10, 1790, 6 Doc Hist at 2060–62. Just as plainly Congress did not view the cession procedure of clause 17 as the only means of acquiring land; state consent was required only to oust state jurisdiction entirely.

B.   Indians

The explosive confrontation between indigenous warriors and encroaching settlers along the western frontier was the proximate cause of the various military measures already discussed. It also gave rise during the First Congress to a series of treaties and statutes specifically directed to Indian relations.

The Fort Harmar Treaty with the Wyandots and other northwestern tribes, which the Senate approved in 1789,[237] confirmed the boundary between the United States and Indian country along the shore of Lake Erie and the release of Indian claims to lands east, south, and west of that boundary in exchange for peace and goods.[238] Article V of the treaty required the Indian nations to deliver up any of their members who robbed or killed a citizen of the United States and promised to punish in accord with "the laws of the state or of the territory wherein the offence was committed" any citizen who robbed or killed an Indian, in order "that nothing may interrupt the peace and harmony now established between the United States and said nations."[239] Article VII provided that "[t]rade sh[ould] be opened with the said nations" but added that no one should be permitted to trade with them without a license, "to the end that they may not be imposed upon in their traffick."[240]

The treaty concluded with the Creek Nation in 1790 was similar in many respects.[241] Instead of providing for licensed traders, however, it declared that no citizen of the United States should enter Creek territory without a passport and that anyone attempting to settle on Creek lands would forfeit the protection of the United States.[242] Finally, the United States promised to provide the Creeks "from time to time" with "domestic animals and instruments of husbandry," in order "[t]hat the Creek nation may be led to a greater degree of civilization, and to become herdsmen and cultivators, instead of remaining in a state of hunters."[243] Encouraging Indians to practice domestic arts, Knox argued, would be cheaper than suppressing them by force.[244]

Both Georgia Senators voted against the Creek Treaty,[245] and Georgia Representative James Jackson assailed it in the House on the ground that it ceded away

---

[237]7 Stat 28 (Jan 9, 1789). See chapter 1.

[238]7 Stat at 28–29, Art II. The Confederation Congress, Secretary Knox explained, had originally assumed that the peace treaty with Great Britain had given us title to lands in the Northwest Territories, but the Fort Harmar treaties acknowledged that we had acquired only sovereignty and that the land had to be purchased from the Indians. See 1 Am St Papers (Indian Affairs) at 7.

[239]7 Stat at 29.

[240]Id at 30. See also the report of the Commissioners appointed to negotiate with the Creeks, 1 Am St Papers (Indian Affairs) at 79, urging licensing in order to avoid the risk that unscrupulous traders might antagonize the Indians.

[241]7 Stat 35 (Aug 7, 1790). The Treaty of Holston River, concluded with the Cherokees and approved by the Senate in 1791, was almost identical to the Creek Treaty. 7 Stat 39 (July 2, 1791).

[242]7 Stat at 36–37, Art VI, VII. As Washington informed the Senate, commerce with the Creeks at the time was "almost exclusively in the hands of a company of British merchants," and the Senators consented in advance to a secret article providing for an orderly transition to commerce through ports of the United States. 1 Annals at 1063–64.

[243]7 Stat at 37, Art XII.

[244]Letter to President Washington, July 28, 1789, 1 Am St Papers (Indian Affairs) at 33.

[245]The vote was 15 to 4; the other dissenters were Butler (South Carolina) and Walker (Virginia). See 1 Annals at 1074.

without compensation "more than three million acres of land . . . guarantied to that State by the Constitution of the United States."[246] Explicitly invoking "those parts" of the document "which secure to every citizen the rights of property," he seemed also to anticipate the Supreme Court's later dictum that the treaty power did not include authority to cede territory within a state without its consent.[247] The House had no say in the formation of treaties, however, and nothing came of Jackson's arguments. The cession of territory was a common subject of treaties; and as Knox's earlier report had made clear, what the treaty confirmed to the Creeks was title, not sovereignty. A treaty giving privately owned land to the Indians might well have triggered compensation once the fifth amendment was ratified; but it is not clear that either the President or the Senate agreed with Jackson's characterization of the facts.[248]

In July 1790, shortly before conclusion of the Creek Treaty, Congress had passed a law "to regulate trade and intercourse with the Indian tribes."[249] Section 1 of this statute provided that no person should carry on such trade without a license and required posting of a bond to ensure compliance with "such rules and regulations as the President sh[ould] prescribe." Not only did the licensing and bonding requirements plainly regulate "commerce . . . with the Indian tribes" as authorized by Article I, § 8; they were just as plainly necessary and proper to implement the corresponding terms of the treaty with the Northwest Indians.[250] Most startling from the perspective of the late twentieth century is the breadth of rulemaking power given to the President, which seemed to delegate to him virtually all of Congress's own authority over Indian commerce.[251]

Section 5 of the statute provided that any citizen or inhabitant of the United States who committed a crime against an Indian in Indian country should be "subject to the same punishment" as if the offense had been committed in the United States.[252] One reading this statute in isolation may be tempted to conclude that the First Congress took quite a broad view of its responsibility to regulate Indian "commerce." Yet the Fort Harmar treaty had promised the Indians the very protection afforded by § 5; this statutory provision too was necessary and proper to carry out the treaty.

Within the states, of course, criminal offenses were basically a matter of state law. The statute did not clearly say whether offenders were to be subject to state or to federal prosecution, though the provision that they were to be "proceeded against in the same manner" as if the offense had occurred within the state or district[253] arguably suggested the

[246]2 Annals at 1839.

[247]Geofroy v Riggs, 133 US 258, 267 (1890).

[248]In other respects both treaties seemed to fit comfortably within traditional conceptions of the treaty power, as their provisions plainly promoted amicable relations with Indian nations and were reasonably related to national defense.

[249]1 Stat 137 (July 22, 1790).

[250]Section 2 of the statute provided for revocation of licenses for violation of the regulations, subject to later judicial review. Evidently Congress thought that to take first and litigate afterwards was consistent in this context with the due process clause of the constitutional amendment it had just proposed.

[251]Section 1 also empowered the President to dispense with the license requirement in the case of tribes "surrounded in their settlements by the citizens of the United States, . . . if he may deem it proper." No standards were set to guide the exercise of this discretionary power. Cf Panama Refining Co. v Ryan, 293 US 388, 414–20 (1935); The Second Century at 216–18.

[252]1 Stat at 138.

[253]Id.

former. In either case Congress appeared to have made it a federal offense to do in Indian territory what state law forbade within the states. In so doing it seemed once again to have made the content of federal law dependent on the future acts of the states[254] and—if the assumption of state prosecution is correct—to have co-opted state officers to enforce federal law as well.[255] To modern eyes these provisions accordingly raise interesting issues of federalism; it may be significant that Congress apparently perceived no constitutional problem.

C.   Pirates

In his Annual Message at the beginning of the second session, President Washington called the attention of Congress to the "distressful" state of trade between the United States and the Mediterranean, adding that "you will not think any deliberations misemployed which may lead to its relief and protection."[256] What this meant was spelled out a few days later in a report from Secretary of State Jefferson to both Houses.[257] Repeated captures of American vessels by Algerian pirates had prevented resumption of a Mediterranean trade that had flourished before the Revolution; it was for Congress to decide whether the appropriate response was tribute, ransom, or war.[258]

A Senate committee responded at once by recommending the establishment of a navy to protect Mediterranean trade as soon as the state of the Treasury allowed.[259] In the meantime the Senate gave advice and consent in advance "that the President . . . take such measures as he may think necessary for the redemption of the citizens of the United States now in captivity at Algiers, provided the expense shall not exceed forty thousand dollars."[260] Appropriately, Washington replied that he would ransom the prisoners "so soon as the moneys necessary shall be appropriated by the Legislature."[261]

Appropriations could be made only by statute, and it would not be long before a request for money to implement a treaty would kindle a great debate over the freedom of the House to refuse its consent.[262] For the moment, however, any such confrontation was postponed by the Senate's agreement to delay any ransom attempt "until the situation of

[254]See the discussion of the inspection law, text at notes 64–74.

[255]The alternative conclusion that Congress had required state legislatures to punish crimes in Indian country would pose equally troublesome questions of federalism. See the discussion of the seamen's law in note 81.

[256]See 2 Annals at 1770, 1772 (Dec 8, 1790).

[257]1 Am St Papers (Foreign Relations) at 104–08.

[258]See also Jefferson's separate report in response to a petition for relief of the hostages taken by the pirates and the President's accompanying letter inviting Congress to "provide on their behalf, what to you shall seem most expedient." Id at 100–04.

[259]Id at 108. Maclay assailed this proposal as a plot to start yet another war and suggested it would be better to spend $35,000 for ransom than $500,000 to build a fleet. 9 Doc Hist at 373. Since he was talking only to his diary, there was no one to remind him that if we didn't build a navy this might not be the last $35,000 we would have to pay.

[260]2 Annals at 1795–96. Since such an exchange would presumably take the form of an international agreement, there was nothing particularly startling in the assumption that this subject fell within the Senate's special authority with respect to foreign affairs. See chapter 1.

[261]2 Annals at 1806.

[262]See chapter 5 (discussing the Jay Treaty).

the Treasury shall more clearly authorize appropriations for that purpose, in light of the large appropriations that had been made for the protection of the Western frontiers."[263]

As Gerhard Casper has observed, both Washington and Jefferson plainly assumed that Congress's powers over appropriations and war gave it ultimate authority to resolve the Algerian controversy, notwithstanding the President's much vaunted responsibility for foreign affairs.[264]

VI.   MISCELLANY

After setting up and financing the new government, and before tackling such critical issues as national defense and the bank, Congress somehow found time to exercise a number of the more mundane powers entrusted it by the Constitution. The second session of the First Congress produced comprehensive legislation on naturalization, patents, copyrights, and crimes. Other legislation of the period dealt with such matters as full faith and credit, the admission of new states, the territories, and the seat of government.

A.   Naturalization

"The Congress shall have power," says Article I, § 8, "to establish an uniform rule of naturalization." On the strength of this authorization Congress enacted a naturalization law in March 1790.[265]

The statute provided that any "free white" alien having resided in the United States for two years could become a citizen upon proving "good character" and promising "to support the constitution." By excluding applicants who did not meet these qualifications Congress demonstrated that, as in the case of taxes, it understood the uniformity require-

---

[263]2 Annals at 1825 (Mar 3, 1791). See also Swanstrom at 120 (suggesting that the true explanation for the Senate's action was its unwillingness "to ask the House of Representatives for advance appropriations and thereby admit that House into a participation in the treaty power"). As Washington had requested, however, Congress did appropriate a sum not to exceed $20,000 "for the purpose of effecting a recognition of the treaty of the United States, with the new emperor of Morocco." 1 Stat 214 (Mar 3, 1791). That treaty, which dated from 1787, required among other things that the emperor set free any Americans so unfortunate as to be captured by Moors. See 8 Stat 100, 101, Art VI (Jan 1787). Why it might require $20,000 to induce the emperor to recognize his obligations was not explained. The President said only that the appropriation was of "importance . . . to the liberty and property of our citizens," and Congress evidently thought it necessary and proper to effectuating the treaty. See 2 Annals at 1806. See also Gerhard Casper, An Essay in Separation of Powers: Some Early Versions and Practices, 30 Wm & Mary L Rev 211, 246 (1989) (explaining that "the Sultan had died and a customary payment was due his successor").

[264]See id. A year later, when the question of ransom arose again, Jefferson advised Washington to consult the House as well as the Senate before making a commitment, since House action would be necessary to authorize any expenditure. Significantly, Jefferson agreed with the President that a treaty would be "obligatory on the Represent[atives] to furnish the money," but he urged Washington not to take the risk that they might "decline to do what was their duty," and Washington obtained an appropriation before beginning negotiations. Anas, 9 Jefferson Writings (Wash ed) at 106–07, 114–15; 23 Jefferson Papers at 256–57, 263–64; 1 Stat 284, 285, § 3 (May 8, 1792); 1 Journal of the Executive Proceedings of the Senate 122–23 (Duff Green, 1828) [hereafter cited as Senate Executive Journal].

[265]1 Stat 103 (Mar 26, 1790).

ment solely in geographic terms.[266] The history of the constitutional provision confirms this conclusion; Congress was given power to adopt a nationwide rule in order to prevent a state with lenient naturalization requirements from foisting off undesirables on other states under the privileges and immunities clause.[267]

In light of this history Representative Sherman urged that the bill be amended to preclude naturalization of Tory emigrants and paupers: The constitutional provision was "meant to guard against an improper mode of naturalization, rather than foreigners should be received upon easier terms than those adopted by the several States."[268] Like the related argument that the commerce power could be employed only to remove obstructions to commerce, this objection got nowhere at the constitutional level;[269] but the historical purpose of the naturalization clause was to play an important part in the later controversy over whether the federal power to grant citizenship was exclusive.[270]

Much of the House debate on naturalization revolved around a provision of the original bill that would have subjected naturalized citizens to an additional residence requirement before they became eligible to hold federal or state office.[271] Laurance understandably doubted whether Congress had authority to add to the qualifications specified for federal legislators in Article I or to tell the states who was entitled to participate in their government.[272] Congress's sole power, Stone added, was to confer citizenship; it was for the states to define the rights of citizens.[273] Jackson responded with a quotation from Blackstone in support of the practice of admitting foreigners to citizenship "progressively," arguing that precedents from "that nation from which we derive most of our ideas on this subject" were highly relevant in interpreting the Constitution.[274] The additional residence requirement was dropped from the bill—whether on constitutional or policy grounds we do not know.

[266]See the discussion of the analogous tax question, text at notes 43–44.

[267]See 3 Story, § 1098; Kent at 397; Agrippa No 9, Dec 28, 1787, in Philip B. Kurland and Ralph Lerner, eds, 2 The Founders' Constitution at 559–60 (Chicago, 1987) (citing Pennsylvania as the most notorious source of infection); Rawle at 84–85. Like the provision limiting military service to males (see text at note 217), the exclusion of non-whites suggests that Congress did not understand the due process clause it had just proposed to contain a general ban on racial or gender discrimination, at least when neither life, liberty, or property in the traditional sense was at stake.

[268]1 Annals at 1148.

[269]However, the bill was amended to require state consent to the naturalization of any person "heretofore proscribed by any state." See 1 Stat at 104.

[270]See Collet v Collet, 6 F Cases 105, 106 (CCD Pa 1792) (No 3001) (holding the power not exclusive); United States v Villato, 28 F Cases 377, 379 (CCD Pa 1797) (No 16,622) (dictum that power exclusive).

[271]1 Annals at 1147.

[272]Id at 1149. Congress had already required that the Attorney General and U.S. Attorneys be lawyers (see chapter 1), but the Constitution was silent as to their qualifications. Cf Powell v McCormack, 395 US 486, 550 (1969); Bond v Floyd, 385 US 116, 132–33 (1966); The Second Century at 442–44, 439–40. But see Edward S. Corwin, The President: Office and Powers 33 (NYU, 1940) (noting that a variety of federal statutes disqualified criminal offenders from holding federal office).

[273]1 Annals at 1156–57.

[274]Id at 1158. See also id at 1155 (Rep. Tucker) (taking the constitutional requirements for members of Congress as evidence that Congress could "make the admission to citizenship progressive"). Provisions imposing additional residence requirements before new citizens could exercise political rights were common in state constitutions adopted during and after the Revolution. See James H. Kettner, The Development of American Citizenship, 1608–1870 214–19 (North Carolina, 1978).

More interesting still was the further provision declaring that "the children of citizens of the United States, that may be born beyond sea, or out of the limits of the United States, shall be considered as natural born citizens"—provided only that their fathers at some point had resided in the United States.[275] Representative Burke had explained to the House that a similar provision had been made in England, but he did not identify the source of congressional authority.[276] In accepting his suggestion, Congress appears to have interpreted the authority to enact "naturalization" laws to give it a general power to define or confer citizenship[277]—a power that Burke might have thought twice about before advocating had he stopped to consider its possible applicability to the numerous individuals euphemistically described in Article IV, § 2 as "persons held to service or labour" in his own state of South Carolina.[278]

Finally, and perhaps most surprisingly from a modern perspective, the statute made naturalization a judicial rather than an executive function. Application was to be made "to any common law court of record" in a state where the applicant had lived.[279] The Act did not specify whether federal courts were included. The terminology was broad enough to include them, but there was no explicit grant of federal jurisdiction; and the Judiciary Act contained no general federal-question provision.[280] To open federal courts to ex parte naturalization petitions would raise the difficult question whether such proceedings fell within Article III's provisions extending the judicial power only to "cases" and "controversies";[281] to rely on the state courts would raise once again the question whether Congress could co-opt state agencies to enforce federal law.[282] There is no evidence that the First Congress was troubled by either of these concerns.

B.   Patents and Copyrights

Barely two weeks after having achieved a quorum, the House received petitions for special legislation granting exclusive rights to publish two books and to exploit scientific dis-

---

[275]1 Stat 104.

[276]1 Annals at 1160.

[277]But see Corwin, The President: Office and Powers at 33 (cited in note 272): "The provision must undoubtedly be referred to the proposition that, as the legislative body of a nation sovereign at international law, Congress is entitled to determine who shall and who shall not be admitted to the body politic." Cf the Chinese Exclusion Case, 130 US 581, 606 (1889); The Second Century at 14–15.

[278]See the discussion in text at notes 82–99 of Southern fears that Congress might attempt to emancipate the slaves; Dred Scott v Sandford, 60 US 393, 405–07 (1857) (declaring the naturalization power limited to foreigners). In the debate over the eligibility of Burke's colleague William Smith for election to Congress (see chapter 1) the consensus had seemed to be that state law determined citizenship in the first instance, but that was not inconsistent with a congressional power to provide otherwise by statute. In urging the House to add a provision permitting aliens to hold property, Representative Clymer seemed to suggest that the naturalization clause gave Congress general authority to regulate the legal status of aliens—a preview of yet another epic controversy that would divide Congress in the next few years. See 1 Annals at 1160; Alien Act, 1 Stat 577 (July 6, 1798), discussed in chapter 6.

[279]1 Stat 103.

[280]See chapter 1.

[281]See Tutun v United States, 270 US 568, 576–78 (1926); The Second Century at 182–83.

[282]See the discussion of offenses against Indians in the text at note 255 and of delinquent sailors in note 81.

coveries relating to the magnetic pole.[283] There was no doubt that Congress had power to grant these requests, for Article I, § 8 authorized it "[t]o promote the progress of science and useful arts, by securing, for limited times, to authors and inventors, the exclusive right to their respective writings and discoveries." A House committee promptly recommended that Congress pass a law securing to the second petitioner "the exclusive pecuniary emolument to be derived from the publication of [his] several inventions."[284]

However, it was not to be. When Washington in his Annual Message the next January urged the legislators to give "effectual encouragement" to "useful inventions,"[285] they responded by authorizing a panel composed of the Attorney General and the Secretaries of State and War to grant a patent for any "invention or discovery" they might deem "sufficiently useful or important."[286] The initial trickle of individual requests had evidently alerted Congress to the inundation it faced if it attempted to grant patents and copyrights by private bill.[287] The discretion delegated was broad but not unrestricted; nobody seems to have thought that Article I required Congress to pass upon individual patent applications.[288]

In contrast to the arguably analogous power to confer citizenship,[289] the authority to grant patents was given to executive officers rather than to the courts. The "district court," however, was empowered upon motion to set aside any patent "obtained surreptitiously by, or upon false suggestion."[290] There was no doubt that this proceeding was properly judicial, since it involved a concrete dispute between adversary parties. There was little doubt that it was properly federal, since the validity of a patent was a federal question.[291] Congress apparently felt no constitutional compulsion to provide judicial review of the determination whether the invention was "sufficiently useful and important,"

[283]See the House Journal in 3 Doc Hist at 22 (Apr 15, 1789).

[284]See 1 Annals at 178.

[285]Id at 970.

[286]1 Stat 109, 110, § 1 (Apr 10, 1790). Faithful to the constitutional injunction that the rights conferred be "for limited times," the statute provided that patents should be issued "for any term not exceeding fourteen years." Id.

[287]See 1 Annals at 985–88, tabling a bill to grant an individual patent pending enactment of a general patent law. Cf Sedgwick's apt objection to the analogous practice of granting individual plots of western land by private bill: "[W]e shall be perpetually employed in a menial business, and which we are greatly incompetent to." 1 Annals at 1109. See also note 412. Similar complaints were made with respect to private bills respecting individual claims against the government. See Gazette of the United States, Mar 13, 1790 (Rep. Bland); New York Daily Gazette, Mar 15, 1790 (Reps. Bland and Boudinot).

[288]On the other hand, despite Marshall's later insistence that the sole province of legislation was "to prescribe general rules for the government of society" (Fletcher v Peck, 10 US 87, 136 (1810)), no one seemed to doubt Congress's *power* to grant individual patents. Indeed the First Congress enacted several private bills providing for the payment of individual claims or pensions and the remission of individual penalties or duties. See 6 Stat 1–3. See also White at 79: "While in general Congress tended to legislate on broad matters of policy, it did nevertheless insist on dealing with some matters which would now be regarded as falling in the proper field of administrative discretion."

[289]See text at notes 279–82.

[290]1 Stat at 111, § 5.

[291]See US Const, Art III, § 2. Arguably, however, the federal question arose only by way of defense to a complaint seeking to establish the common law right to exploit the invention. See Louisville & Nashville R.R. v Mottley, 211 US 149, 152 (1908). The reference to the "district court" seemed to suggest federal jurisdiction, although the statute did not say so expressly.

for it provided none; and it seems to have concluded that the constitutional amendment it had just proposed would not require a jury in such actions, for a jury-trial provision had been deleted in the House after it was suggested that jurors would not be competent to pass on the technical questions involved.[292]

Section 4 provided that infringers should both pay damages and forfeit the offending goods.[293] Nothing was said about the courts in which infringement actions were to be brought, and no other statute provided for federal jurisdiction in the absence of diverse citizenship. Obviously Congress anticipated that state courts would hear them; it did not say they had to. This time, however, the statute expressly provided for jury trial, raising the serious question whether Congress could constitutionally regulate the procedure of state courts enforcing federal law.[294]

A few weeks after passage of the patent law, Congress enacted a comparable statute providing for the issuance of copyrights.[295] In extending protection to "map[s] and chart[s]" as well as books, this law seemed to reflect a rather generous if appropriate interpretation of the constitutional term "writings."[296] Perhaps because there was no requirement in the copyright law that the author's work be "useful and important," there was no provision for executive determination whether the statutory requirements had been met.[297] All the applicant had to do was to deposit copies of his work "in the clerk's office of the district court" and with the Secretary of State,[298] for purposes of public notice. Evidently Congress perceived no constitutional impediment to this convenient use of judicial officers for purely administrative purposes.[299]

As in the patent law, infringement actions were authorized, this time "in any court of record in the United States, wherein the [action] is cognizable."[300] Again there was no provision for federal jurisdiction, and this time nothing was said about jury trial. An interesting provision near the end of the statute added a damage remedy against anyone who should "print or publish any manuscript" without the author's consent.[301] Since remedies had already been provided for infringement of copyrights obtained by depositing books or maps with the district court, the additional provision respecting "manuscript[s]" must have been intended to protect authors who had not yet completed the statutory formali-

---

[292]See 2 Annals at 1463–64. This was the sole issue on which debate on the patent bill was reported.

[293]1 Stat at 111.

[294]For the modern view see Dice v Akron, Canton & Youngstown R.R., 342 US 359, 363 (1952). Cf the question whether Congress could require state courts to act at all, discussed in note 81 and in the text at notes 255, 282. Congress unambiguously gave the circuit courts concurrent jurisdiction of infringement actions in 1793. 1 Stat 318, 322, § 5 (Feb 21, 1793).

[295]1 Stat 124 (May 31, 1790). There was no reported debate on this bill.

[296]Id, § 1. The fluidity of the boundary between "writings" and "discoveries," and thus between copyrights and patents under the statutory scheme, was suggested by the fact that one of the first petitions presented to Congress requested exclusive rights to sell "maps, charts, and tables" based on the "principles of magnetism" whose explanation the applicant had allegedly "invented." 3 Doc Hist at 22.

[297]Contrast the patent law, discussed at note 286.

[298]1 Stat at 125, §§ 3, 4.

[299]Compare the advisory fact-finding duties discussed in chapter 1 (respecting mitigation of certain penalties) that the First Congress entrusted to federal *judges*, whom Article III seems to limit to the decisions of specified types of "cases" and "controversies."

[300]1 Stat at 124–25, § 2.

[301]Id at 125–26, § 6. This remedy too was to be sought in "any court having cognizance thereof." Id.

ties. Protection before deposit was plainly appropriate to promoting the progress of the arts, but one might wonder whether the apparently eternal protection afforded to "manuscript[s]" was consistent with the constitutional requirement that Congress confer exclusive rights only "for limited times."[302]

As noted earlier in this chapter, the petition requesting protection for discoveries respecting the magnetic pole also requested "the patronage of Congress" for "a voyage to Baffin's Bay . . . to ascertain the causes" of the variations that had been observed.[303] Tucker doubted "whether the Legislature ha[d] power . . . to go further in rewarding the inventors of useful machines, or discoveries in sciences, than merely to secure to them for a time the right of making, publishing and vending them."[304] There may have been other bases of congressional authority to finance the proposed expedition, but Tucker was right about the patent clause; the Constitution confers not a general power to "promote the progress of science and the useful arts," but only the power to grant limited exclusive rights in order to accomplish that goal.[305]

C. Crimes

On April 30, 1789, Congress enacted a comprehensive statute defining an impressive variety of federal crimes.[306] As in the case of patents and copyrights, there was little reported debate; yet the statute itself resolved a number of constitutional questions.

Criminal law in general was not a federal subject. Article III, § 3 defined treason restrictively and authorized Congress to "declare" its "punishment." Article I, § 8 empowered Congress to provide for the punishment of "counterfeiting the securities and current coin of the United States," "piracies and felonies committed on the high seas," and "offenses against the law of nations," as well as conferring the power of "exclusive legislation" over the "seat of Government" and other places purchased with state consent "for the erection of forts, magazines, arsenals, dock-yards and other needful buildings." The 1789 statute implemented each of these constitutional provisions while adding several other offenses not expressly mentioned in the Constitution.[307]

---

[302]If the answer is that Congress did not confer this protection but merely provided a remedy for violation of common-law copyright, that raises constitutional questions of its own. Perhaps the clue lies in the term "manuscript": The exclusive right to *publish* a work could be obtained only by following the statutory procedure, and then the right was limited to a renewable term of 14 years. 1 Stat at 124, § 1. For some policy dimensions of copyright in unpublished works see William Landes, Copyright Protection of Letters, Diaries, and Other Unpublished Works: An Economic Approach, 21 J Legal Studies 79 (1992).

[303]See 3 Doc Hist at 22.

[304]1 Annals at 180.

[305]See 1 Tucker's Blackstone at 266–67. Thus while Washington had urged Congress to encourage not only domestic invention but also "the introduction of new and useful inventions from abroad," 1 Annals at 970, even Hamilton had to concede that Congress's authority to give exclusive privileges to "Introducers" of valuable improvements was "not without a question." Report on Manufactures, 10 Hamilton Papers at 230, 308. See also the exchange of letters between Madison and Tench Coxe on the question whether Congress could employ the proceeds of Western land sales for this purpose, 13 Madison Papers at 111, 113, 128–31.

[306]1 Stat 112.

[307]Article I, § 8, cl 14 authorized Congress "to make rules for the government of the land and naval forces" and Article IV, § 3 to "make all needful rules and regulations respecting the territory or other property belonging to the United States." The First Congress provided for crimes under the former clause by ratifying the Articles of War adopted under the Confederation, see text at note 219, and under the

Section 1 repeated the constitutional definition of treason as "levy[ing] war" against the United States or "adher[ing] to their enemies, giving them aid and comfort," and added that the prohibition applied—as seemed implicit in the term itself—only to "persons owing allegiance to the United States."[308] It went on to reiterate the constitutional requirement that the offense be proved by "two witnesses to the same overt act" or by "confession in open court." In specifying that the witnesses testify to a single "overt act of the treason" Congress may have lent support to the argument that the overt act must itself be culpable—a crucial issue that was to divide the Supreme Court a century and a half later.[309] Finally, in accord with Article III's provision authorizing Congress "to declare the punishment of treason," § 1 prescribed that anyone convicted of that offense should "suffer death"—thus conforming to the constitutional strictures restricting "forfeiture" and "corruption of blood"[310] while reinforcing the implication that the ban on cruel and unusual punishment in the proposed eighth amendment did not automatically preclude the deprivation of "life" expressly contemplated by the fifth.

More striking was the following section of the statute, which defined misprision of treason as concealment or failure to disclose the commission of treason by others and provided a punishment of imprisonment and fine.[311] The Constitution said nothing of this offense. Congress may have thought the power to punish misprision implicit in its authority to "declare the punishment of treason" itself; it may have concluded that the provisions setting up the Government implied authority to protect it from destruction. In any event the legislators must have interpreted the narrow definition of treason in Article III not to preclude it from creating lesser related offenses that might otherwise fall within federal purview—although nothing in the misprision provision suggested that Congress had yet considered the possible impact of the treason clause on efforts to punish seditious expression.

As authorized by the exclusive-legislation provision of Article I, § 8, various sections of the statute proscribed such offenses as murder, manslaughter, mayhem, and larceny in any place "under the sole and exclusive jurisdiction of the United States."[312]

---

latter by reaffirming and extending the Northwest Ordinance, which envisioned executive adoption of "such laws of the original states . . . as may be necessary" pending convocation of a territorial legislature. See 1 Stat 50–52 (Aug 7, 1789) (confirming and reprinting the 1787 Ordinance); 1 Stat 123 (May 26, 1790) (extending most of its provisions to the territory south of the Ohio). Section 16 of the 1789 statute, 1 Stat at 116, which made it a federal crime to steal or embezzle military arms or supplies, seemed not only necessary and proper to Congress's power to "raise and support armies"; it too could easily be defended as an exercise of Article IV's authority to "make . . . needful rules and regulations respecting the . . . property of the United States."

[308] 1 Stat at 112. Like Article III itself, the statute was ambiguous as to whether the phrases respecting adherence and aid to enemies established one offense or two. See Cramer v United States, 325 US 1, 29 (1945).

[309] Cramer, 325 US at 29–35 (opinion of the Court); id at 61 (Douglas, J, dissenting). See The Second Century at 294–99.

[310] In emphasizing that no conviction for any offense under the statute should "work corruption of blood, or any forfeiture of estate," § 24 went beyond Article III, § 3, which forbade "corruption of blood, or forfeiture, except during the life of the person attainted" and only in the case of treason.

[311] 1 Stat at 112, § 2.

[312] Id at 113, 115–16, §§ 3, 7, 13, 16, 17. Section 6 provided punishment for misprision of these offenses. Id at 113. No provision was made at this time for the punishment of lesser offenses in federal enclaves;

The most controversial provision of the entire statute was § 4, which authorized the court, after imposing a death sentence for murder, to order "that the body of [the] offender . . . be delivered to a surgeon for dissection."[313] In the House it was argued that dissection "was wounding the feelings of the living, and could do no good."[314] Stone added that it "ma[de] punishment wear the appearance of cruelty,"[315] conjuring up visions of the corresponding amendment that Congress had just proposed.

Dissection was defended both on the ground that it "increased the dread of punishment" and on the ground that it would promote the progress of science.[316] The first argument appeared to confirm Stone's objection, the second to revive the controversy over whether Congress had general authority to promote the advancement of knowledge.[317] So long as the offense occurred within an enclave subject to exclusive federal jurisdiction, however, there could be no doubt that the subject fell within congressional authority.[318]

Sections 8 through 13 implemented Congress's express authority to punish "piracies and felonies committed on the high seas."[319] The statute seemed to take an exceedingly broad view of what constituted piracy, for it branded as a "pirate" both the mariner who "r[a]n away with" a ship or $50 worth of cargo and the mutineer who should "make a revolt in the ship."[320] From the constitutional standpoint no harm was done, since all the acts punished were felonious and Congress's power extended to all felonies on the high seas.[321]

More significantly, the prohibitions were not strictly limited to the high seas but extended as well to crimes committed "in any river, haven, basin or bay, out of the ju-

---

Congress's later assimilation of state laws for this purpose would raise interesting constitutional questions. See United States v Sharpnack, 355 US 286 293–94 (1958).

[313] 1 Stat at 113. For the grisly background of this provision see Steven Robert Wilf, Anatomy and Punishment in Late Eighteenth-Century New York, 22 J Soc Hist 507 (1989). Section 5's further provision of penalties against anyone interfering with such an order was necessary and proper to its effectuation if the dissection itself was constitutional.

[314] 2 Annals at 1572.

[315] Id.

[316] Id.

[317] See text at notes 123–26, 133.

[318] The dissection provision also applied to murder committed on the high seas, for which the statute also provided the death penalty. Congress's power to enact a general code of laws (as contrasted with the punishment of felonies alone) for that realm was not so plain, though the necessary and proper clause in conjunction with the commerce clause or with the admiralty clause of Article III might have provided a basis of authority. See the discussion of the seamen's law in text at notes 75–81.

[319] 1 Stat at 113–15; US Const, Art I, § 8, cl 10.

[320] 1 Stat at 114, § 8. In the former case punishment was imposed only if the act was done "piratically" or "feloniously." Whether in this context "piratically" meant anything more than with felonious intent seems doubtful. See 3 Story, § 1154: "The common law . . . deems piracy to be robbery on the sea."

[321] Section 8 also forbade murder, robbery, and "any other offence which if committed within the body of a county, would be by the laws of the United States be punishable by death." 1 Stat at 113–14. The reference to "laws of the United States" seemed to suggest federal law, but as so construed it was arguably unnecessary; most federal criminal provisions were not restricted in their geographical application. To conclude that Congress meant to incorporate the laws of the several states as they might stand at the time of the offense would present an interesting constitutional question. See text at notes 73–74 and note 312. Possibly Congress intended only to make applicable all criminal laws applying to areas of exclusive federal jurisdiction. See also 1 Stat at 115–16, §§ 12, 13, 16, outlawing manslaughter, mayhem, and larceny on the high seas.

risdiction of any particular state."[322] Whether Congress thought authority over such places included within the ostensibly narrower term "high seas," necessary and proper to the regulation of commerce or to the exercise of admiralty jurisdiction, or implicit in a central government responsible for external affairs is not clear. One can easily imagine the contrary argument that each state was responsible for the actions of its citizens in places neither within any territorial jurisdiction nor upon the high seas. Easier perhaps to sustain were the provisions of sections 10 and 11 punishing anyone on land as well as on sea who aided or abetted the commission of a crime at sea;[323] punishment of earthbound accessories could without much effort be found necessary and proper to prevention of the offense itself.

Section 14, as authorized by Article I, § 8, prescribed the punishment for counterfeiting "any certificate, indent, or other public security of the United States."[324] It was fair enough to construe the constitutional grant to embrace alteration and forgery of securities, assistance to counterfeiters, and perhaps even knowing use of counterfeit instruments, each of which the statute proscribed.[325] What created a small stir in the House was that the punishment provided for all these offenses was death, which some members plausibly suggested might appear excessive even in 1789.[326] Sedgwick was heard to say "that he thought the degrees of punishment ought to be proportioned to the malignity of the offence,"[327] and one day the Supreme Court would interpret the eighth amendment to require just that.[328] For the moment, however, no one tied the argument for proportional penalties to anything in the Constitution.

Sections 25 through 28 of the statute forbade violence against foreign diplomats and judicial seizure of their person or goods.[329] No reliance on inherent or implied powers over foreign affairs was necessary to justify these provisions. The statute plausibly described each of these offenses as a violation of "the law of nations," which Article I, § 8 expressly empowered Congress—within reason, one infers—to define as well as to punish.

This is the point at which explicit constitutional authority for creation of federal crimes runs out. But the statute went on to define additional crimes: theft or falsification of court records, perjury, bribery of federal judges, interference with judicial process, liber-

---

[322]1 Stat at 113, § 8.

[323]Id at 114.

[324]Id at 115. Nothing was said of counterfeiting coins, possibly because at the time—despite yet another exemplary report from the Secretary of the Treasury, 7 Hamilton Papers at 570 (Jan 28, 1791)—the mint had not yet been established. See 1 Stat 246 (Apr 2, 1792) (discussed in chapter 3).

[325]For later views on the breadth of this authority see United States v Marigold, 50 US 560, 566–67 (1850); The First Hundred Years at 234 n 270.

[326]2 Annals at 1573–74.

[327]Id at 1573. Cf W.S. Gilbert, The Mikado, Act II, ll 337–44, in Ian Bradley, ed, 1 The Annotated Gilbert and Sullivan at 325 (Penguin, 1982). Sedgwick was eventually reconciled to the terms of the provision. 2 Annals at 1573.

[328]Weems v United States, 217 US 349 (1910). See also Coker v Georgia, 433 US 584 (1977), Enmund v Florida, 458 US 782 (1982), Solem v Helm, 463 US 277 (1983); Hermelin v Michigan, 501 US 957 (1991); The Second Century at 57, 550 n 315.

[329]1 Stat at 117–18.

ation of federal prisoners.[330] All these provisions were plainly necessary and proper to the operation of the federal courts; Marshall was to cite the perjury section as a precedent for the existence of implicit powers in *McCulloch v. Maryland*.[331] This was not the first time Congress had established criminal penalties for acts outside the specific grants of authority to define federal crimes. Penalties for unloading ships in the dark or without a license[332] were obviously ancillary to collection of customs duties; penalties against census takers who failed to report their findings[333] were plainly appropriate to enumeration of the people. Clearly the First Congress did not view the list of topics of federal criminal law as negating authority to create other offenses when to do so was necessary and proper to the exercise of some other explicit federal power.[334]

D.   States

When the First Congress met in 1789 there were eleven states in the Union. When it adjourned two years later it had made provision for fifteen.

The Articles of Confederation had described the Union they established as "perpetual" and subject to alteration only with the approval of "the legislatures of every state."[335] Knowing that radical Rhode Island was unlikely to endorse the new Constitution, the Framers in Philadelphia had ignored this requirement, providing that that the new Constitution would take effect on ratification by nine of the thirteen original states.[336] They were prescient if revolutionary in doing so, for not only Rhode Island but North Carolina as well initially declined to ratify the Convention's proposal.[337]

The new Congress proceeded to employ both carrot and stick to induce the two delinquents to join the new Union. North Carolina and Rhode Island shipowners were temporarily accorded "all the privileges and advantages to which ships and vessels

---

[330]Id at 115–17, §§ 15, 17, 21–23. The penalties prescribed included whipping for tampering with court records or embezzling government property, id at 115–16, §§ 15, 16, and lifetime disqualification from federal office for a judge who accepted a bribe. Id at 117, § 21. These provisions suggest not only that Congress viewed neither of these punishments as cruel and unusual, but also that it did not understand impeachment to be the sole avenue for future disqualification of current officeholders.

[331]17 US 316, 417 (1819).

[332]1 Stat 29, 39, § 12 (July 31, 1789).

[333]1 Stat at 101, 102, §§ 2– 3 (Mar 1, 1790).

[334]Similarly necessary to operation of the courts were the procedural provisions of § 29, which (pending ratification of the proposed bill of rights) guaranteed the criminal defendant rights to a copy of the indictment, to employ counsel, and to call and subpoena witnesses. The power to enact statutes of limitation for various offenses (§ 32) seems implicit in authority to define the offense itself. See 1 Stat 118–19.

[335]1 Stat 4, 8–9, Art 13.

[336]US Const, Art VII. The Framers also provided for ratification by popular conventions instead of legislatures in order both to increase the chances of approval and to avoid any implication that the new Constitution, like the old, was a mere compact between states that could be dissolved if breached by one of its parties. 2 Farrand at 88–94. Legal justifications for these departures from the Articles ranged from their dissolution by breach to ultimate popular sovereignty. See id at 469 (James Wilson): "We must . . . in this case go to the original powers of Society, The House on fire must be extinguished, without a scrupulous regard to ordinary rights."

[337]See Richard B. Morris, The Forging of the Union, 1781–1789 315–16 (Harper & Row, 1987). Rhode Island had not even sent delegates to the Convention. 1 Farrand at 1–2.

owned by citizens of the United States are by law entitled"[338]—that is, lower tonnage and tariff duties and a federal license.[339] At the same time, however, a variety of goods produced in North Carolina or Rhode Island were subjected to customs duties when "brought into the United States"—just like goods "imported from any foreign state, kingdom, or country."[340]

It did not take long for North Carolina to get the message. A second convention, dominated by Federalists, reversed the initial negative vote, and a new legislature appointed two Federalist Senators.[341] On February 8, 1790, Congress extended the tariff, tonnage, and licensing laws to North Carolina and declared that the sanctions imposed against that state the preceding year had expired on its accession to the Union.[342]

Rhode Island was given two brief months to see the light as its semi-foreign status was extended until April 1.[343] Implicit was the threat that if Rhode Island did not ratify it would be treated as foreign, and thus subject to import duties on all its products as well as discriminatory treatment of its shipping. But as April passed without favorable action the Senate passed a bill that would have gone much further by banning all commercial intercourse between Rhode Island and the United States and requiring the payment of $27,000—that state's purported share of the cost of discharging federal obligations entered into before the new Constitution took effect.[344]

House action on this bill was mooted a few days later when Rhode Island capitulated and swallowed the Constitution.[345] The bill itself nevertheless bristled with troublesome constitutional questions. On its face the ban on intercourse seemed to reflect a conviction that the power to regulate commerce included the power to prohibit it.[346] Yet the preamble to the bill, in declaring the measure "necessary to the security of the Revenue, & other essential interests of the United States,"[347] appeared to argue that it was necessary and proper to the collection of taxes,[348] if not also to national defense.[349] The demand for

[338]1 Stat 69, § 2 (Sept 16, 1789).

[339]See the discussion of the ship licensing law in text at notes 57–63.

[340]1 Stat at 70, § 3. See 1 Annals at 162–63 (Rep. Ames) (urging a stiff tariff on barley and lime because they were "imported in considerable quantities from a neighboring State that had not yet adopted the Constitution; and, perhaps . . . our political situation is such as to make some regulation on this head necessary").

[341]See Morris, Forging of the Union at 315–16 (cited in note 337). Washington reported North Carolina's ratification to the Senate on January 11, 1790. See 1 Annals at 971. Proposal of the Bill of Rights played a significant role in this decision; North Carolina had made constitutional amendments a condition of ratification. See Helen E. Veit, Kenneth R. Bowling, and Charlene Bangs Bickford, eds, Creating the Bill of Rights xi, xvi, 245, 269 (Johns Hopkins, 1991).

[342]1 Stat 99, 99–100, §§ 1–6. The Judiciary Act was extended to North Carolina on June 4. 1 Stat 126.

[343]1 Stat at 100–01, § 7.

[344]See 1 Annals at 1003, 1009, 1012. The bill itself, together with antecedent resolutions and committee reports, appears in 6 Doc Hist at 1810–14.

[345]See 1 Annals at 1018. See also 1 Stat 126 (June 14, 1790); 1 Stat 128 (June 23, 1790) (promptly extending various federal statutes to Rhode Island).

[346]See the discussion of protective tariffs in text at notes 23–25.

[347]See 6 Doc Hist at 1813.

[348]See 1 Annals at 440 (Rep. Ames): "I should be glad to know if any gentleman contemplates the State of Rhode Island disseverered from the Union; a maritime State, situated in the most convenient manner for the purpose of smuggling, and defrauding our revenue." Representative Page argued that the bill would encourage rather than prevent smuggling, since it would shut off the most natural outlet for Rhode Island goods. "It

money seems to have been based on the theory that Rhode Island shared responsibility for debts contracted under the Confederation, to which it was a party. The Articles had required each state to contribute its share toward financing legitimate expenditures, but the Articles seemed to be no longer in force; the prescribed method of finance under the new Constitution was taxation of individuals, not contributions by states.[350] Very likely the Senate thought Congress had implicit authority to collect sums owing to its predecessor, although Article VI, which specifically addressed the status of prior obligations, explicitly preserved only claims *against* the United States—by which it seemed to mean the federal Government, not the individual states.[351]

Supporters of the bill "did not deny," wrote Maclay, that its true purpose was to coerce Rhode Island into the Union;[352] "it was meant to be Used the same Way That a Robber does a dagger or a Highwayman a pistol. & to obtain the end desired by putting the party in fear."[353] This line of reasoning may seem to suggest the further possibility that both the ban on intercourse and the demand for indemnity might have been necessary and proper to the (involuntary) admission of new states under Article IV.[354] Yet Congress at no time considered Rhode Island a "new State" subject to the requirements of Article IV. As in the case of North Carolina, Congress passed no act to admit Rhode Island to the Union; once those states ratified the Constitution, Congress simply extended federal laws to include them.[355] The fact that such legislation was thought necessary seems to refute the alternative hypothesis that Congress thought ratification by nine states made the Constitution binding on all thirteen, which in any event is precluded by the express terms of Article VII; as Maclay insisted, "[t]hey admitted all hands [t]hat Rhode Island was independent."[356] Thus Congress appears to have viewed Article VII as giving all thirteen members of the Confederation, like Canada under the Articles,[357] a right to join the

---

would be thought madness" in Europe, he added, "to interdict all commercial intercourse of neighboring States, merely with a view to prevent smuggling." 2 Annals at 1673.

[349] See Maclay, 9 Doc Hist at 271: "The bill had been assigned to Various Motives. self defense self preservation, self interest . . . ."

[350] Compare Articles of Confederation, Art 8, with US Const, Art I, § 8, cl 1.

[351] See the discussion of Congress's authority to assume state obligations in text at notes 169–70. An alternative explanation might be that the Senate thought the implicit federal power over external affairs empowered it simply to demand tribute from independent states, on the pattern of the Barbary pirates. See text at notes 256–64.

[352] 9 Doc Hist at 264. See also 2 Annals at 1672–74 (Rep. Page).

[353] 9 Doc Hist at 271.

[354] See US Const, Art IV, § 3: "New States may be admitted by the Congress into this Union . . . ."

[355] See notes 342 and 345.

[356] 9 Doc Hist at 264. See US Const, art I, § 7: "The ratification of the Conventions of nine states, shall be sufficient for the establishment of this Constitution between the states so ratifying the same." Congress had acknowledged that neither Rhode Island nor North Carolina was part of the Union in 1789 by providing for the payment of customs duties when certain goods from those states were "brought into the United States." See text at note 340. Indeed, if North Carolina and Rhode Island were part of the United States in 1789, the act for collection of customs duties was arguably unconstitutional, for it named no port in either state as a port of entry for goods imported from other countries; Article I, § 9 forbids Congress in any commercial or revenue measure to give any "preference . . . to the ports of one state over those of another." See 1 Stat at 69–70, § 3. The Articles of Confederation, of course, had protected Rhode Island from being forced to accept any revised plan of union without its consent. See text at note 335.

[357] Articles of Confederation, Art 11.

Union unilaterally at any time. On this hypothesis, coercion seemed to cast a cloud on the validity of Rhode Island's ultimate act of accession; for Article VII seemed to contemplate that each state would make the decision whether or not to ratify as a matter of its own free will.[358]

In contrast, when the President in December 1790 transmitted to Congress a petition from a popularly elected convention seeking the admission of Kentucky as a state,[359] there was no doubt that Article IV provided the appropriate route to statehood. Since Kentucky was a part of Virginia, it could not be admitted without Virginia's consent, but Virginia had benevolently agreed.[360] Interestingly, the petition requested congressional approval no later than November 1791, in order to allow time for the new state to adopt a constitution before June 1, 1792—the date on which Kentucky desired to become a member of the Union.[361] One might have expected Congress to insist on seeing the state constitution before giving its approval, especially in light of the obligation of the United States under the same Article to "guarantee to every State in this Union a Republican form of Government," but it did not; the resulting statute unconditionally declared that Kentucky "shall be received and admitted into this Union" on the appointed date, "as a new and entire member of the United States of America."[362]

But Kentucky was destined to become the fifteenth state, not the fourteenth. For on February 9, five days after the Kentucky bill became law, President Washington transmitted to Congress "authentic documents" received from "the Governor of Vermont . . . expressing the consent of the Legislatures of New York and of the Territory of Vermont, that the said Territory shall be admitted to be a distinct member of our Union."[363] Nine days later the President signed legislation admitting Vermont to the Union as of March 4, 1791—nearly fifteen months before the date set for the admission of Kentucky.[364]

Washington's message had called Vermont a "Territory"; the statute described it,

---

[358]See 2 Annals at 1672 (Rep. Page): "[I]t becomes this House to take care therefore that their sister State, now about to consider of the propriety of adopting the Constitution, shall be as free to judge for herself as was any other State in the Union." Compare the later controversy over ratification of the fourteenth amendment by states that were required to ratify in order to regain their representation in Congress. 14 Stat 428, 429, § 5 (Mar 2, 1867); The First Hundred Years at 296–99.

[359]See 2 Annals at 1773–75 (Dec 9, 1790).

[360]See id at 1774, citing 1789 Va Acts 17; US Const, Art IV, § 3: "[B]ut no new State shall be formed or erected within the jurisdiction of any other State . . . without the Consent of the Legislatures of the States concerned as well as of the Congress."

[361]See 2 Annals at 1774–75.

[362]1 Stat 189, § 2 (Feb 4, 1791). An earlier draft of the bill would have made admission conditional on Kentucky's ratification of the federal Constitution, but this proviso was dropped in the Senate—whether on the expectation that Kentucky would ratify of its own accord or on the assumption that Article IV did not require ratification is not clear. See 5 Doc Hist at 1219. Congress did make some effort to assure that Kentucky would make an acceptable member of the Union, for the Senate Committee repeated the petitioners' assertion that its people were "devoted to the American Union" and added that they were "sufficiently numerous for all the purposes of an independent State." 2 Annals at 1784–85; 5 Doc Hist at 1218. The propriety of some such inquiry is surely implicit in the discretion afforded by Article IV's provision that new states "may be admitted" by Congress. See also 19 Jefferson Papers at 369–70, making comparisons between Kentucky and Vermont on the question of devotion to the Union, to the decided detriment of the latter.

[363]2 Annals at 1798.

[364]1 Stat 191 (Feb 18, 1791).

at the time of its petition, as a "state." Vermont lay within the boundaries of the United States as defined by the Treaty of Paris, but it was not one of the "States" whose sovereignty and independence Great Britain in that treaty confirmed.[365] As indicated by the President's message, Vermont had set up its own government; New York's consent to the application reflects the claim that Vermont was a part of New York.[366] In admitting Kentucky Congress expressly acknowledged Virginia's consent; the Vermont statute said nothing about New York. Thus Congress seems to have thought that state's approval unnecessary and to have implicitly rejected its claim; but since New York had consented, the validity of its claim was no longer of constitutional significance.

As initially drafted the bill provided that, until House seats were apportioned according to the census, Vermont should be entitled to two Representatives.[367] Omitted in the Senate,[368] this provision became part of a separate statute making an identical provision for Kentucky as well.[369] This allotment was reasonably proportioned to each state's estimated population, as Article I, § 2 required;[370] authority to make an interim apportionment seems implicit in the power to admit new states.[371]

On March 2, 1791, two days before Vermont was to become a member of the Union, the President signed a law extending federal laws to the new state, "from and after

---

[365]Definitive Treaty of Peace Between the United States of America and his Britannic Majesty, Art I, II, 8 Stat 80, 81 (Sept 3, 1783).

[366]New York's initial charter of 1664 embraced "all the land from the West side of Connecticut to the East side of Delaware Bay"; a confirmatory charter in 1674 spoke of lands west of "Connecticut River," which plainly included Vermont. Chilton Williamson, Vermont in Quandary: 1763–1825 9–10 (Vermont Historical Society, 1949). Undaunted by a 1764 Privy Council decision fixing the Connecticut River as the boundary between New York and New Hampshire (which, like Massachusetts, also had claims on Vermont territory), Vermont had declared its independence from everybody in 1777. 4 Acts of the Privy Council of England: Colonial Series 673 (July 20, 1764); Matt Bushell Jones, Vermont in the Making: 1750–1777 x, 376 (Harvard, 1939). Vermont's repeated applications for admission to the Confederation were unsuccessful, in part because of its own refusal to submit to Congress the determination of its continuing disputes with New Hampshire and New York, in part because of opposition from New York and from Southern states not wishing to be further outnumbered. William Doyle, The Vermont Political Tradition: And Those Who Helped Make It 49–51 (Northlight Studio, rev ed 1987). Meanwhile Vermont adopted a liberal constitution, coined its own money, set up its own post offices, negotiated with foreign powers, and established a policy of free trade with Quebec. Id at 52. Alarmed at the economic implications of these independent actions, Alexander Hamilton led the campaign for Vermont's admission to the Union, and New York dropped its objections when Vermont agreed to compensate the holders of New York land grants within its borders. See Williamson, supra, at 175–77.

[367]See 6 Doc Hist at 2010.

[368]See 2 Annals at 1799 (Feb 11, 1791).

[369]1 Stat 191 (Feb 25, 1791).

[370]The 1790 census determined the populations of Vermont, Kentucky, and the United States to be 85,539, 73,677, and 3,893,635 persons respectively. Return of the Whole Number of Persons Within the Several Districts of the United States 3, 10, 47 (William Duane, 1802), reprinted as First Census of the United States, 1790 (Arno Press, 1976). After adjusting the slave population pursuant to Art I, § 2, this meant that Vermont comprised 2.4% and Kentucky 1.9% of the U.S. population. Thus by giving each state two of sixty-nine representatives (2.9% of the total representation), the First Congress left Vermont and Kentucky slightly overrepresented in the House.

[371]No such statutory provision had been necessary in the case of Rhode Island or North Carolina, to which Article I, § 2 itself allotted one and five Representatives respectively.

the third day of March next."[372] On March 3 the First Congress expired;[373] the next day Washington called a special session of the Senate to pass upon his nominations to federal offices in Vermont.[374] "The act for the admission of the State of Vermont into this Union, having fixed on this as the day of its admission," the President explained, "it was thought that this would also be the first day on which any officer of the Union might legally perform any act of authority relating to that State."[375] If this left unexplained why Washington had been willing to sign the bill extending the laws to Vermont two days earlier, it showed once again the extreme care he took at all times to conform his conduct to the Constitution.

But the First Congress was not content to incorporate two former states and admit two new ones; it also took time to regulate interstate relations. Article IV, § 1 provided that "full faith and credit sh[ould] be given in each State to the public acts, records, and judicial proceedings of every other State" and empowered Congress "by general laws" to "prescribe the manner in which such acts, records and proceedings shall be proved, and the effect thereof." Acting under this authority, Congress in May 1790 enacted a statute providing that "acts of the [state] legislatures" should be authenticated by affixing the state seal; that state judicial records and proceedings should be "proved or admitted in any other court within the United States" by attestation of the clerk, seal of the court, and certificate of the judge; and that "the said records and judicial proceedings" should be given "such faith and credit . . . in every court within the United States as they have by law or usage in the courts of the state from whence" they were taken.[376]

This brief statute had a number of implications for constitutional interpretation. First of all, Congress seems to have understood Article IV's reference to "public acts" to embrace all "acts of the [state] legislatures"—despite the fact that the inclusion of the

---

[372]1 Stat 197.

[373]See the report of a joint committee, 1 Annals at 1010, concluding that the initial presidential and legislative terms had begun March 4, 1789—the date appointed by the old Congress for the first meeting of the new—and that consequently Representatives and Senators of the first class (those whose terms were to last only two years) would not be entitled by virtue of their initial election "to seats in the next Congress, which will be assembled after the 3d day of March, 1791." As Representative Smith pointed out privately, this meant that North Carolina's representatives, who had not been elected until 1790, would sit for only one year. See Letter of William L. Smith to Edward Rutledge, May 24, 1790, in George C. Rogers, ed, Letters of William Loughton Smith to Edward Rutledge, 69 South Carolina Historical Magazine 101, 116 (1968).

In the House it was objected that Congress had no business making such a determination, since "each successive House must be the sole judge of the qualifications of its Members" (see US Const, Art I, § 5). Others responded that the Constitution plainly contemplated dissolution of one Congress before election of another, and both Houses approved the report. See 1 Annals at 1011; 2 Annals at 1637–38. What the last speaker meant to say was that dissolution of one Congress must precede *installation* of another, and even that did not preclude finding that members could sit until their successors had qualified. The Constitution said only that members should be "chosen every second Year," Art I, 2; to the extent this provision was ambiguous, Congress arguably had implicit authority to flesh it out in order to exercise the responsibilities given it by the Constitution.

[374]See 2 Annals at 1826. Article II, § 3 authorizes the President, "on extraordinary Occasions, [to] convene both Houses, *or either of them*" (emphasis added).

[375]2 Annals at 1827. Until the day of its admission, Jefferson had advised the President, Vermont "will not be a separate and integral member of the U.S. and it is only to integral members of the union that his right of nomination is given by the Constitution." 19 Jefferson Papers at 376, 377.

[376]1 Stat 122 (May 26, 1790).

term had been defended in the Convention on the narrow ground that it was necessary to provide for what we would now call "private" insolvency legislation whose impact was similar to that of a judicial decision.[377] On the other hand, notwithstanding the apparently all-embracing constitutional reference to state "records," the statute seemed to provide for the manner of proving only *judicial* records—whether as a matter of policy or of constitutional interpretation it is impossible to say.

In providing that properly authenticated records and proceedings should be given the same faith and credit everywhere as they had at home, the last sentence of the act raised a number of interesting issues. First, though it would later be argued that the term "faith and credit" referred only to the authenticity of foreign records, this sentence appeared (as the Supreme Court was to hold) to be an exercise of Congress's authority to prescribe the "effect" of one state's judgments in another, and to make those judgments as binding as they were in the court that had rendered them.[378] Furthermore, although Congress made no attempt to go beyond the language of Article IV by prescribing the credit to be given to *federal* judgments, it did require federal courts to respect the judgments of the states[379]—a provision that could easily be explained as necessary and proper to the establishment and operation of federal courts under Article III. Finally, while prescribing the manner of proving state statutes, the act said nothing about the effect that was to be given them. It may have been wise for Congress not to attempt to resolve all the problems of interstate choice of law while it was still wrestling with the difficulties of setting up the Government; it seems less defensible that two centuries later it still had not devoted serious attention to the problem.[380]

E. Territories

The British claims relinquished by the Treaty of Paris reached as far north and west as the Lake of the Woods and the Mississippi River.[381] Maryland had held up ratification of the Articles of Confederation until other states surrendered to Congress their claims to territory north and west of the Ohio,[382] and the Confederation Congress had adopted the celebrated Northwest Ordinance to govern it in 1787.[383]

The most arresting feature of this Ordinance was the audacity of Congress in enacting it at all. One searches the Articles in vain to find even the slimmest reed to support the power of the Confederation Congress to adopt such a measure.[384] Yet under the

---

[377]See 2 Farrand at 447; The Second Century at 70 & n 115.

[378]Mills v Duryee, 11 US 481 (1813); Hampton v McConnell, 16 US 234 (1818); The Second Century at 193 n 261. For the contrary view see *Mills*, 11 US at 485–87 (Johnson, J, dissenting).

[379]1 Stat at 122.

[380]The present statute, enacted in 1948, says unhelpfully that public acts as well as records and proceedings shall be given the same faith and credit everywhere as they have at home; it makes no effort to say when one state must defer to the laws of another. 28 USC § 1738 (1988). See Brainerd Currie, Full Faith and Credit, Chiefly to Judgments: A Role for Congress, 1964 S Ct Rev 89, 90, 121.

[381]Definitive Treaty of Peace Between the United States of America and his Britannic Majesty, 8 Stat 80, 81, Art II (Sept 3, 1783).

[382]See Merrill Jensen, The New Nation: A History of the United States During the Confederation, 1781–1789, 25–26 (Knopf, 1950).

[383]See 32 J Cont Cong 334 (July 12, 1787); 1 Stat 51–53 n (a).

[384]See The Federalist No 38 (Madison).

Ordinance a federal territory was set up and governed with general acquiescence. One lesson of this incident may be that necessity is at least as important a determinant of de facto authority as is any written constitution.

But the Ordinance was as remarkable for what it said as for what it was. Of greatest lasting significance perhaps was the provision in Article V for dividing the Territory into three to five states, to be admitted to the Union as soon as they acquired 60,000 free inhabitants.[385] We were not to retain colonies in our own country. Moreover, the new states were to be admitted "on an equal footing" with the old; there would be no second-class members of the Union. Vital as it was to harmonious relations, the equal footing doctrine was later found implicit in the Philadelphia Constitution;[386] the Ordinance was its source and its inspiration.[387]

Pending statehood, the Ordinance contemplated congressional appointment of a Governor and three judges, who acting jointly were to adopt "such laws of the original States, criminal and civil, as may be necessary and best suited to the circumstances of the district," subject to disapproval by Congress.[388] As soon as the Territory had 5,000 free male inhabitants, a general assembly was to be elected; but its authority to enact laws "for the good government of the district" would be shared with a legislative council selected by Congress from names the assembly submitted and subject to an absolute veto by the Governor, who in turn was removable by Congress.[389] All of this would serve as a precedent under the new Constitution for the delegation of lawmaking authority to local bodies subject to ultimate congressional control, and for federal adoption of state laws to boot. These provisions also established that, despite the Revolution, taxation without representation was not wholly foreign to our system of government. Jefferson's 1784 ordinance for the government of the Territory, which the 1787 enactment superseded, had been considerably more republican.[390]

In addition to these institutional provisions, the Ordinance contained five articles constituting nothing less than a bill of rights for the inhabitants of the Territory. Copied in substantial part from the English Bill of Rights of 1689 with some imaginative additions, these articles were to have a strong influence on the Philadelphia Convention as well as on the amendments proposed by the First Congress. No one "demeaning himself in a peaceable and orderly manner" was to be "molested on account of his mode of worship or religious sentiments."[391] There were guarantees of habeas corpus, jury trial, and "judicial proceedings according to the course of the common law," together with assurances that bail would be allowed in most cases, that fines should be "moderate," and that punishments should not be "cruel or unusual."[392] No one was to be deprived of liberty or property "but by the judgment of his peers, or the law of the land"; "full compensation"

---

[385]32 J Cont Cong at 342, 1 Stat at 53.

[386]Coyle v Smith, 221 US 559, 575–76 (1911); The Second Century at 101 n 71.

[387]The Ordinance, wrote Professor Morris, was thus both "an unprecedented anticolonial measure and a centerpiece of American federalism." Morris, Forging of the Union at 231 (cited in note 337).

[388]32 J Cont Cong at 336, 1 Stat at 51.

[389]32 J Cont Cong at 336–39, 1 Stat at 51–52.

[390]See Jensen, The New Nation at 353–54 (cited in note 382).

[391]32 J Cont Cong at 340, Art I, 1 Stat at 52.

[392]Id, Art II. Bail could be denied only "for capital offences, where the proof shall be evident, or the presumption great."

was required whenever "public exigencies" demanded the taking of property or services; fugitive slaves were to be returned; no law "ought ever to be made, or have force" that should "interfere with, or affect private contracts or engagements . . . previously formed."[393] Most of these provisions found their way, with more or less significant modifications, into either the Constitution or its first eight amendments. The changes that befell the various guarantees during the process of incorporation are most intriguing; in most cases we do not know whether to take the original wording as a guide to the implicit understanding of the often less precise terms later employed or to interpret the change in wording to reflect a desire for substantive change.

The Ordinance's provision for "proportionate representation of the people in the legislature" was picked up at the interstate level by Article I, § 2 of the new Constitution and read into the equal protection clause for intrastate apportionment in *Reynolds v. Sims*.[394] The ban on taxation of federal land found an echo in *McCulloch v. Maryland*;[395] the requirement that the government of the new states be "republican" grew into the universal guarantee of the present Article IV.[396] The proviso that navigation of western waters should be "forever free . . . without any tax, impost, or duty" was to reappear in acts admitting new states and thereby form the basis of at least one important Supreme Court decision.[397] The prohibition of slavery in the Northwest Territory, copied in the Missouri Compromise of 1820, was to provide the focus of controversy in the *Dred Scott* case in 1857.[398] Finally, important provisions conspicuously not echoed in the Constitution imposed on the territorial government the positive obligations to encourage "[s]chools and the means of education" and to enact laws to prevent wrongs against the Indians.[399]

All six Articles attached to the Ordinance, including the promise of prompt admission to the Union, were declared to constitute not a simple statute but a "compact between the original States, and the people and States in the said Territory," unalterable without common consent.[400] Whether this stipulation really bound Congress may be doubtful; it was common ground that the one thing the British Parliament could not do was to divest itself of its powers.[401] But the existence of this clause lent special dignity to

---

[393] 32 J Cont Cong at 340, 343, Arts II, VI, 1 Stat at 52, 53. The curious use of the verb "ought" in the clause last quoted raises the question whether the contract provision, in contrast to the others in this enumeration, may have been intended as hortatory rather than binding.

[394] 377 US 533 (1964); The Second Century at 430–31. See Art II of the Ordinance, 32 J Cont Cong at 340, 1 Stat at 52.

[395] 17 US 316 (1819); The First Hundred Years at 160–68. See Art IV of the Ordinance, 32 J Cont Cong at 341, 1 Stat at 52.

[396] See Art V of the Ordinance, 32 J Cont Cong at 342, 1 Stat at 53; US Const, Art IV, § 4.

[397] Pennsylvania v Wheeling & Belmont Bridge Co., 54 US 518 (1852); The First Hundred Years at 235. See Art IV of the Ordinance, 32 J Cont Cong at 341, 1 Stat at 52.

[398] 60 US 393 (1857); The First Hundred Years at 263–73. See Art VI of the Ordinance, 32 J Cont Cong at 343, 1 Stat at 53.

[399] 32 J Cont Cong at 340, Art III, 1 Stat at 52. See generally David P. Currie, Positive and Negative Constitutional Rights, 53 U Chi L Rev 864 (1986).

[400] 32 J Cont Cong at 339–40, 1 Stat at 52.

[401] See A. V. Dicey, Introduction to the Study of the Law of the Constitution 64–68 (Macmillan, 9th ed 1939). See also Stone v Mississippi, 101 US 814 (1880) (permitting a state to repudiate a contract authorizing the operation of a lottery for a fixed term, despite the contract clause of Article I, § 10, because the state had no right to surrender its police power); The First Hundred Years at 380–81.

the articles and—along with the further requirement that the constitutions of the new states conform to their principles[402]—added force to the later contention that the articles remained in force long after various portions of the Territory had been admitted as states.[403] The compact language also lent some credibility to the argument that, despite its form, the Ordinance was actually an interstate agreement approved by Congress as authorized by the Articles of Confederation, and that therefore its exhaustive provisions were not after all a precedent for interpreting the grant of authority in Article IV, § 3 of the new Constitution to "make all needful rules and regulations respecting the territory or other property belonging to the United States."[404]

In August 1789 the First Congress passed an act whose stated purpose was to "adapt" the Northwest Ordinance "to the present Constitution," in order that it might "continue to have full effect."[405] The Ordinance was not reenacted; Congress plainly assumed it was still in force. A few of its provisions for the territorial government, however, were incompatible with the new division between legislative and executive authority. Originally the territorial officers were responsible to Congress; henceforth they were to be responsible to the President.[406]

In conforming the Ordinance to the Constitution, Congress seems to have been exercising its power under Article IV to make "needful rules and regulations respecting the territory" of the United States. If the Ordinance itself survived, one might think it did so on the theory that in amending it Congress had implicitly confirmed it under the same grant of authority. This interpretation would mean that the power to make "rules and regulations" was, as it appeared to be, a general power to govern the territory.[407] Thus when opponents of the ban on slavery in the Missouri Compromise needed a way to distinguish the Northwest Ordinance they hit upon an alternative explanation: The new Congress had never attempted to enact the Ordinance under the limited authority of Article IV; as an "engagement[] entered into before the adoption of this Constitution," it was "as valid against the United States under [the new] Constitution, as under the Confederation" by virtue of Article VI.[408]

A few months after amending the Northwest Ordinance, Congress accepted a deed from North Carolina ceding to the United States that state's claim to territory west of the

---

[402]32 J Cont Cong at 342, Art V, 1 Stat at 53.

[403]See The First Hundred Years at 268–69.

[404]See Articles of Confederation, Art VI, § 2; Scott v Sandford, 60 US 393, 438–40 (1857); The First Hundred Years at 263–73.

[405]1 Stat 50–51 (Aug 7, 1789).

[406]Compare the provisions of the Ordinance, 32 J Cont Cong at 335–36, 1 Stat at 51, with § 1 of the statute, 1 Stat at 52–53 (providing that the Governor should be appointed by the President with Senate consent, report to the President, and be subject to presidential removal).

[407]In arguing for implicit authority to charter a bank, Ames would soon assert that Article IV conferred a general governmental power not limited, as the words might suggest, to "the management and disposal of property." 2 Annals at 1957. Dismissing the relevance of congressional creation of corporations in the Western Territory, Stone agreed: "[T]o answer this case, nothing more was necessary than to read the clause in the Constitution which gives to Congress expressly the power to make all the rules and regulations" for the Territories. Id at 1985.

[408]See Scott, 60 US at 441–46.

mountains.[409] Whether Congress found authority to acquire territory included in Article IV's grant of power to make regulations respecting it, implicit in the power to admit new states, or inherent in the existence of the Government was left unsaid, but nobody seemed to question Congress's authority. In accordance with the terms of the cession, Congress promptly extended the Ordinance to the new Territory with one conspicuous exception: "[t]hat no regulations made or to be made by Congress, shall tend to emancipate slaves."[410] This time it seemed there could be no doubt about it; the source of governmental authority over the new Territory was not an interstate compact but the Constitution of the United States.[411] It seems fruitless to debate whether the attempt to prevent Congress from interfering with slavery there expressed the fear that Congress otherwise would have such power or reaffirmed the conviction that it would not; the language was well chosen to give slaveowners maximum protection in either event, though once again there was reason to doubt whether Congress could bind itself not to exercise its constitutional powers.[412]

F. The Seat of Government

The first session of the First Congress met in New York, as the Confederation Congress had prescribed.[413] But after Pennsylvania authorities had refused to call out the militia to suppress a mob of unruly soldiers in 1783, the Confederation Congress had felt compelled to abandon Philadelphia. "If any state had the power of legislation over the place where Congress should fix the general government," said Madison in the Virginia ratifying convention, "this would impair the dignity, and hazard the safety, of Congress."[414]

[409]1 Stat 106 (Apr 2, 1790). This territory had been ceded to the United States once before, organized into the incipient state of Franklin, and reclaimed by North Carolina after conditions there had become chaotic. See Jensen, The New Nation at 332–34 (cited in note 382). It would later be admitted to the Union under the name of Tennessee.

[410]1 Stat 123, § 1 (May 26, 1790) (incorporating the conditions of the North Carolina cession statute, as found at 1 Stat 108). This provision, we are told, "occasioned some debate" in the House; "an amendment was proposed and debated, but not adopted." 2 Annals at 1528.

[411]Legal ingenuity being without bounds, opponents of a broad interpretation of Article IV resorted in later analogous cases to notions of a limited extraconstitutional authority difficult to reconcile with the theory of a written constitution. See American Insurance Co. v Canter, 26 US 511 (1828) (leaving the question open); Scott, 60 US at 446–49 (trying to tie power to govern to the authority to admit new states); The First Hundred Years at 119–22, 263–73.

[412]The United States was owner as well as sovereign of most western land, and from the beginning its policy had been to dispose of its title in order to promote settlement and raise money to pay off the revolutionary debt. See Morris, The Forging of the Union at 228–29 (cited in note 337). Debate, the burden of private bills, and a favorable report from Hamilton persuaded the House that Congress ought to set up a land office to dispose of the property under the authority of Article IV; enactment of the law that did so was postponed until the Fourth Congress. See 1 Annals at 646–57, 1104–10; 2 Annals at 1876–80; 1 Stat 464 (May 18, 1796). For land grants made by statute during the First Congress see 1 Stat 182 (Aug 10, 1790) (Virginia veterans); 1 Stat 221 (Mar 3, 1791) (settlers at Vincennes); 6 Doc Hist at 1563–1607.

[413]34 J Cont Cong 521–23 (Sept 13, 1788); 1 Annals at 15, 99.

[414]3 Elliot at 89. See also The Federalist No 43 (Madison); 3 Story, §§ 1213–14. The episode is described in Kenneth R. Bowling, New Light on the Philadelphia Mutiny of 1783: Federal-State Confrontation at the Close of the War for Independence, 101 Pa Magazine of History & Biography 419 (1977). See also George Adams Boyd, Elias Boudinot: Patriot and Statesman 123–26 (Princeton, 1952).

Article I, § 8 of the new Constitution accordingly authorized Congress "[t]o exercise exclusive legislation . . . over such District (not exceeding ten miles square) as may, by cession of particular States, and the acceptance of Congress, become the seat of the Government of the United States." It was common ground that Congress ought to acquire territory for a national capital under this provision. There was monumental disagreement over where it should be.[415]

At the end of its first session the House voted, over southern objections, to locate the capital "at some convenient place on the banks of the river Susquehannah in the state of Pennsylvania."[416] The Senate amended the bill to provide for a capital in the vicinity of Germantown, near Philadelphia.[417] The House agreed to this amendment, but only after attaching an unrelated amendment of its own. The Senate voted to postpone further consideration of the bill, and Congress adjourned without taking final action.[418]

Starting all over in accordance with the decision that unfinished business did not survive the end of a legislative session,[419] a Senate committee in June 1790 proposed that the capital "be placed on the Eastern or North Eastern Bank of the Patomack"[420]—and there, thanks to the need for Virginia and Maryland support for the assumption of state debts, it was to remain.[421] The statute empowered a board of commissioners, appointed by the President and subject to his direction, to define a district "not exceeding ten miles square" between two named points on the Potomac, to acquire "land on the eastern side of the said river" within the district, and to "provide suitable buildings" there to house the various organs of government. All offices "attached to the seat of government" were to be moved to the Potomac in December 1800. In the interim the Government would sit in Philadelphia, and state laws would continue to apply in the new district until Congress otherwise provided. The President was authorized "to accept grants of money" to finance the acquisition of land and the construction of buildings, and "a sufficient sum" was appropriated to cover "the necessary expense of such removal."[422]

---

[415]"[E]normous prestige, financial advantage, and influence on the government hinged on its location." Ralph Ketcham, James Madison, A Biography 271 (MacMillan, 1971). The full story is told in Kenneth R. Bowling, The Creation of Washington, D.C.: The Idea and Location of the American Capital (George Mason, 1991).

[416]See 1 Annals at 946 (Sept 22, 1789); 6 Doc Hist at 1867.

[417]See id at 1869; 1 Annals at 88, 89–90, 91, 955–62. The text of the Senate amendment differs slightly in the sources cited.

[418]See 1 Annals at 962; Bowling, The Creation of Washington, D.C. at 159–60 (cited in note 414).

[419]See chapter 1. The rule itself had been adopted, over Pennsylvania objections, in the context of the capital controversy. "Thus Congress established, and retained for half a century, a joint rule in order to kill a specific bill." Bowling, The Creation of Washington, D.C. at 168 (cited in note 414).

[420]6 Doc Hist at 1779.

[421]See the discussion of the assumption controversy in text at notes 168–81.

[422]1 Stat 130 (July 16, 1790). The next year Congress altered the outer limits of the District in order to permit the inclusion of the East Branch (Anacostia River) and Alexandria, while reaffirming that public buildings should be constructed only "on the Maryland side." 1 Stat 214–15 (Mar 3, 1791). Presidential proclamations actually defining the District appear in 1 Richardson at 100, 102 (Jan 24 and Mar 30, 1791). For the suggestion that motives of pecuniary profit induced Washington to place the District closer to his own property than the original statute allowed see McDonald, Hamilton at 202–04. In fact the first proclamation carefully refrained from incorporating the contested area within the district until corrective legislation was safely passed. See also Kenneth R. Bowling, The Bank Bill, the Capital City and President Washington, 1 Capitol

These provisions evince an appropriately broad congressional understanding of the authority to exercise "exclusive legislation" over the seat of government. Congress interpreted this clause to empower it to acquire not only jurisdiction but also title, to construct buildings, and to accept gifts—in short, to do whatever was necessary and proper to the establishment of a permanent seat of government.[423] In searching for a way to block passage of an earlier bill that would have placed the capital in Pennsylvania, Madison had argued that Congress had no power to fix a temporary capital: Article I, §§ 5 and 7 gave the two Houses of Congress, acting without the President, sole authority to determine where next to meet.[424] Sherman's answer seems to have convinced the bulk of his colleagues: Congress's power to meet where it pleased was unaffected by the bill, since Congress was not required to meet at the seat of government.[425] The express authority conferred by Article I, § 8 extended only to territory ceded by the states, which Philadelphia was not; but providing for the interim location of government offices was plainly necessary and proper to the exercise of their various functions.

From the constitutional viewpoint the most noteworthy feature of the legislation was the breadth of its delegation of authority. Acting through his commissioners, the President was to determine precisely where to locate the District, how large it would be, what land to acquire, and what buildings to erect. When the original bill had provided for a capital somewhere on the Susquehanna, Representative Tucker had objected that Congress itself should fix the location.[426] As adopted the statute was marginally more precise: The District should be located "between the mouths of the Eastern Branch and Connoghochegue" (roughly the distance between Washington and Hagerstown, Maryland).[427] Government needs presumably limited the remaining grants of authority. Under the circumstances it might plausibly be said that in doing what the statute authorized the President was executing the law rather than exercising the power of "exclusive legislation" granted to Congress.

Studies 59, 66 (1972) (citing the suspicions of two Virginia Representatives that Congress held up passage of this bill in order to put pressure on the President not to veto the national bank).

[423] See the debate in 1 Annals at 909–11 over whether the Constitution contemplated that the states would cede title as well as jurisdiction. The statute reflects the consensus that after cession the Government would have to acquire title to any land it intended to occupy.

[424] "[N]either House . . . shall, without the consent of the other, adjourn for more than three days, nor to any other place than that in which the two Houses shall be sitting. . . . [E]very order, resolution, or vote to which the concurrence of the Senate and House of Representatives may be necessary (except on a question of adjournment) shall be presented to the President . . . ." See 1 Annals at 940–42; Bowling, The Creation of Washington, D.C. at 75–76, 152 (cited in note 414) (noting the Convention's rejection of Madison's proposal to *require* a statute to alter the place where Congress met).

[425] 1 Annals at 942. See also id at 942–43 (Rep. Laurance) (pointing out that Madison's argument seemed equally applicable to the fixing of a permanent capital, which the Constitution plainly envisioned). Madison's argument came back to haunt him when others urged Washington to veto the bill on constitutional grounds after the temporary capital had been changed from New York to Philadelphia. At that point both Madison and Jefferson supported the provision's constitutionality, and the President signed the bill. See 17 Jefferson Papers at 163–205. Jefferson's opinion relied heavily on the fact that Congress had twice rejected the constitutional objection: "The sense of Congress itself is always respectable authority." Id at 198.

[426] 1 Annals at 913.

[427] 1 Stat at 130, § 1.

More problematic perhaps were the statutory provisions appropriating whatever sum might be "sufficient" for necessary moving expenses and preserving the applicability of state law pending further congressional action. Other appropriations of the First Congress gave the executive considerable discretion as to how to spend appropriated funds,[428] but it was arguable that Article I, § 9 required Congress at least to prescribe how much money to spend. Finally, the Constitution explicitly deprived the states of authority to legislate for the District; it was not at all clear that Congress had power to give it back.[429] In short, in establishing the seat of government under Article I, § 8 Congress took a very flexible and pragmatic view of its ability to rely on other governmental organs to flesh out its general goals.[430]

VII.   THE BILL OF RIGHTS

In ratifying the Constitution, several states exhorted Congress to have it amended.[431] Many of the suggested amendments were structural changes that would have reversed the Federalist victory at Philadelphia, but others were elements of a Bill of Rights to protect against possible abuses of federal authority.[432]

Hamilton had argued that a Bill of Rights was both unnecessary and dangerous.[433] Some members of the House were loath to interrupt the important business of setting up the Government to consider constitutional amendments,[434] but Madison insisted: Prompt action would show doubters that Congress did care for liberty and might persuade North Carolina and Rhode Island to join the new Union.[435]

[428]See text at notes 100–06.

[429]Compare the discussion of pilots in note 118 and of offenses against Indians in the text at notes 251–55. The provision permitting state law to operate was inserted at Madison's request in order to "prevent the district . . . from being deprived for a time of the benefit of the laws," since "the State relinquished the right of legislation from the moment that Congress accepted of the district." 1 Annals at 961. It was this amendment that had prevented adoption of the bill at the end of the second session. See Bowling, The Creation of Washington, D.C. at 159 (cited in note 414).

[430]As was argued in response to the contention that Congress could not constitutionally delegate authority to designate individual post roads under Article I, § 8, "the principles of conducting the business are established by the House; the mode of carrying those principles into execution is left with the Executive, and this of necessity is done in almost every case whatever." 2 Annals at 1735; see the discussion of the postal controversy in chapter 3.

[431]See 2 Elliot at 177–78 (Massachusetts), 545–46 (Pennsylvania); 4 Elliot at 238–43 (North Carolina); 4 Doc Hist at 12–26; Veit, Creating the Bill of Rights at 14–28 (cited in note 341).

[432]See id at ix-xi. Paranoid antifederalists already perceived in the new Constitution a danger of consolidation of authority. See Letter of Samuel Adams to Elbridge Gerry, Aug 22, 1789, id at 284–85; Letter of Richard Henry Lee and William Grayson to the Speaker of the Virginia House of Delegates, Aug 28, 1789, id at 299. History, of course, has proved them right.

[433]The Federalist No 84 (Hamilton).

[434]See, e.g., 1 Annals at 441 (Rep. Smith). Vining went so far as to suggest that Article V required a two-thirds vote of both Houses even "to take the subject of amendments into consideration." Id at 447. The text did not seem to support him.

[435]Id at 449. Washington had lent significant support by calling attention to the subject of amendments in his inaugural address. See id at 27–29. See also id at 446 (Rep. Page) (warning that if Congress did not act the people would call another constitutional convention). Bland, on behalf of Virginia, had already asked Congress to call such a convention, but dropped his request when Madison (with Tucker contradicente) noted that Article V empowered Congress to call a convention only on application of two thirds of the states. Id at

Carefully culling from the voluminous state suggestions those which would protect basic rights without endangering the "structure" and "stamina" of the Government, Madison proposed a list of amendments that bore a strong resemblance to those ultimately adopted.[436] His further proposals to postpone congressional salary increases and to guard against undue restriction of the number of Representatives were accepted by Congress but never ratified—at least not within the next 200 years.[437] His requests to include a declaration that all governmental authority was derived from the people, a guarantee that no branch would exercise powers granted to another, and a jurisdictional amount for appeals to the Supreme Court all died in Congress, as did others discussed in more detail below.[438] More radical amendments proposed by other members of the House got nowhere at all; in the 1788 elections, which were something of a referendum on the

---

258–61. Formal applications of the Virginia and New York legislatures seeking a second convention are reprinted in Veit, Creating the Bill of Rights at 235, 237 (cited in note 341).

[436]See 1 Annals at 451–53; Veit, Creating the Bill of Rights at xiv (cited in note 341); Letter of James Madison to Edmund Randolph, June 15, 1789, id at 250. Antifederalists recognized that this strategy took much of the wind out of their sails and diminished the chances of structural alterations. See, e.g., Letter of William Grayson to Patrick Henry, June 12, 1789, id at 248–49; Kenneth R. Bowling, "A Tub to the Whale": The Founding Fathers and Adoption of the Federal Bill of Rights, 8 J Early Republic 223, 224 (1988).

[437]See 1 Stat 97. The reason for requiring that an election intervene before a salary raise took effect was, as Vining said, to prevent the members from lining their own pockets. See 1 Annals at 756–57. Cf US Const, Art I, § 6, which makes members of Congress ineligible for appointment to offices created or made more lucrative during their term. The argument for requiring that the number of Representatives initially *equal* one for every 30,000 inhabitants (instead of simply *not exceeding* that number, as provided in Art I, § 2) was that a larger House was more democratic; the counterargument was that it was unwieldy, unqualified, and costly. See 1 Annals at 747–56. For detailed discussion of the background and weaknesses of this latter proposal see Akhil Amar, The Bill of Rights as a Constitution, 100 Yale LJ 1131, 1137–45 (1991).

After languishing unratified for nearly two centuries, the proposed amendment respecting congressional salaries was rediscovered and reintroduced in state legislatures across the country. Michigan became the 38th state to approve the proposal on May 7, 1992, the Archivist certified it as the twenty-seventh amendment, and Congress cravenly passed a resolution declaring it the law of the land. See HR Con Res 320, 102d Cong, 2d Sess, 138 Cong Rec H 3505–06 (May 20, 1992); NY Times, May 8, 1992, p A1; May 21, 1992, p A26.

In upholding the power of Congress to limit the time for ratification of a proposed amendment in 1921, the Supreme Court soundly concluded that the three-fourths requirement of Article V implied that ratification by the various states "must be sufficiently contemporaneous . . . to reflect the will of the people in all sections at relatively the same period." Dillon v Gloss, 256 US 368, 375 (1921); see William Van Alstyne, What Do You Think of the Twenty-Seventh Amendment?, 10 Const Comm 9 (1993). In 1939, alas, the Court added that whether a proposed amendment (like any other offer) expired within a reasonable time in the absence of an explicit limitation was a nonjusticiable "political" question. Coleman v Miller, 307 US 433, 452 (1939). The upshot may be that the amendment is not law but that no court is in a position to say so, or that Congress's unfounded declaration will be treated as final.

[438]The principal objection voiced to amending the Preamble to affirm popular sovereignty was that the same idea was already expressed in the introductory phrase "We, the people." 1 Annals at 734, 745–47. Sherman objected to the proposal to reaffirm the constitution's own version of separation of powers on the reasonable ground that it was already implicit, Livermore on the bizarre ground that it would be "subversive of the constitution." Id at 789. Madison defended the jurisdictional amount to prevent inconvenience to litigants; Benson wisely objected that small cases might involve important questions. Id at 784. The first of these proposals failed to obtain the requisite two-thirds majority in the House; the other two were excised by the Senate. See id at 795; 4 Doc Hist at 38–39.

Constitution, Antifederalists had won only 10 of 59 seats in the House, and only Virginia had sent Antifederalists to the Senate.[439]

Unlike the English Bill of Rights, said Madison, the amendments he proposed would limit the power of the legislature, which was the strongest and most dangerous branch of our federal Government. While "paper barriers" could not provide foolproof protection against the abuse of power, they would tend both "to impress some degree of respect" and to "rouse the attention of the whole community," and they would be enforceable by the courts.[440]

To the argument that a Bill of Rights was unnecessary because the central Government was one of enumerated powers, Madison responded prophetically that much might be found implicit that was not obvious from the face of the enumeration.[441] To the argument that a Bill of Rights was dangerous because it might "disparage" other rights by implying "that those rights which were not singled out, were intended to be assigned into the hands of the General Government," he responded with what became the ninth amendment.[442] Thus in the words of its author this amendment was designed not as a limitation on powers previously granted to the federal Government but as a principle of interpretation: Despite Hamilton's fears, the prohibition of laws abridging freedom of the press was not to be taken to imply that Congress had any power over the press at all.[443]

Given the importance of the Bill of Rights today, there was surprisingly little recorded debate on its provisions; but it should be recalled that the First Congress had plenty of other important things to do. Of greatest interest for present purposes were the

---

[439]Veit, Creating the Bill of Rights at xi–xii (cited in note 341). See, e.g., the long list of proposals by Representative Tucker, 1 Annals at 790–92, ranging from limitation of the terms of federal officeholders and abolition of most lower federal courts to additional restrictions on direct taxes and repeal of Congress's power to regulate its own elections. For a powerful response to the recently resuscitated suggestion of term limits see the article published by Roger Sherman under the pseudonym "A Citizen of New Haven" in the New York Packet, Mar 24, 1789, in Veit, supra, at 220–21, arguing among other things that term limits would deprive the nation of its best qualified servants and "abridge the liberty of the people."

[440]1 Annals at 453–57. See also Letter of Thomas Jefferson to James Madison, Mar 15, 1789, in Veit, Creating the Bill of Rights at 218 (cited in note 341), arguing that one of the principal arguments for a Bill of Rights was "the legal check which it puts into the hands of the judiciary." In the same breath with which he endorsed judicial review, Madison foreshadowed the additional check on congressional usurpation later asserted in the Virginia and Kentucky Resolutions: "[T]he state legislatures will jealously and closely watch the operation of this government, and be able to resist with more effect every assumption of power . . . ." See also Brant, James Madison at 267 (cited in note 122).

[441]1 Annals at 455–56 (arguing by way of example that general warrants might be found necessary and proper to the collection of revenue).

[442]See id at 456; 4 Doc Hist at 11.

[443]This history also helps to clarify the relation between the ninth amendment and the tenth. Madison himself explained the former "as guarding against a latitude of interpretation" and the latter "as excluding every source of power not within the Constitution itself." 2 Annals at 1951. For painstaking corroboration of this understanding see Thomas McAffee, The Original Meaning of the Ninth Amendment, 90 Colum L Rev 1215 (1990). See also Miller at 23.

Arguing that the tenth amendment was salutary though redundant, 1 Annals at 458–59, Madison sensibly opposed Tucker's motion to restore the phrasing of the Articles of Confederation, which had reserved to the states all powers not "expressly" granted to the central authority: "[T]here must necessarily be admitted powers by implication, unless the constitution descended to recount every minutia." Id at 790.

House proceedings bearing on the religion and speech provisions eventually embodied in the first amendment.

As initially presented to the Committee of the Whole, the proposal would have provided that "no religion shall be established by law, nor shall the equal rights of conscience be infringed."[444] What this meant, as Madison understood it, was "that Congress should not establish a religion, and enforce the legal observation of it by law, nor compel men to worship God in any manner contrary to their conscience."[445] The whole purpose of the proposal, he later added, was to quiet fears that "one sect might obtain a pre-eminence, or two combine together, and establish a religion to which they would compel others to conform."[446]

There was nothing either in the text of the provision as it then stood—and the language ultimately adopted was similar—or in Madison's explanation of its meaning to suggest either that it forbade Congress to provide impartial support to religion in general or that it entitled those with religious scruples to exemptions from generally applicable laws. The conclusion that the amendment did not require religious exemptions seemed to be confirmed when Congress rejected a proposal that would have provided explicitly that "no person religiously scrupulous sh[ould] be compelled to bear arms."[447] Adoption of the tenth amendment demonstrated that Congress was not reluctant to say the same thing twice in the interest of avoiding misunderstanding.[448] Yet the principal argument against the exemption for conscientious objectors was that the matter should be "left to the discretion of the Government,"[449] and that argument presupposed that the religion clauses themselves did not take the issue out of the legislature's hands.

Like the amendment finally adopted, the version debated in the Committee of the Whole protected not only freedom of speech and of the press but the right of assembly and petition as well.[450] Sedgwick objected to the inclusion of assembly. "If people freely converse together, they must assemble for that purpose"; one might as well declare "that a man should have a right to wear his hat if he pleased, . . . get up when he pleased, and go to bed when he thought proper"; it was unnecessary to make provision for such "trifles . . . in a Government in which none of them were intended to be infringed."[451]

Sedgwick's motion to omit the reference to assembly failed, but his explanation raised several interesting points about the proper scope of a Bill of Rights. Taken out of context, his characterization of assembly as a "trifle" seems to suggest he thought it unimportant. A little reflection may indicate that neither the right to assemble for the discussion of public issues nor the other rights that Sedgwick so disparagingly invoked

---

[444]1 Annals at 757. Madison's original proposition was similar except that it forbade establishment of any "national" religion, guaranteed "full" as well as equal rights of conscience, and added that "[t]he civil rights of none shall be abridged on account of religious belief or worship." See 4 Doc Hist at 10.

[445]1 Annals at 758.

[446]Id.

[447]Id at 778. Approved by the House in slightly amended form, this proposal was removed in the Senate. See 4 Doc Hist at 36, 37 n 13.

[448]See note 443.

[449]See 1 Annals at 779–80 (Rep Benson).

[450]Id at 759.

[451]Id at 759–60.

could properly be regarded as trivial in that sense.[452] He seems to have been making two distinct arguments: that the right of assembly was not likely to be infringed and that it was implicit in the right to speak. Page was right to warn that experience afforded reason for doubt as to the former conclusion, and Congress was no doubt wise not to leave the latter to the vagaries of litigation. Yet a swarm of modern Supreme Court decisions have confirmed Sedgwick's basic insight that freedom of expression, like the grants of specific powers to Congress, carries with it whatever is necessary to make the provision itself a reality.[453]

The final point to be made about Congress's proposal of the Bill of Rights is a broader one. Except for the first and seventh amendments, all provisions of the Bill as adopted are phrased in general terms that on their face seem equally applicable to both federal and state authorities. This was equally true of the religion, speech, and jury provisions as they were presented to the House.[454] Yet it was abundantly clear from the outset that none of these provisions was meant to limit the actions of state governments. What the state ratifying conventions had sought was assurance that the new central government would not have too much power; they were not asking Congress to protect them against their own state officials.[455]

Most of the provisions that found their way into the Bill of Rights were initially proposed as amendments to Article I, § 9, which a comparison with the following section shows limited only federal authority. The rest were proposed as amendments to Article III, which defines the federal judicial power.[456] The decision to propose the amendments as separate articles, while hotly controverted, was based on stylistic rather than substantive considerations.[4457] Moreover, in dispatching the final draft for ratification Congress duly recited that it did so in response to the desires of the states "at the time of their adopting the Constitution . . . to prevent misconstruction or abuse of its powers."[458]

Finally, both Madison's proposal of a separate amendment to protect expression, religion, and jury trial against state action and its rejection by the Senate tend to corroborate the conclusion that none of the Bill of Rights provisions actually adopted limited state action.[459] For in supporting the proposal its sponsor made clear that he thought state

---

[452]On assembly see Edwards v South Carolina, 372 US 229, 235–38 (1963) (upholding the right to engage in peaceful demonstrations against government policy); on the right not to remove one's hat see West Virginia State Board of Education v Barnette, 319 US 624, 633 n 13 (1943) (invoking the famous cases of William Tell and William Penn).

[453]NAACP v Alabama, 357 US 449, 460–63 (1958) (rights of association and anonymity); Barnette, 319 US at 634–35 (right not to speak); NAACP v Button, 371 US 415, 429 (1963) (right to litigate); Buckley v Valeo, 424 US 1, 39 (1976) (right to spend money in support of candidates); Richmond Newspapers, Inc. v Virginia, 448 US 555, 575–80 (1980) (right of access to criminal trial). See also The Second Century at 382, 318, 421, 510, 525.

[454]See 4 Doc Hist at 10–12; 1 Annals at 757–92.

[455]See, e.g., 2 Elliot at 177–78 (Massachusetts), 545–46 (Pennsylvania); 4 Elliot at 238–43 (North Carolina).

[456]See 4 Doc Hist at 10–11. Compare US Const, Art I, § 9 ("No bill of attainder or ex post facto law shall be passed") with Art I, § 10 ("No State shall . . . pass any bill of attainder [or] ex post facto law").

[457]See 1 Annals at 734–44, 795.

[458]1 Stat 97 (Sept 1789).

[459]See 4 Doc Hist at 11, 39; Barron v Mayor of Baltimore, 32 US 243, 247 (1833); The First Hundred Years at 189–93.

action would not be limited without it,[460] while the sole argument against his suggestion was that it would be "much better . . . to leave the State Governments to themselves."[461]

Significantly, the amendments Congress proposed were sent to the states for ratification without presidential approval despite the Article I, § 7 requirement that the President be given the opportunity to veto not only bills but also (with the exception of adjournment) every other "order, resolution, or vote to which the concurrence of the Senate and House of Representatives may be necessary."[462] The Annals reveal no discussion of this important question. Yet the action of the First Congress was cited to the Supreme Court as a precedent when it upheld the eleventh amendment against the contention that it should have been submitted to the President for approval, and the precedent has been followed with rare exceptions ever since.[463]

[460]See 1 Annals at 784 (Rep. Madison): "If there was any reason to restrain the Government of the United States from infringing upon these essential rights, it was equally necessary that they should be secured against the State Governments."

[461]Id at 783 (Rep. Tucker).

[462]See Hollingsworth v Virginia, 3 US 378, 380 (1798). Neither Congress's resolution (1 Annals at 948) nor Washington's letter of transmittal to the states (30 Washington Writings at 426) said anything of presidential approval.

[463]See *Hollingsworth*, 3 US at 381; The First Hundred Years at 20–23; Edward Campbell Mason, The Veto Power 117–18 (Russell & Russell, 1967) (first published 1890).

Conclusion to Part One

It should be plain from this lengthy summary that both the first President and the First Congress took the Constitution very seriously. Washington set the tone in his inaugural address by referring Congress to "the great, constitutional charter . . . which, in defining your powers, designates the objects to which your attention is to be given."[1] Members of Congress repeatedly acknowledged their obligation to respect constitutional limitations on their powers. "Let us examine the Constitution," said Fisher Ames during the Bank debate, "and if that forbids our proceeding, we must reject the bill . . . ."[2] Boudinot agreed, adding that "[w]hatever power is exercised by Congress must be drawn from the Constitution."[3] Thus the First Congress and President Washington contributed significantly to our understanding of the Constitution as supreme law of the land.

Respect for the Constitution during the First Congress went far beyond ritualistic acknowledgement of its authority; a remarkable proportion of the debate centered on the task of determining its meaning. At the outset Madison admonished the House, as Washington had admonished him, that constitutional issues should be given "careful investigation and full discussion" because "[t]he decision that is at this time made, will become the permanent exposition of the constitution."[4] Constitutional questions cropped up in the House and Senate every time somebody sneezed, and one proposal after another was subjected to intensive debate to determine its compatibility with relevant constitutional provisions. Members of Congress plainly thought it necessary to demonstrate that

[1] 1 Annals at 28.

[2] 2 Annals at 1953.

[3] Id at 1970. "[H]owever expedient it might be," he continued, "if it was clearly unconstitutional, the bill should never receive the sanction of the representatives of the people." Id. See also 1 Annals at 479 (Rep. Madison): "I am clearly of opinion with the gentleman from South Carolina, (Mr. Smith,) that we ought in this, and every other case, to adhere to the constitution . . . ."

[4] 1 Annals at 514. For Washington's earlier letter to Madison see note 7 of the introduction to part 1.

the Constitution supported their actions, and thus everything they did as well as everything they said helps to inform our understanding of particular constitutional provisions.

The arguments employed during the First Congress helped also to develop an understanding of the techniques of constitutional interpretation. Most of the tools of construction we recognize today were employed in the debates: text,[5] structure,[6] history,[7]
purpose,[8] practice,[9] and the avoidance of absurd consequences.[10] Despite the deliberate decision of the Convention not to publish an official record of its proceedings,[11] various
members invoked their recollection of events at Philadelphia to illuminate the meaning of
particular provisions;[12] they were met with very modern arguments for ignoring them.[13]

[5]Textual arguments, of course, were legion. One prominent example was Madison's insistence that the
bank bill fell within neither the power to tax nor the power to borrow because "[i]t laid no tax" and "does not
borrow a shilling." 2 Annals at 1946–47. See also Tucker's powerful argument from the terms of the patent
clause, 1 Annals at 180, noted in the discussion of the Baffin's Bay expedition in chapter 2.

[6]See, e.g., Madison's argument that the enumeration of federal powers implied that those not listed were
reserved to the states. 2 Annals at 1945.

[7]British practice was invoked by Sherman in connection with removal of executive officers, by Lee,
Page, and White in connection with unfinished business, and by Page again (without invocation of the
Constitution) in connection with the right to counsel in an election contest. See 1 Annals at 510–11, 1084–85,
667. Both sides drew on the Articles of Confederation during the Bank debate. Laurance noted that the
Continental Congress had chartered a bank, Boudinot that in accepting the Northwest Territory it had exercised implied powers. Madison responded that Congress had known it had no authority to establish banks and
that the general welfare clause meant no more than its counterpart in the Articles. 2 Annals at 1941, 1946–47,
1975.

[8]See id at 2002 (Rep. Gerry, quoting Blackstone): "'[T]he most universal and effectual way of discover-
ing the true meaning of a law, when the words are dubious, is by considering the reason and spirit of it, or the
cause which moved the Legislature to enact it.'"

[9]"If Congress may not make laws conformably to the powers plainly implied, though not expressed in the
frame of Government, it is rather late in the day to adopt it as a principle of conduct." 2 Annals at 1954 (Rep.
Ames) (citing the taxation of ships, the erection of lighthouses, and the regulation of seamen under the commerce clause as precedents for establishing a national bank). See also id at 2003 (Rep. Gerry): "Does the
gentleman conceive that such [powers] only are delegated as are expressed? If so, he must admit that our
whole code of laws is unconstitutional."

[10]"Where a meaning is clear," said Madison, "the consequences, whatever they may be, are to be admitted—where doubtful, it is fairly triable by its consequences." Id at 1946. To read the general welfare
clause broadly enough to justify establishing a bank, he argued, "would give to Congress an unlimited power"
and "render nugatory the enumeration of particular powers." Id. See also Jefferson's prophetic argument
against the Bank, 19 Jefferson Papers at 276: "He who erects a bank creates a subject of commerce in it's
bills; so does he who makes a bushel of wheat, or digs a dollar out of the mines. Yet neither of these persons
regulates commerce thereby." Cf Wickard v Filburn, 317 US 11 (1942).

[11]2 Farrand at 648.

[12]See, e.g., 1 Annals at 578–79 (Rep. Baldwin in opposition to "mingling the powers of the President and
Senate"); 2 Annals at 1409–10, 1591 (Gerry and Madison on assumption of state debts), 1604 (Sherman on a
national university), 1945 (Madison on the power of incorporation). Similarly, during the debate over presidential removal Jackson invoked James Wilson's argument in the Pennsylvania ratifying convention that the
Senate was to serve as a check on the President, and Smith quoted at some length from the Federalist
Papers—which Jackson and Boudinot also cited on opposite sides of the Bank controversy. 1 Annals at 577–
78, 474; 2 Annals at 1941, 1977. "In controverted cases," said Madison, "the meaning of the parties to the instrument" was "a proper guide" to its interpretation, and "[c]ontemporary and concurrent expositions are a
reasonable evidence of the meaning of the parties." Id at 1946.

[13]See 2 Annals at 2004–05 (Rep. Gerry) (adding similar objections to reliance on the incomplete records
of state ratifying conventions). For a detailed documentation of the various interpretive tools employed during
the 1789 debates see Kent Greenfield, Original Penumbras: Constitutional Interpretation in the First Year of

The quality of the constitutional debates in the First Congress was impressively high. To begin with, the members exhibited an intimate knowledge of what the Constitution actually said. One has the impression they must have had copies of the document at their elbows at all times. Moreover, they had obviously devoted considerable effort to trying to figure out what its various provisions might mean. In the great controversies over removal of cabinet officers and incorporation of the Bank, for example, the House debates brought forth virtually all the constitutional arguments that anyone has come up with in two centuries of second-guessing[14]—as they did on many other issues of greater or lesser importance which as a practical matter they settled for all time.

The debates in the first House were conducted in the main by a strikingly small number of Representatives. Elbridge Gerry, respected by both Jefferson and John Adams, spoke more often during the first session than anyone but Madison.[15] Ames and Sedgwick of Massachusetts, Boudinot of New Jersey, Smith and Tucker of South Carolina were reliably impressive.[16] Benson, Clymer, Fitzsimons, Laurance, Page, Scott, Sherman, Vining, and a few others made significant or frequent contributions.[17] If the record is a fair sample of the whole work of the First Congress, roughly half the members of the House essentially said nothing at all.[18]

Congress, 26 Conn L Rev 79 (1993).

[14]Myers v United States, 272 US 52 (1926); McCulloch v Maryland, 17 US (4 Wheat) 316 (1819). See The Second Century at 193–95; The First Hundred Years at 160–68.

[15]See George Athan Billias, Elbridge Gerry: Founding Father and Republican Statesman 1, 225 (McGraw-Hill, 1976). His efforts, however, were not universally admired. "Gerry took up the Time of the Committee to the hour of adjournment," wrote Maclay after a visit to the House. "[H]e is a tedious & most disagreeable Speaker." 9 Doc Hist at 233.

[16]See, e.g., 1 Annals at 492–96, 559–64, 2 Annals at 1952–60 (Ames on removal and the Bank); 1 id at 1142–43, 2 Annals at 1960–65 (Sedgwick on export regulations and the Bank); 1 Annals at 390–91, 2 Annals at 1970–79 (Boudinot on removal and the Bank); 1 Annals at 828–32 (Smith on inferior federal courts); 1 Annals at 180 (Tucker on the patent clause). Boudinot's biographer, conceding that he lacked the originality of Hamilton or Madison, concluded that he "had ranked among the leaders" of the First Congress. George Adams Boyd, Elias Boudinot: Patriot and Statesman 137, 192 (Princeton, 1952). For an appreciative assessment of Ames's work in that body see Winfred E.A. Bernhard, Fisher Ames: Federalist & Statesman 118, 157 (North Carolina, 1965). See also Richard E. Welch, Jr., Theodore Sedgwick, Federalist: A Political Portrait 77, 106, 251 (Wesleyan, 1965) (finding Sedgwick no great policymaker or statesman but an able legislator and politician who was Hamilton's chief lieutenant in the House); George C. Rogers, Jr., Evolution of a Federalist: William Loughton Smith of Charleston (1758–1812) 208, 219 (South Carolina, 1962) (giving that honor to Smith).

[17]The speeches of James Jackson of Georgia, whom Forrest McDonald described as a "fierce, uncouth rustic" who was "surprisingly learned" (McDonald, Hamilton at 174), tended to be characterized more by their bluster than by their perspicacity. See, e.g., his diatribes on the militia bill (General Advertiser, Dec 24, 1790) (arguing that if conscientious objectors were exempted from service "he did not despair of seeing the whole nation turn quakers"), on the whiskey excise (2 Annals at 1890–91) (foreseeing the time "when a shirt shall not be washed without an excise" and suggesting that Congress might just as well "pass a law interdicting the use of ketchup, because some ignorant persons had been poisoned by eating mushrooms"), and on the Bank (id at 1967–70) (objecting to borrowing generally and asserting that Article IV gave Congress authority only with respect to "property already belonging to the United States").

[18]Madison had predicted this, noting on his way to the first session that the roster of members contained "a very scanty proportion who will share in the drudgery of business." Letter to Edmund Randolph, Mar 1, 1789, 11 Madison Papers at 453. Efforts to identify the most insignificant Member must await investigation of subsequent Congresses. As a preliminary matter one may safely hazard the conclusion that such members as Benjamin Contee, William Floyd, Abiel Foster, Samuel Griffin, Jonathan Grout, Daniel Hiester Jr., Daniel

But the man who dominated constitutional debate in the first House of Representatives was the man who had dominated the Constitutional Convention itself, James Madison. Time and again, after other members had haggled inconclusively over an important issue of constitutional interpretation, Madison would step in and make everything clear. It was he who made the strongest and most careful arguments for presidential removal and against the national bank.[19] It was he who best expounded the considerations relevant to determining the qualifications of Representatives[20] and Congress's authority to acquire information.[21] It was he who took the lead in proposing, explaining, and advocating the Bill of Rights.[22] In the beginning, when he spoke for the Administration, Madison tended to prevail. When he deserted the President on assumption of state debts and establishment of the Bank, he ended up with the minority. But he was at all times a potent force in constitutional debate; and thus the Father of the Constitution played a most significant and constructive role in interpreting and revising the document he had had an equally strong hand in composing.[23]

In construing the Constitution to enable it to assume state debts, establish a bank, regulate the labor relations of seamen, and prescribe the oath to be taken by state officers, the First Congress took a broad though certainly plausible view of its powers. On the other hand, it resisted proposals to do a number of things that might have seemed desir-

---

Huger, George Mathews, Peter Muhlenberg, George Partridge, James Schureman, Thomas Sinnickson, William Smith of Maryland, Jonathan Sturges, Jeremiah Van Rensselaer, and Henry Wynkoop maintained an impressively low profile during the First Congress, since few of them are recorded as ever having opened their mouths. "The way in Which this good Man, can best serve his country," said Maclay of Wynkoop, "is in superintending his farm." 9 Doc Hist at 233. Cf David P. Currie, The Most Insignificant Justice: A Preliminary Inquiry, 50 U Chi L Rev 466 (1983). The list of members is taken from 9 Doc Hist at xxxi–xxxii.

[19]See 1 Annals at 387, 479–82, 514–21 (removal); 2 id at 1944–52 (Bank).

[20]1 Annals at 420–23.

[21]Id at 1115, 1145–46.

[22]Id at 448–62. See Helen E. Veit, Kenneth R. Bowling, and Charlene Bangs Bickford, eds, Creating the Bill of Rights xvi (Johns Hopkins, 1991): "Madison has a greater claim to being known as the father of the Bill of Rights than of the Constitution. Without his commitment there would have been no federal Bill of Rights in 1791."

[23]See McDonald, Washington at 24; Ralph Ketcham, James Madison, A Biography 293 (MacMillan, 1971) (noting that during the first session, "[e]xcept for the judiciary act, fashioned in the Senate, Madison had taken the lead at every stage"); Swanstrom at 267 ("The leading Member of the first Congress was, by all odds, James Madison"). Because of the secrecy of Senate proceedings, we have less knowledge of the performance of individual Senators. One observer tells us that the "outstanding leaders" were Ellsworth, King, Philip Schuyler, and Caleb Strong, and that Monroe joined them among the ten or so members who did most of the committee work after his selection to fill an unexpired term in 1790. Harry Ammon, James Monroe: The Quest for National Identity 83 (McGraw-Hill, 1971). See also Swanstrom at 230–32: "In session after session a handful of Senators bore the major share of the burden of committee work while others were apparently content merely to attend sessions and vote"; id at 268–69 (noting that "[t]he initiative was taken by Oliver Ellsworth . . . , who during his 7 years in the Senate assumed more responsibility, did more work, and exerted more practical leadership in the day-by-day activities of the upper Chamber than any other Member of that body").

If Madison and Ellsworth were de facto leaders of the House and Senate, their talents and industry were at least equalled by those of Hamilton and Jefferson in the Cabinet, as evidenced by the former's impressive reports respecting financial matters and the latter's on weights and measures—all prepared by the Secretaries themselves while attending to the daily responsibilities of office. See Swanstrom at 269–70 (adding that "the impetus behind the major legislative program during Washington's administration did not come from either Madison or Ellsworth—or any other Member of Congress—but from Alexander Hamilton").

able when substantial constitutional doubts were raised—such as financing an expedition to Baffin's Bay or creating a national university.[24] There were policy as well as constitutional arguments against these initiatives, and the latter was postponed rather than rejected. Thus it cannot be said that Congress disapproved them on constitutional grounds; but the tone of the discussion suggests that Congress was sincerely concerned not to do anything it was unauthorized to do.

Repeatedly and without contradiction, members of the First Congress acknowledged that the constitutionality of their actions would be subject to judicial review. "It is said," remarked Laurance during the Bank debate, "we must not pass a problematical bill, which is liable to a supervision by Judges of the Supreme Court; but he conceived there was no force in this, as those Judges are invested by the Constitution with a power to pass their judgment on all laws that may be passed."[25] Boudinot added that "[h]e was so far from controverting this right in the Judiciary, that it was his boast and his confidence. . . . [I]t was the glory of the Constitution that there was a remedy even for the failures of the supreme Legislature itself."[26] "[I]ndependent tribunals of justice," said Madison in introducing the Bill of Rights, "will consider themselves in a peculiar manner the guardians of those rights; they will be an impenetrable bulwark against every assumption of power in the legislative or executive . . . ."[27]

These unchallenged acknowledgements of judicial review are significant not only because they cast light upon contemporaneous understanding of the Constitution but also because they demonstrate the willingness of Congress to accept meaningful limitations on its powers. At the same time, by taking constitutional limitations seriously, Congress earned respect for its own opinion as to their meaning. While not conclusive, congres-

---

[24]Recall also the House's decision not to specify the number of commissioners to be appointed to treat with the Southern Indians once it was suggested that the Constitution left the matter to the discretion of the President and Senate. 1 Annals at 716–30.

[25]2 Annals at 1966.

[26]Id at 1978–79. See also id at 1988 (Rep. Smith) (arguing that legislators had to determine in the first instance whether the Bank was constitutional but that "it was still within the province of the Judiciary to annul the law, if it should be deemed by them not to result by fair construction from the powers vested by the Constitution").

[27]1 Annals at 457. Benson echoed this understanding in arguing against a constitutional exemption of conscientious objectors from military service: "If this stands part of the constitution, it will be a question before the Judiciary on every regulation you make with respect to the organization of the militia, whether it comports with this declaration or not." Id at 780. Far from denying the right of judicial review, opponents of presidential authority to remove executive officers tended to argue that the judiciary played a special role in constitutional interpretation. Thus Representative Smith branded a legislative declaration that the Secretary of Foreign Affairs was "removable from office by the President" (id at 473) "an infringement of the powers of the Judiciary." Id at 488–89. See also id at 491–92 (Rep. Gerry) (arguing that if the President and Senate "do not understand the constitution" the question should be left to "the proper tribunal; the judges are the constitutional umpires on such questions"). Proponents of such a declaration responded not by denying judicial authority but by reaffirming it. "If we declare justly on this point," said Ames, "it will serve for a rule of conduct to the Executive Magistrate; if we declare improperly, the judiciary will revise our decision . . . ." Id at 496. See also id at 520 (Rep. Madison) (arguing that both Congress and the courts were empowered to interpret the Constitution); id at 582 (Rep. Baldwin). Representative White, who thought the President and Senate should be left to determine the relation between their respective powers subject to judicial review, opined that "the Legislature may construe the constitution with respect to the powers annexed to their department, but subject to the decision of the judges." Id at 539. For Gerry's unchallenged assertion that federal courts would also strike down unconstitutional state laws see id at 278.

sional interpretation of the Constitution has traditionally and justly been accorded considerable deference by courts as well as by other organs of government.[28] Nearly all the constitutional interpretations of the First Congress that have been tested in the courts have been sustained.[29]

Legal realists and their successors will remind us that, human nature being what it is, legislators are at least as likely as judges to deduce their reasons from the conclusions they are alleged to support.[30] Members of the First Congress were not wholly disinterested interpreters of the Constitution. Each had a political philosophy of his own; each had constituents to represent.[31] Moreover, in most instances the Members were passing on the extent of their own powers. It is because nobody can be trusted to do that impartially that we have given judges power to review the constitutionality of acts of Congress.[32]

Yet legal realism has not prevented us from taking the reasoning of judges seriously or from evaluating it on its own merits. Nor is it true that legislators, any more than judges, *always* consult only their own preferences or self-interest; there are plenty of examples of public officials who take seriously their oath to support the Constitution. Washington thought a national bank would be good for the country, but he was prepared to veto it until Hamilton persuaded him that it was constitutional.[33] Aedanus Burke thought lower federal courts would make the people "insecure in their liberties and property" but conceded that he could see no "substitute . . . that was not contrary to the constitution."[34] Recognition that legislators' arguments are frequently influenced by interested motives does not require that we simply dismiss them as partisan rhetoric—any

[28]See, e.g., the emphasis placed on congressional understanding and practice in such cases as Martin v Hunter's Lessee, 14 US 304, 378–79 (1816) (The First Hundred Years at 91–96), McCulloch v Maryland, 17 US 316, 422–23 (1819) (The First Hundred Years at 160–68), and Field v Clark, 143 US 649, 672–73 (1892) (The Second Century at 16). See also Justice Frankfurter's famous reference to the "gloss" placed on the Constitution by legislative and executive actions in Youngstown Sheet & Tube Co. v Sawyer, 343 US 579, 610–11 (1952) (concurring opinion) (The Second Century at 365–69).

[29]Famous examples include *Martin*, 14 US 304 (review of state court judgments); *McCulloch*, 17 US 316 (Bank of the United States); and Gibbons v Ogden, 22 US 1 (1824) (ship licensing). See The First Hundred Years at 91–96, 160–68, 168–76. The best known apparent exception is the mandamus provision struck down in Marbury v Madison, 5 US 137, 171–79 (1803) (discussed in chapter 1); but it seems probable that the Court had to misinterpret the statute in order to hold it unconstitutional. See the First Hundred Years at 67–68. See also Mossman v Higginson, 4 US 12 (1800) (The First Hundred Years at 29–30) and Hodgson v Bowerbank, 9 US 303 (1809) (The First Hundred Years at 89–90), giving Congress the benefit of the doubt in construing a provision for federal jurisdiction in cases involving aliens not to go beyond the limitations of Article III.

[30]During the Bank debate Gerry argued that the rules of interpretation Madison had espoused were "the result of his interpretation, and not his interpretation of the rules." 2 Annals at 1998.

[31]The vote on such questions as slavery, the tax on spirits, and the location of the capital was essentially sectional, while "the attitude of the members of Congress toward the assumption of state debts was [generally] determined by the size of the debt of the state they represented." Miller at 46. Representatives like Ames, Benson, Boudinot, Laurance, Sedgwick, and Vining tended to favor a strong central Government with a strong executive; Giles, Jackson, Livermore, Page, Stone, Tucker, and others tended to take the opposite position. Gerry and Smith opposed presidential removal but supported the Bank; Madison's vote was contrary to theirs in both cases. See also 2 Haynes at 1069 (noting that many Senators often voted "in the closest accordance with their own private and class interests").

[32]See The Federalist No 78 (Hamilton), at 524; *Marbury*, 5 US at 178 (1803).

[33]See chapter 2.

[34]1 Annals at 844.

more than we do the arguments of equally human and often equally interested judges.[35]

In short, not only the debates but also the actions taken or rejected by the First Congress constitute a practical interpretation of the Constitution by able and diligent officers sworn to support it and charged with the responsibility to put it into practice. The legislative interpretation was not binding. It was not always unanimous. It was not always convincing. It was not always clear that Congress was even aware of the existence of a constitutional problem. Sometimes, like judges, members of Congress must have been advocates for a predetermined position. Even then their arguments were designed to persuade the impartial observer and thus help us to understand the range of interpretations that would have appeared plausible when the Constitution was new.

Moreover, the sophistication and persuasiveness of the arguments in the First Congress was such as to suggest that on the whole the members performed their obligations both capably and conscientiously. Indeed that is putting it mildly. The truth of the matter is that the achievements of the First Congress were on a plane with those of the Convention whose much admired work it was endeavoring to implement.

But the records of the First Congress do more than help to restore one's sometimes shaky faith in the capacity of republican government to act in the public interest. They also afford important evidence of what thoughtful and responsible public servants close to the adoption of the Constitution thought it meant. What they thought is surely of interest not only to historians but also to anyone trying two hundred years later to figure out what the Constitution means.

[35]"The supposition of universal venality in human nature," wrote Hamilton, "is little less an error in political reasoning than the supposition of universal rectitude." The Federalist No.76, at 513-14.

Part Two

The Federalists
1791–1801

Introduction to Part Two

By the time the Second Congress first assembled in October 1791, the honeymoon was over. Having experienced the intoxication of constructing the machinery of government, Congress and the President settled into the more humdrum task of making it work. /

The rift that had begun to divide the friends of the Constitution during the First Congress was soon to widen into a chasm. Basic philosophical differences separated Hamilton from Jefferson in the Cabinet, Ames from Madison in the House. The intimidating presence of the saintly Washington kept a lid on the cauldron for a time, but the pot seethed with discord that boiled over into public bickering on more than one occasion. Jefferson, then Hamilton left the Government, to be succeeded by pygmies. Madison, the notorious opponent of faction,[1] retired from Congress to organize the opposition party. Washington went back to Mount Vernon in 1797.

With the Father of his Country on the sidelines, his squabbling dependents cast off all restraint.[2] There ensued an era of virulent partisanship, in which the emerging parties seemed to vie with one another for the distinction of most thoroughly losing its head. Constitutional questions were resolved in Congress on strict party lines; the Constitution

---

[1] See The Federalist No 10.

[2] Once Washington was gone, in Jefferson's less than disinterested words,

> these *energumeni* of royalism, kept in check hitherto by the dread of his honesty, his firmness, his patriotism, and the authority of his name, now mounted on the car of State and free from control, like Phaeton on that of the sun, drove headlong and wild, looking neither to right nor left, nor regarding anything but the objects they were driving at; until, displaying these fully, the eyes of the nation were opened, and a general disbandment of them from the public councils took place.

Anas, 9 Jefferson Writings (Wash ed) at 97.

had become a tool, not a guide. Vain, volatile John Adams, who spent much of his Presidency at his home in Quincy,[3] was our closest approximation of a statesman.

The subject of the following chapters is the ten-year period between the adjournment of the First Congress and the inauguration of Jefferson in 1801. This period was dominated by questions of war and peace, first with England, later with France, as Americans chose sides in the conflict that grew out of the French Revolution. Foreign affinities also reflected other divisions in American society. Friends of England tended to be favorable to merchants, manufacturers, and a mighty central Government; friends of France tended to be more agrarian, more democratic, and more sympathetic to states' rights. They also tended to be found in the South.

Congress was safely in the hands of the friends of England during most of the period, and so, with reservations, was the Executive. In the Senate, those who came to be known as Federalists enjoyed a comfortable majority throughout the decade. The popularly apportioned and elected House, always more evenly divided, tilted the other way during the crucial years 1793–97.

Especially after Jefferson's departure in 1793, the Washington Administration consistently took the Federalist line. President Adams, to his sorrow, retained his predecessor's High Federalist Cabinet. Considering himself beholden to no party, he contrived to offend everyone by trying to steer a sensible middle course. To his everlasting credit, he succeeeded in restoring the peace.[4]

Washington seized the initiative with his bold Neutrality Proclamation in 1793, which provoked a major controversy over the locus of authority to set policy in the realm of foreign affairs. Two years later, when he kept us out of war by sending Chief Justice John Jay to London to conclude his famous treaty, Madison and his colleagues sparked another constitutional crisis by creatively insisting, despite the ostensibly plain terms of Article II, that the House had something to say about treaties too. Still later, when it was the French who were harassing our shipping and insulting our diplomats, the Federalists in Congress stirred up additional constitutional dust by abrogating our treaties with France, delegating to the President the power to raise an army he did not want, and creating a "volunteer" force that seemed beastly hard to square with Article I's provisions for state control of the militia.

Not content to overreact to threats from overseas, Federalist Congressmen turned with relish to the task of silencing their critics at home—by deporting them without hearing if they had the misfortune not to be citizens, by locking them up for sedition if they were. But it was not enough to put opponents in jail; they must be expelled from Congress as well, lest they vote against further repressive measures. Before the madness subsided, the Senate could no longer bear to wait for the normal processes of the courts to rid it of Republican journalists but arrogated to itself the power to prosecute, punish, and condemn.

---

[3]See Joseph J. Ellis, Passionate Sage: The Character and Legacy of John Adams 34 (Norton, 1993); Ralph Adams Brown, The Presidency of John Adams 135-37 (Kansas, 1975).

[4]"I desire no other inscription over my gravestone," Adams later wrote, "than: 'Here lies John Adams, who took upon himself the responsibility of the peace with France in the year 1800.'" Letter of John Adams to James Lloyd, Jan 1815, 10 Adams Works at 108, 113.

Finally, anticipating defeat at the polls, congressional Federalists concocted a constitutionally doubtful scheme to proclaim themselves judges of the validity of the electoral vote. When that failed, they exploited a defect in the original Article II in a disreputable last desperate effort to frustrate the popular will.

The Republicans stood up bravely for their rights, but in other respects they were not much better than their opponents. During the French crisis they resolutely refused to vote for anything that might protect the country from aggression.[5] Years earlier, Madison had lent his full energies to a deplorable endeavor to condemn Hamilton for serious misconduct without a trial. Jefferson, who had embarrassingly tried to defend the Reign of Terror,[6] openly risked disunion by calling for state nullification of federal laws.

Amid the storms of war and peace, Congress had also to tend to the ordinary business of government. Additional agencies had to be created: the new Post Office, the Mint, the Militia, the Navy. The first congressional reapportionment prompted the first presidential veto, and it was on constitutional grounds. New exactions on carriages, lands, houses, and slaves generated significant discussions of the meaning and application of the clauses of Article I regarding direct taxes. Proposals to provide relief to New England fishermen, Caribbean refugees, and the victims of a Georgia fire drew renewed attention to the disputed scope of the spending power. Repeated outbreaks of yellow fever produced a federal quarantine law and the first debates over the impact of the commerce clause on state authority.

Important issues respecting the judicial power were also raised by congressional action during this period. Seeking to keep administrative costs under control, Congress authorized the courts to render advisory opinions on pension claims and to pass upon ex parte naturalization petitions. Faced with an embarrassing lacuna in the power to impeach, it took the easy but sleazy way out by passing legislation to transfer the authority of an incompetent judge to another court. The impeachment of Senator William Blount for a conspiracy to detach Louisiana from Spain gave rise to a historic debate over the limits of the impeachment power itself. The shameless attempt of the outgoing Federalists to perpetuate their stranglehold on the federal judiciary by creating a legion of new judgeships set the stage for a major constitutional confrontation after the Republicans took power—but let us not get ahead of our story.

It was not, on the whole, an edifying time. But it teaches us a good deal about the Constitution.

---

[5]"[T]o keep aggressors at bay," says one prominent observer, even the usually sensible Albert Gallatin "advocated reducing the army and suspending work on the frigates." Miller at 208.

[6]Letter of Thomas Jefferson to William Short, Jan. 3, 1793, 25 Jefferson Papers at 14. See also Dumas Malone, Jefferson and the Ordeal of Liberty 186 (1962): "[O]ne wonders how he had managed to overlook the Reign of Terror."

3

The Second Congress, 1791–1793

The Second Congress spent much of its time completing the organization of the Government and began to experiment with supervising governmental operations. It implemented Article IV of the Constitution by passing a law to require the return of fugitives. And once more it debated the scope of its power to spend.

I. CONGRESS

Article I, § 2 provisionally allocated sixty-five House seats among the states, and the First and Second Congresses were elected on the basis of that apportionment. Once the census required by that section was completed, Representatives were to be reallotted among the states "according to their respective numbers," including three fifths of the slaves. The same provision imposed two additional requirements: "The number of Representatives shall not exceed one for every thirty thousand, but each state shall have at least one Representative." When the Second Congress convened, the 1790 census was on its desk, and the House devoted its attention almost immediately to the task.

John Laurance of New York initiated the debate by moving to set the total number of representatives at one for each 30,000 persons.[1] Opponents objected that this ratio would produce a House too large for efficient deliberation and too costly to maintain;[2]

[1] 3 Annals at 148. "The habit of thought in those days was not first to determine the total number of seats or *house size* and then to distribute them, but rather to fix upon some 'ratio of representation,' . . . and then allow the house size to fall where it may." Michel L. Balinski & H. Peyton Young, Fair Representation 11 (Yale, 1982). As in later proposals, it was understood that the population count had to be adjusted downward to include only three fifths of the slaves.

[2] 3 Annals at 154 (Rep. Clark); id at 173 (Rep. Barnwell). See also id at 155 (Rep. Laurance, responding to both objections). Cf The Federalist No 55 (Madison): "Had every Athenian citizen been a Socrates, every Athenian assembly would still have been a mob."

supporters insisted a smaller House would make it impossible for members to know the views of their own constituents and would reduce the influence of the people.[3]

Several speakers invoked the Constitution. Virginia's Alexander White insisted at one point that the Constitution "plainly contemplate[d]" that the ratio would be one to 30,000.[4] What it said, however, was that the number of representatives should not *exceed* one to 30,000, which was by no means the same thing. The difference in phrasing was no accident. The original draft had set a precise ratio; it was altered in response to Madison's argument that as population increased a fixed apportionment formula would produce an unwieldy House.[5]

Representative William Giles (also of Virginia) came close to suggesting that by proposing a constitutional amendment that would have fixed the ratio at exactly one to 30,000 Congress had bound itself not to deviate from that figure.[6] The amendment, however, had not been adopted.[7] Moreover, it would have permitted a less generous ratio once the number of seats reached one hundred, and on the basis of the 1/30,000 ratio that had already occurred.[8]

More to the point was the argument of North Carolina's Hugh Williamson that Congress should employ that ratio which "would leave the fewest fractions,"[9] i.e., would minimize deviations from the basic requirement that representation be proportional to population. Though this contention was not phrased in constitutional terms, it might well have been, for what Williamson was urging was maximum attainment of the constitutional goal.

After approving Laurance's suggestion of a 1/30,000 ratio by a relatively narrow margin,[10] the House passed a bill to that effect[11]—apparently never doubting that, al-

---

[3] 3 Annals at 181 (Rep. Page). Representative Sedgwick reckoned that a 1/30,000 ratio would produce 110 members, 1/33,000 104, 1/34,000 100, and 1/40,000 82. See id at 149.

[4] Id at 201.

[5] See 2 Farrand at 178, 221.

[6] "But, he observed, that Congress had precluded itself from a right to exercise this discretionary power [to alter the ratio], by sending out to the several State Legislatures an amendment on this very subject." 3 Annals at 178.

[7] According to Representative Gerry, eight states had ratified the proposal at the time of this debate. 3 Annals at 169. See also id at 200: "Mr. Macon said he did not conceive that the amendment referred to was to be a guide to the House till it was fully ratified; and, as it was uncertain whether it ever would be, we ought not to be swayed by it on this occasion."

[8] Thereafter "there shall be not less than one hundred Representatives, nor less than one Representative for every forty thousand persons, until the number of Representatives shall amount to two hundred; after which the proportion shall be so regulated by Congress, that there shall not be less than two hundred Representatives, nor more than one Representative for every fifty thousand persons." 1 Stat at 97 (1789). The more plausible argument that Congress ought to comply with the proposed amendment in order to avoid having to revise the law in the event of its adoption (e.g., 3 Annals at 169 (Rep. Gerry); id at 200 (Rep. Bourne)) was not of constitutional dimension. Moreover, a year after ten of the twelve proposals had been approved by the states, adoption of the other two seemed, as Representative Macon suggested (id at 200), a rather remote possibility. In any case, as Gerry ultimately conceded (id at 169), the amendment would have left so much discretion to Congress that most of the ratios under discussion would have satisfied its requirements.

[9] 3 Annals at 154. See also id at 244 (Rep. Sedgwick).

[10] Id at 191. The vote was thirty-five to twenty-three. A subsequent motion to substitute a ratio of 1/34,000 was defeated thirty-eight to twenty-one. Id at 208.

[11] Id at 210.

though Article I, § 2 did not specify who was to make the necessary apportionment, it should be done by statute (presumably as necessary and proper to the operations of Congress) rather than by simple House resolution.[12]

To determine the number of seats for each state, the House divided each state's adjusted population by 30,000 and (because Representatives are indivisible) rounded the quotient down to the nearest whole number. But dividing by 30,000 left eight of the fifteen states with fractions of over 15,000, which the bill ignored. Thus Connecticut, which had a population 7.895 times the divisor, was given only seven seats; Vermont, with a quotient of 2.851, was given two. As Williamson had suggested, the House bill left a number of states substantially underrepresented in relation to their numbers.[13] In the Senate, Vice-President Adams broke a twelve to twelve tie to amend the House bill by substituting a ratio of 1/33,000. The result was to reduce Virginia's share by two seats

[12]After the Senate had amended the ratio to 1/33,000, Representative Findley did protest that apportionment of House seats was basically the House's business (id at 245), but neither he nor anyone else was recorded in the Annals as arguing that the House had power to apportion by resolution or House rule. Neither the House's power to judge "the elections, returns and qualifications of its own members" nor its authority to "determine the rules of its proceedings" appears to cover the case, but one might have argued that the power to apportion, like the power to investigate, was inherent or implied. Cf the question of who was to implement the oath requirement of Article VI, discussed in chapter 1.

[13]The complete figures are shown in the following table:

State	Adj. Pop.	Pop./30,000	Seats
Connecticut	236,841	7.895	7
Delaware	55,540	1.851	1
Georgia	70,835	2.361	2
Kentucky	68,705	2.290	2
Maryland	278,514	9.284	9
Massachusetts	475,327	15.844	15
New Hampshire	141,822	4.727	4
New Jersey	179,570	5.986	5
New York	331,589	11.053	11
North Carolina	353,523	11.784	11
Pennsylvania	432,879	14.429	14
Rhode Island	68,446	2.282	2
South Carolina	206,236	6.875	6
Vermont	85,533	2.851	2
Virginia	630,560	21.019	21
Total	3,615,920	120.531	112

This table and those that follow are adapted from Balinski & Young, Fair Representation at 11–15 (cited in note 1). For the original census figures see US Census Office, Return of the Whole Number of Persons within the Several Districts of the United States 3 (reprinted by Arno, 1976). To understand the political dynamics of the debate it is important to note that small states tended to be the most underrepresented in this allocation.

and those of other large states by one—thus considerably enhancing the relative power of the smaller states.[14]

When the House began consideration of the Senate amendment, Fisher Ames supported it with a more focused version of Williamson's earlier argument. The original House bill, he said, was unconstitutional. For it gave Virginia as many seats as six smaller states with an aggregate of 70,000 more people, in contravention of the requirement that Representatives be allocated on the basis of numbers.[15] Similarly, added Vermont's Nathaniel Niles, both the House and Senate versions produced another "manifest inequality" by awarding Delaware, with its population of 58,000, only a single Representative.[16] The constitutional principle of apportionment according to population, he argued, would be more nearly realized by giving Delaware a second seat.[17]

To do so, replied William Vans Murray of Maryland, would be unconstitutional. Delaware could not be given two Representatives until it had 60,000 inhabitants, because the Constitution forbade giving any state more than one seat for each 30,000 persons.[18] Ames took a different view: The 1/30,000 ratio merely limited the total number of

[14]3 Annals at 46–47. The complete results were as follows:

State	Adj. Pop.	Pop./33,000	Seats
Connecticut	236,841	7.177	7
Delaware	55,540	1.683	1
Georgia	70,835	2.147	2
Kentucky	68,705	2.082	2
Maryland	278,514	8.440	8
Massachusetts	475,327	14.404	14
New Hampshire	141,822	4.298	4
New Jersey	179,570	5.442	5
New York	331,589	10.048	10
North Carolina	353,523	10.713	10
Pennsylvania	432,879	13.118	13
Rhode Island	68,446	2.074	2
South Carolina	206,236	6.250	6
Vermont	85,533	2.592	2
Virginia	630,560	19.108	19
Total	3,615,920	109.573	105

In response to Findley's suggestion that the Senate should defer to the House on questions of its own composition (see note 12), Hillhouse argued that the Senate was more impartial on such issues than the House itself, 3 Annals at 245. Gerry reminded him, significantly in light of the results of the Senate vote, that small states had a disproportionate voice in the upper House. Id. See also id at 244 (Rep. Williamson) (noting that the Senate's ratio would work to the disadvantage of the South).

[15]Id at 246.

[16]Since that figure contained a number of slaves, it should have been reduced to 55,540, but the point remains valid. See 1790 Census (cited in note 13); 23 Jefferson Papers at 370.

[17]3 Annals at 246.

[18]Id at 269. See also id at 264 (Rep. Madison).

Representatives in the House. It had nothing to do with how that number was to be apportioned; apportionment was governed by the independent provision that seats were to be allocated according to population.[19] To apply the ratio to each state rather than to the nation as a whole, added Samuel Livermore of New Hampshire, offended the equality principle.[20]

After an extended deadlock between the two Houses[21] the Senate came up with a new proposal. Without revealing the basis of its apportionment, the new Senate version retained the House ratio of 1/30,000, preserved all the seats originally allotted by the House bill, and awarded an additional eight seats to those states having the largest fractions.[22] One consequence was to raise the number of seats to 120, which was almost exactly 1/30,000 of the total adjusted population.[23] Another was significantly to increase the representation of several of the smaller states. The third was greatly to reduce the deviations from the standard of apportionment according to numbers.[24]

[19]Id at 409–11. See also id at 266 (Rep. Boudinot).

[20]Id at 335. Representative Sedgwick, stressing that direct taxes as well as representatives were to be apportioned according to the census, pointed out that it would hardly comport with that standard to tax Rhode Island twice as much as Delaware, when their populations were practically equal. Id at 248. At the same time, Ames added, parity between benefits and burdens was a fundamental principle of Article I; the Constitution would not permit use of different formulas for apportioning representation and taxes. Id at 255–56.

[21]The whole procedural story is lucidly told in Edmund J. James, The First Apportionment of Federal Representatives in the United States, 9 Annals Am Acad Pol & Soc Sci 1, 9–12 (1897).

[22]3 Annals at 105–06.

[23]The actual census figure was 3,615,920. See note 13. This correspondence led Hamilton to deduce that the Senate had actually reversed the House's approach, beginning by dividing the national adjusted population by 30,000 to determine the number of representatives and then allocating them in proportion to the population of the several states. See 11 Hamilton Papers at 228.

[24]The results were as follows:

State	Adj. Pop.	Pop./30,000	Seats
Connecticut	236,841	7.895	8
Delaware	55,540	1.851	2
Georgia	70,835	2.361	2
Kentucky	68,705	2.290	2
Maryland	278,514	9.284	9
Massachusetts	475,327	15.844	16
New Hampshire	141,822	4.727	5
New Jersey	179,570	5.986	6
New York	331,589	11.053	11
North Carolina	353,523	11.784	12
Pennsylvania	432,879	14.429	14
Rhode Island	68,446	2.282	2
South Carolina	206,236	6.875	7
Vermont	85,533	2.851	3
Virginia	630,560	21.019	21
Total	3,615,920	120.531	120

In this case giving seats to the eight states with the largest fractions amounted to rounding off all fractions to the nearest whole number—a method recommended by Daniel Webster in 1832, utilized on occasion by

The House ultimately acquiesced,[25] but the President did not. After requesting opinions from his four Cabinet officers (who divided evenly on the question),[26] Washington vetoed the bill as unconstitutional:

> First. The Constitution has prescribed that Representatives shall be apportioned among the several States according to their respective numbers; and there is no one proportion or divisor which, applied to the respective numbers of the States, will yield the number and allotment of Representatives proposed by the bill.
>
> Second. The Constitution has also provided that the number of Representatives shall not exceed one for every thirty thousand; which restriction is, by the context, and by fair and obvious construction, to be applied to the separate and respective numbers of the States; and the bill has allotted to eight of the States more than one for every thirty thousand.[27]

In other words, the bill as passed by Congress offended both the requirement that seats be apportioned according to population and the proviso that the number of representatives not exceed one to thirty thousand.

Neither objection seems to hold water. As Justice Story later pointed out in his treatise, nothing in the language of Article I, § 2 appears to require that Congress employ a single ratio to determine the number of seats in each state; what it requires is that seats be apportioned to population.[28] Since the number of representatives from each state must be a whole number,[29] perfect conformity with the constitutional goal cannot be attained;

Congress, and endorsed by a leading modern study as most likely to produce results approximating the constitutional standard. See Balinski & Young, Fair Representation at 30–32, 42, 47, 86 (cited in note 1). Even Jefferson, who urged the President to veto the bill on constitutional grounds, conceded that it produced "a tolerably just result." See 23 Jefferson Papers at 370.

[25]3 Annals at 482–83.

[26]Hamilton and Knox thought the bill was constitutional, Jefferson and Randolph thought it was not. All four opinions are reported in S Doc 234, 22d Cong, 1st Sess (1832). See also 23 Jefferson Papers at 370; 11 Hamilton Papers at 228.

[27]See 1 Richardson at 124; 3 Annals at 539.

[28]Washington had borrowed the ratio argument from Jefferson, who had concocted it by an exercise in synonymy:

> [T]he clause . . . is express that representatives shall be apportioned among the several states according to their *respective numbers*. That is to say, they shall be apportioned by some common ratio. For *proportion*, and ratio, are equivalent words; and it is the definition of *proportion among numbers*, that they have a *ratio common to all*, or in other words *a common divisor*.

23 Jefferson Papers at 371.

[29]See 2 Story, § 676. Article I, § 2 appears to exclude the possibility of representative districts that cross state lines. Not only are members to be chosen "by the people of the several states" and seats apportioned "among the several states"; each Representative is required to be "an inhabitant of that state in which he shall be chosen," and in case of a vacancy "in the representation from any state, the executive authority thereof" is to order a special election. See also Art II, § 1 (providing that when the House selects the President "the votes shall be taken by states, the representation from each state having one vote"). Moreover, though § 2 contains no equivalent of § 3's provision that "each Senator shall have one vote," various provisions of the

unless every state has a population that is an exact multiple of the figure chosen, *any* apportionment will give some states a higher ratio of representatives to inhabitants than others. The most this provision can be held to require is that the apportionment be as nearly proportional to population as is practicable—subject, of course, to other restrictions on the size and apportionment of the House.[30]

Nor does the Constitution say that no state may have more than one representative for 30,000 persons. It says that the number of Representatives shall not exceed one per thirty thousand. As Ames argued, the most natural reading of this language is that it limits the total number of seats, and the history of the provision leaves no doubt that this was its purpose.

The original draft would have prescribed flatly one Representative for each 40,000 persons. When Madison objected that as the population increased this ratio would produce a oversized and unwieldy House, it was amended to require *no more than* one for each 40,000.[31] When Williamson and others objected that at the outset one to 40,000 would produce too few members, it was revised to require no more than one to *30,000*.[32] When critics protested that Congress might be reluctant to increase the number of seats as permitted by this provision, Congress proposed a constitutional amendment that would have assured an increase in the size of the House by *requiring* one Representative for each 30,000, until the total number reached 100 members.[33]

In short, the entire dispute was over the size of the House, not the method of apportionment. While the total number of Representatives was not to exceed one for 30,000, they were to be apportioned as nearly as possible (while assuring that no state went unrepresented) in proportion to population.[34]

On this understanding, not only was Washington wrong in finding the bill invalid as enacted; as Ames argued, the House bill, which conformed to the President's formula, was itself of doubtful constitutionality. For by refusing to award a seat for anything less than a full 30,000 people the House plan produced glaring deviations from the constitutional standard of equal representation for equal numbers—deviations that would have been sharply reduced by approving the Senate plan. If Article I requires that representation

---

Constitution seem to contemplate that the same principle will apply to the House. See, e.g., Art I, § 5 ("one fifth of those present" may demand the yeas and nays); Art II, § 1 (apportioning electoral votes according to "the whole number of Senators and Representatives" to which each state is entitled).

[30]2 Story, §§ 676, 680. See also 11 Hamilton Papers at 230: "If this makes the apportionment not mathematically 'according to the *respective numbers* of the several states' so neither would the opposite principle of construction."

[31]See 2 Farrand at 178, 221.

[32]Id at 511, 553, 612, 643–44.

[33]See note 8. For excerpts from the voluminous debate leading to this proposal see 1 Annals at 734–56.

[34]Hamilton, who argued that the ratio could constitutionally be applied either to each state or to the population of the country as a whole, agreed that the reason for the requirement was "merely to determine a proportional limit which the number of the house of representatives shall not exceed." 11 Hamilton Papers at 230–31. Jefferson said only that "common sense" suggested the ratio should be applied to each state separately and noted that the contrary interpretation had not occurred to anyone until late in the congressional proceedings. 23 Jefferson Papers at 372–73. Despite his recognition that "[t]he object of fixing some limitation was to prevent the future existence of a very numerous and unwieldy house of representatives," Story thought Washington was right on this point, though he did not say why. See 2 Story, §§ 671, 676, 680. To the same effect see Rawle at 42–43.

be apportioned to population as nearly as practicable, it was the House bill, not the Senate version initially passed by both Houses, that failed the constitutional test.[35]

After an attempt to override the veto failed, the House passed a new bill applying a ratio of 1/33,000 to each state and ignoring fractions.[36] The Senate concurred,[37] and the President signed the bill.[38] Delaware still got only one Representative for its 58,000 inhabitants. Two centuries of continued wrestling with the problem have demonstrated the daunting mathematical complexities involved in determining the optimal general formula for eliminating apportionment inequalities.[39] Moreover, the statute finally adopted was much better in this regard than the original House bill it was designed to replace. But the bill that Washington vetoed was better still,[40] and thus the solution that he forced upon Congress in 1792 cannot comfortably be reconciled with the constitutional requirement that states be represented in the House according to their respective numbers.[41]

[35]"The longer the matter was discussed, the plainer did it become that the [House] method [of ignoring fractions] resulted in a decided inequality of representation, and thus in a violation of the constitutional rule that representatives be apportioned according to population." James, The First Apportionment at 13 n * (cited in note 21).

[36]3 Annals at 548, 550. This bill was the equivalent of the Senate amendment to the bill first passed by the House, described at notes 13–14.

[37]3 Annals at 120.

[38]1 Stat 253 (Apr 14, 1792).

[39]See generally Balinski & Young, Fair Representation (cited in note 1); Laurence F. Schmeckebier, Congressional Apportionment (Brookings, 1941); Zechariah Chafee, Congressional Reapportionment, 42 Harv L Rev 1015 (1929); United States Dept of Commerce v Montana, 503 US 442 (1992) (upholding an apportionment in which Montana was given only one Representative for its 803,655 inhabitants although the national average was 1/572,466, on the ground that since no formula was perfect considerable deference was due to the considered judgment of Congress in adopting a reasonable general rule). Contrast the conclusion in Wesberry v Sanders, 376 US 1, 7 (1964), that with respect to districts within a single state—a subject on which the Constitution is silent—the mere command that Representatives be chosen "by the people of the several states" implied that "as nearly as possible one man's vote in a congressional election is to be worth as much as another's."

[40]Rounding to the nearest whole number produces a result closer to true proportionality than rounding down whenever there are fractions greater than 0.5, as there were under the statutory formula.

[41]Two election contests resolved by the House during the Second Congress contributed to our understanding of the constitutional standards governing both elections themselves and the machinery for passing upon them.

Before taking his seat as a Representative from Maryland, William Pinkney sent a letter of resignation to the Governor, who after ordering a special election (as Article I, § 2 requires in case of a "vacanc[y]") certified to the House that John Francis Mercer had been chosen to replace him. Representative Giles, invoking British precedent, denied that a member of the House could create a vacancy by resigning. Echoed by Boudinot and Sedgwick, Giles also argued that only the House itself and not the Governor had authority to determine whether a vacancy existed; for "if the Executive in the present instance judges of the circumstances that cause a vacancy, he may do it in every instance; in which case, the members of the House may be reduced to hold their seats on a very precarious tenure indeed." The House voted to seat Mercer, thus resolving both questions against Giles and in favor of the Governor—and rightly so. Though Article I, § 3 conspicuously contrasts with the House provision by providing for replacement of Senators whenever vacancies happen "by resignation or otherwise," there appears to be no plausible reason for treating the two chambers differently in this regard, and thus every reason to conclude that the difference in phrasing was accidental. As for Giles's fears about Governors going about inventing vacancies in order to unseat uncongenial members of the House, the independence of that body seems adequately assured, as Smith and Gerry argued, by

II. THE PRESIDENT

"On no problem did the Convention of 1789 expend more time," wrote Professor Corwin, "than that of devising a suitable method of choosing a President."[42] Direct popular election was rejected out of fear that the people were incapable of making an informed choice,[43] election by Congress on the basis of concern for the independence of the Executive.[44] Article II, § 1 embodied the ingenious solution: The President would be chosen by "electors," selected in each state "in such manner as the legislature thereof shall direct."[45]

In some respects Article II was quite precise about the electoral process. The electors were to "meet in their respective states" and cast two votes apiece, one of which should be for a candidate from some other state. They were to transmit a signed and certified list of their votes to the President of the Senate, who was to open the envelopes "in the presence of the Senate and House of Representatives," and the votes were then to be counted. The person receiving the most votes became President, if he had a majority; the runner-up became Vice-President. There were detailed provisions for an election by the House of Representatives in case of a tie or the failure of any candidate to receive a majority.

Even these provisions, however, did not resolve all questions about presidential elections. To fill some of the gaps was the purpose of the Presidential Election and Succession Act of 1792.[46]

A.   The Electoral College

Section 2 of the Act provided that the electors should meet to cast their votes on the first

---

the provision of Article I, § 6 making each House "judge of the elections, returns and qualifications of its own members." See 3 Annals at 205–09; Contested Elections at 44–46.

The second controversy arose when former Georgia Representative James Jackson challenged the election in which he had been defeated for reelection by the Revolutionary General Anthony Wayne. A four-day hearing was conducted before the House itself, but not out of a sense of constitutional compulsion; over renewed objections by Livermore that the House could not delegate its responsibility, a standing committee had already been appointed to examine the evidence in election contests and report to the full body. 3 Annals at 144–45. Having found irregularities that invalidated Wayne's election, the House refused to seat him. Giles and Madison argued that, as the candidate with the most valid votes, Jackson should be seated. The House deadlocked on political lines, and the Speaker cast a tie-breaking vote against seating Jackson, thus forcing a new election. Id at 211–12, 458–72, 475–79; Contested Elections at 47–68. Since there was apparently no way of knowing which candidate would have won an untainted election, there is much to be said for this outcome.

[42]Edward S. Corwin, The President: Office and Powers 50 (NYU, 1940).

[43]"[I]t would be as unnatural to refer the choice of a proper character for the Chief Magistrate to the people," said George Mason at the Convention, "as it would, to refer a trial of colours to a blind man." 2 Farrand at 31.

[44]A President chosen by Congress, said Gouverneur Morris, would be "the mere creature of the Legisl[ature]." Id at 29. See also The Federalist No 68 (Hamilton); 3 Story, §§ 1450–51.

[45]To reinforce the President's independence, the same section provided that no member of Congress and no "person holding an office of trust or profit under the United States" was eligible to serve as an elector. See 3 Story, § 1467.

[46]1 Stat 239 (Mar 1, 1792).

Wednesday in December of each election year; section 1 prescribed that the electors themselves should be chosen within the thirty-four days preceding their meeting.[47] So far, so good; Article II, § 1 explicitly empowers Congress to "determine the time of choosing the electors, and the day on which they shall give their votes."[48] But Congress did not stop there, and not everything in the statute can so easily be explained.

The Act further provided that the executive authority of each state should deliver to the electors a certified list of the names of those who had been selected;[49] that the electors should meet at a place designated by their state legislature; that they should make three lists of their votes, attaching copies of the certificate of their own appointments; that one copy should be sent to the President of the Senate by messenger by the first Wednesday in January, another forwarded to the same address by post, and the third delivered to the local federal judge.[50] If no certificate was received by the specified date, the Secretary of State was to send a messenger to fetch it from the judge.[51] For faithful delivery of the certificates the messengers were to receive twenty-five cents per mile; for neglect of their duty they were to forfeit one thousand dollars.[52] Congress was to be in session on the second Wednesday in February for the opening and counting of the votes.[53]

This was all very sensible, and there was an obvious need for regulations of this nature. Embarrassingly, a provision that would expressly have authorized Congress to adopt them was dropped during the Convention—we do not know why—by the Committee of Style.[54] Unaware of this history or deeming it no obstacle, Congress must have concluded that regulating the manner in which the election results were compiled and transmitted was necessary and proper to the duties of Congress and of the Senate President with respect to the opening and counting of votes, or to assure the functioning of the Presidency.[55]

The Annals of Congress reveal only one constitutional objection to any of these provisions. To require the "executive authority" of each state to certify a list of electors, said Representative Niles, involved "a blending of the respective powers" of state and federal governments that was "degrading to the Executives of the several States" and "not

---

[47]Id.

[48]A provision to fix the time for choosing electors had been dropped from an earlier bill during the First Congress after several members argued it would be preferable to leave the matter to the individual states, but no one contested Sherman's assertion that Congress had power to set this date as well as the time on which the electors would meet and cast their votes. See 2 Annals at 1916–18.

[49]1 Stat at 240, § 4.

[50]Id at 239–40, § 2.

[51]Id at 240, § 4.

[52]Id, §§ 7–8.

[53]Id, § 5. The details have been changed, but provisions covering the same ground are still in effect. 3 USC §§ 6, 9–15 (1988).

[54]Before the Committee rewrote it, the draft would have empowered Congress to "determine the time of choosing the Electors, and of their giving their votes; and the manner of certifying and transmitting their votes." 2 Farrand at 529. For the revised version see id at 573. In light of the Framers' clear desire to minimize congressional influence on the selection of the President (see notes 44–45 and accompanying text), the omission may not have been accidental.

[55]Article I, § 4 expressly authorized Congress by statute to fix the date of its own meetings.

warranted by the Constitution."[56] To a modern observer this provision raises an issue of intergovernmental immunity that is the converse of that discussed in *McCulloch v Maryland*.[57] That is not quite the way Niles put it, and the House rejected his objection.[58] At least two provisions adopted by the First Congress had similarly appeared to impose duties on state officers, and no one had perceived any constitutional problem.[59] Niles's argument seems to reflect a growing sensitivity to the need to protect the independence of state governments.

Significantly, the Act made no attempt to regulate the process of choosing the electors themselves. In contrast to Article I, § 4, which authorizes Congress to supersede most state rules governing the time, place, and manner of electing Senators and Representatives, Article II leaves the method of selecting electors entirely to the states, in accordance with the Convention's desire to ensure that the President be independent of Congress.[60]

The Act did, however, have something to say about the number of electors each state was to choose. The Constitution gave the states a number of electors equal to "the whole number of Senators and Representatives to which the state may be entitled in the Congress."[61] The statute specified that this figure should be determined not at the time the electors were chosen but "at the time, when the President and Vice-President, thus to be chosen, should come into office"—that is, under the new apportionment that would be used to elect the next Congress rather than the provisional allotment of seats under which the Congress then sitting had been elected.[62]

This too was an eminently sensible provision. According to Madison, "the Northern interest" (which stood to lose relative strength in the next Congress) argued strongly for the opposite result; but "the intrinsic rectitude" of basing electoral power on the latest census "turned the decision in both houses" in favor of using the new appor-

---

[56] 3 Annals at 279. "[N]o person could be called upon to discharge any duty on behalf of the United States," he added more broadly, "who had not accepted of an appointment under their authority." Id. Niles also worried what could be done "in case those Executives should refuse to comply." Id.

[57] 17 US 316 (1819). See Kentucky v Dennison, 65 US 66 (1860); New York v United States, 505 US 144 (1992).

[58] 3 Annals at 280. See also id at 279: "Mr. Sedgwick observed that if Congress were not authorized to call on the Executives of the several States, he could not conceive what description of persons they were empowered to call upon."

[59] See chapters 1 (form of oath to be taken by state officers under Art VI) and 2 (obligations of justices of the peace under the Seamen's Act). See also the discussion of state prosecution of crimes against Indians in chapter 2.

[60] When a bill to regulate presidential elections was before the First Congress, Representative Giles argued that by prescribing that electors should be chosen "in such manner as the legislature . . . may direct" the Constitution implied that the legislatures were not permitted to make the choice themselves; electors were to be chosen by the people. 2 Annals at 1916–17. See also id at 1916 (Rep. Carroll). Giles was immediately corrected from both ends of the political spectrum. The power was "left discretionary with the state Legislatures," said Jackson of Georgia—as Goodhue of Massachusetts added, "by the express words of the Constitution." Id at 1917. The states took advantage of the latitude thus afforded them to employ a wide variety of methods for choosing electors. In some states they were appointed by the legislature; in others they were elected by the people, sometimes by district and sometimes on a "general ticket," i.e., at large. See 2 Story, § 1466; McPherson v Blacker, 146 US 1 (1892).

[61] US Const, Art II, § 1.

[62] 1 Stat at 239, § 1. This provision remains the law. 3 USC § 3 (1988).

tionment.[63] It is not obvious, however, where Congress got authority to settle this issue. The Constitution was not silent on the question; the problem was to determine what it meant by the number of Representatives to which each state was "entitled." Yet to allow each state to interpret the provision for itself would create an awkward situation when it was time to count the ballots.[64] Did Article II imply that Congress (or the President of the Senate) was to determine the validity of the ballots when they were opened? If so, making more precise the constitutional direction for determining the number of each state's electors might be necessary and proper to the opening and counting function.[65] Nobody seems to have doubted that Congress had power to determine this question; but the theory on which its authority seems to rest was to be the subject of fierce controversy later on.[66]

B.   Succession

The most controversial aspect of the 1792 statute was the provisions it made for a vacancy in the office of President. If the President resigned or died, or if he was removed or unable to discharge his duties, Article II, § 1 provided that his powers and duties should "devolve on the Vice President."[67] The same paragraph went on to authorize Congress to "provide for the case of removal, death, resignation or inability, both of the President and Vice President, declaring what officer shall then act as President, and such officer shall act accordingly, until the disability be removed, or a President shall be elected."

---

[63]Letter of James Madison to Edmund Pendleton, Feb 21, 1792, 14 Madison Papers at 235. See also 3 Annals at 406 (Rep. Murray) (noting that "the present representation in Congress is by no means equal"). Madison was not altogether fair in blaming the pressure to employ the old apportionment on "the Northern interest"; it was Elbridge Gerry of Massachusetts who moved to use the new census, and his motion was adopted "with very little objection." Id at 405.

[64]See id at 406 (Rep. Murray) (arguing that if the states took differing views of how to determine the number of their electors "there might appear before the tribunal of the public two Presidents, or two men of great power claiming the Presidency of America").

[65]It might also have been found necessary and proper to the functioning of the Presidency itself. Alternatively, congressional authority to implement the election provisions might have been found implicit in Article II by analogy to the arguments that prevailed in the First Congress with respect to the details of the oath that Article VI required of state officers, discussed in chapter 1.

[66]See chapter 6 (discussing the Grand Committee proposal of 1800); Charles Fairman, Five Justices and the Electoral Commission of 1877 (Macmillan, 1988) (discussing the 1876 election).

[67]Article II did not say who was to determine whether the President was incapable of performing his functions, and the term "devolve" left it unclear whether the President would resume his duties upon recovering from his disability. The statute did not answer either question. It did provide that a President or Vice-President could resign or decline his office only by delivering a signed written statement to that effect to the Secretary of State. 1 Stat at 241, § 11. The same theories that would sustain this provision—that it was necessary and proper to the regulation of presidential succession or to the exercise of presidential powers, or implicit in Article II—would have justified Congress in specifying who was to make the decision of presidential disability. Yet in true ostrich fashion Congress left this crucial question unregulated until 1971, when the twenty-fifth amendment was adopted. For the variety of views as to the effect of the original provision see Corwin, Office and Powers at 52–53 (cited in note 42) (noting its failure in the cases of Presidents Garfield and Wilson). The subject of disability is discussed in detail in Ruth C. Silva, Presidential Succession, chs 3–4 (Greenwood, 1968).

When the question of presidential succession was initially taken up by the First Congress, William Smith of South Carolina had opened the discussion by moving that in default of both President and Vice-President responsibility should pass to the Secretary of State.[68] Objecting that this resolution would permit the Vice-President in certain circumstances to choose his own successor,[69] Livermore moved to substitute the President pro tempore of the Senate.[70] The objections were numerous and vehement, and most of them were of constitutional dimension.

The President pro tempore, said White, was not an officer within the meaning of Article II and thus could not constitutionally be named. To place the President pro tem in the President's chair would "give one branch of the Legislature the power of electing a President," while the Constitution gave both branches "a right to an equal voice in the appointment"; it would "introduce the very evil intended to be guarded against."[71] Theodore Sedgwick added that the Senate did not always have a President pro tempore; "should the vacancy now happen, there would be no officer in the Senate that could be appointed."[72] Smith complained that to elevate the President pro tem would unconstitutionally "deprive a state of its vote in the Senate";[73] Madison, assuming that he would remain a Senator subject to state instructions, insisted he would "hold two offices at once" in violation of the separation of powers.[74]

Sedgwick suggested that the Chief Justice should be designated to assume the President's duties, as his office "was considered as next to that of President."[75] Madison retorted that this designation "would be blending the Judiciary and Executive,"[76] Smith that the Chief Justice could not be spared from his judicial duties.[77] Livermore had a different objection: If the President was impeached, it was the Chief Justice who presided over his trial.[78] The implication was plain: There should be no possible suspicion that the Chief Justice was influenced in exercising that responsibility by the prospect that he might become President if the incumbent was convicted.[79]

James Jackson of Georgia, objecting to designation of the Chief Justice, suggested the Speaker of the House.[80]

---

[68]2 Annals at 1902.

[69]"If either of the [Cabinet] officers mentioned should be the person designated to supply the vacancy, it would be in the power of the Vice President, by virtue of the power of removing officers, absolutely to appoint a successor, without consulting either branch of the Legislature." Id at 1903.

[70]Id at 1902. As Sherman said, the President pro tem succeeded the Vice-President in presiding over the Senate; it was therefore "very natural" that he should succeed him as President as well. Id at 1912.

[71]Id at 1902.

[72]Id at 1903.

[73]Id.

[74]Id at 1904. Smith echoed both of these objections: If the President pro tem remained in the Senate, he would occupy two incompatible offices; if he resigned he would deprive his state of his vote. Id at 1913.

[75]Id at 1903. See also id (Rep. Benson).

[76]Id at 1904.

[77]Id at 1913.

[78]Id at 1911. See US Const, Art I, § 3.

[79]A congressional committee in 1856 appropriately proposed to add the Chief Justice to the succession list, provided he had not presided at the impeachment of his predecessor. See Charles S. Hamlin, The Presidential Succession Act of 1886, 18 Harv L Rev 182, 187 (1904).

[80]2 Annals at 1904.

Ideally, said Livermore, it might be best to adopt a new constitutional provision "empowering the Electors who had chosen the President and Vice-President, in case of vacancy, to meet again, and make another choice."[81] He did not explain why he thought Congress could not prescribe this procedure by statute; perhaps he read the Constitution to say that only Congress could designate the President's successor.[82] Gerry seemed to think it unnecessary to call the electors together again; the problem could be solved by "filling the blank with the constitutional clause respecting the highest candidates who are primarily voted for as President and Vice President"—which appeared to mean that the House should choose among the candidates who had finished third through fifth in the preceding election.[83]

The First Congress adjourned without resolving the conundrum—even though, as Giles had warned his colleagues, once a double vacancy occurred it would be too late to do anything about it. For succession was to be regulated by statute; no bill could become law without presentation to the President; if there was no President no bill could be presented. "If the event should happen before it was provided for, there would be, he conceived, an end to this Government."[84]

In the Second Congress, the Senate passed a bill providing that, in the event of a double vacancy, the President's duties should be discharged by the President pro tempore, or if that position was vacant, by the Speaker of the House.[85] In the other chamber, Jonathan Sturges of Connecticut renewed the earlier objection that neither the President pro tem nor the Speaker was an "officer" and added that as members of Congress they would be called upon to vote on the President's salary.[86] The implication seemed to be that they might not do so impartially if they foresaw that they might end up receiving that salary themselves.[87]

[81]Id at 1911–12.

[82]He may also have feared that the electors might select someone who was not an "officer," but the proper remedy would appear to be to disallow their choice rather than to deny them jurisdiction.

[83]2 Annals at 1913. Gerry also suggested that succession was not limited, as others had argued, to "officers of the United States"; "[h]e supposed the views of Government may be extended even to 'officers of the several States.'"

[84]Id at 1914.

[85]See 3 Annals at 278, 280.

[86]Id at 281.

[87]This objection may be less serious than it appears, since Article I, § 6 expressly authorizes Congress by statute to determine the compensation of its own members. On the other hand it is arguable that, if the President's salary had been increased during the present term, no member of Congress could constitutionally exercise his powers. See US Const, Art I, § 6 :

> No Senator or Representative shall, during the time for which he was elected, be appointed to any civil office under the authority of the United States, . . . the emoluments whereof shall have been increased during such time.

Whether the assumption of presidential powers under the statute would constitute an "appointment" to a "civil office under the authority of the United States" within this clause is not clear, but there is no doubt that paying the increased salary to the Speaker or President pro tem would offend the spirit of the provision.

Behind the constitutional arguments loomed the political fact that the Secretary of State was Thomas Jefferson.[88] The House, in which Jefferson had many friends, voted largely on what we would now call party lines to place the Secretary of State next in line behind the Vice-President.[89] The Senate, more sympathetic to what would soon be known as the Federalist cause, refused to recede from its preference for its own President pro tempore.[90] The House, as in the reapportionment controversy, finally yielded.[91]

But the constitutional issues that emerged in the House were fascinating and difficult, and the quality of the debate was high.[92] Were the President pro tempore and the Speaker "officer[s]" eligible for designation as the President's surrogate under Article II, § 1? It seems fair enough to assume, contrary to Gerry's suggestion, that the term was intended to limit the choice to someone with the relevant experience that came from current exercise of some federal function. On the other hand, Gerry was right that Article I, § 2 seemed to treat the Speaker as an officer by directing the House to "choose their Speaker and other officers."[93] Article I, § 3 was not so plain with respect to the President pro tem;[94] but as Gerry said of the Speaker, "if he is not an officer, what is he?"[95] Like the Speaker or the Vice-President, the President pro tempore occupied a position of significant authority within one branch of the federal government; he surely met the usual dictionary definition of an officer.

The term "officer," or something like it, appears a number of other times in the Constitution. In Article I, § 6, it plainly excludes both the Speaker and the President pro tem; for in providing that "no person holding any office under the United States shall be a member of either House" the Framers obviously did not mean that Congress would have to select outsiders to preside over its proceedings. An earlier clause of Article II, § 1 itself seems similarly to distinguish sharply between Members of Congress and officers by providing that "no Senator or Representative, or person holding an office of trust or profit under the United States," is eligible to serve as a presidential elector. It would soon be forcefully argued that members of Congress were not "civil officers of the United States" subject to impeachment under Article II, § 4,[96] but that was partly on the ground

---

[88]See 14 Madison Papers at xix; White at 230–31.

[89]3 Annals at 402.

[90]Id at 417.

[91]Id at 417–18. See Hamlin, The Presidential Succession Act at 186 (cited in note 79): "Had it not been for the jealousy of Jefferson entertained by the Federalists, there is little doubt but that the Secretary of State would have been designated . . . ." See also Rawle at 56 (writing in 1829): "[I]t has become usual for the vice president to retire from the senate a few days before the close of the session, in order that a president *pro tempore* may be chosen, to be ready to act on emergencies."

[92]Indeed in the First Congress the partisan nature of the controversy was muted. Both Sedgwick and William Smith, leaders of the developing Federalist faction, spoke against designating the President pro tem at that time, and it was Smith who first suggested the Secretary of State. Both voted for the President pro tem during the Second Congress.

[93]See 3 Annals at 281.

[94]After prescribing that the Vice-President shall be President of the Senate, § 3 adds that "[t]he Senate shall choose their other officers, and also a President pro tempore . . . ."

[95]3 Annals at 281.

[96]Indeed the analogy to impeachment may have been the reason several speakers during the debates on presidential succession provision insisted that the President pro tem was not an "officer of the United States,"

that Article I, § 5 provided a different remedy by empowering each House, by two-thirds vote, to "expel a member."[97] Article I, § 3 provides that judgment in impeachment cases may include disqualification from "any office of honor, trust or profit under the United States," Article I, § 9 that no one holding such an office may accept gifts, emoluments, or titles from any foreign state without congressional consent. It is hard to find anything in the text or purpose of either of these provisions to justify construing them to apply only to executive and judicial officers.[98] Thus it is difficult to say that the Constitution adopts a single meaning of the term "office" or "officer"; each clause employing these terms must be interpreted according to its own context, history, and purpose.

In this light the strongest arguments against permitting Congress to designate its own officers (or the Chief Justice) to step into the President's shoes are those respecting conflict of interest and separation of powers. It is not only the Chief Justice who, if placed in the line of succession, would have a personal stake in removing the President; the Speaker and the President pro tem may be called on to vote on a motion to impeach or condemn.[99] This difficulty might be solved by applying ordinary conflict-of-interest rules to recuse them. To permit one person to exercise executive and legislative functions at the same time, however, would deviate sharply from the general principle underlying Articles I and II and contradict the plain spirit, if not the literal prohibition, of the incompatibility clause.[100]

---

although this terminology does not appear in the succession provision. See, e.g., 2 Annals at 1902 (Rep. White). As reported in the Convention by the Committee of Style, this provision too had spoken expressly of an "officer of the United States." 2 Farrand at 573.

[97] See the discussion of the impeachment of Senator Blount in chapter 6.

[98] See also US Const, Art II, § 2 (empowering the President, with the advice and consent of the Senate, to appoint diplomats, Supreme Court Justices, "and all other officers of the United States, whose appointments are not herein otherwise provided for, and which shall be established by law"); Art II, § 3 (providing that the President "shall commission all the officers of the United States"); Art VI, cl 3 (providing that "no religious test shall ever be required as a qualification to any office or public trust under the United States"). For additional discussion of various analogous provisions see Akhil Reed Amar and Vikram David Amar, Is the Presidential Succession Law Constitutional?, 48 Stan L Rev 113, 114–17 (1995).

[99] See id at 121-24. Ultimately less troubling, though not without weight, is the argument that designating either the Speaker or the President pro tem permits the House or Senate to choose the President, contrary to the basic decision of the Framers as reflected in the electoral-college provisions. The Framers did not exclude Congress from presidential selection entirely; it is the House that chooses the President when the electors fail to do so. US Const, Art II, § 1. But see Amar & Amar, Presidential Succession at 124–25 (cited in note 98) (noting that in the latter case, as also when Congress is asked to confirm the choice of a Vice-President under the twenty-fifth amendment, it chooses only among candidates selected by someone else).

[100] US Const, Art I, § 6, quoted in the text at notes 95–96. See Corwin, Office and Powers at 56 (cited in note 42): "The act thus violated the principle of the separation of powers by investing an officer of the national legislature in his quality as such with the full executive power." See also Amar & Amar, Presidential Succession at 118–21 (cited in note 98).

Professor John Manning argues that the succession provision may be understood as a narrow and justifiable exception to the separation of powers, pointing to the inclusion of the Vice-President in the same clause as evidence that "the Constitution tolerates legislative assumption of the President's duties when the President is unable to serve." John Manning, Not Proved: Some Lingering Questions About Legislative Succession to the Presidency, 48 Stan L Rev 501, 508 (1995). The argument is plausible, but the analogy of the Vice-President is not entirely in point. In the first place, the Vice-President was not a full-fledged member of the Senate, since he could vote only in the case of a tie (US Const, Art I, § 3). Moreover, unlike the officers who were to

At first glance Smith's converse fear that succession by the President pro tem would deprive one state of representation seems unwarranted, for the Constitution makes explicit provision for filling vacancies in both the House and the Senate.[101] But is it clear there would be a vacancy? Curiously, Article II, § 1 does not say that the officer designated by statute shall *become* President; it says he shall "act as President" until the President recovers from his disability or a new President is elected.[102] The implication may be that we are not really dealing with succession at all; the officer who acts as President—"for the time being," as the statute specified—retains his previous position and resumes its duties once his services as surrogate are no longer required. If that is true, then Smith and Madison may have been right on both counts: For the President pro tempore to exercise presidential powers diminishes his state's representation and blurs the separation of powers. Thus it arguably should be constitutional for a member of Congress to act for the President only if he first resigns from the House or Senate;[103] but there was no such requirement in the Act.[104]

C.   Special Elections

One final provision in the 1792 statute warrants our attention. When the offices of President and Vice-President were both vacant, the President pro tempore was not to fill out the President's entire term; unless a new election was already imminent, there was to be a special election.[105] Not only does this provision strengthen the inference that the

---

follow him in the line of succession, he was not to "act" as President; the President's powers and duties (if not the office itself) were to "devolve on" him (id, Art II, § 1). Article I, § 3 made clear that he was not to preside over the Senate at the same time, for there was to be a President pro tempore whenever the Vice-President "shall exercise the Office of President of the United States." Nor did it appear to be contemplated, in the case of removal, death, resignation, or permanent disability, that the Vice-President would ever return to the Senate, since there was no provision permitting Congress to authorize a special presidential election unless the Vice-President (whom the electors had already chosen to succeed the President) was disabled too. In the case of a President who recovered from a temporary disability, however, the Framers' conspicuous failure to say that the Vice-President *became* President may indicate an understanding that, as under the twenty-fifth amendment, the President would resume his powers.

[101]US Const, Art I, §§ 2, 3. See note 41.

[102]This language explains why it is not clear that the President pro tem or Speaker would in fact be "holding" the President's "office," in violation of the incompatibility clause, while exercising his functions.

[103]The suggestion that by resigning one becomes ineligible to act as President because he is no longer an officer, see Amar & Amar, Presidential Succession at 120–21 (cited in note 98), seems unsupported by either the language or the purpose of the provision.

[104]The statute was revised in 1886 to provide that Cabinet officers would fill the President's place in order of the establishment of their offices, beginning with the Secretary of State. 24 Stat 1, § 1 (Jan 19, 1886). Unbeknownst to Secretary of State Alexander Haig (see NY Times, Apr 5, 1981, § 4, p 2), it was revised again in 1948 to restore the Speaker and President pro tem (in that order) to the head of the column—and, appropriately, to require the officer who takes over the President's duties to resign his previous position. 62 Stat 677 (June 25, 1948), 3 USC § 19 (1988). For the difficulties this requirement may cause in finding a willing vicar if the President's difficulty is expected to be brief see Amar & Amar, Presidential Succession at 135–36.

[105]1 Stat at 240, § 10. Interestingly, though Article II spoke only of vacancies occurring by reason of "removal, death, resignation or inability," § 10 provided for an election in the case of all vacancies, including those created by failure to elect a new President or Vice-President—which nearly happened in 1800. See 3 Story, §§ 1476–77 (noting the resultant constitutional question). Section 9 of the statute, which provided for the

President pro tem or Speaker was to return to Congress once the vacancy was filled or the disability removed; it raises constitutional perplexities of its own.

Unlike the second and third sections of Article I, which specifically call for elections to fill vacancies in the House or Senate, Article II does not say whether Congress may provide for special presidential elections. Yet the language of Article II, in contrast to an earlier version proposed during the Convention,[106] does not simply authorize Congress to designate an officer to carry out the President's functions. It begins by stating in general terms that Congress may "provide for the case" of vacancy or incapacity, "declaring what officer shall then act as President." It is unclear from the text whether this designation is meant to be the sole provision Congress makes for the case, or whether Congress may make other provisions as well. There is always a possibility that the change in wording was meant to be merely stylistic; but if the Convention meant to limit Congress to naming an officer to hold the fort, it might better have stuck with the original version. Indeed the Convention records make clear that the final words of the clause, which direct that the designated officer act as President "until the disability be removed, or a President shall be elected," were inserted at Madison's request precisely to avoid the inference that there could be no special election.[107]

Moreover, a special election made perfect sense, and Congress seems to have had no serious doubts as to its authority to prescribe one.[108] But if a new President was to be elected, when would his term expire? In speaking of elections to fill vacancies in the House or Senate, Article I seemed to imply that those who won special election to *Congress* would only complete the terms for which their predecessors had been chosen. This inference was strengthened by the facts that § 2 appeared to contemplate a nation-wide representative election every other year and that under § 3 one third of the Senators'

President pro tem or the Speaker to act pending the new election, applied only in the cases mentioned in Article II.

[106]"The Legislature may declare by law what officer of the United States shall act as President in case of the death, resignation, or disability of the President and vice President . . . ." 2 Farrand at 573.

[107]Randolph had proposed that the officer should serve "until the time of electing a President." "Mr. Madison observed that this, as worded, would prevent a supply of the vacancy by an intermediate election of the President, and moved to substitute—'until such disability be removed, or a President shall be elected.'" Id at 535. In the Virginia ratifying Convention, in answer to an objection by George Mason, Madison insisted that "[w]hen the President and Vice-President die the election of another President will immediately take place." 3 Elliot at 487–88. See also Hamlin, The Presidential Succession Act at 185–86 (cited in note 79): "The above proceedings make it evident that the framers of the Constitution did not intend that the acting President should necessarily serve for the balance of the unexpired term; on the contrary, they so drafted the Constitution that, as regards at least the above clause, an intermediate election of President could be held."

[108]Smith had begun the debate by saying he thought that, "by the Constitution, a new election was not to take place till the term for which the President and Vice President had been elected was expired," 2 Annals at 1902, but no one echoed his concern, and he did not mention it again. See also 3 Story, § 1477, noting that the question had not been resolved:

Every sincere friend of the constitution will naturally feel desirous of upholding the power, as far as he constitutionally may. But it would be more satisfactory, to provide for the case by some suitable amendment, which would clear away every doubt, and thus prevent a crisis dangerous to our future peace, if not to the existence of the government.

terms were to expire every two years; and both Houses had expressly adopted this inter-pretation.[109]

Article II contained no similar provisions. What it did say was that the President should hold office for four years.[110] The Second Congress took this language literally and applied it to a President chosen by special election: "[T]he term of four years for which a President and Vice President shall be elected shall in all cases commence on the fourth day of March next succeeding the day on which the votes of the electors shall have been given."[111]

That is not the only possible interpretation. Arguably the four-year term provision applied only to a President chosen in accord with Article II itself;[112] arguably, since a comparison with Article I's two-year and staggered six-year periods suggested that Presidents should leave office at the end of a congressional term, it implied there were to be no special elections at all.[113]

It may be best not to be too quick to find answers in the Constitution to questions that were never posed. A special election seems a perfectly reasonable exercise of the power to make provision for vacancies in the office of President and Vice-President, and it would have been perfectly reasonable to limit those elected to completing the unfinished term. That is what happens, after all, when the President's duties devolve upon the Vice-President under the same clause of the Constitution; it can hardly be contrary to the con-stitutional plan.[114]

III.   THE POST OFFICE

A.   Delegation

Unable to surmount a difference of opinion over who was to designate the routes over which mail should be carried, the First Congress had passed a temporary measure essen-

---

[109]See 1 Annals at 1010; 2 Annals at 1636–38. Thus William Giles of Virginia, who had been named to succeed Theodorick Bland as a member of the First Congress in 1790, ran for reelection the same year and was returned as a member of the Second Congress. See Dice Robins Anderson, William Branch Giles: A Study in the Politics of Virginia and the Nation from 1790 to 1830 8–9, 16 (George Banta, 1914); Biographical Directory at 1059.

[110]US Const, Art II, § 1.

[111]1 Stat at 241, § 12. For the view that this arrangement was constitutionally required see Silva, Presidential Succession at 148–49 (cited in note 67).

[112]"He shall hold his office during the term of four years, and . . . be elected, as follows."

[113]See Corwin, Office and Powers at 57 (cited in note 42): "[B]y the provisions which [the statute] made for an intermediate election for a full term it set at naught the synchrony evidently demanded by the Constitution in the choice of President with that of a new House of Representatives and one third of the Sen-ate."

[114]"Whether Congress is empowered to provide for such an election is a matter of debate," wrote Professor Corwin in 1940, "but, if it is, then the position is at least plausible that it could limit the term of the President chosen to the unexpired term." Id. Livermore's suggested constitutional amendment would have authorized the electors last chosen to elect a President to complete the unexpired term. 2 Annals at 1912. The provision for a special election was repealed in 1886, but the new law provided for a special session of Congress—presumably to decide, at the worst possible moment, whether a special election should be held. 24 Stat 1–2, §§ 1, 3 (Jan 19, 1886). For the history of this bill and discussions of the problems it raised see Hamlin, The Presidential Succession Act at 187–95 (cited in note 79).

tially keeping in operation the Post Office established under the Confederation.[115] The Second Congress resumed the debate and set up a new Post Office.[116] In so doing it confronted and resolved a number of questions both of federalism and of the separation of powers.

The consuming issue concerned the delegation of authority. The bill first presented to the House in 1790 contained a clause empowering the President to establish post offices and post roads. It was excised after unidentified members objected: "[T]his is a power vested in Congress by an express clause in the Constitution, and therefore cannot be delegated to any person whatever."[117]

Several attempts were made to restore the provision leaving the choice of routes to the executive, especially after the Senate had endorsed such a delegation. Proponents argued that Congress could not intelligently pass upon the merits of particular routes, that local interests would distort the legislative judgment, that Congress would be overburdened with detail.[118] A lengthy squabble over where the main route should cross North Carolina proved them right on all counts.[119] Furthermore, the Confederation Congress had left the matter to the Postmaster General, "and very few complaints were heard."[120] As for the constitutional question, "it was said that the bill proposes no more . . . than is provided for in the other Executive Departments; the principles of conducting the business are established by the House; the mode of carrying those principles into execution is left with the Executive, and this of necessity is done in almost every case whatever."[121]

Both Houses refused to recede on this issue, and the bill was lost.[122]

The debate was resumed in the Second Congress when Representative Sedgwick moved to replace the detailed specification of routes in the House bill with a direction that the mail should be carried between Wiscasset, in the district of Maine, to Savannah, Georgia, "by such route as the President of the United States shall, from time to time, cause to be established."[123] Livermore tied the nondelegation objection to basic democratic principle: "It was provided that the Government should be administered by Representatives, of the people's choice; so that every man, who has the right of voting,

---

[115]1 Stat 70 (Sept 22, 1789) (noted in chapter 2). For the history of postal service before adoption of the Constitution see Lindsay Rogers, The Postal Power of Congress 11–22 (Johns Hopkins, 1916); Gerald Cullinan, The Post Office Department 3–23 (Frederick A. Praeger, 1968).

[116]1 Stat 232 (Feb 20, 1792).

[117]2 Annals at 1579. See US Const, Art I, § 8, cl 7: "The Congress shall have power . . . to establish post offices and post roads." The controversy is concisely recounted in White at 77–79.

[118]2 Annals at 1697, 1734.

[119]Id at 1936–40.

[120]Id at 1734. See Articles of Confederation, Art 4, 1 Stat 4, 7 (July 9, 1778): "The United States, in Congress assembled, shall also have the sole and exclusive right and power of . . . establishing and regulating post offices from one State to another, throughout all the United States . . . ." The 1782 ordinance passed by the Confederation Congress authorized the Postmaster General to establish and maintain "a continued communication of posts throughout these United States," from New Hampshire to Georgia "and to and from such other parts of these United States, as from time to time, he shall judge necessary, or Congress shall direct." 23 J Cont Cong 670 (Oct 18, 1782).

[121]2 Annals at 1735.

[122]See id at 1737, 1743, 1755. The House's attempt to revive the bill in the following Session fizzled after the dispiriting debate over the North Carolina route, text at note 118–19.

[123]3 Annals at 57, 229.

shall be in some measure concerned in making every law of the United States."[124] If the designation of routes was left to the President, added John Page of Virginia, Congress might as well "leave him any other business of legislation; and I may move to adjourn and leave all the objects of legislation to his sole consideration and direction."[125]

Sedgwick responded that he had no desire "to resign all the business of the House to the President, or to anyone else; but he thought that the Executive part of the business ought to be left to Executive officers."

> Congress, he observed, are authorized not only to establish post offices and post roads, but also to borrow money; but is it understood that Congress are to go in a body to borrow every sum that may be requisite? . . . They are also empowered to coin money; and if no part of their power be delegable, he did not know but they might be obliged to turn coiners, and work in the Mint themselves. Nay, they must even act the part of executioners, in punishing piracies committed on the high seas. . . . [T]he whole purpose . . . is answered, when the rules by which the business is to be conducted are pointed out by law . . . .[126]

Besides, said Sedgwick, the House bill itself delegated significant authority, for it authorized the Postmaster General "to establish such other roads as post roads, as to him may seem necessary."[127] Indeed, as Benson added, the parallel question of where to establish post offices was left entirely to executive discretion; "there is not a single post office designated by the bill."[128]

Sedgwick's motion failed; the House ended up listing fifty-three stations through which the main post road should pass, and the Senate fell into line.[129] Similarly, §§ 9 and 10 of the Act prescribed postal rates in hideous detail—hardly the best use, one might have thought, of congressional time.[130] Thus the episode stands as something of a

---

[124]Id at 229–30. The House, Livermore added, might just as well "leave all the rest of the business to the discretion of the Postmaster, and permit him to settle the rates of postage, and every other particular relative to the post office, by saying, at once, 'there shall be a Postmaster General, who shall have the whole government of the post office, under such regulations as he from time to time shall be pleased to enact.'" Id at 230.

[125]Id at 233.

[126]Id at 230–31.

[127]Id at 230.

[128]Id at 236. Madison argued that in this respect too the bill was unconstitutional; for it failed even to specify how many postmasters were to be appointed, and "[t]he Constitution . . . expressly restrains the Executive from appointing officers, except such as are provided for by law." Id at 238. See the discussion of this issue in connection with the establishment of diplomatic offices in chapter 1.

[129]See 3 Annals at 241–42; 1 Stat at 232, § 1. As enacted, this section went on to list a number of side routes in a full page of fine print. Id at 232–33.

[130]See 1 Stat at 235. If the President were permitted to set rates, Representative Hartley implied, he would be able to raise revenue on his own, and Congress would lose its crucial power of the purse. 3 Annals at 231–32. The best answer to this argument is that Congress could limit his discretion by providing that postal fees should not exceed costs and tying expenditures to those prevailing in the market. Congress has since delegated the task of setting rates to the Postal Service, in collaboration with an independent Postal Rate Commission, while providing a standard whereby they shall be determined. 39 USC §§ 404(a), 3621–25 (1988 & Supp 1993).

precedent for an extremely restrictive view of Congress's power to delegate its authority to the executive.

However, as Sedgwick and Benson had noted, it was not a very strong precedent. Not only did the statute as enacted continue to leave it to the Postmaster General to provide for additional roads[131] and, more significantly, to decide where to set up offices;[132] it authorized him to provide for carrying the mail by horse or by carriage, "as he may judge most expedient," and "as often as he . . . shall think proper," in the light of "productiveness" and "other circumstances"; "to prescribe such regulations" for his subordinates "as may be found necessary"; "to superintend the business of the department in all the duties that are, or may be, assigned to it"; and to determine which of two or more routes between points on the statutory list should be designated as a post road.[133]

In other words, the statute basically delegated to the Postmaster General the power to do whatever was necessary to deliver the mail. Congress's insistence on setting the rates and designating the roads was hardly in keeping with the rest of the law.[134] Despite all the crocodile tears, one is tempted to attribute the House's zest for detail more to a taste for pork than to a principled concern for the virtues of representative government.[135]

Moreover, although the principle that Congress may not abdicate its function is an important one (significantly, it was challenged by no one in the post-office debate), Sedgwick's analogies were right on the mark. The nature of the subject, like that of borrowing and coining money, made it seem unlikely that the Framers would have wanted Congress to run the postal enterprise itself. As the statute itself recognized in most respects, management is an executive, not a legislative function. In later years Congress would often go much too far in delegating the power to make basic policy decisions to other organs of government.[136] To conclude that it would have done so by allowing the Postmaster General or the President to decide where the mail should be carried seems little short of absurd.[137]

---

[131]1 Stat at 233, § 2. At Vining's insistence, the original clause authorizing the Postmaster General himself to establish additional roads was replaced by one empowering him to hire contractors to do so, 3 Annals at 251. It is not clear why it mattered.

[132]Section 3 authorized the Postmaster General "to appoint . . . deputy postmasters, at all places where such shall be found necessary"; § 7 required each deputy to keep an office to collect and distribute the mail. 1 Stat at 234.

[133]Id, § 3.

[134]Compare the same Congress's broad delegation of authority to the President with respect to the raising of new troops to protect the frontiers, discussed in note 240.

[135]See Richard E. Welch, Jr., Theodore Sedgwick, Federalist: A Political Portrait 73 (Wesleyan, 1965). The current statute designates as "post roads" all railroads, all waters, canals, air routes, and public roads "during the time the mail is carried thereon," and all "letter carrier routes established for the collection and delivery of mail." 39 USC § 5003 (1988). Under §§ 5203 and 5402 it is the Postal Service that decides where to establish surface mail routes and where to contract for air transportation of the mail. Thus the designation of post roads has now been left essentially to the Postal Service.

[136]See, e.g., The Second Century at 218–19 (discussing Schechter Poultry Corp v United States, 295 US 495 (1935)).

[137]Moreover, the test so ably enunciated by proponents of the delegation was later adopted by the Supreme Court and served us well for many years: The legislature should establish the principle, leaving it to the executive to carry it into effect. See, e.g., 3 Annals at 229 (Rep. Sedgwick); Buttfield v. Stranahan, 192 US 470 (1904); J.W. Hampton, Jr & Co v United States, 276 US 394 (1928); The Second Century at 16–19, 195. Whether the statute as envisioned by Sedgwick would have set forth a "principle" for determining where

B.   Federalism and Other Problems

Issues of states' rights were never far beneath the surface during the 1790's, and when Thomas Fitzsimons of Pennsylvania suggested that mail contractors be authorized also to carry passengers, he was promptly met by the plea of a want of federal power.[138] The Constitution, said Abraham Venable, "was totally silent on the subject of passengers"; the postal clause "simply relates to the transportation of letters."[139] That was fair enough; and it was not enough to make the passenger provision necessary and proper to the exercise of that power, Niles argued, that "by granting to the carrier of your mail the right to carry passengers for hire, the carriage of the mail may be a little less expensive."[140] The usual parade of horribles was trotted out to show that if Congress could authorize the carriage of passengers there was nothing it could not do: "[T]he States might have spared . . . their deliberations on the Constitution, and have constituted a Congress, with general authority to legislate on every subject, and in any matter it might think *proper*."[141]

This time there was force to the objection, and the passenger provision was defeated.[142] In other respects, however, Congress took an appropriately generous view of its postal power. The statute declared it a crime to obstruct, rob, open, embezzle, or abandon the mail, or to demand more than the lawful rate for its delivery.[143] It exempted deputy postmasters and mail carriers from militia duties, reflecting the need to protect postal operation from interference even by the states.[144] Finally, it forbade anyone other than the postmasters and their agents to carry letters or packages for hire, in order, as the statute itself suggested, to prevent the post office from losing revenue.[145] If Congress can ensure

---

to designate post roads is less clear (contrast Steele's proposal, 2 Annals at 1936, that the executive be directed to establish a post road between Wiscasset and Savannah by "the most direct route"), but a sympathetic court could have found it implicit that the decision was to ensure a fair balance of adequate service and reasonable cost.

[138]3 Annals at 303–06.

[139]Id at 310.

[140]Id at 308.

[141]Id at 309 (Rep. Niles). An unidentified speaker also suggested that to grant authority to carry passengers over routes on which the states had granted monopolies would take the property of the franchise holders without compensation, in violation of the fifth amendment. Id at 304. This objection was brushed aside by observing that federal law was supreme, id at 306. This was of course what the Supreme Court was to say of the New York steamboat monopoly in Gibbons v Ogden, 22 US 1 (1824), but *Gibbons* did not address the taking question. The supremacy of federal law would not obviate the need for compensation if the United States condemned land that had been granted by a state; if there is a distinction, it may lie in the difference between appropriating property and taking other actions that may impair its value. Compare Fletcher v Peck, 10 US 87 (1810), with Charles River Bridge v Warren Bridge, 36 US 420 (1837), for an analogous distinction under the contract clause.

[142]See 3 Annals at 311. If the commerce power authorized Congress to license ships, as the First Congress had concluded (see chapter 2), it would seem equally to authorize Congress to license the carriage of interstate passengers on land, as the Supreme Court would ultimately conclude (cf California v Central Pac RR, 127 US 1 (1888)); but no one is reported to have invoked the commerce clause during the passenger debate in 1792.

[143]1 Stat at 234– 37, §§ 5, 11, 16, 17.

[144]Id at 239, § 27. Cf McCulloch v Maryland, 17 US 316 (1819).

[145]Id at 236, § 14. An exception was made to permit the carriage of newspapers, possibly on grounds of freedom of the press. When Livermore moved to strike a clause allowing postal contractors to carry newspapers as well as mail, Page objected on this ground. 3 Annals at 286.

the solvency of the post office by protecting it from competition, it would not be a huge leap to conclude it could do so by authorizing the carriage of passengers; yet most of these measures had antecedents in the ordinances adopted under the Confederation,[146] and no one is recorded as raising constitutional objections to any of them.[147]

There were vehement objections, however, to § 19 of the statute, which authorized free delivery of mail to and from a variety of federal officials, including members of Congress.[148] The Constitution, said Jeremiah Wadsworth of Connecticut, carefully listed the privileges of Senators and Representatives, and franking was not among them.[149] Defenders of the privilege argued that franking was for the benefit of the people, not of the members, since it facilitated the exchange of information, the right of petition, and the intelligent exercise of political rights.[150] In expressing the fear that omission of the privilege threatened freedom of the press (because Congressmen were in the habit of sending newspapers to their constituents), Gerry came close to suggesting that the first amendment entitled publishers to a subsidy, which the language of that provision did not support.[151] But the argument against "privilege" was a red herring. The power to establish a post office implied, as the statute recognized, authority to set postal rates;[152] the power to set rates includes the power to set them at zero.[153] To put it another way, the power to establish a post office is the power to carry the mail, for a fee or for nothing; and in any event free carriage of the mail to and from government offices is plainly necessary and proper to their operation.[154]

Finally, section 26 of the Act, which made provision for sending mail abroad, quietly authorized the Postmaster General to "make arrangements with the postmasters in

---

[146]The 1782 Ordinance had contained both a set of prohibitions limited to postal agents and a monopoly provision, and an earlier ordinance had excused deputy postmasters "from those public duties which may call them from attendance at their offices." See 23 J Cont Cong at 671–74; Rogers, The Postal Power at 15 (cited in note 115).

[147]Chief Justice Marshall invoked the mail-robbery provision as a precedent for Congress's power to establish a national bank in McCulloch v Maryland, 17 US 316, 417 (1819). The postal monopoly was upheld without discussion in United States v Thompson, 28 F Cas 97, 98 (No 16,489) (D Mass 1846); according to Rogers, The Postal Power at 41 (cited in note 115) as of 1916, with one exception in the literature, its constitutionality had never been questioned. See also United States v Kochersperger, 26 F Cas 803, 803 (No 15,541) (CCED Pa 1860): "No government has ever organized a system of posts without securing to itself, to some extent, a monopoly of the carriage of letters and mailable packets."

[148]1 Stat at 237–38, § 19.

[149]3 Annals at 275. See also id at 298–99 (Reps. Murray and Giles).

[150]See 3 Annals at 276–77.

[151]See id at 289–90. See also id at 252, where an unidentified speaker argued that to omit franking "would be levelling a deadly stroke at the liberty of the press." Newspapers were given another subsidy by § 22 of the statute, which set a rate of 1¢ for sending them up to 100 miles and 1 1/2¢ for longer journeys, as compared with 6¢ for sending a letter up to thirty miles. 1 Stat at 235, 238, §§ 9, 22.

[152]See id at 235, §§ 6, 7. The Articles of Confederation had expressly authorized Congress to "exact[] such postage . . . as may be requisite to defray the expenses" of the office (Art 4, 1 Stat at 7), but the Second Congress sensibly inferred that the reason for omitting this language was that it was superfluous.

[153]Cf the exemption of charitable organizations from certain taxes and of indigents from the payment of court costs; and see text at notes 267–84, discussing financial benefits for cod fishermen.

[154]The 1782 ordinance had likewise provided for franking, 23 J Cont Cong at 678. The current franking provisions are found in 39 USC §§ 3210–19 (1988 & Supp 1993). See also Common Cause v Bolger, 574 F Supp 672 (DDC 1982) (upholding the franking privilege against a variety of constitutional objections).

any foreign country for the reciprocal receipt and delivery of letters and packets" between the two nations.[155] Such arrangements were obviously appropriate, and the provision was subject to no reported debate. Yet an "arrangement" with a foreign country looks very much like a treaty, for which Article II requires Senate consent; and the statute said nothing about Senate approval. Congress seems to have concluded, as the Supreme Court has since confirmed, that not every agreement with a foreign nation was a treaty.[156] It would have been helpful if someone had told us when the issue first arose how to distinguish agreements that require Senate consent from those that do not, for the requirement was meant as a significant check on executive authority.[157]

IV.   THE MINT

Compared with the travails of establishing the post office, the mint was a piece of cake.[158] As Sedgwick had predicted in the postal debate, nobody suggested that Congress had to coin money itself. The statute, enacted a few weeks after the postal bill, set up a mint with its own Director and other officers, to be located at the seat of government, "for the purpose of a national coinage."[159] Yet Congress was notably stingy in delegating author-

---

[155]1 Stat at 239, § 23.

[156]See United States v Belmont, 301 US 324 (1937); Corwin, Office & Powers at 235–39 (cited in note 42); Louis Henkin, Constitutionalism, Democracy, and Foreign Affairs 57 (Columbia, 1990). An opinion from Solicitor General William Howard Taft in 1890 affirmed the validity of the postal provision on the ground of "usage since the adoption of the Constitution" while conceding that a different result might be reached by ordinary rules of construction if the issue were new. 19 Op AG 513, 515, 521.

[157]The current provision has eliminated the euphemism, brazenly authorizing the Postal Service with presidential approval to "negotiate and conclude postal treaties or conventions." 39 USC § 407 (1988). One possible way to justify postal conventions might build upon the subject-matter distinction often employed to distinguish "treaties," which the states may not make at all, from "compacts," which they may make with congressional consent (US Const, Art I, § 10). See 1 Tucker's Blackstone at 310 (suggesting that compacts are agreements "concerning transitory or local affairs, or such as cannot possibly affect any other interest but that of the parties"). The prevailing theory, however, seems to be that approval of any agreement by a majority of each House is as good as approval by two thirds of the Senate—a conclusion that to say the least is not easy to square with the terms of the Constitution. See Louis Henkin, Foreign Affairs and the Constitution 173–75, 422–23 (Norton, 1972).

[158]The Articles of Confederation had given Congress exclusive authority to regulate "the alloy and value of coin struck by their own authority, or by that of the respective States." Art 9, § 4, 1 Stat at 7. Pursuant to this provision Congress in 1786 authorized the minting of federal coins, but nothing but pennies and half-pennies was made. See A. Barton Hepburn, A History of Currency in the United States 33–40 (Macmillan, rev ed 1924). For Hamilton's "justly celebrated" 1791 report to the House (see id at 41), which deplored the prevailing "disorder" and laid out detailed specifications for establishment of the Mint, see 7 Hamilton Papers at 570. A few weeks after receiving this report the First Congress by resolution provided that a mint should be established "under such regulations as shall be directed by law" and empowered the President to get started by hiring artists and procuring tools; but it was another year before the necessary "regulations" were adopted. See 1 Stat 225 (Mar 3, 1791). For a glimpse of the difficulties encountered by the Mint in actually producing coins during its early years see White at 139–43.

[159]1 Stat 246, § 1 (April 2, 1792). See US Const, Art I, § 8, cl 5: "The Congress shall have power . . . to coin money, regulate the value thereof, and of foreign coin . . . ." Section 2 of the statute, 1 Stat at 246, authorized the Director to employ "as many clerks, workmen and servants, as he shall from time to time find necessary, subject to the approbation of the President of the United States." Not only did this provision (like the clause respecting deputy postmasters of which Madison complained, see note 128) fail to specify the number of positions to be filled; appointment by the head of a department with presidential approval was not one

ity to the Director; it insisted on specifying not only the precise denominations of coins to be issued (from half cents to ten-dollar eagles) and the exact proportions of gold, silver, and copper they were to contain but even the "devices and legends" that were to appear upon them.[160] Indeed the only debate on the entire bill reported in the Annals concerned the momentous question whether to strike out a clause providing that coins should bear a likeness of the incumbent President, which opponents were quick to describe as yet another "stamp of Royalty."[161]

In accordance with the constitutional authorization to coin money and "regulate the value thereof," Congress went on to set the relative value of gold and silver coins at fifteen to one.[162] More intriguing was § 16 of the statute, which declared all gold and silver coins produced at the mint to be legal tender.[163] Congress was not expressly authorized to declare what was legal tender; when it tried to give that quality to paper money during the Civil War, the Supreme Court initially said it had acted beyond its powers.[164] But paper money is not "coin"; prescribing the legal status of coins may well be necessary and proper to producing them even if it is not a regulation of their "value," and that seems to have been Congress's view.[165]

---

of the methods specified for the appointment of inferior officers under Art II, § 2. The best explanation seems to be that Congress did not consider "clerks, workmen and servants" to be "officers" within the meaning of Article II. See Buckley v Valeo, 421 US 1 (1976).

[160]"Upon one side of each of the said coins there shall be an impression emblematic of liberty, with an inscription of the word Liberty, and the year of the coinage . . . ." 1 Stat at 248–49, §§ 9–10, 12–13. All these matters are still strictly regulated by statute. See 31 USC § 5112 (1988 & Supp 1993). In contrast, § 8 of the 1792 law authorized the President in the most general terms to provide "such buildings . . . as shall appear to him requisite" for the Mint's purposes—a purely managerial task like many of those entrusted in similarly broad terms to the Postmaster General and to the Commissioners for the District of Columbia. 1 Stat at 247–48; see text at notes 131–33 and the discussion of the seat of government in chapter 2. A lot in Philadelphia was promptly purchased and a building constructed—"[t]he first building erected in the United States for public use, under the authority of the Federal Government." See Illustrated History of the United States Mint 14 (George G. Evans, 1888). Thus the executive understanding was that the purchase of land and the construction of buildings were necessary and proper to the coining of money, which of course they were.

[161]3 Annals at 484 (Rep. Page). Even Julius Caesar, Williamson protested, had not dared to put his own face on Roman coins, "but only ventured to cause the figure of an elephant to be impressed thereon; that by a pun on the Carthaginian name of that animal, . . . he might be said to be on the coin." Id. Fortunately for democracy, the enemies of monarchy once again prevailed. Id at 485–86, 489–90. Compare the equally unsuccessful attempt to add to the President's title, discussed in chapter 1. For an amusing account of a similar objection to the choice of an eagle on the ground that it was the "king of birds" and thus a symbol of monarchy see Illustrated History of the Mint at 15 (cited in note 160).

[162]1 Stat at 248–48, § 10. "It has been justly remarked, that the power 'to coin money' would, doubtless, include that of regulating its value, had the latter power not been inserted. But the constitution abounds with pleonasms and repetitions of this nature." 3 Story, § 1112.

[163]1 Stat at 250. See also 1 Stat 300, §§ 1–2 (Feb 9, 1793), which not only regulated the value of foreign coins in accord with the express terms of Art I, § 8 but went on to declare some of them legal tender until the Mint had had three years to produce an adequate supply of domestic money. See 7 Hamilton Papers at 604–05. In fact unexpected delays in minting the new coins combined with other factors to keep foreign coins in circulation for many years. See Hepburn, History of Currency at 46–47 (cited in note 158).

[164]Hepburn v Griswold, 75 US 603 (1870). The Court quickly reversed itself in the Legal Tender Cases, 79 US 457 (1871), after changes in its membership. See The First Hundred Years at 320–29.

[165]See James B. Thayer, Legal Tender, 1 Harv L Rev 73, 75 (1887) (arguing that, in view of "the usual functions of coined money, and the usual powers of a government in regard to it," the power to make "any coin" legal tender "is fairly, although not necessarily, implied in that of coining and regulating the value of

Two final provisions of the Act should be briefly noted. The first required officers and clerks to take an oath to perform their duties faithfully; the second set up a committee to inspect coins in order to verify that they satisfied the statutory standards.[166] Both provisions were plainly necessary and proper to the coining of money.[167] What was striking was that the oath was to be taken before "some judge of the United States," and that the Chief Justice was a member of the committee. Thus the Mint Act was yet another example of an early tendency of Congress to impose nonjudicial duties on federal judges; and it is to a more famous example of that tendency that we now turn.[168]

V. THE COURTS

Just a few days before the statute establishing the Mint became law, President Washington signed an Act whose purpose was, among other things, "to regulate the Claims to Invalid Pensions."[169] Revolutionary veterans disabled in the line of duty were to apply to the Circuit Courts, which were to determine the extent of the injury and

---

coin"). Article I, § 10's provision forbidding the states to "make any thing but gold or silver coin a tender in payment of debts" does not help much in resolving this question. At first glance it appears to imply that the question of legal tender is for Congress to resolve; on closer inspection it may permit the states to make gold and silver legal tender. Whether they may do so exclusively or only until Congress acts seems to depend on the interpretation of the provisions respecting congressional authority.

[166]1 Stat at 247, 250, §§ 4, 18. Similarly, § 5 required three of the Mint's officers to post bonds for faithful and diligent performance. 1 Stat at 247.

[167]So was § 19, which provided stiff punishment for officers debasing coins or embezzling either coins or metal, 1 Stat at 250. In contrast to the statute governing the Post Office, nothing was said about punishing private citizens who robbed the Mint or even those who counterfeited coins, though Article I, § 8, cl 6 expressly made counterfeiting a subject of congressional power. The 1790 statute defining crimes against the United States had penalized counterfeiting securities but not coins. See chapter 2; Letter of John Jay to George Washington, Nov 13, 1790, in Henry P. Johnston, ed, 3 The Correspondence and Public Papers of John Jay 405, 406 (Putnam, 1891) [hereafter cited as Jay Papers] (calling attention to the omission and urging that it be rectified: "It appears to me more expedient that this offence, as it respects current coin, should be punished in a uniform manner throughout the nation, rather than be left to State laws and State courts").

[168]Among the offices created by the Mint statute was that of Chief Coiner, whose duties were just what the name implies. 1 Stat at 246–47, §§ 1, 3. Although Congress remained in session for nearly a week after the President signed the bill, no Coiner was nominated during that period. Not long after Congress went home, Jefferson asked Attorney General Randolph whether in these circumstances the President was authorized to make a recess appointment under Art II, § 2. Randolph replied that he was not. The President was permitted to make such appointments only to fill "vacancies that may happen during the recess of the Senate," and this vacancy had arisen upon creation of the office, when the Senate was still sitting. As an exception to the general principle of Senate participation in appointments, the recess provision was to be strictly construed. 24 Jefferson Papers at 165–67. Accord Letter of Alexander Hamilton to James McHenry, May 3, 1799, 23 Hamilton Papers at 94 (adding that "[i]n my opinion *Vacancy* is a relative term, and presupposes that the Office has once been filled"); Rawle at 163. Cf the Senate's analogous conclusion in the case of Kensey Johns in 1794 that a Governor had no authority to make a recess appointment to that chamber under Art I, § 3 after a legislative session had intervened. 4 Annals at 77. Similarly, when Washington asked Hamilton in 1796 whether he could appoint a special envoy to France during a recess Hamilton said no; as John Marshall later explained, "[d]uring the recess of the Senate, the president can only fill up vacancies; and, consequently, the appointment of a diplomatic character in a case where no previous vacancy existed, transcended his powers." Letter of Alexander Hamilton to George Washington, July 5, 1796, 20 Hamilton Papers at 246; John Marshall, 5 Life of Washington 581 (AMS, 1805); 3 Story, § 1553.

[169]1 Stat 243 (Mar 23, 1792).

transmit their findings and opinion, if favorable to the applicant, to the "Secretary at War."[170] The Secretary, in turn, was to place the applicant's name on the pension list, unless he had "cause to suspect imposition or mistake."[171]

This was the Act that five Justices, sitting on circuit, promptly found unconstitutional in *Hayburn's Case*.[172] To modern eyes the Justices' reasons look highly persuasive: The statute either gave the courts the nonjudicial task of issuing advisory opinions to the Executive or gave the Secretary the judicial task of reviewing court decisions, contrary in either case to the terms and purposes of Article III.[173] Apparently neither objection had occurred to Congress; the Annals reveal no debate of any kind on the pension bill. The Act was a well-intentioned effort to spare Congress the tedious and unsuitable job of passing upon the merits of individual claims;[174] as already noted, this was by no means the first time that Congress had sought to take advantage of the presence of underemployed federal judges in all parts of the country by assigning them duties other than the decision of garden-variety lawsuits.[175]

Rebuffed by the judges, Hayburn turned to Congress for relief.[176] "This being the first instance in which a court of justice had declared a law of Congress to be unconstitutional," the reporter tantalizingly informs us, "the novelty of the case produced a variety of opinions with respect to the measures to be taken on the occasion."[177] Alas, he does not tell us what those opinions were. Though there were reports of considerable private grumbling about the decision,[178] there is no indication in the Annals that any member of Congress publicly challenged either the judges' power to strike down federal statutes or

[170]Id at 244, § 2.

[171]Id, § 4. For the background of this statute see White at 355–58.

[172]2 US 409, 410–14 n (a) (1792). The letter from the Pennsylvania Circuit is also printed in 3 Annals at 572–73, that of the North Carolina judges in id at 1319–22.

[173]Professor Tushnet has suggested that there may have been no executive revision because the Secretary was authorized to find "imposition or mistake" "only in cases where the applicant had not served in the armed forces during the Revolutionary War—an issue not determined by the circuit courts." Mark Tushnet, Dual Office Holding and the Constitution: A View from *Hayburn's Case*, in Maeva Marcus, ed, Origins of the Federal Judiciary: Essays on the Judiciary Act of 1789 196, 201 (Oxford, 1992).

[174]See 3 Annals at 219 (Rep. Parker).

[175]See Tushnet, Dual Office Holding, in Origins of the Federal Judiciary at 196, 197–99 (cited in note 173). In addition to the Mint provisions just cited see text at note 50 (delivery of copy of presidential electors' certificates to the District Court); chapter 2 (deposit of copyrighted material with District Court clerk); chapter 1 (advisory reports by District Judges to Secretary of Treasury respecting mitigation of penalties for nonpayment of tariff and tonnage duties). See also Representative Murray's unsuccessful effort to empower District Judges to grant patents, "for the greater accommodation of the citizens and the more extensive encouragement of genius." 3 Annals at 854–57.

[176]See id at 556.

[177]Id at 557.

[178]Ames wrote to a friend that "[t]he decision of the Judges, on the validity of our pension law, is generally censured as indiscreet and erroneous." Letter of Fisher Ames to Thomas Dwight, Apr 5, 1792, 1 Ames Works at 116, 117. Madison privately intimated that "perhaps [the judges] may be wrong in the exertion of their power" and noted that confirmation of that power was disquieting to "those who do not wish congress to be controuled or doubted whilst its proceedings correspond to their views." Letter of James Madison to Henry Lee, Apr 15, 1792, 14 Madison Papers at 287, 288. Republican newspapers strongly applauded the decision; Federalist papers tended to be noncommittal. See Charles Warren, 1 The Supreme Court in United States History 72–77 (Little, Brown, rev ed 1926).

their conclusion that the pension law was invalid.[179] So far as we can tell, Congress respectfully accepted the Court's decision and set about to find an alternative solution that would withstand judicial scrutiny.

The revised statute, enacted the following year, still provided for evidence to be taken before a federal judge (this time the district judge), and for the judge to send his findings with respect to disability to the Secretary of War. This time, however, authority to take evidence was lodged not in the "courts" but in the "judges." Moreover, the Secretary was not to make a decision; he was to "make a statement of the cases . . . to Congress, with such circumstances and remarks, as may be necessary, in order to enable them to take such order thereon, as they may judge proper."[180] In other words, the judges were not to act in a judicial capacity, and the Secretary was no longer to review their decisions.

From the perspective of the late twentieth century the new statute seems hard to distinguish from the old. The judges were still to be in the business of giving advisory opinions, whether to the Secretary or to Congress. Nevertheless the revisions demonstrate not disregard for the *Hayburn* decision but an honest effort to comply with its limitations. For the new provisions could not be construed to subject judicial decisions to executive or legislative review. The judges themselves had suggested it might be permissible to ask them to step off the bench to perform nonjudicial duties,[181] and Congress clearly continued to think there was no problem.[182]

Unfortunately, there was no reported debate on the revised law either. Thus the congressional proceedings cast little light on the important constitutional questions that were raised by the pension statutes, but they do suggest both a relaxed view of the boundaries between judicial and executive power and early congressional acceptance of judicial review.

---

[179]Representative Murray did suggest to the House the desirability of providing "some regular mode in which the Judges . . . shall give official notice of their refusal to act under any law of Congress, on the ground of unconstitutionality," but nothing came of this sensible proposal. 3 Annals at 557.

[180]1 Stat 324, 324–25, §§ 1–2 (Feb 28, 1793). Section 1, which authorized the judges to appoint three-member commissions to take the evidence as an alternative to hearing it themselves, raised additional questions as to the meaning of Article II's provision permitting Congress to vest the appointment of inferior officers "in the President alone, in the courts of law, or in the heads of departments."

[181]See Hayburn's Case, 2 US at 410 n (a), 413 n (a). Some of the judges had in fact processed claims as "Commissioners" under the earlier law; the 1793 statute preserved whatever rights those determinations established, making it the duty of the Secretary and the Attorney General to seek a Supreme Court determination of the validity of the "Commissioners'" actions. 1 Stat at 325, § 3. The Court held the judges had no authority to act as Commissioners, but whether on statutory or constitutional grounds it did not say. United States v Todd (unreported), discussed in The First Hundred Years at 9–11.

[182]When Washington later that year asked the Justices of the Supreme Court a number of questions respecting our relations to belligerent powers during the war between England and France, they refused to answer; but not all of their reasons were applicable to the lower federal courts. See chapter 4. Conversely, the revised patent law adopted by the Second Congress in 1793 provided for "final" resolution of conflicting claims to the same invention by ad hoc arbitration boards, even though such controversies appeared to fall within the judicial power as defined by Article III, § 2, which § 1 of the same Article says shall be vested in judges with tenure during good behavior. 1 Stat 318, 322–23, § 9 (Feb 29, 1793). The Annals reveal no debate on this provision. Section 5 of the Act, in contrast, explicitly gave the federal circuit courts original but not exclusive jurisdiction of suits for patent infringement. Id at 322.

VI.   THE MILITIA

The First Congress had twice authorized the President to call out the militia in order to protect frontier settlers against Indians.[183] The Second Congress enacted a comprehensive statute to establish a uniform militia[184] and empowered the President to use it to repel invasions, to suppress insurrections, and to enforce federal laws.[185]

A.   Organization

As adopted, the basic Act declared that "every free able-bodied white male citizen" should be enrolled in the militia; that he should provide himself with "a good musket or firelock" and other necessary equipment, which should be exempt from judicial execution; that members of Congress, federal officers and employees, postal contractors, pilots, seamen, and others exempted by state law were not required to serve.[186] Each state's militia was to be "arranged into divisions, brigades, regiments, battalions and companies" as its legislature might direct (with specific suggestions that should be followed if "convenient"), but there were detailed provisions for the number, rank, and duties of officers the states were to appoint and the relative proportions of infantry, artillery, and horse.[187] The "rules of discipline" adopted by the Continental Congress in 1779 were to be observed throughout the United States, and each commanding officer was to see that his troops were exercised and trained agreeably to those rules.[188]

The peculiar mélange of state and federal authority embodied in this statute was the product of the constitutional compromise reflected in the sixteenth clause of Article I, § 8, which provided as follows:

> The Congress shall have power . . . to provide for organizing, arming, and disciplining the militia, and for governing such part of them as may be employed in the service of the United States, reserving to the states respectively the appointment of the officers, and the authority of training the militia according to the discipline prescribed by Congress.[189]

---

[183]1 Stat 95, 97, § 5 (Sept 29, 1789); 1 Stat 119, 121, § 16 (Apr 30, 1790). See chapter 2.

[184]1 Stat 271 (May 8, 1792).

[185]1 Stat 264, §§ 1, 2 (May 2, 1792). See generally Richard H. Kohn, Eagle and Sword: The Federalists and the Creation of the Military Establishment in America, 1783–1802 128–38 (Free Press, 1975).

[186]1 Stat at 271–72, §§ 1–2.

[187]Id at 272–74, §§ 3–6, 10.

[188]Id at 273, § 7. Section 9 (id) provided that any militiaman wounded or disabled while called into federal service should be cared for at public (presumably federal) expense. Plainly this provision was necessary and proper to the purposes for which the militia was to be employed.

For biting criticism of Congress for abandoning the original plan to establish a militia composed of "a select contingent of young men, uniformly and periodically trained," see Frederick Bernays Wiener, The Militia Clause of the Constitution, 54 Harv L Rev 182, 187 (1940). See also Kohn, Eagle and Sword at 137 (cited in note 185), arguing that by passing such a weak and ineffectual statute Congress "had dealt a crushing blow to an already dying militia system."

[189]The Articles of Confederation had required each state to "keep up a well-regulated and disciplined militia, sufficiently armed and accoutred," from which Congress could requisition troops as needed for the common defense. Articles of Confederation, Art 6, § 4; Art 9, § 5, 1 Stat at 5, 7. Complaints about ill-disci-

As the vigorous debates on the uniform militia bill reveal, these provisions leave unresolved a number of questions respecting the boundaries between federal and state authority. Moreover, the advocates of a narrow interpretation of federal powers labored under a peculiar disadvantage in this field; as Sedgwick pointedly observed when strengthening amendments were offered in 1795, the alternative to an effective militia was the detested standing army.[190]

No one had any difficulty with the last clauses of the constitutional provision. As the Constitution requires, the statute left it to the states to select officers and to train the troops according to rules prescribed by Congress.[191] There were scattered objections to requiring militiamen to arm themselves and to exempting their equipment from execution,[192] but they got nowhere; it was only "governing" the militia, not "arming" it, that was reserved to the states until the militia was called into federal service,[193] and soldiers without guns could hardly be expected to perform their functions.[194]

---

plined state militias lay behind the grant of additional authority to Congress in the new Constitution. See 2 Farrand at 330 (Mr. Pinckney), 386–87 (Messrs. Madison and Randolph).

[190]4 Annals at 1069.

[191]"Leaving the appointment of officers to the States," Randolph had said at the Convention, "protects the people ag[ain]st every apprehension [of federal oppression] that could produce murmur." 2 Farrand at 387.

[192]See 3 Annals at 420 (Rep. Sumter) (arguing that Congress could not require troops to arm themselves until they were federalized); 2 Annals at 1867 (Rep. Livermore) (arguing that exemption from civil process was a matter of state police power).

[193]One of the most difficult challenges posed by the militia clause is to draw the line between "disciplining" the militia, for which Congress could provide at any time, and "governing" it, which it could do only when the militia had been called into federal service. At the Convention Rufus King had said that "disciplining" meant "prescribing the, manual exercise evolutions &c" (2 Farrand at 385), and the Constitution itself spoke of "training the militia according to the discipline prescribed by Congress"—thus intimating that "discipline" related to training rather than to a general code of conduct. The 1779 rules of discipline that the 1792 statute made applicable to the militia confirm this interpretation; unlike the old Articles of War that the First Congress had made applicable to the regular Army (see chapter 2), they deal in detail with such military skills as marching, setting up camp, and the use of firearms and say nothing about military offenses. See Regulations for the Order and Discipline of the Troops of the United States, in Joseph R. Riling, ed, Baron von Steuben and his Regulations (Ray Riling, 1966); 13 J Cont Cong 384–85 (Mar 29, 1779).

[194]See 2 Annals at 1867 (Rep. Boudinot) (arguing that authority to exempt from process was incidental and thus implied). The requirement that troops provide their own guns was no more an unapportioned direct tax contrary to Article I, §§ 2, 9 (as Niles contended, 3 Annals at 421) than was their basic obligation to serve. Indeed Sherman had raised the same objection to a provision for penalties for refusal to serve (2 Annals at 1864), but not every civic duty is a "tax," whether or not "direct." Penalties for refusing to respond when the militia was called into federal service were provided by § 5 of the Act dealing with that subject, 1 Stat 264 (May 2, 1792). Penalties for failing to arm oneself, however, were unaccountably omitted, although even such a rabid states'-righter as Giles conceded three years later, when Congress irresponsibly declined to remedy the omission, that since arming was necessary and proper, penalties were too. 4 Annals at 1071; see chapter 4.

Vining went so far as to suggest Congress could require the states to pay for arming the militia (as King had argued in the Convention, 2 Farrand at 385), but Tucker argued it could not (2 Annals at 1855). The Act imposed a number of affirmative duties on state militia officers, and something of the sort may be implicit in the unusual constitutional provision for federal rules to be carried out by the states; yet a relatively innocuous provision that would have required justices of the peace to read a presidential warning to the insurgents was dropped from the companion bill after members complained that state officers could not be compelled to enforce federal law. See 3 Annals at 579 (Reps. Clark and White, opposed by Rep. Gerry).

The question of exemptions from service was hotly debated. A petition from the Quakers asked to be excused on grounds of conscientious objection.[195] Madison supported their request in deference to freedom of conscience, without suggesting that the first amendment required an exemption;[196] Aedanus Burke branded the duty to serve an unconstitutional burden on the free exercise of religion.[197] Jackson retorted that to exempt Quakers would "make the whole community turn Quakers" in order to escape the obligation and thus establish the Quaker religion.[198] Most speakers treated the question as of one of federalism or policy, and it was left to the states.[199]

In a preview of the argument over franking, some argued that an exemption for members of Congress was forbidden because the Constitution contained an exclusive list of their privileges, others that it was required to ensure legislative independence.[200] Exemptions for those engaged in federal business are easy; they are necessary to the functioning of the government.[201] Exemptions for anyone else, Bloodworth argued, had to be left to the states,[202] and most of them were. But exempting seamen and pilots from militia duty was arguably (like lighthouses) necessary and proper to the conduct of interstate and foreign commerce.[203] More generally, by analogy to the case of franking, the power to determine who would be in the militia surely included the power to say who would not;[204] but whether it was for Congress to decide who should serve was the most disputed issue of the entire debate.

Representative Thomas Tucker of South Carolina raised the question in the First Congress by moving to leave the composition of the militia to the states.[205] His motion failed, but so did the bill; and the debate was renewed when the matter was taken up in the Second Congress. Article I gave Congress authority, Sturges noted, only to "organize" the militia, not to create it; Congress's sole task was one of "forming, arming, and arranging" such men and materials as the states might choose to make available.[206] But the term was plainly susceptible of a broader interpretation. Congress's

---

[195] 2 Annals at 1859.

[196] Id at 1871.

[197] Id at 1865.

[198] Id at 1869.

[199] See id at 1868–75. The debates in Congress when the religion clauses were proposed suggested they neither required nor forbade exemptions for conscientious objectors. See chapter 2.

[200] See 2 Annals at 1856–59, 1868.

[201] The postal statute, adopted the same Spring, repeated the exemption for postal workers. See text at note 144.

[202] 2 Annals at 1868.

[203] See the discussion of lighthouses and the labor relations of seamen in chapter 2.

[204] See 2 Annals at 1871 (Rep. Boudinot).

[205] Id at 1885.

[206] 3 Annals at 418–19, 420. Accord id at 419 (Rep. Livermore). Later in the debate Jeremiah Smith objected even to permitting the President to divide the militia into regiments, battalions, and companies, on the ground that federal authority to organize the militia arose only when it was in federal service, 3 Annals at 422. As in the case of arming the militia (see text at 191–94), the text did not support him. Sumter's argument was more plausible: That the Constitution empowered Congress only to *provide for* organizing the militia, leaving execution of its provisions to the states. 3 Annals at 423. But the language may have been chosen only to indicate that Congress may delegate the task to some appropriate federal officer (see text at note 230), and in any event Congress's response to Sumter's argument went beyond his suggestion; for as adopted the statute not only left it to the states to carry out legislative determinations as to how the militia should be structured but

power would be nugatory, Joshua Seney and James Hillhouse protested, if it could not establish a militia. For, as Murray observed, many states had neither militias nor militia laws; and thus the constitutional provision "must respect a militia to be formed or created" by federal authority.[207]

Rufus King had told the Convention that "*organizing* the Committee meant, proportioning the officers and men."[208] But the power to divide state militias into regiments is so trivial that it is difficult to imagine the Convention's taking the trouble to grant it.[209] To the modern eye a grant of power to organize the militia is analogous to the power to establish post offices, to raise armies, or to provide a navy: It is the power to bring an institution, vital to the attainment of important federal interests, into existence. And that is how Congress, after intensive discussion, interpreted the provision. Sturges's motion was defeated; the statute prescribed who was to constitute the militia.

B.   Employment

But the Uniform Militia Act only set up the militia; it did not say how or when it was to be employed. Madison had called attention to the omission when the bill was first debated in 1790.[210] That Article I authorized Congress to provide for calling out the militia seemed to refute any inference that the President could do so without statutory authorization on the basis of his position as Commander in Chief. Indeed, as Madison pointed out, on its face Article II gave the President authority to command the militia only "when called into the actual service of the United States"[211]—just as, we might add, it gave him authority over armies and navies only after Congress had raised or provided them. Contrary to Smith's suggestion,[212] the statutes already enacted did not do the trick, since they authorized use of the militia only to protect the frontiers.[213] Boudinot denied that Congress had power to do what Madison asked: By authorizing Congress "[t]o provide for calling forth the militia to execute the laws of the Union, suppress insurrections and repel invasions," the Constitution contemplated special legislation each time an emergency arose—not a general delegation of power to the President.[214]

Madison's idea was dropped in the First Congress,[215] but when the House passed the militia bill the following year the Senate amended it to empower the President to call

---

provided that the militia should be divided into regiments and other units "as the legislature of each state shall direct." See text at note 187.

[207]3 Annals at 419–20. See also id at 420 (Rep. Wadsworth): "The people in several States already avow the sentiment, that they think that Congress alone has the power to form the militia."

[208]2 Farrand at 385.

[209]One is tempted to add that, if Sturges was right about the narrow scope of congressional power, there was no reason for the explicit reservation of state authority to appoint officers. Yet, when Sherman moved in the Convention to delete the parallel reservation of state authority to train the militia, Ellsworth had opposed him on the ground that both reservations were necessary because "the term discipline was of vast extent and might be so expounded as so include all power on the subject." Id at 385.

[210]2 Annals at 1864.

[211]Id.

[212]Id.

[213]See text at note 183.

[214]2 Annals at 1864. See also 3 Annals at 579 (Rep. Livermore).

[215]See 2 Annals at 1867.

out the militia to execute the laws, suppress insurrections, and repel invasions.[216]
Though these were the precise terms employed in the Constitution, several members of
the House objected, arguing among other things that the delegation was too broad. "It
was surely the duty of Congress," said Murray, who had argued for a broad interpretation
of the power to organize the militia, "to define, with as much accuracy as possible, those
situations which are to justify the execut[ive] in its interposition of a military force."[217]
Moreover, Murray argued, organization and employment of the militia were distinct subjects that ought not to be dealt with in a single bill, and the Senate amendment was
defeated.[218]

A House committee then brought in a separate bill authorizing the President to call
out the militia,[219] and it was attacked from both sides. Egbert Benson of New York preferred the language of the Senate amendment, which tracked the Constitution; Livermore
thought the bill gave too much discretion to the President.[220] Page moved to omit *any*
provision for using the militia to execute the laws: Good laws would be obeyed in any
case, and bad ones ought not to be enforced.[221] John Francis Mercer of Maryland responded with much force that the central government should not have to depend upon the
states to enforce its laws;[222] White explained that every attempt of the committee to make
the clause more definite had "only rendered it more obscure";[223] and Page's motion was
lost.[224]

The opposition to a broad delegation, however, produced significant results. The
law as enacted provided that the President could activate the militia to suppress insurrections only upon state request[225] (as Roger Sherman had argued the Constitution required),[226] and to enforce the laws only if ordinary efforts were unavailing.[227] House
amendments permitted the President to act in the latter case only if the inability to enforce the law was certified by a federal judge and only after issuing a proclamation com-

---

[216]See 3 Annals at 552.

[217]Id at 554.

[218]Id at 554–55.

[219]See id at 555, 557.

[220]Id at 574.

[221]Id. See also id at 576 (Rep. Page) (insisting on "the right of refusing submission to unconstitutional
acts").

[222]Id at 575.

[223]Id at 574.

[224]Id at 576.

[225]1 Stat 264, § 1 (May 2, 1792).

[226]2 Annals at 1867. Since Art I, § 8 contains no such limitation, Sherman must have been referring to Art
IV, § 4:

> The United States shall guarantee to every state in this Union a republican form of government,
> and shall protect each of them against invasion; and on application of the legislature, or of the
> executive (when the legislature cannot be convened) against domestic violence.

Assuming that this provision qualifies the power granted Congress in Art I, § 8, it seems to require a state request only when the insurrection is directed against the state rather than the federal government; the statutory
requirement was broader.

[227]1 Stat at 264, § 2 ("combinations too powerful to be suppressed by the ordinary course of judicial proceedings, or by the powers vested in the marshals by this act").

manding the insurgents to disperse, and to use militiamen from other states only if Congress was not in session.[228]

No one spoke up against the imposition of yet another apparently nonjudicial duty on federal judges,[229] and the nondelegability argument appears misguided. To say that Congress may "provide for" calling for the militia seems to negate the idea that Congress must determine in each case whether the militia shall be employed.[230] As Sedgwick said in the post-roads debate, even the power to "borrow money" did not seem to contemplate that members of Congress would sign the I.O.U.'s.[231] In authorizing the President to employ the militia when necessary to execute the laws, repel invasions, and suppress insurrections Congress was doing exactly what the Constitution empowered it to do. Thus the limits that the statute placed on presidential discretion in this regard may have been a wise exercise of congressional judgment, and the fact that the Constitution did not itself authorize the President to call out the militia suggests Congress was within its rights in imposing them. But since Article I, § 8 plainly contemplates delegation, the argument that delegation is impermissible seems entirely out of place; and the Constitution itself seems to provide adequate standards to guide the President's decision—assuming, as conceded by advocates of delegation in the postal controversy, that standards are constitutionally required.[232]

---

[228]Id, §§ 2, 3; see 3 Annals at 577. Two of these requirements were omitted and the third watered down when the statute was replaced in 1795. 1 Stat 424, §§ 1–3 (Feb 28, 1795). In the case of invasion, the 1792 Act contained no comparable restrictions:

> [W]henever the United States shall be invaded, or be in imminent danger of invasion from any foreign nation or Indian tribe, it shall be lawful for the President of the United States, to call forth such number of the militia of the state or states most convenient to the place of danger or scene of action, as he may judge necessary to repel such invasion.

1 Stat at 264, § 1. Justice Story went out of his way to affirm the constitutionality of a later version of this provision in a case in which it had not been questioned:

> [T]he power to provide for repelling invasions includes the power to provide against the attempt and danger of invasion, as the necessary and proper means to effectuate the object. One of the best means to repel invasion is to provide the requisite force for action before the invader himself has reached the soil.

Martin v Mott, 25 US 19, 28 (1827). The possibility that the Act delegated too much discretion to the President was not even suggested.

[229]See Rawle at 156 (calling attention to the "incongruity" of this provision). In light of the arguments made in the controversy over presidential removal of executive officers during the First Congress (see chapter 1), one might also wonder whether it was consistent with Article II to make the President's ability to ensure execution of the laws dependent upon the action of an officer not subject to presidential control.

[230]Contrast the provision of the same section that "Congress shall have power . . . to declare war." US Const, Art I, § 8, cl 11.

[231]See text at note 126.

[232]See text at notes 116–37. For the current version of the statute see 10 USC § 3500 (1988 & Supp 1993); for a controversial modern method of circumventing Article I's limits on the purposes for which Congress may provide for calling out the militia see Perpich v Department of Defense, 880 F2d 11 (8th Cir 1989).

VII.   THE ARMY

General Harmar, the reader may recall, got roundly thrashed by the Indians while undertaking a punitive mission along the Maumee River in 1790.[233] General Arthur St. Clair, Governor of the Northwest Territory, set out the next year with a larger army for the same purpose, only to suffer an even more humiliating defeat.[234] The House launched a full-scale investigation.[235]

That Congress had implicit investigative powers had been established in 1790, when the House voted to look into Robert Morris's conduct as Superintendent of Finance under the Confederation.[236] The doubts expressed on that occasion seem to have evaporated by 1792; no one in the House was reported as denying its authority to investigate St. Clair's disaster.[237] Little effort was expended in demonstrating that the inquiry served a legitimate legislative purpose. John Vining and John Steele suggested that it might lead to an impeachment;[238] Williamson and Thomas Fitzsimons seemed to think the power to appropriate money implied the power to investigate how it was spent.[239] The obvious argument that investigation might lead to legislation respecting the recruitment, training, supply, or employment of troops was apparently not made.[240]

Without further ado the House referred the matter to a committee, which it empowered "to call for such persons, papers, and records, as may be necessary to assist their in-

[233]See chapter 2.

[234]See James R. Jacobs, The Beginning of the U.S. Army 66–123 (Princeton, 1947); Kohn, Eagle and Sword at 107–16 (cited in note 185).

[235]For a concise account of the entire affair see George C. Chalou, St. Clair's Defeat, 1792, in 1 Arthur M. Schlesinger, Jr. & Roger Bruns, eds, Congress Investigates 3–17 (Chelsea House, 1975).

[236]See chapter 1.

[237]The principal debate was on a motion to request the President to institute the inquiry. After several Members objected that this course would improperly reflect upon the President, the House voted to conduct its own investigation. See 3 Annals at 490–94.

[238]Id at 490, 491. See also id at 681 (Rep. Ames).

[239]Id at 491, 492. Earlier in the Second Congress, when Josiah Parker argued that it was the duty of the House to investigate past expenditures before passing on new appropriations, Madison questioned whether passage of the appropriation bill should be held up pending such an inquiry, but he agreed it was the duty of the Representatives as "guardians of the public money, . . . to satisfy themselves as far as possible of the sources from which money flowed into the Treasury [and] how that money was applied . . . ." Id at 221, 226–27. Arthur Schlesinger, invoking British and colonial precedents, has argued more broadly that "the power to make laws implied the power to see whether they were faithfully executed." Schlesinger & Bruns, Congress Investigates at xix (cited in note 235).

[240]See Philip B. Kurland, Watergate and the Constitution 23 (Chicago, 1978). Before the investigation began, Congress had reacted to St. Clair's defeat by providing for the raising of three additional regiments to help protect the frontiers. 1 Stat 241 (Mar 5, 1792). What is notable about this statute is the breadth of discretion it gave the President. Section 12 permitted him to reduce the number of troops to be raised, or to raise none at all, "in case events shall in his judgment, render his so doing consistent with the public safety"; § 13 authorized him to call into service, at any time and for any period, "such number of cavalry as, in his judgment, may be necessary for the protection of the frontiers." 1 Stat at 243. Many objections were made to the raising of additional troops as a matter of policy (3 Annals at 337–48); in light of the fastidiousness elsewhere displayed by the Second Congress with respect to delegations of authority, it is interesting that no one is recorded in the Annals as having argued that this statute unconstitutionally transferred to the President Congress's power to raise armies. See text at notes 116–37 (discussing the designation of post roads).

quiries."[241] Concerned as always to set the appropriate precedent, President Washington assembled his Cabinet, which unanimously agreed that the House had power both to conduct the investigation and to call for the relevant papers, except for "those, the disclosure of which would injure the public." The Committee was careful to ask only for "papers of a public nature," and the President instructed Secretary Knox to hand them over.[242]

The Committee heard evidence and issued a report exonerating St. Clair and blaming the debacle on mismanagement in the War Department.[243] A motion to invite the Secretaries of War and of the Treasury to appear before the House to discuss the report failed after Abraham Venable complained that they might unduly influence the Members.[244] Page repeated the objection when Knox, feeling besmirched by the report, asked for an opportunity to appear and defend himself against its insinuations.[245] The matter was sent back to the committee,[246] which took additional evidence, corrected a few details, and basically adhered to its original conclusions.[247]

Since the House never acted on the revised report, little of immediate significance came of the St. Clair inquiry.[248] But congressional investigation into the conduct of executive officers under the new Constitution was now firmly accepted not only by the House but by the President and his Cabinet as well.

VIII.   THE TREASURY

The relative harmony that pervaded the discussions surrounding the St. Clair investigation was conspicuously missing a few months later when Representative William Giles presented to the House the first of two groups of proposed resolutions respecting the conduct of the Secretary of the Treasury, Alexander Hamilton.

Hamilton's financial policies, from assumption of state debts and the whiskey excise to the proposed subsidy of manufactures and the national bank, had long been the bane of the budding opposition to a strong central government.[249] Giles, elected to replace the deceased Theodorick Bland as a Representative from Virginia in the waning days of

[241]3 Annals at 493.

[242]See *Anas*, in 9 Jefferson Writings (Wash ed) at 87, 112–13; 23 Jefferson Papers at 261–62. Thus although the groundwork was laid for the doctrine of executive privilege, there was no occasion to determine either its scope or its legitimacy in this case. See Kurland, Watergate at 22 (cited in note 240).

[243]1 Am State Papers (Military Affairs) 36–39; Schlesinger & Bruns, Congress Investigates at 37, 44 (cited in note 235).

[244]See 3 Annals at 679, 683, 684. By refusing to let the Secretaries appear, says one observer, the House "cut off the possible rise of cabinet government in the United States." Irving Brant, James Madison: Father of the Constitution, 1787–1800, 367 (Bobbs-Merrill, 1950).

[245]3 Annals at 685, 688–89. Proposals to ask the Secretary of the Treasury for advice on such matters as raising new revenues and reducing the public debt precipitated a reprise of the heated but unconvincing argument that to ask executive officers for advice similarly gave them too much influence in legislative affairs. See 3 Annals at 437–52, 695–708, 711–22; chapter 1.

[246]3 Annals at 689.

[247]1 Am State Papers (Military Affairs) at 41–44; Schlesinger & Bruns, Congress Investigates at 93–100 (cited in note 235).

[248]See Chalou, St. Clair's Defeat, in id at 17.

[249]See chapter 2.

the First Congress, quickly became one of the Administration's most unbridled critics, and he thought he had got the goods on the despised Secretary. In January 1793, after perusing a report filed by Hamilton at House request, he moved that the House ask the President and the Secretary for a variety of records respecting borrowing, the payment of foreign debts, transactions between the government and the Bank of the United States, the sinking fund established under the assumption law, and unapplied revenues in the Treasury. Casting general aspersions at Hamilton along the way, he intimated that the Secretary might have violated the law in several respects, and the House adopted his resolutions without recorded objection.[250]

Hamilton complied with the House's request, but not to the satisfaction of Representative Giles.[251] Without missing a beat Giles presented a new series of resolutions, this time to inform the President that, among other things, the Secretary of the Treasury had spent money in violation of the appropriation laws and had violated his duty to respond to the House inquiry.[252]

The centerpiece of Giles's charges was that Hamilton had paid off one debt with funds that Congress had appropriated to pay another.[253] The general principle that Giles invoked went to the heart of the separation of powers: When Article I, § 9 said that no money could be drawn from the Treasury without a statutory appropriation, it might or might not permit Congress to make vague lump-sum appropriations;[254] but surely, when Congress specified how the money should be spent, its directions should be obeyed.[255]

Ames and Boudinot responded that the statutes had not set up separate funds, so that Hamilton had acted within the express terms of the law.[256] William Smith agreed but added that "in all Governments a discretionary latitude was implied in all Executive officers, where that discretion resulted from the nature of the office, or was in pursuance of general authority delegated by law."[257] This passage may be taken to suggest that some play in the joints is implicit in even the most precise appropriation law, or in the

---

[250]See 3 Annals at 835–40. Hamilton explained that his supporters had voted for these resolutions in order "to confound the attempt by giving a free course to investigation." Letter of Alexander Hamilton to William Short, Feb 5, 1792, 14 Hamilton Papers at 7. The background of this controversy is briefly sketched in McDonald, Washington at 108–09 (affirming that Jefferson was "directing [Giles's] every move from backstage"), and in Elkins & McKitrick at 295–301 (describing Giles (at 295) as a man of "tempestuous passions" without the intelligence to govern them). For more detail on Jefferson's clandestine role see Note, 25 Jefferson Papers at 280–92.

[251]See 3 Annals at 895. For the most important of Hamilton's responses see 14 Hamilton Papers at 17, 68.

[252]3 Annals at 899–900.

[253]See id at 900 (Resolution 3); id at 918–20 (Rep. Findley); id at 935–39 (Rep. Madison). Hamilton was also charged with having acted without authorization from the President and in one case with having deviated from the President's instructions, but as Boudinot pointed out the President was not complaining. Id at 952.

[254]See chapter 2. In fact the appropriation laws of the Second Congress were much more specific than those of the First, reflecting concerns for legislative control of spending that had been expressed during the First Congress as well as in the controversy over the Giles Resolutions. See 1 Stat 226 (Dec 23, 1791); 1 Stat 325 (Feb 28, 1793). See also Gerhard Casper, Appropriations of Power, 13 U Ark Little Rock L J 1, 13 (1990): "Any attempt to understand the development of the appropriations process in the last decade of the eighteenth century must appreciate that it coincided with the emergence of parties."

[255]See 3 Annals at 920–21 (Rep. Findley). Giles's first two resolutions would have stated this principle in general terms. See id at 900.

[256]Id at 948, 950–51.

[257]See id at 901–02, 911.

Constitution itself.[258] Earlier, however, he had directly challenged Giles's proposition that it was always the Secretary's duty to follow the law. That this was the "general rule" he acknowledged.

> Yet it must be admitted, that there may be cases of a sufficient urgency to justify a departure from it, and to make it the duty of the Legislature to in-demnify an officer; as if an adherence would in particular cases, and under particular circumstances, prove ruinous to the public credit, or prevent the taking measures essential to the public safety, against invasion or insurrec-tion. In cases of that nature, and which cannot be foreseen by the Legislature nor guarded against, a discretionary authority must be deemed to reside in the President, or some other Executive officer, to be exercised for the public good; such exercise instead of being construed into a crime, would always meet with the approbation of the National Legislature. If there be any weight in these remarks, it does not then follow as a general rule, that it is essential to the due administration of the Government, that laws making specific ap-propriations should in all cases whatsoever, and under every circumstance, be strictly observed.[259]

This time Smith seemed to be saying that in some cases the Secretary was justified in violating the law.

Both Madison and William Findley of Pennsylvania, two of Giles's most voluble supporters, agreed with Smith that the law need not always be followed; but they denied that Hamilton had been justified in departing from the law in the case before them.[260] There was some dispute about the facts. But if there was legal room for maneuver, it surely embraced what Hamilton's defenders said he had done, and if there was not he should have been forgiven; for to follow the letter of the law would apparently have re-quired him to transport one sum of money home from Europe and another back to take its place.[261]

---

[258]It is even arguable that if Congress gets too specific in prescribing how money is to be spent it usurps the executive function. Cf United States v Lovett, 328 US 303 (1946) (striking down a law forbidding the payment of the plaintiff's salary as a bill of attainder).

[259]3 Annals at 901–02.

[260]Id at 922, 941. See Lucius Wilmerding, Jr., The Spending Power 3–12 (Yale, 1943) (adding similar statements and actions by early statesmen from Hamilton to Jefferson and concluding (at p 12) that the origi-nal understanding was that "[t]here are certain circumstances which constitute a law of necessity and self-preservation and which render the *salus populi* supreme over the written law").

[261]See 3 Annals at 909–10 (Rep. Barnwell); id at 912–13 (Rep. Smith); id at 925 (Reps. Fitzsimons and Laurance); id at 949 (Rep. Boudinot). For the assertion that Hamilton had not yet replaced the money he had used in Europe see id at 920 (Rep. Findley); id at 939 (Rep. Madison). In 1794, after Hamilton had demanded a further investigation to clear his name, a committee composed largely of unsympathetic Republicans grudgingly gave him a clean bill of health. 1 Am State Papers (Finance) at 281–301; see Note, 25 Jefferson Papers at 280, 291. See also Albert Gallatin's 1796 A Sketch of the Finances of the United States, in Henry Adams, ed, 3 Writings of Albert Gallatin 69, 111 (Antiquarian Press, 1960) (first published in 1879) (concluding that, though Hamilton had offended the letter of the law, his transgression was, "to a certain de-gree, rather a want of form than a substantial violation of the appropriation law").

But the more fundamental question was whether, assuming Hamilton had done something wrong, Giles's resolutions were an acceptable means of correcting him. The reason for sending these resolutions to the President, Smith protested, was "to direct the President to remove the Secretary from office."[262] Thus the consequence of the proceeding was to find Hamilton guilty of criminal offenses and to punish him without trial. "The principles of th[e] Constitution," he continued, "secure to every individual in every class of society, the precious advantage of being heard before he is condemned." Impeachment, Smith added, was the proper course; had Hamilton been impeached, he would have received a fair trial.[263]

Even allowing for the fact that the President would have been under no obligation to discharge Hamilton, Smith's argument strikes a responsive chord. The difficulty is to explain how what Giles proposed differed from what the House had done with general approbation, only a few months before, in the case of General St. Clair.

In each case the House conducted an inquiry into possible official misconduct respecting, among other things, the use of appropriated funds. The information sought in Hamilton's case would have served the same legitimate purposes that had been invoked to justify the St. Clair investigation: possible impeachment and the supervision of federal funds. Moreover, the result of the St. Clair investigation was a legislative finding of executive misbehavior on the part of particular executive officers—which was just what Giles sought in the case of Hamilton.

Yet there were differences between the two cases. Representative Murray called attention to one of them in holding up the St. Clair investigation as a model of what should have been done in the Treasury inquiry: Those suspected of misconduct in the earlier proceeding had been given an opportunity to defend themselves. "Resolutions of conviction," Murray concluded, "might rise out of the report of a committee of inquiry, who would act as a Grand Jury to the House, but could never precede it."[264]

Appealing as Murray's distinction appears, his allusion to the grand jury reveals its weakness; for neither tradition nor the Constitution requires that a suspect be heard before he is indicted. What seems most critical is that the findings of misconduct in St. Clair's case were made in a committee report to the House itself as a prelude to further congressional action; in Hamilton's case they were meant to be an end in themselves. Thus the harm done to individuals by the conclusions in the St. Clair report was incidental to the acquisition of information for the legitimate purpose of possible impeachment; in Hamilton's case condemnation without a hearing was the object of the House's proposed action.

Nobody seriously defended Giles's approach, and all of his resolutions went down in flames. Only four Members besides Giles voted for all of them, and one of the four was James Madison.[265]

---

[262] A draft of the resolutions in Jefferson's handwriting had flatly declared that Hamilton was "guilty of maladministration" and "should, in the opinion of Congress, be removed from his office by the President of the United States." 25 Jefferson Papers at 292, 293.

[263] 3 Annals at 902–03. See also id at 904 (Rep. Murray).

[264] Id at 904.

[265] See id at 955–56, 958–60, 963. The others were Ashe, Baldwin, and Macon. Findley, Mercer, and Parker voted for all save the resolution censuring Hamilton for not providing adequate information to the

Many years later the unlamented House Committee on Un-American Affairs was to emulate Representative Giles by conducting investigations widely believed to be for the sake of exposure.[266] We are but fallible mortals, the best of us; condemnation without trial was no more appropriate when the Father of the Constitution endorsed it in 1793.

IX. CODFISH

The New England cod fisheries, Secretary of State Jefferson reported to the House in early 1791, were in parlous straits as a result of "heavy duties on their produce abroad, and bounties on that of their competitors; and duties at home on several articles particularly used in the fisheries."[267] The First Congress had given some relief in the form of an allowance on fish exports to make up for the customs duties paid on imported salt.[268] But the sum was said to be inadequate, and it was paid to exporting merchants rather than to the fishermen.[269] The Massachusetts legislature had petitioned the House for further relief, and the House had sought Jefferson's advice.[270]

Jefferson saw this occasion as an opportunity to impose retaliatory regulations and duties to counteract British restrictions on American trade.[271] The crux of his recommendation was that the Government should fulfill its "obligation of effectuating free markets" for exported fish by making "friendly arrangements towards those nations whose arrangements are friendly to us." He did not have to add that the result would be arrangements that were less friendly toward Great Britain.[272]

The Senate seized upon a different remedy, sending to the House early in the Second Congress a bill that would provide for paying to the owners of vessels employed in the cod fisheries a "bounty" based upon the size of their boats and the quantity of fish they landed, to be divided among all their crew.[273]

Congress had no authority, said Giles in the House, to grant bounties.[274] Yes it had, said South Carolina's Robert Barnwell; Congress could tax and spend for any pur-

---

House; as Findley explained, he thought that was a matter more appropriately dealt with as a contempt of Congress. Id at 963.

[266]See Watkins v United States, 354 US 178, 200 (1957): "We have no doubt that there is no congressional power to expose for the sake of exposure." Cf. Jenkins v McKeithin, 395 US 411 (1969) (holding similar state proceedings incompatible with due process). Both *Watkins* and *Jenkins*, however, involved investigations into the conduct of private individuals. The Court in *Watkins* added that "[w]e are not concerned with the power of the Congress to inquire into and publicize corruption, maladministration or inefficiency in agencies of the Government," which Woodrow Wilson had vigorously advocated in his influential book Congressional Government 303–04 (Houghton, Mifflin, 1885) (quoted in 354 US at 200 n 33).

[267]Report on the American Fisheries by the Secretary of State, Feb 1, 1791, 19 Jefferson Papers at 206, 207.

[268]1 Stat 24, 27, § 4 (July 4, 1789).

[269]See 3 Annals at 366, 367 (Reps. Goodhue and Ames); Note, 19 Jefferson Papers at 140, 145.

[270]See id at 206.

[271]See Note, id at 163. In the same vein, Madison had labored vainly in the First Congress for discrimination in tonnage duties between British and French vessels to retaliate for British restrictions. See chapter 2.

[272]19 Jefferson Papers at 220.

[273]3 Annals at 66.

[274]Id at 363.

pose that would promote the general welfare.[275] Not so, said Madison; as under the Articles of Confederation, the general welfare clause gave no such power. "[T]he meaning of the general terms in question must either be sought in the subsequent enumeration which limits and details them, or they convert the Government from one limited, as hitherto supposed, into a Government without any limits at all."[276]

Benjamin Goodhue of Massachusetts defended the subsidy as a defensive or commercial measure on the ground that the fishery provided "a copious nursery of hardy seamen" who would protect our commerce.[277] Giles said we didn't need a navy.[278]

Madison offered an olive branch. He was disposed, he said, "to afford every constitutional encouragement to the fisheries";[279] but it was both dangerous and unnecessary to speak of bounties. Defenders of the bill had insisted that all that was involved was reimbursement of the tariffs paid on salt used to cure the fish.[280] Very well; "if, in the allowance, nothing more is proposed than a mere reimbursement of the sum advanced, it is only paying a debt; and when we pay a debt, we ought not to claim the merit of granting a bounty."[281]

The bill was amended accordingly; the fishermen got their money, but the statute spoke of an "allowance" rather than a bounty.[282] Once again Congress had managed to spend money for a purpose it found worthy without accepting Hamilton's broad view of the general welfare clause.[283] But it is not clear that very much was gained for states' rights in the process. For one thing the codfish controversy suggests is that many goals that might be accomplished by subsidy can equally be achieved by selectively refunding taxes; and by passing the statute Congress acknowledged that the power to lay and collect taxes included the power to refund them in order to encourage activities it might not be able to promote directly.[284]

---

[275]Id at 375.

[276]Id at 386–87. See also Letter of James Madison to Henry Lee, Jan 1, 1792, 14 Madison Papers at 179, 180: "If not only the means, but the objects are unlimited, the parchment had better be thrown into the fire at once."

[277]3 Annals at 366. See also id at 369–70 (Rep. Ames).

[278]Id at 364.

[279]Id at 385.

[280]See, e.g., id at 366 (Rep. Goodhue): "We only ask, in another mode, the usual drawback for the salt used on the fish." See also id at 369 (Rep. Ames); id at 376 (Rep. Gerry).

[281]Id at 386. See also id at 367 (Rep. White); id at 397–99 (Rep. Giles).

[282]1 Stat 229, §§ 1–2 (Feb 16, 1792).

[283]For earlier chapters in this ongoing struggle see chapter 2. As Ames recognized, the codfish controversy was a proxy for the federal subsidies proposed in Hamilton's famous Report on Manufactures (also noted in chapter 2), which after resolution of the codfish dispute was never brought to a vote. See Letter of Fisher Ames to Thomas Dwight, Jan 30, 1792, 1 Ames Works at 111, 112; Elkins & McKitrick at 276–77.

[284]See also § 9 of the Indian Commerce Act of 1793, 1 Stat 329, 331 (Mar 1, 1793), authorizing the President to spend up to $20,000 per year "to promote civilization among the friendly Indian tribes, and to secure the continuance of their friendship." Taking this practice as a monument to the inconsistency of those who opposed relief for the cod fishermen, Representative Gerry found no constitutional support for such payments. 3 Annals at 377. The Annals do not reveal what Members of Congress thought was their constitutional basis. Payments made in accordance with a treaty would of course be necessary and proper to its implementation. More generally, civilization promotes commerce, and the power to make war may arguably include authority to keep the peace. See the discussion of payments to the Barbary pirates in chapter 2. Cf 1 Stat 254, 255–56, §§ 2, 3, 7 (Apr 14, 1792), which gave consuls broad powers to administer the estates of citizens

X.   FUGITIVES

A year later Congress passed a law to implement Article IV's provisions requiring the return of fugitives from justice and runaway slaves.[285] The Annals reveal no debate on any of its provisions.

Article IV, § 2 required simply that fugitives of either description should be "delivered up" on the "demand" of the state or the "claim" of the slaveowner.[286] The statute specified that it was the duty of the "executive authority" of the state or territory in which a person charged with crime was found, upon presentation of an indictment or affidavit, to have the fugitive arrested and turned over to the demanding party.[287] With respect to slaves the statutory procedure was different: It was the responsibility of the owner to capture the runaway and bring him before a judge or magistrate, who, upon satisfactory proof, was to issue a certificate entitling the claimant to remove him from the state.[288] To interfere with either process, or to harbor a known fugitive slave, was made a federal crime.[289]

Article IV, § 2 said nothing about any congressional power of implementation. Neither, however, did Article VI, which required state as well as federal officers to take an oath to support the Constitution. Yet the very first statute passed by the First Congress, over predictable constitutional objections, had prescribed the oath to be taken by both state and federal officers on the theory that congressional authority was implicit.[290] This argument was no less applicable to Article IV, and it was the basis on which the Supreme Court in the nineteenth century upheld Congress's power to adopt implementing legislation with respect to both fugitive slaves and fugitives from justice.[291]

There was also nothing entirely new about the fact that the statute imposed an affirmative duty on state executive officers to arrest fleeing criminals and return them; as already noted, both the First and Second Congresses had imposed occasional duties on state officers.[292] Indeed in the case of fugitives, as in the case of the oath, it was arguable that the duty was imposed by the Constitution itself.[293] Yet Representative Niles had protested on constitutional grounds when the Second Congress required Governors to cer-

---

dying abroad, to salvage wrecked ships, and to look after distressed sailors at government expense. Again there is no explanatory debate in the Annals; Congress must have thought it necessary and proper to the appointment of consuls to invest them with their traditional functions.

[285]1 Stat 302 (Feb 12, 1793).

[286]Section 2 went on to state, redundantly, that the laws of the state into which a slave fled were ineffective to set him free.

[287]1 Stat at 302, § 1.

[288]Id at 302–03, § 3. Article IV, § 2 spoke only of persons escaping from one "State" to another. The statute extended the obligation to cases of flight to or from a territory, presumably on the plausible basis of the power to "make all needful rules and regulations respecting the Territory or other property belonging to the United States." US Const, Art IV, § 3. The statute said nothing of flight to or from the district recently designated for the seat of government, over which Congress had the power of "exclusive legislation" under Article I, § 8.

[289]1 Stat at 302, 305, §§ 2, 4.

[290]See chapter 1.

[291]Prigg v Pennsylvania, 41 US 539 (1842); Kentucky v Dennison, 65 US 66, 104 (1860).

[292]See text at notes 55–58 (discussing the electoral college).

[293]See *Dennison*, 65 US at 102–03.

tify who had been chosen to serve as presidential electors,[294] and the Supreme Court made a prophet of him in 1860, reading the executive's obligation out of the 1793 statute to avoid holding it unconstitutional:

> [T]he Federal Government, under the Constitution, has no power to impose on a State officer, as such, any duty whatever, and compel him to perform it; for if it possessed this power, it might overload the officer with duties which would fill up all his time, and disable him from performing his obligations to the State.[295]

The Court changed its mind on this question in 1987,[296] but there are still limits to Congress's power to treat state officers as minions of the federal government.[297]

XI. SUMMARY

With reapportionment according to the first census, regulation of presidential elections and succession, and establishment of the Post Office, the militia, and the Mint, the Second Congress substantially completed the task of setting up the new Government of the United States. With the St. Clair and Hamilton investigations it began to settle into its role as Grand Inquest of the nation.

Sharp ideological differences had not been unknown to the First Congress. But the Giles Resolutions injected a new level of partisan vitriol that was to poison congressional proceedings until after the turn of the century. The quality of constitutional argument—notably by Ames and Sedgwick, Madison, Smith, and Murray—was still impressively high, but increasingly one has the sense that many speakers were tailoring their arguments to their conclusions.

The crucial issues of foreign policy and defense that were about to arise would only make matters worse.

---

[294]Text at notes 55–59. See also note 194 (discussing the abortive proposal to require justices of the peace to publicize a presidential warning to dissolve a rebellious assembly).

[295]*Dennison*, 65 US at 108.

[296]Puerto Rico v Branstad, 483 US 219, 230 (1987).

[297]See New York v United States, 505 US 144 (1992).

4

The Third Congress, 1793–1795

President Washington began his second term on March 4, 1793. Reluctant to run again, he had been persuaded that his country needed him, and he had not been opposed. It has been said, however, that in other respects the election of 1792 was our first "partisan" election. A plan to displace Vice-President Adams with New York Governor George Clinton attracted fifty of the 127 electoral votes; Jefferson rejoiced that there was now a "decided majority" for the "republican interest" in the House.[1] Although it was still perhaps premature to attach firm party labels to individual members of Congress,[2] a number of observers have concluded that at least one chamber of the Third Congress was in Republican hands.[3]

War had broken out in Europe early in 1793, and Washington's first concern was to keep the United States out of it. The first session of the Third Congress was dominated by measures designed to prevent or prepare for war and the ways and means of financing them. Congress enacted a neutrality law; authorized the raising of additional troops, the construction of forts and arsenals, and the establishment of a navy; laid an embargo and a ban on arms exports; debated discriminatory tariffs, nonintercourse with Great Britain, sequestration of British debts, and indemnity for depredations on our shipping. It adopted

---

[1] See Elkins & McKitrick at 288–92; James Roger Sharp, American Politics in the Early Republic 53–60 (Yale, 1993) [hereafter cited as Sharp].

[2] See Miller at 124: "Even as late as the Third Congress . . . almost half the members of the House prided themselves upon being free of party ties and obligations." See also McDonald, Washington at 106–08.

[3] Elkins & McKitrick suggest (at 365) that the Republicans controlled both Houses; most commentators seem to agree that the Federalists still controlled the Senate, though by the narrowest of margins. See, e.g., Swanstrom at 283; Note, 15 Madison Papers at 145, 146. Having been defeated in a bid for reelection, Virginia's Alexander White lamented the hardening of party lines: "I never could reconcile to my mind a maxim which politicians say is necessary in the conduct of public affairs, that of going into all the measures of the Party whose general object you approve." Letter of Alexander White to James Madison, Nov 30, 1793, 15 Madison Papers at 144, 145.

new taxes on carriages, snuff, and sugar and conducted its first debate on the definition of direct taxes.

The second session was held in the shadow of the Whiskey Rebellion. Washington's actions in suppressing the uprising created no constitutional controversy, but his clumsy attempt to implicate the popular Democratic Societies in subversive activities triggered a major brouhaha over first amendment freedoms.

It was the Third Congress that, after rejecting an interesting and little known set of alterations, proposed what became the eleventh amendment, limiting federal jurisdiction over suits against states. At the same time Congress raised serious questions under Article III itself by giving federal judges new responsibilities that were hard to characterize as judicial and by removing jurisdiction from an incompetent judge. And in seating a "Delegate" from the Southwest Territory the House debated important questions concerning the nature of Congress itself.

There was much partisan rancor and wasting of time. The Senate was without a quorum for the first two weeks of the second session, and the House haggled for five days over its reply to the President's speech. Indeed for a time there was considerable uncertainty whether the Third Congress was going to meet at all. An outbreak of yellow fever in Philadelphia lasting into the autumn of 1793 prompted Washington to ask several trusted advisers whether he had authority to move Congress's December session to some safer place. Madison and Jefferson said no: The "extraordinary occasions" on which Art. II, § 3 empowered the President to convene Congress were occasions on which Congress was not scheduled to meet.[4] Fortunately the epidemic subsided in time to permit Congress to assemble in Philadelphia as planned, and Congress avoided future embarrassment by giving the President the authority the Framers had arguably failed to provide.[5]

After admitting the public to the debate over Albert Gallatin's qualifications,[6] the Senate finally voted to open its doors generally during the conduct of "legislative" busi-

---

[4]See Letter of George Washington to James Madison, Oct 14, 1793, 15 Madison Papers at 126; Letter of George Washington to Alexander Hamilton, Oct 14, 1793, 15 Hamilton Papers at 361; Letter of James Madison to George Washington, Oct 24, 1793, 15 Madison Papers at 129; Letter of Thomas Jefferson to George Washington, Oct 17, 1793, in Paul Leicester Ford, ed, 6 The Writings of Thomas Jefferson 436 (Putnam, 1896) [hereafter cited as Jefferson Writings (Ford ed)]. Even Hamilton, who convincingly argued that "[t]he reason of the thing as well as the words of the Constitution" were as applicable to the place as to the time of meeting ("The usual seat of the Government may be in possession of an enemy; it may be swallowed up by an earthquake."), doubted that the President could change the place without also changing the time. Letter of Alexander Hamilton to George Washington, Oct 24, 1793, 15 Hamilton Papers at 373. Noting that some had even questioned whether Congress itself could change a place of meeting it had once established, Washington thought this "a strained construction of the Constitution." Letter of George Washington to Edmund Randolph, Oct 14, 1793, 33 Washington Writings at 127.

[5]See Letter of Thomas Jefferson to James Madison, Nov 2, 1793, 15 Madison Papers at 133; 1 Stat 353 (Apr 3, 1794) (authorizing the President to alter the place of meeting if conditions at the appointed spot were "hazardous to the lives or health of the members"). This provision was obviously necessary and proper to the operations of Congress, and the authority it delegated was confined by a narrow and meaningful standard. Thus it ought to have satisfied anyone but the occasional diehard who refused to accept Congress's 1790 decision that it had power to fix a temporary as well as a permanent seat of government (see chapter 2), and it is still law. See Letter of Edmund Randolph to James Madison, Oct 28, 1793, 15 Madison Papers at 132; 2 USC § 27 (1988).

[6]4 Annals at 43.

ness, but only after "suitable galleries" were built;[7] and it didn't happen during the Third Congress. Moreover, press coverage of House proceedings was skimpier than ever before. Apart from the war issues, there was rather little reported debate; much of the Annals reads like the Senate Journal. But as always much of what Congress did, and much of what we know about what its members said, helps to inform our understanding of the Constitution.

I.   NEUTRALITY

A.   The Proclamation

In the Spring of 1793, after the Second Congress had adjourned, news reached Philadelphia that the revolutionary French government had declared war against Great Britain. On April 22 President Washington issued his famous neutrality proclamation.[8]

"[T]he duty and interest of the United States," wrote the President, required that they "adopt and pursue a conduct friendly and impartial towards the belligerent powers." He therefore deemed it appropriate "to declare the disposition of the United States" to act in a friendly and impartial manner, "and to warn the citizens of the United States carefully to avoid all acts and proceedings whatsoever which may in any manner tend to contravene such disposition." No citizen who offended the law of nations by participating in hostilities or by delivering contraband could count on our government for protection. Finally, said Washington, he had instructed the appropriate officers "to cause prosecutions to be instituted against all persons who shall, within the cognizance of the courts of the United States, violate the law of nations with respect to the powers at war, or any of them."

The President's Cabinet had unanimously approved a declaration along these lines.[9] But Jefferson had expressed serious misgivings along the way, some of which were of a constitutional nature.[10] There followed an epic newspaper battle between Hamilton ("Pacificus") and Madison ("Helvidius") over the relative powers of the President and of Congress in the realm of foreign affairs.[11]

The principal objection to the proclamation was that, since only Congress could declare war, only Congress could commit us to peace. As Jefferson explained in a letter to Madison,

> The procl[a]m[atio]n as first proposed was to have been a declaration of neutrality. It was opposed on the[] ground[] . . . that a declaration of neutrality was a declaration there should be no war, to which the Executive was not competent.[12]

---

[7]Id at 47. For the background of this decision see Swanstrom at 245–49.

[8]1 Richardson at 156. The story is told concisely in Elkins & McKitrick at 336–41, and in Abraham D. Sofaer, War, Foreign Affairs and Constitutional Power: The Origins 103–16 (Ballinger, 1976). For a more detailed account see Charles M. Thomas, American Neutrality in 1793: A Study in Cabinet Government 13–52 (Columbia, 1931).

[9]See Jefferson's memorandum of this meeting, 25 Jefferson Papers at 570.

[10]See Miller at 128–29; Editorial Note, 25 Jefferson Papers at 571.

[11]These articles, which can be found in volume 15 of the Hamilton and Madison Papers respectively, were also published together by J. and G.S. Gideon in 1845 under the title The Letters of Pacificus and Helvidius (reprinted by Delmar, 1976).

[12]Letter of Thomas Jefferson to James Madison, June 23, 1793, 15 Madison Papers at 37.

In response to Jefferson's concerns, however, the word "neutrality" (which was "understood to respect the future") was omitted from the proclamation. Thus Hamilton was able to argue with considerable force in his first Pacificus essay that there was nothing to the objection:

> The Proclamation . . . only proclaims a *fact* with regard to the *existing state* of the Nation, informs the citizens of what the laws previously established require of them in that state, & warns them that these laws will be put into execution against [offenders].[13]

Congress remained "free to perform its own duties" as it saw fit;[14] it could declare war or not, as it chose.

Hamilton's argument was powerful but not quite decisive. For Washington had not stopped at declaring our present condition of peace; he had proclaimed the "disposition" of the United States to pursue a friendly and impartial policy in accordance with his view of our "duty and interest." In a letter to Jefferson, Madison took the position that in so doing Washington had gone too far.[15] Speaking to the public as Helvidius, Madison toned down his objection to avoid making it an attack on the popular President, explaining why use of the unfortunate term "disposition" did not justify interpreting the proclamation to declare a policy of peace:

> Had the Proclamation prejudged the question on either side, and *proclaimed the decision to the world*; the Legislature, instead of being as free as it ought, might be thrown under the dilemma, of either sacrificing its judgment to that of the Executive; or by opposing the Executive judgment, of producing a relation between the two departments, extremely delicate among ourselves, and of the worst influence on the national character and interest abroad.[16]

Madison's concern should not be dismissed out of hand. In the converse situation Washington and his Cabinet scrupulously insisted on several early occasions that no one outside the executive branch communicate directly with foreign governments lest the President be embarrassed in his conduct of foreign affairs.[17] Moreover, Hamilton's argu-

---

[13]Pacificus No 1, 15 Hamilton Papers at 43.

[14]Id at 41.

[15]See Letter of James Madison to Thomas Jefferson, June 13, 1793, 15 Madison Papers at 28, 29:

> A] proclamation on the subject could not properly go beyond a declaration of the fact that the U.S. were at war or peace, and an enjunction [sic] of a suitable conduct on the Citizens. The right to decide the question whether the duty & interest of the U.S. require war or peace under any given circumstances, and whether their disposition be towards the one or the other seems to be essentially & exclusively involved in the right vested in the Legislature, of declaring war in time of peace; and in the P[resident] & S[enate] of making peace in time of war.

See also Madison's letter of June 19 to Jefferson, id at 33, arguing that the proclamation "seems to violate the forms & spirit of the Constitution, by making the executive Magistrate the organ of the disposition the duty & the interest of the Nation in relation to war & peace, subjects appropriated to other departments of the Government."

[16]Helvidius No 5, 15 Madison Papers at 113, 116.

[17]When the House exuberantly voiced its approval of the new French constitution in 1792, Washington

ment that the President had merely declared "the existing state of the Nation" seems not to have been entirely candid. In a later meeting to discuss what Washington should say to Congress about the proclamation, Hamilton was reported as saying that it had been intended as an expression of the President's opinion that war was contrary to our interests, and that the President had every right to express his opinion.[18]

However, Washington himself read the proclamation narrowly. "The President," Jefferson reported, "declared he never had an idea that he could bind Congress against declaring war, or that anything contained in his proclamation could look beyond the first day of their meeting." Sharing this interpretation, Jefferson said he was satisfied that the proclamation did not interfere with Congress's prerogatives: "I admitted the President, having received the nation at the close of Congress in a state of peace, was bound to preserve them in that state till Congress should meet again, and might proclaim anything that went no further."[19] Hamilton had made the same point in Pacificus: The fact that only Congress could declare war meant that the President had a "duty . . . to preserve Peace"; Washington would have intruded on legislative authority if he had *not* taken steps to prevent individuals from provoking a war that Congress had not declared.[20]

It is easy to see how hostile acts by the President himself may improperly interfere with Congress's power to determine whether or not to declare war.[21] Before we can find that the President has a duty to take affirmative action to prevent similar actions by private parties, however, we must find that he has power to do so, and it is not so obvious that he has.

---

expressed concern that "the legislature would be endeavoring to invade the executive." Jefferson persuaded him not to protest, arguing that the House "had a right, independently of legislation, to express sentiments on other subjects" so long as, "instead of a direct communication, they should pass their sentiments through the President." See 3 Annals at 100, 106–07, 456–57; *Anas*, Mar 12, 1792, 9 Jefferson Writings (Wash ed) at 110–12; Editorial Note, 23 Jefferson Papers at 221–22. When the House unanimously voted felicitations to France four years later on the adoption of a new flag, the resolution respectfully requested the President to forward the House's sentiments to the French authorities, and he did. See 5 Annals at 195–99; Letter of George Washington to the President of the Directory of the French Republic, Jan 7, 1796, 34 Washington Writings at 418, 419. When Citizen Genêt brazenly persisted in addressing a French consul's credentials to Congress rather than to the President, Jefferson returned them with the curt reminder that the President was "the only channel of communication between this country and foreign nations": "[B]ound to enforce respect to the order of things established by our Constitution, the President will issue no Exequatur to any consul or vice-consul, not directed to him in the usual form . . . ." Letter of Thomas Jefferson to Mr. Genêt, Nov 22, 1793, 4 Jefferson Writings (Wash ed) at 84–85, 1 Am State Papers (Foreign Relations) at 184; see Edward S. Corwin, The President: Office and Powers 208–09 (NYU, 1940). In 1799 Congress recognized this principle by making it a crime for private citizens to negotiate with foreign governments without the President's consent. Logan Act, 1 Stat 613 (Jan 30, 1798) (now 18 USC § 953 (1988)).

[18]*Anas*, Nov 8, 1793, 9 Jefferson Writings (Wash ed) at 177, 178. See Sofaer, War, Foreign Affairs and Constitutional Power at 115 (cited in note 8) (arguing that by issuing and enforcing the proclamation without calling Congress into special session the President and his Cabinet unilaterally determined a policy of neutrality "for about a seven-month period").

[19]*Anas*, 9 Jefferson Writings (Wash ed) at 179.

[20]Pacificus No. 1, 15 Hamilton Papers at 40. See also Rawle at 197: "It is the office of the legislature to declare war; the duty of the executive, so long as it is practicable to preserve peace."

[21]Compare the congressional debate over President Polk's provocative actions toward Mexico in 1846 and the resulting preliminary vote to condemn him for forcing the United States into an undeclared war. Cong Globe, 30th Cong, 1st Sess 95 (Jan 3, 1848). See also David Gray Adler, The President's War-Making Power, in Thomas E. Cronin, ed, Inventing the American Presidency 119, 138–39 (Kansas, 1989).

Hamilton took the occasion to argue for the broadest possible interpretation of the opening clause of Article II, § 1, which declares that "the executive power shall be vested in [the] President." This grant of authority, Hamilton argued, was not limited to the particular powers enumerated in the provisions that followed. "[T]he difficulty of a complete and perfect specification of all the cases of Executive authority . . . would render it improbable" in any event that the general terms of the vesting clause were meant to be restricted by the enumeration. Moreover, this inference was reinforced by the contrast in phrasing between Articles I and II. For the first article conspicuously conferred on Congress only the "legislative powers herein granted"; the second contained no such restriction. Since the executive was the traditional "*organ* of intercourse . . . [with] foreign Nations," proclaiming our neutrality was an executive function; and since it fell within none of the exceptions to the general principle expressed in the vesting clause, the President had acted within his powers.[22]

To this day the crucial controversy over Hamilton's interpretation of the vesting clause has never been authoritatively resolved.[23] The difference in phrasing between Articles I and II is suggestive but not decisive; like other differences in phrasing, it may well have been accidental. The vesting clause was plainly designed to codify James Wilson's suggestion "that the Executive consist of a single person" rather than a committee;[24] the "herein provided" language in Article I was added without explanation by the Committee of Style, which was not supposed to make substantive changes.[25] Indeed to take the omission of similar language from Article II seriously might suggest that the President could exercise executive powers that have always been understood not to be federal at all, for the "herein granted" language of Article I is a principal source of the basic tenet that legislative powers not enumerated are reserved to the states. There is thus much to be said for concluding that, as has recently been urged, "[t]he Vesting Clause does nothing more than show who . . . is to exercise the executive power, and not what that power is."[26]

But the validity of the neutrality proclamation does not stand or fall with Hamilton's all-encompassing approach to the vesting clause. To begin with, assuming that the declaration did not invade the powers of Congress, it would have sufficed to

---

[22]Pacificus No 1, 15 Hamilton Papers at 37–40. Madison did not attack Hamilton's general principle that the vesting clause empowered the President to exercise all powers of federal concern that were properly classed as executive; he argued that the provisions for making treaties and declaring war were not narrow exceptions to the general principle but evidence that both powers were legislative rather than executive. Helvidius No. 1, 15 Madison Papers at 67–73. With respect to foreign affairs, however, Jefferson had already taken Hamilton's position. See Opinion on the Powers of the Senate Respecting Diplomatic Appointments, Apr 24, 1790, 16 Jefferson Papers at 378, 379: "The transaction of business with foreign nations is Executive altogether. It belongs then to the head of that department, *except* as to such portions of it as are specially submitted to the Senate."

[23]The question was debated in the opinions in the *Steel Seizure* case, but enough Justices found that Congress had implicitly forbidden the President's action to make it impossible to say that a majority either embraced or rejected Hamilton's interpretation. See Youngstown Sheet & Tube Co. v Sawyer, 343 US 579 (1952); The Second Century at 367–69.

[24]See 1 Farrand at 64–66, 88–89, 96–97; 2 id at 134, 145, 171, 401, 597.

[25]See 1 Farrand at 291; 2 id at 151, 152, 163, 565, 590. See also id at 547 ("a Committee of five to revise the style of and to arrange the articles agreed to by the House").

[26]See Lawrence Lessig & Cass Sunstein, The President and the Administration, 94 Colum L Rev 1, 48 (1994).

show that, as the Supreme Court has since concluded, the President had broad implicit authority over foreign affairs.[27] The widespread conviction that foreign relations was meant to be essentially a federal matter, as it had been under the Articles of Confederation;[28] the conspicuous advantages possessed by the executive in terms of the secrecy and dispatch essential to the conduct of foreign affairs;[29] the fact that foreign affairs remained a matter of royal prerogative in Great Britain;[30] and the meager list of foreign affairs powers expressly given to other branches all lend support to this conclusion. The express grants of foreign-affairs authority to the President, of course, were equally sparse. Madison's Helvidius papers demonstrated that he took no such latitudinarian view of presidential powers in foreign affairs;[31] and even Hamilton's assumption that the federal government as a whole had plenary authority in this area would be hotly disputed in the debates over the controversial Alien Act five years later.[32]

But there was no need to adopt a broad view of the President's implicit or inherent foreign-affairs powers in order to sustain the proclamation. Both Hamilton and Madison ultimately defended it as an exercise of his express constitutional duty to "take care that the laws be faithfully executed." Hamilton made this point at the end of his first Pacificus paper,[33] and Madison acknowledged it in Helvidius. The danger that indiscreet actions might involve us in an undeclared war and "the duty of the Executive to preserve peace by enforcing its laws," wrote Madison, "might have been sufficient grounds" for the President's action.[34]

In bowing to the President's obligation to "enforce [the] laws," Madison may have given away the strongest argument against the neutrality proclamation. Of course Article II, § 3 required the President to enforce the laws. But Article I, § 8 empowered Congress, not the President, to "define and punish . . . offenses against the law of nations"; and,

---

[27]United States v. Curtiss-Wright Corp., 299 US 304, 315–19 (1936); The Second Century at 231 n 140. See also Louis Henkin, Foreign Affairs and the Constitution 44 (Norton, 1972).

[28]"It will not be disputed," wrote Hamilton, "that the management of the affairs of this country with foreign nations is confided to the Government of the U[nited] States." Pacificus No 1, 15 Hamilton Papers at 36. See also Fong Yue Ting v United States, 149 US 698, 711 (1893); Henkin, Foreign Affairs and the Constitution at 15–16 (cited in note 27) ("Foreign affairs are national affairs"). On the Confederation and its antecedents see Richard B. Morris, The Forging of the Union 1781–1789 63 (Harper & Row, 1987): "Congress's right to conduct foreign relations—wartime defense and diplomacy, including the negotiation of treaties—stood unchallenged throughout the Revolutionary period." The foreign-affairs powers of the Confederation Congress, which on their face were no broader than those granted to the President and Congress under the new Constitution, are listed in Art 9, § 1 of the Articles of Confederation, 1 Stat at 6.

[29]See The Federalist Nos 64, 75.

[30]See 1 Blackstone at 252–61; Sofaer, War, Foreign Affairs and Constitutional Power at 10 (cited in note 8).

[31]See also Bruce Stein, The Framers' Intent and the Early Years of the Republic, 11 Hofstra L Rev 413, 511 (1982) (arguing that "the distribution of power shows clearly that the Framers intended the Congress to predominate in foreign policy").

[32]1 Stat 577 (July 6, 1798). Nevertheless, wrote Professor Corwin a century and a half afterward, "Hamilton's contention that the 'executive power' clause of the Constitution embraces a prerogative in the diplomatic field which is plenary except as it is curtailed by more specific clauses of the Constitution has consistently prospered." Corwin, Office and Powers at 252–53 (cited in note 17).

[33]See Pacificus No 1, 15 Hamilton Papers at 43.

[34]Helvidius No 5, 15 Madison Papers at 115. See also 3 Story, § 1564. Not only the institution of criminal procedings but also the withdrawal of diplomatic protection from offending citizens might arguably have been defended as a means of executing the laws.

with minor exceptions not here relevant,[35] Congress had not done so. Thus in threatening to prosecute individuals who offended the law of nations the President was arguably arrogating to himself or to the courts a power the Constitution had placed in Congress.[36]

Congress had, of course, given the federal circuit courts jurisdiction of "all crimes and offences cognizable under the authority of the United States."[37] The law of nations, as the Supreme Court was soon to hold, was binding on the United States of its own force.[38] Indeed the Second Circuit recently concluded, in upholding a provision of the 1789 Judiciary Act giving federal courts jurisdiction over certain tort actions arising under international law, that the law of nations was a law of the United States within the meaning of Article III.[39] It arguably follows, as Hamilton argued in Pacificus, that the law of nations was one of the "laws" the President was bound to enforce under Article II even in the absence of congressional action.[40]

There are at least two difficulties in the way of applying these arguments in the context of criminal prosecution.[41] First, authority to enforce customary international law in criminal cases is difficult to reconcile with the Supreme Court's rejection of a federal common law of crimes[42] and with the concern for fair warning that helps to explain that

---

[35]Sections 25–28 of the 1790 Crimes Act, 1 Stat. 112, 117–18, forbade interference with foreign diplomats. See chapter 2.

[36]See Stein, 11 Hofstra L Rev at 468, 475–76 (cited in note 31). That the United States is bound by the law of nations, of course, does not prove that the President has authority to enforce it by criminal proceedings without statutory authorization.

[37]Judiciary Act of 1789, § 11, 1 Stat 73, 78–79 (Sept. 24, 1789). For the argument that Senate deletion of the restrictive words "and defined by the laws of the same" from an earlier draft shows that this provision was meant to embrace nonstatutory crimes see Charles Warren, New Light on the History of the Federal Judiciary Act of 1789, 37 Harv L Rev 49, 73 (1923).

[38]Glass v The Sloop Betsy, 3 US 6 (1794) (ordering a French prize restored to its owners after concluding that France had no right to erect prize courts in U.S. territory); Charles Warren, 1 The Supreme Court in United States History 116–18 (Little, Brown, rev ed 1926). See also 1 Op AG 26, 27 (June 26, 1792): "The law of nations, although not specifically adopted by the constitution or any municipal act, is essentially a part of the law of the land." Accord Louis Henkin, International Law as Law in the United States, 82 Mich L Rev 1555, 1561 (1984).

[39]Filartiga v Pena-Irala, 630 F2d 876, 885 (2d Cir 1980) (discussed in chapter 1).

[40]Pacificus No 1, 15 Hamilton Papers at 43. See also Restatement (3d), Foreign Relations Law, § 111 comment c (1987); Louis Henkin, The President and International Law, 80 Am J Intl Law 930, 934 (1986): "The President's duty to take care that the laws be faithfully executed includes not only statutes of Congress and judge-made law, but also treaties and principles of customary law." Jefferson, in a letter to Monroe, acknowledged that those who committed hostile acts against nations with which we were at peace could be punished even in the absence of statute. Letter of Thomas Jefferson to James Monroe, July 14, 1793, 4 Jefferson Writings (Wash ed) at 17, 19. For the contrary view see Arthur Weisburd, The Executive Branch and International Law, 41 Vand L Rev 1205, 1233 (1988).

[41]The argument that the alien-tort provision might be explained on the narrower ground that it implicitly federalized the law of nations or authorized the federal courts to do so (cf Textile Workers Union v Lincoln Mills, 353 US 448, 450 (1957)), however anachronistic, could equally be made in the criminal context on the basis of § 11 of the same statute (see note 37), which gave the courts jurisdiction over federal crimes.

[42]United States v Hudson, 11 US 32, 33 (1812): "The legislative authority of the Union must first make an act a crime, affix a punishment to it, and declare the court that shall have jurisdiction of the offence." Justice Chase had taken this position on circuit as early as 1798; Judge Peters disagreed with him, and somehow the defendant was convicted. Worrall's Case, 28 F Cas 774, 778–80 (No 16,766), Wharton's State Trials 189, 196–99 (CCD Pa 1798).

decision.[43] Second, if offenses against the law of nations were already punishable, one wonders why Congress was given power to proscribe them.

The Convention record suggests possible answers to this question. The power to "punish" offenses seems to have been included in order to make clear that the subject was one of federal rather than state concern;[44] the power to "define" them was added because of a conviction that the law of nations was "often too vague and deficient to be a rule."[45] Neither of these explanations is necessarily inconsistent with the conclusion that the law of nations is binding on the courts of its own force in cases in which it can be fairly ascertained or that the President may take steps to enforce it even though Congress has not acted.[46]

Moreover, the Supreme Court did not reject the notion of a federal common law of crimes until *United States v. Hudson* in 1812,[47] and even then the law of nations was arguably distinguishable. For *Hudson* was a garden-variety libel case, explainable in part by the legitimate fear that federal prosecution would undermine states' rights; no one argued that foreign relations should be left to the states.[48] The opinion that the law of nations was one of the "laws" the President was bound to execute was widespread in 1793, and the text of the proclamation demonstrates that Washington shared that conviction. Thus, even if he was ultimately wrong on this question, his action did not represent a claim of presidential authority to create new criminal offenses; he was merely asserting the right to do his duty by enforcing preexisting law.

B.   The Aftermath

Proclaiming neutrality, however, was one thing; enforcing it was another. Since the law of nations had not been codified, its contours remained murky. On Washington's orders, Jefferson posed a famous list of clarifying questions to the Justices of the Supreme

---

[43]See Zephaniah Swift, A System of the Laws of the State of Connecticut 365–66 (Windham, CT, 1795) (arguing that punishment for common-law crimes "manifestly partakes of the odious nature of an ex post facto law, and subjects a man to an inconvenience which he could not possibly foresee, or calculate upon, at the time of doing the act"); Stewart Jay, Origins of Federal Common Law: Part One, 133 U Pa LR 1003, 1061 (1985).

[44]See 2 Farrand at 316 (Madison) (arguing in support of the provision of the same clause respecting piracy and felonies on the high seas that there would be "neither uniformity nor stability in the law" if the matter were left to the states); The Federalist No 42 (Madison) (complaining that by making no provision for offenses against the law of nations the Articles of Confederation "leave it in the power of any indiscreet member to embroil the confederacy with foreign nations"); 3 Story, §§ 1158, 1160.

[45]2 Farrand at 615 (Gouverneur Morris).

[46]In civil admiralty cases, for example, the federal courts have long been held to have authority to develop a general maritime law despite the fact that Congress may legislate in the same field. Compare The Lottawanna, 88 US 558, 574–75 (1875), with Butler v Boston & Savannah SS Co, 130 US 527, 557 (1889).

[47]See note 42.

[48]See Stewart Jay, The Status of the Law of Nations in Early American Law, 42 Vand L Rev 819, 843–44 (1989). Cf United States v Coolidge, 25 F Cas 619, 621 (No 14,857) (CCD Mass 1813), where Justice Story distinguished *Hudson* on the ground that federal judges had traditionally had power to enforce nonstatutory rules in admiralty. Accord 1 Kent at 318–21. In the Supreme Court, despite an invitation by several Justices to reexamine the question, the Attorney General declared that he considered *Hudson* controlling, and "[u]nder these circumstances" the Court elected to follow *Hudson*. United States v Coolidge, 14 US 415, 416–17 (1816).

Court.[49] Stymied by their refusal to render advisory opinions,[50] the Cabinet then formulated a set of "regulations"[51] reflecting an executive interpretation of international law—for the President cannot fulfill his obligation to take care that the law is enforced without making a preliminary determination of what it means.[52]

Even before the regulations were adopted, at Jefferson's request[53] a U.S. citizen named Gideon Henfield was indicted in federal court for serving as prize-master aboard a French privateer that preyed upon British shipping. Echoed by the Republican press, the defendant argued that he had violated no enforceable law, but the court disagreed. By taking part in hostilities against nations with which we were at peace, Justice Wilson instructed the jury, Henfield had offended both the law of nations and treaties declaring a state of peace, and thus he had committed an offense against the United States.[54]

Henfield was nevertheless acquitted. Jefferson thought the jury had been unwilling to punish a man who had not known he was breaking the law.[55] Some observers have hinted at nullification by "a pro-French jury,"[56] others that the jury may have accepted the argument that there could be no punishment in the absence of statute.[57]

[49]Jefferson's covering letter to the Justices is reprinted in 4 Jefferson Writings (Wash ed) at 22, the questions themselves in 33 Washington Writings at 15–19.

[50]3 Jay Papers at 488–89; 15 Hamilton Papers at 111 n 1. The entire correspondence appears in Paul M. Bator, et al, ed, Hart & Wechsler's The Federal Courts and the Federal System 65–67 (Foundation, 3d ed 1988). For discussion of this incident see Russell Wheeler, Extrajudicial Actions of the Early Supreme Court, 1973 Sup Ct Rev 123, 144–55; The First Hundred Years at 11–14. The Justices' refusal was the more striking in that, only a few months before, Jay had responded (privately) to an inquiry from Hamilton by composing a draft of a neutrality proclamation for the President's use. See Letter of Alexander Hamilton to John Jay, Apr 9, 1793, 14 Hamilton Papers at 299; Letter of John Jay to Alexander Hamilton, Apr 11, 1793, id at 307, 308. See Wheeler, supra, at 145: "The general understanding during that period was that federal judges, like their English counterparts, were to render advice to the executive and legislative branches."

[51]See 9 Jefferson Writings (Wash ed) at 440–41; 1 Am St Papers (Foreign Relations) at 141. See Elkins & McKitrick at 352–53.

[52]See Pacificus No 1, 15 Hamilton Papers at 43. But see Stein, 11 Hofstra L Rev at 473 (cited in note 31): "The administration's neutrality measures resemble a legislative enactment rather than a mere executive enforcement of the laws."

[53]Despite his qualms about the proclamation itself, Jefferson enforced neutrality vigorously; he had no more desire to see the United States dragged into war than anyone else. See Thomas, American Neutrality at 35, 51 (cited in note 8); Dumas Malone, Jefferson and the Ordeal of Liberty 69–73 (Little, Brown, 1962).

[54]Henfield's Case, 11 Fed Cas 1099 (No 6,350), Wharton's State Trials 49 (CCD Pa 1793). See also Chief Justice Jay's similar charge to a grand jury in the District of Virginia, printed in 11 Fed Cas at 1100–03, Wharton's State Trials at 49, and 3 Jay Papers at 478; Julius Goebel, Jr, 1 History of the Supreme Court of the United States: Antecedents and Beginnings to 1801 624–27 (Macmillan, 1971). Attorney General Randolph, in an opinion rendered to the Secretary of State, had concluded that Henfield's actions were punishable as violations of the peace treaties and of "the common law . . . of disturbing the peace." 1 Am St Papers (Foreign Relations) at 152. Article VI made treaties, as Randolph called them, the law of the land; whether their peace provisions should be construed as self-executing was a more difficult matter. See Henkin, Foreign Affairs and the Constitution at 156–60 (cited in note 27).

[55]See Letter of Thomas Jefferson to Gouverneur Morris, Aug 16, 1793, 4 Jefferson Writings (Wash ed) at 31, 38, reprinted in 11 Fed Cas at 1122.

[56]Elkins & McKitrick at 353; cf Miller at 135 (a jury "strongly predisposed in favor of France").

[57]See Jules Lobel, The Rise and Decline of the Neutrality Act: Sovereignty and Congressional War Powers in United States Foreign Policy, 24 Harv Int'l LJ 1, 14 (1983); Thomas, American Neutrality at 173 (cited in note 8) (semble).

In any event the acquittal of Henfield was a severe blow to the policy of neutrality.[58] Accepting the view of the majority of his Cabinet that there was no need to call Congress into special session,[59] Washington made neutrality his first order of business when the Third Congress met in December 1793, informing the lawmakers of what he had done to preserve the peace and urging them "to extend the legal code and the jurisdiction of the Courts of the United States to many cases which, though dependent on principles already recognised, demand some further provisions."[60] Without recorded objection each House promptly praised the President for issuing his proclamation,[61] and Congress prescribed punishment for a number of crimes including those with which Henfield had been charged[62]—in exercise of its indisputable authority "to define and punish . . . offenses against the law of nations."[63]

[58]See John Marshall, 5 Life of Washington 358 (AMS, 1805).

[59]Jefferson had favored a special session, in part "[b]ecause several Legislative provisions are wanting to enable the government to steer steadily through the difficulties daily produced by the war of Europe, and to prevent our being involved in it by the incidents and perplexities to which it is constantly giving birth." Opinion of Aug 4, 1793, relative to the propriety of convening the Legislature at an earlier period than that fixed by law, 9 Jefferson Writings (Wash ed) at 441–42.

[60]4 Annals at 10–11.

[61]Id at 17–18 (Senate), 138 (House). As early as August Jefferson, recognizing the breadth of popular support for neutrality, had advised Madison that congressional Republicans should endorse neutrality without quibbling over who had the power to proclaim it. Letter of Thomas Jefferson to James Madison, Aug 11, 1793, 15 Madison Papers at 56, 57.

[62]1 Stat 381 (June 5, 1794). Despite Jefferson's admonition (see note 61), support for the legislation was far from unanimous; the House divided sharply over many details of the bill, and Vice-President Adams had to break a tie to pass it in the Senate. See 4 Annals at 68, 743–57. The current version of this statute, originally intended to be temporary, is found at 18 USC § § 958–66 (1988 & Supp 1993).

On March 24, 1794, Washington issued a second proclamation warning that the enlistment of troops in Kentucky to attack the territories of a friendly power (Spain) was "contrary to the laws of nations" and calling on "courts, magistrates, and other officers" to suppress it. 1 Richardson at 157–58. Since the Neutrality Act had not yet been adopted, this proclamation too was based on the theory that the President had authority to enforce the unwritten law of nations. For a brief sketch of the background of this proclamation see Thomas, American Neutrality at 177–86 (cited in note 8).

[63]See United States v Arjona, 120 US 479, 488 (1887) (dictum); Letter of James Madison to Thomas Jefferson, Apr 2, 1798, 17 Madison Papers at 104–05. For the argument that the Neutrality Act went beyond the existing requirements of the law of nations see Lobel, The Rise and Decline of the Neutrality Act at 16–29 (cited in note 57); for the view that the true basis of the statute lies in Congress's war powers see id at 28.

Other issues of presidential authority over foreign affairs were debated within the executive branch during the same period. In April, 1793, as it approved Washington's neutrality proclamation, the Cabinet unanimously agreed that he should receive the new French minister, Edmond Genêt. Although Hamilton argued that to receive Genêt was to recognize the new French government, no one suggested consulting Congress—though Madison was soon to argue that the President's authority to "receive ambassadors and other foreign ministers" (Art II, § 3) was purely ceremonial. See Anas, 25 Jefferson Papers at 666, 9 Jefferson Writings (Wash ed) at 142–43; Helvidius No 3, 15 Madison Papers at 96–98 (quoting Hamilton's Federalist No 69); Thomas, American Neutrality 68–77 (cited in note 8); Corwin, Office and Powers at 213 (cited in note 17); Miller at 129 & n 5 (noting that Jefferson had already instructed Gouverneur Morris (in a letter dated Mar 12, 1793, 25 Jefferson Papers at 367) to deal with the new French government).

After receiving written opinions from the Cabinet, Washington also rejected Hamilton's suggestion that the change of government had "suspended" U.S. obligations under the 1778 treaties with France, thus avoiding the difficult constitutional question whether the President alone could terminate a treaty. See Anas, 25 Jefferson Papers at 666, 9 Jefferson Writings (Wash ed) at 143; Pacificus No 1, 15 Hamilton Papers at 41–42; Helvidius No 3, 15 Madison Papers at 98–101; Thomas, supra, at 54–66; Goldwater v Carter, 444 US 996 (1979). Finally, when it became necessary to ask for recall of the impossible Genêt for continually flouting

II. DEFENSE

At the same time President Washington informed the House and Senate of what he had done to keep us out of war, he urged them to strengthen our defenses. For our best efforts to stay out of trouble might not succeed, and in any event, "[i]f we desire to avoid insult, we must repel it; if we desire to secure peace, . . . it must be known that we are at all times ready for war."[64] Congress took its time in responding, but ultimately it enacted a package of defense measures that illuminated a number of aspects of congressional war powers.

A.   The Scope of Federal Authority

Acting pursuant to its explicit authority "to raise and support armies,"[65] Congress provided for the fortification of designated harbors,[66] the establishment of arsenals and armories,[67] and the enlistment of additional troops.[68] Similarly, although no Navy Department was yet established,[69] Congress laid the foundation of the Navy by authoriz-

---

our neutrality, it was Washington as arbiter of our diplomatic relations (again presumably under the authority to receive foreign envoys) who made the decision on the basis of a unanimous Cabinet recommendation and Jefferson who willingly carried it out, without suggesting that Congress should have any say in the matter. See *Anas,* Aug 1, 1793, 9 Jefferson Writings Wash ed) at 162; Corwin, supra, at 213; Miller at 131–39; Elkins & McKitrick at 351–52.

[64]4 Annals at 12.

[65]US Const, Art I, § 8, cl 12.

[66]1 Stat 345 (Mar 20, 1794). Section 3 of the statute authorized the President to accept any land ceded for this purpose by a state under Art I, § 8, cl 17, which expressly mentions "forts, magazines, arsenals, [and] dock-yards." Recognizing that national defenses ought not to depend on the will of any individual state, the same section added authority to acquire the necessary land by purchase, indicating an understanding that clause 17 was not meant to limit the authority implicit in other provisions but only to provide a means for acquiring the power of "exclusive legislation" over areas acquired for the stated purposes. See Fort Leavenworth RR v Lowe, 114 US 525 (1885).

A different question of the meaning of clause 17 was raised when the President called Congress's attention to the fact that several states had qualified their cessions of lighthouses to the United States by reserving the right to serve process within the ceded areas. 4 Annals at 36. Congress responded by approving these reservations, suggesting that it read the constitutional provision giving it the power of "exclusive legislation" over such areas not to require it to exclude state authority entirely. 1 Stat 426 (Mar 2, 1795). Compare the discussion in chapter 2 of Congress's decision to leave state law temporarily in force in the District set aside for the seat of government.

[67]1 Stat 352 (Apr 2, 1794).

[68]1 Stat 366 (May 9, 1794). See also 1 Stat 430 (Mar 3, 1795). In a paragraph largely devoted to improvement of the militia Washington alluded to the desirability of providing "an opportunity for the study of those branches of the military art which can scarcely ever be attained by practice alone." 4 Annals at 12. Jefferson had advised the President a few days earlier that Congress had no authority to establish a military academy, though it seems preposterous to deny that the power to raise and support armies includes the power to train them. See *Anas,* Nov 23, 1793, 9 Jefferson Writings (Wash ed) at 182. Congress did not act on Washington's suggestion; it was not until 1802 that the academy at West Point was founded, and then on the initiative of President Jefferson. See 2 Stat 132, 137, § 27 (Mar 16, 1802); James Ripley Jacobs, The Beginning of the U.S. Army, 1783–1812 280, 288–89, 297–99 (Princeton, 1947).

[69]Earlier in the session Madison had bravely opposed the creation of a Navy on the ground that it would be cheaper to go on paying tribute to the Barbary pirates. 4 Annals at 433. See also id at 434 (Rep. Baldwin); White at 156–57.

ing the construction or purchase of six frigates[70] and ten galleys[71] under its power "to provide and maintain a navy."[72] In addition, Congress authorized the President to require the executives of the various states to hold a specified number of militiamen "in readiness to march at a moment's warning,"[73] presumably as an incident to calling them out, under the authority provided two years earlier, to repel any possible invasion.[74]

Less obvious perhaps in their constitutional bases were two further measures taken by the Third Congress: a ban on arms exports[75] and an embargo on the departure of ships bound for foreign ports.[76] In the literal sense both were regulations of foreign commerce, unless one is prepared to accept a distinction between regulations and prohibitions that is more verbal than substantial[77] and that cannot be justified in terms of the known purposes of the commerce clause.[78] The protective tariff provisions enacted in 1789 had established without dissent that the power to regulate commerce included the power to restrict it.[79] Moreover, both the ban on arms exports and the embargo could be defended as exercises of the war powers, the former to ensure an adequate supply of arms for our own defense[80] and both to prevent incidents that belligerent nations might view as cause for war.[81] What

[70]1 Stat 350 (Mar 27, 1794).

[71]1 Stat 376 (June 5, 1794).

[72]US Const, Art I, § 8, cl 13.

[73]1 Stat 367 (May 9, 1794).

[74]See chapter 3; US Const, Art I, § 8, cl 15. The modern eye may be struck by the fact that this statute imposed affirmative obligations on state officers, but Congress had done so before in the militia context (also discussed in chapter 3), and this time too there was no constitutional objection.

[75]1 Stat 369 (May 22, 1794).

[76]The embargo was first imposed for thirty days and then extended for thirty-seven more. 1 Stat 400 (Mar 26, 1794); 1 Stat 401 (Apr 18, 1794).

[77]Every regulation prohibits something, and every prohibition of one aspect of commerce is a regulation of commerce as a whole.

[78]See chapter 2. Madison emphasized those purposes in moving to protect our foreign commerce by enacting retaliatory tariff, tonnage, and trade restrictions against Britain, as Jefferson had recently proposed. See 4 Annals at 155–56, 209; 1 Am St Papers (Foreign Relations) at 300; Elkins & McKitrick at 375–88.

Madison would have used the resulting revenue to indemnify victims of British depredations. 4 Annals at 156, 157. Others advocated indemnity as well. See id at 535 (Rep. Dayton), 614 (Rep. Goodhue). No one challenged Congress's authority to provide it. Madison defended indemnity on the basis of the law of nations without saying why that was a source of congressional power; he might have argued it was necessary and proper to the encouragement of commerce. Compare the arguments for indemnity of officers and others injured in the Whiskey Rebellion, which was defended as a means of encouraging support for suppressing the insurrection and thus as necessary and proper to enforcing the laws. See 4 Annals at 984–1002; text at note 128.

Dayton would have established a fund for indemnification by sequestering debts owed to British subjects, defending his proposal as part of the overall defense package. 4 Annals at 535. Boudinot, who opposed this measure on policy grounds, conceded that the power to sequester debts in reprisal for hostile acts was both recognized by the law of nations and implicit in the greater power to declare war. Id at 537. See Miller at 151–52 (adding that Hamilton "did not doubt that sequestration would lead to war . . . in the worst of causes—to enable debtors to escape from paying their creditors their just dues").

[79]See chapter 2.

[80]The title of the Act described one of its purposes as "encouraging the importation" of arms, and § 5 removed import duties on arms for a period of two years. See 1 Stat at 369, 370.

[81]Representative Sedgwick, who proposed the embargo, defended it as a means of preventing Great Britain from supplying her Caribbean possessions in the event of an attack on the French West Indies. See 4 Annals at 500–04. In 1793, however, Jefferson had denied that either the law of nations or U.S. policy required a ban on selling arms to belligerents; it was enough that the proclamation had warned arms traders that

was significant, as so often is the case, was the nonbarking dog. Though the Federalists were to scream constitutional objections to Jefferson's embargo in 1807,[82] nobody even hinted that an embargo was beyond Congress's power in 1794.[83]

In order to finance this array of defense measures[84] Congress increased tariffs on specified imports[85] and imposed excises on retailers of wines and foreign spirits,[86] on snuff and refined sugar,[87] and on auction sales.[88] There was no serious constitutional objection to any of these measures. Tariffs had been enacted in 1789, and the new excises were indistinguishable from that assessed on whiskey producers in 1791.[89]

A levy of one to ten dollars to be paid by the owners of carriages, attacked as a "direct" tax not apportioned among the states according to population as required by Article I, §§ 2 and 9, provoked a significant debate over the meaning of the vague constitutional term. Samuel Dexter and John Nicholas agreed that (as Dexter put it) "all taxes are direct which are paid by the citizen without being recompensed by the consumer" but differed as to whether the carriage tax could be passed on.[90] Murray thought the tax on carriages no different from that previously imposed on stills; Samuel Smith responded that, unlike carriages, stills were taxed only when they were used.[91] Sedgwick anticipated the argument that was to dominate the opinions of the several Justices when the tax was upheld by the Supreme Court: "[I]t would astonish the people of America to learn that they had made a Constitution by which pleasure carriages and other objects of luxury were excepted from contributing to the public exigencies"; and "[a]s several of the States

---

the Government would not protect them. See Letter of Thomas Jefferson to George Hammond, May 15, 1793, 3 Jefferson Writings (Wash ed) at 557, 558–59; Thomas, American Neutrality at 247–50 (cited in note 8). See also Miller at 154, arguing that the embargo was "[i]ntended to prevent the capture of American ships by British cruisers."

[82]See United States v The Brigantine William, 28 Fed Cas 614 (No 16,700) (D Mass 1808) (upholding the embargo on both commerce and war-power grounds); Warren, 1 The Supreme Court at 341–51 (cited in note 38).

[83]Alexander White, who had recently left Congress, defended the embargo as "connected with War as with commerce": "Congress having the sole power in both these cases, their right to lay an Embargo will hardly be disputed." Letter of Alexander White to James Madison, Mar 30, 1794, 15 Madison Papers at 297, 298.

[84]House members whined so over the inequity of each proposal for new taxes that Representative Dexter was moved at one point to remind his colleagues that "[i]f we have the benefits of Government, we must pay for them." 4 Annals at 628.

[85]1 Stat 390 (June 7, 1794).

[86]1 Stat 376 (June 5, 1794).

[87]1 Stat 384 (June 5, 1794).

[88]1 Stat 397 (June 9, 1794).

[89]See chapter 2.

[90]4 Annals at 646. Dexter was a Massachusetts lawyer who served one term in the House; he later became a Federalist Senator and briefly served under President Adams as Secretary of War and of the Treasury. Nicholas, a freshman from Virginia, served until 1801 and became an important Republican spokesman. See also Letter of Alexander White to James Madison, May 19, 1794, 15 Madison Papers at 335–36 (agreeing with Nicholas that the tax could not be passed on); 1 Tucker's Blackstone at 233–34 (concluding on this basis that a tax on wheels would be indirect if assessed against the wheelwright but not if assessed against the carriage owner).

[91]4 Annals at 653. See also id at 730 (Rep. Ames) (insisting that "the [carriage] duty falls not on the possession, but the use").

had few or no carriages, no such apportionment could be made."[92] The tax was enacted;[93] the debates do not reveal a consensus as to why it was not "direct."

B.   The President and Congress

More important at the time than the questions of federalism raised by the defense measures taken by the Third Congress were those of the separation of powers.

Representative Sedgwick had originally proposed that the decision whether to impose an embargo be left to the President: "On great occasions, confidence must be reposed in the Executive."[94] Congress's decision to impose the embargo by joint resolution suggests a preference for reserving to itself the basic policy decision. Yet before adjourning Congress delegated to the President authority to lay a new embargo during the legislative recess "whenever, in his opinion, the public safety shall so require" and "under such regulations as the circumstances . . . may require,"[95] and no one is reported as suggesting any constitutional problem.[96] Similarly, although the number of galleys the President could construct or acquire was limited to ten after Madison insisted the statute must specify a number,[97] no one is recorded as having objected to the fact that the President was given virtually unlimited discretion to resolve the more fundamental question whether to build them at all, the statute authorizing him to do so if it "shall appear to him necessary for the protection of the United States."[98]

The absence of objection was the more notable because, just a few days before, the House had emphatically rejected a bill that would have authorized but not required the President to raise an additional 10,000 troops after Giles and Madison had complained that it effectively transferred to the President Congress's power "to raise . . . armies"[99]— an especially dangerous delegation, Madison added, in view of the Framers' clear decision to separate the power to raise troops from the power to command them.[100]

---

[92]Id at 644–45. Cf Hylton v United States, 3 US 171 (1796); The First Hundred Years at 31–37. A direct tax, which several members assumed would fall upon land, was rejected on policy grounds. See 4 Annals at 640–47.

[93]1 Stat 373 (June 5, 1794).

[94]4 Annals at 502, 503.

[95]1 Stat 372 (June 4, 1794). The discretion given by this statute was far broader than than upheld in the famous case of The Aurora, 11 US 382 (1813), where the Court struggled to demonstrate that in determining whether England or France had ceased violating our neutrality the President was merely making a finding of fact. See The First Hundred Years at 118–19.

[96]Alexander White, noting the inconvenience of requiring passage of a statute when Congress might not be in session, wrote Madison that he saw "no objection" to authorizing the President to lay an embargo "under proper regulations." Letter of Alexander White to James Madison, Mar 30, 1794, 15 Madison Papers at 297, 298. Along the same lines, just before its final adjournment the Third Congress empowered the President to permit the export of arms, despite the statute it had earlier enacted, "in cases connected with the security of the commercial interest of the United States." 1 Stat 444 (Mar 3, 1795).

[97]4 Annals at 762. See also id at 764 (Rep. Dayton). Neither Madison nor Dayton expressly invoked the Constitution.

[98]1 Stat 376, § 1 (June 5, 1794).

[99]4 Annals at 735, 738.

[100]Id at 738. See also Madison's "Political Observations" of Apr 20, 1795, 15 Madison Papers at 511, 521. Most of the appropriation laws of the Third Congress followed the pattern of specificity set by the Second Congress. See 1 Stat 342 (Mar 14, 1794); 1 Stat 346 (Mar 21, 1794); 1 Stat 394 (June 9, 1794); 1 Stat 405 (Jan 2, 1795); 1 Stat 438 (Mar 3, 1795). An unexplained exception was the provision of "a sum not exceeding five

Madison thus succeeded in preventing a delegation to the President of discretion whether or not to raise troops, but not in his further effort to provide that the troops that were raised "should only be employed for the protection of the frontier."[101] He did not argue that the Constitution limited the discretion the President could be given in determining how the troops should be employed, and indeed one can make the converse argument that his proposal would impermissibly have *limited* the President's constitutional authority as Commander in Chief.[102] The same policy of separation that Madison invoked to deny that the President could raise troops, combined with the Framers' patent desire to avoid the inefficiencies and dangers of entrusting tactical and strategic decisions to a committee,[103] suggests that Congress infringes the President's powers if it attempts to exercise the power of command. The counterargument is that defining the purposes for which troops can be used is not a question of military tactics or strategy but rather one of those basic policy decisions reserved to Congress by the various grants of legislative war powers. Arguably the question whether to employ troops is implicit in the question whether to fight, which Congress makes under its authority to declare war; arguably the power to raise troops includes authority to determine the purposes for which they may be used.[104]

Yet another kind of separation-of-powers objection was raised when Abraham Clark of New Jersey asked the House to go beyond the embargo to forbid the importation of any articles produced in Great Britain or Ireland.[105] Defended as a classic regulation of commerce, which it was,[106] this "nonintercourse" proposal was assailed as an invasion of the power of the President and Senate to make treaties. For the preamble of Clark's resolution revealed that its purpose was to put economic pressure on Britain to make reparations for violations of our neutral rights and to evacuate forts within our territory still occupied in defiance of the 1783 peace treaty.[107] President Washington, as Sedgwick observed, had just sent a special envoy to England to negotiate on those very issues; to ban imports until Britain yielded on those points would dictate to the President what treaty to make.[108]

If this argument sounds familiar, it is because it is essentially the converse of the ar-

---

hundred thousand dollars . . . towards defraying the expense of the military establishment" during 1795, 1 Stat 404, 405, § 2 (Dec 31, 1793). See also chapter 3.

[101]His proposed amendment to this effect received only 26 votes. See 4 Annals at 1221.

[102]US Const, Art II, § 2. This argument was apparently not made either; both sides treated the question as one purely of policy.

[103]"Of all the cares or concerns of government, the direction of war most peculiarly demands those qualities which distinguish the exercise of power by a single hand." The Federalist No 74 (Hamilton).

[104]Interesting arguments on both sides of this question were made during the Fifth Congress when Republicans endeavored to limit the uses to which the President could put new ships that he was authorized to build or acquire. See 7 Annals at 289–97, 364–67; 8 Annals at 1440–59.

[105]4 Annals at 561. Passed by the House, the proposal was defeated by the Vice-President's tiebreaking vote in the Senate. See 4 Annals at 605, 90; Miller at 154.

[106]See The Federalist Nos 11, 22 (Hamilton) (defending the grant of authority over foreign commerce as a means of enabling Congress to retaliate for foreign commercial restrictions).

[107]4 Annals at 561. Washington had complained of interference with our commerce by both Britain and France in a letter to Congress at the beginning of the session, 4 Annals at 15.

[108]4 Annals at 569–70. See also id at 584 (Rep. William Smith), 589 (Rep. Dexter). Since the President had already appointed a negotiator, an unidentified speaker added, Congress had no right to interfere. Id at 600.

guments the friends of France had made against the Neutrality Proclamation.[109] By committing us to peace, it was then urged, the President obstructed Congress's authority to declare war; by cutting off trade, it was now insisted, Congress would impede the President in exercising the treaty power.

One can distinguish the cases, if one likes, on the ground that in issuing his proclamation President Washington disclaimed any intention of committing the country to anything more than an observance of its international obligations pending Congress's decision whether or not to declare war. On a more fundamental plane, however, both incidents demonstrate the perspicacity of Hamilton's insight in defense of the proclamation: In many matters involving foreign relations the President and Congress have overlapping powers.[110] Congress's authority to regulate commerce is as explicit as the President's authority to negotiate treaties. What one may do may frustrate the exercise of authority by the other. But there is no warrant in the Constitution for giving precedence to either; this is one of those situations in which, for better or worse, the Framers knowingly sacrificed coherence and efficiency in the interest of separation of powers.

III.   ST. DOMINGO

The most important spending controversy during the Third Congress concerned appropriations for the relief of refugees from disturbances in the French colony on the West Indian island of Hispaniola, known in the debates by the name of St. Domingo.

A number of French citizens had landed in Baltimore in the last days of 1793,[111] where they had been supported by private and state contributions. Responding to a petition for federal assistance, a House committee urged that federal funds be made available,[112] and they were;[113] but not until after yet another debate on the limits of the power to spend.

Virtually everyone wanted to help. John Nicholas of Virginia, doubting that Congress had authority "to bestow the money of their constituents on an act of charity," declared his willingness to tell the voters he had exceeded his powers and throw himself on their mercy.[114] "In a case of this kind," Clark trumpeted, "we were not to be tied up by the Constitution."[115]

Elias Boudinot, always an exponent of broad federal authority, trotted out the general welfare clause once again.[116] But although he professed to think it obvious that relief of Caribbean refugees came within that provision, it was not; even so generous an interpreter as Justice Story would later express doubt that the "general welfare of the United States" would be served by expenditures for building foreign palaces or "for propagating Mahometanism among the Turks."[117]

---

[109]See text at notes 11–16.

[110]Pacificus No 1, 15 Hamilton Papers at 40–42.

[111]See 4 Annals at 169–70 (Rep. Samuel Smith).

[112]See 1 Am St Papers (Foreign Relations) at 308 (Jan 10, 1794).

[113]6 Stat 13 (Feb 12, 1794).

[114]4 Annals at 170, 172.

[115]Id at 350. Cf William Smith's argument, in opposition to the Giles Resolutions, respecting the right to ignore limitations in appropriation laws in an emergency (discussed in chapter 3).

[116]4 Annals at 172.

[117]2 Story, § 919.

As in the recent codfish controversy,[118] Madison found a way out of the dilemma that would enable Congress to satisfy the obligations of fraternité without "establishing a dangerous precedent, which might hereafter be perverted to the countenance of purposes very different from those of charity." The United States owed money to France for assistance provided during the Revolution; Congress should authorize relief for the refugees in partial payment of this obligation.[119] That is what Congress did,[120] and thus the question of the meaning of the general welfare clause was avoided once again.[121]

IV. INSURRECTION

Congress was not in session in August 1794, when resistance to the liquor excise in western Pennsylvania became ugly. Pursuant to the authority Congress had given him two years before,[122] President Washington recited Justice Wilson's finding that ordinary processes were insufficient to enforce the laws, ordered the insurgents to disperse, and gave notice that he was taking steps to call out the militia.[123] When this warning was ignored he marched the militia to the rebellious counties in person, and the insurrection melted before him.[124]

By the time Congress reassembled in November it was all over. The President told Congress what he had done.[125] Congress commended him[126] and appropriated money to cover the cost of the expedition, which he had properly undertaken in the expectation that Congress would pay for it later.[127] Congress also authorized the expenditure of $8,500 to indemnify federal officers and citizens who had supported them for property destroyed by the mob—an expenditure obviously necessary and proper, like the officers' salaries, to the execution of the laws.[128] The President sensibly pardoned all who had taken part in the

[118]See chapter 3.

[119]4 Annals at 170–71. One of the express purposes for which taxes may be laid and collected is "to pay the debts . . . of the United States." US Const, Art I, § 8, cl 1.

[120]See 6 Stat at 13, § 3: "[T]he amount thereof shall be provisionally charged to the debit of the French Republic, subject to such future arrangements as shall be made thereon, between the government of the United States and the said Republic."

[121]A month later, following the precedent of subsidy by tax forgiveness established in the codfish case, Congress also forgave the tonnage duties assessed on the ship that had brought the refugees to this country. 1 Stat 342 (Mar 7, 1794).

[122]See chapter 3.

[123]See 1 Richardson at 158 (Aug 7, 1794). As early as 1792 the President had warned against obstruction of the laws and directed federal officers to enforce them. Id at 124 (Apr 5, 1792).

[124]See Washington's proclamation of Sept 25, 1794, id at 161, announcing that the militia was on its way. The story is told concisely in Miller at 155–59 and in Sharp at 93–98, and less so in Elkins & McKitrick at 461–88. The most complete account is Thomas P. Slaughter, The Whiskey Rebellion (Oxford, 1986).

[125]4 Annals at 787–91.

[126]See id at 794 (Senate), 947–48 (House). At the President's request Congress authorized him to call up additional militiamen to prevent a new outbreak of violence, 1 Stat 403 (Nov 29, 1794), since the obligations of those initially summoned were about to expire. See 4 Annals at 790.

[127]1 Stat 404 (Dec 31, 1794). Gallatin thought Washington should have called a special session of Congress, since the funds he used had been appropriated for the army, not for the militia. A Sketch of the Finances of the United States, 3 Gallatin Writings at 69, 117–18. See the discussion of this problem in connection with the Giles Resolutions in chapter 3.

[128]1 Stat 423 (Feb 27, 1795). See 4 Annals at 996 (Rep. Hartley): "When the officers know that they are to be protected in their persons and property—when the *posse comitatus* are informed that they are to be regarded in like manner—we may expect energy in the execution of the laws." Congress also amended the law

uprising,[129] including—in accord with the understanding expressed in the Philadelphia Convention—those who had not yet been put on trial.[130]

Thus the Whiskey Rebellion came to a happy end; the new Government had survived its first crisis, to nearly everyone's satisfaction, and it had acted in full compliance with the Constitution. Along the way, however, the President had made one serious mistake. In his otherwise measured address to Congress he had accused "certain self-created societies" of encouraging the insurrection.[131]

Everyone knew what "societies" the President had in mind: the Democratic Societies, sometimes disparagingly called Jacobin Clubs, which had sprung up all over the country in the enthusiasm created by the French Revolution.[132] When Fitzsimons moved to insert in the House's ceremonial reply to the President's speech a paragraph expressing "reprobation" of these societies,[133] the friends of France exploded in wrath. If the societies offended the law, said Giles, let them be brought to justice; but it was not the House's business to act as a board of censure or "to attempt checking public opinion."[134] The Constitution gave Congress no authority to denounce private associations; members of the Societies had "the inalienable privilege of thinking, of speaking, or writing, and of printing"; the proposal "confounded the innocent with the guilty" and condemned them all without a hearing.[135] Madison, who had voted with Giles less than two years earlier to condemn Alexander Hamilton without a hearing,[136] called the measure a

---

defining the occasions on which the President could call out the militia, eliminating some of the restrictions enacted in 1792. 1 Stat 424 (Feb 28, 1795); see also chapter 3. Washington's plea that Congress also strengthen the provisions respecting organization of the militia, however, fell on deaf ears despite powerful arguments by Sedgwick and others in favor of a vigorous exercise of congressional authority. See 4 Annals at 791, 1067–71. The principal problem, spelled out in a report from the Secretary of War, was that Congress had required militiamen to arm themselves but provided no penalties to enforce the requirement, as even Giles conceded it had power to do. See id at 1396–97, 1071.

[129]In his proclamation Washington had branded the insurrection as "treason," 1 Richardson at 158, and two of the insurgents were convicted of that offense after Justice Paterson charged the jury that if the object of the revolt was "to suppress the excise offices and prevent the execution of an act of Congress," it met the constitutional definition of treason. United States v Mitchell, 26 F Cas 1277, 1281 (No 15,788), Wharton's State Trials 176, 182 (CCD Pa 1795). As an original matter there seems to have been something to the argument of the defense (id at 179, 26 F Cas at 1279) that not every case of organized resistance to the laws rose to the level of "levying war" against the United States, as Article III, § 3 required.

[130]See 1 Richardson at 181 (July 10, 1795); 2 Farrand at 426; Philip B. Kurland, Watergate and the Constitution 136–48 (Chicago, 1978). See also Forrest McDonald, The American Presidency: An Intellectual History 240 (Kansas, 1994) (arguing that by issuing a blanket amnesty Washington construed the pardon power to give him authority to make general dispensations of the laws); Corwin, Office and Powers at 137 (cited in note 17) (arguing that in light of common law tradition the pardon power should not have been construed to embrace a general amnesty).

[131]4 Annals at 788. See Letter of James Madison to James Monroe, Dec 4, 1794, 15 Madison Papers at 405, 406 ("perhaps the greatest error of his political life"). For the depth of Washington's feelings against these societies see his letters in 33 Washington Writings at 475–76, 506–07, 524.

[132]See Miller at 160–62; Elkins & McKitrick at 451–61; Sharp at 85–89.

[133]4 Annals at 899.

[134]Id at 899–901. See also id at 905 (Rep. Nicholas): "I cannot agree to persecution for the sake of opinions." "There was not an individual in America," Giles added, "who might not come under the charge of being a member of some one or other self-created society. Associations of this kind, religious, political, and philosophical, were to be found in every quarter of the Continent." Id at 899–900.

[135]Id at 916–19.

[136]See chapter 3.

bill of attainder;[137] Thomas Carnes of Georgia said it would infringe freedom of speech and assembly.[138]

For a week the House debated nothing but its reply to the President's speech. The occasion was trivial but the principle important; the debate was a preview of the arguments over the Sedition Act.[139] Murray said he would not vote to abolish the Democratic Societies, but he saw nothing wrong in warning the people against them;[140] Madison responded that, as the infamous list of "subversive" organizations compiled by the Attorney General taught us a century and a half later, denunciation was punishment too.[141] Dexter's defense of the censure proposal was even more sinister. Ames had already argued, with considerable justice, that the right of assembly did not embrace a conspiracy to obstruct the laws;[142] Dexter asserted that the Constitution gave no one "the precious right of vilifying and misrepresenting their own Government and laws."[143] Ames assailed the Societies for their secrecy[144] and professed to find the very existence of private associations as intermediaries between citizens and their government a threat to republican principles.[145]

[137]4 Annals at 934. Madison did not advert to the effort to besmirch Hamilton, but he distinguished the investigation of General St. Clair on the ground that, unlike the Democratic Societies, St. Clair was employed "in the public service." Id at 935.

[138]"Sir, by this amendment you would prevent the freedom of speech, and lock the mouths of men." Id at 941. See also Letter of Thomas Jefferson to James Madison, Dec 28, 1794, 15 Madison Papers at 426–27: "It is wonderful indeed that the President should have permitted himself to be the organ of such an attack on the freedom of discussion, the freedom of writing, printing & publishing."

[139]See Irving Brant, James Madison: Father of the Constitution, 1787–1800 419 (Bobbs-Merrill, 1950).

[140]4 Annals at 906–07. William Smith added that the House had had no hesitation in expressing opinions on matters outside its legislative competence when, at the insistence of many of those who objected to criticizing the Democratic Societies, it had applauded the new French constitution. Id at 942; see note 17.

[141]4 Annals at 934. Madison was even more emphatic in private:

> It must be seen that no two principles can be either more indefensible in reason, or more dangerous in practice—than that 1. arbitrary denunciations may punish, what the law permits, & what the Legislature has no right, by law, to prohibit—and that 2. the Govt. may stifle all censures on its misdoings; for if it be itself the Judge it will never allow any censures to be just, and if it can suppress censures flowing from one lawful source it may those flowing from any other—from the press and from individuals as well as from Societies, &c.

Letter of James Madison to James Monroe, Dec 4, 1794, 15 Madison Papers at 405, 407. For the Attorney General's list see The Second Century at 357.

[142]4 Annals at 922.

[143]Id at 937. See also id at 923 (Rep. Ames) (accusing the Societies of spreading, in Washington's words, "'jealousies, suspicions, and accusations of the Government'").

[144]"I would just ask, however, [w]hether they meet in darkness; whether they hide their names, their numbers, and their doings; whether they shut their doors to admit information?" 4 Annals at 923. See also id at 902 (Rep. William Smith). "Is there no other place," Giles asked in reply, "where people bolt their doors, and vote in the dark? Is there not a branch of our Legislature which transacts its business in this way?" Id at 919. The Senate, the reader will recall, still had not admitted the public to its deliberations.

[145]Political societies, he argued, served as "a substitute for representation"; when they acted in the name of those who were not members, they committed "an usurpation"; the result was "the power of the few over the many"; "[i]f the clubs prevail, they will be the Government." 4 Annals at 923–25. See also id at 910 (Rep. Dexter): "Such societies are proper in a country where Government is despotic, but it is improper that such societies should exist in a free country [sic] like the United States." For discussion of this point of view see Sharp at 100–03.

Cooler heads ultimately prevailed, and the response was watered down by a large majority:

> And we learn, with the greatest concern, that any misrepresentations whatever, of the Government and its proceedings, either by individuals or combinations of men, should have been made, and so far credited as to foment the flagrant outrage which has been committed on the laws.[146]

There was no denunciation of the Democratic Societies as such, by name or by innuendo; there was no disparagement of the right to associate; "concern" over "misrepresentations" is not necessarily inconsistent with the right to criticize the Government. But the gulf between the developing parties in Congress was deeper and more hostile than ever, and it was clear that some members had a pretty narrow view of what the first amendment meant by freedom of speech.

V.   CITIZENSHIP

Congress had passed a hospitable naturalization law in 1790.[147] It passed a more niggardly one in 1795.[148]

The new statute clarified two important points left unanswered in 1790. First, it mooted the controversy whether Congress's naturalization power was exclusive, as its purpose seemed to suggest,[149] by providing that citizenship could be acquired only as provided in the Act itself.[150] The uncontested assumption seemed to be that exclusivity was necessary and proper to the exercise of congressional authority to provide a "uniform" rule, as it clearly was.

The second clarification was to make it explicit that naturalization proceedings could be brought in federal as well as state courts.[151] It was surely appropriate that some federal agency share the burden of passing upon applications for national citizenship. To the twentieth-century observer it is less obvious that that agency should be the courts. As under the pension law, which the courts had struck down for other reasons,[152] the typical proceeding was ex parte; unless the Government chose to oppose a particular application—which the 1795 statute did not say it had the right to do—, it was difficult to see how there was a "case" or "controversy" of the adversarial nature we have come to understand that Article III requires.[153] There is no suggestion in the Annals that anyone in Congress shared this understanding in 1795.

---

[146]4 Annals at 947.

[147]1 Stat 103 (Mar 26, 1790). See chapter 2.

[148]1 Stat 414 (Jan 29, 1795).

[149]See the materials cited in chapter 2.

[150]1 Stat 414, § 1.

[151]Id. The earlier statute had ambiguously provided for application to "any common law court of record, in any one of [several] states." See chapter 2.

[152]See Hayburn's Case, 2 US 409, 410–14 n (a) (1792) (discussed in chapter 3).

[153]Justice Brandeis would have to strain mightily to find a case or controversy when the question finally reached the Supreme Court a century and a quarter later. See Tutun v United States, 270 US 568 (1926); The Second Century at 182–83; Wheeler, 1973 S Ct Rev at 134 & n 61 (cited in note 50). The traditional judicial authority to issue search and arrest warrants, see US Const, Amend 4, seems difficult to reconcile with the modern perception that adversary proceedings are required; it seems to be understood today as a historical exception to the general rule.

But the main point of the new statute was to make it more difficult to become a citizen.[154] The two-year residence requirement was extended to five years. The applicant was required to announce his intention to become a citizen three years in advance and to renounce allegiance to his former sovereign.[155] More interesting to the constitutional scholar were two additional restrictions: The applicant was required to disclaim any foreign title or order of nobility and to have "behaved as a man of good moral character, attached to the principles of the constitution of the United States, and well disposed to [their] good order and happiness."[156]

The latter condition enjoyed broad support. Sedgwick had begun the debate by warning of the perils of unchecked immigration from despotic and war-torn Europe: People who had not been brought up in a republic could not be expected to absorb its virtues overnight, and people from nations at war with one another could not be expected to get along.[157] Giles, from the opposite end of the political spectrum, moved to require proof that the applicant was "attached to a Republican form of Government," in order "to prevent those poisonous communications from Europe, of which gentlemen were so much afraid."[158] There was much quibbling over the word "Republican," which had been appropriated by Madison and Jefferson's party; there was some objection to requiring the testimony of two witnesses, which was alleged to impose an undue burden on the poor.[159] Only Madison called attention to the more fundamental problem:

> It is hard to make a man swear that he preferred the Constitution of the United States, or to give any general opinion, because he may, in his own private judgment, think Monarchy or Aristocracy better and yet be honestly determined to support this Government as he finds it.[160]

He did not put this objection on constitutional grounds, but the bitter lessons of the McCarthy period enable us to do so: A test of political orthodoxy for dispensing government benefits impinges on values protected by the first amendment.[161]

Possibly in response to Madison's criticism, the requirement of actual endorsement of constitutional principles was replaced by the more innocuous insistence on a finding

---

[154]Dexter, in a speech badly truncated in the Annals, is said to have "described the present easy access to citizenship as dangerous and insufficient to prevent improper persons from being incorporated with the American people." Frank George Franklin, The Legislative History of Naturalization in the United States 49 (Chicago, 1906). Fears of unsuitable immigrants had been increased by the flood of refugees from the wars that broke out in the wake of the French Revolution. See the remarks of Representative Sedgwick noted in the text at note 155; James H. Kettner, The Development of American Citizenship, 1608–1870 240 (North Carolina, 1978).

[155]1 Stat at 414, § 1. The first two of these requirements, but not the third, were made inapplicable to persons already resident in the United States. Id at 415, § 2.

[156]Id at 414, § 1. The 1790 act had required only that the applicant be "of good character" and swear "to support the constitution of the United States." 1 Stat at 103, § 1.

[157]4 Annals at 1005–09.

[158]Id at 1021.

[159]Id at 1021–23.

[160]Id at 1022–23.

[161]See, e.g., Keyishian v Board of Regents, 385 US 589 (1967); The Second Century at 355–58; Harry Kalven, A Worthy Tradition: Freedom of Speech in America, ch 23 (Harper & Row, 1988). The tension was highlighted by Giles's frank admission that the purpose of his proposal was to keep out "poisonous" ideas. See text at note 158.

that the applicant had *behaved* like a person attached to our Constitution[162]—which was perhaps to say only that he must have been a law-abiding denizen. The doctrinal foundation for a constitutional attack on the original political test, moreover, was laid when the irrepressible Giles moved to add the requirement that the applicant renounce any preexisting titles.[163]

William Smith protested that Congress had no power to deprive anyone of his titles.[164] Dexter added the analogy that constitutionalized Madison's objection to a political test: "An alien might as well be obliged to make a renunciation of his connexions with the Jacobin club. The one was fully as abhorrent to the Constitution as the other."[165] Giles, echoed by Page, gave the response later made familiar by Justice Holmes: No one was being deprived of anything; the nobleman could keep his title by not becoming a citizen.[166]

Dexter threw the House into an uproar by blandly announcing that he would be happy to vote for the proposal if Giles would agree to an amendment requiring the applicant to renounce not only his titles but also his slaves.[167] Giles affected injury: "He was sorry to see slavery made a jest of in that House. . . . It had no proper connexion with the subject before the House."[168] John Heath of Virginia, who seldom spoke, swallowed the bait in a single gulp: Since Congress could not forbid the importation of slaves, it could not require their renunciation as a condition of citizenship.[169] That, of course, was pre-

---

[162]See text at note 156.

[163]4 Annals at 1030.

[164]Id at 1030–31.

[165]Id at 1031.

[166]Id at 1034 (Rep. Giles), 1035 (Rep. Page). Cf McAuliffe v Mayor of New Bedford, 155 Mass 216, 220, 29 NE 517, 517 (1892) (Holmes, J) ("no constitutional right to be a policeman"). Madison, who appeared to perceive the dangers of this approach, took a different tack that served to distinguish the Jacobin example: It was proper to require renunciation of hereditary titles because they were "proscribed by the Constitution." 4 Annals at 1035. See also id at 1039 (Rep. Scott). Uriah Tracy (Connecticut) set them straight: While Article I, § 9 forbade the United States to grant titles and federal officers to accept them, nothing in the Constitution prevented private citizens from receiving foreign titles, much less retaining those they had previously possessed. 4 Annals at 1053.

[167]Id at 1039. Thatcher twisted the knife by moving, as a second amendment, "and that he never will possess them." Id.

[168]Id at 1039. Similarly, when an unidentified member of the House suggested dropping the requirement that the militia be limited to white persons he was greeted with a cold reminder of political correctness: "[T]he subject was obviously and extremely improper for public discussion." Id at 1233–34. Yet it was the Third Congress that, in response to yet another petition from the Quakers (id at 249), forbade sailing from the United States for the purpose of exporting slaves or of transporting inhabitants of one foreign country into slavery in another. 1 Stat 347 (Mar 22, 1794). Neither of these provisions fell within the twenty-year moratorium on congressional powers contained in Article I, § 9; Congress evidently surmounted any doubts as to whether such provisions came within the commerce power, as the House had concluded in 1790. See chapter 2. The Annals report no debate on these interesting provisions.

[169]4 Annals at 1040. See also id at 1042 (Rep. McDowell). McDowell made a second and distinct argument against requiring renunciation of slaves: "What right had the House to say to a particular class of people, you shall not have that kind of property which other people have?" Id at 1042–43. He seemed to be suggesting that "naturalization" implied that new citizens, like new "states" under the Northwest Ordinance and the Supreme Court's interpretation of Article IV, were to be admitted on an equal footing with old ones. See Coyle v Oklahoma, 221 US 559 (1911), and the discussion of the Ordinance in chapter 2. The argument is quite plausible: There is no reason to think the Framers would have looked kindly on the prospect of second-class citizens. The same principle of equality may help to explain the cold shoulder the House had given in

cisely Dexter's point: Since Congress could not strip individuals of their titles directly, it could not do so by indirection.

Dexter's conclusion was not unavoidable; some discretion as to who is an acceptable member of the community is obviously implicit in the authority to enact a uniform naturalization rule. Yet Dexter's reminder that this discretion must be limited if it was not to impinge on individual or state rights was welcome. The House had already debated the difficult problem of unconstitutional conditions in 1791, when it voted down a proposal to limit the political activities of revenue officers.[170] The Third Congress decreed that new citizens renounce their titles but not their slaves;[171] its successors would have ample opportunities to wrestle with the analogous question of what conditions could permissibly be attached to federal grants[172] or to the admission of new states.[173]

VI.   THE ELEVENTH AMENDMENT

For the second time in two years a judicial interpretation of the Constitution commanded congressional attention. When the Justices had struck down the pension law in *Hayburn's Case*, Congress had amended the statute.[174] When the Supreme Court held in *Chisholm v Georgia* that one state could be sued by the citizens of another,[175] Congress decided it was the Constitution that needed amending.

The text of Article III seemed to support the *Chisholm* decision: "The judicial power shall extend to . . . controversies . . . between a state and citizens of another state." Suits against unconsenting sovereigns, however, were unknown when the Constitution was written; and prominent framers from Madison to Marshall had assured the country that nothing in Article III would permit the states to be sued.[176]

1790 to the suggestion that new citizens be denied the right to hold public office. See chapter 2; Kettner, The Development of American Citizenship at 237 (cited in note 154): "Congress generally agreed [in 1790] that the Constitution barred attempts to establish gradations of rights among the mass of citizens . . . ." See also 4 Annals at 1026–27 (Rep. Sedgwick) (hoping but doubting that Congress could find some way to permit aliens to hold property without giving them the right to vote).

[170]See chapter 2.

[171]See 1 Stat 414, § 1; 4 Annals at 1057.

[172]See United States v Butler, 297 US 1 (1936); South Dakota v Dole, 483 US 203 (1987); The Second Century at 227–31.

[173]See, e.g., the extensive debates leading to the Missouri Compromise, 35 Annals at 467–69; 36 Annals at 1576–88. Proposals to require state or congressional consent to restore U.S. citizenship to those who had renounced it (as Loyalists had done during the Revolution, and others had done in 1793 in order to fight for France without running afoul of the neutrality laws) produced a variety of constitutional objections. Madison, in a preview of the *Dred Scott* case, argued that Congress had no power to readmit American citizens, since only "aliens" could be naturalized. 4 Annals at 1027. Cf Scott v Sandford, 60 US 393 (1857). In denying that expatriates were "aliens" Madison may have assumed, as Dexter asserted, that citizens could not renounce their allegiance at all; Murray reminded the House that the country had been built on the contrary principle. 4 Annals at 1028–29. (For a reprise of these arguments during the Fifth Congress see 7 Annals at 348–55.) The proposal to require special legislation was questioned on various grounds: Mingling of federal and state authority, interference with exclusive federal and state prerogatives, and violation of the apparent requirement that naturalization laws be uniform. Id at 1005. It was not enacted.

[174]See chapter 3.

[175]2 US 419 (1793). See The First Hundred Years at 14–20.

[176]3 Elliot at 533 (Madison); id at 555 (Marshall). See also The Federalist No 81 (Hamilton).

The decision, as one commentator has written, "fell upon the country with a profound shock." Newspapers representing a rainbow of opinion protested what they viewed as an unexpected blow to state sovereignty. Others spoke more concretely of prospective raids on state treasuries. Georgia's House of Representatives passed a bill providing that anyone attempting to execute process in the *Chisholm* case should be "guilty of felony and shall suffer death, without benefit of clergy, by being hanged."[177]

The adverse reaction was not universal.[178] But other state legislatures called for a constitutional amendment to reverse the Court's decision,[179] and one was introduced in the House the day after *Chisholm* was announced.[180] Amendment was one of the Senate's first priorities when Congress reconvened in December 1793, and by mid-March the proposal was on its way to the states.[181] President Adams proclaimed its ratification in 1798.[182] Thenceforth, said the eleventh amendment, "the judicial power of the United States sh[ould] not be construed to extend to any suit in law or equity commenced or prosecuted against one of the United States by citizens of another state, or of any foreign state."

The Annals report no debate on the amendment. Each House discussed and endorsed it in a single day, almost without dissent.[183] It is plain that just about everybody in Congress agreed the Supreme Court had misread the Constitution.[184]

There were three revealing attempts to water down the proposal. An unidentified Senator moved to limit the amendment to suits in which "the cause of action shall have arisen before the ratification of the amendment." An unidentified Representative moved to close the federal courts only "where such State shall have previously made provision in their own Courts, whereby such suit may be prosecuted to effect." Albert Gallatin, sitting briefly as a Pennsylvania Senator before succeeding Madison as opposition leader in the

---

[177]See Warren, 1 The Supreme Court at 96–101 (cited in note 38).

[178]See Maeva Marcus and Natalie Wexler, Suits Against States: Diversity of Opinion in the 1790s, 1993 Journal of Supreme Court History 73 (noting, among other things, that Maryland had not protested when it was sued, before *Chisholm*, in the Supreme Court).

[179]The Massachusetts legislature, for example, finding the *Chisholm* decision "repugnant to the first principles of a federal government," requested the state's Representatives and instructed its Senators to take all necessary steps to bring about an amendment that would "remove any clause of the Constitution, which can be construed to imply or justify a decision, that a State is compellable to answer in any suit by an individual or individuals in any Court of the United States." 15 Hamilton Papers at 314. See also Goebel, 1 History of the Supreme Court of the United States at 734–36 (cited in note 54).

[180]See Warren, 1 The Supreme Court at 99–101 (cited in note 38).

[181]The amendment was proposed in the Senate on January 2, 1794, in the terms in which it was adopted. It passed the Senate January 14 and the House March 4; a joint resolution of March 12 requested the President to forward the proposal to the states. See 4 Annals at 25, 30, 477, 499; 1 Stat 402 (1794). As in the case of the twelve amendments that had been proposed in 1789, neither Congress nor the President suggested that proposed amendments had to be presented for presidential approval or veto under Article I, § 7. See chapter 2; Hollingsworth v Virginia, 3 US 378 (1798); The First Hundred Years at 20–23.

[182]1 Richardson at 260. For the curiously careless manner in which ratifications were recorded and proclaimed see Warren, 1 The Supreme Court at 101–02 n 2 (cited in note 38).

[183]The Senate vote was 23 to 2, the House vote 81 to 9. See 4 Annals at 30–31, 476–78.

[184]See also 1 Kent at 415. Story, writing like Kent a generation and a half later, seemed to think *Chisholm* had been rightly decided. 3 Story, § 1677.

House,[185] moved to make an exception permitting states to be sued "in cases arising under treaties made under the authority of the United States."[186]

All three of these limiting proposals were rejected.[187] Congress was unwilling to permit suits against states on future causes of action, or in cases in which no other forum was available, or even in cases arising under treaties. Only a handful of members —including Gallatin and Boudinot but not Madison or even Ames—thought the Constitution should provide a mechanism to ensure that the states paid their debts.

Sovereign immunity is not fashionable today. Nor is it an attractive principle. When governments commit wrongs, they ought to be brought to book. When they violate federal rights, or the rights of citizens of other states or nations, they ought to be suable in federal court. But that was not the view of the Third Congress nor of the state legislatures that approved its proposal.

The fate of Gallatin's modest request not to leave our foreign relations at the mercy of individual states should put to rest the modern heresy that the eleventh amendment does not apply to federal-question cases.[188] One can imagine a scenario in which a motion

---

[185]Born in Switzerland, Gallatin had come to the United States in 1780, engaged in farming, fought in the Revolution, taught French at Harvard, and taken an oath of allegiance to Virginia in 1785. When named to the Senate in 1793 he was challenged and unseated (after the Senate had taken action on the proposed amendment) on the ground that he had not been nine years a citizen of the United States, as Article I, § 3 required. See 4 Annals at 19, 47–62. Like the case of William Smith (see chapter 1), Gallatin's exclusion raised difficult questions of defining citizenship before the new Constitution took effect. As in Smith's case, the result was inconclusive; Gallatin lost by an unexplained vote of 14 to 12 that appeared to be on what we would now call party lines. 4 Annals at 57. He was elected to the House as a member of the Fourth Congress and served until he became Secretary of the Treasury in 1801. See Raymond Walters, Jr., Albert Gallatin: Jeffersonian Financier and Diplomat 59–63 (Macmillan, 1957); Kettner, The Development of American Citizenship at 232–35 (cited in note 154); Biographical Directory at 1038.

Two contests over House elections during the Third Congress made clear that, in exercising its responsibility to judge the elections of its members, the House was generally to apply state law. See 4 Annals at 145–48, 442–43, 453–55; Contested Elections at 69–77. As a general matter there was nothing surprising in this conclusion, since as was pointed out in debate (4 Annals at 147) Article I, § 4 expressly provided that state law should regulate the "times, places and manner" of holding congressional elections until Congress legislated a federal rule. The Delaware law that the House applied in the second case, however, required voters to pick two candidates for Representative, one of whom resided outside their own county. Cf Art II, § 1, which makes analogous provision for presidential elections. Whether the residence clause related to the "manner" of holding elections or to the qualifications of the candidate, and whether the states had authority to add to the qualifications of age, citizenship, and residence prescribed in Article I, § 2, the House apparently did not discuss.

The Annals also report a brief contretemps over the seating of one Gabriel Duvall, who had presented credentials as a Representative from Maryland in the place of John Francis Mercer, whose election had created a controversy only two years before. See chapter 3. Once a committee report was read finding that Mercer had resigned, Duvall was awarded his seat, which he occupied for the next sixteen months without ever opening his mouth—suggesting that his brief service in the House was a fertile training ground for the exemplary record of insignificance he was to compile in the twenty-five years he spent on the Supreme Court. See 4 Annals at 873–74; Biographical Directory at 941; David P. Currie, The Most Insignificant Justice: A Preliminary Inquiry, 50 U Chi L Rev 466 (1983).

[186]See 4 Annals at 30, 476.

[187]Id.

[188]The trouble started with Justice Brennan's unfortunate dissenting opinion in Employees v Department of Public Health & Welfare, 411 US 279, 315–21 (1973), attacking the well-settled proposition (see Hans v Louisiana, 134 US 1 (1890)) that the arising-under clause of Article III, § 2 contained an implied exception for suits against states. The argument was soon extended to the point of contending that federal-question cases

to exempt treaty cases is voted down as unnecessary because the amendment itself is inapplicable to cases arising under federal law. But the language of the actual amendment is not conducive to such an interpretation; it flatly bars "any suit in law or equity" by diverse plaintiffs against a state. More important, the historical context belies any attempt at wishful thinking: As the prompt rejection of all ameliorating alterations shows, Congress was in no mood to permit *any* federal suit against a state by a citizen of another state or of a foreign country.

VII.   THE DISTRICT OF NEW HAMPSHIRE

On April 3, 1794, President Washington signed into law an obscure little bill transferring the jurisdiction of the United States District Court for New Hampshire to the Circuit Court of that district, "until the next session of Congress, or until a new district judge be appointed, and no longer."[189] In so doing it dealt a grave setback to the independence of the judiciary.

If the office of District Judge for New Hampshire had been vacant, we could have relegated the incident to a footnote as an example of ingenuity in ensuring that federal judicial business not be interrupted—wondering aloud why the President did not see that the vacancy was filled and whether in designating the Circuit Court to exercise jurisdiction Congress was not effectively usurping the power of appointment. But the office was not vacant. It had been occupied since 1789 by one John Sullivan, who for some time had been unable to perform his duties.

John Sullivan was a war hero. Fighting beside Washington at battles from Long Island to Brandywine, he had risen to the rank of Major-General. When the Revolution was over he served in the Confederation Congress and as President (Governor) of New Hampshire and was a leader in the struggle to ratify the Philadelphia Constitution.[190] He was "a logical choice" for appointment as the state's first federal judge[191]—"the only position in the appointment of the President," one biographer ominously observes, "his health permitted him to accept."[192]

At the time of his appointment Sullivan was still President of New Hampshire, and he did not immediately resign. The state legislature protested that it was improper for him to hold both offices at once but did nothing.[193] The federal Constitution makes clear that federal judges cannot simultaneously be members of Congress;[194] it says nothing

---

were not barred even when they fell within the explicit terms of the eleventh amendment. See Atascadero State Hospital v Scanlon, 473 US 234, 290 (1985) (Brennan, J, joined by Marshall, Blackmun, and Stevens, JJ, dissenting). For a defense of *Hans* see The Second Century at 7–9.

[189]1 Stat 352, §§ 1, 3. Section 2 of the Act transferred the nonjudicial duties of the District Judge under the latest version of the pension act (see chapter 3) to the federal district attorney. 1 Stat at 353.

[190]See Charles P. Whittemore, A General of the Revolution: John Sullivan of New Hampshire (Columbia, 1961) [hereafter cited as Whittemore]; Thomas C. Amory, Military Services and Public Life of Major-General John Sullivan (Wiggin & Lunt, 1868) [hereafter cited as Amory].

[191]Whittemore at 222.

[192]Amory at 241.

[193]Whittemore at 223.

[194]US Const, Art I, § 6.

about holding federal and state offices at the same time. One is tempted to mumble something about the spirit of the Constitution.

Sullivan resigned his state office in June 1790. It was not until a year later that the first case came before his federal court. Even then he was "not . . . particularly occupied by his judicial duties," and by 1792 he had reached such a state of drunkenness and senility that he was incapable of sitting at all.[195]

At the urging of his "friends," Sullivan elected not to resign. Some person "over eager for the advancement of a friend" suggested that Washington do something about Sullivan; the President is said to have replied that "there was no man in the country he would not sooner remove than General Sullivan."[196]

The truth of the matter was that the Framers had arguably made a mistake: In their commendable zeal to ensure an independent judicial branch[197] they had neglected to provide any tools for removing an incompetent judge.

Impeachment, of course, required proof of "high crimes [or] misdemeanors," not mere inability to fulfill one's duties.[198] Later judges who approached Sullivan's lamentable condition were coaxed off the bench by their colleagues, though they did not always react with grace.[199] But there was no way of making them go, and President Washington was unwilling even to try.

It was in this pitiful state of affairs that a House committee was charged with the task of devising a remedy in the event of the incapacity of a federal judge.[200] The result we know already: a bill to transfer Sullivan's duties to the Circuit Court,[201] which was adopted without recorded debate.[202]

The crisis was real, the temptation great, the benefit clear: Federal judicial business could once again be done in New Hampshire. The cost was greater, the action unforgivable: All Congress had to do to rid itself of a judge of whose opinions it disapproved was to transfer his jurisdiction to another court. It is true that, since Article III vests the judicial power in the Supreme Court and "such inferior courts as the Congress shall, from time to time, ordain and establish," the legislature has a good deal of discretion in defining the jurisdiction of the lower federal courts.[203] But unbridled legislative authority to

---

[195]See Whittemore at 223–24 .

[196]Amory at 245.

[197]See The Federalist No 78 (Hamilton).

[198]US Const, Art II, § 4. For the improbable conclusion that judges may be impeached for disability see Raoul Berger, Impeachment: The Constitutional Problems 181–87 (Harvard, 1973).

[199]Holmes wrote his letter of resignation on the day Chief Justice Hughes suggested it was time to hang up his robe. Sheldon M. Novick, Honorable Justice: The Life of Oliver Wendell Holmes 375 (Little, Brown, 1989). Field, when reminded by his executioner that thirty years before he had been chosen to give the fatal word to Justice Grier, observed that he had never done a dirtier day's work in his life. Charles Evans Hughes, The Supreme Court 76 (1928). Justice Douglas is said to have asserted the right to participate in deciding cases after he had been persuaded to retire. James M. Simon, Independent Journey: The Life of William O. Douglas 452–53 (Harper & Row, 1980).

[200]See 4 Annals at 457, 468–69.

[201]See id at 482.

[202]Id at 528 (noting that "some time" was spent on the proposition in Committee of the Whole but reporting nothing of what was said). The yeas and nays were not taken.

[203]See Sheldon v Sill, 49 US 441 (1850).

transfer cases from one court to another makes a mockery of the constitutional guarantee that federal judges hold office "during good behavior."[204]

The obvious remedy was to amend the impeachment clause to make incapacity a basis for the removal of a federal judge. Only a month had passed since Congress had proposed another amendment to correct a perceived deficiency in the jurisdictional provisions of Article III.[205] To be sure, a willful House and Senate could always cook up "incapacity" where none existed;[206] but they could cook up "high crimes and misdemeanors" too, as they demonstrated in removing Sullivan's unhappy successor in 1804.[207] What Congress did to Sullivan in 1794 was subject to greater abuse than any plausible impeachment standard, for no finding of misconduct or even inadequacy—and no two-thirds vote of the Senate—was necessary to transfer jurisdiction from one court to another.

Perhaps the most charitable explanation for Congress's unfortunate action is that time was of the essence: Judicial business in New Hampshire could not comfortably await ratification by three fourths of the states. It seems not to have occurred to Congress in 1794, as it later would, that the "good behavior" standard might permit the creation of statutory machinery for circumventing an incompetent judge by the action of his judicial peers[208]—a procedure that, while diminishing the independence of the individual judge, does no violence to the central principle that the judiciary must be free from interference by other branches that it is expected to police.[209]

VIII.   THE SOUTHWEST DELEGATE

When the Third Congress convened for the second time in Philadelphia in November 1794, James White laid before the House his credentials as "Representative of the Territory of the United States South of the river Ohio, in the Congress of the United

---

[204]US Const, Art III, § 1.

[205]See text at notes 174–88.

[206]See 3 Story, § 1619: "An attempt to fix the boundary between the region of ability and inability would much oftener give rise to personal, or party attachments and hostilities, than advance the interests of justice, or the public good. And instances of absolute imbecility would be too rare to justify the introduction of so dangerous a provision." The first sentence of this passage is taken verbatim from Hamilton's Federalist No 79. In place of the second Hamilton had written, less convincingly, that "insanity without any formal or express provision, may be safely pronounced to be a virtual disqualification."

[207]See Eleanore Bushnell, Crimes, Follies, and Misfortunes: The Federal Impeachment Trials 43–55 (Illinois, 1992) (describing the successful impeachment of the equally deficient and alcoholic Judge Pickering, also of the luckless District of New Hampshire).

[208]The short-lived Judiciary Act of 1801 authorized the circuit court to appoint one of its own members to perform the duties of a district judge it found incompetent, and this procedure was employed in Pickering's case before he was impeached and the statute repealed. 2 Stat 89, 97, § 25 (Feb 13, 1801); see 2 Haynes at 850. See also 28 USC § 372(c) (1988 & Supp 1993); Symposium, Disciplining the Federal Judiciary, 142 U Pa L Rev 1 (1993); and 28 USC § 372(b), which authorizes appointment of an additional judge (not to be replaced after the need disappears) in case a disabled judge declines to retire.

[209]For sobering doubts as to the constitutionality of removing judges without impeachment see Philip B. Kurland, The Constitution and the Tenure of Federal Judges: Some Notes from History, 36 U Chi L Rev 665 (1969). "When dealing with so fundamental and so fragile a notion as the independence of the judiciary, one ought to tread warily lest the ultimate cost far outweigh the immediate gains." Id at 666.

States."[210] He was eventually seated, but only after a heated debate that went to the very nature of the House.

It was Zephaniah Swift, a new member from Connecticut, who raised the objection:

> The Constitution made no provision for such a member as this person is intended to be. If we can admit a Delegate to Congress or a member of the House of Representatives, we may with equal propriety admit a stranger from any part of the world.[211]

Article I, § 2 seemed to support him: "The House of Representative shall be composed of members chosen . . . by the people of the several states."[212]

There were two arguments for seating the gentleman from the Southwest Territory, and William Smith espoused them both. First, he said, Mr. White was entitled to a seat "by the terms of an express compact with the people."[213] What that meant was spelled out in the report of an ad hoc committee.[214] The Northwest Ordinance had promised the residents of the Territory Northwest of the Ohio, once they established a legislature, the right to send "a Delegate to Congress, . . . with a right of debating, but not of voting."[215] After the new Constitution took effect Congress had passed a statute giving this ordinance "[f]ull effect."[216] In conformity with the Act whereby North Carolina ceded to the United States the area that became the Southwest Territory,[217] the Act of Congress establishing that territory granted its inhabitants "all the privileges, benefits, and advantages" set forth in the Northwest Ordinance."[218]

Of course no "compact" or Act of Congress could authorize what the Constitution forbade; and Article I seemed pretty clear that only the people of the states were entitled to representation in Congress. As far as the Northwest Territory was concerned, the promise in the Ordinance could plausibly be viewed as an "engagement[] entered into before the adoption of this Constitution" and thus, under Article VI, "as valid . . . under this Constitution, as under the Confederation." It is true that the entire Northwest Ordinance seemed to be unauthorized by the Articles of Confederation,[219] but it was generally accepted as valid; and thus there was a respectable argument that Article VI required Congress to seat a delegate sent by the Northwest Territory.

No delegate from that territory, however, appeared until 1799, when young William

---

[210]4 Annals at 873.

[211]Id at 884.

[212]Moreover, said Swift, if White was a member he could not be denied the right to vote, as had been proposed. The Constitution, he seemed to be saying, did not envision two distinct classes of members. 4 Annals at 884.

[213]Id at 885. See also id at 886 (Rep. Dayton); id at 887 (Rep. Baldwin).

[214]Id at 888–89.

[215]See 1 Stat 50, 51, 52 n (a) (Aug 7, 1789).

[216]Id at 51.

[217]See 1 Stat 106, 108 (April 2, 1790).

[218]1 Stat 123, § 1 (May 26, 1790). See chapter 2. Some difficulty was engendered by the fact that the Ordinance provided for a delegate to "Congress," which had originally meant the Congress of the Confederation. As Swift pointed out, the House of Representatives was not Congress. Boudinot contended that, since White had been elected by the territorial legislature, his proper place was in the Senate; Murray suggested that as a delegate to "Congress" he might be "entitled to a seat in both Houses." 4 Annals at 884, 886.

[219]See chapter 2.

Henry Harrison presented his credentials to the Sixth Congress.[220] James White came from the Southwest Territory, which had not been organized until 1790. It had no "engagement" antedating the Constitution and thus could derive no comfort from Article VI.

The argument based on the Northwest Ordinance therefore boils down to an argument based on tradition, however brief. If the seating of a nonvoting territorial delegate was consistent with the Articles of Confederation provision for selection of congressional delegates "in such manner as the legislature of each State shall direct,"[221] it was consistent with Article I, § 2 as well.

Smith's second argument helps to explain how the admission of a nonvoting delegate can be reconciled with that provision. The House could admit anyone it liked for purposes of debate; it could admit the Secretary of State.[222] Indeed, Dayton added, the House had often called upon Cabinet officers for advice.[223] In other words, Article I, § 2 spoke only to the method of selecting "members" of the House; and, as Madison observed in arguing that White was not required to take the oath prescribed by Article VI,[224] he was not a "member."[225]

This argument posed in starkest form the question of what it meant to be a "member" of Congress. Only the people of the states were entitled to elect "members"; but members engaged in a variety of activities. They introduced bills, sat on committees, made motions, spoke in debate, and cast votes. The question was which of these functions were so central to the operation of the House that they could be exercised only by representatives chosen in accordance with Article I, § 2.

Voting, it seemed to be agreed, was at the core of the member's office;[226] and the Ordinance was careful to make clear that territorial delegates would not have the right to vote.[227] For voting is the act whereby Congress makes decisions and thus actually exercises its various powers; anyone who can vote on the floor of Congress is pretty clearly a "member."

Mere speaking, it was argued, was another matter. But when the House had innocuously asked the Secretary of the Treasury even for written advice, there had been a storm

---

[220]Under the terms of the Ordinance the delegate was to be chosen by the territorial legislature, which was not to be elected until the territory had a population of 5,000 free adult males. Settlement was retarded by repeated Indian depredations until General Wayne's victory at Fallen Timbers in 1794 and evacuation of the forts held by the British in defiance of the Peace Treaty, which occurred only after the Jay Treaty was approved in 1795. Consequently the population threshold was not reached until 1798, and the legislature first met in 1799. See Charles B. Galbreath, 1 History of Ohio 197–99 (American Historical Society, 1925); Dorothy Burne Goebel, William Henry Harrison: A Political Biography 41–42 (Indiana Historical Bureau, 1926); Robert M. Taylor, Jr., ed, The Northwest Ordinance 1787: A Bicentennial Handbook 52–53 (Indiana Historical Society, 1987); Elkins & McKitrick at 436–39.

[221]Articles of Confederation, Art 5, § 1, 1 Stat at 4.

[222]4 Annals at 885–86. See also id at 885 (Rep. Giles): "If the House chose to admit the *gallery*—a resource for information that he should never wish to see adopted—they had a right to consult it, or to ask advice from any other quarter, notwithstanding the assertion of the gentleman from Connecticut" (Rep. Swift).

[223]Id at 886.

[224]"The Senators and Representatives . . . shall be bound by oath or affirmation, to support this Constitution . . . ." See chapter 1.

[225]4 Annals at 889.

[226]See id at 885 (Rep. Dexter); id at 887 (Rep. Baldwin); id at 890 (Rep. Dayton).

[227]See text at note 215.

of protest;[228] and in the investigation of General St. Clair the House had insisted on hearing from Cabinet members in committee, not before the House itself.[229] Admitting executive officers to congressional proceedings raises separation-of-powers concerns not present in the case of the Southwest Delegate.[230] But as Swift pointed out, it was one thing "[t]o admit a person within the bar for the purpose of consulting him"; it was quite another to let him "take a permanent seat among the members, for the purpose of regularly debating."[231] Conceding that the Delegate's position was "infinitely higher" than "that of an advocate allowed to plead at the bar of the House," Baldwin insisted that it was nevertheless "extremely short of the situation of a member of Congress."[232]

The House agreed with Baldwin; White was seated as a nonvoting Delegate from the Southwest Territory, in accordance with the tradition created by the Northwest Ordinance and the "compact" made when the territory was established.[233] Since he was not a member of the House, White was neither required to take the oath nor entitled to a member's rights;[234] Congress passed a law to provide him with franking privileges, reimbursement of expenses, and a salary[235]—all, one surmises, as necessary and proper to the operation of the House. It all made very good sense;[236] and so long as the Delegate was not given powers so extensive as to make him effectively a member of the House, it was not impossible to reconcile it with the Constitution.[237]

[228]See chapter 1.

[229]See chapter 3.

[230]Cf also the furor over the right of cabinet officers to introduce bills, which was heatedly denied. See chapter 1.

[231]4 Annals at 888.

[232]Id at 887. It should not follow from the conclusion that nonmembers may be permitted to speak that members may be denied that privilege; membership implies the right to speak as well as to vote, and it ought to imply a basic equality among members. See chapter 1.

[233]Dexter and Boudinot thought White could not be seated without an Act of Congress; Smith responded that the House "ought to decide their elections on their own authority," apparently under the power given each House by Article I, § 5 to judge "the elections, returns and qualifications of its own members." 4 Annals at 885–86. Since the best argument for seating the delegate was that he was not a "member," Smith might better have invoked the further provision of the same section empowering each House to "determine the rules of its proceedings." White was seated by a simple vote of the House, as Smith had suggested. Id at 888.

[234]See id at 889–90 (Reps. Madison, Smith, Giles, and Dayton). A motion to require him to take the oath was rejected forty-two to thirty-two. Id at 890.

[235]1 Stat 403 (Dec 3, 1794).

[236]At one point Giles moved to limit the Delegate to speaking on "any question touching the rights and interests of the people in the Territory," as to which it made most sense to permit him to speak; but he was happy to withdraw this motion when it attracted no support, saying he had advanced the idea only to make it easier to "get the resolution through the House." 4 Annals at 887.

[237]This issue arose again in heightened form in 1993, when the House extended to five Delegates (who had been given the right to vote in standing committees in 1970) the right also to vote in the Committee of the Whole—except that, if their votes were decisive, a new vote would be taken without them. The District of Columbia Circuit upheld this arrangement in Michel v Anderson, 14 F3d 623 (1994), relying largely on the First Congress's endorsement of the provision for a Delegate in the Northwest Ordinance and the powers exercised by William Henry Harrison (which included making motions and serving on committees) after his election to that position in 1799. Id at 631. (The more significant decision to seat the Southwest Delegate, after the constitutional question had been fully debated, was not mentioned in the opinion.) The court warned that the House had gone to the limit: Similar rights for mayors, or a power to affect the result in the Committee of the Whole, or a vote of any kind on the floor of the House itself, would be unconstitutional. Id at 630. These distinctions were all stated as a matter of fiat, and of course no voting rights followed from the eighteenth-century experience; the prevailing argument in 1794 was that all the Delegate could do was speak—a right

IX.   THE FLAG

Let us close this survey of the work of the Third Congress by retracing our steps for a moment to the opening days of its first session in January 1794, when the House was asked to take a breather from momentous issues of war and peace to endorse a Senate bill to add two stars and two stripes to the national flag.

There was some grumbling about the expense of replacing existing flags, and several members without souls complained that the matter was too trivial to deserve congressional attention. Benjamin Goodhue protested that if the bill passed it would not be long before the flag became hopelessly unwieldy: "It is very likely, before fifteen years elapse, we shall consist of twenty States." Boudinot pointed out that "the citizens of Vermont and Kentucky . . . might be affronted" if they were not acknowledged by stars and stripes of their own, and the bill became law.[238] No one questioned Congress's authority to enact it.

The Constitution says nothing about flags. Congress must have understood the power to prescribe one to be inherent in nationhood: Every country needs a flag, and the states were in no position to provide it.[239] Tradition supports this interpretation, as it supported the Third Congress in seating the Southwest Delegate; for the original flag of thirteen stars and stripes was adopted in 1777 by the Continental Congress, which had no express authority in the premises either.[240]

The banner that Congress approved in 1794 was to remain our national emblem until 1818. It was this flag that inspired Francis Scott Key during the War of 1812, long after its fifteen stars and stripes had ceased to represent the true state of the Union.[241] When the number of states reached twenty, Congress was moved to act once more, and this time it made sure it would never have to be bothered again. From then on the flag was to consist of thirteen stripes and twenty stars, with a new star to be added on the admission of each new state.[242] Thus the stars were to represent all the states of the Union, the

---

that could be afforded to anyone.

[238]See 4 Annals at 164–66; 1 Stat 341 (Jan 13, 1794). The House vote was a miserly fifty to forty-two.

[239]See Frederick C. Hicks, The Flag of the United States 20, 87 (Washington, D.C., 1926):

> From the sculptures and paintings on the monuments of Egypt it is evident that the use of standards and flags was common in the Valley of the Nile thousands of years before the Christian era. . . . [Yet t]he use of a particular emblem to symbolize the authority and unity of a nation is of comparatively modern origin, and has been so used only during the last three or four centuries.

The German constitution (Basic Law) of 1949 prescribes the colors of the national flag; authority to define other national symbols is understood to be inherent in the central government despite the fact that, as in the United States, all powers not delegated to the Federation are reserved to the constituent states. See Basic Law of the Federal Republic of Germany, Art 22, 30, 70; Theodor Maunz et al, Grundgesetz Kommentar, Art 70, Rdnr 46 (1989).

[240]See 8 J Cont Cong 464 (June 14[!], 1777); Hicks, The Flag of the United States at 99–100 (cited in note 239). See also id at 101–05 (debunking the legend of Betsy Ross).

[241]See id at 145–46.

[242]3 Stat 415 (Apr 4, 1818). "A further increase in the number of stripes," wrote Congressman Hicks, "would have made the width of the flag disproportionate to its length, unless the stripes were narrowed, and this would have impaired its distinctness." Hicks, The Flag of the United States at 147 (cited in note 239). Goodhue, the reader will surely recall, had foreseen this problem in 1794. See text at note 238.

stripes the original thirteen, and as far as the flag was concerned we could all live happily ever after.

Most of the Representatives who voted for the new flag in 1794 were associated with the faction that was soon to become the Republican party. The doctrine of inherent federal authority that justified their innocent action would come back to haunt them in 1798.[243]

[243]See chapter 6 (discussing the Alien Act, 1 Stat 570). An alternative theory might be that, since armies and navies needed symbols to facilitate distinguishing friends from foes, adoption of the flag was necessary and proper to the various war powers; but, of course, the flag was not confined to military uses.

5

The Fourth Congress, 1795–1797

By the time the Fourth Congress met in Philadelphia in December 1795, President Washington had an entirely new Cabinet. Jefferson had resigned on the last day of 1793 to go back to Monticello; Hamilton followed him into retirement thirteen months later. Edmund Randolph served briefly as Secretary of State until questionable dealings with the French minister forced him to yield the office to Timothy Pickering of Massachusetts, who had taken Knox's position in the War Department. William Bradford and then Charles Lee succeeded Randolph as Attorney General; James McHenry became Secretary of War. For Secretary of the Treasury Washington picked Oliver Wolcott of Connecticut, who had previously served as Comptroller.[1]

Washington himself was fast approaching his last year as President, and a number of Federalist leaders left the Senate.[2] In the House, both Ames and Madison were beginning their last term; neither would run for reelection in 1796. Already the mantle of opposition leadership was passing to Albert Gallatin, the brilliant new member from Pennsylvania.[3]

---

[1] A table illustrating these changes appears in White at 517–18. For Randolph's difficulties see Elkins & McKitrick at 422–31; Miller at 169–71. "The offices are now filled," John Adams reportedly said, "but how differently than when Jefferson, Hamilton, Jay, etc., were here." Quoted in James Thomas Flexner, George Washington: Anguish and Farewell (1793–1799) 251 (Little, Brown, 1972). See also White at 264: "The Cabinet changes required in 1795 revealed a strong reluctance on the part of leading men to serve in high federal posts."

[2] Ellsworth, Morris, Rufus King, and the two Massachusetts Senators, Caleb Strong and George Cabot, all departed "during the 16 months following Hamilton's resignation" in early 1795. Swanstrom at 276.

[3] See Elkins & McKitrick at 449; Miller at 163. After deciding to retire, Madison played little part in the second session of the Fourth Congress. See Editorial Note, 16 Madison Papers at 141, 150–51. Ames was ill during most of the first session and, apart from one stirring speech on the merits of the Jay Treaty, said relatively little during the Fourth Congress; his "role as spokesman and defender of the Federalist faith was being

The capital was witnessing a gradual changing of the guard.[4]

In terms of ordinary legislation the Fourth Congress was relatively quiescent. Constitutional issues were raised in connection with the admission of Tennessee and by a number of legislative proposals that were debated but not adopted, from direct taxation to penalties for kidnapping blacks to relief for victims of the great Savannah fire. Like its predecessors, the Fourth Congress spent an inordinate amount of time impersonating an administrative agency by passing on individual claims against the United States,[5] but it took one momentous step in the right direction by finally setting up a land office to dispose of Western real estate under its authority "to dispose of . . . the territory or other property of the United States,"[6] and this time nobody said it had to manage all the details itself.[7]

In matters internal to the legislative branch, an attempt to bribe members of the House provoked the assertion of a broad inherent contempt power, and the Senate finally opened its doors.[8] Yet after an initial squabble over the Senate's answer to the President's speech[9] and its right to congratulate France on the adoption of a new flag[10] there still were no significant reports of Senate debates; years of exclusion had apparently convinced the fourth estate that the House was where the action was, and the Senate was largely ignored.[11]

---

assumed by William L. Smith of Charleston." Winfred E.A. Bernhard, Fisher Ames: Federalist and Statesman, 1758–1808, 268, 286, 287 (North Carolina, 1965).

[4]As in the previous Congress, the House was safely in Republican hands. See Letter of Fisher Ames to Thomas Dwight, Dec 30, 1795, 1 Ames Works at 180: "I count fifty-six *antis*, forty-nine feds, of the one hundred and five members of the House of Representatives."

[5]See, e.g., 6 Stat 27 (May 17, 1796) ("An Act to authorize Ebenezer Zane to locate certain lands in the territory of the United States northwest of the river Ohio"); id at 28 (June 1, 1796) ("An Act to indemnify the estate of the late Major-General Nathaniel Greene, for a certain bond entered into by him during the late war"); id at 29 (Mar 2, 1797) ("An Act granting a certain sum of money to the widow and children of John de Neufville, deceased"); 5 Annals at 161–64, 235–36 (debating the merits of divers private claims). When named to continue as Chairman of the Committee of Claims, Representative Uriah Tracy asked to be excused because "he had been extremely hard employed last year, and had undergone much trouble about this business"; his colleagues, unctuously praising his ability and experience, refused to let him go. 5 Annals at 130. See also 1 Stat 490, 491, § 5 (June 1, 1796), which directed the Surveyor General to convey a specified tract of land to "the society of United Brethren for propagating the gospel among the heathen" in accordance with an ordinance of the Confederation Congress—suggesting that Congress believed either that a land grant for this purpose did not run afoul of the first amendment prohibition of laws respecting an establishment of religion or that the acknowledgement of preexisting obligations in Article VI enabled the new government to carry out a promise it could not have made.

[6]1 Stat 464 (May 18, 1796). See US Const, Art IV, § 3. At the House's request, Hamilton had submitted a plan for a General Land Office as early as 1790. 1 Am St Papers (Public Lands) at 8–9.

[7]See also 6 Stat at 23 (Apr 20, 1796) (adding to the pension list a multitude of names certified by district judges under the statute passed in the wake of *Hayburn's Case* (discussed in chapter 3)); 1 Stat 463 (May 12, 1796) (authorizing payment of former officers' claims for horses killed in battle on presentation of proof to the Secretary of War).

[8]5 Annals at 14.

[9]Id at 15–22.

[10]Id at 28–36. This controversy is briefly described in note 17 of chapter 4.

[11]See Swanstrom at 249–51.

President Washington interposed his only policy veto,[12] and the House sustained him.[13]

In proposing that the President be asked to ascertain whether the proposed constitutional amendment limiting suits against states had been ratified by "three fourths of the several states" as required by Article 5,[14] a Senate committee solemnly concluded that nine states out of thirteen had sufficed to ratify the Bill of Rights,[15] but a House committee set the record straight:[16] Nine was not even the closest whole number to 9.75, much less enough to satisfy the evident requirement of at least three fourths of the states. Representative Robert Goodloe Harper went so far as to deny that eleven was three fourths of fourteen,[17] but he was virtually laughed off the floor. As Gallatin demonstrated in what was described as a rare display of humor,[18] to insist that there be three fourths not of the actual number of states but of some integer divisible by four could lead to cases in which three fourths was more than the whole; it was enough that eleven was more than 10.5, which was the constitutional standard.[19]

But the Fourth Congress was dominated by the epic battle over the House's role in implementing the Jay Treaty, and it is with that controversy that we begin.

---

[12]1 Richardson at 211 (Feb 28, 1797); 6 Annals at 1567, 2328. Among other things, the bill (id at 2330–31) would have abolished two companies of light dragoons. Washington objected that the dragoons should not be dismissed and that in any case they should be compensated so long as they remained in actual service.

[13]The House, the reporter tells us, voted fifty-five to twenty-six in favor of repassing the bill. That was more than two thirds of those voting on the motion, but without explanation the bill was declared lost, and a new bill was promptly enacted without the offending provision. 6 Annals at 2332; 1 Stat 507 (Mar 3, 1797). In contrast to Article II, § 2, which requires that treaties be approved by "two thirds of the Senators present," Article I, § 7 requires approval by two thirds of the "House"; if the reporter's tally is correct, it suggests that the Representatives understood this to mean two thirds of all members, whether or not present or voting. But Article V similarly requires "two thirds of both Houses" to propose constitutional amendments, and both the House and the Senate had considered it sufficient that two thirds of those present had endorsed the Bill of Rights. See Senate Journal, 1st Cong, 2d Sess 116–41, 148, 150. Many years later, invoking long and consistent congressional practice, the Supreme Court confirmed that in the case of vetoed bills as well the Constitution required only two thirds of a quorum, which Article I, § 5 defines as a majority of the elected members. Missouri Pac Ry v Kansas, 248 US 276, 280–81 (1919). Counting the yeas and nays on the dragoon provision for oneself resolves the puzzle: There were thirty-six negative votes, not twenty-six, and the motion failed for want of two thirds of those present and voting.

[14]See 1 Stat 519 (Mar 2, 1797). Though seven years had passed, the Senate committee seemed to concede the two additional amendments proposed along with the Bill of Rights in 1789 were still alive: Having received only seven votes before the admission of Vermont and three thereafter, the first proposal (which Congress declared "ratified" in 1992) had "not yet," the report said, been approved. 6 Annals at 1537.

[15]6 Annals at 1537.

[16]Id at 2163.

[17]"[H]e believed there must be twelve ratifying states to be three-fourths, as intended, by the Constitution, because that number would be three-fourths of sixteen, which was the nearest number to fourteen capable of four equal divisions." Id at 2281.

[18]Id at 2284.

[19]Id at 2281–83. After the 1796 Presidential election William Smith had the foresight to perceive there was a risk of mischief in the original provisions of Article II, § 1, id at 1824; but his suggestion that electors vote separately for President and Vice-President got nowhere until the election of 1800 showed how right he was. See the discussion in chapter 6. For a glimpse of some of the shenanigans encouraged by the original provisions see McDonald, Washington at 178–79, 183.

I. THE JAY TREATY

A. Negotiation and Approval

The United States were close to war with Great Britain in 1794, and in April President Washington sent John Jay to London to try to forestall it.[20] The Senate approved Jay's appointment, but not without protest.[21] For at the time of his nomination John Jay was Chief Justice of the United States, and some Senators had the temerity to suggest that he belonged on the Bench.[22]

"Who is to supply the Chief Justices [sic] place in the Courts in the mean time . . . [?]," inquired one of Madison's correspondents, complaining also that Jay was to be paid for not performing his judicial duties.[23] But the objections went beyond mere policy; the Senate narrowly defeated a resolution that would have declared that to permit a Supreme Court Justice simultaneously to hold an office "emanating from and holden at the pleasure of the Executive" was "contrary to the spirit of the Constitution."[24]

Madison wrote Jefferson that there would be no difficulty if Jay resigned as Chief Justice; nothing in the Constitution made a judge ineligible to change jobs. But it began to look, Madison said, as if Jay intended to hold both positions at once, and that was another story.[25] Madison's judicious former colleague Alexander White still saw no constitutional problem: While Article I, § 6 forbade members of Congress to hold other federal offices, it said nothing about judges.[26]

Jay went to England, and he did not resign until the following year, after he was elected Governor of New York.[27] This was not the first time a federal judge had been given nonjudicial responsibilities, and it would not be the last;[28] it certainly went beyond

[20]See Elkins & McKitrick at 388–96. The background is depicted at great length in Samuel Flagg Bemis, Jay's Treaty: A Study in Commerce and Diplomacy (Yale, rev ed 1962), and in Jerald A. Combs, The Jay Treaty: Political Battleground of the Founding Fathers (California, 1970).

[21]Sen Exec Journal at 152.

[22]The office to which Jay was named had not been created by statute, but that presented no problem. The First Congress had established, and the Fourth Congress confirmed, that the President could nominate diplomatic officers without prior congressional action. See chapter 1 and text at note 93.

[23]Letter of Joseph Jones to James Madison, Nov 16, 1794, in 15 Madison Papers at 382, 383.

[24]1 Sen Exec Journal at 152. See also the May 29 letter of Charles Cotesworth Pinckney to his brother Thomas, the regular Minister to Britain, who understandably felt slighted by Jay's appointment (noting that "the appointment of a Judge to that office has been generally deemed inconsistent with the spirit of our Constitution"). Quoted in George C. Rogers, Jr., Evolution of a Federalist: William Loughton Smith of Charleston (1758–1812) 264 (South Carolina, 1962). Other similar objections are cited in 1 Warren at 118–21.

[25]Letter of James Madison to Thomas Jefferson, April 28, 1794, 15 Madison Papers at 315, 316.

[26]Letter of Alexander White to James Madison, May 5, 1794, 15 Madison Papers at 325.

[27]Letter of John Jay to George Washington, June 29, 1795, 4 Jay Papers at 177. See Charles Warren, 1 The Supreme Court in United States History 121, 124 (Little, Brown, rev ed 1926); Julius Goebel, Jr., 1 History of the Supreme Court of the United States: Antecedents and Beginnings to 1801 747 (Macmillan, 1971). John Rutledge, given an interim appointment to take Jay's place as Chief Justice, was not confirmed—for reasons having as much to do with his outspoken opposition to the treaty as with rumors of his mental instability. See 1 Warren at 128–39. Oliver Ellsworth, the most talented and influential member of the Senate, left to become Chief Justice in March 1796. See 5 Annals at 50.

[28]Cf the comparable and equally controversial appointment of Justice Robert Jackson as chief prosecutor for the Nuremberg trials after World War II, which necessitated his absence from the Supreme Court during the entire 1945 Term, and Chief Justice Warren's chairmanship of the commission that investigated the assassination of President Kennedy. See Ann Tusa and John Tusa, The Nuremberg Trial 68–70 (Atheneum,

the precedents in the significance and time-consuming nature of the extracurricular duties he was expected to perform.[29]

Meanwhile Jay's labors had borne fruit; Washington submitted the treaty he had negotiated to a special session of the Senate in June 1795.[30] Like its author, the treaty encountered heavy weather in the Senate.

The first hurdle was a two-pronged Republican challenge to its constitutionality. Article IX of the treaty, which guaranteed the right of British subjects to own land, was attacked as beyond federal authority; various commercial provisions—including Article XV, which promised that neither country would impose higher duties on the other's ships or goods than upon those of other nations—were alleged to imply "a power in the President and Senate, to control, and even annihilate the constitutional right of the Congress of the United States over their commercial intercourse with foreign nations."[31] Though he was no longer in the Government, Hamilton in yet another brilliant set of essays (under the name Camillus) reminded his readers that the Confederation Congress, under a similar treaty provision, had made agreements that likewise regulated subjects otherwise reserved to the states[32] and demonstrated that the treaty power would be essentially hollow if it were limited by every grant of legislative authority.[33] In the meantime the Senate rejected the constitutional challenge by a bare 20–10 vote on what has been described as strict party lines.[34]

The second difficulty came from the Federalists, who had provided the votes to sustain the treaty's validity. Article XII purported to reopen trade between the United States and the British West Indies, but on onerous terms: It permitted U.S. citizens to transport

---

1984); Jack Harrison Pollack, Earl Warren: The Judge Who Changed America 228–30 (Prentice-Hall, 1979). Earlier examples are cited in chapters 1, 3, and 4.

[29]For the contention that Jay's acceptance of the position was inconsistent with the position he had taken with respect to advisory opinions both in the neutrality crisis (discussed in chapter 4) and under the pension law (discussed in chapter 3) see Richard B. Morris, John Jay, the Nation, and the Court 92 (Boston U, 1967). Whatever constitutional difficulties may attend a judge's simultaneous occupancy of a nonjudicial office, however, the problem is not the same as that which arises when nonjudicial functions are vested in the courts themselves, for Article III seems to limit federal courts to resolving "cases" or "controversies" of a "judicial" nature. Jay himself, while concluding that the pension act unconstitutionally conferred nonjudicial power on the courts, agreed to exercise the same authority as a "commissioner." Hayburn's Case, 2 US 408, 409 n (a) (1792).

[30]4 Annals at 855. The treaty itself appears at 8 Stat 116 (Nov 19, 1794).

[31]See 8 Stat at 122, 124; 1 Sen Exec Journal at 185, 4 Annals at 861–62. Senator Butler also suggested, at least privately, that the treaty was procedurally infirm because Washington had not properly consulted the Senate in advance. See Letter of Pierce Butler to James Madison, June 12, 1795, 16 Madison Papers at 14, 15; Swanstrom at 121–22. But although Washington on occasion had asked the Senate's advice before negotiating a treaty (see the discussion of the Southern Indians in chapter 1), it is not clear either from the text of Article II or from its history that he did so as a matter of constitutional compulsion.

[32]Camillus (The Defence) No 38, 20 Hamilton Papers at 22, 25–31. See also Camillus No 36, id at 3, 6: "[W]hatever is a proper subject of compact between Nation & Nation may be embraced by a Treaty between the President of the U States, with the advice and consent of the Senate, and the correspondent Organ of a foreign state"; 5 Annals at 516 (Rep. Sedgwick); 3 Story, § 1502; Geofroy v Riggs, 13 US 258, 266 (1890); Missouri v Holland, 252 US 416, 435 (1920); The Second Century at 100–01.

[33]Camillus No 37, 20 Hamilton Papers at 13, 18–22. See also Louis Henkin, Foreign Affairs and the Constitution 149 (Norton, 1972) ("Treaties have dealt with many matters that were also subject to legislation . . . .").

[34]4 Annals at 863, 1 Sen Exec Journal at 186.

West Indian goods only in small vessels and only to the United States and could even be read (contrary to its probable intention) to forbid American ships to carry American cotton.[35] The upper House disapproved this article and gave only conditional consent to the treaty.[36]

The Constitution said nothing about conditional consent; Article II could easily have been read to make Senate approval, like Presidential approval of a bill passed by Congress, an all-or-nothing affair.[37] Before obtaining British agreement to suspend the offending provision[38] Washington prudently consulted his Cabinet, which (after an initial expression of doubt by Randolph) unanimously concluded that he was under no obligation to resubmit the treaty to the Senate:[39] By conditionally endorsing the original draft, the Senate had consented in advance to the revision.[40] Like most of Washington's interpretations of ambiguous constitutional provisions, this was an eminently sensible resolution under the circumstances, for it satisfied the spirit of the consent requirement while avoiding an unnecessary burden.[41]

B.   The Role of the House

Serious pressure was brought to bear on the President not to sign the treaty even after the Senate had approved it,[42] confirming the understanding (which had prevailed since the First Congress)[43] that ratification was a separate and discretionary act. Overcoming doubts as to the desirability of the treaty, Washington gave his final approval,[44] and the battle shifted to the House of Representatives.

For, in addition to renouncing U.S. claims of freedom to trade with France in exchange for a promise by the British to evacuate forts in the Northwest Territory that they had continued to occupy in violation of the peace treaty of 1783,[45] Jay's agreement provided for the establishment of bilateral commissions to resolve a New England border dispute, the rights of British creditors, and claims for depredations against U.S. ship-

---

[35]See 8 Stat at 122–23; Elkins & McKitrick at 418–19; Miller at 166–67; Hamilton's Remarks [to Washington] on the Treaty, 18 Hamilton Papers at 404, 432.

[36]1 Sen Exec Journal at 185, 4 Annals at 861–62.

[37]See US Const, Art II, § 2: "He shall have power, by and with the advice and consent of the Senate, to make treaties . . . ." Cf id, Art I, § 7: "If he approve [the bill] he shall sign it, but if not he shall return it, with his objections . . . ."

[38]See 8 Stat at 130 (May 4, 1796).

[39]See Elkins & McKitrick at 423.

[40]See Henkin, Foreign Affairs at 133–34 (cited in note 33). In contrast, when the Senate in 1798 approved a treaty with Tunis on condition that it be made consistent with most-favored-nation clauses in other agreements, President Adams resubmitted the revised treaty to the Senate, and the Senate gave its approval. See 1 Sen Exec J at 263–64, 328–30; Ralston Hayden, The Senate and Treaties, 1789–1817 108–12. (Macmillan, 1920)

[41]"The practice of qualifying its advice and consent to the ratification of treaties, thus begun during Washington's Presidency, has been continued to the present day." 2 Haynes at 608.

[42]See Elkins & McKitrick at 420–21.

[43]See chapter 1.

[44]See 5 Annals at 48.

[45]Art II, XVIII, 8 Stat at 117, 125–26; cf Definitive Treaty of Peace Between the United States of America and his Britannic Majesty, Art VII, 8 Stat 80, 83 (Sept 3, 1783); see Miller at 165–66.

ping.[46] The President sent the fully ratified treaty to both Houses of Congress, in the evident expectation that they would appropriate money to cover the attendant expenses.[47]

Before anyone moved to do so, however, Representative Edward Livingston of New York fired the first shot by offering a resolution requesting the President to provide the House with the instructions that Jay had been given when he undertook his mission to England, as well as other documents and correspondence relevant to the treaty.[48] The debate on this resolution lasted an entire month and was one of the most impressive and fundamental ever conducted in Congress.

The House had no right to seek information, said Representative Murray, without indicating how it related to some subject within the House's purview.[49] The House had nothing to do with treaties, since Article II, § 2 expressly empowered the President to make them with Senate consent.[50] Impeachment, he acknowledged, would be a legitimate purpose;[51] but as Harper noted no one had suggested that Jay or anyone else should be impeached.[52]

Gallatin took the lead in defending Livingston's proposal, and he made two distinct arguments. First, no treaty affecting any subject over which Congress had legislative authority could take effect without congressional approval, and several provisions of Jay's agreement regulated commerce between the United States and Great Britain.[53] Second,

[46]Art V–VII, 8 Stat at 119–22. Among other things the United States agreed to pay British claims against U.S. citizens that, owing to "various lawful impediments," could not be recovered "by the ordinary course of judicial proceedings." Art VI, id at 119. During the House debate Representative Page attacked this provision as vesting judicial power outside the federal courts in violation of Article III, § 1. 5 Annals at 1099. Representative Bourne's response that the matter fell outside that Article because "the Judicial authority is incompetent to take cognizance of controversies between independent nations" (id at 1102) was clever but incomplete. For although the United States was substituted for the original debtor as defendant, individual British subjects were still to prosecute their own claims; the modern view is that private suits against the Government, when authorized, are "Controversies to which the United States shall be a party" within the meaning of Article III, § 2. See Glidden v Zdanok, 370 US 530 (1962). On the other hand, Congress is still recognized as having the option to create alternative tribunals for such claims on the ground that it did not have to consent to be sued at all. Id; see Ex parte Bakelite Corp, 279 US 438 (1929). A better answer to the Article III objection might be that an international tribunal, like a state court, does not exercise the judicial power of the United States. See Henkin, Foreign Affairs at 196–200 (cited in note 33).

[47]1 Richardson at 192, 5 Annals at 394.

[48]Id at 426. Livingston soon amended his motion to except any information that pending negotiations required to be kept secret (id), but modern notions of executive privilege are broader. See United States v Nixon, 418 US 683 (1974) (recognizing the need to keep certain communications confidential in order not to discourage the frank interchange of views). A motion by Madison to except any papers the President thought it "not . . . consistent with the interest of the United States to disclose" was defeated. Id at 438.

[49]5 Annals at 429.

[50]Id at 429–30. See also id at 518 (Rep. Sedgwick); id at 455 (Rep. Nathaniel Smith). Both Pennsylvania and Virginia, William Smith added, had proposed amendments to make treaties subject to House approval, indicating a recognition that the Constitution gave the House no say in the matter. Id at 495, 497; see 2 Elliot at 546; 3 id at 660. Similar proposals had been made and defeated in the Philadelphia Convention. See 2 Farrand at 538; 4 id at 58. The reasons for excluding the House from the treaty-making process are detailed in The Federalist No 75 (Hamilton).

[51]5 Annals at 429.

[52]Id at 461.

[53]Id at 465–69, 473. See also id at 493 (Rep. Madison); id at 562 (Rep. Page). Jefferson had suggested this line of argument in a letter to Giles (Dec 31, 1795), 4 Jefferson Writings (Wash ed) at 125, and he repeated it in the Manual of Parliamentary Practice he compiled as Vice-President, 9 id at 81. Representative Havens went further: Since Article VI described treaties as "law" and Article I vested all legislative powers in

Congress had a right to the information because even if the treaty was valid it could not be carried out without appropriations, which under Article I, § 9 only a statute could provide.[54]

Not so, said the treaty's supporters; Article VI made a treaty duly concluded the law of the land, as binding on the House as on anyone else.[55] The House could no more refuse to implement a treaty than a tax collector could refuse to enforce the law;[56] it might as plausibly withhold the salaries of the President and the judges[57] or decline to call a constitutional convention at the request of two thirds of the states.[58] Congressional discretion to refuse an appropriation, in short, would undermine the treaty power.[59]

Wrong, said Pennsylvania's John Swanwick; discretion was implied in every grant of legislative authority.[60] To hold that the House was bound to vote funds to implement a treaty would destroy the appropriation power[61]—which, Giles added, was intended as a check on the powers given to other branches.[62] The two-year limit on military appropriations, Madison noted in support of this conclusion, was designed to permit the people's representatives to review on regular occasions the desirability of maintaining an army.[63]

Congress, Congressional approval was required before *any* treaty could become law. 5 Annals at 483–84. This argument is refuted by the language and purposes of the treaty and supremacy clauses, which by unambiguously giving the President and Senate power to make "law" demonstrate that treaty-making is not a "legislative" power within the meaning of Article I.

[54]5 Annals at 466. See also id at 448 (Rep. Heath).

[55]Id at 438–39 (Rep. William Smith); id at 479 (Rep. Griswold). If the treaty was unconstitutional, Smith conceded, Congress might refuse to enforce it; but no constitutional doubts had been raised in the House, and in any event "the question of constitutionality should be determined from the face of the instrument," not from extraneous materials. Id at 438.

[56]Id at 541 (Rep. Cooper).

[57]Id at 480 (Rep. Griswold): "The Constitution declares, that these compensations shall be paid; and yet they cannot be paid without Legislative appropriation. It therefore becomes the duty of the Legislature to make the necessary appropriations . . . ." See also id at 456 (Rep. Nathaniel Smith); id at 529–30 (Rep. Sedgwick). Hamilton had made the same point in a letter to William Smith (Mar 10, 1796), 20 Hamilton Papers at 72.

[58]5 Annals at 498 (Rep. William Smith).

[59]Accord Rawle at 73–74; Henkin, Foreign Affairs at 162 n * (cited in note 33) (acknowledging that the question has never been authoritatively resolved). In 1792, in connection with the ransom of U.S. citizens captured by Barbary pirates, both Washington and Jefferson had concluded that Congress would be bound to appropriate money to implement a treaty but that prudence dictated consulting the House in advance to avoid the possibility that it might fail to do its duty. See *Anas*, 9 Jefferson Writings (Wash ed) at 106–07, 114–15, 23 Jefferson Papers at 256–57, 263–64; see note 264 of chapter 2. No one contended that a treaty itself could appropriate money; even Hamilton acknowledged that a statute was required. Camillus No 37, 20 Hamilton Papers at 13, 21.

[60]5 Annals at 449.

[61]"In such a case the House become mere automatons, mere Mandarine members, like those who nod on a chimney-piece, as directed by a power foreign to themselves." Id at 450.

[62]Id at 509. See also id at 466, 473 (Rep. Gallatin). Representatives Hillhouse and Harper, while opposing both Livingston's resolution and the more extravagant assertions of its advocates, conceded that Congress had discretion not to appropriate money. Id at 671–72 (Rep. Hillhouse); id at 758 (Rep. Harper). John Marshall, who coaxed a resolution in support of the treaty through the Virginia legislature, took the same position. Letter of John Marshall to Alexander Hamilton, Apr 25, 1796, 20 Hamilton Papers at 137, 138. Accord Turner v American Baptist Missionary Union, 24 Fed Cas 344, 345–46 (No 14,251) (CC D Mich 1852) (McLean, J.); Edward S. Corwin, The President's Control of Foreign Relations 95–97 (Princeton, 1917); Edward S. Corwin, The Constitution and What it Means Today 91 (Princeton, 6th ed 1938).

[63]5 Annals at 492. See also id at 445–46 (Rep. Nicholas); id at 508 (Rep. Giles).

The clauses expressly requiring payment of the salaries of the President and the judges,[64] Gallatin explained, were narrow exceptions to the general principle. There was no comparable provision with respect to treaties;[65] the supremacy clause served only to establish the subordinate status of state law[66] and (in Swanwick's words) "does not affect the powers of this House, as a component part of the General Legislature, and authority of the United States."[67] Finally, Gallatin invoked British precedent: Though Blackstone described treaties as law, it was universally acknowledged that Parliament had discretion not to appropriate money to implement them.[68]

At length the House approved Livingston's resolution by the lopsided vote of sixty-two to thirty-seven,[69] suggesting that a substantial majority agreed that the House had discretion in implementing the treaty. But the President refused to turn over the requested information. Not content to lecture the House on the need for secrecy in treaty negotiations,[70] he denied that the inquiry was related to any legitimate legislative function. As a member of the Constitutional Convention he knew that action by the President and the Senate was enough to make a treaty the law of the land; the Convention Journal revealed that a motion to require congressional ratification of treaties had been defeated. Thus the Constitution, he extravagantly concluded, *forbade* him to accede to the House's request.[71]

Representative Thomas Blount responded by proposing another resolution, which the House promptly adopted by a similarly decisive vote, affirming its discretion to refuse

---

[64]US Const, Art II, § 1: "The President shall . . . receive for his services, a compensation, which shall neither be increased nor diminished during the period for which he shall have been elected . . ."; Art 3, § 1: "The judges . . . shall . . . receive for their services, a compensation, which shall not be diminished during their continuance in office."

[65]5 Annals at 472–73. See also id at 509 (Rep. Giles). William Smith turned this argument around: The clause respecting military appropriations was a narrow exception to the general duty to provide funds to meet obligations lawfully incurred. Id at 498.

[66]Id at 468–69.

[67]Id at 450.

[68]Id at 469–72; see also id at 450–51 (Rep. Swanwick). Blackstone's assertion that it was within the king's prerogative "to make treaties . . . binding upon the whole community" and Dicey's that "not a penny of revenue can be legally expended except under the authority of some Act of Parliament" show that in Britain, as in the United States, the problem lay at the intersection of two competing principles; Holdsworth's flat statement that one of the "limitations" on the king's authority was that no treaty provisions involving "the imposition of any charge on the subject, or an alteration in the rules of law" could take effect "without the sanction of Parliament" seems to imply discretion not to give the requisite approval. See 1 Blackstone at 257; A.V. Dicey, Introduction to the Study of the Law of the Constitution 203 (Macmillan, 8th ed 1915); W.S. Holdsworth, The Treaty-Making Power of the Crown, 58 LQ Rev 175, 175 (1942). British precedent, Nathaniel Smith replied, was not in point; Britain had no counterpart of our written Constitution, and Parliament could do anything it liked. 5 Annals at 454–55; see also id at 481 (Rep. Griswold).

[69]Id at 759.

[70]Madison conceded that the President had "a right . . . to withhold information, when of a nature that did not permit disclosure of it at the time." Id at 773.

[71]1 Richardson at 194–96, 5 Annals at 760–61. See also Letter of George Washington to Charles Carroll, May 1, 1796, 35 Washington Papers at 29, 30. Hamilton had spelled out these arguments in much greater detail in a draft message prepared at Washington's behest, 20 Hamilton Papers at 85–102. In the House both Gallatin and Madison made the usual arguments against relying on what had happened at the Constitutional Convention. 5 Annals at 734–35, 775–76. See also Letter of James Madison to Thomas Jefferson, Apr 4, 1796, 16 Madison Papers at 285, 286 (complaining that the Convention had voted to keep its Journal secret).

to implement any treaty affecting a subject within congressional power and its right to request information without giving reasons.[72]

Deprived of the materials it professed to find crucial to its deliberations, the House proceeded to debate the merits of the treaty. As it did so petitions began to pour in, most significantly from the Republican West, urging that Congress appropriate the necessary funds.[73] For control of the northwestern forts was critical to the prevention of Indian raids and thus to settlement of the Northwest Territory.[74] With their constituents vociferously against them, a number of House opponents gave up the fight; having asserted its right not to appropriate money, the House voted to do so after all.[75]

There was no inconsistency between these two positions. In fact, although the episode ended in a standoff on the constitutional questions between the President and the House, the latter seems to have been substantially right in both its decisions. For the treaty was apparently a good one under the circumstances and deserved to be carried out,[76] but the appropriation power *was* intended as a check on other branches.

The text of the provision is suggestive: "No money shall be drawn from the Treasury, but in consequence of appropriations made by law . . . ." This language reads like a limitation on the powers given to other branches. The natural inference, when an Act of Congress is required, is that Congress has discretion to vote the money or not, as it sees fit.[77] Analogous provisions include those requiring Senate consent to appointments and treaties, presidential approval of bills not repassed over the veto, and state ratification of constitutional amendments.[78] The contrast with the President's duty to "take

---

[72]5 Annals at 771–72, 782. "It cannot be mentioned, at this day, without equal regret and astonishment," wrote Chancellor Kent in 1826, "that such a resolution passed the house of representatives . . . ." 1 Kent at 268.

[73]See Elkins & McKitrick at 445–47.

[74]Once the forts were in U.S. hands and General Wayne had defeated the Indians at Fallen Timbers, Ohio's population rose dramatically, and it was admitted to the Union in 1803. See the Treaty of Peace with the Northwestern Indians, 7 Stat 49 (Aug 3, 1795) (extinguishing Indian claims to much of the future state); Elkins & McKitrick at 436–39. A popular treaty concluded with Spain by Thomas Pinckney about the same time also promoted Western development by settling our southern boundary and opening the mouth of the Mississippi. 8 Stat 138 (Oct 27, 1795); see Elkins & McKitrick at 439–40.

[75]5 Annals at 1279, 1291, 1295; see Elkins & McKitrick at 447–49. The appropriation law appears at 1 Stat 459 (May 6, 1796).

[76]See Elkins & McKitrick at 410–14; McDonald, Washington at 153–55. Hamilton summed it up in his response to the President's request for advice in July 1795, 18 Hamilton Papers at 404, 451–52:

> The truly important side of this Treaty is that it closes and upon the whole as reasonably as could have been expected the controverted points between the two Countries—and thereby gives us the prospect of repossessing our Western Posts, an object of primary consequence in our affairs—of escaping finally from being implicated in the dreadful war which is ruining Europe—and of preserving ourselves in a state of peace for a considerable time to come.
>
> Well considered, the greatest interest of this Country in its external relations is that of peace.

Less favorable assessments, of course, abound. See, e.g., Raymond Walters, Jr., Albert Gallatin: Jeffersonian Financier and Diplomat 96 (Macmillan, 1957) (arguing that the treaty was "a complete triumph for British diplomacy" that gave the United States "modest concessions at a humiliating price").

[77]See 5 Annals at 493 (Rep. Madison): "[T]his House, in its Legislative capacity, must exercise its reason; it must deliberate; for deliberation is implied in legislation."

[78]US Const, Art II, § 2; Art I, § 7; Art V.

care that the laws be faithfully executed"[79] is equally illuminating: By phrasing that clause in terms of obligation, the Framers indicated that they were content merely to protect the people against lawless action by separating the power to make laws from the power to enforce them; the President's sole check on unwise but constitutional legislation is his suspensive veto.[80]

The textual inference that Congress normally has discretion whether or not to appropriate funds is confirmed by extrinsic evidence of the Framers' thinking. There was no relevant debate in the Constitutional Convention; the sole controversy was whether appropriation bills, like revenue bills, would have to originate in the House.[81] But Hamilton left no room for doubt in his explanation of the Article I, § 8 provision that no appropriation to support armies should be "for a longer term than two years." Not satisfied with having forbidden the President to raise armies without congressional authorization,[82] the Founders had guarded even against congressional abdication of its control over military expenditures:[83]

> [T]he Legislature of the United States will be obliged by this provision, once at least in every two years, to deliberate upon the propriety of keeping a military force on foot; to come to a new resolution on the point; and to declare their sense of the matter, by a formal vote in the face of their constituents.[84]

The explicit assumption of this passage is that the appropriation process *typically* entails deliberation over the desirability of supporting the activity in question, even if already authorized by law; the clause limiting military appropriations is an exception only in that it requires Congress to deliberate on that subject every two years.[85]

---

[79]Id, Art II, § 3.

[80]Congress's express duty to call a constitutional convention at the request of two thirds of the states (id, Art V), invoked as an analogy by Representative William Smith (see note 57), was distinguishable on the same ground.

[81]See 1 Farrand at 538; 2 id at 200, 545.

[82]"[T]he whole power of raising armies was lodged in the *legislature*, not in the *executive* . . . ." The Federalist No 24.

[83]Id.

[84]Id, No 26.

[85]At least two early commentators on the Constitution reached the same conclusion. St. George Tucker, emphasizing that the appropriation clause was meant to ensure that no money was spent without the approval of the people's representatives, lamented that it meant Congress could frustrate the satisfaction of judicial judgments recognizing claims against the United States. 1 Tucker's Blackstone at 362–64. Story, thirty years later, took issue with Tucker on the desirability of exempting judgments from the appropriation requirement but agreed it implied discretion to refuse to vote money. 3 Story, §§ 1342–43. The assumption that Congress had such discretion was an important factor in Chief Justice Taney's draft opinion in Gordon v United States, 74 US 188 (1868) (arguing that the Supreme Court could not review a decision of the Court of Claims). See also Williams v United States, 289 US 553 (1933) (making the same assumption in concluding that suits against the United States were not "controversies to which the United States shall be a party" within the meaning of Article III, § 2). Discretion not to pay judgments against the United States no longer is thought to take suits against the Government outside either the judicial power or the list of federal matters in Article III, but the assumption of congressional discretion has never been repudiated. See United States v Jones, 119 US 477 (1886); Glidden v Zdanok, 370 US 530 (1962).

This passage and others like it likewise justify Gallatin's insistence that no treaty could bind Congress to raise armies, to levy taxes, or to declare war.[86] Those powers too were demonstrably given to Congress in order to require a legislative decision on the merits.[87]

Gallatin was on shakier ground, however, in extending this argument to treaty provisions affecting foreign commerce. There is nothing in the history of the commerce clause to suggest that it, like the fiscal and military powers, was designed to limit the authority elsewhere given to the President and Senate; inspired by the embarrassments engendered by state regulations on the subject, the Framers made clear that their purpose was to ensure that foreign commerce was subject to federal control.[88] That is not to say that the President may legislate generally on matters of interstate or foreign commerce, for he essentially is given only executive powers. To accomplish its evident purpose of providing a mechanism for the resolution of disputes with other nations, however, the treaty power must be construed (as it has been) to embrace all subjects of legitimate international concern[89]—limited only by such provisions as were intended as a check on powers otherwise granted, not by every grant of congressional authority. Thus in the field of foreign commerce, as in other areas of foreign affairs, there may be a significant overlap between executive and legislative powers.[90]

II.   TENNESSEE

The arguments over discretion in the exercise of congressional authority so ably presented in the controversy over the Jay Treaty were repeated in a variety of additional contexts during the Fourth Congress. Consistently, Gallatin, Giles, and other budding

[86]5 Annals at 739–40.

[87]On raising armies see the sources just cited. On taxes we can begin with the English Bill of Rights, 1 W&M Sess 2 c 2 (1688) ("The levying money for or to the use of the crown, . . . without grant of parliament, . . . is illegal") and the Stamp Act Congress, Journal of the First Congress of the American Colonies in Opposition to the Tyrannical Acts of the British Parliament 28 (E. Winchester, 1845) ("the undoubted rights of Englishmen, that no taxes should be imposed upon them, but with their own consent, given personally, or by their representatives") and move on to the Constitutional Convention, where advocates of the Article I, § 7 provision forbidding even the Senate to initiate revenue bills explained that "the people ought to hold the purse strings" (Gerry, 1 Farrand at 233) and that only "the immediate representatives of the people" should have "the power of giving away the peoples [sic] money" (Mason, id at 544). See also id at 546 (Franklin) (arguing that "money affairs" should be "confined to the immediate representatives of the people"); 2 Farrand at 275 (Gerry): "Taxation & representation are strongly associated in the minds of the people, and they will not agree that any but their immediate representatives shall meddle with their purses"; The Federalist No 58 (Hamilton). On the power to declare war see, e.g., id, No 69 (Hamilton) (explaining that the President's authority as Commander in Chief "would amount to nothing more than the supreme command and direction of the military and naval forces, as first General and Admiral of the Confederacy; while that of the British King extends to the *declaring* of war and to the *raising* of fleets and armies; all of which by the Constitution under consideration would appertain to the Legislature"). See also 2 Farrand at 318–19; 1 Tucker's Blackstone at 269–70; 1 Kent at 53; and the views of Washington and Jefferson quoted in chapter 2.

[88]"[B]ecause the States individually are incompetent to the purpose that the United-States should also regulate the Commerce of the United-States foreign and internal, is I believe a matter of general Consent." 4 Farrand at 23 (Luther Martin). See also Madison's preface to the Convention debates, 3 Farrand at 547–48; The Federalist No 22.

[89]See note 32.

[90]See Hamilton's argument with respect to neutrality in Pacificus No 1, 15 Hamilton Papers at 33, discussed in chapter 4.

Republicans insisted that the House was free to refuse to appropriate money for the operations of the mint,[91] for completion of the *Constitution* and other frigates authorized by
statute,[92] and for the salaries of foreign ministers whom the President (with Senate consent) had conceded authority to appoint.[93] Predictably, proto-Federalists like Sedgwick,
Murray, Ames, and William Smith took the opposite position[94]—but not without significant concessions as to the existence of legislative discretion.[95] In each case, as in the
treaty controversy, Congress ultimately voted to provide the money;[96] in each case it was
perfectly consistent to vote appropriations while asserting the right to deny them.[97]

The admission of Tennessee to the Union raised a closely analogous question, and
some of the same arguments were made. But this time the parties changed sides: Those
who had most adamantly defended Congress's discretion not to implement the treaty insisted that Tennessee had a right to admission, while those who had maintained that the

[91] 5 Annals at 254 (Rep. Gallatin) (insisting that "there was certainly a discretionary power in the House to
appropriate or not to appropriate for any object whatever, . . . for the purpose of checking the other branches
of Government"); id at 261 (Rep Giles).

[92] 6 Annals at 2055 (Rep. Giles); id at 2204 (Rep. Venable). Representatives Varnum and Nicholas made
the same argument in respect to appropriations for the horses and equipment of a unit of cavalry that
Congress (following Washington's veto, see note 12) had just authorized the President to retain. Id at 2337,
2239.

[93] 5 Annals at 1488, 1492 (Rep. Gallatin); id at 1491 (Rep. Giles). As Giles noted, the First Congress had
acquiesced in the President's assertion of the appointment authority. See chapter 1. The debate over
Congress's right not to provide funds for the President's envoys was repeated at great length during the Fifth
Congress, when Republicans vainly sought to use the appropriation power to reduce the rank and salary of
our Ministers to Spain and Portugal and to frustrate Adams's decision to send a representative to Prussia. 7
Annals at 435–40, 849–945, 1083–1216; 8 Annals at 1217–34. It was in the course of the former debate that
the usually sensible and intelligent George Nicholas of Virginia obtusely declared that "we ought to have no
political connexion with Europe" at all. 7 Annals at 922.

[94] See, e.g., 5 Annals at 253 (Rep. Smith); id at 254–55 (Rep. Sedgwick); id at 258–60 (Rep. Murray)
(arguing that refusing to fund an activity authorized by statute was tantamount to repealing the law and thus
beyond the competence of a single House); 6 Annals at 2343–44 (Rep. Ames).

[95] Smith acknowledged (as he had argued during the First Congress, see note 263 of chapter 1) that
Congress had power to refuse to appropriate money for ministers' salaries while arguing it should not do so
without "very strong reasons." 5 Annals at 1494. Ames, having posed the rhetorical question whether it was
not necessary to repeal the law authorizing construction of frigates before deciding not to build them (6
Annals at 2343–44), later denied having said that the House "had not a discretion"; he had meant only that in
exercising their discretion the members "ought to be regulated by duty." Id at 2347.

[96] See 1 Stat 445, 446–47, § 1 (Feb 5, 1796) (Mint); 1 Stat 508, 509 (Mar 3, 1797) (frigates); 1 Stat 493, § 3
(June 1, 1796) (ministers' salaries). See also 5 Annals at 1496.

[97] Representative Buck, who had argued that Congress was bound to appropriate money to carry out the
treaty, contended that statutes were different. To refuse to vote money to implement a statute, he seemed to
be saying, did not undermine anyone else's powers, since the House did not have to pass the law in the first
place. 6 Annals at 2204. See also Louis Henkin, Constitutionalism, Democracy, and Foreign Affairs 31
(Columbia, 1990): "[W]here the President has independent constitutional authority to act, Congress, I believe,
is constitutionally bound to implement his actions, notably by appropriating the necessary funds . . . ." The opposite distinction is arguably more plausible, since the appropriation power was specifically designed as a
congressional check on *other* branches; but the text of the provision and the statements of the Framers suggest
that no money was to be spent to satisfy *any* obligation until Congress had specifically addressed the question
of the expenditure itself.

treaty left no room for legislative judgment tended to argue that Congress was not obliged to admit the new state.[98]

In April 1796 President Washington laid before Congress a communication from Governor William Blount of the Territory South of the River Ohio containing a new state constitution and the results of a local census purporting to show that the Territory had a population of more than sixty thousand persons. The statute establishing the Territory, Washington reminded the legislators, had extended to its inhabitants all the privileges set forth in the Northwest Ordinance, which appeared to include the right to join the Union when they reached that number and adopted a form of government consistent with the Ordinance and the Constitution.[99]

A House committee accordingly found that the citizens of the Territory, "now formed into a State . . . by the name of Tennessee," were "entitled to all the rights and privileges to which the citizens of other States in the Union are entitled" and that Tennessee ought therefore to be "declared to be one of the sixteen United States of America."[100]

William Smith, who had taken the lead in arguing that Congress was obliged to implement the treaty with Great Britain, began to quibble. The Ordinance provided for dividing the Northwest Territory into three to five states, each of which was to be admitted when it attained a population of sixty thousand; the deed by which North Carolina ceded the area that was to be Tennessee contemplated its division into "a state or states." Thus no state could be admitted until Congress had determined how many states there should be; and by separating the Territory into two states Congress might "leave less than sixty thousand inhabitants in either, and consequently deprive them of any claim whatever to an admission into the Union at this time."[101]

Harper acknowledged that he thought it "doubtful whether the people of the Southwestern Territory had a right to erect themselves, by their own act, into a State," but he argued that Congress should admit them anyway in the interest of popular sovereignty—leaving the number of Representatives to be determined by a subsequent federal census.[102]

Madison, Gallatin, and a number of others insisted that Tennessee had a right to admission.[103] Jonathan Dayton of New Jersey, the Speaker, met them head on:

---

[98]The story is ably told in Samuel C. Williams, The Admission of Tennessee into the Union, 4 Tenn Hist Q 291 (1945).

[99]1 Richardson at 197, 5 Annals at 68, 891. For the statute incorporating the Territory see 1 Stat 123, § 1 (May 26, 1790); for the relevant provisions of the Ordinance see 1 Stat 50, 53 n (a), Art V.

[100]5 Annals at 1300.

[101]Id at 1300–02. See also id at 1306–08 (Rep. Sedgwick); id at 1323–27 (Rep. Sitgreaves). Smith also contended that only Congress could conduct the census needed to determine whether the condition for admission had been met, since territorial authority extended only to "internal concerns," and that several provisions of the state constitution were inconsistent with the Ordinance or with the Constitution. Id at 1302–04. Sedgwick added that the census was inaccurate because it had included not only inhabitants but everyone present within the Territory, and because some of them might have been counted more than once. Id at 1307.

[102]Id at 1304–06.

[103]Id at 1308 (Rep. Madison); id at 1311 (Rep. Nicholas); id at 1315 (Rep. Blount); id at 1316 (Rep. Lyman); id at 1318 (Reps. Macon and Baldwin); id at 1320 (Rep. Gallatin).

He could never give his assent to any proposition which expressly or even impliedly admitted that the people inhabiting either of the Territories of the United States could, at their own will and pleasure, and without the declared consent of Congress, erect themselves into a separate and independent State. Yet this seemed to be the spirit of the report under consideration, and what was still worse, it went, as he understood it, to renounce any right in Congress even to deliberate whether they should become a member of the Union.[104]

Dayton was badly outnumbered; the House adopted the resolution recognizing a right to admission by a vote of forty-three to thirty.[105] The Senate disagreed, resolving for the reasons given by Representative Smith that Tennessee was "not at this time entitled to be received as a new State"[106] and passing a bill to provide for a federal census prior to admission.[107] The House stuck to its guns,[108] and the Senate ultimately receded.[109] Proclaiming that by accepting the Territory Congress had "bound" itself to lay it out into one or more states, the statute flatly declared Tennessee a state "on an equal footing with the original states."[110]

Thus the House of Representatives, barely a month after ceremoniously declaring that no treaty could bind it to appropriate money, just as unequivocally announced that the statute establishing the Southwest Territory deprived it of discretion to determine whether or not Tennessee should become a state.

The Articles of Confederation had given Canada a right to join the Union without asking its consent,[111] but Article IV of the Constitution says that "[n]ew states may be admitted by the Congress into this Union."[112] Even without this contrast, the term "may" reeks of discretion; the natural inference is that in admitting states, as in appropriating money, Congress is to determine for itself what the public interest demands. Moreover, no clause of the Constitution expressly requires the United States to live up to its obligations; the contract clause applies only to the individual states.[113] If Congress

[104]Id at 1313–14.

[105]Id at 1328–29.

[106]Id at 94.

[107]Id at 94, 108–09.

[108]Id at 1473–74.

[109]Id at 117.

[110]1 Stat 491 (June 1, 1796). The "equal footing" language was taken from the Northwest Ordinance, which provided that the states carved from the Northwest Territory should be admitted on that basis. 1 Stat at 53 n (a), Art V. Representative Macon had moved that Tennessee be given two House seats (5 Annals at 1474), the territorial census having shown a population twice the established quota of 33,000 even without adding 3/5 of the slaves. See id at 1312 (Rep. Blount). Yet Macon's motion "was opposed on all sides, as giving an advantage to this State over all others, whose representation was fixed in the year 1790" (id at 1474), and the statute allowed the new state only one Representative. 1 Stat at 492.

[111]"Canada acceding to this confederation, and joining in the measures of the United States, shall be admitted into, and entitled to all the advantages of this Union . . . ." Articles of Confederation, Art 11, 1 Stat at 8.

[112]US Const, Art IV, § 3.

[113]Id, Art I, § 10. Even pre-existing engagements, as explained in connection with Hamilton's public-credit plan in chapter 2, are made only "as valid against the United States under this Constitution, as under the Confederation." Id, Art VI.

may renege on promises to other nations, as the House concluded in the treaty dispute, it is difficult to see why it cannot equally renege on promises to its own constituents. Indeed it is not at all obvious that Congress *can* promise not to exercise its constitutional discretion. The one thing Parliament is concededly unable to do is to surrender its authority;[114] even states bound by the contract clause, the Supreme Court has held, cannot bargain away their police powers.[115]

Possibly the strongest argument in favor of the House's position that Congress had no right to examine the merits of Tennessee's admission was that it had already done so when it established the Southwest Territory in 1790. For by incorporating the Northwest Ordinance provisions respecting statehood into the territorial statute Congress seems to have made the policy decision, as Article IV required, that Tennessee should become a state; arguably Congress had conditionally admitted Tennessee to the Union.[116]

As Article II is silent about conditional approval of treaties, Article IV says nothing about conditional admission; it may be that Congress must either admit a state or not, as a President must sign or reject a bill.[117] But the precedents did not entirely fit this model. Neither Kentucky or Vermont was simply admitted by statute; Congress decreed that both "shall be . . . admitted" at a prescribed date in the future.[118] If admission may be conditioned on the passage of time, maybe it can be subjected to other conditions as well. On the other hand, time will pass of its own accord; whether a state constitution is consistent with the Northwest Ordinance or "republican," as the Southwest statute required, can be determined only by the exercise of judgment. Yet Congress reserved the right to make that determination for itself; it is not clear why it should have to determine all questions respecting a state's admission at the same time. Indeed, if the provision is read to require Congress to determine at the time of admission whether a territory deserves to become a state, the earlier statutes may have been the more questionable. For in Tennessee's case Congress at least read the state constitution before passing upon its adequacy; Kentucky's admission was irreversibly approved before its constitution was even written.[119]

The final question is what all the shouting was about. In the Jay controversy what lay behind the assertions of congressional discretion was a desire to torpedo the agreement; nobody denied that Tennessee belonged in the Union. What the opponents of a right to admission were after was delay. With the presidential election approaching and Washington unlikely to accept a third term, the last thing the emerging Federalists wanted was that Tennessee, with its known Republican sympathies, should be admitted in time to cast its electoral votes. The results confirmed their apprehensions; with the

[114]See Dicey, The Law of the Constitution at 23 (cited in note 68).

[115]Stone v Mississippi, 101 US 814, 817–19 (1880).

[116]Both the House resolution and the 1796 statute suggest this interpretation, for both simply declare Tennessee a state and eschew the term "admission." The statutes respecting Kentucky and Vermont, in contrast, had expressly said those states were to be "admitted" to the Union. 1 Stat 189, § 2 (Feb 4, 1791) (Kentucky); id at 191 (Feb 18, 1791) (Vermont). The biggest obstacle to this line of reasoning may be that the Ordinance provision that Congress wrote into the territorial statute prescribed that states meeting the prescribed criteria "shall be admitted" to the Union; that is the language of promise, not of conditional admission.

[117]US Const, Art I, § 7. See text at note 36–41 (discussing treaties).

[118]See 1 Stat at 189 (Kentucky); id at 191 (Vermont).

[119]See chapter 2.

unanimous support of the new state's electors, Jefferson fell short of Adams by the har-rowing margin of three votes.[120]

Why then did the Senate give in and accept immediate admission? Dark rumblings in the House debate may provide a clue; it may be the Senate feared that if left outside the Union the new state—which had presumptuously set up its own government before its admission was approved—might declare its independence or even take up with Spain.[121]

In one last defiant gesture, on the last day of its session the Senate refused to seat the two Senators certified by the new state, although on that very day the President signed the bill admitting it to the Union.[122] We are not told why. When Vermont was admitted in 1791, Washington had called the Senate into special session to approve his nominations to federal offices there, reasoning that he had no authority to make appoint-ments until Vermont actually became a state.[123] The Senate may have taken an analogous position in 1796: Only a state legislature was entitled to elect Senators,[124] and Tennessee had no state legislature until it was admitted to the Union.[125]

III.   CONGRESSIONAL POWERS

A.   Spending—Again

In his last State of the Union address President Washington renewed his recommendation that Congress establish a university and proposed that it set up a board to promote agri-culture.[126] The House looked coldly on both suggestions.

A committee report endorsing the agricultural board[127] was never brought to debate. Unless one agreed with Hamilton that the general welfare clause empowered Congress to tax and spend for whatever was good for the country,[128] it was hard to find a plausible ar-gument for federal authority.[129] The committee had cleverly proposed that the Board have its headquarters at the seat of government, where Congress had the power of "exclusive

[120]See Williams, 4 Tenn Hist Q at 304–05, 316 (cited in note 98); Stanley J. Folmsbee, Robert E. Corlew, and Enoch L. Mitchell, Tennessee: A Short History 110–12 (Tennessee, 1969); 6 Annals at 1543.

[121]See 5 Annals at 1317 (Rep. Dayton); Williams, 4 Tenn Hist Q at 311–12 (cited in note 98).

[122]5 Annals at 120–21.

[123]See chapter 2.

[124]US Const, Art I, § 3.

[125]The same individuals, duly reelected, took their seats in the following session. See Folmsbee, et al, Tennessee History at 112 (cited in note 120).

[126]6 Annals at 1592, 1594–95 (Dec 7, 1796). To instruct farmers how to take care of their soil, Washington explained, was "a great national object." Letter of George Washington to Alexander Hamilton, Nov 2, 1796, 35 Washington Writings at 251, 254. For the fate of earlier efforts to establish a university see chapter 2.

[127]6 Annals at 1835.

[128]See Hamilton's Report on Manufactures, noted in chapter 2.

[129]"You know," Jefferson wrote a few years later, "some have proposed to Congress to incorporate [an agricultural] society. I am against that, because I think Congress cannot in all the enumerated powers find one which authorizes the act, much less the giving the public money to that use." Letter of Thomas Jefferson to Robert Livingston, Feb 16, 1801, 7 Jefferson Writings (Ford ed) at 492, 493.

legislation";[130] but if that was enough to sustain the proposal there was very little Congress might not do despite the Constitution's careful reservation of unenumerated powers to the states.[131]

The university fared little better despite the support of Madison, who had long since ceased to be—if he ever had been—an advocate of expansive federal powers. His committee modestly proposed that Congress authorize the acceptance of private donations toward an institution at the seat of government,[132] but the House would have none of it.[133] Assurances that nobody was asking for federal dollars[134] fell on deaf ears; the proposal was denounced by suspicious opponents as a nose in the tent,[135] and the university was shelved again.[136]

William Smith made a serious effort to persuade Congress not only to establish a naval yard (which was plainly necessary and proper to providing a navy) but also to ban timber exports and buy timberland to ensure the availability of building materials, and even to provide subsidies for the construction of private vessels that could be converted to government use in an emergency.[137] The export ban would also have been a regulation of commerce,[138] but the timberland proposal reminds the reader of Jefferson's parade of horribles: Next Congress would go into mining to provide the copper too.[139] Indeed

---

[130]US Const, Art I, § 8, cl 17.

[131]Id, Amend 10.

[132]6 Annals at 1694–95.

[133]See, e.g., id at 1699–1700 (Reps. Lyman and Nicholas) (distinguishing between local schools and a national university). That Washington had no mere local institution in mind is suggested by a will he had drawn up (and later altered) that would have left a number of shares of canal stock to a university to be established in the Federal District for "young men from all parts of the United States." See Flexner, Anguish and Farewell at 199, 201 (cited in note 1). See also his letters to the Commissioners of the District of Columbia, Jan 28, 1795, 34 Washington Writings at 106, and to Alexander Hamilton, Sept 1, 1796, 35 id at 198, 199–200.

[134]See 6 Annals at 1698 (Reps. Harper and Craik); id at 1702 (Rep. Madison); id at 1704–05 (Rep. Murray); id at 1710 (Rep. Brent). Brent conceded that Congress had no power to appropriate money for a university; why he thought it could take other steps for the same purpose he did not say.

[135]See id at 1699 (Rep. Lyman) ("If we take this step, I shall very much wonder if our next is not to be called upon to produce money"); id at 1697–98 (Rep. Nicholas); id at 1700 (Rep. Dayton); id at 1701–02 (Rep. Livingston). See also the caustic assessment of Madison's own biographer:

> Nobody pointed out to Madison that the visible part of his project contravened his contention that Congress had no power to set up corporations, and that the invisible part of it was out of harmony with his strict interpretation of the "general welfare" clause.

3 Brant at 448.

[136]6 Annals at 1711.

[137]5 Annals at 887; 6 Annals at 2131, 2154.

[138]On prohibitions as regulations see chapters 2 and 4.

[139]See Letter of Thomas Jefferson to Edward Livingston, Apr 30, 1800, 7 Jefferson Writings (Ford ed) at 443, 444:

> Congress are authorized to defend the nation. Ships are necessary for defence; copper is necessary for ships; mines, necessary for copper; a company necessary to work mines; and who can doubt this reasoning who has ever played at "This is the House that Jack Built"?

"We are here engaged in improving our constitution by construction," he wrote to Robert Livingston the same day, "so as to make it what the majority thinks it should have been." Id at 444, 445.

Congress asked the President to look into that very thing a few years later—in the Territories, where there should have been no doubt of federal authority.[140] In the meantime nothing came of Smith's ambitious proposals.[141]

A fire that devastated the Georgia port city of Savannah presented a spectacular opportunity for Hamilton's disciples, for the idea of aiding the victims had obvious emotional appeal for Southern Representatives, many of whom were ideologically allergic to federal spending.[142] Supporters generally avoided the inflammatory term "general welfare," invoking the distinguishable precedent of aid to the refugees from St. Domingo[143] and muttering vaguely about restoring commerce, revenue, and defenses without clearly identifying the source of congressional authority.[144] Tiptoeing cautiously around the general welfare clause, poor Abraham Baldwin (of Georgia!) repeated in best Madisonian terms that Congress could spend only to pay the debts, to provide for the common defense, and for the other purposes listed in Article I, § 8 and came perilously close to asking Congress to overlook the limitations on its power.[145]

One has the sense the wily Federalists were hoping to slip this one by on sympathy grounds, only to employ it mercilessly as a precedent later on.[146] But the Republicans refused the bait. Macon and Nicholas flatly denied Congress's authority;[147] Giles reminded Baldwin that Congress had no right to ignore the Constitution.[148] Even some Members with an expansive view of federal power were unwilling to open the Treasury

---

[140]2 Stat 87 (Apr 16, 1800). See US Const, Art IV, § 3: "The Congress shall have power to dispose of and make all needful rules and regulations respecting the territory or other property belonging to the United States . . . ." A bill to incorporate a company to mine copper (in New Jersey!) passed the House the same year but did not become law. 10 Annals at 987–89. It was of this bill that Jefferson (see the preceding note) complained.

[141]The Fifth Congress authorized the President both to buy timberlands (1 Stat 622 (Feb 25, 1799)) and to manufacture cannon and other arms if they could not conveniently be purchased (1 Stat 555, § 2 (May 4, 1798))—as Washington had also suggested in his 1797 address. See 6 Annals at 1594.

[142]See id at 1696 (Rep. William Smith) (proposing federal assistance).

[143]Id at 1712 (Rep. Smith); id at 1714 (Rep. Hartley). Representative Macon reminded the House that the St. Domingo outlay had been carefully crafted as a payment on the debt to France in order to allay widespread doubts as to the authority to make a gift of federal funds. Id at 1717; see the discussion of the St. Domingo incident in chapter 4. Smith also relied on the earlier decision to compensate victims of the Whiskey Rebellion. Id at 1724. But that measure, as Coit observed, was "a very different thing; the grant was in consequence of exertions in favor of Government," id at 1726, and it was defended as necessary to promote the enforcement of the laws. See chapter 4.

[144]See 6 Annals at 1716 (Rep. Smith); id at 1719 (Rep. Murray); id at 1726 (Rep. Claiborne). Harper was less cautious: "The present case might justly be included under the head of promoting the general welfare of the country." Id at 1721.

[145]6 Annals at 1721–22. Cf Madison's remarks in the debate over the Bank of the United States, noted in chapter 2.

[146]They had carefully left little handholds for use in later argument: Smith said it was in the "general interest" to help Savannah, 6 Annals at 1716, Murray called the fire a "national calamity," id at 1719, and Claiborne slipped the dreaded GW words into a plea to help restore revenue and trade. Id at 1726. See also Harper's unequivocal statement, quoted in note 144.

[147]Id at 1717 (Rep. Macon); id at 1723 (Rep. Nicholas).

[148]Id at 1724.

for this purpose;[149] and the proposal, like the city itself, went down (up?) in flames.[150]

B. Direct Taxes

Nobody denied that Congress had power to impose direct taxes,[151] but they were not popular. When the Ways and Means Committee in March 1796 proposed to ask the Secretary of the Treasury to prepare a plan for raising $2,000,000 by direct taxation to help cover an anticipated deficit,[152] doubts were expressed whether a direct tax should be levied at all.[153] When, after receiving the Secretary's detailed report,[154] the Committee recommended that a direct tax actually be laid,[155] serious issues were raised as to how it could or should be done.

The first question was what should be taxed. Secretary Wolcott had identified three possible approaches: Congress might specify the objects to be taxed everywhere, tax whatever the various states taxed directly, or leave it to each state to collect and pay over its share.[156] Representative Varnum advocated the last option,[157] but Wolcott had listed it only to condemn it as bad policy: "[I]t partakes of the system of requisitions upon the States, which utterly failed under the late Confederation, and to remedy which, was one great object of establishing the present Government."[158] The Committee, which had originally proposed asking the Secretary for a scheme incorporating state law,[159] opted for a tax on land, improvements, and slaves.[160] But neither Varnum nor Wolcott nor the Committee perceived any constitutional impediment to laying taxes that differed from one

---

[149]Even if Hamilton was right that Congress could spend for anything that would enhance the general welfare, Savannah's plight was arguably not "general" but local. See 2 Story, § 919: "[I]f the welfare be not general but special, or local, as contradistinguished from national, it is not within the scope of the constitution."

[150]The vote was fifty-five to twenty-four. 6 Annals at 1727. A proposal by Madison for a survey of existing post roads and an estimate of the expense of making them "fit" provoked an anguished response from his vigilant friend in Monticello on an issue that would soon divide the nation: The power to "establish" post roads, wrote Jefferson, was the power only to designate routes, not to build them. Madison replied without elaboration that he proposed to open new roads "so far only as may be necessary for the transportation of the mail," and "[t]his I think fairly within the object of the Const[itutio]n." See 5 Annals at 298, 314–15; Letter of Thomas Jefferson to James Madison, Mar 6, 1796, 16 Madison Papers at 249, 251; Letter of James Madison to Thomas Jefferson, Apr 4, 1796, id at 285.

[151]See US Const, Art I, §§ 2, 8, 9.

[152]5 Annals at 791–94.

[153]E.g., id at 843–44 (Rep. Williams) (noting that land taxes were hard on farmers "in cases of bad crops"). See also 6 Annals at 1865 (Rep. Cooper) (arguing that the Framers had anticipated direct taxes only as a last resort); id (Rep. Harper) (arguing that direct taxes were difficult to apportion and to collect).

[154]See id at 2635–2713.

[155]Id at 1843.

[156]Id at 2699.

[157]Id at 1881. A land tax, Varnum complained, would fall most heavily on farmers. Id.

[158]Id at 2699. For the Federal Government to collect the taxes only in case of state delinquency, Wolcott added, would result in "unavoidable collision with the State Governments." Id at 2699.

[159]5 Annals at 793.

[160]6 Annals at 1843. Southerners had argued in the debate over the Quakers' anti-slavery petition in 1790 that the requirement that direct taxes be apportioned according to the census was designed to prevent federal taxes on slaves (see chapter 2), but the point was not repeated in 1796; the addition of land and improvements as objects of taxation assured that free states would pay their prescribed share.

state to another,[161] or to delegating to the states authority to define and collect federal taxes.

The most serious question, however, was how to apportion the tax among the states "according to their respective numbers" and "in proportion to the census," as the second and ninth sections of Article I required.

Adopting Wolcott's figures, the Committee proposed that the apportionment be based upon the previous census, which had been taken in 1790.[162] But that enumeration was already more than six years old, and several members objected that it would saddle states that had not increased significantly in population with more than their share of the burden. A new census must be taken, it was argued, to ensure that the tax be apportioned according to actual "numbers."[163]

A new census, replied New York's Jonathan Havens, would not do; representation and taxation must be apportioned by the same standard, and House seats had been allotted under the old enumeration.[164] Very well, said Zephaniah Swift of Connecticut, let there be a new census for both purposes.[165] But as Havens had already pointed out,[166] under Article I, § 2 the census was to be taken once every ten years.[167] Although the obvious purpose of this provision was to require that the population be counted *at least* that frequently, it was not clear it permitted the expense of more frequent enumeration; and in any event § 9 expressly (though perhaps not deliberately) tied direct taxation to the census "herein before *directed* to be taken."[168]

When the hubbub subsided, the House approved the tax in principle and directed the committee to bring in an appropriate bill.[169] But the Fourth Congress had only six more weeks to sit, and no bill appeared. The following year, after a second report from the Secretary[170] and a reprise of the plea for a new enumeration,[171] the Fifth Congress enacted a direct tax on land, houses, and slaves, apportioned according to the 1790 census.[172] Although it might be excessively literal to say that the Constitution precluded an

[161]See also 1 Tucker's Blackstone at 238.

[162]See 6 Annals at 1843–44; id at 2645.

[163]"In the report of the Secretary of the Treasury," said Representative Swift, "Connecticut was apportioned $98,000 of the estimated tax, and New York $140,000; the latter being only about $40,000 more than the former, though it contained double the number of inhabitants." Id at 1915–16. See also id at 1855, 1856 (Rep. Christie); id at 1918 (Rep. Holland).

[164]Id at 1917–18. See also id at 1919 (Rep. Gilbert) ("representation & taxation must go together").

[165]Id at 1922.

[166]Id at 1917.

[167]"The actual enumeration shall be made within three years after the first meeting of the Congress . . . , and within every subsequent term of ten years . . . ."

[168]Even if there was a new census, Gallatin added, no tax could be assessed under it until the term of the newly apportioned Congress began, since taxation was to be proportional to actual representation. 6 Annals at 1926. Dayton's response that taxation and representation were to be apportioned "by one common standard, but not by each other" (id at 1927) missed the mark; things equal to the same thing, as we learned in elementary geometry, are equal to each other.

[169]Id at 1941.

[170]9 Annals at 3594.

[171]See 8 Annals at 1597 (Rep. Bayard).

[172]1 Stat 597 (July 14, 1798). With minor exceptions the quotas allotted to each state by the statute were taken from Wolcott's most recent report, and he said he had based them on the 1790 figures. See 1 Stat at 597–98, § 1; 9 Annals at 3594.

interim census, Congress seems right in concluding that it could base the direct tax on the old one; for the requirement that the people be counted only once in ten years suggests that the Framers were willing to permit some deviation from the ideal of equal apportionment in the interest of reducing administrative expense, so long as taxation and representation were tied to the same standard.[173]

C. Perils of the Deep

Two proposals for legislation during the Fourth Congress engendered debates over the interpretation of the commerce clause. The first concerned the quarantine of foreign ships, the second the regulation of pilots in Chesapeake Bay.

Representative Samuel Smith of Maryland ignited the first controversy by proposing that the President be authorized to impose such quarantine requirements as he thought necessary.[174] There were objections on grounds both of separation of powers[175] and of federalism. In the end a bill was enacted merely empowering the President to enforce state quarantine laws;[176] the result was yet another victory for states' rights in the House.

Quarantine was a health matter, argued Representative Hiester, and it ought to be left to the states.[177] No, said Smith, it was a commercial regulation and therefore within federal power.[178] Indeed, added Samuel Sitgreaves of Pennsylvania, because quarantine fell within the commerce power, it could not be left to the states.[179] The answer was not that,

---

In accord with Wolcott's report, the bill initially provided for paying to the United States any excess above a state's quota that resulted from applying the statutory formulas for determining the tax to be paid by individual owners of houses, land, and slaves. When Representative Holmes rightly objected that states could not be obliged to contribute more than their apportioned share, the bill was amended to make each state's apportionment a ceiling on its obligation. See id at 2060, 2061; 1 Stat at 599, § 3.

[173]Like the whiskey excise of 1791 (see chapter 2), the direct tax provoked a minor revolt, this time in the Pennsylvania Dutch country of southeastern Pennsylvania. Adams sent in the troops. See 1 Richardson at 286–87. John Fries, leader of a mob that had compelled federal officers to release imprisoned resisters, was convicted of treason on the same shaky theory that had been employed against leaders of the Whiskey Rebellion five years before (see chapter 4). Like the earlier defendants, he was ultimately pardoned, after the President expressed doubt whether every case of resistance to the enforcement of federal law amounted to "levying war" against the United States within the meaning of Article III. See Wharton's State Trials at 458, 641–48; Elkins & McKitrick at 696–99; Miller at 246–49; Ralph Adams Brown, The Presidency of John Adams 128–29 (Kansas, 1975); Letter of John Adams to the Heads of Departments, May 20, 1800, in Charles Francis Adams, ed, 9 The Works of John Adams 57, 58 (Little, Brown, 1853); Letter of John Adams to Charles Lee, May 21, 1800, id at 60.

[174]5 Annals at 1228.

[175]See, e.g., id at 1357 (Rep. Page) (condemning the bill as "an attempt to extend the power of the Executive").

[176]1 Stat 474 (May 27, 1796).

[177]5 Annals at 1347.

[178]Id at 1348.

[179]Id at 1350. Others offered a more modest version of the same argument: The states might enact quarantine regulations, but they could not enforce them without federal assistance; for only Congress had authority to provide for preventing vessels from entering port. Id at 1348 (Reps. Samuel Smith and William Smith); id at 1349 (Rep. Bourne) ("[I]t being of the nature of a commercial regulation, to which, by the Constitution, Congress alone were competent").

as the language suggested, Congress had concurrent rather than exclusive power;[180] it was that the regulation concerned health and not commerce and thus was not within congressional authority at all.[181] It seemed to be understood that, if quarantine rules were regulations of commerce, only Congress could make them.[182]

But the argument that quarantine was a matter of health rather than commerce (though to a modern observer it is pretty clearly both)[183] seems to have carried the day. The bill was amended by a whopping majority[184] to authorize the President only to enforce state law, as in the earlier statute respecting the inspection of goods for export[185]— apparently on the theory that interfering with the passage of ships *was* a regulation of commerce and therefore beyond state power.[186]

Swanwick's proposal to require Virginia to license Maryland pilots[187] raised a very different question. Nobody denied that what was proposed was a regulation of interstate and foreign commerce, although after the quarantine debate one might have expected an argument that safety, like health, was a matter reserved to the states.[188] Joshua Coit of Connecticut opposed the bill on the understandable and modern ground (asserted not for the first time) that Congress could not tell the states what to do.[189] Samuel Smith responded that state officers "might be directed to grant licenses . . . on the same ground that the Judges and Justices of States are directed to do the business of the United States."[190] Although the Judiciary Act had carefully refrained from requiring state courts to hear federal cases,[191] there was indeed precedent for imposing affirmative obligations on state judges—and on other state officers as well.[192] Sitgreaves replied (without reported explanation) that Smith had chosen the wrong analogy: Congress should *ask* Virginia to

[180]Contrast US Const, Art I, § 8, cl 17 (power of "exclusive legislation" over seat of government); id, Art I, § 10 (states forbidden to make war under most circumstances, to enter treaties, or to coin money). See The First Hundred Years at 173–74.

[181]5 Annals at 1352, 1354 (Rep. Lyman); id at 1358 (Rep. Holland). Any adverse effect on commerce, Lyman added, was merely incidental. Id at 1354. The states had so understood the Constitution from the beginning, said Representative Brent, as they had enacted and enforced their own quarantine laws. Id at 1359.

[182]Both Tucker and Rawle asserted that Congress's commerce powers were exclusive. See 1 Tucker's Blackstone at 180; Rawle at 81–82.

[183]See Gibbons v Ogden, 22 US 1, 235 (Johnson, J, concurring).

[184]See 5 Annals at 1359.

[185]See chapter 2.

[186]See note 179. Occasional Members asserted that states had the right to stop ships but still needed federal help. See 5 Annals at 1352 (Rep. Williams); id at 1355 (Rep. Swanwick).

[187]The problem, Swanwick explained, was that Maryland pilots refused to assist distressed vessels bound for Virginia ports because Virginia would not permit them to collect a fee for their services, "so that many had been lost for want of pilots, as the Virginia pilots scarcely ever went out to sea." 6 Annals at 1982–83.

[188]The distinction may be that pilotage regulations are designed to ensure the safety of commerce itself, while a quarantine protects the general population. The Supreme Court confirmed that pilotage was a commercial matter in Cooley v Board of Wardens, 53 US 299 (1852).

[189]6 Annals at 1983. For earlier objections along the same lines see the discussions of the certification of electors and of warnings to insurgents in chapter 3.

[190]6 Annals at 1983.

[191]See chapter 1. Much later the Supreme Court would uphold Congress's authority to impose such duties on state judges, but it has never satisfactorily distinguished them from executive officers for this purpose. Compare Testa v Katt, 330 US 386 (1947), with New York v United States, 505 US 144 (1992).

[192]See the discussion of the oath to be taken by state officers (chapter 1), the obligations of justices of the peace under the seamen's act (chapter 2), the duty to certify the selection of presidential electors (chapter 3), and the duty to apprehend and return fugitives (chapter 3).

license Maryland pilots, as the First Congress had asked the states to provide cells for persons convicted of federal crimes.[193]

At this point the House adjourned for the day, and the bill was not taken up again.

D.   Kidnapping and the Right to Petition

In April 1796, in response to a memorial from the state of Delaware, Representative Gallatin asked that the Committee of Commerce and Manufactures explore the possibility of "making effectual provision for preventing the kidnapping of negroes and mulattoes, and of carrying them from their respective States" in violation of state law.[194] The difficulty, Swanwick explained after the committee had made a favorable report, was that state laws were inadequate to prevent the evil; for the victims were spirited away in ships, and the states "had no power on the water."[195] The remedy the committee suggested was to require that every ship captain "have a certificate of the number and situation of any negroes or mulattoes he may have on board."[196]

Murray inquired whether the intention was to prevent "the taking of free negroes and selling them as slaves, or the taking slaves to make them free."[197] Swanwick said both.[198]

William Smith, who had just insisted that Congress had power to buy timberland, impose quarantines, and aid victims of the Savannah fire, suddenly was revealed as a defender of states' rights: Kidnapping was a matter for "municipal regulation, and not at all connected with trade or commerce"; he did not think Congress could meddle with the subject at all.[199]

Isaac Smith of New Jersey replied that he was "sure" that the committee's proposal was constitutional, but he did not say why; and no one attempted to explain the basis of congressional authority. Insofar as the idea was to prevent the freeing of slaves, it might conceivably have been defended as necessary to implement the fugitive-slave clause of Article IV, although there were difficulties in fitting the proposal to the language of that provision.[200] But if Congress was to deal with the problem of stealing slaves from their masters to resell them, or with the enslavement of free blacks, the best hope of justification lay in the commerce clause, and that seems to have been what the sponsors of the proposal had in mind.[201]

[193]6 Annals at 1983. For the prisoner provision see 1 Stat 96 (Sept 23, 1789), noted in chapter 2.

[194]5 Annals at 1025. For reference to the state's memorial see 6 Annals at 1730.

[195]Id at 1731.

[196]Id at 1730.

[197]Id at 1731.

[198]Id. See also id at 1732 (Rep. Sitgreaves) (declaring that the purpose was to protect free blacks but that he was prepared to combat the freeing of slaves, too).

[199]Id at 1731–32. Moreover, he added, there was no obstacle to the application of state law on shipboard: "The laws of the States could prevent robbery on water as well as on land, if within the jurisdiction of the United States." Id at 1732.

[200]Article IV speaks of persons held to service in one state and "escaping into another." Maybe one who is "kidnapped" for his own good can be said to be "escaping," and maybe one can be in the process of escaping to another state before one gets there; but there were references in the debate to persons being transported "to the West Indies and other parts of the world" as well. See 6 Annals at 1732 (Rep. Isaac Smith).

[201]The memorial had been sent to the Committee of Commerce and Manufactures, and William Smith pointedly argued that the proposal had nothing to do with commerce. The transportation of kidnapped persons

There are unspoken analogies both to the quarantine statute that Congress had enacted a few months prior to this debate[202] and to the 1790 law forbidding ships to leave port without complying with state inspection laws.[203] In all three cases Congress was asked to regulate the operation of vessels on navigable waters in the interest of enforcing state law. Smith's argument notwithstanding, legislative precedent thus appeared to support Congress's authority to take this limited step against kidnapping; but Swanwick reluctantly reported after yet another reference to the committee that its members had been "pretty unanimous" in concluding that it was "not expedient" for the House to take action on the subject,[204] and the proposal was not heard from again.

Less than two weeks later Swanwick presented a petition from four persons "of African descent, late inhabitants and natives of North Carolina," complaining that after having been set free by their masters they had been forced to flee the state to avoid being returned to slavery in accordance with a new state law. Others in the same position, the petition continued, had actually been enslaved or, in one case, apprehended under the Fugitive Slave Act. Appealing to the members of the House and Senate as "fellow-men . . . who can admit that black people . . . have natural affections, social and domestic attachments and sensibilities," the petitioners compared their situation with that of citizens held in captivity by Algerian pirates and inquired eloquently if unspecifically whether there was not "some remedy for an evil of such magnitude" worthy of consideration by "the supreme Legislative body of a free and enlightened people."[205]

As they had done when petitions respecting the slave trade were presented to the First Congress,[206] Southern Representatives argued that the petition should not even be received, and this time they prevailed. In 1790, while finding that the relief requested was within congressional authority, the House appeared to acknowledge that otherwise it would have had no jurisdiction to entertain the petition. In 1797 the House seems to have concluded that the petition was not within its purview.

There were three distinct objections: The subject was judicial;[207] it was reserved to the states;[208] and slaves had no right to petition.[209] None of these objections was persuasive.

Whether the petitioners were slaves, as Sitgreaves noted, could not be ascertained without inquiry; the petition asserted that they were free.[210] Similarly, he argued, only committee consideration could determine whether the matter was one for a state court rather than Congress to resolve.[211] More fundamentally, as several speakers insisted, the petition implicitly sought relief that only Congress could grant: If as alleged the Fugitive

---

over the ocean might well have been punishable under Congress's power "to define and punish piracy and felonies on the high seas" (US Const, Art I, § 8, cl 10), but nothing was said in the debate about making anything a federal crime.

[202]See notes 174–86.

[203]See chapter 2.

[204]6 Annals at 1895–96.

[205]Id at 2015–18.

[206]See chapter 2.

[207]6 Annals at 2020 (Rep. Madison); id at 2022 (Rep. Holland).

[208]Id at 2020 (Rep. Heath); id at 2022–23 (Rep. Macon).

[209]Id at 2019 (Rep. Blount); id at 2021 (Rep. William Smith).

[210]Id at 2019–20.

[211]Id at 2020.

Slave Law had been employed to deprive free people of their liberty, it was Congress that should amend it.[212]

Swanwick went further: Everyone had a right to petition; it did not matter whether they were slaves.[213] There was even precedent for this remarkable position. The Connecticut legislature had not only entertained a petition by a slave seeking emancipation from a master who had fought against independence but had granted it,[214] while the Virginia House of Burgesses had formally resolved to consider "the propositions and grievances . . . of all and every person and persons."[215] The first amendment, which was not cited in the House debate, is inconclusive on this score but hardly promising; for although this history suggests it would not have been inconceivable to include slaves within the "people" whose right to "petition the Government for a redress of grievances" was protected against congressional abridgment, it seems highly improbable that they would have been given the right "peaceably to assemble," which was extended to the same "people" by the same clause.[216]

Tradition did not answer the question whether, as everyone seemed to concede, the right to petition Congress extended only to matters that Congress had power to resolve.[217] The earliest colonial codification of the right, in the Massachusetts Body of

[212]Id at 2019 (Reps. Thatcher and Swanwick); id at 2023 (Rep. Varnum).

[213]"Mr. Swanwick . . . could not have thought . . . that the gentleman was so far from acknowledging the rights of man, as to prevent any class of men from petitioning. If men were aggrieved, and conceive that they have claim to attention, petitioning was their sacred right . . . ." Id at 2019. See also id at 2021–22 (Rep. Thatcher) (semble).

[214]2 Pub Recs of CT, 1778–80 at 427–28.

[215]3 Hening's Va Stats at 246. See Raymond C. Bailey, Popular Influence upon Public Policy: Petitioning in Eighteenth-Century Virginia 6, 43–45 (Greenwood, 1979) (noting that the Burgesses too had entertained petitions from slaves).

[216]Moreover, it was not obvious that the amendment required Congress to accept and consider petitions, or that the petitioners were proper parties to seek redress for wrongs allegedly done to other individuals. What the amendment forbade was the passage of laws abridging the right to petition, and history suggested that the danger to be avoided was that petitioners might be punished for attempting to communicate with the Government. See the English Bill of Rights, 1 W&M Sess 2, c 2 (1688) ("it is the right of the subjects to petition the king, and all commitments and prosecutions for such petitioning are illegal"); the Declaration and Resolves of the First Continental Congress, 1 J Cont Cong at 63 (Oct 14, 1774) ("a right peaceably to assemble, consider of their grievances, and petition the King; and that all prosecutions, prohibitory proclamations, and commitments for the same, are illegal"). The Supreme Court has since flatly stated (although in a context that did not require such a broad conclusion) that the petition clause imposes no duty on the Government to listen or to respond. Smith v Arkansas State Highway Employees, 441 US 463 (1979); Minnesota State Board for Community Colleges v Knight, 465 US 271, 284 (1984). For a brief defense of this conclusion see Norman B. Smith, "Shall Make No Law Abridging . . .": An Analysis of the Neglected, but Nearly Absolute, Right of Petition, 54 U Cin LR 1153, 1190–91 (1986); for criticism see Note, 96 Yale LJ 142 (1986) (noting that colonial assemblies had recognized a duty to respond).

The possible argument that "grievances" should be read—in accordance with notions of judicial standing—to mean the petitioners' own injuries seems less convincing, since petitions traditionally served not only to secure redress of individual harms but also as a source of information for the Government. Indeed petitioning was defended in Congress as an alternative to the proposed right of the people to instruct their representatives that assured public input on legislative issues without compromising the principle of representative government. See 1 Annals at 736, 737–38.

[217]There are so few limits to Congress's power to propose constitutional amendments that almost anything could fall within Congress's cognizance if phrased as a request that the Constitution be amended, but it is not at all clear that the first amendment requires the House to entertain petitions in order to consider granting relief that is not even requested.

Liberties of 1642, expressly required that the subject be within the jurisdiction of the body to which the petition was addressed.[218] Later restatements of the right contained no such explicit limitation, but it may be implicit: There is arguably little point in requiring an agency to consider a petition for redress it has no power to grant.[219]

Despite the fragility of the arguments for rejecting the petition out of hand, the House voted fifty to thirty-three to do so.[220] It is not clear which of the three objections had most force with the Members. The following year, however, when a petition complaining of similar grievances was filed not by manumitted slaves but by a group of Quakers, it was not dismissed summarily; it was referred to a committee, which after requesting additional documentation concluded that the relief sought could be granted only by a court.[221] The contrasting treatment of the two cases, together with the fact that the earlier petition implicitly sought amendment of the Fugitive Slave Act, suggests that dismissal of the first petition was heavily influenced by the identity of the petitioners—though as already indicated it seemed premature to conclude that they were in fact still slaves.

IV.   RANDALL AND WHITNEY

Robert Randall was interested in acquiring federal land—the entire lower peninsula of what is now the state of Michigan. He wanted it badly enough to inform several Representatives that substantial portions of the land would be set aside for those Members of Congress who supported his plan.[222] Representative Buck said he had received a similar proposal from a man named Whitney, who was reported to be a part of the same consortium, before the session began.[223]

Congressman William Smith had reported the incident to the President,[224] but the House was determined to deal with the matter itself. The Sergeant-at-Arms was sent to arrest both Randall and Whitney.[225] After hearing and debate Randall was found guilty of "contempt and of a breach of the privileges of the House" and imprisoned for a week.[226]

---

[218]Colonial Laws of Massachusetts (1887) (reprinted from the edition of 1672).

[219]On the other hand, to reject the jurisdictional limitation would encourage communication by preventing sanctions against persons who guessed wrong in deciding whom to petition.

[220]6 Annals at 2024.

[221]7 Annals at 65, 670, 945, 1032–33.

[222]5 Annals at 166 (Rep. William Smith); id at 167–68 (Reps. Murray and Giles). Giles added that Randall had told him "he had already secured thirty or forty members of this House." Id at 168.

[223]Id at 168. The background is briefly recounted in 16 Madison Papers at 175.

[224]5 Annals at 167. Giles questioned the propriety of communicating the matter to the President, id at 177. He gave no reasons, but Members on the other side of the political fence were to expand on his doubts a few years later in connection with an incident in which several army officers allegedly harassed Representative John Randolph. See chapter 6.

[225]5 Annals at 169–70. President Washington had already issued a warrant for Randall's arrest (for violation of what law is unclear), and he had apparently been apprehended by the City Marshal. The supremacy clause does not seem to answer Representative Venable's question whether the House had power to take Randall from the Marshal's custody since the latter was acting under a federal warrant, but a conflict was avoided when the Sergeant-at-Arms and the Marshal joined forces to bring him before the House. See id at 167, 169, 173.

[226]Id at 220, 244.

Whitney, after cooling his heels in custody while the House considered his case, was discharged.[227]

A statute penalizing attempts to bribe members of Congress would have been necessary and proper to the operations of Congress,[228] but there was no such law. Smith inferred the House's authority to act on its own from the existence of the House itself:

> The present inquiry was of a special and peculiar nature, resulting from the rights and privileges which belonged to every Legislative institution, and without which such institution could not exist. As every jurisdiction had certain powers necessary for its preservation, so the Legislature possessed certain privileges incident to its nature, and essential for its very existence. This is called in England the parliamentary law; and as from that law are derived the usages and proceedings of the several State Legislatures, so will the proceedings of this House be generally guided by the long-established usages of the State Legislatures.[229]

Smith's theory of incidental powers had already been invoked to justify congressional investigations,[230] and there was ample precedent from other legislative bodies for applying it to support House proceedings against Randall and Whitney. Under the rubric of "privilege" the British Parliament had long asserted not only freedom of speech and debate and freedom from civil arrest but also the power to punish bribery or any other interference with its functions,[231] and colonial assemblies had been quick to follow its ex-

---

[227]Id at 226.

[228]Cf the various provisions outlawing interference with federal courts enacted by the First Congress in 1789, discussed in chapter 2. A statute making it a crime to refuse to answer questions in the course of a legitimate legislative investigation was upheld in In re Chapman, 166 US 661, 671–72 (1897).

[229]5 Annals at 181. See also id at 189 (Rep. Isaac Smith): "I will presume to assert that it is a necessary and competent power lodged in this House, *ex necessitate rei*, by which we are enabled to defend ourselves against insult from within and contamination from without." Accord Rawle at 47–48; 2 Story, § 842: "[U]nless such a power, to some extent, exists by implication, it is utterly impossible for either house to perform its constitutional functions"; Luther Sterns Cushing, Law and Practice of Legislative Assemblies 221 (Little, Brown, 9th ed 1874):

> It may be laid down as the first rule on this subject, that the establishment, in general terms, of a legislative department, is equivalent to an express grant, to each branch composing it, of all the powers and privileges which are necessarily incident to a legislative assembly.

[230]See the discussions of the investigations of Robert Morris and of General St. Clair in chapters 1 and 3. The power to investigate strongly implies authority to enforce orders by contempt in that setting, see McGrain v Daugherty, 273 US 135 (1927), but a more general power to punish interference with House operations is a different question.

[231]See Erskine May, Treatise on the Law, Privileges, Proceedings, and Usage of Parliament 143 (Butterworths, 20th ed 1983):

> It may be stated generally that any act or omission which obstructs or impedes either House of Parliament in the performance of its functions, or which obstructs or impedes any Member or officer of such House in the discharge of his duty, or which has a tendency, directly or indirectly, to produce such results may be treated as a contempt even though there is no precedent for the offence.

ample.[232] In some colonies privilege was spelled out by statute or fundamental law; in others, as in England, it was based on necessity and tradition alone.[233]

Several Representatives denied or doubted the House's authority over Randall, and several more questioned its authority over Whitney. No one directly challenged Smith's exposition of the powers of British and colonial assemblies.[234] To the extent they gave reasons, several of those who disputed the House's jurisdiction seemed to embrace Randall's argument that the Constitution had "considerably narrowed" the privileges of Congress.[235] Representative Page was the most explicit in this regard. Parliamentary precedents respecting breach of privilege, he argued, had no relevance to the congressional powers; "the Constitution had defined those powers, and he hoped never to exceed them."[236]

There was more than one way in which the Constitution might have restricted congressional privilege. St. George Tucker, criticizing the House's action a few years later, took the most straightforward and most extreme position: Having codified certain aspects of parliamentary privilege, including the right to discipline members and protect them from official harassment,[237] the Constitution must be taken to have rejected those aspects it did not mention—such as the power to punish private citizens for bribery and other interference with congressional functions.[238] Indeed, although no one mentioned it in the

---

See also id at 70 (defining privilege as "the sum of the peculiar rights enjoyed by the House collectively as a constituent part of the High Court of Parliament, and by members of each House individually, without which they could not discharge their functions"); id at 156–57 (citing pre-1789 bribery cases); 1 Blackstone at 164–66; William Holdsworth, 6 History of English Law 95 (Little, Brown, 1937). Rawle specifically defended the House's jurisdiction in a case of attempted bribery. See Rawle at 47–48.

[232]See Mary Patterson Clarke, Parliamentary Privilege in the American Colonies 63–130 (Da Capo, 1971); 2 Story, § 843 ("No man ever doubted, or denied [the] existence [of parliamentary privilege] as to our colonial assemblies in general, whatever may have been thought, as to particular exercises of it.").

[233]See Clarke, Privilege in the Colonies at 81–82 (cited in note 232). In several colonies, as in England, the Speaker began each session by petitioning the Crown or its representative to confirm the House's privileges, but from an early date the petition was recognized as "an act only of manners," not a prerequisite for the exercise of authority. See May, Parliamentary Privilege at 74 (cited in note 231); Clarke, Privilege in the Colonies at 61–87.

[234]Randall's counsel did argue that the practice of Parliament at the time was to refer such cases to the Attorney General for trial before a jury, 5 Annals at 216, but that practice was not inconsistent with the existence of authority to proceed independently.

[235]See id at 215 (Tilghman's argument for Randall). Representative Brent, in contrast, stated merely that "he had his doubts" whether the House had power to arrest Randall and Whitney; "he was suspicious that they exceeded the limits of their authority." Id at 193. Representative Freeman voted to discharge both prisoners on the ground that "even an outrage upon [the House itself] could be as well punished by a Justice of the Peace as by ourselves." Id at 224. Representative Giles maintained over and over that the evidence did not prove Whitney had committed a breach of privilege, but he staunchly declined to say why. Id at 222–23, 226, 228.

[236]Id at 227–28. See also Letter of James Madison to Thomas Jefferson, Jan 10, 1796, 16 Madison Papers at 180, 181: "[I]t will be difficult, I believe, to deduce the privilege from the Constitution, or limit it in practice, or even to find a precedent for it in the arbitrary claims of the British House of Commons."

[237]US Const, Art I, §§ 5, 6.

[238]1 Tucker's Blackstone at 200–01 n § (also invoking the tenth amendment). Tilghman had hinted at this reasoning in his argument for Randall, 5 Annals at 214. The revolutionary constitutions of Maryland and Massachusetts, in contrast, spelled out the power of legislative chambers to punish a variety of offenses committed by ordinary citizens as well as members and officials—but not in circumstances like those of Randall or Whitney. See Francis Newton Thorpe, ed, 3 The Federal and State Constitutions, Colonial Charters, and Other Organic Laws of the States, Teritories, and Colonies Now or Heretofore Forming the United States

House, the Convention had rejected a proposal to add to the Constitution a clause declaring each House "judge of the privileges of its Members."[239] But the reasons given for this rejection tend to rebut Tucker's contention that the list of privileges in Article I was meant to be exhaustive. Wilson thought an express provision "needless" since all necessary privileges were implicit without it;[240] Madison complained that making the House "judge" of its own privileges might enable it to extend its rights beyond those "previously & duly established."[241]

However, as Tucker also noted, the Constitution did not stop at enumerating certain congressional privileges. Article III, § 1 vested all judicial authority in courts whose judges were made independent by constitutional guarantees of tenure and compensation. The fifth amendment forbade deprivation of life, liberty, or property without due process of law, which Tucker interpreted to require judicial proceedings. It also prohibited punishment for any "infamous crime" without indictment or presentment by a grand jury, while Article III and the sixth amendment required jury trial of all "crimes" or "criminal prosecutions." Legislative punishment for breach of privilege, Tucker intimated, offended all these provisions.[242]

Without mentioning the Constitution, several speakers in the House adverted to additional dimensions of what we would call the due-process problem. Representative Harper, declaring that the privilege doctrine "violated the rights of the people," argued that it made Members of Congress judges in their own cause;[243] Representative Sherburne suggested that punishment for violating vague unwritten law offended the principle of fair warning.[244]

---

of America 1693, 1899 (GPO, 1909); Philip B. Kurland & Ralph Lerner, 2 The Founders' Constitution 288 (Chicago, 1987).

[239]See 2 Farrand at 502–03.

[240]Id at 503.

[241]Id. The English Bill of Rights likewise codified only a part of the traditional parliamentary privilege, yet no one seems to have suggested that in so doing it restricted Parliament's authority. See 1 W&M Sess 2, c 2 (1688) (freedom of speech and debate). The Supreme Court, in upholding congressional contempt powers a generation after the present incident, dismissed Tucker's *inclusio unius* argument by noting that it would equally prevent Congress from defining crimes not explicitly listed in Article I, contrary to longstanding precedent. Anderson v Dunn, 19 US 204, 232–33 (1821); see the discussion of the 1789 Crimes Act in chapter 2.

[242]See 1 Tucker's Blackstone at 203–05 n §. In support of this conclusion Tucker suggested, as have other scholars, that the authority of the House of Commons to punish breaches of privilege was derived from the fact that, at least at one time, that House had been not only a legislative body but also "a judicial court." Id at 203 n §. Accord May, Parliamentary Privilege at 124 (cited in note 231); Carl Wittke, History of English Parliamentary Practice 13 (Ohio State, 1921). See also Randall's related argument (5 Annals at 216) that British precedents were inapposite because of the omnipotence of Parliament.

Although the Supreme Court has accepted Tucker's historical argument (see Kilbourn v Thompson, 103 US 168, 183–85 (1881); Marshall v Gordon, 243 US 521, 533–34 (1917)), it has not gone undisputed. Not only did the House of Commons exercise its contempt power long after it ceased to function in other respects as a court; it has been argued that it did not even begin to punish for contempt until after it had lost its traditional judicial authority. See C. S. Potts, Power of Legislative Bodies to Punish for Contempt, 74 U Pa L Rev 691, 697 (1926). But the fact remains that the House of Commons was never subject to written constitutional limitations like those found in the Constitution of the United States.

[243]5 Annals at 194, 224. See also id at 223 (Rep. Sedgwick); id at 228 (Rep. Page). Cf Tumey v Ohio, 273 US 510 (1927).

[244]5 Annals at 190. See United States v L. Cohen Grocery Co., 255 US 81 (1921) (striking down a criminal statute as unconstitutionally vague). The same concern helps to explain both the constitutional prohibitions

William Smith had answered the jury-trial contention before it was made, arguing that to hold the Constitution entitled Randall to a jury would leave the House at the mercy of other branches.[245] The same argument can be made with equal force against the application of most of the other provisions on which Tucker relied. Indeed analogous implicit exceptions to the judicial and jury requirements have since been recognized; it is arguable that in enacting general provisions to govern run-of-the-mill proceedings the Framers no more intended to deny Congress the right of self-defense than to require grand juries in impeachment cases or abolish courts-martial.[246]

Implicitly conceding that the Constitution did not do away with unwritten privilege entirely, Representative Nicholas took a narrower position: The House should not have arrested Randall because "[t]he right of privilege had been given up, unless in cases of absolute necessity."[247] What he meant by necessity may be suggested by the earlier argument of Randall's counsel: The House might punish "violence, or open insult," but since "the safety of the House [was] not in danger" in his case it should be left to the courts.[248] The Supreme Court has developed a similarly strict test of necessity under the due process clause to limit summary proceedings for contempt of court,[249] but the absence of an emergency does not refute the need for legislative contempt powers; as Smith said, to remit the matter to the ordinary processes of law would leave the House "altogether dependent on the other branches of the Government" to ensure the integrity of its own proceedings.[250]

Whitney's offense, unlike Randall's, had been committed in Vermont before the House had convened, and several Members denied that the House had authority to punish offenses committed before its session began. "It is admitted," said Representative John Milledge of Georgia, "that the utmost which can be done to the prisoners is confinement till the rising of the session; if our power does not go beyond the end, it seems not to extend previous to the beginning of the session."[251]

---

of ex post facto criminal legislation (US Const, Art I, §§ 9, 10) and the Supreme Court's rejection of a federal common law of crimes. See the discussion of this point in connection with the Neutrality Proclamation in chapter 4. Parliament's steadfast refusal to define its privileges, echoed during the Randall debate by Representative Isaac Smith (5 Annals at 189), doubtless helped to protect legislative deliberations against novel encroachments (see 1 Blackstone at 164), but it heightened the tension between privilege and the requirement of fair warning.

[245]5 Annals at 181–82.

[246]See Rawle at 48 (invoking the impeachment analogy); Dynes v Hoover, 61 US 65 (1857) (finding courts-martial consistent with Article III's provision vesting "judicial power" in independent courts). Article III's jury provision contains an express exception for impeachment cases, but the fifth and sixth amendments do not; "cases arising in the land or naval forces" are explicitly exempted from the grand jury requirement, but not from Article III or the sixth amendment.

[247]5 Annals at 219. Madison and Harper both repeated that privilege could be justified only by "necessity." Harper added that, "it being so liable to misapprehension and misconstruction, he wished to see as little of it as possible." Id at 223–24 .

[248]Id at 215–16 (Tilghman and Lewis's arguments for Randall).

[249]Cooke v United States, 267 US 517 (1925); In re Oliver, 333 US 257, 274–78 (1948).

[250]5 Annals at 182. Both Parliament and colonial assemblies had punished breaches of privilege occurring outside their presence. See May, Parliamentary Privilege at 122 (cited in note 231); Clarke, Privilege in the Colonies at 93–131 (cited in note 232).

[251]5 Annals at 183. See also id at 223 (Rep. Sedgwick); id at 223–24 (Rep. Harper); id at 225 (Rep. Nathaniel Smith).

The analogy is flawed. Confinement had indeed traditionally ended when the legislature went home,[252] but both British and colonial assemblies (though not without opposition) had imposed sanctions for acts that took place before they convened.[253] Furthermore, as several Members pointed out, the injury to Congress is just as great wherever and whenever the attempt at corruption is made.[254] Efforts by Harper and Smith to specify that the reason for releasing Whitney was the timing of his offense were defeated;[255] yet for all its weakness the fact that the House was not yet in session seems the only plausible basis for distinguishing the two cases.

The final battle in Randall's case was over the procedure the House was to follow. After considerable debate Randall was afforded a hearing before the full House rather than a committee. He was permitted to be represented by counsel and to cross-examine Representatives who gave evidence against him, all of whom were put under oath.[256] In the House's view, however, all these procedural safeguards were extended as a matter of grace and not of constitutional compulsion.[257] William Smith immediately challenged Sedgwick's suggestion that the Constitution gave Randall the right to counsel,[258] and the Constitution did not surface again during the entire procedural debate.

When the Supreme Court upheld implied congressional contempt powers a quarter century afterward, it did so on the narrowest possible ground. The case was a carbon copy of Randall's, and counsel argued (as Randall had suggested) that the House could punish only those breaches of privilege which occurred in its presence.[259] But the issue had arisen on demurrer in an action for trespass against the Sergeant-at-Arms, and there was no allegation in the complaint that his warrant had not been based upon "an offence committed in the immediate presence of the house."[260] That was enough to resolve the case; "that such an assembly should not possess the power to suppress rudeness, or repel insult, is a supposition too wild to be suggested."[261]

---

[252]The Supreme Court confirmed this limitation in dictum in *Anderson*, 19 US at 231.

[253]See May, Parliamentary Privilege at 61, 168 (cited in note 231); Clarke, Privilege in the Colonies at 218–21 (cited in note 232) (noting that this practice was unsettled in England at the time of the Revolution, disputed in the colonies, and denied by the Privy Council).

[254]See 5 Annals at 223 (Reps. William Smith, Hillhouse, and Madison); id at 227 (Rep. Venable); id at 228 (Rep. Page). Several of those who denied the distinction argued that Randall should not have been punished either.

[255]See id at 225–27. The final resolution was only "that Charles Whitney be discharged from the custody of the Sergeant-at-Arms." Id at 229.

[256]See the resolutions to this effect, id at 194–95, 206–07. For discussion of the various procedural questions see id at 179–83 (counsel); 185–94 (oath); id at 187 (cross-examination); id at 188–90 (hearing before full House); for the questions actually propounded to House Members see id at 207.

[257]Nor had a right to counsel traditionally been recognized in breach of privilege proceedings in Parliament. See May, Parliamentary Privilege at 170 (cited in note 231).

[258]The counsel provision, Smith argued, was no more applicable than the following clause of the same amendment, which guaranteed a right to jury trial. See 5 Annals at 180, 181.

[259]See 5 Annals at 215, 2 Hinds' Precedents at 1058; *Anderson*, 19 US at 215:

The impunity of the offence being the only possible reason of the necessity, if the offender may be adequately punished by the courts of justice, in the ordinary mode of proceeding, the supposed necessity ceases. Bribery of a member of congress is punishable in the state courts, and in the circuit court of the district of Columbia, according to the course of the common law.

[260]Id at 229.

[261]Id. See also The First Hundred Years at 184–85.

There was language in the opinion suggesting support for a broader power as well.[262] But in discussing the limits of the punishment the House might impose the Court left a handhold that could be grasped to support Randall's argument of necessity in an appropriate case: The House had only "'the least possible power adequate to the end proposed.'"[263] Half a century later, indeed, the Court would cast considerable doubt on the authority of the House in a case like Randall's.[264]

The argument of necessity is strong, and the current practice of referring contempt-of-Congress cases to the U.S. Attorney for prosecution[265] does not disprove it; there may come another day when the legislature cannot rely on other branches for protection. Yet later invocations of congressional contempt powers during the Federalist period would soon highlight the degree of tension between conventions of parliamentary privilege and the policies underlying a variety of constitutional provisions. As in the cases of judicial contempt,[266] courts-martial,[267] and legislative investigation,[268] one might well conclude (as the Supreme Court has since concluded)[269] that there were limits to the extent to which the Framers would have wanted such principles as fair hearing and free expression to yield when they came into conflict with traditional legislative privilege.[270]

[262]Acceptance of the power to punish contempts in the House itself, Justice Johnson added, destroyed the principal argument against a more extensive contempt power: "For why should the house be at liberty to exercise an ungranted, unlimited, and undefined power, within their walls, any more than without them?" *Anderson*, 19 US at 229.

[263]Id at 230–31.

[264]Kilbourn v Thompson, 103 US 168, 182, 189–90 (1881) (dictum) (assuming that each House had authority to punish contumacious witnesses in proceedings to determine the elections of its members or to impeach officers but emphasizing that due process embraced both a guarantee that proceedings be governed by "rules of law previously established" and "the strongest implication against punishment by order of the legislative body").

[265]See Ronald L. Goldfarb, The Contempt Power 40–42 (Columbia, 1963); Powers of Congress 188 (Congressional Quarterly, 2d ed 1982): "The last time either chamber punished someone for contempt was in 1932." The refusal to respond to congressional inquiry was made criminal by statute in 1857, 11 Stat 155 (Jan 24, 1857) (now 2 USC § 192); 2 USC § 194 requires that violations be referred to the United States Attorney, "whose duty it shall be to bring the matter before the grand jury . . . ." Bribery and attempted bribery of Members of Congress or other federal officials are also punishable in court under 18 USC § 201 (b) and (c) (1988) [amended 1994].

[266]For due process limitations see note 249; see also Bridges v California, 314 US 252, 260 (1941) (freedom of expression).

[267]Reid v Covert, 354 US 1 (1957); United States ex rel Toth v Quarles, 350 US 11 (1955).

[268]E.g., Watkins v United States, 354 US 178, 188 (1957); Gibson v Florida Legislative Investigation Committee, 372 US 539 (1963).

[269]See Marshall v Gordon, 243 US 521, 545–46 (1917) (holding the House without power to punish a defamatory letter sent to one of its members); Groppi v Leslie, 404 US 496, 502–07 (1972) (holding that even in the case of physical disruption of legislative proceedings due process required a state legislature to afford notice and an opportunity to be heard if it did not take immediate action).

[270]A second incident involving House privileges occurred a few months later when Senator James Gunn of Georgia challenged Representative Baldwin to a duel in the course of a controversy arising out of Gunn's participation in the notorious Yazoo land scheme. Gunn argued that the matter was strictly personal and thus no offense to the House. A committee found that both Gunn and his second, Senator Frelinghuysen of New Jersey, had infringed House privileges but recommended that no further action be taken in light of their apologies. See 5 Annals at 532–33, 786–91, 795–98; Note, 16 Madison Papers at 268.

6

The Fifth and Sixth Congresses, 1797–1801

Less than ten weeks after John Adams took the constitutionally prescribed oath as second President of the United States[1] the Fifth Congress met in special session at his behest to consider what to do about deteriorating relations with France.[2]

Matters arising out of our French troubles would occupy most of the attention of the Fifth Congress.[3]

I. TROUBLES WITH FRANCE

The French, Adams told Congress, had refused to receive our new Minister, Charles Cotesworth Pinckney. They had also issued a decree "injurious to our lawful commerce" and contrary to the Treaty of Amity and Commerce entered into between the two countries in 1778.[4] In fact, like the British a few years before, the French had been preying on American shipping; and they had gone so far as to brand as pirates U.S. citizens who had had the misfortune to be impressed into the British Navy.[5]

Adams determined to deal with these injuries as his predecessor had dealt with comparable problems with Great Britain: by negotiating while strengthening our defenses.[6]

---

[1]See 6 Annals at 1586 (Mar 4, 1797).

[2]See 7 Annals at 9, 49.

[3]For a comprehensive account of the relevant events see Elkins & McKitrick at 529–690.

[4]7 Annals at 54, 55–56. The decree itself, which announced that France would no longer respect the "free ships, free goods" provision of the treaty, can be found in 2 Am St Papers (Foreign Relations) at 30–31.

[5]For a comprehensive account of French depredations see Secretary Pickering's report of June 21, 1797, in id at 28–29, 55–63; for the piracy provision see id at 31. The decree justified both this proision and the abrogation of the "free ships, free goods" principle on the basis of similar provisions in the Jay Treaty and a most-favored-nation clause in the French treaty with the United States. Id. See also Miller at 205–06.

[6]See Elkins & McKitrick at 552. Hamilton, before he left office, had urged Washington to pursue the

The day before his inauguration Adams had consulted Jefferson about the composition of a new three-member commission to be sent to France in the hope of restoring acceptable relations. Adams would have preferred to send Jefferson himself along with Pinckney and Elbridge Gerry, the former Congressman from Massachusetts. But as Jefferson tells it Adams "supposed it was out of the question, as it did not seem justifiable for him to send away the person destined to take his place in case of accident to himself, nor decent to remove from competition one who was a rival in the public favor."[7] Jefferson concurred as to the "impropriety" of leaving his post and agreed to ask Madison, who also declined.[8]

Neither Adams nor Jefferson phrased his misgivings in constitutional terms, but Jefferson's correspondence suggested he perceived constitutional difficulties in the way of accepting a new assignment to France. Adams and Jefferson, the reader may recall, had once been fast friends. Though they had drifted apart in recent years, they had exchanged warm sentiments after finishing first and second in the 1796 election, and Adams had written Jefferson, in the latter's words, of his "satisfaction in the prospect of administering the government in concurrence with me." Fearing that Adams might be thinking of asking him to take on executive duties, Jefferson expressed constitutional qualms: "[T]he constitution will know me only as the member of a legislative body; and it's [sic] principle is that of a separation of legislative, executive & judiciary functions, except in cases specified."[9]

In 1789 William Maclay had seen the Vice-President as an executive interloper whose presence endangered the independence of the Senate.[10] Eight years later Jefferson viewed him as a purely legislative officer who could not constitutionally perform executive functions.[11]

In any event it was John Marshall, not Jefferson or Madison, who sailed for France

---

same course. See letter of Alexander Hamilton to George Washington, Jan 19, 1797, 20 Hamilton Papers at 469, 470; Elkins & McKitrick at 544–45.

[7]*Anas*, 9 Jefferson Writings (Wash ed) at 185.

[8]Id (adding, id at 186, that thereafter Adams "never . . . consulted me as to any measures of the government"). Apparently both Jefferson and Madison were motivated in part by political considerations; neither wanted to take any responsibility for dealing with our intractable problems with France. See Elkins & McKitrick at 546.

[9]Letter of Thomas Jefferson to James Madison, Jan 22, 1797, 7 Jefferson Writings (Ford ed) at 107, 108. Adams put a somewhat different twist on the argument: "The nation has chosen Jefferson, and commanded him to a certain station. The President, therefore, has no right to command him to another or to take him off from that." Letter of John Adams to Elbridge Gerry, Apr 6, 1797, Charles Francis Adams, ed, 8 The Works of John Adams 538, 539 (Little, Brown, 1853).

[10]See chapter 1. But Vice-President Adams had taken little more part in executive business than his successor did. The Adams papers contain only three requests for his advice in eight years (see 8 Works of John Adams 489, 496, 515 (cited in note 9)); Jefferson reported in his *Anas* that only once did Washington suggest to the Cabinet that Adams be consulted. 9 Jefferson Writings (Wash ed) at 96.

[11]At the same time Jefferson took a narrow literal view of the functions that Article I, § 3 gave him as "President of the Senate," "[r]egarding himself as a presiding officer pure and simple" and devoting much of his energy to compiling a much-admired "Manual of Parliamentary Procedure" (9 Jefferson Writings (Wash ed) at 3–86), based largely on the practice of Parliament, which was still being printed in the Senate Manual "more than a century and a half after he left his chair." Dumas Malone, Jefferson and the Ordeal of Liberty 452–53 (Little, Brown, 1962).

with Pinckney and Gerry in the summer of 1797,[12] and in the meantime Congress was left to haggle over Adams's request to strengthen the armed forces, particularly the Navy.[13]

A. Declaring the Peace

Little came of the President's plea during the special session. Congress did authorize him to man and employ the three frigates that were under construction,[14] and—in response to another suggestion in his address[15]—forbade U.S. citizens to engage in privateering against nations with which we were at peace, or against their fellow citizens.[16] The House preferred to expend its energy in debating its wholly ceremonial reply to the President's speech[17]—the rejected Republican version of which Representative Griswold actually challenged as unconstitutionally dictating the President's conduct of foreign affairs.[18]

The next regular session, which began in November 1797, dragged on for four months in the same desultory way until President Adams informed Congress that letters from our envoys had revealed that there was "no ground for expectation that the objects of their mission can be accomplished on terms compatible with the safety, honor, or the essential interests of the nation" and reiterated his request for additional defensive measures.[19] Alarmed by the tone of the President's message, Representative Richard Sprigg, a Republican from Maryland, proposed that Congress resolve that the United States *not* go to war with France.[20]

The President had neither declared war nor asked Congress to do so, replied Samuel Sewall of Massachusetts; there was no reason to say anything on the subject.[21] It was not the business of the legislature, Sitgreaves added, "to pass mere negative resolutions"; Congress might just as well adopt a statute declaring it inexpedient to enact a bankruptcy law.[22]

Not so, said Baldwin. The whole country was "agitating this question of peace and war," and it was up to Congress to set the record straight by declaring that we were at

[12]See 1 Sen Exec J at 243–45.

[13]7 Annals at 57–58.

[14]1 Stat 523 (July 1, 1797). Nine months later, however, Congress was still appropriating money to complete and equip these vessels "with all convenient speed." Id at 547 (Mar 27, 1798). Earlier stages in the genesis of the frigates are related in chapters 4 and 5.

[15]See 7 Annals at 58.

[16]1 Stat 520 (June 14, 1797). In part, like the Neutrality Act discussed in chapter 4, this statute was apparently an exercise of Congress's power to define and punish offenses against the law of nations, US Const, Art I, § 8, cl 10. Insofar as it dealt with matters of purely domestic concern by protecting citizens against other citizens, it could most plausibly be justified under the authority to punish piracies and felonies committed on the high seas (id), although it was not expressly so limited.

[17]7 Annals at 67–137 [!].

[18]Id at 94. Cf the earlier controversies over congressional reactions to the adoption of the French constitution and flag, noted in chapter 4. Two Representatives had the wit to recognize that the entire exercise was a colossal waste of time. See id at 97 (Rep. Baldwin); id at 110 (Rep. Swanwick).

[19]8 Annals at 1271–72 (Mar 19, 1798).

[20]Id at 1319.

[21]Id at 1327.

[22]Id at 1320. Moreover, said Sitgreaves, under the existing circumstances war might soon prove necessary. Id. At the very least, Brooks added, the resolution ought to distinguish between offensive and defensive war: In no case should we promise not to defend ourselves if attacked. Id at 1325.

peace. "He did not believe it was intended that this House should merely be the instrument to give the sound of war; the subject seemed to be placed wholly in the hands of the Legislature."[23] Gallatin went a step further: By dismissing our Minister and seizing our ships, France had given us just cause to go to war; it was Congress's responsibility to decide whether or not we should do so.[24] Nicholas went further still: By announcing that he would no longer enforce an executive order forbidding the arming of private vessels,[25] the President had taken a step that would lead to war. "Many discussions had heretofore taken place on the Constitution," said Nicholas, "but he had never heard it doubted that Congress had the power over the progress of what led to war, as well as the power of declaring war; but if the President could take the measures which he had taken, with respect to the arming of merchant vessels, he, and not Congress, had the power of making war."[26]

We encountered this question from the opposite perspective in connection with President Washington's neutrality proclamation of five years before.[27] At that time Madison (echoed half-heartedly by Jefferson) had intimated that the President had no authority to proclaim peace; now their adversaries argued that Congress had no power to do so. They can hardly have both been right; it would be very odd if the Constitution empowered no one to decide that the country would not go to war.[28] More likely both were wrong: As Hamilton said, the President may announce the fact that we are at peace and must preserve it until Congress otherwise decides; but as Baldwin argued the grant of authority to declare war was intended to give Congress power to determine whether or not to resort to force.[29]

[23]Id at 1321.

[24]Id at 1328. See also id at 1323 (Rep. Giles); id at 1324 (Rep. Nicholas).

[25]See id at 1272. Adams had previously asked Congress to consider whether the ban should be lifted. 7 Annals at 57.

[26]8 Annals at 1324. In March 1798 Jefferson wrote to Madison, lamenting the "inefficiency of Constitutional guards":

> We had relied with great security on that provision which requires two thirds of the Legislature to declare war. But this is completely eluded by a majority's taking such measures as will be sure to produce war.

Letter of Thomas Jefferson to James Madison, Mar 21, 1798, 17 Madison Papers at 99. Madison reminded him that a declaration of war required only a simple majority of Congress but added that Jefferson's remark was nonetheless pertinent as applied to executive actions. Letter of James Madison to Thomas Jefferson, Apr 2, 1798, id at 104, 105.

[27]See the discussion in chapter 4.

[28]Whether once a war has been declared it can be ended by statute or only by treaty is a different question neither presented nor debated in 1798.

[29]See the authorities cited to this effect in note 235 of chapter 2. Normally one would think a formal declaration of peaceful intentions unnecessary; if Washington, Jefferson, and Madison were right that only Congress or a foreign attack could take the country into war, Congress should be able to achieve the same result by simply declining to declare war. See 8 Annals at 1320 (Rep. Sitgreaves). But see Madison's letter to Jefferson, Apr 15, 1798 (17 Madison Papers at 112, 113–14), listing extraordinary cases in which Congress as repository of "the War prerogative" should declare the nation's pacific intent.

More important in light of subsequent events (and suggested by Nicholas's argument, text at note 26) was the question whether Congress had power to forbid the President to take actions that might lead to war—a power that one would think implicit in the authorization to declare war, given the purpose of that provision. Cf the twentieth-century controversy over the War Powers Resolution, 50 USC § 1541 (1988 & Supp 1994), and Congress's power to order the President to refrain from further military action.

Meanwhile the Republican press had been clamoring for release of the letters from the disappointed envoys, and a motion was made to ask the President to produce them.[30] As in the Jay Treaty debate, another controversy broke out over whether the resolution should call for only such information "as considerations of public safety and interest," in the President's opinion, might permit to be disclosed.[31] The power to declare war, said Nicholas, implied authority to obtain all relevant information.[32] Without the entire correspondence, said Livingston, the House could not make an intelligent decision between peace and war; if the President was allowed to decide what to withhold he could frustrate the House's inquiry.[33] John Allen of Connecticut, the Federalist who had originally asked that the request be limited, offered to withdraw his objection: The Constitution gave the President the right to withhold any information he thought it improper to divulge, and thus no exception was required.[34]

The request was adopted without limiting language.[35] Disdaining to press the question of executive privilege, Adams turned over the entire correspondence, which revealed how (through the agency of the notorious anonymes who have come down to us as X, Y, and Z) our ambassadors had been insulted, ignored, and asked for a bribe.[36] This coup de théâtre knocked the wind out of the opposition. Sprigg's resolution to declare peace was put on the back burner to boil away; as Nicholas said, it would not do to give the impression that we were prepared to accept peace on such humiliating terms.[37]

Congress then embarked upon a feeding frenzy, giving the President all the defense measures he had asked for and several that he had not. It provided for additional warships[38] and for recruitment of the first Marines[39] and created a new Navy Department to manage them.[40] It enlarged the Army by twelve infantry regiments and six troops of light

---

[30]8 Annals at 1358 (Rep. Allen).

[31]Id. See the discussion of the earlier controversy in chapter 5.

[32]Id at 1368.

[33]Id at 1359.

[34]Id at 1368–69. See also id at 1369 (Rep. Harper).

[35]Id at 1371.

[36]See Elkins & McKitrick at 571–75.

[37]8 Annals at 1380–81.

[38]1 Stat 552 (Apr 27, 1798); 1 Stat 556 (May 4, 1798); 1 Stat 575 (June 30, 1798).

[39]1 Stat 594 (July 11, 1798).

[40]1 Stat 553 (Apr 30, 1798). Such naval forces as had existed previously had been within the jurisdiction of the War Department. As Secretary of the Navy Adams appointed Benjamin Stoddert, a Baltimore merchant, who has been described as an excellent Secretary. See White at 156–63.

In its third and final session the Fifth Congress enacted a naval code. 1 Stat 709 (Mar 2, 1799). In addition to defining a panoply of offenses subject to court-martial (which, no doubt for sound historical reasons, nobody suggested was inconsistent with Article III's provision vesting judicial authority in independent courts), this statute required that (absent bad weather or other "extraordinary accidents") divine services be performed twice daily on board ships that were provided with chaplains. Id, § 1, Art. 2. There was no reported debate on this provision, but plainly Congress did not think it an establishment of religion. We might add that not to provide such services would raise a serious question under the free-exercise clause, since by confining sailors to a ship without religious facilities the Government had made it impossible for them to provide services for themselves. Cf Cruz v Beto, 405 US 319, 322 (1972); see The Second Century at 347.

When this statute was rewritten the following year, the impetuous John Randolph objected to courts-martial on the ground that Article III and the fifth amendment required petty and grand juries in all criminal proceedings. But the very text he quoted contradicted him, his motion was defeated "by a large majority," and the court-martial provisions were retained. See 10 Annals at 655–56; 2 Stat 45 (Apr 23, 1800).

dragoons.[41] It empowered the President to accept companies of volunteer soldiers[42] and to raise an additional 10,000 regular troops in case of emergency.[43] It authorized the construction of more forts[44] and the purchase or manufacture of arms.[45] It barred intercourse with France and its possessions,[46] authorized merchant ships to defend themselves,[47] and gave the President permission to capture French warships[48] and commission privateers.[49] Finally, just before adjourning in July 1798, Congress declared that, because of repeated French infractions, the treaties and conventions previously concluded between the United States and France "shall not henceforth be regarded as legally obligatory on the government or citizens of the United States."[50]

Most of these measures could easily be traced to one or another of Congress's war powers; with the possible exception of the treaty provision, all were plainly related to national defense.[51] Much of the constitutional debate in the House revolved once again around questions of the separation of powers.

B.   The Provisional Army

The bellicose legislation of the Fifth Congress was riddled with broad delegations of authority. The President was empowered to build whatever fortifications the public safety

---

[41]1 Stat 604 (July 16, 1798). It was this "New Army," not the "Provisional Army" authorized by the statute next described in the text, that the aged Washington was nominally to command and on which Hamilton was to expend the bulk of his energies until Congress provided for its dissolution in 1800. 2 Stat 85 (May 14, 1800). See also 1 Stat 552 (Apr 27, 1798) (providing for an additional regiment of "artillerists and engineers"). The relationships among the various armies in existence or authorized during this period are explained in Richard H. Kohn, Eagle and Sword 229 n * (Free Press, 1975).

[42]1 Stat 558, § 3 (May 28, 1798).

[43]Id, § 1. A similar provision for "eventual" raising of yet another batch of soldiers was adopted the following year. 1 Stat 725, § 1 (Mar 2, 1799). The later provision for military hospitals (1 Stat 721 (Mar 2, 1799)) was necessary and proper to the raising and supporting of armies, as the statute providing for the care of disabled merchant seamen (1 Stat 605 (July 16, 1798)) arguably was to the regulation of commerce. Cf the seamen's labor code promulgated by the First Congress, discussed in chapter 2.

[44]1 Stat 554 (May 3, 1798).

[45]1 Stat 555 (May 4, 1798). To finance these and other military measures the Fifth Congress adopted the first direct tax, 1 Stat 597 (July 14, 1798), which is discussed in the preceding chapter. It also adopted a stamp tax on a variety of documents from wills, banknotes, and stock shares to patents and naturalization certificates. 1 Stat 527 (July 6, 1797). A provision of the original bill that would have prohibited the use of unstamped paper for pleadings or proof in state courts, defended as necessary to collect the tax, disappeared (along with the tax on evidence and pleadings) after Nicholas and Venable raised the expected constitutional objection. See 7 Annals at 417–18.

[46]1 Stat 565 (June 13, 1798). This Act was yet another Federalist precedent for Jefferson's controversial embargo. See also the discussion of earlier embargo provisions in chapter 4.

[47]1 Stat 572 (June 25, 1798).

[48]1 Stat 561 (May 28, 1798); 1 Stat 578, § 1 (July 9, 1798). The first statute applied only to vessels committing "depredations" on American ships or "hovering on the coasts" for that purpose; the second was general.

[49]Id, § 2.

[50]1 Stat 578 (July 7, 1798).

[51]On the strength of all this legislation Attorney General Lee advised the Secretary of State that "there exists not only an *actual* maritime war between France and the United States, but a maritime war *authorized* by both nations," and consequently that for a US citizen to aid, assist, or abet France in its efforts would constitute treason. 1 Op AG 84 (1798). See also id at 85, 86.

might require,[52] to build more ships if he found them necessary to protect the United States,[53] to discontinue the statutory ban on intercourse with France if it ceased to violate our neutrality,[54] to make rules for the training of volunteer companies,[55] and even to authorize the capture of French warships,[56] which looked suspiciously like a delegation of the power to determine whether or not to go to war.[57] The loudest howls of protest, however, were provoked by the proposal to authorize the President to raise a provisional army.

When the Senate bill for this purpose reached the House, it contained no restrictions on the President's discretion save that he find such an army required by the public safety and that he enlist no more than 20,000 men.[58] Representative Nicholas immediately raised the obvious objection: The bill would transfer to the President "the highest act of Legislative power, . . . the power to raise an army, which he was to exercise at his pleasure."[59] If Congress could give the President its power to raise armies, Gallatin added, it might equally empower him to raise taxes; "and if Congress were once to admit the principle that they have a right to vest in the President powers placed in their hands by the Constitution, that instrument would become a piece of blank paper."[60]

Sewall, a second-term Representative who had already become one of the principal Federalist spokesmen, attempted to justify the delegation as a matter of principle. Surely Congress could authorize the President to raise an army "two months from this time," and thus it could authorize him to do so on other "contingencies" as well.[61] This was not much of an argument, since the bill under consideration would make the army dependent upon the President's judgment while a time provision would leave him no discretion at all.[62] For the most part the bill's defenders relied on precedent.[63]

[52]1 Stat 554, 555, § 1 (May 3, 1798).

[53]1 Stat 556, § 1 (May 4, 1798).

[54]1 Stat 565, 566, § 5 (June 13, 1798). A later tintype of this provision was upheld against constitutional challenge in The Aurora, 11 US 382 (1813). See The First Hundred Years at 119.

[55]1 Stat 569, 570, § 1 (June 22, 1798).

[56]1 Stat 578, § 1.

[57]If the statute could be interpreted to express Congress's policy decision that such action *ought* to be taken, there would be no problem; Congress would not have left the basic decision to presidential discretion. Representative Davis, who opposed the privateering provision, clearly viewed it as an expression of congressional policy. See 8 Annals at 1878. But cf Panama Refining Corp v Ryan, 293 US 388 (1935), where the Supreme Court in its most fastidious mode refused to construe a comparably worded grant of authority as suggested in this note, despite an exemplary Cardozo dissent that showed how it could be done. See The Second Century at 216–18.

[58]8 Annals at 1525, 1631.

[59]Id at 1525. He went on, as Republicans were wont to do, to insist that we didn't need an army. Id. The reader should perhaps resist the urge to retort that it made obvious sense for a nation contemplating war to have an army, since the President had not asked for a significant increase in troops and his War Secretary had told Congress they were not needed; the chances of a French invasion were understandably slim. See 1 Am St P (Military Affairs) at 120–23; Elkins & McKitrick at 595–96.

[60]8 Annals at 1526. See also id at 1532 (Rep. Baldwin). A similar proposal had been defeated after similar objections during the 1794 crisis. See chapter 4.

[61]8 Annals at 1528. See also id at 1529 (Rep. Harper): "[I]f they had the power to authorize the President to raise troops immediately, they could certainly do it under such contingencies as they thought proper."

[62]See id at 1649 (Rep. Robert Williams): "No person has said Congress could not authorize the President to raise an army for the defence of the country; but it was denied that the power could be transferred from Congress to him, to determine whether it should or should not be raised."

[63]In so doing, Gallatin argued, they had demonstrated the weakness of their position. Id at 1538.

John Rutledge, Jr., freshman South Carolina Federalist and son of the unconfirmed Chief Justice, pointed out that Congress had given the President broad authority to determine when to call out the militia.[64] The analogy was not propitious, since in authorizing Congress to "provide for" mobilization the Constitution appeared to contemplate that Congress would not have to make the individual decision itself;[65] but there were plenty of other examples. Harper noted that Congress had entrusted the President with "the discretionary power of borrowing money" and of "fixing salaries";[66] William Craik cited statutes "authorizing the President, if he shall judge it expedient, to alter the usual place of meeting of Congress" or to build galleys, as well as "the law for regulating and revoking embargoes."[67] Most pertinently, earlier statutes had directed the President to raise troops "except he should think it necessary to forbear raising them," and "he believed this was the first time that granting the power had ever been questioned."[68]

Baldwin strove bravely to distinguish this last example. Even in that case, he said, Congress itself had made the decision "that circumstances required the troops to be raised"; it had authorized the President not to raise them "if circumstances should alter so as to make the troops unnecessary"; it had given him "power to disband the Army, but not to raise one."[69]

There may be something in Baldwin's distinctions. In light of the fear of military power that impelled the Framers to vest the authority to raise armies in Congress, it seems much less worrisome to authorize the President *not* to do so.[70] Moreover, though it may make little theoretical difference whether one is authorized to take action that is necessary or to refrain from action that is not, the President's discretion may well have been narrower under the 1795 statute than under the provisional-army bill. For in the past he had been expected only to determine whether the circumstances that had led to Congress's original decision to raise troops still existed; now it was proposed to permit him to make the more open-ended initial determination on his own.

Gallatin dismissed the precedents as innocuous and for the most part irrelevant. The only one that "came near to the present bill" was the provision authorizing the President to forbear to enlist troops, and that had been a mistake; "when this was shown, it proved that they had heretofore done wrong, and that they ought to be more careful in future."[71]

Gallatin was right that Members of Congress had sworn to support the Constitution rather than their own erroneous precedents, but prior congressional actions were entitled to some respect as evidence of what the Constitution was understood to mean. On the question of delegation the record was mixed. Congress had in fact given the President a

---

[64]Id at 1534.

[65]See chapter 3.

[66]8 Annals at 1529. Less than a year before, the House had voted to authorize the President to set seamen's wages despite constitutional objections. See 7 Annals at 367, 376.

[67]8 Annals at 1535. Craik was a Federalist from Maryland who had served since the Fourth Congress.

[68]Id. See also id at 1527 (Rep. Dana). See 1 Stat 241, 243, § 12 (Mar 5, 1792) (discussed in note 240 of chapter 3); 1 Stat 430, 432, § 16 (Mar 3, 1795). Indeed, although no one mentioned it during the 1798 debate, the 1792 Act had gone even further, authorizing the President to call into service "such number of cavalry as, in his judgment, may be necessary for the protection of the frontiers." 1 Stat at 243, § 13.

[69]8 Annals at 1532.

[70]See The Federalist Nos 24, 26 (Hamilton).

[71]8 Annals at 1538–39. See also id at 1638 (Rep. Brent): "Error will continue to be error however frequently it is repeated."

great deal of discretion in a variety of different fields that Article I committed to Congress, and often without apparent objection.[72] On other occasions, however, lingering misgivings bubbled to the surface, and Congress could be parsimonious indeed with its authority—as, when after an acrimonious constitutional debate, it had insisted on designating individual post roads.[73] Even the proponents of broad delegation had acknowledged that there had to be limits if Congress was not to abdicate its intended functions; as Sedgwick said in the postal debate, it was up to Congress to lay down guiding principles for the executive to apply.[74] Congress ultimately did just that with respect to the provisional army.

At Sewall's request the bill was sent to committee.[75] It emerged with significant limitations on executive discretion: Now the President was to be authorized to raise troops "in the event of a declaration of war against the United States, or of actual invasion of their territory by a foreign Power, or of imminent danger of such invasion."[76] Gallatin conceded that the bill had been much improved. Since "a declaration of war or actual invasion were definite," the first two conditions were unobjectionable; but to let the President be the judge of when an invasion was imminent still went too far, as it left it to him "to decide the proper time of raising an army."[77]

Sewall replied that "the fact of the existence of imminent danger was as ascertainable as the other two,"[78] and the revised bill was adopted.[79] Obviously there was room for legitimate disagreement as to the permissibility of this provision. As delegations went, this one was pretty narrowly confined; it could hardly be doubted that Congress itself had laid down the basic policy that was to guide the President's determination.

It is the nature of the subject matter that is likely nonetheless to give pause. Gallatin's analogy to the tax power is suggestive, and Richard Brent offered an even more sobering comparison: "[I]f a proposition was made to transfer to the President the right of declaring war in certain contingencies, the measure would at once appear so outrageous, that it would meet with immediate opposition."[80] Like the power to tax and to declare war, the power to raise armies was given to Congress in order to ensure that the decision was made by a representative assembly;[81] it may be that delegation is more suspect, and must accordingly be more narrowly defined, when the authority in question is one the Framers specifically meant to keep out of executive hands.[82]

---

[72]See, e.g., the examples cited in notes 66 and 68; the laws respecting Indian commerce and the seat of government noted in chapter 2; the postal provisions discussed in chapter 3; and the naval and embargo measures described in chapter 4 .

[73]See chapter 3.

[74]3 Annals at 329. See also id at 330–31 (Rep. Sedgwick): "[T]he whole purpose . . . is answered, when the rules by which the business is to be conducted are pointed out by law . . . ."

[75]8 Annals at 1561.

[76]Id at 1631.

[77]Id at 1631–32. See also id at 1674 (Rep. Brent).

[78]Id at 1635.

[79]1 Stat 558, § 1 (May 28, 1798); see 8 Annals at 1689. The President's discretion was further narrowed by limiting his authority to emergencies arising during the next recess of Congress. 1 Stat at 558, § 1; see 8 Annals at 1671, 1684–85.

[80]Id at 1638. Brent was a second-term Representative from Virginia.

[81]See the discussion in connection with the Jay Treaty controversy in chapter 5.

[82]It was just as unacceptable to alter the constitutional distribution of authority by abdication, said Gallatin, as by usurpation; in either case the effect was "precisely the same." 8 Annals at 1655.

But the residue of disagreement over the permissible breadth of presidential authority should not be allowed to obscure the significant area of consensus achieved in the
course of this rather impressive debate.[83] In defending the rewritten bill on the ground that
it permitted the President to act only in three clearly defined situations, Sewall seemed to
acknowledge that Congress could not simply transfer its authority to anyone else;[84] on
the other side Gallatin conceded that the President could be allowed to find the facts if the
governing principle was sufficiently precise. There was plenty of room to argue over the
adequacy of a particular set of congressional standards for the exercise of delegated authority, but there seemed to be broad agreement that Congress was neither required to dot
every "i" itself nor permitted to give away the store.[85]

C.   Volunteers

The dust kicked up by the storm over the provisional army had not settled before an
equally fierce confrontation arose over the provision of the same bill authorizing the
President, if in his opinion the public interest so required, "to accept of any company or
companies of volunteers . . . who may associate and offer themselves for the service."
Such volunteers would be "liable to be called upon to do military duty at any time the
President shall judge proper," and the President would appoint their officers.[86] This proposal was ultimately enacted without amendment, but by no means without protest.[87]

Two objections were raised: Under Article I, § 8 the militia could be called into
federal service only "to execute the laws of the Union, suppress insurrections, and repel
invasions,"[88] and the appointment of their officers was expressly reserved to the states.[89]

Friends of the bill replied that the volunteers were not a militia but federal troops
and that the proposal was an exercise of Congress's power to raise armies.[90] The debate

[83]See id at 1671: "Mr. J. Williams believed there was but little difference of opinion . . . ."

[84]See also id at 1660 (Rep. Pinckney) (conceding the point expressly); id at 1637 (Rep. Dana)
(acknowledging that it was up to Congress "to define the number of troops to be raised, and the manner and
the time of their service").

[85]The provisional army was never raised, although the President did appoint several of its officers. See
Editorial Note, 22 Hamilton Papers at 383, 387; 1 Sen Exec J at 291, 293.

[86]See 8 Annals at 1703.

[87]1 Stat 558, § 3 (May 28, 1798).

[88]See 8 Annals at 1740 (Rep. McDowell); US Const, Art I, § 8, cl 15. Gallatin (8 Annals at 1728) did not
put this objection in constitutional terms, but he did argue that permitting the President to call on volunteers for
any purpose would enable him to circumvent the limitations of clause 15, which were designed as a major
barrier to the dangers of a standing army. Sitgreaves seemed to suggest at one point that the fact that volunteers could be called up for purposes not listed in clause 15 demonstrated that they were not militiamen, id at
1730, but Congress cannot evade constitutional limitations simply by offending them.

[89]See 8 Annals at 1703 (Rep. Harrison); id at 1704 (Rep. Sumter); US Const, Art I, § 8, cl 16. A committee
proposal to authorize the President to call out 20,000 militiamen for "training and discipline" received only
eleven votes after it was pointed out that these were not purposes listed in clause 15 and that clause 16 reserved actual training to the states. 8 Annals at 1701–02.

[90]See id at 1704 (Rep. Dana). See also id at 1729 (Rep. Sitgreaves): "[I]f they are a standing army, the
Constitutional doubt must be at an end." Varnum disagreed: In that case the proposal was subject to the same
objection that had been levelled against the provisional army, since "the power of raising armies is placed in
the Legislature; but if this power is given to the President, he might raise an army to any extent he pleases,
without the consent of Congress." Id at 1739.

turned on determining just what distinguished a militia from an army within the meaning of Article I.

"If there be any characteristic marks by which to distinguish a militia from regulars," said Samuel Dana of Connecticut, "it is that the former are compelled to serve, and the latter enter voluntarily into the service."[91] Representative McDowell disagreed: The essence of a militia was that its members were not full-time federal troops; "these men could not be considered any other than militia, until they were enlisted into the service of the United States."[92]

To Gallatin the proposed volunteers were neither fish nor fowl:

> They are, in some degree, similar to the militia, inasmuch as they are to remain at home, except upon special calls of the President to do duty. . . . In other respects, [they] very much resemble the Army of the United States; inasmuch as they are to be enlisted . . . , they are also to be considered as making part of the Army, though remaining at home . . . , [and] their officers are not appointed by themselves, or by the individual States, as in the militia, but by the President of the United States . . . .[93]

The Constitution recognized only two kinds of soldiers, and the volunteers were neither; "[i]f the principle proposed to be adopted in this section be admitted, the consequence may be, that all the regulations provided in the Constitution for securing a good militia may be evaded, and the whole of the militia be turned into a kind of Public Standing Army."[94]

The militia provisions of the Constitution, as noted in an earlier chapter, represent an awkward compromise between state and federal authority.[95] Significant areas of competence were reserved to the states, presumably out of the usual jealousy of federal power; yet Congress remained free at any time to displace the states entirely by providing for a completely federal army. If we can understand why it was thought important nevertheless to limit federal authority over the militia, we may be in a better position to evaluate the arguments regarding the constitutionality of the volunteer army.

Unfortunately the possible explanations seem to cut in opposing directions. Among the fears expressed during the House debate was that creating a volunteer force might impair the militia by enticing away its most valuable members.[96] One possible consequence, though not mentioned at the time, might be to deprive the states of their only means of self-defense—a right acknowledged by Article I, § 10 and arguably guaranteed

---

[91] 8 Annals at 1704. See also id at 1705–06 (Rep. Harper); id at 1733 (Rep. Otis). Carter Harrison of Virginia suggested that the volunteers would qualify as militiamen because "they would be included in the census of citizenship," id at 1703, but as Harper observed there was no reason to think regular soldiers would lose the right to be counted or any other rights of citizens. Id at 1706.

[92] Id at 1705. Accord 1 Tucker's Blackstone at 274–75. Joseph McDowell was a freshman Republican from North Carolina.

[93] 8 Annals at 1725–26.

[94] Id at 1726.

[95] See chapter 3.

[96] See 8 Annals at 1703–04 (Rep. Varnum); id at 1705 (Rep. McDowell); id at 1726 (Rep. Gallatin).

them by the second amendment.[97] But if this was one of the reasons for limiting federal control of the militia, the fact that the proposed force was one of volunteers suggested that, as its defenders argued, it was not a militia; for it meant that no one could be removed from the state's service without his consent.[98]

On the other hand, a dominant theme both before and after adoption of the Constitution was the fear of federal power in general and of federal military might in particular. The existence of a militia reduced the need for a standing army, while the limitations on federal control diminished the risk that it would become one. What is more, the existence of a militia created a powerful disincentive to the establishment of federal forces by making a reserve of military power available at greatly reduced cost. Indeed one of the benefits most emphasized by advocates of the volunteer army was that it would do just that[99]—at the expense, as Gallatin astutely responded, of the crucial incentive not to create a federal force.[100]

Thus there was much to be said for the contention that the essence of a militia was that it was composed of part-time soldiers, but a comfortable majority of the House was of a different opinion; the motion to expunge the provision for a volunteer Army was defeated by a vote of fifty-six to thirty-seven,[101] and the bill was enacted into law.[102]

D.   The French Treaties

During the Revolution, when France was the dearest friend and strongest bulwark of the embattled new nation, the United States and France entered into two treaties, one of alliance and the other of commerce.[103] Ten years later, as the first elections were being held under the new Constitution, they added a consular convention, which the new Senate promptly approved.[104] In 1793, during the controversy over the reception of the French minister Edmond Genêt, Jefferson and Hamilton engaged in an inconclusive sparring

[97]One of the complaints against permitting the President to send what was assumed to be a militia to Canada during the War of 1812 was that to do so would "leave the State unprotected." 23 Annals at 730 (Rep. Grundy); see also id at 761 (Rep. Key).

[98]If this argument prevailed, it would mean that Congress could not have recourse to a draft, which would otherwise appear, as it was later held to be, necessary and proper to the raising of armies. See Selective Draft Law Cases, 245 US 366 (1918). Thus the suggested distinction does not even sound plausible today, and it certainly does not reflect the current understanding.

[99]See 8 Annals at 1706 (Rep. Harper): "The country would have the advantage of a large body of troops, who would receive no pay except in time of service."

[100]See id at 1728:

He knew it was not in our power (our revenues not being sufficient for it) to raise a standing army in the ordinary way, large enough to prove dangerous to the liberties of the country; but the manner in which this force is proposed to be raised, removes the great security which we otherwise would have from our inability to pay a large standing army.

[101]Id at 1758.

[102]"[M]any" volunteer companies, it is said, were formed; only one of them was called into actual service, to help suppress Fries' rebellion against the direct tax (noted in chapter 5). See Editorial Note, 22 Hamilton Papers at 383, 388. This use of the volunteers did not rest on the President's constitutional authority as Commander in Chief; it was expressly authorized by statute. 1 Stat 725, 726, § 7 (Mar 2, 1799).

[103]8 Stat 6 (Feb 6, 1778); 8 Stat 12 (Feb 6, 1778).

[104]8 Stat 106 (Nov 14, 1788). See the discussion of ratification in chapter 1.

match over the status and effect of the treaties in light of the French Revolution and the ensuing European war.[105] In 1798, ceremoniously reciting that the treaties had been "repeatedly violated on the part of the French government," just reparation claims rejected, and efforts at negotiation "repelled with indignity," Congress declared that the United States were "freed and exonerated" from all three agreements, "and that the same shall not henceforth be regarded as legally obligatory on the government or citizens of the United States."[106]

Whether this action was consistent with international law this is not the place to decide.[107] It is difficult enough to square it with the Constitution.

There was little discussion of the bill in the House.[108] When Dwight Foster of Massachusetts introduced the idea,[109] Robert Williams objected: "[H]e did not believe that this House has the power to annul a treaty; if they had, it appeared to him that they would have the power of defeating the treaty-making power as laid down by the Constitution."[110] William Claiborne and Samuel Sewall, from opposite sides of the political divide, took issue with him;[111] but neither they nor anyone else explained where congressional authority to abrogate treaties could be found in the basic law.

Williams's argument that legislative repeal would undermine the treaty power was reminiscent of the Federalist position, during the Jay Treaty debate, that Congress would undercut the authority of the President and the Senate if it did not appropriate funds to carry out a treaty.[112] It thus sounds a little out of place in the mouth of a freshman North Carolina Republican. Yet in opposing the British treaty on the ground that it would deprive Congress of its commerce power[113] Senate Republicans had seemed to assume, as others flatly asserted, that treaties took precedence over ordinary laws, which was another way of stating Williams's conclusion. The Supreme Court, of course, has since concluded that the last in time prevails.[114] That means that Congress can supersede a treaty by enacting an inconsistent statute, but it does not answer our question. For the sole purpose of the 1798 statute was to abrogate the French treaty, and there was a prior question as to its power to pass it at all.

The analogy that leaps to mind is the great debate in the First Congress over the

---

[105]See note 63 of chapter 4.

[106]1 Stat 578 (July 7, 1798).

[107]See 8 Annals at 1889–90 (Rep. John Williams): "[I]t was clear from the writers on the laws of nations, that when one nation breaks a treaty, it is no longer obligatory on the other party."

[108]As usual, the Annals contain no report of the Senate debates.

[109]8 Annals at 1870.

[110]Id at 1880.

[111]Id at 1882 (Rep. Claiborne); id at 2120 (Rep. Sewall). Claiborne was a freshman Republican from Tennessee, born in 1775, who contrived to serve from 1797 until 1801 "in spite of the fact that he was still initially under the constitutional age requirement of twenty-five years." See Biographical Directory at 778.

[112]See chapter 5.

[113]See chapter 5.

[114]E.g., The Cherokee Tobacco, 78 US 616 (1871). That the text of the supremacy clause seems to equate treaties with statutes is suggestive but not decisive; on its face the clause can also be read to equate the Constitution with statutes and treaties, to both of which it has been held supreme. More convincing is the fact that there seems to be no reason to think the Framers would have wanted treaties to have more weight than statutes, or vice-versa. For the contrary position see Louis Henkin, Constitutionalism, Democracy, and Foreign Affairs 64 (Columbia, 1990).

removal of executive officers.[115] Both the power to appoint officers and the power to make treaties are given expressly to the President and Senate;[116] in both cases there is a plausible argument that authority to undo an action is implicit in the authority to take it.[117] The stronger argument in the removal context was that the one-way phrasing of the provision was deliberate: There was greater need for a check on the appointment than on the removal of officers, and the President could remove without Senate approval. The same argument has since been made with respect to treaties: The Framers were more leery of contracting entangling alliances than of dissolving them, and thus the President may terminate treaties in the exercise of his residual authority over foreign affairs.[118]

Neither the power of the President and the Senate nor that of the President alone to terminate treaties was before the House in 1798, and neither is necessarily inconsistent with concurrent congressional authority. Nevertheless the fact that someone else may have such authority reduces the force of the argument that it must be implicit in Congress.[119] In fact it has long been understood that the President and the Senate together may terminate a treaty,[120] and the District of Columbia Circuit held just the other day[121] that the President could do so all by himself.[122] So what about Congress?

The commercial treaty is the easiest case. To the extent that a treaty regulates foreign commerce, so does a law repealing it; the commerce clause supports congressional action.[123]

If, as was soon to be argued, Congress had implicit general authority over foreign relations,[124] that would justify it in setting aside treaties of any description; but such an argument was not easy to reconcile with the basic principle of enumerated powers.[125] An argument that congressional abrogation was necessary and proper to the exercise of the treaty power or of the President's individual responsibility for foreign affairs is also conceivable; but legislative renunciation without executive request is easier to characterize as undermining than as promoting the executive agenda.[126]

More promising perhaps is the argument that treaty termination is implicit in the

[115]See chapter 1.

[116]US Const, Art II, § 2.

[117]Indeed no one seems ever to have doubted that the President and the Senate might repeal one treaty by making another. See Goldwater v Carter, 617 F2d 697, 706 n 19 (DC Cir 1979).

[118]See id at 709; Louis Henkin, Foreign Affairs and the Constitution 169 (Norton, 1972).

[119]The possibility that the failure to grant explicit authority to declare treaties no longer binding means that no one can do so is so contrary to expectations that one is likely to take a good deal of persuading that any such conclusion was intended. Cf the fate of the argument that impeachment was the exclusive means of removing an executive officer, discussed in chapter 1.

[120]See the 1856 congressional debate over abrogation of a treaty with Denmark concerning commerce and navigation, discussed in 2 Haynes at 670–71.

[121]We speak in glacial time. This is after all History.

[122]Goldwater v Carter, 617 F2d 697 (DC Cir 1979). The Supreme Court found the case nonjusticiable, 444 US 996 (1979); Justice Brennan, who would have decided the merits, would have upheld the President's authority on narrower and less convincing grounds. Id at 1006–07.

[123]See Taylor v Morton, 23 F Cas 784, 786 (CC D Mass 1855), and the Chinese Exclusion Case, 130 US 581, 600 (1889) (both recognizing that Congress can effectively repeal a treaty respecting a subject within its legislative authority).

[124]See text at notes 167–84, discussing the Alien Act.

[125]See The Second Century at 231 n 140, discussing United States v Curtiss-Wright Corp, 299 US 304 (1936).

[126]See Henkin, Foreign Affairs at 413–14 n 117 (cited in note 118).

power to declare war.[127] It may have been hyperbolic for Gallatin to assert that denouncing the treaties was tantamount to declaring war,[128] but it certainly seemed likely to provoke hostility.[129] As Nicholas had argued in support of congressional authority to declare peace, the power to decide whether to start a fight ought to include authority over actions that make it unavoidable;[130] if the President (with or without Senate consent) had announced that the nation would no longer respect its obligations to France, there would have been a good argument that he had interfered with congressional prerogative.[131]

In short, it is not entirely clear where Congress got the authority to nullify treaties; yet since it first exercised that authority in 1798 few have seriously questioned its right to do so.[132]

II. THE ENEMY WITHIN

When we have enemies abroad, they must have friends inside our gates; and thus there must be enemies among us as well.[133] In the twentieth century the grain of truth in this seductive perception gave us the Espionage Act, the internment of Japanese-Americans, and the witch hunts of Senator Joseph McCarthy. In the eighteenth it gave us, among other things, the Alien and Sedition Laws.[134]

---

[127]See Rawle at 68. But see Henkin, Foreign Affairs at 170 (cited in note 118) (arguing that in the future "Congress will probably be unable to claim plausibly that the maintenance or termination of treaties is intimately related to war or peace").

[128]8 Annals at 2118.

[129]See id at 1882 (Rep. Claiborne). See also Sitgreaves's suggestion that Congress not bother discussing the treaties but move directly to the question whether or not to declare war: A declaration would automatically put an end to the treaties since "it is the major proposition, and, of course, includes all the minor propositions." Id at 2117.

[130]See text at notes 26, 29.

[131]See Jefferson's suggestion to this effect in connection with the reception of Citizen Genêt, 9 Jefferson Writings (Wash ed) at 142–43. Professor Corwin once extravagantly suggested that congressional power to abrogate treaties could be derived from its authority to "define and punish . . . offenses against the law of nations" (US Const, Art I, § 8, cl 10), which, "it has been generally held," included a general "power to define International Law." Edward S. Corwin, The President's Control of Foreign Relations 115 (Princeton, 1917).

[132]See Quincy Wright, The Control of American Foreign Relations 260 (Macmillan, 1922). In the disputes over termination of treaties with Denmark in 1856 and with Taiwan in 1979 Congress's power to abrogate treaties was generally taken for granted. See, e.g., S Rep No 97, 34th Cong, 1st Sess (1856), reprinted in 58 Cong Rec 8126, 8127 (1919); Goldwater v Carter, 617 F2d 697, 705–06 (DC Cir 1979); id at 717 (MacKinnon, J, dissenting). But see Cong Globe, 34th Cong, 1st Sess 1151 (1856) (Sen. Clayton) (arguing that treaties could be rescinded only by those who had made them). See also Jefferson's Manual, § 60, 9 Jefferson Writings (Wash ed) at 81: "Treaties being declared, equally with the laws of the United States, to be the supreme law of the land, it is understood that an act of the Legislature alone can declare them infringed and rescinded. This was accordingly the process adopted in the case of France, 1798."

[133]See 8 Annals at 1577: "Mr. Sitgreaves . . . believed the business of defence would be very imperfectly done, if they confined their operations of defence to land and naval forces, and neglected to destroy the cankerworm that is corroding in the heart of the country." See also id at 1961 (Rep. Otis): "[A]n army of soldiers would not be so dangerous to the country, as an army of spies and incendiaries scattered through the Continent."

[134]The debates on the entire package of anti-subversive legislation are recounted in detail in James Morton Smith, Freedom's Fetters: The Alien and Sedition Laws and American Civil Liberties (Cornell, 1956). See id at 21: "Under the guise of patriotic purpose and internal security, the Federalists enacted a program designed to cripple, if not destroy, the Jeffersonian party."

A. Aliens

The first order of the day was to keep matters from getting worse. It was bad enough that there were people of foreign extraction already in the United States; the door must be shut against a further infusion of the human capital that had made us a nation.[135]

A few hotheads wanted to ban naturalization entirely,[136] but Congress was not ready for that. It was content to extend the residence requirement for new citizens from five to fourteen years and to forbid naturalization of anyone from a country with which the United States was "at war"—whether in the formal or practical sense the statute did not say.[137] This was all pretty distressing as a matter of policy, but not even the most francophile Virginian ventured to question it on constitutional grounds; Congress had indisputable authority to enact uniform naturalization laws.[138]

While it was up, Congress required registration of aliens already in the country.[139] This was a significant restriction of privacy, but nothing in the Bill of Rights seemed to prevent it. It did not occur to anyone in the House to argue that it was an unreasonable search or an unreasonable interference with liberty, or that the due process clause invalidated all unreasonable laws.

More challenging once again was the issue of where Congress got the power to require aliens to register; we shall confront it when we come to the extensive debates on the more controversial and more burdensome measures that followed.

In a logical sense the next question was what to do about French citizens in the United States. No war had yet been declared, but it might break out at any time. It was not hard to find a connection between protection from alien enemies and the conduct of war,[140] and before it went home Congress passed a statute to deal with the problem.[141] If the President proclaimed that war had been declared or an invasion "perpetrated, attempted, or threatened," male citizens or subjects of the hostile nation over the age of

---

[135]Immigrants, it has been said, tended to become Republicans; the naturalization law was "a political maneuver by the Federalists designed to cut off an increasingly important source of Republican strength." Smith, Freedom's Fetters at 22–23 (cited in note 134).

[136]See, e.g., 8 Annals at 1567 (Rep. Harper). Harper also suggested that persons naturalized in the future should not be permitted to vote in federal or state elections, Otis that they should be barred from holding federal office. Id at 1568, 1570. Venable and Macon responded that Congress could not discriminate against naturalized citizens or add to the qualifications for Congressmen laid down in Article I, §§ 2, 3; Otis replied that since Congress could withhold citizenship it could grant it on conditions. Id at 1570–71. Earlier naturalization provisions, and Congressional rejections of previous attempts to create two classes of citizens, are discussed in chapters 2 and 4.

[137]1 Stat 566, § 1 (June 18, 1798). There was a grandfather clause for persons who had been in the United States before the first day of 1795. Id at 567, § 1.

[138]US Const, Art I, § 8, cl 4. No one suggested that the requirement that the rules be "uniform" precluded Congress from making distinctions as to those persons eligible for naturalization. The history of the provision suggested that the idea was that naturalization rules (like bankruptcy laws under the express terms of the same clause and duties, excises, and imposts under the first clause of the same section) should be identical "throughout the United States." See the discussion of the whiskey excise in chapter 2.

[139]1 Stat at 567, § 4. Registration was to be made, if convenient, with the clerk of the nearest district court—yet another example of the efficient early practice of giving judicial officers nonjudicial functions. Id.

[140]Gallatin conceded that the power to declare war "includes that of making prisoners of war, and of making regulations with respect to alien enemies, who are liable to be treated as prisoners of war." 8 Annals at 1980. See also Rawle at 100.

[141]1 Stat 577 (July 6, 1798).

fourteen would be liable to possible arrest and deportation.[142] What to do with them was up to the President;[143] there were virtually no limits to this remarkable delegation of authority.[144]

Republicans sputtered over the vagueness of the alien enemies bill when it was first introduced[145] but did not attack it in principle,[146] and it was they who finally insisted on its enactment once some of its more objectionable features were withdrawn.[147] But that did not happen until after the guardians of our national security had succeeded in ramming through Congress their next brilliant idea, which was that *all* aliens should be subject to expulsion without enemy status, without wrongdoing, and without trial.[148]

The heart of the statute lay in its first section:

[I]t shall be lawful for the President of the United States at any time during the continuance of this act, to order all such aliens as he shall judge dangerous to the peace and safety of the United States, or shall have reasonable grounds to suspect are concerned in any treasonable or secret machinations against the government thereof to depart out of the territory of the United States . . . .[149]

[142]Id, § 1.

[143]Id.

[144]Resident aliens who had not participated in actual hostilities were to be given a "reasonable time," or the time prescribed by treaty, in which to arrange their affairs. One close student of the Act has argued that § 2 (id at 577–78), which made it the "duty" of state as well as federal courts to entertain enforcement proceedings under the act and directed them to conduct hearings, significantly narrowed the area of discretion. See Smith, Freedom's Fetters, at 48–49 (cited in note 134). Nowhere in the statute, however, were substantive standards laid down to govern either the President's or the court's decision; in contrast to the law next to be discussed, there was not even a requirement that the President find an individual dangerous before ordering him expelled.

[145]Matthew Lyon argued that the clause respecting "threatened" invasion, like the comparable terms in the provisional-army bill, delegated excessive authority to the President (8 Annals at 1786, 1792); Gallatin complained that the bill gave the President too much discretion to determine what to do with enemy aliens, id at 1793. Otis defended the delegation on the ground that Congress was in no position to determine which individuals ought to be deported; since the President would have power to impound all French citizens the moment war began, the bill should be seen as "an amelioration or modification of those powers which the President already possesses, as Commander in Chief . . . ." Id at 1790–91.

Gallatin also objected to a provision authorizing retaliation for inhuman treatment of captured Americans, on the convincing grounds that the United States ought to behave in a civilized fashion and that the eighth amendment forbade cruel and unusual punishments, id at 1794. Dropped from the alien-enemies bill, this obnoxious provision was enacted separately at the end of the following session. 1 Stat 743 (Mar 3, 1799).

[146]See, e.g., 8 Annals at 1795: Mr. Gallatin "was ready to acknowledge that the power of regulating this business was in the power of Government, as it was a power possessed by every nation, which it had a right to exercise for its own security; but it ought to be exercised according to law." See also note 140 (his argument based on the war powers).

[147]See 8 Annals at 2034–35; Smith, Freedom's Fetters at 48 (cited in note 134): "Although the *Annals* contain no debates on the Alien Enemies Law during its final stages of passage, it appears to have been virtually a Republican measure." See also id at 49: "The Alien Enemies Law . . . has remained a fundamental part of American wartime policy." See 50 USC §§ 21–24 (1988).

[148]1 Stat 570 (June 25, 1798). Of the entire package of anti-subversive legislation, say Elkins & McKitrick (at 591), the Alien Act may have been "the most farfetched and misbegotten."

[149]1 Stat at 570–71. Criminal penalties and permanent disqualification from citizenship were prescribed for violation of such an order. Id at 571, § 1. Any deportee who returned without permission was to be imprisoned, upon conviction, "so long as, in the opinion of the President, the public safety may require." Id, § 2.

Aliens ordered to leave the country might in the President's discretion be granted a "license" to remain upon demonstrating "to the satisfaction of the President, by evidence to be taken before such person or persons as the President shall direct," that they posed no danger to the United States.[150]

Republican legislators understandably went ballistic over this proposal.

From the standpoint of modern civil liberties it was a nightmare. There was no right to jury trial or to proceedings before an independent judge. The normal burden of proof was reversed. The President was to define what circumstances sufficed to make an individual "dangerous," investigate individuals he thought might meet the standard, and determine for himself whether they did. The potential for arbitrary or discriminatory administration was great, and the consequences were severe: Any foreigner the President thought dangerous would have to leave the country.

None of these blemishes escaped the sharp-eyed critics in the House. Gallatin raised the judge and jury objections and invoked due process.[151] Robert Williams said the bill would give the President "arbitrary power."[152] Gallatin was more specific: The bill permitted "civil rights, the personal liberty, [and] the property of aliens" to be taken away "upon suspicion, and . . . at the will of one man."[153]

Livingston, arriving like an avenging angel in the midst of the battle, delivered the full broadside. The bill would grant the President a combination of legislative, executive, and judicial powers.[154] It would afford even less notice of what conduct was forbidden than the "detestable contrivance of the Decemvirs," who "hung the tables of their laws so high that few could read them." For in that case "a tall man," he said, "might reach them, a short one might climb and learn their contents, but here the law is equally inaccessible to high and low."[155] And that was not all.

> Judicial power is taken from courts, and given to the Executive, the previous safeguard of a presentment by a grand inquest is removed; the trial by jury is abolished, the "public trial" required by the Constitution is changed into a secret and worse than inquisitorial tribunal; instead of giving "information on the nature and cause of the accusation," the criminal, igno-

---

Needless to say this last provision raised the question whether Congress had transferred to the executive not only its own lawmaking authority but also the judicial power of sentencing.

[150] 1 Stat at 571, § 1 (adding that the President might prescribe the duration and situs of the licensee's stay, require a bond for his "good behavior," and revoke the license whenever he thought proper). Section 3 required ship captains to make full reports respecting aliens brought into the country; § 4 gave federal courts jurisdiction over offenses defined by the statute. Id at 571–72.

[151] 8 Annals at 1956, 1981–82. Gallatin also contended that the bill suspended habeas corpus without making the findings required by Article I, § 9 (id at 1956), but here he was not on solid ground. As Otis observed, habeas corpus is a procedural device that affords a prisoner a judicial determination of the legality of his custody; substantive limitations on what may be made a legal justification for that custody must be sought elsewhere. Id at 1960. See also id at 1858 (Rep. Sewall). See the Judiciary Act of 1789, 1 Stat 73, 82, § 14 (Sept 24, 1789), giving federal judges "power to grant writs of *habeas corpus* for the purpose of an inquiry into the cause of commitment."

[152] 8 Annals at 1995.

[153] Id at 1983.

[154] Id at 2007–08.

[155] Id at 2008–09.

rant of his offense and the danger to which he is exposed, never hears of either until the judgment is passed and the sentence is executed; instead of being "confronted with his accusers," he is kept alike ignorant of their names and their existence; and even the forms of a trial being dispensed with, it would be a mockery to talk of "proofs for witnesses," or the "assistance of counsel for the defence"—thus are all the barriers which the wisdom and humanity of our country had placed between accused innocence and oppressed power, at once forced and broken down. Not a vestige of their form remains.[156]

Some of Livingston's more colorful arguments depended upon his assumption that the bill envisioned deportation as punishment for crime,[157] which as Allen pointed out it did not appear to do.[158] More generally, Harrison Gray Otis of Massachusetts insisted that constitutional safeguards were only for citizens and that because aliens could be kept out altogether they could be admitted on whatever terms Congress might choose to prescribe.[159]

Otis's first argument seems simply wrong.[160] His second, which has enjoyed much currency in the immigration field,[161] was recognized as a recipe for mischief as early as the First Congress;[162] fortunately it is in relative disrepute today.[163]

But the infringement of civil liberties and the rule of law was not the principal objection to the Alien Act. Most of the opponents' ammunition was employed to demonstrate that Congress was the wrong body to deal with the problem.

Republican speakers made much of the fact that Article I, § 9 forbade Congress until 1808 to prohibit "[t]he migration or importation of such persons as any of the states now existing shall think proper to admit." If Congress could expel immigrants as soon as they arrived, Gallatin argued, it could defeat the whole purpose of this provision.[164] This polit-

---

[156]Id at 2010.

[157]Id at 2011–12.

[158]Id at 1984. Nevertheless the modern Supreme Court has appropriately concluded that due process requires a fair hearing in deportation proceedings. Wong Yang Sung v McGrath, 339 US 33, 49 (1950).

[159]8 Annals at 2018. Otis, serving the first of his two terms in the House, had been elected as a Federalist to replace Fisher Ames. See also id at 1984–85 (Rep. Gordon).

[160]"[U]pon reading the Constitution," said Otis, "he found that 'we, the people of the United States,' were the only parties concerned in making that instrument. He found nothing in it which bound us to fraternize with the whole world." Id. Had he read on he would have discovered that Article III vested the judicial power of the United States in tribunals whose judges were independent of other branches, that the fifth amendment provided that "no person" should be deprived of life, liberty, or property without due process, and that the sixth amendment applied to "all criminal prosecutions." See 8 Annals at 2012 (Rep. Livingston). Contrast US Const, Amend 14: "No state shall make or enforce any law which shall abridge the privileges or immunities of citizens of the United States . . . ."

[161]See, e.g., Harisiades v Shaughnessy, 342 US 580 (1952); United States v Macintosh, 283 US 605, 615 (1931); United States ex rel Turner v Williams, 194 US 279 (1904); T. Alexander Aleinikoff, Federal Regulation of Aliens and the Constitution, 853 AJIL 862, 862–65 (1989).

[162]See the discussion of the proposal to limit the political rights of federal revenue agents in chapter 2.

[163]See, e.g., Elrod v Burns, 427 US 347 (1976); FCC v League of Women Voters, 468 US 364, 399–401 (1984); The Second Century at 355–58, 473–75.

[164]8 Annals at 1956–57. If Congress could deport dangerous aliens, said Robert Williams, it could deport slaves too, for they could be regarded as equally dangerous. Id at 1963.

ically prickly clause was subjected to the most minute scrutiny,[165] but supporters of the bill seemed to have the better of the argument this time. "It is one thing," said Otis, "to banish all aliens indiscriminately, and a very different thing to banish a few individuals of suspicious character." One might as well argue that no alien could be convicted of crime "because the Courts might imprison or hang up aliens as fast as they are admitted to any State."[166]

The § 9 argument was a diversion. Gallatin had issued the fundamental challenge at the outset of the debate: What provision of the Constitution gave Congress authority to order the deportation of nonenemy aliens?[167]

The commerce clause, said Sewall; "foreigners who came here generally [came] for commercial purposes."[168] That was ridiculous. "If Congress has any power which they can exercise on the persons of alien merchants," said Gallatin, "it must relate to them as merchants"; nothing in the bill would "in any way determine how commerce shall be carried on with foreign countries, or from one state to another."[169]

The general welfare clause, said Dana, for "what relates to the Union generally, must be done by the Government of the United States."[170] That was preposterous. As Baldwin said, such an interpretation would make the enumeration of other congressional powers "surplusage" and license Congress to abolish slavery.[171] Gallatin quoted the Federalist and James Wilson in the Pennsylvania ratifying convention: "[T]he obvious and universally received meaning of the last words was . . . to define the purpose for which taxes should be laid."[172]

---

[165]Otis argued that the clause was meant only to allow the importation of slaves, id at 1960; Gallatin and Williams said the additional reference to "migration" showed that free persons were included, id at 1979, 1964. Baldwin and Dayton, both of whom had been there, sparred over what the Convention had intended. Id at 1968–69, 2003–04 (Rep. Baldwin); id at 1992–93 (Rep. Dayton). Otis insisted that no state had passed a law expressly admitting dangerous aliens (id at 1959), but as Gallatin replied "whatever is not prohibited is permitted." Id at 1978.

[166]Id at 1987. See also id at 1967 (Rep. Bayard). No one denied, said Sewall, that Congress could order the deportation of alien enemies (id at 1959); surely, Otis added, § 9 did not mean Congress could not keep out the French army. Id at 1961. Sewall made the mistake of arguing that the migration clause "implies that the Congress has the power to regulate this business respecting aliens, or why does the clause suspend the power until 1808?" Id at 1958. Gallatin blew him out of the water with a reference to the ninth amendment that was right on the money: "[T]he Constitution . . . had expressly guarded against the danger of a similar construction, by declaring . . . that 'the enumeration in the Constitution of certain rights, shall not be construed to deny or disparage others retained by the people.'" Id at 1979. See the discussion of this amendment in chapter 2.

[167]8 Annals 1955–56.

[168]Id at 1958.

[169]Id at 1974–75. Cf Gibbons v Ogden, 22 US 1, 196 (1824): "What is this power? It is the power to regulate; that is, to prescribe the rule by which commerce is to be governed." See also Keller v United States, 213 US 138, 148 (1909), where the Court struck down a congressional effort to punish a citizen for harboring an alien prostitute, concluding that the power to control immigration did not extend to "all the dealings of our citizens with resident aliens"; and the overdue decision in United States v Lopez, 115 SCt 1624 (1995) (denying that the commerce power extended so far as to permit Congress to forbid firearms in schools). See also 8 Annals at 1963 (Rep. Robert Williams) (denying that immigrants were "articles of commerce").

[170]Id at 1969. See also id at 1959 (Rep. Otis); id at 1965 (Rep. Bayard).

[171]Id at 1967–68. See also id at 1962 (Rep. Robert Williams) (making the same response to Sewall's invocation of the Preamble, text at note 181). Otis, who had his own arguments in support of federal power over aliens, conceded that "to provide for the common defence and general welfare" was merely "the end of the powers recited" in the preceding clause. 8 Annals at 1986.

[172]Id at 1975. Accord 2 Story, § 908; United States v Butler, 297 US 1 (1936).

The war powers, said Otis.[173] Gallatin had conceded that the power to declare war justified deporting alien enemies,[174] and other aliens might pose an equal threat to national security. That was scary. So might citizens, opponents countered ominously,[175] or for that matter slaves.[176] If Congress could do anything that might contribute to national defense, there would be little left for the tenth amendment to reserve to the states.

The necessary and proper clause, said Bayard.[177] That was unconvincing as phrased, since as Bayard himself noted one must identify the particular grant of power whose execution the measure promotes. The best he could do was to argue that deporting dangerous aliens was necessary "for the common defence and general welfare,"[178] and as already indicated that language in Article I, § 8 was not an independent grant of authority. However, as others were soon to argue with respect to the Sedition Act,[179] if prohibiting mail robbery was necessary and proper to carrying the mail and punishing perjury to the decision of a lawsuit, deporting aliens who endangered the whole country was arguably necessary and proper to the exercise of *all* federal powers; for none of them could be exercised if the government itself was destroyed.

The whole structure of the Constitution, said Dana; "the power of preserving itself" was "inherent . . . in every form of Government."[180] That was dangerous and contrary to the basic principle that the federal government was one of enumerated powers.

The Preamble, said Sewall, for it demonstrated that the United States were sovereign, and that meant the central government had general authority over "intercourse with foreign nations."[181] That was misguided, since the Preamble did nothing of the sort. Stripped of this infelicitous attribution, the argument boils down to a variant of Dana's notion of inherent authority,[182] and in that form the Supreme Court has accepted it;[183] as John Marshall might have put it, surely the Framers would have wanted the central government rather than the states to manage foreign affairs.[184]

The House passed the Alien Act by a vote of forty-six to forty,[185] and the President signed it into law.

[173]8 Annals at 1986–87, 2018. See also id at 1959 (Rep. Sewall) (invoking Congress's "sovereign power to preserve peace and tranquillity").

[174]Id at 1980.

[175]Id at 1981, 2026 (Rep. Gallatin).

[176]Id at 1996 (Rep. Robert Williams).

[177]Id at 1965.

[178]Id at 1965–66.

[179]See text at note 191.

[180]8 Annals at 1969.

[181]Id at 1957. The express authority to appoint foreign ministers, he added, went a long way; but it could not explain everything that Congress had done in the realm of foreign affairs. Id at 1957–58.

[182]See id at 1957 (Rep. Sewall) (prefacing his invocation of the Preamble with a reference to "the general nature of the Constitution itself").

[183]Chinese Exclusion Case, 130 US 581 (1889); United States v Curtiss-Wright Export Corp, 299 US 304, 315–18 (1936); The Second Century at 14–16, 231 n 140. See also the discussion of this point in connection with the Neutrality Proclamation in chapter 4.

[184]Compare Marshall's use of the argument from unacceptable consequences in such cases as Marbury v Madison, 5 US 137 (1803), and Cohens v Virginia, 19 US 264 (1821); see The First Hundred Years at 71, 97. As Otis put the argument for Dana's conclusion, a government without power to protect itself from "intrigues and malpractices" that endangered its "welfare" and "very existence" would not "be worth a farthing." 8 Annals at 1960.

[185]Id at 2028.

B.   Sedition

It was not only foreigners who might weaken the nation in its struggle against French aggression. Something had also to be done about citizens who went out of their way to undermine the government.

Citizens could not very well be deported.[186] They could be fined and imprisoned, and that is what Congress provided:

> [A]ny person [who] shall write, print, utter or publish . . . any false, scandalous and malicious writing . . . against the government of the United States, or either house of the Congress of the United States, or the President of the United States, with intent to defame [them] . . . or to bring them . . . into contempt or disrepute . . . . shall be punished by a fine not exceeding two thousand dollars, and by imprisonment not exceeding two years.[187]

Truth was made a defense, and the jury was to determine both "the law and the fact, under the direction of the court, as in other cases."[188]

There were two constitutional objections to this bill, said Nicholas in the House: No provision gave Congress power to adopt it, and it was forbidden by the first amendment.[189]

Supporters of the proposal expended little effort to identify the source of congressional authority. To Otis the power was inherent: "[E]very independent Government has a right to preserve and defend itself" against insurrection and obstruction, and thus against "all means calculated to produce" them.[190] Harper found the answer once again in the necessary and proper clause: "[C]an the powers of a Government be carried into execution, if sedition for opposing its laws, and libels against its officers, itself, and its proceedings, are to pass unpunished?"[191]

So much for Hamilton's argument that no amendment was necessary to protect free-

---

[186]Responding to an earlier motion he characterized as contemplating the deportation of seditious citizens, Gallatin denied that Congress "had power to remove any citizen out of the United States," id at 1746. He did not identify the provision or provisions on which he relied.

[187]1 Stat 596, 596–97, § 2 (July 14, 1798). There was more verbiage about publications designed to excite "hatred" against the government, "to stir up sedition," "to excite . . . unlawful combinations" to oppose or resist federal laws or presidential acts, or to "aid, encourage or abet any hostile designs of any foreign nation against the United States." Id. Section 1 less controversially proscribed instigation of insurrection and what may charitably be interpreted as conspiracy to obstruct ("oppose") the enforcement of federal law. Id at 596.

[188]1 Stat at 597, § 3. Harper argued there was no need to provide that the jury would determine the law, since that was understood. 8 Annals at 2135. Bayard contradicted him: The judge determined the law. Id at 2136. As Gallatin said, this difference of opinion called for a clarifying amendment, which was approved by the one-sided tally of 67–15. Id at 2137–38. Since there was no consensus as to what the jury's function was "in other cases," the inclusion of this phrase makes one wonder how well the amendment performed its intended function.

[189]Id at 2139–40. Macon argued at one point that Congress had no power to punish crimes other than those expressly listed in the Constitution. 8 Annals at 2152. Jefferson repeated this argument in his Kentucky Resolutions, 4 Elliot at 540, but he had lost that battle in the First Congress, and rightly so. As Gallatin conceded, Congress could proscribe any offenses whose punishment was necessary and proper to the exercise of federal powers. 8 Annals at 2158. See the discussion of this question in chapter 2.

[190]8 Annals at 2146.

[191]Id at 2167.

dom of the press because Congress had no power over the press to begin with.[192] And thank goodness for old Jemmy Madison![193]

But the defenders of national security had arguments for getting around the first amendment as well. Harper's was the worst: "[T]he true meaning" of freedom of the press was that "a man shall be at liberty to print what he pleases, provided he does not offend against the laws . . . ."[194] That would not do; the first amendment was expressly phrased as a limitation on the laws that Congress might pass.[195]

Others invoked the obvious historical arguments: Freedom of expression protected only against previous restraints;[196] it had never been understood to embrace sedition or slander.[197]

To challenge this view of history would have been an uphill battle,[198] and opponents of the bill did not try. Their arguments were consequential, textual, and ultimately teleological. "It was striking at the root of free republican Government," said Nicholas, "to restrict the use of speaking and writing."[199] "To restrict the press, would be to destroy the elective principle, by taking away the information necessary to election. . . ."[200] It was "preposterous to say," said Gallatin, "that to punish a certain act was not an abridgement of the liberty of doing [it]."[201]

---

[192]The Federalist No 84. See also 2 Farrand at 618 (Roger Sherman); 2 Elliot at 449 (James Wilson in the Pennsylvania ratifying convention).

[193]See 1 Annals at 455–56 and text at note 441 of chapter 2.

[194]8 Annals at 2102.

[195]See US Const, Amend 1: "Congress shall make no law . . . ." Harper's argument, Livingston noted, would enable Congress to ban printing altogether. 8 Annals at 2105.

[196]Id at 2148 (Rep. Otis) (citing Blackstone).

[197]Id at 2097 (Rep. Allen); id at 2112 (Rep. Dana); id at 2148–49 (Rep. Otis) (citing numerous examples from states with constitutional guarantees of free expression); id at 2167–68 (Rep. Harper). See also Rawle at 124:

> A previous superintendency of the press, an arbitrary power to direct or prohibit its publications are withheld, but the punishment of dangerous or offensive publications, which on a fair and impartial trial are found to have a pernicious tendency, is necessary for the peace and order of government . . . .

Accord 3 Story, §§ 1881–82. On the "different" question whether such offenses came within federal cognizance Story expressed no opinion. Id, § 1885.

[198]See Leonard Levy, Emergence of a Free Press (Oxford, 1985), passim. The most that could be said, according to Professor Levy's exhaustive study, was that there was some dispute whether, in addition to forbidding prior restraints, freedom of the press had come to require (as the Sedition Act provided) that truth be recognized as a defense and that the jury be permitted to determine whether the statement was defamatory; "[f]reedom of speech and press . . . was not understood to include a right to broadcast sedition by words." Id at 268–69. For an earlier, rosier, and less well documented view of history see Zechariah Chafee, Jr., Free Speech in America 16–22 (Harvard, 1948) (concluding (at 21) that the authors of the amendment "intended to wipe out the common law of sedition, and make further prosecutions for criticism of the government . . . forever impossible in the United States . . .").

[199]8 Annals at 2104. See also id at 2140.

[200]Id at 2144. See also id at 2110 (Rep. Gallatin): "If you put the press under any restraint in respect to the measures of members of Government; if you thus deprive the people of the means of obtaining information of their conduct, you in fact render their right of electing nugatory . . . ."

[201]Id at 2160. "It would seem a mockery to say," wrote Madison in his "Report of 1800" defending the Virginia Resolutions (discussed at notes 257–85), "that no law should be passed, preventing publications from being made, but that laws might be passed for punishing them in case they should be made." 17 Madison Papers at 307, 336.

Others have said it again since, but it was all there in 1798: Criticism of the Government was essential to the democratic process, and it was that process that the guarantee of free expression was intended to serve.[202]

Not to worry, said Dana. Truth was a defense; only falsehood would be deterred, as it should be.[203] But the bill applied to opinions as well as to facts; "[a]nd how," Gallatin asked, "could the truth of opinions be proven by evidence?"[204] "[T]he determining a political question, true or false," said Nicholas, "would rest upon a variety of considerations; and the doctrine, in its extent, would have the effect to suppress useful truths."[205] "[T]he proper weapon to combat error," Gallatin added, "was truth," not suppression.[206]

The Senate passed the sedition bill on July 4, 1798.[207] Happy birthday, America![208]

In the same report Madison made the broader argument that the first amendment was a states'-rights provision:

> [T]he article of amendment, instead of supposing in Congress, a power that might be exercised over the press, provided its freedom be not abridged, was meant as a positive denial to Congress, of any power whatever on the subject.

Id at 339. See also Letter of Thomas Jefferson to James Madison, June 7, 1798, id at 143; Levy, Emergence of a Free Press at 269–70 (cited in note 198). Attractive as this position may appear at first glance, the copyright and seat-of-government clauses, as well as the phrasing of the amendment itself, cut against it; and of course it has never been the position of the Supreme Court. See The Second Century at 118–19.

[202]Cf Whitney v California, 274 US 357, 375 (1927) (Brandeis, J, concurring); New York Times Co v Sullivan, 376 US 254 (1964); Alexander Meiklejohn, Free Speech and its Relation to Self-Government (Harper, 1948), passim. It is true that, as Walter Berns has emphasized, a principal concern of opponents of the Sedition Act was states' rights and that their commitment to a libertarian view of press freedom was compromised by their frequent concession (or insistence) that state courts could punish seditious libel. See, e.g., 8 Annals at 2106 (Rep. Macon); id at 2153–54 (Rep. Livingston); Walter Berns, Freedom of the Press and the Alien and Sedition Laws: A Reappraisal, 1970 SCt Rev 109. It remains equally true, as Leonard Levy has argued, that the Republicans in the Sedition Act debates were the first to develop a full-blown modern theory for protecting political speech, even if they did not entirely believe it or later practice what they preached. See Levy, Emergence of a Free Press at 282, 302–04 (cited in note 198).

[203]8 Annals at 2112.

[204]Id at 2162.

[205]Id at 2113. See also id at 2140–41. Only one jury acquitted a defendant under the Sedition Act. See Levy, Emergence of a Free Press at 203 (cited in note 198).

[206]8 Annals at 2164. See also id at 2106 (Rep. Macon); id at 2109 (Rep. Gallatin). Cf Whitney v California, 274 US 357, 377 (1927) (Brandeis, J, concurring).

[207]7 Annals at 599.

[208]The Logan Act, 1 Stat 613 (Jan 30, 1799), made it a crime for any unauthorized U.S. citizen to "carry on any verbal or written correspondence or intercourse with any foreign government . . . with an intent to influence [its] measures or conduct . . . in relation to any disputes or controversies with the United States." This legislation, which is still on the books (18 USC § 953 (1988)), was a reaction to well-meaning private efforts by George Logan, a prominent Philadelphia physician, to explore possibilities of improving relations between the United States and France. Logan returned with tidings of French willingness to talk, and Adams received him. Before long, over Federalist opposition, the President sent a new team of negotiators to France, and peace was restored. See 9 Annals at 2502–05, 2519–25 (Rep. Harper); Elkins & McKitrick at 614.

Federalists in Congress perceived Logan's mission as an interference with executive conduct of foreign affairs. E.g., 9 Annals at 2494, 2607 (Rep. Griswold); id at 2501 (Rep. Pinckney); id at 2504 (Rep. Harper). Rutledge termed the Act yet another defense measure, id at 2496, but the principal arguments employed to justify it suggest it should properly be understood as necessary and proper to the President's authority to negotiate with foreign nations. Gallatin opposed the bill on policy grounds, id at 2497–99, and it was amended to

C.   The Expulsion of Matthew Lyon

It was no coincidence that the first person convicted under the Sedition Act was Representative Matthew Lyon of Vermont.[209] Representative Lyon had been in trouble before.[210]

Elected as a Republican in 1796, Lyon had promptly attracted attention by spitting in the face of his colleague Roger Griswold, who had not so subtly accused him of cowardice under enemy fire.[211] A select committee had recommended that Lyon be expelled from the House,[212] and a lively debate had ensued.

Article I, § 5 is singularly uninformative about the circumstances under which the House or the Senate "may . . . expel a member." A two-thirds vote is explicitly required, but nothing is said about the procedure to be followed or the grounds on which expulsion may be based. The Senate, as we shall see, had recently had occasion to expel one of its members,[213] but it had acted in great haste and under its usual veil of darkness; Lyon's case produced the first significant exploration of the expulsion provision.

At Lyon's request several members (along with a visiting Senator from Vermont) were put under oath and testified orally before the entire House sitting as a Committee of the Whole.[214] Christopher Champlin of Rhode Island then stated the case for expulsion: Lyon had committed "an offence of a gross and injurious nature," and nothing short of expulsion could "vindicate the honor" of the House.[215]

Lyon's principal defense, ably elaborated by Robert Williams, was that the House had not been in session at the time of the undisputed events.[216] That was important because it meant he had not interrupted the business of the House. If any member "acted so as to disturb the peace and order of the House," said Williams, the House had a right to turn him out; but a member could not be expelled for anything done outside the House "except it rendered him infamous."[217]

---

make clear it did not prevent citizens from seeking redress of individual injuries, id at 2677–79. Constitutional qualms were rare. Nicholas extravagantly asserted that because Article III narrowly defined treason Congress was powerless to create other offenses "of this kind." Id at 2495. Samuel Smith apparently argued that the bill would abridge the freedom of speech; Edmond responded that one might as plausibly argue that the Constitution protected perjury. 9 Annals at 2647. As in the Sedition Act controversy, the House was not convinced that the first amendment guaranteed the right to say whatever one pleased.

[209]See 15 F Cas 1183 (No 8646) (CC D Vt 1798); Wharton's State Trials at 333.

[210]See Elkins & McKitrick at 706–11; Miller at 208–09; Aleine Austin, Matthew Lyon (Pennsylvania State, 1981), passim.

[211]See 7 Annals at 961–62, 1025–29. According to the committee report, Lyon had started the quarrel by making disparaging remarks in Griswold's presence about Connecticut Representatives, of whom Griswold was one. Id at 961. The incident is described in Austin, Matthew Lyon at 96–102 (cited in note 210).

[212]Id at 962.

[213]See the discussion of the case of Senator Blount at notes 315–59.

[214]7 Annals at 962, 964–65. A transcription of the testimony appears in id at 1009–29. Nicholas perceived a risk of embarrassment in that "a majority of the committee might come to a decision which, according to the Constitution, it would require a two-thirds vote of the House to confirm," but he yielded on the point, and the reference was approved by a vote of eighty-eight to four. Id at 964.

[215]Id at 975.

[216]Id at 971–72 (Rep. Lyon); id at 977 (Rep. Williams). See also id at 983–85 (Rep. Nicholas). According to the committee report, the members were marking time while tellers counted the ballots for selection of managers to present the impeachment case against Senator Blount, and Lyon himself was "standing without the bar of the House." Id at 961.

[217]Id at 977. Cf 2 Story, § 835 (defending the expulsion provision on the ground that "a member might be

The power of expulsion, Williams argued, was a dangerous one and should be interpreted narrowly. For in a case such as Lyon's the House was victim, prosecutor, jury, and judge, all rolled into one; there was a serious risk that it might abuse its authority.[218] Moreover, the consequences of expulsion were grave: It affected not only "the person and character of the member himself" but also "all the citizens of a large district of country— his constituents."[219]

Gallatin summed up the argument against expulsion with his usual brilliance:

> Our Government, he said, was a Government of representation. . . . This being the case, said Mr. G., we, the representatives of the people, have only a limited power over individual representatives in our body. . . . He conceived that the power of expulsion had not been given . . . for the purpose of impairing the principle of representation, but for the purpose of enforcing that principle; and two cases might exist in which the power of expulsion . . . might be considered as a safeguard to the principle of representation. These two cases were, when the House discovered a person to be disqualified by some infamous conduct from voting, and when a member pertinaciously interrupted and prevented public business from being carried on.[220]

Lyon's case fell into neither category. Whether or not the House had been technically in session, Lyon had not disrupted its proceedings; and his conduct had displayed not corruption but only "a want of good breeding."[221] If Lyon was expelled, "one-half of the State of Vermont would be deprived of a representation" in the House "for the remainder of the session"; that was too high a price to exact "in order to gratify our sensibilities."[222]

Fire-eating Federalists who perceived the opportunity to enhance their majority piously insisted that the House had indeed been in session[223] and that Lyon's conduct proved him utterly unfit to serve.[224] Sewall invoked British precedent, maintained that

---

so lost to all sense of dignity or duty, as to disgrace the house by the grossness of his conduct, or interrupt its deliberations by perpetual violence or clamour").

Representative Findley argued that expulsion was proper only for crimes that would justify impeachment "in other bodies where impeachments could be brought." Id at 1000–01. The text of the Constitution did not help him; while Article II, § 4 left room for argument over just what besides treason and bribery constituted "high crimes and misdemeanors" sufficient to justify removing federal officers who had been impeached, it departed suggestively from the silence of the expulsion provision.

[218] 7 Annals at 976.

[219] Id at 978. In apparent response to this concern for democracy, Sitgreaves suggested that if Lyon's constituents approved of his conduct they were free to elect him again. Id at 995. The implication seemed to be, as the case of John Wilkes was said to have established in England, that a legislator could not properly be expelled twice for the same misconduct (see Erskine May, Treatise on the Law, Privileges, Proceedings, and Usage of Parliament 141 (Butterworths, 20th ed 1983)); but there was no occasion to explore the point further.

[220] 7 Annals at 997.

[221] Id at 997–98. See also id at 987 (Rep. Nicholas).

[222] Id at 999.

[223] Id at 979–80 (Rep. Harper); id at 989 (Rep. Otis).

[224] Id at 980 (Rep. Harper) ("unworthy of a seat in that House"); id at 988 (Rep. Otis) ("conduct which could not be suffered in a brothel or in a den of robbers").

the silence of the constitutional provision left the grounds for expulsion to legislative discretion, and chillingly contended that the voters should not be able to elect anyone repugnant to two thirds of the House.[225] But Gallatin was dead right, and cooler heads prevailed; the motion to expel fell comfortably short of the required two-thirds majority.[226]

It was almost exactly a year later that the House learned of Lyon's conviction for sedition. Now we've got him, Bayard exulted; now he can be expelled. Subverting the Government was a political offense of the first magnitude. It was immaterial that the crime had been committed outside the House; "a man who does not keep the laws ought not to be allowed to make them."[227]

Nicholas leapt to the defense. Vermonters had a right to be represented by whomever they chose. Lyon's conduct was not infamous. He should not be punished twice for the same offense. The House was not bound by the judicial decision but should reexamine the facts for itself. The offending statements had been written before the Sedition Act was in force. Since Nicholas believed the statute unconstitutional, he would not vote to punish its breach.[228]

Some of this scattershot was off the mark;[229] some of it tickles our fancy.[230] But Nicholas struck paydirt when he read to the House the statements for which Lyon had been condemned. The Senate, Lyon had said, was servile, the Executive power hungry,

[225]Id at 1001. Both British and colonial assemblies had often expelled members for extracurricular sins as well as for offenses against the assembly itself. See May, Parliamentary Privileges at 139–40 (cited in note 219); Mary Patterson Clarke, Parliamentary Privilege in the American Colonies 194–96 (Da Capo, 1971) (first published in 1943). Cf the use of British practice to sustain a broad power in the House to punish nonmembers for attempted bribery in the earlier case of Randall and Whitney, discussed in chapter 5.

[226]7 Annals at 1008. Griswold was not content to let the matter drop. Three days later he attacked Lyon with a walking stick, and Lyon responded by grabbing the tongs from the fire. Id at 1034. Thomas Davis of Kentucky moved to expel them both on the ground that "neither the dignity, the honor, or peace of that House could be preserved whilst these members remained in it." Id at 1036. Thatcher responded that Lyon had only defended himself and that when Griswold attacked him the House was not in session. Id at 1037. The committee recommended against expulsion, and the House by a lopsided vote agreed. Id at 1048, 1065. Boys, the House seemed to be saying, will always be boys.

[227]9 Annals at 2954, 2960–61.

[228]Id at 2961–65. Gallatin echoed several of these arguments, id at 2969–73.

[229]Both the double-jeopardy argument and the position that the voters could be represented by anyone they liked would read the expulsion provision out of the Constitution. As Bayard said, expulsion was not punishment within the meaning of the double-jeopardy clause; the House was protecting its processes from perceived corruption. 9 Annals at 2968. Moreover, Bayard said, it was irrelevant that Lyon had written the letter in question before the Act was passed; what counted was when it was published, and he had published it afterward. Id.

[230]Since the integrity of the House's processes was at stake, there was considerable appeal to the argument that it must be free to make its own decision, especially to the extent that the standards for expulsion differed from those for conviction; one would not expect the House to accept an acquittal as foreclosing the possibility of expulsion. Nicholas's determination to exercise his own judgment as to the constitutionality of the law has impressive support: Both Abraham Lincoln and Andrew Jackson are famous for declaring that even the Supreme Court's imprimatur does not bind other branches, and both Jefferson and Madison were about to go on record with analogous statements in the context of the Alien and Sedition Laws. See Lincoln's remarks respecting the *Dred Scott* decision in his debates with Stephen Douglas, in Basler, ed, 3 The Collected Works of Abraham Lincoln 255 (1953); Jackson's message explaining his veto of the legislation extending the charter of the Bank of the United States, 2 Richardson at 576, 581–83. For Jefferson and Madison's views as expressed in the Virginia and Kentucky Resolutions see text at note 274.

pompous, and riddled with patronage. Most of what he had said was a matter of opinion, not fact, and there was no way it could be proved true or false.[231] "[I]f a man is to be convicted because his opinions and those of a jury are at variance, there is an end to all security."[232] That Lyon was a Member of Congress only made matters worse: It was "incumbent on a Representative to disclose his opinions on public affairs to his constituents, and this disclosure will become more necessary, in proportion as such opinions may be offensive to the administrators of the Government."[233] "If this resolution should be adopted," Gallatin added, "it would follow . . . that every member who shall write anything which is contrary to the opinion of a majority of this House, whether what he writes be founded in truth or not, will be liable to be expelled, in order to purify the House."[234]

The House voted forty-nine to forty-four in favor of expulsion. Lyon thus won his war; the Federalists never succeeded in expelling him. But it was a sour victory; Lyon was saved only by the two-thirds requirement whose wisdom the incident so graphically proved. A majority of those voting on the motion were prepared to remove a colleague from his seat, and to deprive his constituents of representation, because he had dared to criticize the Government.

It is hard to believe that the expulsion clause was intended thus to frustrate both the election provisions of Article I and the purposes of what was to be the first amendment.

D.   The Cases of Duane and Randolph

The persecution of the incontinent Lyon was indefensible enough, but at least the House failed in its effort to compound the penalties already inflicted on him in federal court. Two incidents that occurred during the Sixth Congress illustrate the extent to which a majority of Federalists in each House were prepared to pervert instruments designed to protect the integrity of the legislative process into weapons for suppressing dissent.

On February 19, 1800 the *Aurora*, a shrill Republican mouthpiece in Philadelphia, published a critical article respecting, among other things, a Senate bill to regulate the process by which the President and Vice-President were elected.[235] A week later Senator Uriah Tracy of Connecticut proposed that the newly established Committee of Privileges find out who was the editor of the *Aurora*, how he had obtained a copy of the bill, and "by what authority" he had made "sundry assertions" in the paper about the bill, the Senate, and its members.[236]

Various Senators repeated the arguments that had been made in the House against

---

[231] 9 Annals at 2962–64. "The words called seditious," Jefferson had written to Madison after the trial, "were only general censures of the proceedings of Congress & of the President." Letter of Thomas Jefferson to James Madison, Nov 3, 1798, 17 Madison Papers at 173.

[232] 9 Annals at 2964.

[233] Id.

[234] Id at 2972.

[235] The article is printed in its entirely in 10 Annals at 113–15; the incident is related in detail in Smith, Freedom's Fetters, ch 13 (cited in note 134). See also Swanstrom at 217–22; Austin, Matthew Lyon at 127–28 (cited in note 210). The bill itself is discussed at notes 433–58.

[236] 10 Annals at 63. "Heretical doctrines maintained in Senate," Jefferson wrote in his *Anas* for March 1800, summarizing Federalist arguments in favor of this motion. 9 Jefferson Writings (Wash. ed) at 198–99.

the Sedition Act[237] and the punishment of Randall and Whitney.[238] The Constitution had limited legislative privileges by enumerating them; no law had defined the alleged offenses in advance; the Senate was acting as judge in its own cause; since Congress had no power over the press, neither had the Senate; the information the *Aurora* had published was not confidential; no one would print the debates if he could be punished for so doing.[239] Declaring that the newspaper had incorrectly stated that one of the members of the committee appointed to draft the bill had not been consulted and that the Senate had already passed it, the Senate by a vote of nineteen to eleven asked the committee to determine what ought to be done.[240]

Finding that the article contained "false, defamatory, scandalous, and malicious" statements "tending to defame the Senate of the United States, and to bring them into contempt and disrepute," the committee concluded that it constituted "a high breach of the privileges of this House." It recommended that William Duane, editor of the offending paper, be ordered to appear and given the opportunity "to make any proper defence for his conduct, in publishing the aforesaid false, defamatory, scandalous, and malicious assertions."[241]

Apart from its other difficulties, this proposal seemed an uncanny precedent for the Queen of Hearts' notorious insistence on judgment before trial;[242] yet the Senate approved the report in its entirety by a series of similarly overwhelming votes.[243]

Duane appeared and requested the right to be heard by counsel.[244] Over Republican objections the majority granted his request on such restrictive terms that Duane refused to appear again, asserting that he had been effectively "deprived of professional assistance."[245] For this refusal the Senate held him in contempt and ordered him arrested until further notice.[246]

Yes, as noted in connection with the contempt proceedings against Randall and

[237]See text at notes 186–208.

[238]See the discussion in chapter 5. Jefferson summarized the arguments on both sides of Duane's case in his Manual of Parliamentary Practice, 9 Jefferson Writings (Wash ed) at 9–11, adding that each future Senate would have to decide the question for itself. Id at 11.

[239]10 Annals at 68, 684–85, 690–91 (Sen. Cocke); id at 69–84 [!] (Sen. Pinckney); id at 88–90 (Sens. Bloodworth and Mason). Charles Pinckney, South Carolina's freshman Senator, was as the citation suggests a total windbag. As the *Aurora*'s principal defender in this controversy he had a special pipeline to the press, and that newspaper was the principal source of the Annals during this period. Thus throughout the Sixth Congress the otherwise familiarly barren record of the Senate proceedings is peppered with pretentious and cloying formal addresses by Pinckney, which make for bad reading but afford a rare insight into the issues ventilated in the still largely unilluminated upper House.

[240]10 Annals at 105.

[241]Id at 115.

[242]See Lewis Carroll, Alice in Wonderland, ch. 12.

[243]10 Annals at 111–15.

[244]Id at 118.

[245]Id at 122. The Senate had graciously allowed Duane to be heard by counsel "in denial of any facts charged against [him], or in excuse and extenuation of his offense," but not to challenge the Senate's authority. Id at 119.

[246]Id at 122–23. Duane went into hiding, and the Sergeant-at-Arms never found him. Just before it adjourned the Senate formally requested the President "to instruct the proper law officer to commence and carry on a prosecution" against Duane for his "false, defamatory, scandalous, and malicious publications." Id at 184. He was duly indicted but managed to put off the trial until after Jefferson became President, and the case was eventually dismissed. See Smith, Freedom's Fetters at 298–306 (cited in note 134).

Whitney, there was precedent for all of this in England and the colonies.[247] There was precedent for just about any excess a legislative body might commit. But it was not obvious that such precedents could be incorporated wholesale into a document that expressly guaranteed freedom of the press, due process, and the right to trial by jury.

Just a few weeks before the Duane incident the House of Representatives had been confronted with a very different challenge to its integrity. John Randolph of Roanoke, who had just begun his long service as a Republican from Virginia, complained to President Adams that while attending the theater he had been insulted and harassed by two Marine officers for having spoken in the House in favor of reducing the size of the Army. Adams had referred the complaint to the House, which sent it to committee.[248]

Affidavits of other House members fully confirmed Randolph's allegations.[249] Military intimidation, someone soundly observed, meant "an end to all legislation"[250]—i.e., of legislative independence and popular sovereignty.[251] Yet the committee exonerated the officers and attacked Randolph for taking the matter to the President, for in so doing he had derogated from the rights of the House.[252]

This was a new pinnacle of unadulterated chutzpah even for the Federalist Congress. Criticism of the majority was to be punished; intimidation of the opposition was to be condoned.[253] In vain did Randolph and his friends protest that the same conduct could be both a breach of privilege and a criminal offense,[254] and that the Commander in Chief had a responsibility to discipline his subordinates.[255] Ultimately the committee's proposal was amended to say that the officers' conduct had been "indiscreet and improper." But the resolution itself was narrowly defeated; an opposition motion to censure the officers' action was ruled out of order, and the matter was dropped without a decision.[256]

---

[247]See chapter 5. Instances of legislative punishment for reflections on the legislature or its members are given in May, Parliamentary Privileges at 152 (cited in note 219), and in Clarke, Parliamentary Privilege at 117–29 (cited in note 225); see also Levy, Emergence of a Free Press at 13–14, 17–18 (cited in note 198). For cases involving false reports or premature disclosure of parliamentary proceedings see May, Parliamentary Privileges at 152–54. Disobedience of lawful orders, of course, was an independent ground for imposing sanctions. See id at 146; Clarke, Parliamentary Privilege at 207 (cited in note 225). John Marshall, who thought it politically foolish to pursue Duane, acknowledged that public sentiment favored the existence of legislative authority to punish breaches of privilege and insisted that, "[i]f the privilege of members extends beyond the walls of their hall, & such seems to have been the opinion of both parties, it was unquestionably violated by Duane." Letter of John Marshall to James Markham Marshall, Apr 4, 1800, in Charles T. Cullen, ed, 4 The Papers of John Marshall 121, 122–23 (North Carolina, 1984).

[248]10 Annals at 372–73. See Miller at 249–50; William Cabell Bruce, 1 John Randolph of Roanoke 156–65 (Octagon, 1970).

[249]10 Annals at 378–82.

[250]Id at 374.

[251]There was ample precedent for treating both prior intimidation and subsequent molestation of members as breaches of privilege subject to legislative sanction. See May, Parliamentary Privileges at 157–59 (cited in note 219); Clarke, Parliamentary Privilege at 108–09 (cited in note 225).

[252]10 Annals at 504–05.

[253]Bayard went so far as to maintain that it was worse to attack a legislator in print than in person, since the printed word was permanent; the only limitation was that those who accosted a Representative in the theater must refrain from what we would call fighting words. Id at 435–36.

[254]Id at 442 (Rep. Davis).

[255]Id at 373 (Rep. Randolph); id at 446 (Rep. Jones); id at 488 (Rep. Gallatin).

[256]Id at 505–06. The following year the House came down hard on an unsuspecting Maryland magistrate who had had the misfortune to exercise jurisdiction over a complaint filed by a spectator whom the Sergeant-at-Arms had arrested on the Speaker's orders for applauding in the gallery. As Bayard said, the House (like a

E.   All's Well That Ends Well

The Alien and Sedition Acts were adopted in June and July of 1798, just before the second session of the Fifth Congress adjourned. When that Congress returned to
Philadelphia for its final session in December it was inundated by petitions demanding
their repeal.

The most disturbing challenges came from the legislatures of Kentucky and
Virginia.[257] Resuming the arguments that had been stated during the House debate, both
assemblies declared the acts unconstitutional.[258] That was fair enough; they may well
have been. What was troubling was the proposed remedy. Madison's Virginia
Resolutions proclaimed that the states, as parties to the constitutional "compact," had
the right and the duty, "in case of a deliberate, palpable, and dangerous" federal usurpation of authority, "to interpose, for arresting the progress of the evil, and for maintaining,
within their respective limits, the authorities, rights, and liberties, appertaining to
them."[259] Characteristically, a supplementary set of Kentucky pronouncements inspired
byJefferson was even more reckless, trumpeting "that [state] nullification . . . of all
unauthorized acts . . . is the rightful remedy."[260]

If you were wondering where John C. Calhoun and Ross Barnett got their weird notions about disobedience of federal law, you can stop looking.

Just what the Resolutions meant by "interpos[ition]" and "nullification," of course,
has been the subject of dispute. Madison at one point sternly reminded Jefferson that it
did not follow from the premise that the state was "the ultimate judge of infractions" that
the legislature was "the legitimate organ" to make the decision.[261] Virginia pointedly refrained from declaring the statutes "void," as Kentucky had done,[262] and Madison's later
official defense of the Virginia Resolutions—his famous Report of 1800—insisted that
they had been mere "expressions of opinion, unaccompanied with any other effect than

---

court) had authority to punish for contempt in order to preserve order; the magistrate was found to have
breached the House's privileges but was not punished for his actions. See id at 851, 880–90.

[257]The Kentucky and Virginia Resolutions, together with the negative responses of other states and
Madison's committee report in rejoinder, are collected (with some errors) in 4 Elliot at 528–80. Additional
legislative responses are printed in Frank Maloy Anderson, Contemporary Opinion of the Virginia and
Kentucky Resolutions, 5 Am Hist Rev 225, 244–52 (1899); the debates in the Virginia House of Delegates,
which retraced the arguments made in Congress, can be found in S Doc No 873, 62d Cong, 2d Sess (1912).

[258]4 Elliott at 528–29 (Virginia); id at 540–42, 544 (Kentucky). Both added that Congress had tended to
exceed its authority in other instances by taking an unwarrantedly broad view of the general welfare and
necessary and proper clauses, but as the Kentucky legislature put it that subject could be taken up "at a time
of greater tranquillity, while those specified in the preceding resolutions call for immediate redress." Id at
528, 542.

[259]Id at 528. Madison had given a foretaste of this when he introduced the Bill of Rights, arguing that not
only the courts but also the states would watch over their enforcement. 1 Annals at 457; see chapter 2.

[260]4 Elliot at 545. Jefferson's biographer called the supplementary resolutions "the work of an unknown
draftsman." Malone, Jefferson and the Ordeal of Liberty at 406 n 27 (cited in note 11). Elkins and McKitrick
(at 722), writing a long generation later, flatly attribute them to Jefferson. In any case Jefferson's draft of the
initial resolutions had contained a similar reference to nullification, which the legislature had omitted for the
time being. 7 Jefferson Writings (Ford ed) at 301.

[261]Letter of James Madison to Thomas Jefferson, Dec 29, 1798, 17 Madison Papers at 191 (adding (id at
191–92) that the Resolutions ought to leave other states a wide choice of remedies so as to "shield the Genl.
Assembly agst. the charge of Usurpation in the very act of protesting agst the usurpations of Congress").

[262]4 Elliott at 528–29 (Virginia); id at 540, 541, 542, 544 (Kentucky).

what they may produce on opinion, by exciting reflection."[263] Even the less guarded Kentucky Resolutions concluded with a meek request that other states, after declaring the laws "void and of no force," "unite with this commonwealth in requesting their repeal,"[264] while the same later broadside that brandished the dread word "nullification" conceded that "this commonwealth . . . will bow to the laws of the Union."[265] Thus it has been argued, not without force, that neither state actually endorsed "individual states' resistance to federal authority."[266]

Maybe not. It takes pretty close parsing, however, to arrive at this conclusion; critics may perhaps be forgiven for perceiving more in the Resolutions than an innocuous argument for repeal.[267] In any event Jefferson was plainly prepared to go a good deal further. Not only had his draft of the first Kentucky Resolutions contained a reference to "nullification" unalloyed by professions of obeisance to federal laws;[268] it had concluded with an incendiary invitation to each state to "take measures of its own for providing that neither these acts, nor any other of the General Government not plainly and intentionally authorized by the Constitution, shall be exercised within their respective territories."[269] Nay, more: In his initial suggestions to Madison respecting the second round of Resolutions Jefferson had proposed to warn that, if the country did not return to "true principles," the offended states were prepared "to sever ourselves from th[e] union."[270]

Central to the Virginia and Kentucky position was the argument that, there being no tribunal above the states to determine whether their "compact" had been violated, it was up to them to decide[271]—"as in all other cases of compact among parties [e.g., independent nations] having no common judge."[272] But, you ask, what about the Supreme Court? "It belongs not to state legislatures," the Vermont House of Representatives re-

---

[263]Id at 546, 578.

[264]Id at 544.

[265]Id at 545.

[266]See Jefferson Powell, The Principles of '98: An Essay in Historical Retrieval, 80 Va L Rev 689, 721 (1994) (adding, id at 718, that what Madison envisioned was a "collective" right of imposition that "could be exercised only in concert through the electoral process or by a quasi-revolutionary act of the people themselves"). See also Adrienne Koch & Harry Ammon, The Virginia and Kentucky Resolutions: An Episode in Jefferson's and Madison's Defense of Civil Liberties, 5 Wm & Mary Q (3d series) 145, 173 (1948) (terming it "difficult to imagine" that Senator Hayne could later interpret the 1800 Report as an argument for nullification).

[267]The historian Henry Adams referred to the Virginia Resolutions as "nullification resolves" and called them "a foundation for revolution"; Theodore Sedgwick said they (and their Kentucky cousins) were "little, if at all, short of a declaration of war." See Henry Adams, The Life of Albert Gallatin 212 (Lippincott, 1880); Letter of Theodore Sedgwick to Rufus King, Mar 20, 1799, in Charles R. King, ed, 2 The Life and Correspondence of Rufus King 579, 581 (Putnam, 1895). See also Berns, Freedom of the Press, 1970 Sup Ct Rev at 125–30 (cited in note 202). The modern skeptic may also be forgiven for observing that the Kentucky legislature, which so piously promised to respect "the laws of the Union," had just solemnly declared both the Alien and Sedition Acts "void and of no force" and therefore not laws at all.

[268]See note 260.

[269]7 Jefferson Writings (Ford ed) at 306.

[270]Letter of Thomas Jefferson to James Madison, Aug 23, 1799, 17 Madison Papers at 257, 258. In light of Madison's apparently horrified response, Jefferson omitted this language before sending the otherwise largely unchanged recommendations on to Kentucky. See Letter of Thomas Jefferson to Wilson Cary Nicholas, Sept 5, 1799, 7 Jefferson Writings (Ford ed) at 389, 390.

[271]4 Elliot at 548 (Virginia).

[272]Id at 540 (Kentucky).

torted, "to decide on the constitutionality of laws made by the general government; this power being exclusively vested in the judiciary courts of the Union."[273] But the federal courts, Madison and Jefferson insisted, were after all federal; to make the central government the ultimate judge of the extent of its own authority "would have made its discretion, and not the Constitution, the measure of its powers."[274] Massachusetts turned the argument around: If each state were to determine when its reserved rights had been infringed, "the Constitution"—more properly the federal Government—"would be reduced to a mere cipher."[275]

Both, of course, were right. If the states had had the final say, we would never have had *Wickard v Filburn*;[276] but we might never have had *McCulloch v Maryland*[277] either. But the last word must reside somewhere, or the result is chaos. In agreeing to the basic law, with its provision for Supreme Court review of cases arising under the Constitution, the states accepted the Court's authority to decide.[278] It is one thing for a President to veto a law the Court has found constitutional, as Jackson would later do;[279] he is free to reject it for any reason. It may even be acceptable within limits, as Lincoln was to argue, for a legislator to vote to reenact a law the Supreme Court has struck down, in the hope that the judges will change their minds.[280] But to defy a law that has been enacted and upheld, as Representative Allen said when Livingston urged the people to disobey the Alien Act,[281] is nothing short of rebellion; it can be justified only by the extralegal right of revolution on which we relied in breaking with England[282] and in discarding the Articles of Confederation.[283] Madison seemed indeed to invoke that right in his subsequent report on the Virginia Resolutions:

> [T]he proper answer to the objection [that constitutionality is for the courts to determine] is, that the resolution of the General Assembly relates to those great and extraordinary cases, in which all the forms of the Constitution may prove ineffectual against infractions dangerous to the essential rights of the parties . . . .[284]

Many years later Madison would insist that was what Jefferson had had in mind too.[285]

---

[273]Id at 539. See also id at 533 (Rhode Island); id at 534 (Massachusetts); id at 537–38 (New York Senate); id at 539 (New Hampshire).

[274]Id at 540 (Kentucky). See also id at 549 (Virginia Report of 1800).

[275]Id at 534.

[276]317 US 111 (1942).

[277]17 US 316 (1819).

[278]This is another way of saying that *Martin v Hunter's Lessee* was right; the Convention debates leave no doubt that Article III contemplated Supreme Court review of state judgments respecting federal rights. See *Martin*, 14 US 304 (1816); The First Hundred Years at 91–96.

[279]See 2 Richardson at 576, 581–83 (renewal of the charter of the Bank of the United States).

[280]See Basler, ed, 3 The Collected Works of Abraham Lincoln at 255 (1953).

[281]8 Annals at 2095–96.

[282]Declaration of Independence, 1 Stat 1 (July 4, 1776).

[283]See 2 Farrand at 469 (James Wilson): "The House on fire must be extinguished, without a scrupulous regard to ordinary rights."

[284]4 Elliot at 549, 17 Madison Papers at 311.

[285]"[T]he right of nullification meant by Mr. Jefferson is the natural right, which all admit to be a remedy against insupportable oppression." Notes on Nullification (1835–36), reprinted in Marvin Myers, ed, The Mind of the Founder: Sources of the Political Thought of James Madison 428–29 (Univ Press of New England,

The situation, as the frog said when the carriage rolled over him, was a little taut over the eyeballs. Harper ranted about a campaign of misrepresentation to discredit the Alien and Sedition Acts and demanded that copies of the statutes be distributed to dispel the misunderstanding.[286] Federalists were heard to argue that petitions seeking repeal of the laws were libelous and insurrectionary and ought to be rejected out of hand.[287] The Constitution guaranteed the right to complain about unconstitutional legislation, Livingston responded;[288] having silenced the press, said Gallatin, now you want to destroy the right to petition.[289]

Similar arguments had been made a few months before when a company of Virginia grenadiers had politely petitioned to protest government policy toward France and argue against expanding the armed forces.[290] In addition to labeling that petition indecent, scandalous, and calumnious, Federalists had argued that petitioners had no right to insult Congress or to say that the Government had neglected its duty, and that even if the grenadiers had a right to send their petition the House had a right not to receive it.[291] Fortunately in both cases the objections were overruled; the grenadiers' petition, as well as the protests against the Alien and Sedition Acts, was referred to committee for consideration.[292]

The grenadiers' petition never emerged from committee. Those attacking the Alien and Sedition Acts prompted a detailed report restating the arguments in favor of the constitutionality of the laws and advising against their repeal.[293] By this time the Federalists had settled on their story. The Alien Act was a defense measure.[294] So was the Sedition Act, which was also necessary and proper to the execution of all federal powers.[295]

Opponents repeated their arguments and urged repeal.[296] A couple of border-state Federalists defected; the votes were close, but no cigar.[297] A motion to repeal the Sedition

---

rev ed 1981). Jefferson had indeed employed the term "natural right." See 7 Jefferson Writings (Ford ed) at 301, 306.

[286]9 Annals at 2426–27. Dawson suggested that the Constitution be distributed at the same time so that citizens could make their own comparison, but the House rejected his request. Id at 2245, 2253. Indeed a number of Federalists voted against publication of the statutes too after Thatcher said the sole result would be to encourage people to determine for themselves the constitutionality of the laws, which was a matter for the courts. Id at 2454–56.

[287]See id at 2798 (Rep. Gordon); id at 2884, 2886 (Rep. Sewall); id at 2957 (Rep. Harper).

[288]Id at 2800; see US Const, Amend 1.

[289]9 Annals at 2958. See also id at 2801.

[290]8 Annals at 1707–08.

[291]See id at 1708–09 (Rep. Sitgreaves); id at 1709 (Rep. Brooks); id at 1713 (Rep. Sewall); id at 1714 (Rep. Otis); id at 1716–17 (Rep. Rutledge); id at 1719 (Rep. Thatcher). Dana made the usual objection that the petition was misdirected since the House had no authority to punish crimes, id at 1710; Gallatin appropriately replied that the petition made specific recommendations with regard to congressional policy. Id at 1711.

[292]Id at 1724; 9 Annals at 2959.

[293]Id at 2985–93.

[294]Id at 2986.

[295]Id at 2988, 2990–91.

[296]See id at 2993–3001 (Rep. Gallatin); id at 3003–13 (Rep. Nicholas).

[297]Both votes were fifty-two to forty-eight. George Dent of Maryland and Josiah Parker of Virginia voted with the Republicans for repeal. Id at 3016.

Act actually passed the House early in the Sixth Congress,[298] but a clever Federalist amendment made the cure seem worse than the disease, and the Republicans abandoned their own proposal.[299]

For the saving grace of both the Alien Act and the Sedition Act was that they were temporary; each was to expire by its own terms after less than three years.[300] As Bayard had remarked during the earlier repeal debate, although President Adams had signed the Alien Act he had never expelled anyone under it;[301] its sponsors let it die in peace. The Sedition Act was another matter; during the Sixth Congress a House committee recommended that it be extended for another two years.[302] The courts had upheld it, said Platt and Griswold; its constitutionality was settled.[303] Benjamin Huger, a South Carolina Federalist who usually held his peace, said he would vote against his friends on this one. Harsh measures like the Sedition Act should be reserved for times of crisis, and the storm had passed. The public was against the law; the line between liberty and license was fuzzy enough that in normal times it was better to take the bad speech with the good.[304] After a confusing series of close votes Huger's view prevailed; the House voted fifty-three to forty-nine not to engross the bill.[305]

One of Jefferson's first acts as President was to pardon those who had been convicted under the Sedition Act and to reimburse them for the fines they had paid.[306] The Supreme Court declared it unconstitutional in 1964.[307]

---

[298]10 Annals at 419.

[299]The Federalist amendment provided that after repeal the crimes the statute had defined would remain punishable at common law. 10 Annals at 410. Republicans were not prepared to concede that there *was* a federal common law, much less that it included the harsh English notion of sedition—which, as Federalists had noted in arguing that the statute made the law less stringent, neither made truth a defense (as the amendment generously would have done) nor provided for a jury determination of the ultimate question of fact. See id at 410–11 (Rep. Nicholas). Gallatin objected to the whole idea of a federal common law on positivistic grounds that sound quite modern after all that has been said about Erie v Tompkins, 304 US 1 (1938), and Swift v Tyson, 41 US 1 (1842): Recognition of common law crimes would permit the courts to adopt laws never passed by Congress, and indeed on subjects beyond Congress's power. 10 Annals at 413. Hartley, who had spoken for repeal, and John Marshall, who had criticized the Alien and Sedition Acts as useless and divisive (Letter to a Freeholder, Oct 2, 1798, in 3 Marshall Papers at 503, 505–06), voted against their party's indigestible amendment, see 10 Annals at 419, 423; the final vote to leave well enough alone was 87–11. Id.

[300]1 Stat at 572, § 6 (aliens) (two years from the date of passage, or June 25, 1800); 1 Stat at 597, § 4 (sedition) (Mar 3, 1801).

[301]9 Annals at 2895; see Elkins & McKitrick at 591–92. A number of foreigners, however, had left the country to avoid the risk of expulsion. In addition, although he resisted Cabinet pressure for vigorous enforcement of the Act, Adams actually signed three warrants under it, and the affected individuals left the country before further action could be taken. See Ralph Adams Brown, The Presidency of John Adams 125 (Kansas, 1975); Smith, Freedom's Fetters at 159–76 (cited in note 134).

[302]10 Annals at 874, 877.

[303]Id at 916, 920. Conceding that the courts had power to pass upon the validity of statutes, Thomas Davis of Kentucky argued that in this instance they had not decided "with all the moderation and solemnity that usually attend judicial decisions" and that therefore their conclusions were not entitled to deference. Id at 917–18

[304]Id at 925–28.

[305]Id at 975–76, 1038–39, 1049–50.

[306]See Dumas Malone, Jefferson the President: First Term, 1801–1805 35 (Little, Brown, 1970).

[307]New York Times Co. v Sullivan, 376 US 254, 273–77(1964) (dictum).

III. ODDS AND ENDS

We are fast approaching the end. The Federalists won one last victory in 1798. John Marshall put in a brief appearance in the House before going off to be Secretary of State and then Chief Justice and acquitted himself well.[308] Opposed at every turn by truculent High Federalists in the Cabinet, President Adams ultimately appointed his own team[309] and made peace with France.[310]

Congress finally passed a bankruptcy act,[311] and the Government moved to the

---

[308]Despite his glaring lack of seniority, it was Marshall who took the lead in drafting the House's response to the President's Annual Address, 10 Annals at 191, 193–96, and in honoring the departed Washington, see note 313. More substantively, it was he who mounted the principal defense of President Adams in the brouhaha over his role in the extradition of Thomas Nash (alias Jonathan Robbins), who had been charged with committing murder on board a British vessel. Livingston (10 Annals at 532) had branded the President's action an interference with the judicial function and with the right of jury trial. Marshall, in one of the most effective speeches of this uninspired session, maintained that whether an individual was extraditable under a treaty was a question for the President to decide in the exercise of his duty to take care that the treaty was faithfully executed. Id at 597–618. This incident is exhaustively analyzed in Ruth Wedgwood, The Revolutionary Martyrdom of Jonathan Robbins, 100 Yale LJ 229 (1990). On Marshall's role in the Sixth Congress see Editorial Note, 4 Marshall Papers at 31–38 (cited in note 247); Albert Beveridge, 2 The Life of John Marshall 432–84 (Houghton Mifflin, 1916); Elkins & McKitrick at 728–32.

[309]In addition to Marshall in the State Department, Samuel Dexter served concurrently as Secretary of the Treasury and Secretary of War.

[310]As in the case of the recent treaty with Great Britain (see chapter 5), one of the negotiators was Chief Justice of the United States—in this instance former Senator Oliver Ellsworth, who like his predecessor did not resign his judicial office until he had been abroad for some time. Senator Charles Pinckney, who voted against Ellsworth's appointment (1 Sen Exec J at 318), proposed first a constitutional amendment and then a statute that would forbid federal judges to hold any other federal or state office (10 Annals at 41–42, 96–97), supporting the latter proposal with persuasive arguments respecting judicial independence, impartiality, and attention to judicial duties. Id at 97–102. Livingston, in the House, offered a more restrictive amendment that would have made judges ineligible for other appointments for six months after they left office, id at 523. Congress took no action on any of these proposals. See Charles Warren, 1 The Supreme Court in United States History 156, 167–68, 172 (Little, Brown, rev ed 1926).

As in the case of Jay's Treaty, the Senate gave only conditional consent to the resulting convention with France. See 8 Stat 178 (Sept 30, 1800); 10 Annals at 777–78. Adams ratified the agreement as the Senate had approved it, just as his term expired. France then accepted the Senate's revisions, adding a proviso of its own. France's ratification "not being pure and simple," President Jefferson resubmitted the convention to the Senate for final approval, but the Senate insouciantly responded that it considered the convention "fully ratified"—implying it saw no need for further consent even in the face of French action that arguably altered the agreement the Senate had approved. See 10 Annals at 1206–07; 1 Richardson at 315, 332; Ralston Hayden, The Senate and Treaties, 1789–1817 124 (Macmillan, 1920).

[311]2 Stat 19 (Apr 4, 1800). For efforts along this line in the First Congress see introduction to part I, note 9. During the Fifth Congress, when a bankruptcy bill was narrowly defeated in the House (see 9 Annals at 2676), several constitutional questions were raised. There was a flurry of concern about the discharge of debts contracted before enactment, which Bayard said some Members argued was inconsistent with the ex post facto clause of Article I, § 9. See id at 2579. The majority was rightly unimpressed, id (the need to discharge preexisting debts having been one reason the contract clause applied only to the states, see Michael W. McConnell, Contract Rights and Property Rights, 76 Cal L Rev 267, 286 (1988)) but apparently uninformed, for nobody mentioned the definitive decision in Calder v. Bull, 3 US 386 (1798), The First Hundred Years at 41–49. Differing views were expressed as to state authority. Bayard asserted that federal power was exclusive, 9 Annals at 2656. Baldwin denied it, id at 2670–71 (noting that the states had continued to regulate the subject in the absence of congressional action), and the statute itself preserved the rights under state insolvency laws of debtors not covered by the federal provisions. 2 Stat at 36, § 61. Nobody mentioned the analogy of the commerce clause, whose exclusivity had just been debated in the quarantine context. See chapter 5.

District of Columbia.[312] George Washington did not live to see the Government established in the new city that he had worked so hard to create and that bore his name; he had been carried off by a chill in 1799.[313]

Washington was gone, the temporary capital was gone, the undeclared war was gone, and with it the Alien and Sedition Acts. It would not be long before the Federalists were gone too.[314] The big news of the Sixth Congress was their stubborn and unscrupulous fight to forestall the inevitable. But first we must tie up a few loose ends.

A.   The Impeachment of Senator Blount

A year before the House first sought to rid itself of the raging Lyon, the Senate had unceremoniously expelled one of its own members. The House had already voted to impeach him, but after an illuminating argument the Senate dismissed the charges for lack of jurisdiction. Unfortunately we do not quite know why.

Six weeks after the Fifth Congress first met in 1797, President Adams transmitted to each House a letter purportedly written by William Blount, former Governor of the Southwest Territory, who had just been selected as Senator from the new state of Tennessee.[315] The letter was oblique but plainly implicated Senator Blount in a cloak-and-dagger scheme involving the British and the Indians in the Southwest.[316] It turned

---

Pinckney repeated the improbable argument that Congress was *required* to adopt a bankruptcy law; Baldwin refuted him. 9 Annals at 2581, 2670–71. Compare US Const, Art I, § 8, cl 4 ("The Congress shall have power . . . to establish . . . uniform laws on the subject of bankruptcies . . .") with id, Art I, § 5 ("Each House shall keep a journal of its proceedings . . .").

[312]See 2 Stat 55 (Apr 24, 1800); 10 Annals at 721, 781.

[313]"Our Washington," John Marshall told the House, "is no more." 10 Annals at 203. The House adopted Marshall's resolution dubbing him (really!) "first in war, first in peace, and first in the hearts of his countrymen." Id at 204. Congress resolved to conduct a funeral procession and other appropriate ceremonies, to recommend that citizens wear black armbands for thirty days and assemble on his next birthday to remember him, and to construct a monument in his honor. 2 Stat 86 (Dec 24, 1799); 2 Stat 87 (Jan 6, 1800).

It seems churlish to question any of this, but that is what this book is about. A resolution passed by the same Congress to provide a medal to the Captain of the "Constellation" (2 Stat 87 (Mar 29, 1800)) suggests that recognition for services rendered may be necessary and proper to the functioning of public offices (not least, to attract qualified persons and encourage their best efforts). In any event, the monument was to be erected in the District of Columbia, over which Congress had the power of "exclusive legislation." US Const, Art I, § 8, cl 17.

[314]Before they left, the Federalists pushed through a new judiciary act, designed to extend federal jurisdiction (subject to a four hundred dollar minimum) to all classes of cases within Article III and to spare Supreme Court Justices the burden of circuit riding by creating a new set of circuit courts, each with judges of its own for the outgoing President to appoint. 2 Stat 89, 90, 92, §§ 6, 7, 11 (Feb 13, 1801). The only constitutional question of interest was raised by a provision specifying that two of the seats in the Sixth Circuit (comprising Kentucky, Tennessee, and the future state of Ohio) were to be occupied by the present District Judges for Kentucky and Tennessee. Id at 90, § 7. One is tempted to argue that in so providing Congress usurped the power of appointment given the President (with Senate consent) by Article II, § 2. Yet the designated judges had tenure during good behavior, and § 24 of the Act abolished the courts on which they sat (id at 97); it may be that Congress perceived a constitutional obligation to give them a new court on which to exercise their authority. The Republicans, it should be noted, were not so punctilious; when they abolished the new circuit courts the following year they put the new judges out on the street, and the Supreme Court never passed on the constitutional question. See 2 Stat 132, §§ 1, 4 (Mar 8, 1802); Stuart v Laird, 5 US 299 (1803); The First Hundred Years at 74–77.

[315]7 Annals at 33, 440.

[316]See id at 41–43.

out that his plan was to wrest Louisiana and the Floridas from Spain,[317] in blatant violation of the Neutrality Act.[318]

Two of his colleagues having verified Blount's handwriting, a Senate committee found him "guilty of a high misdemeanor, entirely inconsistent with his public trust and duty as a Senator," and he was expelled on the spot by a vote of twenty-five to one.[319] Nothing in the House debates over Matthew Lyon affords any reason to doubt that Blount's was a proper case for expulsion.[320]

In the meantime, after a brief debate, Blount had also been impeached by the House. Nicholas and Gallatin had expressed doubt whether Senators were "civil officers of the United States" subject to impeachment under Article II, § 4.[321] Dana had responded that legislators fell within the clause's purpose of enabling the Government "to protect itself by displacing from its counsels men who were faithless and unworthy."[322] He had also invoked analogies: Surely the "office[s]" that under Article I, § 3 a person could be disqualified from holding after successful impeachment included seats in Congress; surely a Senator was "a person holding . . . office" whom § 9 of the same Article forbade to accept emoluments or titles from foreign governments without congressional consent.[323] Gallatin had allowed that Dana "had removed a part of his doubts,"[324] and the motion to impeach had been agreed to without a division.[325]

---

[317]See Stanley J. Folmsbee, Robert E. Corlew, & Enoch L. Mitchell, Tennessee: A Short History 127–31 (Tennessee, 1969); William H. Masterson, William Blount 302–15 (LSU, 1954); Miller at 189–91. The evidence collected by the House committee, which is quite convincing, appears in 8 Annals at 2324–2416.

[318]1 Stat 381, 384, § 5 (June 5, 1794); see chapter 4.

[319]7 Annals at 41, 43–44. Senator Tazewell's lone dissenting vote, we are told, was based on "a technicality of procedure." Masterson, William Blount at 322 (cited in note 317).

[320]At the time the Senate was in the dark as to the precise nature of Blount's conspiracy; the committee thought it sufficient that the letter showed he had attempted "to seduce" a federal Indian agent "from his duty" and "to alienate the affections and confidence of the Indians." Id at 43. Noting that this action was neither "a statuteable offence," nor "committed in his official character," nor "during the session of congress; nor at the seat of government," Story cited Blount's case as demonstrating the Senate's view that "expulsion may be for any misdemeanor, which, although not punishable by any statute, is inconsistent with the trust and duty of a senator." 2 Story, § 836. See also In re Chapman, 166 US 661, 669–70 (1897) (citing the Blount case and endorsing Story's interpretation). As for the question of procedure, the committee reported that Blount had failed to appear to defend himself. Id at 41.

[321]7 Annals at 450 (Rep. Nicholas); id at 451 (Rep. Gallatin).

[322]Id at 453.

[323]Id. As we shall see, the Senate soon had occasion to construe this clause as well. See text at notes 360–93.

[324]7 Annals at 457.

[325]Id at 459. Sitgreaves was careful to point out that, except in cases of corruption, the speech or debate clause (US Const, Art I, § 6) forbade impeaching a Senator "for anything he might do as a legislator," id at 449; Gallatin thought the clause forbade impeachment even for a vote cast in exchange for a bribe. Id at 451. Representative Brooks inquired at one point whether the House "could proceed to impeach a man, if he were not present," id at 458, but there was no recorded reply. His concern seems to have been misplaced, since impeachment is only accusation, not conviction; potential defendants generally have no right to appear before the grand jury. United States v Fritz, 852 F2d 1175, 1178 (9th Cir 1988); Daniels v United States, 26 F3d 706, 711 (7th Cir 1994). When Nicholas doubted the need to ask the Senate to take steps to ensure Blount's presence at the coming trial, Harper responded that he could not be tried in absentia; Venable's sensible rejoinder that a man ought not to be able to frustrate justice by running away fell for the moment on deaf ears. Id at 461. This exchange was twice repeated at later stages of the proceeding, see id at 837–39; 9 Annals at 2472–85, and Blount was not present for any of the Senate proceedings. Not surprisingly, in resolving procedural questions respecting impeachment House members tended to rely on British precedents, with

Six months passed before the House presented its formal articles of impeachment,[326] ten more before the Senate proceedings began.[327] Blount's lawyers, Jared Ingersoll and Alexander Dallas, challenged the Senate's jurisdiction on three distinct grounds: Having been expelled from the upper House, Blount was no longer a Senator; he had never been a "civil officer of the United States"; and he was not charged with having committed any offense in the execution of his duties. They also noted that in all criminal prosecutions the sixth amendment required, among other things, a jury trial.[328]

An earlier effort by Senator Tazewell to require a jury in impeachment cases had attracted only three votes.[329] James Bayard of Delaware, lead counsel for the House, brought out the heavy artillery to show why. Article I, § 3 expressly gave the Senate "the sole power to try all impeachments" and provided for conviction upon the vote of "two thirds of the Members present." Article III's provision for jury trial contained an explicit exception for "cases of impeachment." The sixth amendment guarantee of a jury "[i]n all criminal prosecutions" must be read in the context of other constitutional provisions; otherwise there would have to be a jury in courts-martial, too, and that would mean "an end of discipline in the army and navy." Impeachment was not a "criminal prosecution" but "a proceeding purely of a political nature," which the Senate (as the Framers, we might add, had perceived) was "peculiarly and exclusively the proper tribunal to try."[330]

Dallas hastened to explain: The defense had not meant to suggest that there was a right to jury trial if the case was a proper one for impeachment.[331] On the contrary, the fact that there was no jury in impeachment cases was a reason for construing the impeachment power narrowly; for to find an offense impeachable was to subject the defendant to condemnation without jury trial.[332]

---

which they were intimately familiar. See, e.g., 7 Annals at 459 (Rep. Sitgreaves); id at 464 (Rep. Rutledge); id at 952 (Rep. Sitgreaves).

[326]See id at 498–502. Congress had adjourned four days after having voted to impeach, and Venable had doubted whether the committee appointed to draft the articles could be authorized to sit during the recess. Id at 464. No one is reported to have responded to his concern, which sounds highly technical today; the committee was expressly authorized to do its work while the House was away. Id at 466.

[327]A Senate bill to regulate procedure in impeachment cases was read twice, sent to committee for refinement, and debated, only to be denied a third reading, id at 491, 508–09; the Senate later adopted rules without consulting the House or the President, 8 Annals at 2196, 2197. One may speculate that, although a statute for this purpose would have been necessary and proper to the trial of impeachments, the Senate thought it more appropriate to deal with the matter itself under its authority to determine its own procedures. US Const, Art I, § 5. Cf Sitgreaves's argument, 7 Annals at 683–84, that to prescribe by statute the method of taking testimony in disputes over House elections "would give to the President and Senate a power over the rules for governing [House] proceedings, which, by the Constitution, they were alone the judges of." That statute was adopted despite Sitgreaves's reservations, possibly on the ground that because it conferred authority on state and federal judges it was not entirely a matter of House procedure. 1 Stat 537 (Jan 23, 1798). This explanation, however, is more difficult to apply to the statute enacted later in the same session to authorize congressional leaders themselves to administer oaths. 1 Stat 554 (May 3, 1798).

[328]8 Annals at 2247–48.

[329]See 7 Annals at 508.

[330]8 Annals at 2250–51. See also 2 Farrand at 551 (Messrs. Gouverneur Morris and Sherman); The Federalist No 65 (Hamilton). Cf the disposition of the jury-trial question in the comparable contempt case of Randall and Whitney, discussed in chapter 5.

[331]8 Annals at 2278.

[332]Id at 2279, 2281. Jefferson, on the other hand, had written that Blount would ask for a jury, calling attention to the contrast between Article III, which contained an express exception for impeachment cases, and the sixth amendment, which did not. Letter of Thomas Jefferson to James Madison, Jan 24, 1798, 17 Madison

Bayard next turned to Blount's three arguments against Senate jurisdiction. The first was easily disposed of, and Blount's counsel did not press it.[333] The fact that Blount was no longer a Senator, said Bayard, was immaterial: If events subsequent to commission of the offense could defeat jurisdiction, a defendant could frustrate impeachment by resigning, contrary to the maxim "that does not allow a man to derive a benefit from his own wrong."[334] Dallas tried weakly to distinguish between resignation and expulsion,[335] but the objection went deeper. Neither resignation nor expulsion removed the need for impeachment, for as Bayard noted Article II, § 4 permitted disqualification as well as removal from office upon conviction.[336]

The defense worked harder to demonstrate that impeachment was a remedy only for abuse of authority. Conceding that "[i]n theory" impeachment was not limited to official acts in England, Ingersoll insisted that it had been so employed in practice;[337] Dallas quoted limiting language from a number of state constitutions.[338] Bayard replied that "there [wa]s not a syllable in the Constitution which confines impeachment to official acts," and for good reason; a judge who stepped off the Bench to join an insurrection would be as unfit to continue in office as if he had abused the office itself.[339] For as Harper argued, one purpose of the impeachment provisions was "to remove persons whose misconduct may have rendered them unworthy of retaining their office."[340] While not every extracurricular offense would necessarily meet this standard, Blount's did and thus can

---

Papers at 71. Madison was skeptical: "My impression has always been that impeachments were somewhat sui generis, and excluded the use of Juries." Letter of James Madison to Thomas Jefferson, Mar 4, 1798, id at 88.

[333]In the course of an argument that consumes sixteen columns of small print in the Annals, Dallas said only "that there was room for argument, whether an officer could be impeached after he was out of office," 8 Annals at 2278, and Ingersoll did not mention the issue at all.

[334]Id at 2261.

[335]Id at 2278.

[336]Id at 2260–61. Rawle, without discussion, declared in his treatise that "those who are or have been in public office" were liable to impeachment. Rawle at 213. Justice Story, suggesting that Article II's provision for removal implied that the offender must still be in office, insisted he did not mean to resolve the question. 2 Story, §§ 801, 803. The House, we are told, has often dismissed impeachment proceedings after the offending officer's resignation, see 2 Haynes at 868, but that does not prove it was required to do so; it may have concluded that further proceedings were not worth the trouble.

[337]8 Annals at 2287–88 (citing numerous examples). See also id at 2266–67 (Mr. Dallas). Harper came up with a single counterexample: Doctor Sacheverell (see W.S. Gilbert, Patience, Act I) had once been "impeached for preaching an improper sermon." 8 Annals at 2299. See May, Parliamentary Privileges at 69 (cited in note 219): "By the law of Parliament, all persons, whether peers or commoners, may be impeached for any crimes whatever although impeachments have generally been reserved for extraordinary crimes and extraordinary offenders."

[338]8 Annals at 2269.

[339]Id at 2261–62. See also id at 2316 (Rep. Harper) (giving the example of a judge who committed perjury or theft). Bayard's offhand suggestion that the charges against Blount did involve a violation of his official trust (id at 2261) was less effective; as Ingersoll observed, if it sufficed that the act was "contrary to his duty as a Senator" the distinction would evaporate, for "so is every impropriety." Id at 2287.

[340]Id at 2316. Rawle opined without explanation that, except for bribery and treason, "all offences not immediately connected with office" were beyond the reach of impeachment. Story, adumbrating the competing contentions, declined to take a position of his own. See Rawle at 215; 2 Story, §§ 802–03. See also Raoul Berger, Impeachment: The Constitutional Problems 200 (Harvard, 1973) (arguing that the test should be not whether the offense was committed in the course of official duties but "whether it has a destructive impact upon confidence in public administration").

readily be classed as a "high crime or misdemeanor" within the meaning of Article II, §
4.[341]

The defense placed most of its money on the argument that a Senator was not a
"civil officer of the United States" under that provision and thus not subject to impeachment at all.

The prosecution had the audacity to suggest that *everyone* could be impeached, as
had been the case in England.[342] Article II, said Bayard, did not restrict the unlimited
grant of jurisdiction in Article I, § 3; its purpose was merely to make removal from office
mandatory in the case of "[t]he President, Vice-President, and all civil officers of the
United States."[343] Dallas responded convincingly that such an unnatural interpretation
would "overthrow[] the boundaries of Federal and State authority" and "annihilate the
trial by jury" and thus could not have been intended.[344] Impeachment was designed to
purge the Government of disreputable officeholders, which the ordinary courts were unable
to do. Article I merely allocated authority over impeachment cases; Article II defined who
was subject to impeachment and for what cause.[345]

Most of the argument over the real question whether Senators were "civil officers"
was a reprise of the textual analogies that had been paraded a few years earlier to demonstrate that the President pro tempore or the Speaker of the House was or was not an
"officer" eligible to assume presidential responsibilities if both the President and Vice-
President disappeared.[346] There were, of course, analogies to support either position.[347] As
Bayard pointed out, there was a new one: Congress had concluded the earlier exercise by
deciding that legislators *were* officers for purposes of the presidential succession provision.[348] That was different, said Dallas: The simple term "officer" in that clause—as contrasted with "officers of the United States" in the impeachment provision—"seems to be
employed to admit the very case of the Speaker of the House of Representatives," who

---

[341]Since the House had clearly charged Blount with (among other things) a violation of the Neutrality Act,
the Senate did not have to face the converse question (to be much mooted in the case of President Nixon)
whether an officer could be impeached for official misconduct that did not offend the criminal code. Harper
did make the general observation that a second reason for the impeachment power was to permit punishment
of "offenses of a political nature" that were "not susceptible of that exact definition whereby they might be
brought within the sphere of ordinary tribunals." 8 Annals at 2316. Dallas, on the other side, denied that there
was any such thing as a federal common law of crimes (id at 2264–65), but that was not a complete answer to
the argument that common-law tradition defined what was meant by "high crimes and misdemeanors" in
Article II. For Bayard's excellent exposition of the role of common law in the interpretation of constitutional
provisions see id at 2251–53.

[342]For the broad English view see note 337.

[343]8 Annals at 2251–54. See also id at 2298–99 (Rep. Harper).

[344]Id at 2263–64, 2267.

[345]Id at 2267. Jefferson, it is said, later expressed sympathy for Bayard's position that ordinary citizens
were subject to impeachment. Madison was appalled: "The universality of the impeachment power is the most
extravagant novelty that has yet been broached." Letter of James Madison to Thomas Jefferson, Mar 4, 1798,
17 Madison Papers at 89; see 2 Haynes at 862. Tucker, Rawle, and Story all agreed that only officers could
be impeached. See 4 Tucker's Blackstone at 57, 58; Rawle at 213; 2 Story, § 788.

[346]8 Annals at 2254–61 (Rep. Bayard); id at 2269–75 (Mr. Dallas); id at 2288–93 (Mr. Ingersoll); id at
2304–14 (Rep. Harper). See the discussion of these analogies in chapter 3.

[347]See Berger, Impeachment at 215 (cited in note 340): "[O]ne can only admire the tireless acuteness that
produced such a plethora of examples cutting both ways."

[348]8 Annals at 2258.

under Article I, § 2 was an officer of the House but not of the United States.[349]

Since the textual arguments were inconclusive, the crucial challenge for Blount's defenders was to show that Senators did not come within the purpose that Dallas had correctly attributed to the impeachment provisions; for as Harper said each clause of the Constitution should be construed in light of its own purpose.[350] Prima facie they did; impeaching a Senator could oust an unworthy legislator from a position of public authority.[351] But so, said Blount's attorneys, could expulsion;[352] there was no need to resort to the more cumbersome process of impeachment when, as Blount's own case had demonstrated, the Senate could expel the offender on identical grounds and by the identical two-thirds vote.[353]

The argument was not airtight. Harper pointed out the obvious difference: Only after impeachment could the offending Senator be disqualified from holding future office.[354] Dallas thought this fact cut the other way. "[O]n the principles of the Constitution, without any express prohibition," no member of Congress could be expelled twice for the same cause; if his constituents chose to reelect him, "he ha[d] a perfect title to his seat."[355] To permit impeachment and disqualification of a Senator would undermine the purpose of the expulsion clause to leave the question of future service to the democratic process.[356]

After these splendid arguments the Senate debated for four days whether Blount had stated an adequate defense to the charges and voted fourteen to eleven to dismiss them.[357] Alas, it did so in secret; the public record does not reveal how many Senators were per-

---

[349]Id at 2275. See US Const, Art I, § 2: "The House of Representatives shall choose their Speaker, and other officers."

[350]8 Annals at 2312–13.

[351]Id at 2316 (Rep. Harper). See also Rawle at 214.

[352]8 Annals at 2274–76 (Mr. Dallas); id at 2283, 2290 (Mr. Ingersoll). Dallas noted also that the people themselves could dispose of undeserving legislators by refusing to reelect them, id at 2274. See also 2 Story, § 262. Apart from Harper's riposte (8 Annals at 2315) that the same was true of the President and Vice-President (both of whom were expressly made subject to impeachment and removal) and that Senators were less subject than either of them to direct popular control, defeat at the polls often comes too late to be an adequate substitute for instant removal from office.

[353]Accord James Monroe, Observations Upon the Proposed Plan of Federal Government (Hunter & Prentis, 1788), 1 Monroe Writings at 361–62, reprinted in Philip B. Kurland & Ralph Lerner, 2 The Founders' Constitution 160 (Chicago, 1987). Less persuasive was the further suggestion that impeachment of Senators would give the House too much power over the Senate or make the Senators judges in their own cause. Id at 2271 (Mr. Dallas); id at 2290 (Mr. Ingersoll). For in the case of impeachment as well as expulsion no sanction can be imposed without a two-thirds vote of the Senate, and in expulsion cases too the Senate is in the same sense judge in its own cause.

[354]8 Annals at 2317.

[355]Id at 2274. The case of John Wilkes, as already noted, had been widely taken to establish this proposition. See note 219.

[356]Randolph and C.C. Pinckney in the ratification debates (3 Elliot at 202; 4 id at 265) and three Government attorneys in response to Adams's inquiry in Blount's case (see 2 Haynes at 862–63) had opined that Senators were subject to impeachment. Other "friends of the constitution," Story tells us, were of the contrary opinion. See 2 Story, § 791 (doubting the existence of jurisdiction). Raoul Berger, finding impeachability of legislators the predominant view among the Framers and in accord with English practice, argues that Members of Congress can be impeached. See Berger, Impeachment at 214–23 (cited in note 340).

[357]8 Annals at 2318–19.

suaded by each of his three arguments,[358] however much the acknowledged weakness of two of them may lead us to surmise that the dominant conclusion was that members of Congress are not "officers of the United States." It is that proposition that Blount's case, for better or worse, is commonly cited to have established.[359]

B.   Mr. Pinckney's Gifts

There were a lot of Pinckneys. Charles and his cousin Charles Cotesworth had both represented South Carolina at the Philadelphia Convention.[360] Charles became a Senator in 1798.[361] Charles Cotesworth had been twice sent by President Adams to France, where he had been twice rejected.[362] His brother Thomas, Federalist favorite for Vice-President in 1796, had served as Minister to Great Britain and negotiated a popular treaty with Spain.[363] South Carolina voters sent him to the House in the summer of 1797 to replace William Loughton Smith, who had resigned.[364]

When Thomas Pinckney left Europe, the Kings of Britain and Spain presented him with the customary tokens of esteem for departing diplomats—unidentified, but assumed to be on the order of a snuffbox, a portrait, or a golden chain.[365] When he got back he asked Congress for permission to keep them,[366] for Article I, § 9 forbade a "person holding any office of profit or trust" under the United States to "accept of any present, emolument, office, or title . . . from any king, prince, or foreign state," without the consent of Congress.

The Senate said yes,[367] the House no.[368] Pinckney had to do without his snuffboxes.[369]

---

[358]See Swanstrom at 55; 2 Haynes at 862, 865.

[359]See, e.g., 2 Story, § 791; Rawle at 213–14; Miller at 191.

[360]See 1 Farrand at 2.

[361]See note 239.

[362]See text at notes 4, 12, 36.

[363]See chapter 5.

[364]This William Smith, the prominent Federalist, had been appointed Minister to Portugal. See 1 Sen Exec J at 248, 249. Another William Smith from South Carolina, a Republican, served throughout the Fifth Congress. See Biographical Directory at 1839, 1840. This explains why "William Smith" voted not only against consent to Pinckney's gifts but also against the Sedition Act, and why the better known William L. Smith was sometimes referred to in the Annals as "William Smith, of Charleston." None of the Pinckneys, of course, is to be confused (good luck!) with William Pinkney of Maryland, whose resignation from the Second Congress had given rise to debate over the meaning of the Article I, § 2 provision respecting vacancies in the House. See note 41 of chapter 3.

[365]See 8 Annals at 1589 (Rep. Bayard) (reporting the results of his inquiry into what gifts were customary on such occasions).

[366]Id at 1558.

[367]7 Annals at 553.

[368]8 Annals at 1593.

[369]If the House had concurred with the Senate resolution, presumably it would have been presented to the President for approval or veto under Article I, § 7, which applies not only to bills but also to "[e]very order, resolution, or vote [except adjournment] to which the concurrence of the Senate and House . . . may be necessary." The contrary conclusion with respect to constitutional amendments (see chapter 2) reminds us that here as elsewhere surprises are possible in constitutional interpretation; the negative House vote made it unnecessary to confront the question.

Nobody had anything against Pinckney. Members could not say enough to commend him, especially for his highly favorable Spanish treaty.[370] But the purpose of the constitutional provision, said William Claiborne of Tennessee, was "to lock up every door to foreign influence" within the Government, which "could not but prove baneful to every free country."[371]

Pinckney was no longer a government officer when the gifts were offered, said Bayard; he was already on his way home, and the constitutional restriction did not apply.[372] Wrong, said Claiborne, and immaterial. The presents "were offered to him when he was about to take leave" and thus still in office, and in any event they were "meant as a compliment to him as Minister."[373] Thus they fell within the purpose of the provision; as our friend Matthew Lyon growled, no American officer should be paid by a foreign government for his service.[374]

There was no harm in these particular gifts, said Bayard; they were "trifling" and "could have no possible operation upon any man."[375] There was no suggestion, Otis added, that Pinckney had been bribed.[376] "[S]o far from the Constitution insinuating that it would be bad policy to allow these presents to be received," Bayard continued, the consent provision "proves that they might be received if inconvenience . . . could be avoided"; the purpose was publicity, which would "make it impossible for [officers] to be unduly influenced" in favor of their foreign friends.[377] Besides, an envoy might create ill feeling if he spurned the common trappings of hospitality;[378] American diplomats had accepted presents in the past "because they could not refuse them without giving umbrage to the Courts which presented them."[379]

Not so, said Venable; "it was well known to the European courts that our

---

[370]See 8 Annals at 1582 (Rep. McDowell); id at 1584 (Rep. Claiborne); id at 1586 (Rep. Macon); id at 1594 (Rep. Harper).

[371]Id at 1584. See also id at 1587.

[372]Id at 1583. See also id at 1585 (Rep. Otis) (suggesting that Pinckney might *now* accept the gifts, "for he is at present no officer of the United States"). As Gallatin noted in response, however (id at 1593), he was a member of Congress. Otis's suggestion thus raised the same question with respect to foreign gifts that Blount's case had raised under the impeachment clauses. It did not have to receive the same answer. Gallatin's uncharacteristically inconsistent reply was that Congress could not even consent to the acceptance of a gift by one of its own members. Id.

[373]Id at 1584, 1588.

[374]Id at 1589. Gallatin, noting that Pinckney had still been Minister to England at the time he left Spain, argued that the consent requirement applied only to the Spanish gift. Id at 1592.

[375]Id at 1583. In fact it is not so clear that this was the case. When Jefferson asked Benjamin Franklin's grandson about international practice in this regard upon becoming Secretary of State, he was told that the standard present for a Minister Plenipotentiary in France was worth "about one thousand Louis d'ors," that its value varied according to "the personal respect entertained for the Negotiator," and that Franklin himself had received "a large Miniature of the King, set with four hundred and eight Diamonds," of an estimated value of 1,500 louis. Letter of William Temple Franklin to Thomas Jefferson, Apr 27, 1790, 16 Jefferson Papers at 364, 365.

[376]8 Annals at 1585.

[377]Id at 1583. Bayard shot himself in the foot by going on to say that a minister who had received a foreign gift would bend over backward to avoid the suspicion of bias (id); presumably we expect our officers to be prejudiced neither for or against any foreign country.

[378]Id at 1583.

[379]Id at 1585 (Rep. Otis). Indeed, Otis added, the old Congress had routinely acquiesced in such gifts even though the Articles of Confederation (Art VI, § 1) had contained an absolute ban on them with no provision for congressional consent. Id.

Government is established on principles totally different from theirs; and when our Ministers informed them that their Government did not permit them to receive presents, it must be a satisfactory reason for not accepting them."[380] The reason for giving presents to foreign officers, McDowell supposed, was "to gain their friendly offices and good wishes towards the country who gave them," and that was "improper"; "he believed it would be well now to put a stop to the business."[381] Claiborne allowed that there might be extraordinary instances—such as when a naval officer assisted "the vessel of a foreign Power in distress on the high seas"—in which it would be appropriate to permit "any suitable present as a reward"; but "in all ordinary cases, every present ought to be rejected."[382]

Robert Williams urged Congress to lay down a firm rule one way or the other to avoid the burden of case-by-case determination; "if this was not done, there would be no end of the business."[383] He too would prefer to forbid gifts entirely. If the House was not prepared to do so, "he would rather that our Ministers should be at liberty to receive all the presents offered to them, than that the thing should stand upon its present footing"; and he would propose legislation to that effect.[384] Congress could not constitutionally pass such a law, said Bayard; he did not say why.[385]

Claiborne was quite right about the purpose of the constitutional provision. Ironically, it was one of the Pinckneys (Madison does not tell us which) who proposed it to the Convention, citing "the necessity of preserving foreign Ministers & other officers of the U.S. independent of external influence."[386] Bayard was equally right that the provision for congressional consent showed the Framers had not meant that permission to accept gifts had always to be denied—even if, as in the modern case of favors extended to legislators by lobbyists, that might well be the best policy. Rather the matter was left to the judgment of Congress, and the general purpose of the clause does not dictate how Congress should make its decision. Thatcher's position that consent should be given unless there was evidence of impropriety[387] was as consistent with that purpose as Claiborne's that it should be given only in exceptional cases.[388] Nor was it obvious from the text or policy of the clause that, as Bayard seemed to imply, it required Congress to

[380]Id at 1587.

[381]Id at 1583. Besides, said McDowell, if our envoys accepted presents, we would have to give them too, and that would be expensive. Id at 1582–83. See also id at 1586 (Rep. Macon). But see id at 1587 (Rep. Bayard): "[T]he amount would be very trifling."

[382]Id at 1584. Claiborne also argued that approving Pinckney's gifts would create a precedent for accepting more troublesome foreign titles. Id. Otis negligently responded that Congress could not consent to the acceptance of titles, and Claiborne corrected him, id at 1585. Bayard conceded that Congress had authority to consent to a foreign title, "but he could not apprehend that they would ever do so." Id at 1586.

[383]Id at 1589. See also id at 1586 (Rep. Macon).

[384]Id at 1588–89.

[385]Id at 1590.

[386]2 Farrand at 389. See also 3 Story, § 1346; Rawle at 119–20 (lamenting the fact that the Constitution did not specify "[d]isfranchisement, or a deprivation of all the rights of a citizen," for violation of the clause: "There cannot be too much jealousy in respect to foreign influence").

[387]8 Annals at 1588.

[388]Cf the provisions of Article I, § 10, requiring congressional consent for such matters as interstate compacts and state duties on imports or ships (see note 6 of chapter 2), as well as the provisions for presidential veto of legislation (Art I, § 7) and for Senate approval of appointments and treaties (Art II, § 2).

assume the burden of passing on each individual gift; a blanket decision that trinkets whose value did not exceed a specified value, or that were in accord with prevailing international custom, would appear equally consonant with the Framers' intentions.[389]

Having voted forty-nine to thirty-seven to deny Pinckney permission to accept his presents,[390] the House after some rather unseemly haggling[391] had the decency to explain, formally and unanimously, that in so doing it had been influenced "solely by motives of general policy, and not by any view personal to the said Thomas Pinckney."[392]

St. George Tucker cited Pinckney's case as "a precedent which we may reasonably hope will be remembered by all *future* ministers, and ensure a proper respect to this clause of the constitution."[393]

C.   The Mississippi Territory

One of the accomplishments of Thomas Pinckney's 1795 treaty with Spain was to settle the southern boundary of the United States at a latitude of thirty-one degrees, the northernmost point of the present state of Florida.[394] North of that line, in what is now Mississippi, lay the Spanish settlement of Natchez. In accordance with the treaty, the Spanish authorities retired from Natchez in 1797. Even before their departure, President Adams urged Congress to consider setting up a territorial government for "the district of the Natchez" on the model of the Northwest Ordinance.[395]

There was just one difficulty, said Representative Nicholas: the area in question was part of Georgia.[396] John Williams took issue with Nicholas's view of the facts: The territory belonged to the United States.[397] That approach was debatable but dull.[398] The alternative argument was a zinger.

---

[389]Cf Prudential Ins. Co. v Benjamin, 328 US 408 (1946) (permitting Congress to consent generally to state regulation of interstate insurance that otherwise might have offended the commerce clause). See also In re Rahrer, 140 US 545 (1891); The Second Century at 34–35.

[390]8 Annals at 1593.

[391]See id at 1594–95, 1612.

[392]Id at 1775–76. Pinckney himself had reluctantly asked the House for such an explanation, arguing that otherwise, "considering this power to have been intended as a check upon the improper conduct of officers, it must strike the minds of the public when they are told that an officer was refused this privilege, that he had not done his duty . . . ." Id at 1613.

[393]1 Tucker's Blackstone at 296. Congress has since taken the path indicated by Representative Williams, consenting in advance to gifts of "minimal value" (one hundred dollars or less) and of certain travel expenses, and authorizing acceptance of more significant presents "on behalf of the United States" if "to refuse the gift would likely cause offense or embarrassment or otherwise adversely affect the foreign relations of the United States." 5 USC § 7342 (1988 & Supp 1994).

[394]8 Stat 138, 138–39, Art II (Oct 27, 1795). See chapter 5.

[395]7 Annals at 21–22 (June 12, 1797). See Jack D.L. Holmes, A Spanish Province: 1779–1798, in Richard Aubrey McLemore, ed, 1 A History of Mississippi 158, 171–73 (Mississippi, 1973); Robert Haynes, The Formation of the Territory, in id at 174.

[396]8 Annals at 1283–84. See also id at 1299 (Rep. Milledge).

[397]Id at 1302. See also id at 1300–01 (Rep. Harper).

[398]According to a 1797 House report, Georgia's original grant from George II in 1732 included all the land between the Savannah and Altamaha rivers, and from their headwaters westward to the Pacific. 1 Am St Papers (Public Lands) 79 (Mar 2, 1797). See also Kenneth Coleman, ed, A History of Georgia 16–17 (Georgia, 2d ed 1991). After Spain ceded its claims to territory east of the Mississippi to Great Britain in 1763, a royal proclamation establishing the provinces of East and West Florida (printed in 1 Am St Papers (Public

In extraordinary circumstances, said Dayton, Congress had authority to set up a new government "even within the ordinary jurisdiction of a State."[399] If a member of the Union left any part of its territory "in a defenceless state," Harper explained, Congress would be obliged to step in to preserve it against foreign ambitions, ensure freedom of navigation, and prevent anarchy.[400]

Where was this authority found in the Constitution? Harper did not say. His first two arguments suggest that the establishment of a government might be necessary and proper to national defense or to the promotion of various branches of commerce.[401] The reference to anarchy suggests he may have been thinking of Article IV, § 4, which requires the United States to "guarantee to every state in this Union a republican form of government"—and thus arguably to provide one if the state does not.[402]

Nicholas was appalled. Harper's argument struck at the core of state sovereignty. Congress had no more right to set up a government in Georgia's western wilderness than in some part of Virginia that it might decide was not well governed.[403]

Congress was unimpressed. Milledge's motion to postpone the establishment of the government until Georgia consented failed,[404] and the bill became law.[405] Winthrop Sargent set up shop as the first territorial Governor in August 1798;[406] Georgia did not relinquish its claim until 1802.[407]

Lands) at 36) added to Georgia "all the lands lying between the rivers Altamaha and St. Mary's"—the present boundary between Georgia and Florida. The same proclamation, however, reserved to the Crown, for use of the Indians, "all the land and territories lying to the westward of the sources of the rivers which fall into the sea from the west and northwest," id at 37. The committee understood this to have extinguished Georgia's claim to lands west of the sources of the Savannah and the Altamaha. Id at 80. Moreover, the committee found, Georgia had not objected when Britain later extended the boundary of West Florida north of the thirty-first meridian to the mouth of the Yazoo River; if the disputed territory had ever been a part of Georgia, it had ceased to be before the British released their claims in 1783. Id. Congress, be it noted, was not a disinterested party in this controversy; the real issue was what compensation Georgia would receive for relinquishing its claim. See 8 Annals at 1281 (Rep. Milledge) (of Georgia): "The country to be negotiated for, is an amazing tract of country of sixty or seventy millions of acres of land, as valuable as any in the world, which the State of Georgia could not be expected to surrender . . . without an equivalent." For an earlier attempt to negotiate a cession of Georgia's claims see Coleman, A History of Georgia at 94 (cited in this note).

[399]8 Annals at 1284.

[400]Id at 1300–01. Kittera took a neutral position: The United States should "hold[] the territory until the existing dispute was settled." Id at 1303–04.

[401]See also Gordon's argument, id at 1305–06, that the United States was "bound to protect all its citizens."

[402]The same section also requires Congress to protect the states against invasion.

[403]8 Annals at 1302.

[404]See id at 1283, 1306.

[405]1 Stat 549, 549–50, § 3 (Apr 7, 1798). Section 5 of the Act, id at 550, preserved Georgia's claims to the territory; § 1 provided for commissioners to negotiate with Georgia over the conflicting claims.

[406]See Haynes, Formation of the Territory at 178 (cited in note 395).

[407]Ga Laws 1800–1810, 48 (June 15, 1802). Georgia was given $1,250,000 in return for relinquishing its claims. Id at 48–49; 1 Am St Papers (Public Lands) at 125, 126.

A somewhat similar situation confronted the Sixth Congress in the case of the so-called Western Reserve. This area, the northeast corner of the present state of Ohio, had been claimed by four states under overlapping colonial charters; with congressional consent, Connecticut had excepted it from its cession of other western claims in 1786. See 30 J Cont Cong 310–11 (May 23, 1786); 31 J Cont Cong 654–55 (Sept 14, 1786). After Jay's Treaty made it possible to suppress hostile Indians by removing their British protectors, Connecticut opened the Reserve to settlement, sold off the land, and left the settlers to their own devices. Bereft of all government, the inhabitants petitioned Congress to incorporate them into the Northwest Territory. To assert

Seventy years later Harper's theory would be employed to justify displacing the duly elected governments of ten Southern states.[408]

Like the former Southwest Territory, the new Mississippi Territory was to be administered in conformity to the Northwest Ordinance, with the same significant exception: The provision forbidding slavery was not to apply.[409]

When the bill was debated in the House, George Thatcher of Massachusetts moved to ban slavery in Mississippi as well.[410] There was a chorus of opposition. To outlaw slavery would "banish" many present inhabitants;[411] it would prejudice Georgia's claim to the territory, which the statute expressly preserved;[412] it would lead to "insurrection" and "war";[413] it would be better for slaves to be spread over a larger area rather than crowded together in the existing states.[414] Thatcher's motion received the paltry total of twelve votes.[415]

Significantly, not one speaker doubted Congress's authority to ban slavery in the territory, and Gallatin expressly affirmed it: Congress had jurisdiction over Mississippi, and that meant it could decide whether or not there should be slaves.[416]

D.   The District of Columbia

In the case of Mississippi the federal government was accused of assuming plenary authority within the borders of a state. An 1800 bill relating to the District of Columbia confronted Congress with the opposite problem.

When the seat of government was established in 1790, Congress did not enact a code of laws to govern the new district, as it obviously could have done;[417] it provided

---

jurisdiction without a formal cession of the area, however, would have endangered existing land titles by implying that Connecticut had had no right to grant them. Congress accordingly authorized acceptance of a cession of jurisdiction, 2 Stat 56 (Apr 28, 1800), and the Western Reserve became a part of the Northwest Territory.

As in the case of Mississippi, the transfer of power did not go as smoothly as one might have hoped. The federal statute providing for acceptance of the territory took effect in April 1800, but Connecticut waited until May of the next year to cede it. Nevertheless the territorial government began to govern the Reserve six weeks after the statute was passed, and even before its enactment had proceeded to divide the area into counties—"by what right has never been known, as at that time that part of the Reserve did not belong to the Northwest Territory." P.P. Cherry, The Western Reserve and Early Ohio 70 (R.L. Fouse, 1921). See generally id at 56–63, 68–71; Beverly W. Bond, Jr., The Foundations of Ohio 356–61, 454–55 (Ohio State Archaeological Society, 1941); Forrest Morgan, et al, 2 Connecticut as a Colony and as a State, or One of the Original Thirteen 225–29 (Publishing Society of Connecticut, 1904); and John Marshall's detailed committee report of Mar 20, 1800, 1 Am St Papers (Public Lands) at 94–98.

[408] 14 Stat 428 (Mar 2, 1867); see The First Hundred Years at 296–99.

[409] 1 Stat at 550, §§ 3, 6. The corresponding provisions respecting the Southwest Territory are discussed in chapter 2.

[410] 8 Annals at 1306.

[411] Id at 1306 (Rep. Harper).

[412] Id at 1308 (Rep. Gordon).

[413] Id at 1307–08 (Rep. Otis).

[414] Id at 1309 (Rep. Giles). It upsets us when you talk about slavery, Rutledge added; it's uncivil of you to bring it up. Id at 1307–08.

[415] Id at 1312.

[416] Id at 1309. See US Const, Art IV, § 3: "The Congress shall have power to . . . make all needful rules and regulations respecting the territory or other property belonging to the United States . . . ." The Act did ban importation of slaves from abroad, 1 Stat at 550, § 7, but that was arguably foreign commerce (assuming that

that state laws should continue to apply until the Government moved there and Congress took further action.[418] In 1800, after the move was completed, Representative Henry Lee proposed to continue existing Maryland and Virginia laws in force and to leave sitting state judges in office until the President removed them.[419]

Nicholas raised the standard objection to static conformity: The bill would saddle the District with obsolete laws, "without those improvements which experience may suggest."[420] Otis protested that no federal code was necessary,[421] but that was not what Nicholas had in mind. He seems to have thought that if Congress did nothing Maryland and Virginia would govern the District as they had before ceding the area to the United States.[422]

Harper complained that Nicholas's position would make the constitutional provision for establishment of the seat of government "a dead letter."[423] The states had proved unable or unwilling to protect the earlier Congress from harassment; "[i]t was to protect [Congress] from such outrages as had occurred" in the past that the provision had been adopted.[424] Nicholas responded that Congress's authority did not have to be exercised: It was "like a suit of armor, intended to protect the Government in periods of danger, and not to be worn at all times for parade or show."[425]

The difficulty with this argument was the language of Article I, § 8, which as Representative Bird said seemed to mean that once the states ceded the area their authority was at an end.[426] Nicholas strove hard to avoid this conclusion: "The Constitution does not say Congress shall possess exclusive power of legislation; but that they shall have power of exercising exclusive legislation."[427] By this he apparently meant that the effect of the provision was only to make federal statutes relating to the District supreme once they were enacted. Since that was already true of all federal laws under Article VI, there was not much to be said for his unnatural interpretation.

Congress did not buy Nicholas's argument that state law applied in the District of its own force, and it was unwilling (if not unable) to delegate its legislative authority to the states.[428] It avoided the constitutional problem by enacting Lee's proposal to keep

---

slaves were articles of commerce, which would itself be disputed). The moratorium on banning the importation of slaves before 1808 (US Const, Art I, § 9) applied only to the original states.

[417]See US Const, Art I, § 8, cl 17.

[418]See chapter 2.

[419]10 Annals at 825.

[420]Id at 869. Smilie objected to Lee's proposal on the ground that it would deprive District residents of representation in Congress (id at 996), implying that they had theretofore voted in state elections, which seems hard to reconcile with a cession of jurisdiction that appeared to mean the area was no longer part of any state.

[421]10 Annals at 869.

[422]See id at 872. The 1790 statute had provided that "the operation of the laws of the state within such district shall not be affected" by acceptance of the cession, suggesting that new as well as old state laws would apply. 1 Stat 130, § 1 (July 16, 1790).

[423]10 Annals at 872.

[424]Id at 873.

[425]Id.

[426]Id at 870–71.

[427]Id at 872.

[428]At one point, when the House was considering a version of the bill that would have set up a local government in the District, Macon doubted that Congress could constitutionally delegate its powers to a local legislature. 10 Annals at 1000. Why it would be any less troublesome to delegate the same authority to the states is not clear.

state laws in force "as they now exist," which could be interpreted as incorporating them into federal law.[429]

But Congress did not accept Lee's idea of permitting state judges to exercise judicial power until the President removed them. No discussion of this provision was recorded in the Annals, but even if state officers can be allowed to exercise judicial authority in an area over which Congress has the power of "exclusive legislation," the notion of judges subject to presidential removal contrasts sharply with the provisions for independent federal judges in Article III.

The statute provided instead for a federal circuit court whose judges were to be appointed during "good behavior."[430] If adoption of this Article III standard suggested that Congress thought that Article applied to the District of Columbia, there was contrary evidence elsewhere in the same law; for the statute also provided that small claims be resolved by justices of the peace who were to serve for a period of five years.[431] The Supreme Court would soon specify that they could not be removed until that term had expired,[432] but five years is a long way from the essentially lifetime tenure the Constitution guarantees to those who exercise "the judicial power of the United States."

IV.   THE ELECTION OF 1800

A.   The Grand Committee

As the election of 1800 drew nigh, Federalist Senator James Ross of Pennsylvania blandly moved that a committee be appointed to consider what provisions, if any, should be made "for deciding disputed elections for President and Vice President of the United States, and for determining the legality of the votes given for those officers in the different States."[433] For questions might arise, he explained, as to the legality either of the electors' appointment or of their votes, and the Constitution did not say how such questions were to be resolved.[434]

Congress had no authority in the premises, said Senator John Brown of Kentucky.[435] Indeed it had not, said Pinckney. The Convention had taken great pains to keep Congress out of the business of choosing the President; the whole matter of appointing electors was expressly entrusted to the state legislatures, which could make ample provision for resolving disputes.[436] Abraham Baldwin, who had recently moved from the lower to the upper House, had an alternative theory: The electors should resolve such

---

[429]2 Stat 103, § 1 (Feb 27, 1801). There was no obvious basis for Randolph's argument (10 Annals at 871) that if Congress acted it must adopt a uniform law for the entire district.

[430]2 Stat at 105, § 3.

[431]Id at 107, § 11.

[432]Marbury v Madison, 5 US 137 (1803).

[433]10 Annals at 29.

[434]Id. It has been said that the motivating cause was the fear that Pennsylvania's new Republican Governor, in the face of a divided legislature, might take it upon himself to appoint a slate of electors of his own persuasion. See Tadahisa Kuroda, The Origins of the Twelfth Amendment 78 (Greenwood, 1994). See also Letter of John Marshall to James Markham Marshall, Apr 4, 1800, 4 Marshall Papers at 121, 123 (cited in note 247); Malone, Jefferson and the Ordeal of Liberty at 463 (cited in note 11).

[435]10 Annals at 29.

[436]Id.

questions themselves, just as the House and Senate resolved controversies respecting the elections and qualifications of their own members.[437]

The contemplated regulations, Dexter argued, were necessary and proper to the election of the President.[438] Baldwin disagreed: Congress was authorized to enact only those laws which were necessary and proper to carry into execution the powers elsewhere granted to the central government; elections involved the organization of the government, not the exercise of its powers.[439]

A committee appointed pursuant to Ross's motion reported a bill to establish a "Grand Committee" composed of members of both Houses to resolve disputes over the credentials of electors and the validity of their votes.[440]

In a windy canned speech that spans twenty columns of small print in the Annals, Pinckney fulminated against this proposal.[441] To authorize members of Congress to determine the validity of electoral votes would effectively give the majority party in Congress power to decide who was to be President. For it was easy to fabricate election disputes, and it was obvious that members of the Committee would be guided by "party spirit" in resolving them.[442] The consequence would be to deprive the states of their "sacred right" to elect the President and to make him the "creature" of Congress—the very result the Framers had worked so hard to avoid.[443]

The Senate passed the bill by a vote of sixteen to twelve.[444] The House adopted an amended version, which the Senate in turn amended; neither House was willing to recede from its position, and the bill was lost.[445]

The Grand Committee thus remained a gleam in the eye of its sponsors. But the questions it raised went to the heart of the presidential selection process, and the debate served as a trial run when a somewhat similar Electoral Commission was created in 1877.[446]

What is one to think of the merits? On its face the necessary and proper clause would appear adequate to support the Grand Committee proposal. Baldwin's distinction between organization of the government and exercise of its powers seems artificial. There

[437]Id at 31–32. See US Const, Art I, § 5.

[438]10 Annals at 30.

[439]Id at 32.

[440]See id at 33, 47, 124–25, 129. The one limitation was that the Committee was not to "draw into question the number of votes on which any Elector . . . shall have been declared appointed." Id at 125.

[441]Id at 126–46.

[442]Id at 130–31.

[443]Id at 127–31. "Should the Spirit of the Bill be followed up," wrote Madison to Jefferson (Mar 15, 1800), "it is impossible to say, how far the choice of the Ex: may be drawn out of the Constitutional hands, and subjected to the management of the Legislature." 17 Madison Papers at 372–73.

[444]10 Annals at 146.

[445]See id at 177, 179. The House version would have given the two Chambers equal representation on the Committee and made its role ministerial, requiring a majority of each House to reject an elector's vote. The Senate voted to require a majority of each House to *accept* a challenged vote. See Kuroda, The Twelfth Amendment at 80–82 (cited in note 434). See also Elkins & McKitrick at 730 (crediting Marshall with sabotaging this "unconstitutional, . . . disreputable, and politically demented" scheme). For a change it was the debate in the House, not in the Senate, that was unreported; Marshall's draft of the House bill appears in 4 Marshall Papers at 138–45 (cited in note 247).

[446]See generally Charles Fairman, Five Justices and the Electoral Commission of 1877 (Macmillan, 1988). As the title of Fairman's book indicates, the 1877 Commission included not only members of Congress but also Supreme Court Justices, thereby raising additional constitutional questions.

is as much need for incidental legislation in setting up the government as in the exercise of other authority, and the argument is that creation of the Committee was necessary and proper to the exercise of federal *powers* respecting the Presidency. If the votes are to be counted before a joint session of Congress, as Article II provides, there must be some procedure for determining which votes are to be considered; therefore the Committee is necessary to the counting of votes in Congress.[447] If there is to be a President, there must be some means of determining who he is; therefore the Committee is necessary to the exercise of all the President's powers. Dexter's suggestion that it was necessary to "the power of appointing the President" raises yet another intriguing possibility: The Electoral College may itself be a federal agency within the meaning of the necessary and proper clause.[448]

One or another of these theories must underlie the much more modest provisions of the Presidential Election and Succession Act of 1792 regarding the manner of certifying election results to Congress, which were adopted without reported complaint.[449] But that may be an instance in which an easy case made bad law—or at least pointed in a dangerous direction. For the Convention record is abundantly plain that, as Pinckney argued, the Framers did not want Congress—unless the electors were unable to make a choice—to decide who was to be President.[450] Electors were to be selected as the state legislatures saw fit, with no provision—as in the case of congressional elections—for Congress to regulate the "times, places and manner of holding elections."[451] Members of Congress were the only people, apart from other federal officers, who were disqualified from serving as electors.[452] And Pinckney was quite right as to the hazards involved in allowing Congress to decide which electoral votes should be counted; the experience of 1877 illus-

---

[447]"I maintain that the authority granted in general terms to 'count' the electoral 'votes' embraces, by a proper application of the rule of implied powers, authority to ascertain what electoral votes have been lawfully given . . . ." George Ticknor Curtis, 2 Constitutional History of the United States 103 (Harper, 1896). It should be noted that Article II does not say who is to count the votes once the President of the Senate has opened them; the provision speaks irritatingly in the passive voice.

[448]But see In re Green, 134 US 377, 379–80 (1890) (upholding state power to punish illegal participation in the choice of electors):

> Although the electors are appointed and act under and pursuant to the Constitution of the United States, they are no more officers or agents of the United States than are members of the State legislatures when acting as electors of federal Senators, or the people of the States when acting as electors of representatives in Congress.

[449]See chapter 3. See also Justice Black's argument, in casting the decisive vote to uphold congressional power to lower the voting age to eighteen in presidential elections, that authority "to insure that [national] officers represent their national constituency" was "inherent in the very concept of a supreme national government." Oregon v Mitchell, 400 US 112, 124 n 7 (1970); see The Second Century at 562–63. No other Justice agreed with this reasoning.

[450]See the discussion in chapter 3. Because the purely technical provisions of the earlier law posed no substantial risk of this nature, the precedent may well be distinguishable. Indeed Pinckney cited the failure of the earlier Congress to include provisions respecting the resolution of electoral disputes in its otherwise comprehensive legislation as evidence of an understanding that the subject was beyond Congress's power. 10 Annals at 135–36.

[451]US Const, Art I, § 4. Pinckney made much of this contrast, 10 Annals at 128–29.

[452]US Const, Art II, § 1.

trates how easy it is to turn the question of who was elected into the question of who ought to have been.[453]

The provision for House election of the President in default of a decision by the electors demonstrates, of course, that the Framers were not absolute about keeping Congress out of the process.[454] If there were no other way to determine which votes should be counted, presumably the Framers would have allowed Congress to do the job; it is plainly better to compromise the principle against legislative interference than to risk having no President at all. But the arguments of Pinckney and Baldwin suggest that alternative solutions were available that were more consonant with the constitutional plan.

Baldwin's proposal that the electors themselves resolve these disputes is convincing only in part. He seems quite right in suggesting that the electors were in the best position to authenticate their own acts, and that there was no reason to think Congress would do a better job of determining whether the votes they cast complied with constitutional requirements than the electors themselves.[455] Nor is there any difficulty with his argument that the electors in each state, like each House of Congress, pass upon the elections and qualifications of individual members.[456] But Baldwin's solution will not work when, as Pinckney hypothesized (and as happened in 1876), two competing slates claim to have been selected.[457] Since Article II requires the electors to meet separately in their respective states, there is no nationwide "College" to which the question can be referred. Who is to judge the election depends on who has been elected; Alphonse and Gaston will never get through the door.

But there is no such objection to Pinckney's alternative thesis. Pursuant to the authority recognized by Article II, § 1 to determine the manner of appointing electors, each state may establish such tribunals and such procedures as it likes for resolving disputes over their selection, and in counting the votes the certificate of the designated authority should be accepted as binding.[458]

Congressional censorship of the Electoral College was avoided in 1800, but not because Pinckney's arguments prevailed; a majority in each House thought it was constitutional to make Congress judge of the validity both of the electors' appointment and of their votes.

---

[453]The Electoral Commission, with eight Republican members, voted eight to seven to accept the Republican votes from each of the disputed states. The Republican Senate voted to accept the Commission's report, the Democratic House to reject it. See Fairman, Five Justices and the Electoral Commission at 114–19 (cited in note 446).

[454]US Const, Art II, § 1.

[455]10 Annals at 31.

[456]Id.

[457]See id at 134–35; Fairman, Five Justices and the Electoral Commission at 58, 116–17 (cited in note 446).

[458]That is the essence of the present statutory solution, which dates from 1887. See 3 USC §§ 5, 15 (1988 & Supp 1994); 24 Stat 373, 373–74, §§ 2, 4 (Feb 3, 1887). It was also the basis of Justice Bradley's decisive vote to accept the Republican electoral votes in 1876, and it had been the position of prominent legislators of both parties before the 1876 election. See Fairman, Five Justices and the Electoral Commission at 96–106 (cited in note 446).

B.   Mr. Bayard's Conscience

As it turned out, there were no challenges to the electoral votes in the election of 1800. President Adams was given sixty-five votes, his running-mate Charles Cotesworth Pinckney, sixty-four. There was one for John Jay. Vice-President Jefferson received seventy-three votes, a clear if slender majority. But so did Aaron Burr.[459]

"[T]he numbers . . . being equal," the reporter records, "no choice was made by the people; and . . . consequently, the remaining duties devolve on the House of Representatives."[460]

The House's duty was clear. Everyone knew that the electors had voted for Jefferson as President and Burr as Vice-President, although the poorly drafted constitutional provision did not permit them to say so.[461] The people had not failed to make a choice; they had merely been prevented from expressing it. The House ought to have instantly ratified the electors' decision; the provision for an independent House determination[462] was designed for a wholly different case.

But the defeated Federalists preferred to play games. Petty, self-serving games, for they hoped that by throwing the election to Burr they would be in a position to control him[463]—or perhaps, as their opponents feared, that by preventing a decision they might somehow manage to keep the Presidency for themselves.[464] Dangerous games, for before the election was over there were ominous rumblings from the Republicans about extra-

---

[459]See 10 Annals at 744.

[460]Id. See US Const, Art II, § 1.

[461]A New York correspondent, distressed by the rumor that Virginia electors might withhold votes from Burr in order to ensure that Jefferson became President, assured Madison that it was "the general voice as well as the individual wish that Mr. J. should succeed as Presidt and Mr. B. as V. Presdt. . . ." Letter of David Gelston to James Madison, Nov 21, 1800, 17 Madison Papers at 438. See also Letter of Albert Gallatin to his wife, May 12, 1800, in Adams, Life of Gallatin at 243 (cited in note 267): "We had last night a very large meeting of Republicans, in which it was unanimously agreed to support Burr for Vice-President"; Letter of Thomas Jefferson to John Breckenridge, Dec 18, 1800, 7 Jefferson Writings (Ford ed) at 468, 469; Editorial Note, in Mary-Jo Kline, ed, 1 Political Correspondence and Public Papers of Aaron Burr 430–34 (Princeton, 1983).

[462]See Representative Harper's explanatory letter to his constituents, Feb 24, 1801, in Elizabeth Donnan, ed, Papers of James A. Bayard, 1796–1815, 2 Annual Report of the American Historical Ass'n 132, 134 (1913):

> I was of opinion that the two candidates, in a constitutional and legal view, stood precisely equal, having an equal number of votes from those whom the people had appointed to act for them in the elections; and that my choice between them ought to be governed, entirely, by my opinion of their respective fitness and qualification for the office.

[463]See Letter of Theodore Sedgwick to Alexander Hamilton, Jan 10, 1801, 25 Hamilton Papers at 310, 312; Letter of Henry Lee to Alexander Hamilton, Feb 6, 1801, id at 331; Letter of Alexander Hamilton to John Rutledge, Jr., Jan 4, 1801. id at 293, 294 (warning them not to count on it); Elkins & McKitrick at 747.

[464]Id. See Letter of Albert Gallatin to his wife, Jan 15, 1801, in Adams, Life of Gallatin at 252, 253–54 (cited in note 267); Letter of Timothy Pickering to Rufus King, Jan 5, 1801, 3 King Papers at 366 (cited in note 267); Letter of Samuel Bayard to Allan McLane, Feb 17, 1801, Bayard Papers at 128–29 (cited in note 462): "The New England Gentlemen declared they meant to go without a constitution and take the risk of a Civil War."

constitutional action;[465] those who tamper with the democratic process are playing with fire.[466]

For thirty-five ballots, over a period of a week, the Federalists voted for Burr. Hamilton had protested loudly,[467] to no immediate avail; his former henchmen were out of control. Under Article II each state's delegation had one vote, and a majority was needed for election. Eight states went for Jefferson, six for Burr, and two were divided.[468] The *National Intelligencer* reported that a plan had been put forward for designation of a President pro tem, for which the Constitution made no provision.[469]

On the thirty-sixth ballot the Federalists flinched, and Jefferson was elected. James Bayard of Delaware—always a reluctant supporter of the Federalist strategy, by his account[470]—had had a change of heart. He was prepared, he said, to vote for Jefferson on the next ballot, putting the decisive ninth state into Jefferson's column. He did not have to; facing certain defeat, the party caucus agreed that Federalist Representatives in the divided states of Maryland and Vermont would abstain, as did Bayard himself and those from South Carolina. Maryland and Vermont thus went for Jefferson, and the final vote was ten to four.[471]

Thus the crisis was avoided, and the transition took place—leaving a goodly portion of egg on the face of virtually every Federalist in the House and more on that of the insupportable Mr. Burr, who could have avoided the whole fiasco by making clear that he would not accept the Presidency.[472]

[465]Gallatin drew up a written plan of action recommending that Republicans acquiesce in a new election if it promised to be fair but refuse to respect the acts of a "usurper" who assumed presidential authority. See Plan at Time of Balloting for Jefferson and Burr, Communicated to Nicholas and Mr. Jefferson, in Henry Adams, ed, 1 The Writings of Albert Gallatin 18, 19 (Antiquarian Press, 1960) (first published in 1879). See also Letter of Thomas Jefferson to James Monroe, Feb 15, 1801, 7 Jefferson Writings (Ford ed) at 490, 491:

> If they could have been permitted to pass a law for putting the government into the hands of an officer, they would certainly have prevented an election. But we thought it best to declare openly and firmly, one & all, that the day such an act passed, the middle States would arm, & that no such usurpation, even for a single day, should be submitted to.

[466]All of this amply confirmed the wisdom of the Framers in attempting to keep Congress out of the selection process to the extent they could.

[467]See the barrage of letters he sent to a number of Federalist leaders on the subject, in 25 Hamilton Papers at 257, 269, 271, 275, 280, 286, 292, 293, 319; Elkins & McKitrick at 747–49. Hamilton did not contend that Jefferson had a right to be President; his argument was that Burr was a scoundrel. See, e.g., the detailed indictment he attached to his letter of Jan 4, 1801 to John Rutledge, Jr, 25 Hamilton Papers at 293, 295–98.

[468]See 10 Annals at 1024–34.

[469]Id at 1031.

[470]See his deposition in a later libel action brought by Burr, in Bayard Papers at 122 n 1 (cited in note 462).

[471]See 10 Annals at 1028, 1033; Elkins & McKitrick at 749–50. Burr was declared Vice-President without further ado, as the Constitution provides: "In every case, after the election of the President, the person having the greatest number of votes of the electors shall be the Vice President." US Const, Art II, § 1; see 10 Annals at 746.

[472]See Irving Brant, James Madison: Secretary of State 1800–1809 34 (Bobbs-Merrill, 1953). Burr did write Samuel Smith in December 1800 that he would "disclaim all competition" in the event of a tie, insisting that he would never "be instrumental in Counteracting the Wishes & expectations of the U.S.," and Smith had the letter published. Letter of Aaron Burr to Samuel Smith, Dec 16, 1800, in 1 Burr Papers at 471 (cited in

What would have happened if the House had been unable to reach a decision? Adams's term came to an end on March 4, 1801; there was no way he could continue in office thereafter. Madison, in retirement in Virginia, sensibly suggested that Adams call a special session of the new (Republican) House to make the choice if the old House did not, adding more grotesquely that if he failed to do so Jefferson and Burr should summon Congress by "joint proclamation," since "the prerogative of convening the Legislature must reside in one or other of them."[473] The 1792 act provided that the Senate President pro tem should act as President in case of the removal, death, resignation, or incapacity of both President and Vice-President, but neither that statute nor the constitutional provision on which it was based made provision for the failure to elect a President in the first place.[474] The same statute provided for a special election whenever the Presidency and Vice-Presidency were both "vacant,"[475] but its constitutional basis was shaky.[476] Would a statutory provision for a President pro tem, as bruited about by some of Burr's supporters, have been necessary and proper to the functioning of the government? Or was it precluded by negative implication from the express authority to provide for other contingencies?[477] Fortunately it proved unnecessary to answer that question, thanks to Mr. Bayard's belated act of conscience—or was it cold feet?[478]

---

note 461); see 17 Madison Papers at 453. But that was before the votes were counted and the House balloting began; he did not repeat his disclaimer when it would have made a difference. Indeed less than two weeks later he wrote again to Smith, suggesting that he would be willing to serve as President if the House chose him. Letter of Aaron Burr to Samuel Smith, Dec 29, 1800, 1 Burr Papers at 478, 479 (cited in note 461); see also the Editorial Note in id at 481–87.

[473]If as a constitutional matter this daffy expedient was "not strictly regular," he added, it was more nearly so than any alternative that had been proposed. Letter of James Madison to Thomas Jefferson, Jan 10, 1801, 17 Madison Papers at 453–54. Cf W.S. Gilbert, The Gondoliers, Act I: "[U]ntil it is ascertained which of you is to be king, I have arranged that you will reign jointly, so that no question can arise hereafter as to the validity of any of your acts." But in Gilbert's comic opera it was assumed that one of the individuals who were to reign jointly was already the King; in Madison's the one thing that was certain was that neither Jefferson nor Burr was President until somebody chose between them.

[474]See 1 Stat 239, 240, § 9 (Mar 1, 1792); US Const, Art II, § 1. For either the President pro tem or any other officer designated by statute to assume presidential authority, Gallatin argued, would accordingly be unconstitutional: "For the constitution has not provided any mode by which the Presidential power can be exercised except in the specific cases of vacancy therein enumerated." Plan at Time of Balloting, 1 Gallatin Writings at 18, 19 (cited in note 465). Moreover, so long as the Vice-President was in the chair there was no President pro tem, and Jefferson was determined to remain there in order to prevent the Senate from electing one. See Letter of Samuel Smith to Aaron Burr, Jan 11, 1801, id at 487, 488.

[475]1 Stat at 240, § 10.

[476]See note 105 of chapter 3.

[477]For the suggestion that (three constitutional amendments later) there are still gaps in the procedure for selecting a President, and for imaginative proposals for filling them by statute, see Akhil Reed Amar, Presidents, Vice Presidents, and Death: Closing the Constitution's Succession Gap, 48 Ark L Rev 215 (1995).

[478]"Being perfectly resolved not to risk the constitution or a civil war," Bayard explained at the time, "I . . . considered it the time to announce my intention of voting for Jefferson." Letter of James Bayard to Richard Bassett, Feb 16, 1801, Bayard Papers at 126–27 (cited in note 462). His contemporaneous reference to the New Englanders' stubborn determination "to exclude Jefferson at the expense of the constitution" seems to suggest not that it was unconstitutional to vote for Burr (as he himself had been doing), but that to prolong the impasse would threaten the Union; for in the same breath he repeated his own "inflexible intention to run no risk of the constitution." Letter of James Bayard to Samuel Bayard, Feb 22, 1801, id at 131–32. Bayard said afterward that he had been "chiefly influenced by the current of public sentiment, which I thought it neither safe nor politic to counteract." He had also received two impassioned letters from Hamilton urging him not to vote for Burr. See Letters of Alexander Hamilton to James Bayard, Dec 27, 1800 and Jan

Jefferson's conciliatory inaugural address was a breath of fresh air:

> Let us, then, fellow-citizens, unite with one heart and one mind. Let us restore to social intercourse that harmony and affection without which liberty and even life itself are but dreary things. And let us reflect that, having banished from our land that religious intolerance under which mankind so long bled, we have yet gained little if we countenance a political intolerance as despotic, as wicked, and capable of as bitter and bloody persecutions. . . .
>
> We are all republicans, we are all federalists. If there be any among us who would wish to dissolve this Union or to change its republican form, let them stand undisturbed as monuments of the safety with which error of opinion may be tolerated where reason is left free to combat it. . . .[479]

Amen.

16, 1801, 25 Hamilton Papers at 275, 319; Elkins & McKitrick at 748–49; Malone, Jefferson and the Ordeal of Liberty at 504–05 (cited in note 11).

[479] 1 Richardson at 321, 322, 324.

Conclusion

It is hard to believe that the kaleidoscope we have been viewing represents the work of only twelve years. During a period in which the Supreme Court wrote opinions in only a handful of constitutional cases,[1] Congress and the executive resolved a breathtaking variety of constitutional issues great and small, left us a legacy of penetrating and provocative constitutional arguments, and developed a sophisticated glossary of the meaning of a whole host of constitutional provisions. It was in the legislative and executive branches, not in the courts, that the original understanding of the Constitution was forged.

One element of that understanding was the identification of a list of critical issues on which there were irreconcilable differences of opinion. Battle lines were clearly drawn on such recurring questions as the permissible degree of delegation of discretionary authority, the interpretation of the general welfare provision, and the application of the necessary and proper clause. All these conundrums still plague us, however the Supreme Court may for the moment have resolved them. Everything that has since been said about them, or that needed to be said, can be found in the congressional and executive records of the Federalist period.

After the relative honeymoon of the First Congress, debates became more partisan; one is less confident that many of the participants were dispassionately seeking to determine what the Constitution meant. Yet the quality of argument remained astoundingly high, and on the whole there is considerable cause for satisfaction with the results. Most of the time, despite extreme statements on one side or the other, Congress and the President seem to have been faithful to the Constitution. Most of the time Congress displayed both a willingness to exercise the authority the Framers had given it and a sensitivity to the demands of federalism and the separation of powers.

The most troublesome exceptions are those surrounding the Alien and Sedition

---

[1]See The First Hundred Years, chs 1–2.

Acts. During the Fifth Congress many Federalists exhibited a ruthlessness in pursuit of their goals that seems to call into question their concern for limitations on their authority and makes one thankful they were not permitted to remain in power. Yet the principal lesson of that lamentable experience is to demonstrate how malleable the Constitution is, how much it leaves to the good faith of those whose conduct it governs and to their commitment to the principles it represents.[2] For neither the Alien Act nor the Sedition Act was clearly unconstitutional, though they ought to have been. Moreover, although the Republicans lost the fight over the Sedition Act, they ultimately won the war. For not only did they prevail in the elections of the next generation while their proud adversaries sank into self-induced oblivion; they also gave us all that really matters in our modern theory of free expression—the indispensability of speech to the political process and the marketplace of ideas.

Many talented individuals graced the House and Senate during the Federalist period. A handful were truly distinguished: Ames, Gallatin, and of course Madison.[3] In the Cabinet Jefferson and Hamilton were as gifted as one could possibly hope, and their divergent views ensured a lively and stimulating debate on most of the controversial questions of the time.[4] John Adams was a man of real substance and independence and a worthy occupant of the Presidency.[5]

And then there was President Washington.

Nobody seems to think he could compete with Madison, Hamilton, or Jefferson at the intellectual level. He has not been identified as the source of original ideas or renowned for the ingenuity of his constitutional thought. But he was the indispensable focal point, the glue that held the uncertain enterprise together. He had what was needed to make it work: An unconditional commitment to the Constitution, an unswerving integrity, and the unalloyed confidence of the people.[6]

---

[2] See 2 Story, § 425.

[3] See Gallatin's assessment of the members on the other side of the House:

> I may say that though there were, during my six years of Congressional service, many clever men in the Federal party in the House (Griswold, Bayard, Harper, Otis, Smith of South Carolina, Dana, Tracy, Hillhouse, Sitgreaves, etc.) I met with but two superior men. Ames . . . and John Marshall.

Quoted in Winfred E.A. Bernhard, Fisher Ames: Federalist and Statesman, 1758–1808 273 (North Carolina, 1965). Marshall's service in the House was too brief to permit his inclusion in our list of titans of the early Congress; his vocation lay elsewhere.

[4] "Hamilton and Jefferson were, by any standards, great men. . . We cannot see how America could have become the America we know without both of them." Andrew McLaughlin, A Constitutional History of the United States 242 (Appleton-Century-Crofts, 1935).

[5] One recent study has labeled Adams the "most misconstrued and unappreciated 'great man' in American history." Joseph J. Ellis, Passionate Sage: The Character and Legacy of John Adams 12 (Norton, 1993).

[6] See McDonald, Washington at ix; White at 101; James Thomas Flexner, George Washington and the New Nation 501 (Little, Brown, 1969–70). As Jefferson later wrote:

> His integrity was most pure, his justice the most inflexible I have ever known, no motives of interest or consanguinity, of friendship or hatred, being able to bias his decision. He was indeed, in every sense of the words, a wise, a good and a great man. . . .

A minor incident near the end of the Third Congress illustrates Washington's abiding respect for the rule of law and his determination to set an example for others even at the cost of personal embarrassment. On February 27, 1793 he nominated William Paterson, then Governor of New Jersey, to be an Associate Justice on the Supreme Court in place of Thomas Johnson, who had resigned. The next day he sent a second message effectively withdrawing the nomination:

> It has since occurred that he was a member of the Senate when the law creating that office was passed, and that the time for which he was elected is not yet expired. I think it my duty, therefore, to declare that I deem the nomination to have been null by the Constitution.

On March 4, after the Third Congress (and with it Paterson's Senate term) had expired, Washington sent the nomination in again, and it was immediately confirmed.[7]

When President Washington rendered his last great service to his country by announcing that he would not accept reelection in 1796, he took the occasion to remind his fellow citizens of the importance of the union, to warn them against the spirit of party, and to advocate peace with all nations. He added a word of advice about respect for the Constitution that has lost nothing in the ensuing years:

> If in the opinion of the people the distribution or modification of the constitutional powers be in any particular wrong, let it be corrected by an amendment in the way which the Constitution designates. But let there be no change by usurpation; for though this in one instance may be the instrument of good, it is the customary weapon by which free governments are destroyed. The precedent must always greatly overbalance in permanent evil any partial or transient benefit which the use can at any time yield.[8]

Letter of Thomas Jefferson to Walter Jones, Jan 2, 1814, 9 Jefferson Writings (Ford ed) at 448.

[7]See 1 Sen Exec J at 134, 135, 138; Glenn A. Phelps, George Washington and American Constitutionalism 136–37 (Kansas, 1993); US Const, Art I, § 6.

[8]1 Richardson at 213, 220.

Appendix

The Constitution of the United States

We the people of the United States, in order to form a more perfect union, establish justice, insure domestic tranquility, provide for the common defense, promote the general welfare, and secure the blessings of liberty to ourselves and our posterity, do ordain and establish this Constitution for the United States of America.

ARTICLE I

Section 1. All legislative powers herein granted shall be vested in a Congress of the United States, which shall consist of a Senate and House of Representatives.

Section 2. The House of Representatives shall be composed of members chosen every second year by the people of the several States, and the electors in each State shall have the qualifications requisite for electors of the most numerous branch of the State legislature.

No person shall be a representative who shall not have attained to the age of twenty-five years, and been seven years a citizen of the United States, and who shall not, when elected, be an inhabitant of that State in which he shall be chosen.

Representatives and direct taxes shall be apportioned among the several States which may be included within this Union, according to their respective numbers, which shall be determined by adding to the whole number of free persons, including those bound to service for a term of years, and excluding Indians not taxed, three fifths of all other persons. The actual enumeration shall be made within three years after the first meeting of the Congress of the United States, and within every subsequent term of ten years, in such manner as they shall by law direct. The number of Representatives shall not exceed one for every thirty thousand, but each State shall have at least one Representative; and until such enumeration shall be made, the State of New Hampshire shall be entitled to choose three, Massachusetts eight, Rhode Island and Providence Plantations one, Connecticut five, New York six, New Jersey four, Pennsylvania eight, Delaware one, Maryland six, Virginia ten, North Carolina five, South Carolina five, and Georgia three.

When vacancies happen in the representation from any State, the executive authority thereof shall issue writs of election to full such vacancies.

The House of Representatives shall choose their Speaker and other officers; and shall have the sole power of impeachment.

Section 3. The Senate of the United States shall be composed of two Senators from each State, chosen by the legislature thereof, for six years; and each Senator shall have one vote.

Immediately after they shall be assembled in consequence of the first election, they shall be divided as equally as may be into three classes. The seats of the Senators of the first class shall be vacated at the expiration of the second year, of the second class at the expiration of the fourth year, and of the third class at the expiration of the sixth year, so that one third may be chosen every second year; and if vacancies happen by resignation, or otherwise, during the recess of the legislature of any State, the executive thereof may make temporary appointments until the next meeting of the legislature, which shall then fill such vacancies.

No person shall be a Senator who shall not have attained to the age of thirty years, and been nine years a citizen of the United States, and who shall not, when elected, be an inhabitant of that State for which he shall be chosen.

The Vice-President of the United States shall be President of the Senate, but shall have no vote, unless they be equally divided.

The Senate shall choose their other officers, and also a President pro tempore, in the absence of the Vice-President, or when he shall exercise the office of President of the United States.

The Senate shall have the sole power to try all impeachments. When sitting for that purpose, they shall be on oath or affirmation. When the President of the United States is tried, the Chief Justice shall preside: And no person shall be convicted without the concurrence of two thirds of the Members present.

Judgment in cases of impeachment shall not extend further than to removal from office, and disqualification to hold and enjoy any office of honor, trust or profit under the United States: but the party convicted shall nevertheless be liable and subject to indictment, trial, judgment and punishment, according to law.

Section 4. The times, places and manner of holding elections for Senators and Representatives shall be prescribed in each State by the legislature thereof; but the Congress may at any time by law make or alter such regulations, except as to the place of choosing Senators.

The Congress shall assemble at least once in every year, and such meeting shall be on the first Monday in December, unless they shall by law appoint a different day.

Section 5. Each House shall be the judge of the elections, returns and qualifications of its own Members, and a majority of each shall constitute a quorum to do business; but a smaller number may adjourn from day to day, and may be authorized to compel the attendance of absent Members, in such manner, and under such penalties as each House may provide.

Each House may determine the rules of its proceedings, punish its Members for disorderly behavior, and, with the concurrence of two thirds, expel a Member.

Each House shall keep a journal of its proceedings, and from time to time publish the same, excepting such parts as may in their judgment require secrecy; and the yeas and nays of the Members of either House on any question shall, at the desire of one fifth of those present, be entered on the journal.

Neither House, during the session of Congress, shall, without the consent of the other, adjourn for more than three days, nor to any other place than that in which the two Houses shall be sitting.

Section 6. The Senators and Representatives shall receive a compensation for their services, to be ascertained by law, and paid out of the Treasury of the United States. They shall in all cases, except treason, felony and breach of the peace, be privileged from arrest during their attendance at the session of their respective Houses, and in going to and returning from the same; and for any speech or debate in either House, they shall not be questioned in any other place.

No Senator or Representative shall, during the time for which he was elected, be appointed to any civil office under the authority of the United States, which shall have been created, or the emoluments whereof shall have been increased during such time; and no person holding any office under the United States, shall be a Member of either House during his continuance in office.

Section 7. All bills for raising revenue shall originate in the House of Representatives; but the Senate may propose or concur with amendments as on other bills.

Every bill which shall have passed the House of Representatives and the Senate, shall, before it become a law, be presented to the President of the United States. If he approve he shall sign it, but if not he shall return it, with his objections, to that House in which it shall have originated, who shall enter the objections at large on their journal, and proceed to reconsider it. If after such reconsideration two thirds of that House shall agree to pass the bill, it shall be sent, together with the objections, to the other House, by which it shall likewise be reconsidered, and if approved by two thirds of that House, it shall become a law. But in all such cases the votes of both Houses shall be determined by yeas and nays, and the names of the persons voting for and against the bill shall be entered on the journal of each House respectively. If any bill shall not be returned by the President within ten days (Sundays excepted) after it shall have been presented to him, the same shall be a law, in like manner as if he had signed it, unless the Congress by their adjournment prevent its return, in which case it shall not be a law.

Every order, resolution, or vote to which the concurrence of the Senate and House of Representatives may be necessary (except on a question of adjournment) shall be presented to the President of the United States; and before the same shall take effect, shall be approved by him, or being disapproved by him, shall be repassed by two thirds of the Senate and House of Representatives, according to the rules and limitations prescribed in the case of a bill.

Section 8. The Congress shall have power to lay and collect taxes, duties, imposts and excises, to pay the debts and provide for the common defense and general welfare of the United States; but all duties, imposts and excises shall be uniform throughout the United States;

To borrow money on the credit of the United States;

To regulate commerce with foreign nations, and among the several States, and with the Indian tribes;

To establish a uniform rule of naturalization, and uniform laws on the subject of bankruptcies throughout the United States;

To coin money, regulate the value thereof, and of foreign coin, and fix the standard of weights and measures;

To provide for the punishment of counterfeiting the securities and current coin of the United States;

To establish post offices and post roads;

To promote the progress of science and useful arts, by securing for limited times to authors and inventors the exclusive right to their respective writings and discoveries;

To constitute tribunals inferior to the Supreme Court;

To define and punish piracies and felonies committed on the high seas, and offenses against the law of nations;

To declare war, grant letters of marque and reprisal, and make rules concerning captures on land and water;

To raise and support armies, but no appropriation of money to that use shall be for a longer term than two years;

To provide and maintain a navy;

To make rules for the government and regulation of the land and naval forces;

To provide for calling forth the militia to execute the laws of the Union, suppress insurrections and repel invasions;

To provide for organizing, arming, and disciplining the militia, and for governing such part of them as may be employed in the service of the United States, reserving to the States respectively, the appointment of the officers, and the authority of training the militia according to the discipline prescribed by Congress;

To exercise exclusive legislation in all cases whatsoever, over such District (not exceeding ten miles square) as may, by cession of particular States, and the acceptance of Congress, become the seat of the Government of the United States, and to exercise like authority over all places purchased by the consent of the legislature of the State in which the same shall be, for the erection of forts, magazines, arsenals, dockyards, and other needful buildings;—And

To make all laws which shall be necessary and proper for carrying into execution the foregoing powers, and all other powers vested by this Constitution in the Government of the United States, or in any department or officer thereof.

Section 9. The migration or importation of such persons as any of the States now existing shall think proper to admit, shall not be prohibited by the Congress prior to the year one thousand eight hundred and eight, but a tax or duty may be imposed on such importation, not exceeding ten dollars for each person.

The privilege of the writ of habeas corpus shall not be suspended, unless when in cases of rebellion or invasion the public safety may require it.

No bill of attainder or ex post facto law shall be passed.

No capitation, or other direct, tax shall be laid, unless in proportion to the census or enumeration herein before directed to be taken.

To tax or duty shall be laid on articles exported from any State.

No preference shall be given by any regulation of commerce or revenue to the ports of one state over those of another; nor shall vessels bound to, or from, one state, be obliged to enter, clear, or pay duties in another.

No money shall be drawn from the Treasury, but in consequence of appropriations made by law: and a regular statement and account of the receipts and expenditures of all public money shall be published from time to time.

No title of nobility shall be granted by the United States: And no person holding any office of profit or trust under them, shall, without the consent of the Congress, accept of any present, emolument, office, or title, of any kind whatever, from any king, prince, or foreign State.

Section 10. No State shall enter into any treaty, alliance, or confederation; grant letters of marque and reprisal; coin money; emit bills of credit; make any thing but gold and silver coin a tender in payment of debts; pass any bill of attainder, ex post facto law, or law impairing the obligation of contracts, or grant any title of nobility.

No State shall, without the consent of the Congress, lay any imposts or duties on imports or exports, except what may be absolutely necessary for executing its inspection laws: and the net produce of all duties and imposts, laid by any State on imports or exports, shall be for the use of the Treasury of the United States; and all such laws shall be subject to the revision and control of the Congress.

No State shall, without the consent of Congress, lay any duty of tonnage, keep troops, or ships of war in time of peace, enter into any agreement or compact with another State or with a foreign power, or engage in war, unless actually invaded, or in such imminent danger as will not admit of delay.

ARTICLE II

Section 1. The executive power shall be vested in a President of the United States of America. He shall hold his office during the term of four years, and, together with the Vice-President, chosen for the same term, be elected, as follows.

Each State shall appoint, in such manner as the legislature thereof may direct, a number of electors equal to the whole number of Senators and Representatives to which the State may be entitled in the Congress: but no Senator or Representative, or person holding an office of trust or profit under the United States, shall be appointed an elector.

The electors shall meet in their respective States, and vote by ballot for two persons, of whom one at least shall not be an inhabitant of the same State with themselves. And they shall make a list of all the persons voted for, and of the number of votes for each; which list they shall sign and certify, and transmit sealed to the seat of the Government of the United States, directed to the President of the Senate. The President of the Senate shall, in the presence of the Senate and House of Representatives, open all the certificates, and the votes shall then be counted. The person having the greatest number of votes shall be the President, if such number be a majority of the whole number of electors appointed; and if there be more than one who have such majority, and have an equal number of votes, then the House of Reprsentatives shall immediately choose by ballot one of them for President; and if no person have a majority, then from the five highest on the list the said House shall in like manner choose the President. But in choosing the President, the votes shall be taken by States, the representation from each State having one vote; a quorum for this purpose shall consist of a Member or Members from two thirds of the States, and a majority of all the States shall be necessary to a choice. In every case, after the choice of the President, the person having the greatest number of votes of the electors shall be the Vice-President. But if there should remain two or more who have equal votes, the Senate shall choose from them by ballot the Vice-President.

The Congress may determine the time of choosing the electors, and the day on which they shall give their votes; which day shall be the same throughout the United States.

No person except a natural born citizen, or a citizen of the United States, at the time of the adoption of this Constitution, shall be eligible to the office of President; neither shall any person be eligible to that office who shall not have attained to the age of thirty-five years, and been fourteen years a resident within the United States.

In case of the removal of the President from office, or of his death, resignation, or inability to discharge the powers and duties of the said office, the same shall devolve on the Vice-President, and the Congress may by law provide for the case of removal, death, resignation or inability, both of the President and Vice President, declaring what officer shall then act as President, and such officer shall act accordingly, until the disability be removed, or a President shall be elected.

The President shall, at stated times, receive for his services, a compensation, which shall neither be increased nor diminished during the period for which he shall have been elected, and he shall not receive within that period any other emolument from the United States, or any of them.

Before he enter on the execution of his office, he shall take the following oath or affirmation:—"I do solemnly swear (or affirm) that I will faithfully execute the office of President of the United States, and will to the best of my ability preserve, protect and defend the Constitution of the United States."

Section 2. The President shall be Commander in Chief of the Army and Navy of the United States, and of the militia of the several States, when called into the actual service of the United States; he may require the opinion in writing, of the principal officer in each of the executive departments, upon any subject relating to the duties of their respective offices, and he shall have power to grant reprieves and pardons for offenses against the United States, except in cases of impeachment.

He shall have power, by and with the advice and consent of the Senate, to make treaties, provided two thirds of the Senators present concur; and he shall nominate, and by and with the advice and consent of the Senate, shall appoint ambassadors, other public ministers and consuls, judges of the Supreme Court, and all other officers of the United States, whose appointments are not herein otherwise provided for, and which shall be established by law: but the Congress may by law vest the appointment of such inferior officers, as they think proper, in the President alone, in the courts of law, or in the heads of departments.

The President shall have power to fill up all vacancies that may happen during the recess of the Senate, by granting commissions which shall expire at the end of their next session.

Section 3. He shall from time to time give to the Congress information of the state of the Union, and recommend to their consideration such measures as he shall judge necessary and expedient; he may, on extraordinary occasions, convene both Houses, or either of them, and in case of disagreement between them, with respect to the time of adjournment, he may adjourn them to such time as he shall think proper; he shall receive ambassadors and other public ministers; he shall take care that the laws be faithfully executed, and shall commission all the officers of the United States.

Section 4. The President, Vice President and all civil officers of the United States shall be removed from office on impeachment for, and conviction of, treason, bribery, or other high crimes and misdemeanors.

ARTICLE III

Section 1. The judicial power of the United States shall be vested in one Supreme Court, and in such inferior courts as the Congress may from time to time ordain and establish. The judges, both of the supreme and inferior courts, shall hold their offices during good behavior, and shall, at stated times, receive for their services, a compensation, which shall not be diminished during their continuance in office.

Section 2. The judicial power shall extend to all cases, in law and equity, arising under this Constitution, the laws of the United States, and treaties made, or which shall be made, under their authority;—to all cases affecting ambassadors, other public ministers, and consuls;—to all cases of admiralty and maritime jurisdiction;—to controversies to which the United States shall be a party;—to controversies between two or more States;—between a State and citizens of another State;—between citizens of different States;—between citizens of the same State claiming lands under grants of different States, and between a State, or the citizens thereof, and foreign states, citizens or subjects.

In all cases affecting ambassadors, other public ministers, and consuls, and those in which a State shall be party, the Supreme Court shall have original jurisdiction. In all the other cases before mentioned, the Supreme Court shall have appellate jurisdiction, both as to law and fact, with such exceptions, and under such regulations, as the Congress shall make.

The trial of all crimes, except in cases of impeachment, shall be by jury; and such trial shall be held in the State where the said crimes shall have been committed; but when no committed within any State, the trial shall be at such place or places as the Congress may by law have directed.

Section 3. Treason against the United States, shall consist only in levying war against them, or in adhering to their enemies, giving them aid and comfort. No person shall be convicted of treason unless on the testimony of two witnesses to the same overt act, or on confession in open court.

The Congress shall have power to declare the punishment of treason, but no attainder of treason shall work corruption of blood, or forfeiture except during the life of the person attainted.

ARTICLE IV

Section 1. Full faith and credit shall be given in each State to the public acts, records, and judicial proceedings of every other State. And the Congress may by general laws prescribe the manner in which such acts, records and proceedings shall be proved, and the effect thereof.

Section 2. The citizens of each State shall be entitled to all privileges and immunities of citizens in the several States.

A person charged in any State with treason, felony, or other crime, who shall flee from justice, and be found in another State, shall on demand of the executive authority of the

State from which he fled, be delivered up to be removed to the State having jurisdiction of the crime.

No person held to service or labor in one State, under the Laws thereof, escaping into another, shall, in consequence of any law or regulation therein, be discharged from such service or labor, but shall be delivered up on claim of the party to whom such service or labor may be due.

Section 3. New States may be admitted by the Congress into this Union; but no new State shall be formed or erected within the jurisdiction of any other State; nor any State be formed by the junction of two or more States, or parts of States, without the consent of the legislatures of the States concerned as well as of the Congress.

The Congress shall have power to dispose of and make all needful rules and regulations respecting the territory or other property belonging to the United States; and nothing in this Constitution shall be so construed as to prejudice any claims of the United States, or of any particular State.

Section 4. The United States shall guarantee to every State in this Union a republican form of government, and shall protect each of them against invasion; and on application of the legislature, or of the executive (when the legislature cannot be convened) against domestic violence.

ARTICLE V

The Congress, whenever two thirds of both Houses shall deem it necessary, shall propose amendments to this Constitution, or, on the application of the legislatures of two thirds of the several States, shall call a convention for proposing amendments, which, in either case, shall be valid to all intents and purposes, as part of this Constitution, when ratified by the legislatures of three fourths of the several States, or by conventions in three fourths thereof, as the one or the other mode of ratification may be proposed by the Congress: Provided that no amendment which may be made prior to the year one thousand eight hundred and eight shall in any manner affect the first and fourth clauses in the ninth section of the first Article; and that no State, without its consent, shall be deprived of its equal suffrage in the Senate.

ARTICLE VI

All debts contracted and engagements entered into, before the adoption of this Constitution, shall be as valid against the United States under this Constitution, as under the Confederation.

This Constitution, and the laws of the United States which shall be made in pursuance thereof; and all treaties made, or which shall be made, under the authority of the United States, shall be the supreme law of the land, and the judges in every State shall be bound thereby, any thing in the Constitution or laws of any State to the contrary notwithstanding.

The Senators and Representatives before mentioned, and the members of the several state legislatures, and all executive and judicial officers, both of the United States and of the several States, shall be bound by oath or affirmation, to support this Constitution: but no religious test shall ever be required as a qualification to any office or public trust under the United States.

ARTICLE VII

The ratification of the conventions of nine States shall be sufficient for the establishment of this Constitution between the States so ratifying the same.

AMENDMENT I (1791)

Congress shall make no law respecting an establishment of religion, or prohibiting the free exercise thereof; or abridging the freedom of speech, or of the press; or the right of the people peaceably to assemble, and to petition the Government for a redress of grievances.

AMENDMENT II (1791)

A well regulated militia being necessary to the security of a free State, the right of the people to keep and bear arms shall not be infringed.

AMENDMENT III (1791)

No soldier shall, in time of peace, be quartered in any house, without the consent of the owner, nor in time of war, but in a manner to be prescribed by law.

AMENDMENT IV (1791)

The right of the people to be secure in their persons, houses, papers, and effects, against unreasonable searches and seizures, shall not be violated, and no warrants shall issue, but upon probable cause, supported by oath or affirmation, and particularly describing the place to be searched, and the persons or things to be seized.

AMENDMENT V (1791)

No person shall be held to answer for a capital, or otherwise infamous crime, unless on a presentment or indictment of a grand jury, except in cases arising in the land or naval forces, or in the militia, when in actual service in time of war or public danger; nor shall any person be subject for the same offense to be twice put in jeopardy of life or limb; nor shall be compelled in any criminal case to be a witness against himself, nor be deprived of life, liberty, or property, without due process of law; nor shall private property be taken for public use, without just compensation.

AMENDMENT VI (1791)

In all criminal prosecutions, the accused shall enjoy the right to a speedy and public trial, by an impartial jury of the State and district wherein the crime shall have been committed, which district shall have been previously ascertained by law, and to be informed of the nature and cause of the accusation; to be confronted with the witnesses against him; to have compulsory process for obtaining witnesses in his favor, and to have the assistance of counsel for his defense.

AMENDMENT VII (1791)

In suits at common law, where the value in controversy shall exceed twenty dollars, the right of trial by jury shall be preserved, and no fact tried by a jury shall be otherwise re-examined in any court of the United States, than according to the rules of the common law.

AMENDMENT VIII (1791)

Excessive bail shall not be required, nor excessive fines imposed, nor cruel and unusual punishments inflicted.

AMENDMENT IX (1791)

The enumeration in the Constitution, of certain rights, shall not be construed to deny or disparage others retained by the people.

AMENDMENT X (1791)

The powers not delegated to the United States by the Constitution, nor prohibited by it to the States, are reserved to the States respectively, or to the people.

AMENDMENT XI (1798)

The judicial power of the United States shall not be construed to extend to any suit in law or equity, commenced or prosecuted against one of the United States by citizens of another State, or by citizens or subjects of any foreign state.

AMENDMENT XII (1804)

The electors shall meet in their respective States and vote by ballot for President and Vice President, one of whom, at least, shall not be an inhabitant of the same State with themselves: they shall name in their ballots the person voted for as President, and in distinct ballots the person voted for as Vice-President, and they shall make distinct lists of all persons voted for as President, and of all persons voted for as Vice-President, and of the number of votes for each, which lists they shall sign and certify, and transmit sealed to the seat of the Government of the United States, directed to the President of the Senate;—The President of the Senate shall, in presence of the Senate and House of Representatives, open all the certificates and the votes shall then be counted.—The person having the greatest number of votes for President, shall be the President, if such number be a majority of the whole number of electors appointed; and if no person have such majority, then from the persons having the highest numbers not exceeding three on the list of those voted for as President, the House of Representatives shall choose immediately, by ballot, the President. But choosing the President, the votes shall be taken by States, the representation from each State having one vote; a quorum for this purpose shall consist of a member or members from two thirds of the States, and a majority of all the States shall be necessary to a choice. And if the House of Representatives shall not choose a President whenever the right of choice shall devolve upon them, before the fourth day of March next following, then the Vice-President shall act as President, as in the case of the death or other constitutional disability of the President.

The person having the greatest number of votes as Vice-President shall be the Vice-President, if such number be a majority of the whole number of electors appointed; and if no person have a majority, then from the two highest numbers on the list the Senate shall choose the Vice-President; a quorum for the purpose shall consist of two thirds of the whole number of Senators, and a majority of the whole number shall be necessary to a choice. But no person constitutionally ineligible to the office of President shall be eligible to that of Vice-President of the United States.

AMENDMENT XIII (1865)

Section 1. Neither slavery nor involuntary servitude, except as a punishment for crime whereof the party shall have been duly convicted, shall exist within the United States, or any place subject to their jurisdiction.

Section 2. Congress shall have power to enforce this article by appropriate legislation.

AMENDMENT XIV (1868)

Section 1. All persons born or naturalized in the United States, and subject to the jurisdiction thereof, are citizens of the United States and of the State wherein they reside. No State shall make or enforce any law which shall abridge the privileges or immunities of citizens of the United States; nor shall any State deprive any person of life, liberty, or property, without due process of law; nor deny to any person within its jurisdiction the equal protection of the laws.

Section 2. Representatives shall be apportioned among the several States according to their respective numbers, counting the whole number of persons in each State, excluding Indians not taxed. But when the right to vote at any election for the choice of electors for President and Vice-President of the United States, Representatives in Congress, the executive and judicial officers of a State, or the members of the legislature thereof, is denied to any of the male inhabitants of such State, being twenty-one years of age, and citizens of the United States, or in any way abridged, except for participation in rebellion, or other crime, the basis of representation therein shall be reduced in the proportion which the number of such male citizens shall bear to the whole number of male citizens twenty-one years of age in such State.

Section 3. No person shall be a Senator or Representative in Congress, or elector of President and Vice-President, or hold any office, civil or military, under the United States, or under any State, who, having previously taken an oath, as a member of Congress, or as an officer of the United States, or as a member of any state legislature, or as an executive or judicial officer of any State to support the Constitution of the United States, shall have engaged in insurrection or rebellion against the same, or given aid or comfort to the enemies thereof. But Congress may, by a vote of two thirds of each House, remove such disability.

Section 4. The validity of the public debt of the United States, authorized by law, including debts incurred for payment of pensions and bounties for services in suppressing insurrection or rebellion, shall not be questioned. But neither the United States nor any State shall assume or pay any debt or obligation incurred in aid of insurrection or rebellion against the United States, or any claim for the loss or emancipation of any slave; but all such debts, obligations and claims shall be held illegal and void.

Section 5. The Congress shall have power to enforce, by appropriate legislation, the provisions of this article.

AMENDMENT XV (1870)

Section 1. The right of citizens of the United States to vote shall not be denied or abridged by the United States or by any State on account of race, color, or previous condition of servitude.

Section 2. The Congress shall have power to enforce this article by appropriate legislation.

AMENDMENT XVI (1913)

The Congress shall have power to lay and collect taxes on incomes, from whatever source derived, without apportionment among the several States, and without regard to any census or enumeration.

AMENDMENT XVII (1913)

The Senate of the United States shall be composed of two Senators from each State, elected by the people thereof, for six years; and each Senator shall have one vote. The electors in each State shall have the qualifications requisite for electors of the most numerous branch of the state legislatures.

When vacancies happen in the representation of any State in the Senate, the executive authority of such State shall issue writs of election to fill such vacancies: Provided, that the legislature of any State may empower the executive thereof to make temporary appointments until the people fill the vacancies by election as the legislature may direct.

This amendment shall not be so construed as to affect the election or term of any Senator chosen before it becomes valid as part of the Constitution.

AMENDMENT XVIII (1919)

Section 1. After one year from the ratification of this article the manufacture, sale, or transportation of intoxicating liquors within, the importation thereof into, or the exportation thereof from the United States and all territory subject to the jurisdiction thereof for beverage purposes is hereby prohibited.

Section 2. The Congress and the several States shall have concurrent power to enforce this article by appropriate legislation.

Section 3. This article shall be inoperative unless it shall have been ratified as an amendment to the Constitution by the legislatures of the several States as provided in the

Constitution, within seven years from the date of the submission hereof to the States by the Congress.

AMENDMENT XIX (1920)

Section 1. The right of citizens of the United States to vote shall not be denied or abridged by the United States or by any State on account of sex.

Section 2. Congress shall have power to enforce this article by appropriate legislation.

AMENDMENT XX (1933)

Section 1. The terms of the President and Vice-President shall end at noon on the 20th day of January, and the terms of Senators and Representatives at noon on the 3d day of January, of the years in which such terms would have ended if this article had not been ratified; and the terms of their successors shall then begin.

Section 2. The Congress shall assemble at least once in every year, and such meeting shall begin at noon on the 3d day of January, unless they shall by law appoint a different day.

Section 3. If, at the time fixed for the beginning of the term of the President, the President elect shall have died, the Vice-President shall become President. If a President shall not have been chosen before the time fixed for the beginning of his term, or if the President elect shall have failed to qualify, then the Vice-President elect shall act as President until a President shall have qualified; and the Congress may by law provide for the case wherein neither a President elect nor a Vice-President elect shall have qualified, declaring who shall then act as President, or the manner in which one who is to act shall be selected, and such person shall act accordingly until a President or Vice-President shall have qualified.

Section 4. The Congress may by law provide for the case of the death of any of the persons from whom the House of Representatives may choose a President whenever the right of choice shall have devolved upon them, and for the case of the death of any of the persons from whom the Senate may choose a Vice-President whenever the right of choice shall have devolved upon them.

Section 5. Sections 1 and 2 shall take effect on the 15th day of October following the ratification of this article.

Section 6. This article shall be inoperative unless it shall have been ratified as an amendment to the Constitution by the legislatures of three fourths of the several States within seven years from the date of its submission.

AMENDMENT XXI (1933)

Section 1. The eighteenth article of amendment to the Constitution of the United States is hereby repealed.

Section 2. The transportation or importation into any State, Territory, or possession of the United States for delivery or use therein of intoxicating liquors, in violation of the laws thereof, is hereby prohibited.

Section 3. This article shall be inoperative unless it shall have been ratified as an amendment to the Constitution by conventions in the several States, as provided in the Constitution, within seven years from the date of the submission hereof to the States by the Congress.

AMENDMENT XXII (1951)

Section 1. No person shall be elected to the office of the President more than twice, and no person who has held the office of President, or acted as President, for more than two years of a term to which some other person was elected President shall be elected to the office of the President more than once. But this Article shall not apply to any person holding the office of President when this Article was proposed by the Congress, and shall not prevent any person who may be holding the office of President, or acting as President, during the term within which this Article becomes operative from holding the office of President or acting as President during the remainder of such term.

Section 2. This article shall be inoperative unless it shall have been ratified as an amendment to the Constitution by the legislatures of three fourths of the several States within seven years from the date of its submission to the States by the Congress.

AMENDMENT XXIII (1961)

Section 1. The District constituting the seat of Government of the United States shall appoint in such manner as the Congress may direct:

A number of electors of President and Vice-President equal to the whole number of Senators and Representatives in Congress to which the District would be entitled if it were a State, but in no event more than the least populous State; they shall be in addition to those appointed by the States, but they shall be considered, for the purposes of the election of President and Vice-President, to be electors appointed by a State: and they shall meet in the District and perform such duties as provided by the twelfth article of amendment.

Section 2. The Congress shall have power to enforce this article by appropriate legislation.

AMENDMENT XXIV (1964)

Section 1. The right of citizens of the United States to vote in any primary or other election for President or Vice-President, for electors for President or Vice-President, or for Senator or Representative in Congress, shall not be denied or abridged by the United States or any State by reason of failure to pay any poll tax or other tax.

Section 2. The Congress shall have power to enforce this article by appropriate legislation.

AMENDMENT XXV (1967)

Section 1. In case of the removal of the President from office or of his death or resignation, the Vice-President shall become President.

Section 2. Whenever there is a vacancy in the office of the Vice-President, the

President shall nominate a Vice-President who shall take office upon confirmation by a majority vote of both Houses of Congress.

Section 3. Whenever the President transmits to the President pro tempore of the Senate and the Speaker of the House of Representatives his written declaration that he is unable to discharge the powers and duties of his office, and until he transmits to them a written declaration to the contrary, such powers and duties shall be discharged by the Vice-President as Acting President.

Section 4. Whenever the Vice-President and a majority of either the principal officers of the executive departments or of such other body as Congress may by law provide, transmit to the President pro tempore of the Senate and the Speaker of the House of Representatives their written declaration that the President is unable to discharge the powers and duties of his office, the Vice-President shall immediately assume the powers and duties of the office as Acting President.

Thereafter, when the President transmits to the President pro tempore of the Senate and the Speaker of the House of Representatives his written declaration that no inability exists, he shall resume the powers and duties of his office unless the Vice-President and a majority of either the principal officers of the executive department or of such other body as Congress may by law provide, transmit within four days to the President pro tempore of the Senate and the Speaker of the House of Representatives their written declaration that the President is unable to discharge the powers and duties of his office. Thereupon Congress shall decide the issue, assembling within forty-eight hours for that purpose if not in session. If the Congress, within twenty-one days after receipt of the latter written declaration, or, if Congress is not in session, within twenty-one days after Congress is required to assemble, determines by two-thirds vote of both Houses that the President is unable to discharge the powers and duties of his office, the Vice-President shall continue to discharge the same as Acting President; otherwise, the President shall resume the powers and duties of his office.

AMENDMENT XXVI (1971)

Section 1. The right of citizens of the United States, who are eighteen years of age or older, to vote shall not be denied or abridged by the United States or by any State on account of age.

Section 2. The Congress shall have power to enforce this article by appropriate legislation.

AMENDMENT XXVII (1992)[1]

No law varying the compensation for the services of the Senators and Representatives shall take effect until an election of Representatives has intervened.

[1]Proposed in 1789, this amendment was not ratified by three fourths of the states until 1992. Although both Congress and the Executive proclaimed that the amendment had been adopted, doubts as to its validity persist because of the long delay betwen proposal and ultimate ratification.

Index

Adams, John 4, 10, 11, 34, 35, 41, 126, 130, 172, 196, 211, 222, 239, 240, 241, 243, 273, 274, 275, 284, 292, 294, 297
Advisory opinions. *See* Federal courts
Agriculture
  congressional authority 222
Alien and Sedition Acts 253, 269, 296
Aliens
  constitutional rights 257
  delegation of authority 255
  enemy aliens 254
  expulsion 255
  federal jurisdiction 51, 52
  migration clause 257
  naturalization 88, 192, 254
  registration 254
  unconstitutional conditions 257
Allen, John 243, 257, 271
Ambassadors
  appointment 44
  compensation 45, 218
  power to receive 45, 182
Amendment. *See also particular provisions*
  Bill of Rights 110
  conscientious objectors 113
  constitutional conventions 110
  instruction of representatives 16
  limits on state action 114
  number of Representatives 111
  presidential veto 115, 196
  ratification 208

  rejected proposals 111
  salary increases 111
Ames, Fisher 18, 34, 39, 57, 59, 62, 73, 75, 78, 98, 106, 116, 117, 118, 121, 125, 131, 134, 155, 165, 171, 185, 191, 197, 206, 218, 257, 297
Appointments
  ambassadors and consuls 44
  circuit judges 275
  Ellsworth, Oliver 274
  employees 153
  extension of duties 43
  Fishbourn, Benjamin 23
  Foreign Affairs Secretary 36
  incompatibility 198, 209, 274
  inferior officers 36, 43, 156
  Jay, John 209
  military officers 81
  nonstatutory offices 43
  presidential approval 152
  procedure 23, 25, 36
  recess appointments 154
  Short, William 22
  Vermont officers 102
Appropriations. *See also* Spending
  Barbary pirates 87
  check on other branches 215
  diplomatic salaries 46, 218
  discretion of Congress 88, 215, 218
  District of Columbia 108
  Giles Resolutions 165
  military purposes 83

Appropriations (*continued*)
  Mint 218
  naval vessels 218
  specificity of 46, 68, 110, 165
  treaty implementation 212
  unauthorized spending 165, 189
  Whiskey Rebellion 189
Armed forces. *See* War powers
Articles of Confederation
  admission of states 220
  Articles of War 82
  coinage 152
  flag 204
  foreign affairs 178
  general welfare clause 79, 169
  militia 157
  negotiable notes 74
  Northwest Ordinance 103
  payment of debts 75
  Post Office 147, 151
  treaties 210
Assumption of State Debts 76
Attorney General 43

Baldwin, Abraham 33, 66, 117, 203, 224, 241, 242,
  246, 258, 274, 275, 288, 289, 291
Bank of the United States 78
Bankruptcy
  Act of 1800 274
  discretion of Congress 4, 275
  exclusivity of power 274
  First Congress 4
  merchants' debts 4
  preexisting debts 274
  scope of authority 4
  state authority 274
Barbary pirates 25, 87
Barnwell, Robert 168
Bayard, James 259, 260, 265, 268, 273, 274, 277,
  278, 279, 282, 293, 297
Benson, Egbert 37, 40, 46, 47, 111, 118, 120, 121,
  148, 161
Bill of Rights. *See also particular provisions*
  adoption 110
  inapplicability to states 114
  judicial enforcement 112
  Northwest Ordinance 104
  ratification 208
Bills of attainder 191
Bird, John 287
Bland, Theodorick 37, 57, 60, 110, 164
Blount, Thomas 214
Blount, William 219, 275
  impeachment 275

Borrowing
  delegation of authority 73
  national bank 79
  negotiable notes 74
Boudinot, Elias 14, 17, 18, 36, 67, 72, 75, 79, 116,
  117, 118, 120, 121, 135, 158, 160, 165, 184, 188,
  197, 201, 203, 204
Bourne, Benjamin 212, 227
Bradford, William 206
Brent, Richard 223, 228, 234, 246, 247
British precedents
  advisory opinions 181
  appropriations 214
  committees 9
  election contests 18
  expulsion of members 264
  foreign affairs 178
  impeachment 278, 279
  legislative vacancy 135
  naturalization 89
  parliamentary privilege 233, 268
  unfinished business 8
Brooks, David 241, 276
Brown, John 288
Buck, Daniel 218, 232
Burke, Aedanus 7, 67, 121, 159
Burr, Aaron 292
Butler, Pierce 210

Cabot, George 206
Carnes, Thomas 191
Carroll, Daniel 57
Cases and controversies
  advisory opinions 51, 181
  Correspondence of the Justices 181
  ex parte proceedings 192
  executive review 155
  finality 155
  naturalization 90, 192
  pension claims 155
Census
  direct taxes 226
  frequency 226
  penalties 97
  scope of questions 19
Champlin, Christopher 263
Circuit Courts 54, 275
Citizenship
  children born abroad 90
  naturalization 88, 192, 254
  renunciation 195
  state and federal law 17
Claiborne, Thomas 224
Claiborne, William 251, 282, 283
Clark, Abraham 187, 188

Clymer, George 38, 57, 90, 118
Coins. *See* Money
Coit, Joshua 224, 228
Commander in Chief
    militia, employment of 160
    offensive operations 84
    troops, employment of 81, 187
Commerce clause
    federal authority
        alien expulsion 258
        arms exports 184
        codfish subsidy 169
        commerce between foreign countries 67, 194
        delegation of authority 227
        delegation to states 70
        disabled seamen 244
        embargo 184
        enforcement of state law 64, 228, 230
        exclusivity 70, 227
        export regulations 63
        glass factory 72
        health and safety 227
        Indian commerce 86
        inspection laws 63
        kidnapping 229
        lighthouses 69
        militia exemptions 159
        Mississippi Territory 285
        national bank 79
        noncommercial purposes 59
        nonintercourse 187
        offenses outside states 96
        pilots 228
        postal passengers 150
        power to prohibit commerce 59, 98
        power to restrict commerce 57
        protective tariff 57
        quarantine 227
        relation to tax power 63
        relation to treaty power 210, 212, 217
        Rhode Island commerce 98
        scientific expeditions 71
        seamen's labor law 65
        ship licensing 62
        slave trade 66, 194, 286
        timber exports 223
        treaty abrogation 252
    state authority
        lighthouses 70
        pilots 70
        quarantine 227
Common law
    crimes 179, 273
Compromise of 1790 77, 108
Congress. *See also* House of Representatives,

Senate, *and particular powers*
    Annals 11
    bribery of 232
    chaplains 12
    compensation 7, 111
    conflict of interest 9
    contempt of Congress 232, 266, 268
    delegation. *See* Delegation of authority
    election contests
        Duvall, Gabriel 197
        Gallatin, Albert 197
        Johns, Kensey 154
        Mercer, John Francis 135
        New Jersey delegation 18
        procedure 18
        Smith, William 17
        state law, applicability 197
        Tennessee Senators 222
        Wayne, Anthony 136
    executive influence 30, 164
    expiration of terms 102
    expulsion of members 263, 276
    foreign gifts 281
    impeachment of members 276
    implied and inherent powers
        aliens 259
        contempt 233, 266
        flag 204
        foreign affairs 252, 259
        fugitives 170
        investigation 20
        necessary and proper clause. *See* Necessary
            and proper clause
        oath of office 14
        Sedition Act 260
        self-preservation 260
    intimidation of members 268
    investigations
        Army 163
        executive privilege 164
        exposure as goal 167
        Giles Resolutions 164
        Hamilton 164
        Morris, Robert 20
        St. Clair expedition 163
        Treasury 164
    journal 10
    oath of office 13
    officers 11
    place of meeting 173
    private bills 91
    privileges
        contempt power 232, 266
        Duane's case 267
        franking 151

privileges (*continued*)
    militia exemption 159
    Randall and Whitney 232
    Randolph's case 268
  public sessions 10, 173, 207
  qualifications of members 16, 197
  recess appointments 154
  reporting of debates 10, 174, 207
  resignation of member 135
  rules 9, 277
  sessions 8
  special sessions 8, 102, 173, 239, 294
  term limits 112
  territorial delegate 200
  unfinished business 8, 108
  vacancies 135
Consuls
  credentials 175
  duties 169
  French Consular Convention 22
Contempt of Congress
  Duane's case 266
  Randall and Whitney 232
  Randolph's case 268
Contract clause
  federal obligations 75
  Northwest Ordinance 105
Cooper, William 225
Copyrights. *See* Patents and copyrights
Corporations
  national bank 78
  power to establish 78
Counsel, right to
  contempt of Congress 237, 267
  election contests 18
Courts-martial 243
Craik, William 246
Crimes
  Articles of War 93
  bribery 96
  coins, debasing or stealing 154
  common law offenses 179, 273
  counterfeiting 96, 154
  courts-martial 243
  cruel and unusual punishment 94, 95, 96, 104, 255
  death penalty 94, 96
  dissection 95
  extradition 170, 274
  federal enclaves 94
  fugitives 170
  high seas, offenses on 95, 241
  impeachment. *See* Impeachment
  implied powers 97, 260
  Indians, offenses against 85, 86
  law of nations, offenses against 96, 174, 241

  military and naval offenses 93, 243
  misprision of treason 94
  perjury 96
  piracy 95
  postal offenses 150
  private prosecution 65
  procedural provisions 97
  sedition 260
  territories 93
  treason 94
Cruel and unusual punishment
  death penalty 94
  dissection 95
  Northwest Ordinance 104
  proportionality 96
  retaliation 255

Dana, Samuel 248, 249, 258, 259, 262, 272, 276, 297
Davis, Thomas 245, 265, 273
Dawson, John 272
Dayton, Jonathan 184, 202, 219, 226, 258, 285
Debts
  assumption of state debts 76
  borrowing. *See* Borrowing
  claims against United States 207
  contract clause 75
  ex post facto clause 75
  full payment 74
  national bank 79
  preconstitutional obligations 74
  private bills 207
  public credit 73
  Rhode Island's responsibility 99
  sequestration 184
  St. Domingo 189
  taking clause 75
Delegation of authority
  alien enemies 255
  appropriations 165
  arms exports 186
  borrowing 73
  capture of vessels 244
  coinage 152
  congressional meeting place 173
  crimes against Indians 87
  District of Columbia 109, 110, 286
  embargo 186
  fortifications 244
  Indian commerce 86
  inspection laws 64
  land office 207
  militia, employment of 160
  naval vessels 186, 244
  nonintercourse 244
  Northwest Ordinance 104

patents 91
pilots 70
post roads 146
Provisional Army 245
quarantine 227
state laws 70, 87, 104, 110, 286
territories 104
troops, raising of 163, 186, 245
Democratic Societies 190
Dent, George 272
Dexter, Samuel 185, 191, 193, 194, 195, 203, 274,
289, 290
District Attorneys. *See* Officers
District of Columbia. *See* Seat of government
Duane, William 266
Due process
Alien Act 256
contempt of Congress 235
postdeprivation hearing 86
Duvall, Gabriel 197

Edmond, William 263
Education
national university 71, 222
Elections. *See also* Congress, President
election of 1788 4
election of 1792 172
election of 1796 221
election of 1800 288
Eleventh amendment 195
Ellsworth, Oliver 15, 39, 47, 119, 160, 206, 274
Enumeration. *See* Census
Equal footing doctrine 104
Ex post facto laws
bankruptcy 274
contractual obligations 75
Excises. *See* Taxation
Executive power. *See* President
Executive privilege. *See* President
Exports. *See* Commerce clause, Taxation
Extradition. *See* Crimes

Federal courts
advisory opinions 51, 154, 181
cases and controversies 50, 90, 154, 181, 192
Conformity Act 51
Correspondence of the Justices 181
eleventh amendment 195
ex parte proceedings 192
executive review 155
finality 155
full faith and credit 103
inferior courts
discretion of Congress 48
jurisdiction

admiralty 48
alien a party 51
alien tort statute 52
copyright infringement 92
diversity cases 48
exclusivity 49, 50, 212
federal questions 52, 275
naturalization 90, 192
patent cases 91, 156
pension claims 154
judges
appointment 275
disability 198
District of Columbia 288
dual office-holding 198
eligibility 298
incompatibility 198
nonjudicial duties 51, 154, 162, 209, 274
removal 199
judicial review 14, 112, 120, 271
Judiciary Act of 1789 47
Judiciary Act of 1801 275
nonjudicial duties 92, 254
offenses against 96
procedural rules 51
review of administrative action 91, 156
sovereign immunity 195
suits against states 195
Supreme Court. *See* Supreme Court
transfer of jurisdiction 198
Federal enclaves
crimes 94
state law in 183
Federal jurisdiction. *See* Federal courts
Federal taxes. *See* Taxation
Findley, William 130, 166, 264
First amendment,. *See* Petitions, Religion, Speech and
press
Fitzsimons, Thomas 30, 56, 57, 59, 66, 70, 118, 150,
163, 190
Flag 204
Foreign affairs
alien acts 254
ambassadors 44, 182, 218
Articles of Confederation 178
Barbary pirates 25, 87
Citizen Genêt 176, 182
congressional powers 252, 259
consular credentials 176
contact with foreign governments 175, 262
Correspondence of the Justices 181
delegation of authority 255
department of 36
diplomatic salaries 45, 218
diplomats, offenses against 96

Foreign affairs (*continued*)
  enemy aliens 254
  extradition 274
  federal powers 178
  French constitution 175
  French flag 176
  law of nations
    as law of U.S. 52
    offenses against 96, 174
    presidential enforcement 179
  Logan Act 262
  Neutrality Proclamation 174
  presidential powers 36, 175, 178, 241, 262, 274
  receiving ambassadors 45, 182
  recognition of governments 45, 182
  Secretary of State 42
  special agents 44
  treaties. *See* Treaties
  XYZ Affair 243
Foster, Dwight 251
Freeman, Nathaniel Jr. 234
Fugitives. *See* Crimes, Slavery
Full faith and credit
  congressional implementation 102
  federal courts 103
  public acts 102

Gallatin, Albert 189, 196, 197, 206, 208, 212, 214,
  217, 218, 219, 226, 229, 242, 245, 246, 247, 248,
  249, 250, 253, 254, 255, 256, 257, 258, 259, 260,
  261, 262, 263, 265, 266, 272, 273, 276, 282, 286,
  292, 293, 294, 297
General welfare clause. *See* Spending
Gerry, Elbridge 7, 11, 14, 20, 38, 42, 43, 44, 67, 77,
  78, 79, 117, 118, 120, 121, 129, 135, 139, 141,
  142, 151, 240
Gilbert, Ezekiel 226
Giles, William 80, 121, 129, 135, 138, 141, 146, 158,
  164, 168, 186, 190, 191, 193, 194, 202, 203, 213,
  217, 218, 224, 232, 234
Giles resolutions 164
Goodhue, Benjamin 138, 169, 204
Gordon, William 285
Grand Committee 288
Griswold, Roger 213, 241, 263, 273, 297
Grout, Jonathan 17
Guarantee clause. *See* States

Habeas corpus 256
Hamilton, Alexander 31, 33, 38, 42, 50, 68, 72, 73,
  74, 75, 76, 77, 78, 80, 83, 93, 110, 119, 121, 122,
  125, 133, 134, 152, 154, 164, 169, 173, 174, 175,
  176, 177, 178, 179, 182, 184, 188, 206, 207, 210,
  213, 214, 215, 216, 222, 242, 250, 260, 293, 297

Harper, Robert Goodloe 208, 212, 213, 219, 224,
  225, 235, 236, 237, 245, 246, 249, 250, 254, 260,
  261, 264, 272, 276, 278, 279, 280, 285, 287, 292,
  297
Harrison, Carter 249
Harrison, William Henry 202
Hartley, Thomas 4, 8, 38, 56, 148, 189, 273
Havens, Jonathan 212, 226
Health and safety 228
Heath, John 194
Hiester, Daniel 57, 227
Hillhouse, James 160, 213, 297
Holmes, David 227
Home Department 42
House of Representatives. *See also* Congress
  apportionment of seats 101, 128, 220
  number of seats 111, 129, 131, 134
  presidential election 292
  Speaker 11
  treaties 211
Huger, Benjamin 273
Huntington, Benjamin 37, 42, 73

Impeachment
  Blount, William 275
  exclusivity of remedy 37
  grounds for 277
  jury trial 277
  members of Congress 276
  persons subject to 276
  procedure 276, 277
  trial in absentia 276
Indians
  crimes against 85, 86
  St. Clair expedition 163
  subsidies 169
  Superintendent of Indian Affairs 43
  trade and commerce 85, 86
  treaties 21, 24, 26, 85
Intellectual property. *See* Patents and copyrights
Intergovernmental immunity
  extradition 170
  insurrection 158
  militia readiness 184
  naturalization cases 90
  Northwest Ordinance 105
  oath of office 15
  offenses against Indians 87
  pilot licensing 228
  presidential electors 138
  seamen's labor law 65
Interpretation 117
Investigations. *See* Congress
Izard, Ralph 15

Jackson, James 17, 46, 48, 62, 66, 85, 89, 117, 118, 121, 136, 138, 140, 159
Jay, John 22, 126, 181, 209
Jay Treaty 209
Jefferson, Thomas 4, 9, 22, 77, 80, 87, 102, 104, 109, 112, 117, 119, 125, 126, 127, 133, 134, 142, 154, 167, 168, 172, 173, 174, 176, 177, 179, 180, 181, 182, 183, 184, 191, 206, 212, 213, 222, 223, 225, 240, 242, 250, 253, 260, 266, 267, 269, 270, 271, 273, 277, 279, 292, 293, 295, 297
Judges. *See* Federal courts, State courts
Judicial review
    administrative action 91
    Bill of Rights 112
    federal legislation 120, 271
    state legislation 14
Judiciary Act of 1789 47
Judiciary Act of 1801 275
Jury trial
    contempt of Congress 235
    courts-martial 243
    impeachment cases 277
    military and naval offenses 243
    Northwest Ordinance 104
    patent cases 92
    state courts 92

Kentucky
    admission to Union 100
Kentucky and Virginia Resolutions 269
Kidnapping 229
King, Rufus 119, 158, 160, 206
Kittera, John Wilkes 285
Knox, Henry 22, 24, 26, 82, 84, 85, 133, 164, 206

Langdon, John 11
Laurance, John 14, 17, 18, 33, 38, 43, 44, 46, 74, 75, 89, 109, 117, 118, 120, 121, 128, 129
Law of nations
    Alien Tort Statute 52
    as law of U.S. 52
    offenses against 96, 174
    presidential enforcement 179
Lee, Charles 206
Lee, Henry 287
Lee, Richard Bland 8, 17, 18, 36, 46
Livermore, Samuel 18, 34, 37, 47, 50, 62, 64, 74, 111, 121, 132, 136, 140, 141, 146, 147, 150, 158, 161
Livingston, Edward 212, 256, 261, 271, 272, 274
Livingston, Robert 43
Logan Act 262
Lyman, Samuel 228
Lyon, Matthew 255, 263, 282
    expulsion 263

Maclay, William 4, 10, 12, 15, 20, 24, 26, 30, 35, 36, 37, 44, 48, 68, 82, 84, 87, 99, 240
Macon, Nathaniel 129, 220, 224, 260, 287
Madison, James 17, 19, 35, 36, 38, 39, 40, 41, 44, 56, 59, 60, 66, 67, 70, 71, 73, 75, 76, 77, 78, 79, 81, 107, 109, 110, 111, 112, 113, 114, 116, 117, 118, 119, 120, 121, 125, 126, 127, 134, 135, 138, 140, 144, 148, 155, 159, 160, 163, 166, 167, 168, 169, 171, 173, 174, 175, 178, 180, 182, 184, 186, 187, 189, 190, 191, 194, 195, 197, 202, 206, 209, 213, 214, 219, 223, 225, 234, 235, 236, 242, 261, 269, 271, 278, 279, 289, 294, 297
Mandamus
    Supreme Court 53
Marshall, John 195, 213, 240, 268, 273, 274, 289, 297
McDowell, Joseph 194, 249, 283
McHenry, James 206
Mercer, John Francis 135, 161, 197
Militia. *See* War powers
Milledge, John 285
Mining
    congressional authority 223
Mint
    appropriations 218
    establishment 152
Mississippi Territory 284
Money. *See also* Appropriations, Borrowing, Debts
    coinage 153
    coins, value of 153
    counterfeiting 96, 154
    foreign coins 153
    legal tender 153
    Mint 152, 218
    paper money 74
Monroe, James 119
Moore, Andrew 57
Morris, Gouverneur 44
Morris, Robert 15, 201, 206
    investigation of 20
Muhlenberg, Frederick Augustus 11
Murray, William Vans 131, 139, 155, 156, 160, 161, 167, 171, 185, 191, 195, 201, 212, 218, 224, 229

Naturalization
    1790 law 88
    1795 law 192
    1798 law 254
    attachment to Constitution 193
    case or controversy 90, 192
    disclaimer of titles 193
    equal footing 194
    exclusivity of federal power 192
    expatriates 195
    public office 89, 194, 254
    unconstitutional conditions 193

Naturalization (*continued*)
    uniformity requirement 88, 254
Navy. *See* War powers
Necessary and proper clause
    Alien Act 259
    buildings and land 153
    census questions 20
    consular functions 170
    creation of offices 44
    customs collection 97
    diplomatic salaries 47
    District of Columbia 109
    full faith and credit 103
    indemnity 189
    medals and monuments 275
    military pensions 82
    national bank 79
    national university 71
    oath of office 14
    offenses against courts 97
    postal passengers 150
    presidential elections 137, 139, 289
    removal of officers 38
    Sedition Act 260, 272
    territorial delegate 203
    treaty implementation 86
Neutrality Proclamation 174
Nicholas, John 185, 188, 190, 218, 224, 236, 242,
    243, 245, 253, 260, 261, 262, 263, 265, 276, 284,
    285, 287
Niles, Nathaniel 131, 137, 150, 170
Ninth amendment 112, 258
North Carolina
    cession of territory 106
    ratification of Constitution 97
Northwest Ordinance 103
    affirmative duties 105
    amendment by First Congress 106
    authority to adopt 103
    bill of rights 104
    compact status 105
    delegate to Congress 201
    legislative apportionment 105
    slavery 105
    statehood provisions 219

Oath of office 13
Officers
    ambassadors and consuls 44, 169, 218
    appointment. *See* Appointments
    Attorney General 43
    Chief Coiner 154
    compensation 45, 218
    Comptroller 41
    creation of offices 36, 43, 152

District Attorneys 43
impeachment 37, 275
incompatibility 209, 274
inferior officers 36, 37, 43
legislative officers. *See* House of
    Representatives, Senate
military officers 81
militia exemptions 159
naturalized citizens 89, 195, 254
nonstatutory offices 43
oath of office 14
political activities 62
President. *See* President
presidential succession 140
qualifications 43, 89
quasi-judicial duties 156
recess appointments 154
removal 37
Secretary of Foreign Affairs 36
Secretary of Treasury 41
Secretary of War 41
special agents 44
Superintendent of Indian Affairs 43
territorial officers 106
Vermont officers 102
Vice-President. *See* Vice-President
Otis, Harrison Gray 253, 254, 255, 257, 258, 259,
    260, 264, 282, 287, 297

Page, John 8, 18, 34, 35, 71, 98, 100, 110, 114, 117,
    118, 121, 148, 150, 153, 161, 164, 212, 227, 234
Pardon
    before trial 190
    Fries' Rebellion 227
    general amnesty 190
    Sedition Act 273
    Whiskey Rebellion 189
Parker, Josiah 57, 61, 163, 272
Patents and copyrights
    Baffin's Bay 71, 93
    conflicting claims 156
    copyright law 92
    delegation of authority 91
    federal jurisdiction 91, 92, 156
    jury trial 92
    loan of federal funds 72
    national university 71
    patent law 91, 156
    scientific expeditions 71, 93
    special legislation 90
Paterson, William 298
Petitions
    Alien and Sedition Acts 272
    duty to consider 231, 272
    jurisdiction to entertain 230

slavery and slave trade 66, 230
  Virginia grenadiers 272
  who may file 230
Pickering, Timothy 206
Pinckney, Charles 267, 274, 281, 288, 289, 290, 291
Pinckney, Charles Cotesworth 239, 240, 281, 292
Pinckney, Thomas 248, 281
Platt, Jonas 273
Post Office
  Articles of Confederation 43, 147, 151
  carriage of passengers 150
  criminal offenses 150
  delegation of authority 146
  establishment 146
  franking privilege 151
  militia exemptions 150
  monopoly 150
  newspapers 150, 151
  post roads 146, 225
  postal conventions 151
  temporary office 43
Preamble 259
President
  advisors 25
  appointments. See Appointments
  Commander in Chief 81, 84, 160, 187, 255
  compensation 32
  creation of offices 43
  election 136
    congressional role 288, 292
    disputed elections 288
    election of 1788 4
    election of 1796 221
    election of 1800 288
    Grand Committee proposal 288
    House of Representatives, election by 292
    number of electors 138
    procedure 136
    special elections 144
  execution of laws 39, 178, 274
  executive privilege 23, 164, 214, 243
  foreign affairs 36, 175, 178, 241, 262, 274
  immunity from process 28
  inability to elect 294
  inherent and implicit powers 36, 178
  legislative proposals 29
  militia, employment of 160, 189
  Neutrality Proclamation 174
  oath of office 13
  pardons 189, 227, 273
  receiving ambassadors 45, 182
  recognition of governments 45, 182
  removal of officers 37
  resignation 139
  succession and disability 139

take care clause 39, 178, 274
term of office 145
titles 34
treaties. See Treaties
troops, employment of 81, 187
vesting clause 39, 177
veto
  apportionment bill 133
  constitutional amendments 115, 196
  foreign gifts 281
  item veto 32
  light dragoons 208
  time limit 31
  vote to override 208
  Washington's view 31
Privileges and immunities
  naturalization 89
Property clause
  land office 107, 207
  national bank 79
  theft of US property 94
Provisional Army 244
Public credit 73

Quarantine 227

Randall and Whitney 232
Randolph, Edmund 80, 133, 154, 206, 211
Randolph, John
  intimidation of 268
Read, George 40
Religion
  establishment
    census questions 20
    chaplains 12
    conscientious objectors 159
    land grant to church 207
    shipboard services 243
    Thanksgiving 13
  free exercise
    conscientious objectors 113, 159
    Northwest Ordinance 104
  legislative history 113
  limits on state power 114
Republican form of government. See States
Rhode Island
  commerce ban 98
  federal debts 98
  ratification of Constitution 97
Robbins, Jonathan
  extradition 274
Ross, James 288
Rutledge, John 52, 209
Rutledge, John Jr. 246, 263

Savannah fire 224
Schuyler, Philip 119
Scott, Thomas 43, 46, 67, 75, 118
Searches and seizures
    tariff and tonnage laws 61
    whiskey excise 61
Seat of government 107, 286
    agricultural board 222
    delegation of authority 109
    establishment 108
    exclusive power 110, 287
    interim capital 108
    location 108
    national bank 79
    national university 72, 223
    representation in Congress 287
    state judges 288
    state laws in 110, 286
    Washington monument 275
Sedgwick, Theodore 34, 40, 46, 63, 76, 77, 79, 113,
    118, 121, 132, 135, 138, 140, 142, 147, 148, 149,
    152, 158, 162, 171, 184, 185, 186, 193, 218, 237,
    247
Sedition Act 260, 269
Senate. *See also* Congress
    appointments 22, 23, 25
    Executive Journal 21
    Instructions 15
    President pro tempore 11, 140
    treaties 21, 211, 251, 274
    Vice-President's role 11, 240
Seney, Joshua 62, 72, 75, 160
Sewall, Samuel 241, 245, 247, 248, 251, 258, 259,
    264
Sherburne, John 235
Sherman, Roger 20, 44, 46, 57, 62, 72, 77, 89, 109,
    111, 112, 117, 118, 137, 140, 158, 160, 161
Sitgreaves, Samuel 227, 228, 229, 230, 241, 248, 253,
    264, 276, 297
Slavery
    emancipation 66
    fugitive slaves 15, 105, 170
    kidnapping 229
    manumission 230
    Northwest Ordinance 105
    petitions 66, 230
    slave trade 66, 194, 286
    territories 67, 105, 107, 286
Smilie, John 287
Smith, Isaac 229, 233, 236
Smith, Jeremiah 159
Smith, Nathaniel 213
Smith, Samuel 185, 227, 228
Smith, William Loughton 4, 11, 17, 18, 36, 37, 38, 39,
    44, 46, 47, 48, 66, 67, 72, 75, 117, 118, 120, 121,

    135, 140, 142, 144, 145, 160, 165, 167, 171, 191,
    194, 201, 202, 203, 207, 208, 212, 213, 216, 218,
    219, 223, 224, 229, 232, 233, 236, 237, 281, 297
Southwest Territory
    delegate to Congress 200
    establishment 106
    statehood 219
Sovereign immunity 195
Speech and press
    attachment to Constitution 193
    criticism of government 191
    defamation of Senate 267
    Democratic Societies 190
    denunciation by President 191
    Duane's case 266
    foreign negotiations 262
    franking privilege 151
    Hatch Act 62
    legislative history 113
    limits on state power 114
    Logan Act 262
    Lyon, expulsion of 265
    naturalization 193
    newspapers in mail 150
    revenue agents 62
    Sedition Act 260, 269, 296
    unconstitutional conditions 62, 193
    Virginia and Kentucky Resolutions 269
Spending
    agricultural board 222
    appropriations. *See* Appropriations
    arms manufacture 224
    Articles of Confederation 79, 169
    assumption of state debts 77
    Baffin's Bay expedition 71
    Barbary Pirates 88
    Caribbean refugees 188
    cod fisheries 168
    glass factory 72
    indemnity 184, 189
    Indian subsidies 169
    lighthouses 69
    loan of federal funds 72
    manufacturing subsidies 72, 169
    post roads 225
    Savannah fire 224
    scientific expeditions 71
    St. Domingo 188
    tax refund 169
    university 71, 222
Sprigg, Richard Jr. 241, 243
St. Domingo 188
State courts
    full faith and credit 102
    jurisdiction in Art. III cases 48, 50

jury trial 92
naturalization 90
patent infringement 92
review by Supreme Court 52
State officers
  federal duties 15, 65, 87, 90, 137, 158, 170, 184,
    228
  naturalized citizens 89
  oath of office 14
State taxes. *See* Taxation
States
  admission to Union
    Articles of Confederation 220
    conditional admission 221
    discretion of Congress 218
    Kentucky 100
    Northwest Ordinance provisions 104, 219
    Tennessee 218
    Vermont 100
  equal footing doctrine 104, 220
  full faith and credit 102
  intergovernmental immunity 15, 65, 87, 90, 137,
    158, 170, 184, 228
  interposition 269
  nullification 269
  presidential elections 291
  ratification of Constitution
    North Carolina 97
    Rhode Island 97
  Republican form of Government 100, 285
  secession 270
  sovereign immunity 195
  suits against 195
  territorial government within 285
  Virginia and Kentucky Resolutions 269
Steele, John 163
Stoddert, Benjamin 243
Stone, Michael 34, 46, 49, 72, 76, 77, 89, 95, 121
Strong, Caleb 119, 206
Sturges, Jonathan 141
Sullivan, John 198
Sumter, Thomas 158, 159
Supremacy clause
  treaties 213
Supreme Court
  advisory opinions 26, 180
  appellate jurisdiction
    exceptions 52
    jurisdictional amount 111
    review of state courts 52
  Justices
    circuit duties 54
    nonjudicial duties 181, 209, 274
    number 54
  organization 52

original jurisdiction 53
Paterson nomination 298
Swanwick, John 213, 214, 228, 229, 230, 231
Swift, Zephaniah 201, 203, 226

Take care clause. *See* President
Taking of property
  Creek treaty 86
  federal obligations 75
  Northwest Ordinance 105
  postal monopoly 150
Tariffs. *See* Taxation
Taxation
  federal taxes
    apportionment 226
    carriage tax 185
    direct taxes 66, 158, 185, 225, 244
    enforcement provisions 97, 98
    excises 60, 185, 244
    export taxes 64
    importation of slaves 66
    land, improvements, and slaves 225
    nonrevenue purposes 56
    rebate as subsidy 169
    relation to commerce power 63
    stamp tax 244
    tariffs 56, 184, 185
    tonnage duties 56
    uniformity 60
    whiskey excise 60, 189
    Whiskey Rebellion 189
  intergovernmental immunity 105
  state taxes
    congressional consent 56, 70
    tonnage duties 56, 70
Tazewell, Henry 276
Tennessee
  admission to Union 218
  Senators, refusal to seat 222
Territories
  copper mining 224
  crimes 93
  delegate to Congress 200
  fugitives 170
  government 104
  land office 107, 207
  Mississippi Territory 284
  national bank 79
  Northwest Ordinance 103
  officers 106
  slavery 67, 105, 107, 286
  Southwest Territory 106, 200, 219
  state laws in 104
  Western Reserve 285
Thatcher, George 18, 194, 265, 286

Tonnage duties. *See* Taxation
Tracy, Uriah 194, 207, 266, 297
Treason
    definition and punishment 94
    Fries' Rebellion 227
    misprision of 94
    resistance to laws 190, 227
    Whiskey Rebellion 190
Treasury
    appropriations. *See* Appropriations
    Comptroller 41
    establishment 41
    Giles Resolutions 164
    investigation of 164
    relation to Congress 42
    reports to Congress 31
Treaties 85
    advice and consent 22, 24, 152, 210, 274
    alien land ownership 210
    appropriations to implement 88, 212
    Articles of Confederation 210
    cession of territory 86
    commercial provisions 210
    conditional consent 211, 274
    congressional interference 187
    Cherokees 85
    Creek Nation 85
    Fort Harmar Treaties 21, 26, 85
    French Consular Convention 22
    French treaties 250, 274
    Holston River Treaty 85
    House's role 211
    implementation by statute 86, 212
    Indian treaties 21, 24, 26, 85, 215
    Jay Treaty 209
    law of the land 213
    Northwestern Indians 215
    peace with France 274
    postal conventions 151
    preconstitutional treaties 22
    ratification 22, 27, 211
    relation to commerce power 210, 212, 217
    scope of authority 210, 217
    Southern Indians 24
    Spanish treaty 215, 284
    suits against states 197
    termination 182, 250
    Tunisian treaty 211
Tucker, Thomas 16, 35, 47, 66, 67, 70, 93, 112, 117,
    118, 121, 158, 159
Twenty-seventh Amendment 7, 111

Unconstitutional conditions
    aliens 257
    Hatch Act 62

    naturalization 194
    officers and politics 62
    revenue agents 62
University
    authority to establish 71, 222

Varnum, Joseph 218, 225, 248
Venable, Abraham 150, 164, 218, 232, 276, 282
Vermont
    admission to Union 100
    appointments 102
    special session 102
Vesting clause. *See* President
Veto. *See* President
Vice-President
    casting vote 11
    compensation 34
    election 293
    executive duties 240
    resignation 139
    Senate President 11, 240
    succession to presidency 139
Vining, John 42, 62, 72, 110, 118, 121, 149, 158, 163
Virginia and Kentucky Resolutions 269

Wadsworth, Jeremiah 160
War powers
    acquisition of property 84, 183
    Alien Act 259, 272
    alien enemies 254
    appropriations 68, 83, 218
    arms exports 184
    arms manufacture 224, 244
    Army, establishment of 81
    Articles of War 82, 93
    Barbary Pirates 88
    codfish subsidy 169
    Commander in Chief. *See* Commander in Chief
    conscientious objectors 113
    copper mining 223
    declaration of war 82, 174, 187, 242
    delegation of authority 163, 186, 244, 255
    embargo 184
    flag 205
    glass factory 72
    Harmar expedition 84
    Indian subsidies 169
    lighthouses 70
    Marines 243
    military academy 183
    military offenses 93, 243
    militia
        Articles of Confederation 157
        composition 159
        delegation of authority 160

discipline 158
employment 81, 82, 160, 189, 248
exemptions from service 150, 159
officers, appointment of 248
organization 157
readiness requirement 184
regular army distinguished 248
state authority 158, 248
volunteer army 248
Mississippi Territory 285
national bank 79
naval code 243
naval hospitals 244
naval vessels 184, 241, 243
naval yard 223
navy 87, 183
Navy Department 243
neutrality 174
nonintercourse 187
peace declaration 241
peacetime armies 83
pension claims 154
Provisional Army 244
Sedition Act 272
sequestration of debts 184
shipping, encouragement of 58
St. Clair expedition 163
standing armies 83
state cession of property 69, 84

timber exports 223
timberland 223
treaty termination 253
troops, employment of 81, 187
troops, raising of 163, 183, 186, 243
volunteer army 248
War Department 41
West Point 84, 183
Whiskey Rebellion 189
Washington, George 4, 21, 23, 24, 26, 27, 29, 32, 33,
   44, 71, 80, 81, 84, 85, 87, 91, 93, 100, 102, 108,
   110, 116, 121, 125, 126, 133, 134, 154, 164, 172,
   173, 174, 175, 176, 180, 182, 183, 187, 189, 190,
   198, 206, 208, 209, 211, 213, 214, 219, 221, 224,
   232, 242, 275, 297, 298
Weights and measures 4
Western Reserve 285
Whiskey Rebellion 189
White, Alexander 8, 34, 39, 120, 129, 140, 161, 172,
   185, 186, 209
White, James 200
Williams, John 251, 284
Williams, Robert 225, 245, 251, 256, 257, 263, 283
Williamson, Hugh 60, 129, 130, 134, 153, 163
Wilson, James 48, 189, 235
Wolcott, Oliver 206, 225
Wynkoop, Henry 119

XYZ Affair 243